COME HELL OR HIGH FEVER

READYING THE WORLD'S MEGACITIES FOR DISASTER

COME HELL OR HIGH FEVER

READYING THE WORLD'S MEGACITIES FOR DISASTER

RUSSELL W. GLENN

Australian
National
University

ANU PRESS

For those who render aid in disaster's wake … or whose preparations strive to render disasters no more than nuisances.

To Sid Heal, friend, colleague and passionate servant of urban residents everywhere. You passed far too early.

And to my father, Colonel (US Army) Russell A. Glenn, whose works sought to ensure disaster never visited.

Australian
National
University

ANU PRESS

Published by ANU Press
The Australian National University
Canberra ACT 2600, Australia
Email: anupress@anu.edu.au

Available to download for free at press.anu.edu.au

ISBN (print): 9781760465537
ISBN (online): 9781760465544

WorldCat (print): 1354992433
WorldCat (online): 1354993959

DOI: 10.22459/CHHF.2023

Printed by Lightning Source
ingramcontent.com/publishers-page/environmental-responsibility

Cover design and layout by ANU Press. Cover photograph: NASA/NOAA

This book is published under the aegis of the Asia-Pacific Security Studies Editorial
Board of ANU Press.

Contents

Abbreviations

AI	artificial intelligence
CBD	central business district
CDC	US Centers for Disease Control and Prevention
DRC	Democratic Republic of Congo
FBI	Federal Bureau of Investigation (US)
FEMA	Federal Emergency Management Agency (US)
GDP	gross domestic product
GPS	global positioning system
IDF	Israel Defense Forces
IDP	internally displaced person
IED	improvised explosive device
IGO	intergovernmental organisation
ISIS	Islamic State of Iraq and Syria
MSF	Médicins Sans Frontières
NATO	North Atlantic Treaty Organization
NGO	nongovernmental organisation
NYPD	New York Police Department
RAMSI	Regional Assistance Mission to Solomon Islands
SARS	severe acute respiratory syndrome
SWAT	special weapons and tactics
TEWG	Terrorism Early Warning Group (US)
UAV	unmanned aerial vehicle

UN	United Nations
UNHCR	United Nations High Commissioner for Refugees
USAID	United States Agency for International Development
WHO	World Health Organization

Foreword

Read this book to gain insight into subjects no-one wishes to discuss: disasters that are catastrophic in nature with consequences unbearable to comprehend. They can and will happen. Cities must be prepared to thwart the high-impact event, mitigate the catastrophe once it begins and respond appropriately after the calamity takes place. This timely, well-thought-out book is the answer to world cities grappling with how to protect their citizens, infrastructure and information in today's threat environment. It additionally provides valuable insight into how cities should spend their limited funds to secure these assets. I highly recommend it to leaders such as those on city councils, managers, security planners and first responders.

I served as the US security representative to the Olympic Games in Rio de Janeiro, Brazil, with the State Department's Diplomatic Security Service. In that role, I was leading many of the crisis management exercises sponsored by the US Government and an active participant in the Government of Brazil's crisis exercises during which we sought to plan for every contingency that could affect not only the Olympic Games, but also the city of Rio de Janeiro. This book delves into many of the problem sets we planned for to ensure a safe and secure Olympics.

Though the book focuses on the most challenging of urban environments, megacities, its insights apply to urban areas of any size and, in fact, contingencies beyond urban bounds as well. The interconnectedness of the world's megacities with one another, their nations and their immediate surroundings means disaster-readiness serves not only the millions in a stricken urban area but also many tens of millions beyond. Preparing for sudden disasters of any type—pandemic, hurricane, earthquake, war, terrorism or another—goes far in being ready for those due to other causes. In short, urban disasters of any sort offer lessons of value regardless of their origin. As such, the pages of this book will be of value to organisations and leaders helping Ukraine's urban areas as they rebuild no less than those who will confront future crises. Climate change, including sea-level rise, will continue to threaten many of the planet's urban millions for decades to come via both direct impacts and magnifying the effects of other events. The pages herein make clear that readiness for tomorrow's disasters necessitates considering and taking steps to mitigate climate change's influences today. Urban preparedness is an alpha to omega (or A to Z) process. Preparing for, responding to and recovering from a megacity disaster will be more effective if all three are considered parts of a single preparedness whole (system?) rather than pieces in isolation. Every urban area is unique in terms of its social makeup, political influences and threat profile, but with a bit of well-considered contemplation, lessons from virtually any megacity crisis have value for others yet to come. First responders and those whose responsibilities include urban preparedness and response are invaluable. But we must not overlook the crucial role of the man and woman on the street when readying for and later dealing with ill fortune's visits. The unfortunate truth is that urban catastrophes are inevitable. This is the case whether they are due to nature's vagaries, mismanagement that exacerbates a natural phenomenon or humankind's malevolence. The offering here is a step forward in identifying what leaders and other citizens can do to reduce the harm when disaster calls.

Peter D. Ford
Arlington, Virginia

Preface

It was August 1993. After five years of military service in Europe, I was driving across the United States for a year-long research fellowship with a West Coast think tank. The focus of the year would be, I had been told, left pretty much to whatever security topic I thought might be of value to the US Army. West Texas gives one plenty of time to think. Operation Just Cause had taken place less than four years earlier; most of its operations had involved Panama's urban areas. The planet would soon pass the hallmark of half its human population living in such environments. My suggestion that investigating operations therein would be time well spent fell on deaf ears back in the nation's capital. Two months passed. The loss of two Blackhawk helicopters and 18 US soldiers' lives in Mogadishu, Somalia, caused reconsideration. Contemplation of urban undertakings became worthy.

So, it is nearly a generation later, after well over a thousand formal interviews and many less-formal discussions have granted me insights 10 lifetimes of personal experience could not provide, that I hope via this offering to repay the wisdom of those many people with whom I spoke. Men and women providing thoughts and sharing experiences did so from around the world. Iraq, Afghanistan, East Africa, Japan, the Republic of China (Taiwan), the Philippines, much of Europe, Canada, Australia, New Zealand, Republic of Korea and the United States are an incomplete list of countries whose individuals from virtually every walk of life cast light on these most complex of challenges. It very quickly became evident that consideration of military concerns alone was insufficient. It likewise was obvious that very different types of disasters—earthquakes, typhoons, hurricanes, flooding, war's devastation, terrorism, disease and others—offer lessons of value to them all. Equally evident: the exceptional phenomena that are megacities likewise provide perspectives applicable to urban areas of any size—and often to catastrophes in other environments as well. The hope is that the following pages prove valuable to those whose responsibilities include preparing for, responding to or recovering from urban tragedy.

It has become popular among some to forecast the death or, at a minimum, the diminishment of cities. Pundits foreseeing their demise will find the detrimental effects of remote work, Covid-19 flight or increasing costs of urban living greatly exaggerated. Cities are here to stay. The twenty-first century is far more likely to prove prescient those declaring it the urban century than those ready to see tumbleweeds roaming Madison Avenue or Shibuya Crossing. Urban areas have proven—continue to prove—adept at evolving to serve their occupants' needs. It is therefore essential to be ever-ready to address the inevitable calamities to come.

I would like to individually thank each of those more than one thousand interviewed, hundreds of authors and many others who have given so much and continue to enhance our understanding of Earth's most influential environs. It is a desirable but impossible goal given the passage of years and imperfect memory. Please allow this too brief list to represent the far greater whole, including those I have surely overlooked and regret not naming. Many thanks to John, Bob, Lise, Clif, Bill, Ed, Dave, Jesse, Chris, Junichi, Jenny, Jim, Robert, Ken, Andrew, Bill, Pehr, Nick, JJ, Mohammed, Koji, Akiko, Mike, Rick, Aaron, Sheri, Ben, Randy, Gideon, Doug, Pam, Larry, Myron, Mike, Kevin, Cullen, Fred, Ernie, Drew, Suzanne, Gerry, Scott, Rick, Ted, Kazuaki, Jamie, Brian, Sherilyn, Kent, Gary, Ian, Allan, Peter, Todd, Paul, Jason, Steve, Simeon, Gretchen, Tetsu, Eric, Leonard, Dionne, Vinson, Don, Tristan, Lou, Claudia, Carl, Shane, Megan, Angus, Fenner, Ryoichi, Alex, Harrison, Pat, Lester, Kelly, Barbara, Noboru, Beth, Arthur, Joel, Tim, Henk, James, Donna, Shigeru, Brenton, Christine, Colin, Matt, Roger, Caleb, Greg, Alessandro, Patrice, Adam, Phyllis, Shannon, Nicole, Becky, Shoko, Sidney, Ann, Chua Jin, Geri, Tom, Dan, Marcus, Gene, Ernst, Joshua, Darren, Al, Will, Andy, Mark, Jaime, Duncan, Liu, Kei, Duane, Ross, Sid, Sean, Luc, Yuna, Jody, Harry, Hugh, Jeremy, Les, Horacio, Stephen, Tim, Chuck, Karl, Jonathan, Rodney, Singe, Joan, Nikki, Lisa, Irena, Clint, Ralph, Ingred, Phil, Liz, Ashleigh, Gina, Johnny, JB, Sandy, George, Howard, Carl, Stuart, Marilyn, Alain, Luke, Tony, Ron, David, Joe, Gordon, Keith, Julie, Rod, Martin, Lois, Erik, Susan, Lance, Rusty, Jay, Barak, Melissa, Mary, Ronald, Charles, Johan, Houston, Amy, Jeff, Frank, Nigel, Marygail, Terri, Gayle, Alison, Ralph, Marion and Michele. A particular nod to

Jan Borrie for her most excellent editing of these pages, Greg Raymond for escorting the manuscript through the early stages of its publication process, and Emily Tinker and Elouise Ball for doing so during those later.

A special thanks to family for inspiration and patience over the many years: mother, Priscilla, the artist for several report covers over the years; father, Russell Alger; sons, Drew and Russell Andrew; daughter-in-law, Steffi; grandson, Huck; loyal canine workmate, Tuxedo; and, of course, my lovely, talented and beautiful Dee.

1
The nature of megacities

What is the city but the people?[1]
—William Shakespeare, 'The Tragedy of Coriolanus', Act 3, Scene 1

The city was rough on migrants, terrible sometimes, and also better than anywhere else.[2]
—Katherine Boo, *Behind the Beautiful Forevers*

They are verbs as well as nouns.[3]
—Merlin Sheldrake, *Entangled Life*

Haruki Akamatsu had not felt the ocean crust heave 10 metres upward. He was not there to see the 6-metre tsunami surge inland, drowning thousands and clawing the earth bare with its retreat. He had, however, clutched the carpet beneath his desk as the twenty-first-floor office in Tokyo swayed sickeningly, thinking the worst was over when the swaying stopped. It was not, but Haruki would not know that until later, for he did not hear the nuclear power station reactors 274 kilometres north of Tokyo explode after cooling pumps failed and nuclear cores superheated. The pumps' reserve generators failed as well, submerged as they were beneath tsunami waters. He could not see, nor smell, nor taste, nor hear the radiation in the air, but it was there. He knew he should not be able to

1   William Shakespeare, 'The Tragedy of Coriolanus', Act 3, Scene 1, Line 198, in *Shakespeare, The Complete Works*, G.B. Harrison (ed.), New York, NY: Harcourt, Brace & World, 1968, 1292.
2   Katherine Boo, *Behind the Beautiful Forevers: Life, Death, and Hope in a Mumbai Undercity*, New York, NY: Random House, 2012, 41.
3   Merlin Sheldrake, *Entangled Life: How Fungi Make Our Worlds, Change Our Minds, & Shape Our Futures*, New York, NY: Random House, 2020, 88.

feel it, but his skin prickled, nonetheless. Yes, it was there, being inhaled into millions—no, tens of millions—of lungs, for this was the most populous urban area in the world.

Haruki was one of the many millions trying and failing to flee Tokyo. They sat trapped behind steering wheels, in bus seats, on trains. He rubbed his eyes, which were dry from staring skyward at the invisible radiation, and returned his gaze to the gridlocked road. Cars packed every lane in shared motionlessness. Even the righthand lanes—normally filled with vehicles coming into Tokyo—had been recruited and were now part of the failure.

He had thought the Shutoko, Tokyo's system of elevated and underground highways, was a better choice than the surface streets. Haruki looked down. The traffic below was as still as that above. Only pedestrians moved; open doors and vacant seats told him that some drivers had abandoned their vehicles to join them. He wondered whether the same had happened ahead, whether people had run from their cars and down exit ramps, blocking everyone behind. It had not surprised him when the Tokyo metropolitan police officer directed traffic on to both sides of the highway three hours ago. Why not? No-one would seek to enter Tokyo other than police, firefighters, soldiers and others whose duties demanded they turn their faces into the disaster everyone else was fleeing. Trying to flee. Streets would be open for them. Everyone knew disaster reaction plans reserved certain passageways for that purpose.

The flow of people had started from the north, trickling, then building into a stream before becoming a deluge that quickly settled into this anxious but motionless lake. The flow had been smooth but slow when he set out four hours ago. He had moved only 8 kilometres since then, covering the first 5 before the traffic slowed to a crawl, then oozing to a halt. That had surprised him. He had travelled to many other cities for work: Singapore, Manila, Jakarta, Los Angeles, Bangkok. None had adapted to the daily tides of humankind as well as Tokyo. Well, maybe Singapore, but none of the other big cities. Most were overwhelmed on a typical workday. Only today, after the government belatedly admitted that the wrecked reactors' radiation was advancing directly on the capital, did the flood of the desperate clog every passageway and with it hope of outrunning the unseen rider on Honshu Island's southbound winds. He could only hope his parents had made good the exit he now could not. They lived—had lived, he corrected himself, for surely none would return to the capital for some time to come—in Tokyo's southern suburbs rather than one of the more posh and exciting commercial centres. He had called once and texted countlessly after the prime minister's announcement, receiving two messages in response before phones and Facebook, the internet, Instagram, Twitter and, well, everything, stopped working, smothered by the hundreds of millions of calls, texts, tweets, updates, photos and other desperate attempts to reassure, be assured, share and reshare. Yes, he assured himself, Sone and Tetsu Akamatsu must have made good their escape.

Haruki figured he was one of more than 38 million people trying to bolt from the world's largest megacity. There must be, he thought as he glanced up again, another 10 million fleeing from further north or north-east or north-west. Most of those, too, would have coursed into Tokyo along roads built primarily for going to or departing from the city. Where would they go, those who successfully escaped? Who would feed them? How would they shelter from the March cold? Where would they find the stuff of daily life once hastily packed bags and hurriedly filled cars emptied? Could the millions be decontaminated and treated for radiation exposure? How would they decide whom to treat first? The more vulnerable elderly? The increasingly rare young as Japan continued to age? The workers like him without whom the economy would surely collapse? Some would have relatives or friends who might take them in. What risk did kindness bring with it? Was contamination transmissible?

The above did not happen on 11 March 2011, of course, though the events behind this notional scenario merited labelling as Japan's '3/11'.[4] But it was a close-run thing. The 9.0 Richter scale earthquake centred

---

4   Sources for material about the Fukushima disaster include Yale-Tulane ESF-8 Planning and Response Network, *Yale/Tulane ESF-8 Planning and Response Program Special Report (Japan Earthquake and Tsunami), as of 2200 hours EST, March 25, 2011*, [Online], available from: slideplayer.com/ slide/5350222/; World Nuclear Association, 'Fukushima Daiichi Accident', London: World Nuclear Association, June 2018, [Updated May 2022], available from: www.world-nuclear.org/information-library/safety-and-security/safety-of-plants/fukushima-accident.aspx; 'Mission impossible: Fukushima Dai-ichi', *The Economist*, [London], 7 February 2015, 22; NPR Staff and Wires, 'Food, gas shortages amid relief efforts in Japan', *KPBS*, [San Diego, CA], 17 March 2011, available from: www.kpbs. org/news/2011/mar/17/food-gas-shortages-amid-relief-efforts-japan/; Lucy Birmingham and David McNeill, *Strong in the Rain: Surviving Japan's Earthquake, Tsunami, and Fukushima Nuclear Disaster*, New York, NY: Palgrave, 2012; Nathan Hall, 'Fukushima-Daiichi: Multinational disaster response & longterm crisis management', Briefing slides, Santa Monica, CA: RAND Corporation, 14 May 2013; Mark Willacy, *Fukushima: Japan's Tsunami and the Inside Story of the Nuclear Meltdowns*, Sydney: Macmillan, 2013; The Saskawa Peace Foundation (SPF), *The Fukushima Nuclear Accident and Crisis Management: Lessons for Japan–US Alliance Cooperation*, Tokyo: SPF, September 2012, available from: www.spf.org/jpus/img/investigation/book_fukushima.pdf; Nuclear Energy Agency of the Organisation for Economic Co-operation and Development (NEA), 'Timeline for the Fukushima Daiichi Nuclear Power Plant Accident', *News*, 7 March 2012, Paris: NEA, available from: www.oecd-nea.org/news/2011/ NEWS-04.html; and National Diet of Japan, *The Official Report of the Fukushima Nuclear Accident Independent Investigation Commission: Executive Summary*, Tokyo: Government of Japan, 2012.

under the sea 400 kilometres north-east of Tokyo—the largest to strike the country since modern instruments began recording such events more than 130 years earlier—did create a series of tsunamis that ripped bare much of Honshu's north-eastern shores. Nineteen thousand people died. Three of the six nuclear reactor cores at the Fukushima Daiichi power plant did melt down after the one–two punch of shaking and flooding knocked out power to both their primary and backup cooling systems. Reserve generators, batteries and supporting equipment designed to come online lay useless, destroyed, as they were positioned too low to escape the invading waters.[5] The loss of those batteries and generators meant workers within the damaged plants—the men responsible for gauging the condition of the reactors—were literally in the dark as to their status. Three meltdowns; a fourth reactor badly damaged. Units 1 and 3 at the facility suffered the first explosions. Unit 3's reactor building was 'bent like candy'.[6] Unit 4 had been shut down and its fuel rods removed before the quake. Its refuelling had only just started. But hydrogen from the neighbouring Unit 3, the experts would later guess, made its way through shared ducts to feed another explosion there. The explosions in Units 1 and 3 scattered radiation about the site and beyond. The damaged Unit 2 added to the contamination. Fortunately, reactors 5 and 6 were shut when the tremors hit.

Officials from the country's Nuclear and Industrial Safety Agency tracked the radiation plume as it drifted from the site. They chose not to share its route with the public. Thousands of those fleeing unwittingly drove into the contamination. There were procedures for coordinating relief organisations that could have rendered aid, but the guidance dictated policies only for international catastrophes, not those at home. Disaster centres sent out advice via the internet, but loss of power when the reactors failed meant many had no access to its offerings. The elderly tended not to use computers anyway, so they would not have received the guidance unless someone passed the information along. Reports did eventually inform Tokyo's residents that slightly contaminated air and water had reached them. Deciding what to do was left to residents. Reports regarding safe levels of radiation were conflicting and inconclusive. To the north, emergency vehicles trying to reach the reactor site ran into a secondary

---

5   Birmingham and McNeill, *Strong in the Rain*, 12, 16; and World Nuclear Association, 'Fukushima Daiichi Accident'.

6   The words are those of Japanese nuclear reactor designer Setsuo Fujiwara.

tsunami—of vehicles fleeing the danger. Many never reached the disaster site. Officials celebrated reports of a generator truck finally succeeding. Joy quickly gave way to despair. The vehicle's electrical plugs did not fit those at Fukushima Daiichi. Little matter: the truck's cables were too short to reach the equipment needing power.

No, Haruki's traffic jam never took place. There was no panicked flight from Tokyo despite contamination of the capital's air and water. That it did not occur does not mean it could not have occurred. Just how close was the megacity's brush with catastrophic radiation in lieu of its minor contamination? Japan's prime minister at the time, Naoto Kan, recalled:

> [T]he future existence of Japan as a whole was at stake … We were able to halt the spread of radiation … by a wafer-thin margin thanks to the efforts of people who risked their lives. Next time, we might not be so lucky.[7]

A cold front lingering off eastern Honshu could have refused the radiation cloud's western drift that spared the tens of millions to the south. Tokyo would then have been the bullseye for its invisible poison. It seems at least a partial evacuation of the capital would have been inevitable had Fukushima Daiichi plant operators not disobeyed orders to stop pumping seawater into the failing reactors. Their managers feared 'the water would destroy the reactors and create an enormous commercial loss'.[8] The disobedience was no small feat of social assertiveness in Japan's hierarchical society. William Saito, an advisor to Japan's government, concluded that the men's decision to keep pumping 'basically totalled the plant … but saved the country'.[9] Just how momentous was the brush with catastrophe? The event caused Emperor Akihito to broadcast live for the first time since the end of World War II;[10] more than 100,000 members of the Japan Self-Defense Forces deployed to assist recovery—Japan's largest

7   Andrew Gilligan, 'Fukushima: Tokyo was on the brink of nuclear catastrophe, admits former prime minister', *The Telegraph*, [London], 4 March 2016, available from: www.telegraph.co.uk/news/worldnews/asia/japan/12184114/Fukushima-Tokyo-was-on-the-brink-of-nuclear-catastrophe-admits-former-prime-minister.html.
8   Judith Rodin, *The Resilience Dividend: Being Strong in a World Where Things Go Wrong*, New York, NY: PublicAffairs, 2014, 214.
9   ibid., 214.
10   Birmingham and McNeill, *Strong in the Rain*, 82.

military deployment since that conflict.[11] Those men and women were joined by 17,000 personnel from the US military supporting Operation Tomodachi ('Friendship') and representatives from 19 other countries.[12]

Despite Tokyo escaping the worst of the catastrophe, the combination of earthquake, tsunami and reactor failure stands as the world's most costly natural disaster ... if one believes that any disaster today can be completely laid at the feet of Mother Nature. Estimates of direct and indirect losses exceed US$54 billion.[13] Japan's National Diet, the country's legislature, found that 'although triggered by these cataclysmic events, the subsequent accident at the Fukushima Daiichi Nuclear Power Plant cannot be regarded as a natural disaster. It was a profoundly manmade disaster that could and should have been foreseen and prevented.'[14] The same is true more often than not for other urban catastrophes. Though the term 'natural disaster' will appear in the following pages on occasion, it is a rare urban crisis that is not intensified by some form of human error, misjudgement or outright deliberate malice even given the presence of natural forces. In no few cases it is legitimate to ask whether the calamity would have occurred had those errors not been made or had judgements been wiser.

The horrendous physical, economic, social and emotional devastation within Japan was soon forgotten by most of the rest of the world, aside from an occasional reminder when a news report sought to entertain by reporting exotic debris washing ashore in the eastern Pacific months afterward. News reports intrigued with near-fantastic stories such as the US Coast Guard sinking the wreck of the Japanese fishing trawler *Ryou-Un Maru*. The ghost ship had taken more than a year to drift across the ocean after being cast out to sea by the March 2011 tsunamis. Approaching another shoreline, it had become a danger to marine traffic.[15] Such diversions distracted from

11   ibid., 126; Willacy, *Fukushima*, 43.
12   Japan Joint Staff, 'Lessons learned from the Great East Japan Earthquake', Briefing slides, Disaster Relief Operation, J-3, Japan Joint Staff, 7 February 2012; and Ryoichi Oriki [General, Japan Ground Self-Defense Force, retired], Keynote presentation to Current and Future Operations in Megacities Conference, Tokyo, 17 July 2019.
13   Willacy, *Fukushima*, 271; and Dick K. Nanto, William H. Cooper, J. Michael Donnelly and Renée Johnson, *Japan's 2011 Earthquake and Tsunami: Economic Effects and Implications for the United States*, CRS Report for Congress R41702, Washington, DC: Congressional Research Service, 6 April 2011, available from: sgp.fas.org/crs/row/R41702.pdf.
14   National Diet of Japan, *The Official Report of the Fukushima Nuclear Accident*, 9.
15   CNN Wire Staff, 'US Coast Guard sinks Japanese fishing trawler near Alaska', *CNN*, 5 April 2012, [Updated 6 April 2012], available from: www.cnn.com/2012/04/05/us/japan-tsunami-ship/index.html.

the occasional academic writing contemplating the extent of calamity had Tokyo been forced to evacuate. The logistics alone boggle the mind. Haruki Akamatsu was right to wonder where the urban area's 38 million residents could go.[16] How would the government have provided them with food, drink, shelter, medical care and other necessities of life? From where would the massive amounts of those resources have come given the loss of the megacity's ports, trains and truck traffic? Some 50,000 evacuees from the Fukushima area were still living in temporary housing six years after the reactor explosions. They represented one in three of the 150,000 people who lost their homes in March 2011.[17]

The economic shock alone would have devastated Japan for years. Tokyo's is the largest urban economy on the planet. The megacity would rank as the 17th largest economy in the world were it a country—just a fraction less than South Korea's and almost twice that of Australia's.[18] The city's budget is greater than that of Sweden. The capital is home to more than one-quarter of the country's population—on only 4 per cent of Japan's landmass.[19] It hosts more foreign companies than any other urban area on Earth and is responsible for more than one-third of the country's national gross domestic product (GDP). Fukushima's radiation might have been invisible, but its crippling of Japan's capital would have visibly ravaged both the country's and the world's economies just as waves had ransacked north-eastern Honshu on 11 March 2011.

---

16   While the political entity of Tokyo includes islands more than 1,600 kilometres distant, the megacity of Tokyo encompasses only the extensive urban area on the island of Honshu. In the case of Japan's capital, the following prefectures fall completely or largely within the megacity: Tokyo, Kanagawa, Chiba and Saitama. Lesser portions of Gunma, Tochigi and Ibaraki prefectures also do so. Demographia, *Demographia World Urban Areas*, 15th annual edition, Belleville, IL: Wendell Cox Consultancy, April 2019, 17.

17   Becky Oskin, 'Japan earthquake & tsunami of 2011: Facts and information', *Live Science*, [New York], 13 September 2017, [Updated 26 February 2022], available from: www.livescience.com/39110-japan-2011-earthquake-tsunami-facts.html.

18   Richard Florida, 'The economic power of cities compared to nations', [*CityLab*], *Bloomberg*, 17 March 2017, available from: www.citylab.com/life/2017/03/the-economic-power-of-global-cities-compared-to-nations/519294/; PricewaterhouseCoopers (PwC), 'Which are the largest city economies in the world and how might this change by 2025?', *PricewaterhouseCoopers UK Economic Outlook November 2009*, London: PwC, 22, 23, available from: pwc.blogs.com/files/global-city-gdp-rankings-2008-2025.pdf; Schumpeter, 'Global cities revisited: Where businesses locate now—and where they will go', *The Economist*, [London], 3 October 2013, available from: www.economist.com/blogs/schumpeter/2013/10/geography-business; and Tokyo Metropolitan Government, 'About our city', [Online], 2006, available from: www.metro.tokyo.lg.jp/english/about/index.html.

19   Somik V. Lall and Uwe Deichmann, *Density and disasters: Economics of urban hazard risk*, Policy Research Working Paper No. 5161, Washington, DC: The World Bank, January 2010, 9, doi.org/10.1596/1813-9450-5161.

What are the chances of a megadisaster striking this largest of megacities? Greater than you might think. Japan suffers about one in every five of the Earth's magnitude 6.0 or above earthquakes.[20] Tokyo is near the junction of four active tectonic plates.[21] In 2012, the country's joint military staff estimated the city had a 70 per cent chance of experiencing a major earthquake within the next 30 years.[22] The military is not alone in their concerns. That same year, scientists determined that portions of Japan including Tokyo were vulnerable to earthquakes twice as large and tsunamis three times as high as previously estimated.[23] Subsidence would compound the effects of a major shock thanks in part to withdrawal of groundwater beneath the city. Then there is the matter of the still-active Mount Fuji volcano that provides so striking a panorama from the city. The world's largest reinsurance company, Swiss Re, puts the Tokyo–Yokohama region at the top of the list for the number of people exposed to natural disasters among the 616 urban areas it considered.[24] Sure, that is partly due to its being the world's largest urban area—more people means greater exposure—but it is also because of the number and potential magnitude of possible disasters. And the character of daily life.

The suffering of Tokyo's urban-dwellers will not end when future tremors cease, winds abate, waters recede, soil stops its sliding or ash ceases falling. Tokyo's combined subway and other rail use exceeds an estimated 14 billion-plus riders annually—nearly twice the entire population of the

20   Justin McCurry, 'Tokyo "has 70% chance of powerful earthquake within four years"', *The Guardian*, 23 January 2012, available from: www.theguardian.com/world/2012/jan/23/tokyo-powerful-earthquake-four-years.
21   Yoshio Kumagai and Yoshiteru Nojima, 'Urbanization and Disaster Mitigation in Tokyo', in *Crucibles of Hazard: Mega-Cities and Disasters in Transition*, James K. Mitchell (ed.), New York, NY: United Nations University, 1999, 64. Another source states: 'Tokyo sits above two fault lines and [is] near another [while] just southwest of the city the Philippine Sea plate dives down under the Eurasian continental plate; right under that, the Pacific plate dives under that.' Banyan, 'When the Earth wobbled: An earthquake in Japan', *The Economist*, [London], 11 March 2011, available from: www.economist.com/banyan/2011/03/11/when-the-earth-wobbled.
22   Japan Joint Staff, 'Lessons learned from the Great East Japan Earthquake'; McCurry, 'Tokyo "has 70% chance of powerful earthquake within four years"'.
23   David Lochbaum, Edwin Lyman and Susan Q. Stranahan, *Fukushima: The Story of a Nuclear Disaster*, New York, NY: The New Press, 2014, 229.
24   Lukas Sundermann, Oliver Schelske and Peter Hausmann, *Mind the Risk: A Global Ranking of Cities under Threat from Natural Disasters*, Zürich: Swiss Re, 2014, 18–19, available from: www.swissre.com/dam/jcr:1609aced-968f-4faf-beeb-96e6a2969d79/Swiss_Re_Mind_the_risk.pdf.

world.[25] The sum of public transportation users riding on *all* forms of mass transit in the United States is roughly two-thirds of that for Tokyo alone[26] (by comparison, New York City's five boroughs account for about 30 per cent of public transportation commuters in the United States).[27] Though the physical damage to Tokyo was minimal in the aftermath of the 2011 disaster, tens of thousands of commuters walked long distances to return home as subways and trains automatically shut in response to the earthquake tremors that triggered the tsunami. Other residents were simply stranded and unable to notify family given overloaded mobile phone networks.[28] The issues go beyond mere inconvenience. Researchers looking into indirect causes of death after the 1995 Great Hanshin Earthquake that struck the Osaka–Kobe–Kyoto area (one of two urban agglomerations in Japan with a population of more than 10 million) found that more than 900 survivors later died after catching the flu in public shelters. It is no surprise that many people chose to sleep in their cars following another of the country's earthquakes in 2016. That decision came with its own problems; some suffered deep-vein thrombosis (better known as 'economy-class syndrome') thanks to remaining in a semi-reclined position for long periods as do passengers on long flights.[29]

25   Statistics regarding rail ridership to, from and within the megacity of Tokyo are inconsistent and difficult to compare. This is in large part attributable to statistics varying in terms of what parts of the urban area they measure, the large number of private and public rail companies serving those various parts, differing years for which data are collected and contrasting ways of measuring usage—for example, whether a single trip commuting to the office is counted once or multiple times if it involves transfers. Daily ridership estimates range from roughly 8 million to more than 12 million, with estimations of annual ridership similarly ranging from between 4 and 5 billion (for only two primary rail companies) to nearly 15 billion. The 14 billion-plus number for Tokyo's annual ridership comes from a source that could not be independently substantiated. However, the following provides a 2013 value of more than 9.6 billion: Statistics Japan, 'Railway passenger transport', *Prefecture Comparisons*, Tokyo: Statistics Japan, 2010, [Updated 2022], available from: stats-japan.com/t/kiji/10796. Given other sources reflecting a significant increase in Tokyo's rail ridership over recent years, the 14 billion estimate seems reasonable. A very small sample of additional sources addressing the topic includes Ramon Brasser, 'Tokyo's rush hour by the numbers', *ELSI Blog*, Tokyo: Earth–Life Science Institute, Tokyo Institute of Technology, 26 November 2015, available from: old.elsi.jp/en/blog/2015/11/blog1126.html; and Geradi Yudhistira, Muhammad Iqbal Firdaus and Lira Agushinta, 'Transportation system in Japan: A literature study', *Journal of Management and Logistics* 2(3) (2015): 333–52, doi.org/10.25292/j.mtl.v2i3.108.
26   American Public Transportation Association, *Public Transportation Facts, 2020*, Washington, DC: APTA, 2022, www.apta.com/news-publications/public-transportation-facts/. The source reports: 'Americans took 9.9 billion trips on public transportation' in 2019.
27   Edward Glaeser, *Triumph of the City: How Our Greatest Invention Makes Us Richer, Smarter, Greener, Healthier, and Happier*, New York, NY: Penguin, 2011, 14.
28   McCurry, 'Tokyo "has 70% chance of powerful earthquake within four years"'; Banyan, 'When the Earth wobbled'.
29   '"Indirect" deaths from disasters', [Editorial], *The Japan Times*, [Tokyo], 23 March 2019, available from: www.japantimes.co.jp/opinion/2019/03/23/editorials/indirect-deaths-disasters/#.XLz2v-tKhn4. The author thanks Keisuke Ogawa for bringing this article to his attention.

Officials worry that they have no means of finding out where the millions of stranded evacuees will be or what aid they will need when calamity visits a megacity (remembering that mobile phone networks may be overloaded even if they remain operational). We will come back to this challenge later when looking at the weeks following Hurricane Sandy's devastation in New York City.[30]

This book is meant for those interested in protecting the world's urban areas from the worst effects of disasters. These include but are not limited to city administrators; police, fire and medical personnel; commercial interests; soldiers who could find themselves called on in times of emergency; members of local and international nongovernmental organisations (NGOs) and intergovernmental organisations (IGOs); and the many others whose responsibilities are key to preparing for, reacting to and assisting with recovery from calamity. It also includes those on whom a neighbourhood initially relies in troubling times—usually individuals other than the men and women bearing the label 'first responder'. Important as formal emergency response personnel are, it was not firefighters who first escorted occupants of the World Trade Center's Twin Towers down the smoke-choked staircases and on to concrete-powdered streets on 9/11. It was not the police or medical personnel on whom hundreds would rely when buried beneath rubble after an earthquake struck Japan's second largest megacity in early 1995. Nor was it ambulances or squad cars that rushed most victims to medical facilities when terrorists attacked Tokyo's subway system only two months later. It was neighbours—sometimes friends, occasionally relatives, but often strangers—who found themselves delivering lifesaving aid thanks primarily to proximity. More than one-third of those suffering during that 1995 Tokyo sarin nerve agent event were transported to hospitals by good Samaritans in their private vehicles or taxi drivers cut from the same cloth.[31] Another third walked. This was not due to negligence or lack of caring on the part of emergency responders. Rather, the sheer number of people suffering during a megacity catastrophe quickly overwhelms. We will see in later chapters that Japan has come to recognise this as the norm. The Tokyo megacity's

30   The author also thanks Keisuke Ogawa for summarising this information, taken from Japan's 13 April 2019 edition of *Yomiuri Shinbun* (newspaper).
31   Tetsu Okumura, Kouichiro Suzuki, Atsuhiro Fukuda, Akitsugu Kohama, Nobukatsu Takasu, Shinichi Ishimatsu and Shigeaki Hinohar, 'The Tokyo subway sarin attack: Disaster management, part 1—Community emergency response', *Academic Emergency Medicine* 5(6) (1998): 613–17, at 614, doi.org/10.1111/j.1553-2712.1998.tb02470.x.

many urban governments prepare information, public spaces and stocks of tools and other supplies in recognition of the citizen as saviour or aid provider. The importance of formal aid providers should by no means be underestimated, but it is also important to recognise and prepare the *first* first responders on whom thousands will also rely in the immediate aftermath of a mass tragedy and in the days, weeks and months to follow when food, water, shelter and care for the injured are in short supply.

A first look at the world's largest urban areas

The five zip codes that occupy the mile of Manhattan between Forty-first and Fifty-ninth streets employ six hundred thousand workers (more than New Hampshire or Maine).[32]

—Edward Glaeser, *Triumph of the City*

25 percent of businesses do not reopen at all after a major disaster.[33]

—Judith Rodin, *The Resilience Dividend*

Besides these peacetime calamities, there is always the possibility of war.[34]

—Francis Gies and Joseph Gies, *Life in a Medieval City*

As the most populous urban area in the world, Tokyo is certainly an outlier. Further, more than half the world's 35 largest urban areas are cities in developing countries that often do not share Tokyo's government effectiveness, quality of infrastructure or similar resources in preparing their residents for calamity. Japan's capital therefore provides an admittedly optimistic view of things to come. Yet, it in many ways provides an example others can seek to match in preparing for, responding to and recovering from disaster.

Tokyo might be an outlier, but it is not alone. More than half of those 35 largest urban areas are in the Indo-Pacific region, which extends from the eastern Pacific Rim to the western border of India. Many, like Tokyo,

---

32 Glaeser, *Triumph of the City*, 5.
33 Rodin, *The Resilience Dividend*, 294.
34 Francis Gies and Joseph Gies, *Life in a Medieval City*, New York, NY: Harper Perennial, 2016, 193.

sit atop or close to the 'Ring of Fire' that traces the edges of the Pacific Ocean. These are likely to share one or more of Tokyo's vulnerabilities to natural threats. More than 6,000 people lost their lives and another 400,000 were injured in the Great Hanshin Earthquake of 1995. Most were lost to crush injuries, which reflected changes to Japan's building codes after the 1923 Tokyo quake in which 140,000 people died—nearly nine of every 10 of whom were killed by fire. Those fires burned for 40 hours and scorched 44 per cent of the city.[35] It was primarily on older, less well-to-do neighbourhoods that the later Great Hanshin quake visited its damage, while newer, better constructed and more wealthy neighbourhoods remained all but intact.[36] An ocean away, Los Angeles shares Tokyo's threat of seismic activity; geologists expect a major quake on the San Andreas Fault to occur every 150 years;[37] it has been more than 300 years since the last. Manila, Lagos, Mumbai and Dhaka are by no means unique in terms of megacities that regularly suffer extensive flooding, while 40 per cent of Jakarta is below sea level. Pumps for ridding that city of floodwaters failed in early 2020. In what seems too common a story (and one we have not heard the end of), they had been submerged and were inoperable as a result.[38] Dhaka, Bangladesh's capital, experienced nine major floods in the half-century from 1954 to 2004. Its 40 canals could do much to lessen the megacity's notorious susceptibility to floodwater—if city leaders stopped permitting encroachments and tolerating other mismanagement of its channels.[39] Were floods not enough, Dhaka has the Indian and Eurasian tectonic plates as near neighbours. Estimates put damage at more than one-third of the megacity's buildings and deaths at 25,000 should an earthquake of 7.0 or greater on the Richter scale

---

35   Kumagai and Nojima, 'Urbanization and disaster mitigation in Tokyo', 66; and Iware Matsuda, 'Two surveys for taking measures to cope with the coming earthquake to the Tokyo Metropolis', *GeoJournal* 38 (March 1996): 349–53, at 349, doi.org/10.1007/BF00204728.

36   Birmingham and McNeill, *Strong in the Rain*, xiv.

37   Suzanne Perry, Dale A. Cox, Lucile Jones, Richard Lewis Bernknopf, James Goltz, Kenneth W. Hudnut, Dennis Mileti, Daniel Ponti, Keith Porter, Michael Reichle, Hope A. Seligson, Kimberley Shoaf, Jerry Treiman and Anne Wein, *The Shakeout Earthquake Scenario: A Story That Southern Californians Are Writing*, USGS Circular 1324, Reston, VA: US Geological Survey, 2008, doi.org/10.3133/cir1324.

38   'The incredible sinking city: Jakarta submerged', *The Economist*, [London], 11 January 2020, 32.

39   Helmut Breitmeier, Judith Kuhn and Sandra Schwindenhammer, 'Analyzing urban adaptation strategies to climate change: A comparison of the coastal cities of Dhaka, Lagos and Hamburg', Paper contributed to DVPW Congress 21: Politics in Climate Change—No Power for Just Solutions?, 2009, 14, 17.

strike.[40] Taking an example from outside the Indo-Pacific region, Türkiye's megacity of Istanbul shares Tokyo's discomfort of sitting amid several major fault lines. As Constantinople, it suffered multiple massive tremors in just over a century from 447 to 558 CE—the last collapsing the city walls and exposing the people within to attacking Huns. Another tremor struck so severely roughly a millennium later that residents labelled it 'Little Judgement Day'.[41]

It is a fair argument that nothing has changed the human experience more than urbanisation. Bear with me for a brief torrent of numbers that help us better understand what makes cities—particularly the largest and most influential of them—crucial to humankind. The 1920 census reflected the fact that the US population had become more urban than rural. The world followed suit during the first decade of this millennium. The majority of the 35 urban areas with a population of more than 10 million abut the coast, adding cyclones/hurricanes and tsunamis to whatever other threats confront a particular city. The interconnectedness of the most influential of these megalopolises means a catastrophe dramatically impacts the lives not only of their own residents but also of other millions living thousands of kilometres distant. Cities in the United Kingdom collectively account for 78 per cent of that country's jobs—impressive, but in the United States, the figure is 84 per cent.[42] The United Nations estimates that urban areas generate 80 per cent of the world's GDP; in some countries, a single city is responsible for more than half of national wealth creation.[43] Beirut accounts for 75 per cent of Lebanon's GDP, while Amman in nearby Jordan provides some 55 per cent of that country's employment.[44] With nearly 13 million people, the capital of Democratic Republic of Congo (DRC), Kinshasa, houses, coincidentally, only 13 per cent of the country's population but generates 85 per cent of its income.[45] With the occasional exception, the world at large continues its march towards more people living in cities. (India is de-urbanising in some locations given public

40   Imtiaz Ahmed, 'Dhaka: Stressed but Alive!', in *Building Resilience in Cities under Stress*, Francesco Mancini and Andrea Ó Súilleabháin (eds), New York, NY: International Peace Institute, June 2016, 17, available from: www.academia.edu/27153738/Building_Resilience_in_Cities_under_Stress.
41   Bettany Hughes, *Istanbul: A Tale of Three Cities*, London: Weidenfeld & Nicolson, 2017, 252, 408, 442.
42   United Nations Human Settlement Programme (UN-Habitat), *Urbanization and Development: Emerging Futures*, World Cities Report 2016, Nairobi: UN-Habitat, 2016, 27, 33, available from: unhabitat.org/sites/default/files/download-manager-files/WCR-2016-WEB.pdf.
43   ibid., 27.
44   John de Boar, 'Resilience and the fragile city', *Stability: International Journal of Security & Development* 4(1) (2015), Art. 17, doi.org/10.5334/sta.fk.
45   UN-Habitat, *Urbanization and Development*, 7.

policies guaranteeing minimum income to farmers.) This is somewhat ironic from a historical perspective. Dispersing critical national assets seemed wise during the Cold War given the destructive power of nuclear weapons. Virtually all countries have now cast aside such fears in the face of urban efficiencies of scale and inexorable human migration to cities, but with these concentrations comes the possibility of national calamity should a dominant city suffer devastation.[46] The largest urban area in a country often dominates not only economically, but also politically and socially.

The twenty-first century may or may not prove to be the Asian Century. It already is and will continue to be the Urban Century. Unfortunately, governments have no deep history on which to draw when it comes to readying for megacity disasters. There were only 16 urban areas with more than *1* million residents in 1900—less than half of the 35 with populations 10 times greater or more today.[47] The fact that more than half of Earth's population resides in urban areas means 3.5 billion people call these phenomena home. Some estimate the number will rise to 6.4 billion—70 per cent of the planet's men, women and children— by 2050. Ninety-five per cent of the increase will be in the developing world.[48] Seventy-five per cent of those living in Latin America and the Caribbean are already urban types.[49] China alone has more people living in towns and cities than the combined total populations of the United States and Japan.[50]

Those 3.5 billion people in today's urban areas occupy only about 3 per cent of our planet's land area. They are responsible not only for 80 per cent of Earth's economic productivity, but also for between 60 and 80 per cent of its energy consumption (depending on whom you ask)

---

46   United States Army Training and Doctrine Command (TRADOC), *The Changing Character of Warfare: The Urban Operational Environment*, TRADOC Pamphlet 525-92-1, Fort Eustis, VA: TRADOC, April 2020, 8, available from: adminpubs.tradoc.army.mil/pamphlets/TP525-92-1.pdf.
47   PwC, 'Which are the largest city economies in the world', 20.
48   Jo da Silva, Sam Kernaghan and Andrés Luque, 'A systems approach to meeting the challenges of urban climate change', *Journal of Urban Sustainable Development* 4(2) (2012): 125–45, at 125, doi. org/10.1080/19463138.2012.718279; and United Nations, 'Goal 11: Make Cities Inclusive, Safe, Resilient and Sustainable', *Sustainable Development Goals*, New York, NY: United Nations, 2015, available from: www.un.org/sustainabledevelopment/cities/.
49   Paul Teng, Margarita Escaler and Mely Caballero-Anthony, 'Urban food security: Feeding tomorrow's cities', *Significance* 8(2) (2011): 57–60, at 57, doi.org/10.1111/j.1740-9713.2011.00486.x.
50   Peilin Wu and Minghong Tan, 'Challenges for sustainable urbanization: A case study of water shortage and water environment changes in Shandong, China', *Procedia Environmental Sciences* 13 (2012): 919–27, at 920, doi.org/10.1016/j.proenv.2012.01.085.

and three-quarters of humankind's carbon dioxide pollution.[51] But do not let that 'only about 3 per cent' fool you into thinking urban tenants are crammed cheek-by-jowl into living spaces. The megacity of New York is the largest in the world in terms of area—three times the size of Rhode Island (and, by the way, it is not the United States' densest major urban area; that is Los Angeles).[52]

It would be comforting to think that at least the developed world's largest urban areas are ready for coming disasters. The examples of 2011 Tokyo (Fukushima) and New York make it clear that even the best prepared fall short. New York City had crisis plans in place before Hurricane Sandy paid its October 2013 visit. Despite what we will see was a decidedly mixed performance, it was and remains among the world's most disaster-prepared urban areas—a situation helped by its police force and fire department being larger than many countries' armed forces. Plans notwithstanding, the city was unready for Sandy's severity and long-range consequences. Outages left some neighbourhoods without electricity for more than two weeks (and therefore without heating, refrigeration, elevators, water and several ways to receive information)—no small matter for the semi-mobile or immobile living in high-rise apartment buildings. Garbage was not collected. Medical services fell short of need. People could not cook or flush toilets. Those already suffering health issues were thus put at further risk as they went without proper nutrition, ran short of water, failed to receive required medications and lacked heat as temperatures dipped into the mid-40s Fahrenheit (6–8°C) when a chilling storm hit the city with a second punch a week after Sandy's departure.[53]

51   United Nations Conference on Housing and Sustainable Urban Development (Habitat III), *Urban ecosystems and resource management*, Habitat III Issue Paper 16, New York, NY: United Nations, 31 May 2015, 2, available from: habitat3.org/wp-content/uploads/Habitat-III-Issue-Paper-16_Urban-Ecosystem-and-Resource-Management-2.0.pdf.

52   Demographia, *Demographia World Urban Areas*, 16th Annual Edition, Belleville, IL: Wendell Cox Consultancy, April 2020, 40, 74. Other sources claim New York is the country's densest city. Presumably, those so doing are looking at the city only in terms of its five boroughs. Such apparent discrepancies are common in discussions of urban areas. They are generally the result of differing definitions (Los Angeles megacity's suburbs tend to be denser than those of New York City), year of data collection or similar differences in the underlying analysis.

53   Michael T. Schmeltz, Sonia K. González, Liza Fuentes, Amy Kwan, Anna Ortega-Williams and Lisa Pilar Cowan, 'Lessons from Hurricane Sandy: A community response in Brooklyn, New York', *Journal of Urban Health* 90 (2013): 799–809, doi.org/10.1007/s11524-013-9832-9.

One in every 12 of Earth's people lives in a city of more than 10 million.[54] What follows is a look at how occupants in the largest, most widely connected and most influential urban areas prepare for, survive and rebound from a calamity. Ours will not be a look at creeping disasters like those arising from higher sea levels or economic disparity (though we will consider how ocean rises make disasters even worse, as was the case with Sandy. New York City is one area where sea levels are rising about 50 per cent faster than the global average).[55] Nor will the pages to come contemplate similarly gradual challenges such as India's already critical shortage of urban water.[56] Likewise, ours is not a concern with long-term dangers due to urban pollution such as the abysmal air quality that shortens lives in Delhi and Beijing. Crime and corruption can make the bad worse, but these day-to-day plagues will only concern us in terms of how they aggravate megadisasters. We will instead reflect on tragedies that are more like a boxer's punch than a slow strangling. The culprits include both Mother Nature and humans. The disasters we cover include deliberate abuses of urban humankind: the 9/11 attacks, Mumbai's 2008 terrorist attacks and the already mentioned sarin nerve agent attack on Tokyo's subway in 1995. We will also include suffering brought about by the misfortunes imposed by war—a source of lessons rarely thought of when the focus is on urban perils brought about by nature's unkindness or acts of the misguided fringe. The nature of war's punishments differs somewhat from that inflicted by other means, but preparations for and recovery from disasters spawned by combat's brutality share much with those brought about in other ways. Thus, those responsible for the waging of war in a city and its subsequent recovery can learn much from civil calamity no less than urban warfare can provide lessons in readiness for disasters brought about by other means. I hope that what follows offers some value during the recovery of Ukraine's urban areas from the tragedies ongoing as this book goes to print.

---

54 *Demographia World Urban Areas*, 15th edn, 3, 4.
55 Jeff Goodell, *The Water Will Come: Rising Seas, Sinking Cities, and the Remaking of the Civilized World*, New York, NY: Little, Brown & Company, 2017, 149.
56 Jessie Yeung, Swati Gupta and Michael Guy, 'Experts: India has just five years to solve its water crisis—Groundwater has been steadily decreasing', *CNN*, 27 June 2019, [Updated 4 July 2019], available from: edition.cnn.com/2019/06/27/india/india-water-crisis-intl-hnk/index.html.

Timing *is* everything: The why and what of this book

> Nations appear and fall, but cities endure and rediscover how to succeed. Their longevity gives them time to develop free institutions and a loyal citizenry. Beijing, Athens, Damascus, Philadelphia, Cairo, Delhi, and Rome, to name just a few, have seen empires come and go while they remain. The fall of the Roman Empire never entailed the fall of Rome. The Prussian empire and then the Third Reich were vanquished, but Berlin, though bombed into rubble, survived.[57]

—Benjamin R. Barber, *If Mayors Ruled the World*

> It's notable that most of Karachi's violence is not blamed on Islamist extremist groups. But extremists have established a presence in Karachi, attracted by many of the same factors that make the city rich … Taliban fighters are believed to visit Karachi when they need places to hide … Al Qaeda used the city as a receiving station for militant recruits and a base for attacks outside Pakistan. This should not surprise; the international airport and financial system offer links to the outside world while some universities and religious schools have become centers of Islamist political thought.[58]

—Steve Inskeep, *Instant City*

No city of size and influence comparable with today's megacities has ever experienced major combat operations or a catastrophic citywide act of terror. This is true despite the multiple locations suffering the latter in Mumbai, Paris and London in recent years. Hopefully none ever will. But hope cannot replace preparation or a diligent response. These pages therefore seek to offer something to those responsible for disaster readiness, from leaders of international response organisations and nations to the individual on the street, no matter what a catastrophe's cause. The largest and most influential of urban areas have known their share of disasters. Many, too, are the lessons from other environments that will prove valuable when preparing for megacity misfortunes to come. We will therefore plunder knowledge drawn from events in smaller cities, towns and even rural areas when they offer ore rich in preparedness

---

57   Benjamin R. Barber, *If Mayors Ruled the World: Dysfunctional Nations, Rising Cities*, New Haven, CT: Yale University Press, 2013, 222.

58   Steve Inskeep, *Instant City: Life and Death in Karachi*, New York, NY: Penguin, 2011, 11.

value. In return, it is fortunate that understanding how better to ready for megacity catastrophes will advise those preparing for disaster response elsewhere.

The why behind this book

> Cities have always been cradles of culture, technology, and commerce, where history's most luminous minds and civilizations converged.[59]
>
> —Janette Sadik-Khan, *Street Fight*

> One hundred thousand soldiers encircled—but did not isolate— IS [Islamic State] in Mosul.[60]
>
> —Thomas D. Arnold and Nicolas Fiore, 'Five operational lessons from the battle for Mosul'

> We overbuild, and we built it wrong.[61]
>
> —Yu Kongjian, Peking University landscape architect, commenting on the fact that 70 per cent of Chinese cities are on floodplains

It was August 1993. My family and I were driving across the United States to California after five years in Europe and the Middle East. The new assignment was a year-long fellowship at an American think tank. Phone conversations with my soon-to-be colleagues informed me that I would be able to work on whatever topic we thought would be of value to those sponsoring my research. Interminable miles across west Texas provided plenty of time to contemplate. It struck me that as the planet became more and more urbanised, I might be able to offer something of value for when disaster struck built-up areas. On arriving in California, I proposed that my year should focus on the challenges posed by what we called 'urban operations'. My colleagues seemed enthused, not so much my sponsors. I was told to find another topic.

59 Janette Sadik-Khan, *Street Fight: Handbook for an Urban Revolution*, New York, NY: Viking, 2016, 2.

60 Thomas D. Arnold and Nicolas Fiore, 'Five operational lessons from the battle for Mosul', *Military Review: The Professional Journal of the US Army* 99 (January–February 2019): 56–71, at 60, Fort Leavenworth, KS: Army University Press, available from: www.armyupress.army.mil/Journals/Military-Review/English-Edition-Archives/Jan-Feb-2019/Arnold-Mosul/.

61 'Soaking it up: Flood-proofing cities', *The Economist*, [London], 20 November 2021, 42.

Five weeks later, 18 US soldiers died when Somali militia shot down two helicopters in Mogadishu and ground forces rushed to the crews' rescue. My colleagues came back to me. My sponsors had reconsidered. I spent the bulk of what remained of that fellowship year considering urban areas' wartime concerns. Later years saw a return to the think tank community on a permanent basis. The scope of urban considerations became more inclusive. This book is a culmination of a quarter of a century's study of the topic—invaluably aided by insights graciously offered by the more than 1,000 individuals who granted interviews during that period and whose paths I have been lucky enough to cross since those ill-starred days of 3–4 October 1993 on Mogadishu's streets.

The what of this book

> Once the battle has started, commanders at all levels will often experience the frustration of being out of contact with their subordinates. By the very nature of the terrain, communications will be difficult. These difficulties will be compounded by the fact that in this type of fighting, there will be a mass of individual fire fights out of sight of each other.[62]
>
> —R.D. Jenkins, 'Notes on fighting in built-up areas (FIBUA)'

> The cities most at risk are those where these events are already common—although there is some evidence of the geographic range of some extreme weather events expanding. Coastal cities will be doubly at risk as sea-level rise increases hazards from coastal flooding and erosion. For any city, the scale of the risk from these extreme weather events is also much influenced by the quality of housing and infrastructure in that city and the level of preparedness among the city's population and key emergency services.[63]
>
> —David Satterthwaite et al., *Adapting to climate change in urban areas*

It quickly became obvious during those years of study that the men and women called to aid a city in times of distress were far more likely to find themselves helping in the aftermath of a disaster outside the bounds

---

62   R.D. Jenkins, 'Some notes on fighting in built-up areas (FIBUA)', *British Army Review Special Report: Urban Operations Report 1*, Winter 2018, 28–37, at 32.
63   David Satterthwaite, Saleemul Huq, Mark Pelling, Hannah Reid and Patricia Romero Lankao, *Adapting to climate change in urban areas: The possibilities and constraints in low- and middle-income nations*, Human Settlements Discussion Paper Series, London: International Institute for Environment and Development, January 2007, 17, available from:pubs.iied.org/pdfs/10549IIED.pdf.

of war. What was no less obvious was that any such help would require a team featuring a wide range of expertise regardless of the disaster's underlying cause. This book strives to provide value to all who seek to minimise the suffering of anyone experiencing an urban catastrophe. This first chapter begins to set the table regarding what urban areas and megacities are—a less straightforward undertaking than one might think. Chapter 2 picks up where Chapter 1 leaves off, delving deeper into the megacity's character and the implications when calamity visits. It is in this second chapter that we challenge the common (and historically inconsistent) understanding of what qualifies as a megacity and why they present disaster planners and responders with exceptional challenges. The next three chapters contemplate the challenges and opportunities inherent when calamity strikes these largest and most influential urban areas (Chapter 3), the role of information and influence during such events (Chapter 4) and the essentiality of bringing all relevant parties together when addressing catastrophe and its aftermath (Chapter 5). The three succeeding chapters offer thoughts, respectively, on preparing for, responding to and recovering from megacity crises, each doing so in terms of:

- context
- how the urban area functions as a system and part of systems greater than itself
- maintaining control in terms of safety and security during and in the wake of misfortune
- orchestrating the efforts of those with a role to play when adversity calls
- exceptional considerations when disaster involves military combat operations
- final thoughts given the above.

If you are one for alliteration, you might think of these six elements as context, collectiveness, control, cooperation, additional considerations and concluding thoughts.

Chapters 9 and 10 bring the whole to a close, sweeping up what the previous eight did not and casting our minds forward to deliberate on what the future could offer in the way of urban disaster preparedness and recovery.

2

More on megacities

Except for the disasters of 1923 and 1945, there have since the end of Meiji been no fires of the good old type, taking away buildings by the thousands and tens of thousands within a few hours. The number of fires did not fall remarkably, but losses, with the two great exceptions, were kept to a few thousand buildings per year.[1]

—Edward Seidensticker, *Tokyo from Edo to Showa, 1867–1989*

During the 1980s the world's business community was startled by predictions that a large earthquake in Tokyo could precipitate a collapse of the global economic system.[2]

—Dennis J. Parker, 'Disaster Response in London'

Even today it is the earthquake's impeccable timing that receives the blame: two minutes before noon on 1 September 1923. It was as though Mother Nature waited until Tokyo's residents had kindled their lunch fires and the city's breezes stiffened in expectation of the tremors to come.[3] Yet, it was not Mother Nature who had scattered chemical storage sites about the city, built gas mains unable to withstand the shaking and strung

---

1   Edward Seidensticker, *Tokyo from Edo to Showa, 1867–1989: The Emergence of the World's Greatest City*, Singapore: Tuttle, 2010, 318.
2   Dennis J. Parker, 'Disaster Response in London: A Case of Learning Constrained by History and Experience', in *Crucibles of Hazard: Mega-Cities and Disasters in Transition*, James K. Mitchell (ed.), New York, NY: United Nations University, 1999, 200.
3   Three sources provided material for this vignette: Seidensticker, *Tokyo from Edo to Showa*; Joshua Hammer, 'The Great Japan Earthquake of 1923', *Smithsonian Magazine*, May 2011, available from: www.smithsonianmag.com/history/the-great-japan-earthquake-of-1923-1764539/; and Daniel Hurst, 'This is not a "what if" story: Tokyo braces for the earthquake of a century', *The Guardian*, 11 June 2019, available from: www.theguardian.com/cities/2019/jun/12/this-is-not-a-what-if-story-tokyo-braces-for-the-earthquake-of-a-century.

electrical lines whose sparks found willing tinder in the wood and paper structures built in surrender to the capital's inevitable conflagrations—fires that regularly swept away homes and shops easily destroyed yet so readily replaced. The 1923 earthquake's damage and suffering were thanks not to ill timing alone but to a witches' brew of factors consequent of both humans and nature. The quake shattered Tokyo's wood and shoji-paper structures, creating plentiful surface area for the slightest spark to find a home. Five of the city's 15 wards lost 90 per cent of their buildings; a sixth suffered but a fraction less. Only one was untouched, sheltered as it was in the western hills. Accounts from the period suggest three-quarters of Tokyo's buildings were destroyed or badly damaged in the aftermath, with two-thirds of the total falling victim to fire. Tokyo was not the only major urban area to suffer. The nearby port city of Yokohama—today part of the megacity's unbroken sprawl—felt the same shaking when the Philippine Sea Plate ruptured and slammed into its Eurasian counterpart in Sagami Bay 48 kilometres to the city's south. In took only 14 seconds for nearly every one of the port city's buildings to be flattened. Yokohama's piers gave way—the cars and people on them instantly disappearing into the sea. Minutes later, a 12-metre-high tsunami washed ashore, drowning thousands. Ensuing waves followed, pulsing inland to recede with more men, women and children in their grasp. US Navy Ensign Thomas Ryan was one of many on the ground who saved lives otherwise forfeit. He freed a woman trapped beneath the rubble in Yokohama's Grand Hotel. Realising both of her legs were broken, he carried her to safety as flames consumed the building's tattered remains.

Recovery began even as embers cooled. It was believed that any shop that did not reopen within three days never would. Stalls and emergency markets sprang up almost instantly, many built using lumber stored in fireproof warehouses for just that purpose. 'The Reconstruction Song', sung in the months after the catastrophe, celebrated the recovery. One verse proclaimed: 'Completely burned out, But see: The son of Edo has not lost its spirit.' Resident-driven rebuilding occurred so quickly that intentions for grander redesigns had, at best, to compromise with actions already taken. Many such plans died on design tables, overwhelmed by the pace of grassroots recovery.

The devastation had effects both immediate and reaching deeper in time. The extent of damage again spurred calls to move the national government out of quake and fire-prone Tokyo. It was a recurring argument after any such catastrophe. The emperor quickly laid the appeals to rest: the capital would rebuild. The quake's consequences nonetheless lingered long after its last aftershocks. Officials blamed the economic panic of 1927 on the quake. Demands to repay debts associated with recovery were repeatedly put off, which weakened the Bank of Japan and, by extension, the country's commercial financial institutions. Historians suggest the relatively democratic national government's mishandling of the recovery fed the rise of autocracy that took the country into World War II.

The next major quake looms over every Tokyo resident's life. Playing of the children's tune *Yuyake Koyake* in the city's Minato ward welcomes the arrival of each evening; it is also a daily test of the community warning system. As in Los Angeles, in Tokyo, residents' bookshelves and other heavy furniture come with brackets to secure them to walls. Governments advise citizens to keep extra water and canned food on hand, ensure they have flashlights and radios with working batteries in homes and offices and maintain a sufficient supply of necessary medications. Stores offer toilet bags to affix to regular commodes when water supplies falter. Numerous publications and permanent signage provide response guidance and identify particularly vulnerable areas. The streets that our notional Haruki Akamatsu knew were designated for post-disaster emergency use also act as firebreaks. Buildings must meet design standards to forever deny a repeat of the havoc wrought by fire in 1923. There are phone apps to instruct Japanese residents in times of disaster. International residents receive invitations to emergency response training; it, like that offered to Japanese speakers, addresses preparations, survival tips and guidance on how to assist victims post quake. It is impossible to overstate the importance of the last. 'After the huge earthquake that struck modern, supposedly quake-proof Kobe in 1995,' writes one author, 'about four in five people requiring rescue were helped by other members of the public rather than the city's official disaster responders.'[4]

What, me worry?

> It was divine nature which gave us the country, and man's skills that built the cities.[5]
>
> —Marcus Tarentius Varro, *On Agriculture*

---

4   Hurst, 'This is not a "what if" story'.
5   Marcus Tarentius Varro, *On Agriculture. Book III*, London: Loeb Classical Library, 1934, 425, available from: penelope.uchicago.edu/Thayer/E/Roman/Texts/Varro/de_Re_Rustica/3*.html.

> Even among rich, industrialized nations, the size of a city is no longer a measure of its importance.[6]
> —Witold Rybczynski, *City Life*

History and common sense tell us that megacities will very likely be the sites of the world's greatest disasters to come. They are, after all, where concentrations of millions upon millions of people live and work. We already noted that they are also in some of the most vulnerable spots on the planet. Humankind has too often done little to make the situation otherwise. If being in the 'wrong' place was not problem enough, we often double the negative by relegating those least able to prepare for or recover from disaster to the most disaster-exposed urban localities. Add a fair dose of human cruelty, as in the 2008 Mumbai terrorist attacks or 11 September 2001 in Manhattan, and it makes it a fool's bet to believe there is not more to come. We fortunately have yet to see a truly devastating megacity disaster in which the casualties measure not in the hundreds or thousands but in the hundreds of thousands or millions. The longer the reprieve, the greater is the opportunity to ensure losses— human, economic and structural—are less than at present. Preparing before the fact ensures fewer buildings topple, are engulfed in flames, suffer flooding or otherwise wreak avoidable deaths.

A few recent catastrophes

> No city is an island. Improving urban infrastructure in one city may attract immigration from other cities, and a negative shock in one location may be mitigated because people can move to another location.[7]
> —Klaus Desmet and Esteban Rossi-Hansberg, *Analyzing urban systems*

> Cairo writes. Beirut prints. Baghdad reads.[8]
> —Arab proverb

---

6   Witold Rybczynski, *City Life: Urban Expectations in a New World*, New York, NY: Scribner, 1995, 40.

7   Klaus Desmet and Esteban Rossi-Hansberg, *Analyzing urban systems: Have mega-cities become too large?*, Paper, Princeton University, Princeton, NJ, 20 October 2014, 2, available from: www.princeton.edu/~erossi/WBChapterKD%26ERH.pdf.

8   'The age of mechanical reproduction as a work of art', *The Economist*, [London], 21 December 2019, 23.

In May 2017, Armed Forces of the Philippines units moved into the Mindanao city of Marawi with plans to seize the leader of the Jihadist Abu Sayyaf Group. The arrival surprised the insurgents and disrupted their plans to take over the provincial capital. Fighting in the city wouldn't end until five months later. Much of the city lay demolished in the aftermath, as had been the case in World War II fighting for Manila nearly three-quarters of a century before[9] (in the latter case, noncombatant *deaths*—as contrasted with total casualties—totalled an estimated 100,000, from a population of 1.1 million).[10] Too little had changed since the earlier struggle for the country's capital. Lightly armoured vehicles and infantry advanced in the same deliberate, symbiotic relationship seen in Manila—one later repeated in Seoul in 1950, Hue in 1968, Grozny in 1999 and elsewhere. Foot soldiers advanced beside their steel-encased partners, the former protecting the latter from an enemy who might dash out from an adjacent building to attach a mine or engage with an anti-tank weapon at close range. The fighting vehicles would in turn fire on foes who threatened the vulnerable infantrymen. Filipino soldiers and marines quickly learned what their predecessors worldwide had discovered at the cost of fellow fighters' lives: innovation and adaptation are the key to not joining those unfortunates. Lacking the smoke grenades necessary to blind snipers too well-positioned for vehicle and infantry fire to eliminate, foot soldiers carried long pieces of fabric, sending a runner to dash across alleyway or street with one end to anchor it on the other side of the gap so their comrades could follow unobserved. Their enemy likewise learned to improvise. It took little time for the insurgents to recognise that hiding until aircraft departed to refuel did much to improve one's chances of survival. Validating lessons repeatedly learned and an equal number of times forgotten in those previous urban contests, the attackers found anti-tank and high-explosive tank rounds were not the munitions of choice for holing walls. Another lesson re-realised: rubble created by bombs and artillery hindered both infantry and vehicle progress while sheltering defenders. So much debris clogged Marawi's streets that bulldozers had to clear lanes for trailing fighting vehicles. This delaying power was magnified when an adversary seeded the debris with booby-traps (more recently referred to as improvised explosive devices or IEDs).

---

9   Much of this description regarding the Battle of Marawi draws on James Lewis, 'The battle of Marawi: Small team lessons learned for the close fight', *Small Wars Journal*, 23 January 2019, available from: smallwarsjournal.com/index.php/blog/battle-marawi-small-team-lessons-learned-close-fight.
10   Russell W. Glenn, Randall Steeb and John Matsumura, *Corralling the Trojan Horse: A Proposal for Improving U.S. Urban Operations Preparedness in the Period 2000–2025*, Santa Monica, CA: RAND Corporation, 2001, 7.

Also in common with urban combat of decades, centuries and even millennia before, men, women and children huddled in their homes or fleeing lethality could not escape death's reach, maiming or—for the lucky—struggling to survive post battle. World Bank estimates figure Marawi may not recover its pre-disaster standing for two decades. Though the city itself originally housed only 200,000 people, twice that number was displaced thanks to the nearby fighting, manoeuvring and scavenging that accompanied the lengthy battle. Their numbers included 90 per cent of the city's precombat inhabitants.[11] Marawi thus reminds us that while the number of those calling an urban area home is important, cities—especially the world's largest—are equally significant for the influence they have on the communities beyond. Any city is a system. Megacities are systems extraordinaire. Any urban area is a subsystem of one or more larger systems. More-populous cities tend to be the more influential. Just 20 urban areas host the headquarters for one-third of the world's largest companies.[12] More amazing yet: those urban residents who occupy only 3 per cent of our planet's land area draw water from 41 per cent of its ground surface.[13] Obviously, these urban-dwellers have much to give. They take in return. With just less than 8 per cent of the world's total population, megacities tend to both give and take in extraordinary amounts.

The examples of Manila and Marawi reinforce the conclusion that war is particularly unkind to those in urban areas. Fighting and its knock-on effects in built-up areas of Iraq and Syria between March 2017 and July 2018 accounted for eight times more fatalities than that in rural environments in those countries.[14] Manila's 1.1 million people made it a large city in 1945. Even Berlin, the largest city to see street fighting of significance during World War II, housed but 4 million people at the start

11   Joseph Franco, *The battle for Marawi: Urban warfare lessons for the AFP*, SRI Working Paper, Manila: Security Reform Initiative, 4 October 2017, available from: www.researchgate.net/publication/337076300_The_Battle_for_Marawi_Urban_Warfare_Lessons_for_the_AFP.
12   Richard Dobbs, Jaana Remes, Sven Smit, James Manyika, Jonathan Woetzel and Yaw Agyenim-Boateng, *Urban World: The Shifting Global Business Landscape*, McKinsey Global Institute Report, Washington, DC: McKinsey Global Institute, 1 October 2013, 3, available from: www.mckinsey.com/featured-insights/urbanization/urban-world-the-shifting-global-business-landscape.
13   Habitat III, *Urban ecosystems and resource management*, 4.
14   International Committee of the Red Cross (ICRC), 'New research shows urban warfare 8 times more deadly for civilians in Syria and Iraq', News release, Geneva: ICRC, 1 October 2018, available from: www.icrc.org/en/document/new-research-shows-urban-warfare-eight-times-more-deadly-civilians-syria-iraq.

of that conflict.[15] It is a gross understatement to say that the ripples from a major calamity in a megacity today, regardless of cause, would quickly beget a tsunami of consequences.

Megacities and social influence

> Resilient ecosystems have greater diversity of species. It is no accident that successful cities are those that offer a greater spectrum of job opportunities and businesses.[16]
> —Geoffrey West, *Scale*

> Whatever brought you here, you are part of the neighborhood now.[17]
> —T.R. Reid, *Confucius Lives Next Door*

Urban areas, and megacities in particular, have more varied economic, social and political systems than their rural counterparts—a diversity that offers advantages to those living within. Shoppers have more choice and more opportunity for bargains. Entertainment runs the gamut from sport of all types to live theatre and film, and more base offerings. Employers more readily find the skills they need at competitive wage levels and in the numbers they require. All these touch on a point that provides larger urban areas a resilience those smaller lack: redundancy. The decline, even the complete demise, of a given economic sector in larger cities need not impose undue suffering much less collapse as the affected will find employment in another. Urban areas by their very character practise what nature has long tried to tell a too-often unlistening human race: redundancy is crucial to wellbeing, even survival. Entire banana plantations turned from green to black virtually overnight in Central America when ravaged by Panama disease (or fusarium wilt, for the more botanically minded)— a malady that thrived thanks to the industry's deliberate cultivation of the genetically identical plants preferred by consumers.[18] Smaller populations mean villages and towns cannot match the diversity of religions, languages, ethnicities, work skills, innovation and other features their larger cousins

15 World Population Review, 'Berlin population 2018', [Online], Walnut, CA: World Population Review, 19 October 2018, available from: worldpopulationreview.com/world-cities/berlin-population/.
16 Geoffrey West, *Scale: The Universal Laws of Growth, Innovation, Sustainability, and the Pace of Life in Organisms, Cities, Economies, and Companies*, New York, NY: Penguin, 2017, 143.
17 T.R. Reid, *Confucius Lives Next Door: What Living in the East Teaches Us about Living in the West*, New York, NY, Vintage, 1999, 75.
18 Rob Dunn, *Never Out of Season: How Having the Food We Want When We Want It Threatens Our Food Supply and Our Future*, New York, NY: Little, Brown & Company, 2017, 7–8.

possess. Experts estimate that New York City is home to some 800 languages. Roughly half the families it counts as resident do not rely on the English tongue at home as their primary means of communication. Students in the City of Los Angeles school system (never mind those in the larger megacity of which that city is the core) speak one or more of 199 languages.[19] With these different voices come different cultures. With varied cultures come the different perspectives fundamental to developing innovative approaches to meeting challenges.

What drove (and continues to drive) people to live where so many others unlike themselves lived, to leave the comfort of the familiar for the strange, even incomprehensible? For many centuries, it certainly was not the promise of a longer or more pleasant life. Cities were unhealthy in the extreme. With their thousands and tens of thousands and—very occasionally—hundreds of thousands packed together and sharing impure water and one another's waste, disease was the order of the day. British countryfolk lived more than 10 years longer in 1841 than their fellow citizens in the industrial cities of Manchester and Liverpool.[20] A boy born in New York City in 1901 could expect to live seven fewer years than a young American male elsewhere.[21] Cholera was so devastating during the nineteenth century that riots broke out in New York, Liverpool and other urban areas to protest government incompetence in addressing sanitation failures.[22] These death rates exceeded those for births. Continued existence depended on human inflow from elsewhere.[23]

As alien as their populations might be, and as dangerous as they were to live in, cities attracted people anyway. Marked by great differences internally, the largest urban areas nonetheless became distillers that gave countries common languages and shared social standards. One historian offers that London and Paris promoted English and French to the top of their respective countries' language hierarchies thanks to how much

---

19   Charles S. Heal, 'Best practices for securing a megacity during a major world event 1', Presentation to Current and Future Operations in Megacities Conference, Tokyo, 18 July 2019.
20   As quoted in Thomas J. Bollyky, *Plagues and the Paradox of Progress: Why the World is Getting Healthier in Worrisome Ways*, Cambridge, MA: MIT Press, 2018, 28–29, 115, doi.org/10.7551/mitpress/11750.001.0001.
21   Glaeser, *Triumph of the City*, 10.
22   As quoted in Bollyky, *Plagues and the Paradox of Progress*, 30.
23   Sean Fox, 'Urbanisation as a Global Historical Process: Theory and Evidence from Sub-Saharan Africa', in *Africa's Urban Revolution*, Susan Parnell and Edgar Pieterse (eds), New York, NY: Bloomsbury Academic, 2014, 257–83, at 261, doi.org/10.5040/9781350218246.ch-014.

the two urban areas dominated culturally.[24] People immersed themselves in those urban cultures if they wanted to reach the top in government, business or another part of society. That included learning the local lingo. It seems Frank Sinatra was right when it comes to dominant cities: 'If you can make it here, you can make it anywhere.' Little wonder that urban areas continue to attract now that cities are healthier places to live than those formerly superior rural areas, especially in developing countries.

Urban areas are also more efficient places to work. City infrastructure is built to move people, link them, concentrate them, supply them, serve them, inform them and protect them.[25] Manager and worker, provided and provider, served and server will tend to find they can accomplish sought-after ends more efficiently in terms of labour exerted and time spent than in rural environments. As we noted in terms of entertainment variety, urban mobility, internal connections, proximity to others, availability of goods and services, and limits on exposure to physical harshness also offer a more interesting life during nonworking hours. People do not flee megacities to escape boredom. Sheer volume of resources means urban environments are easier to survive in than rural areas during times of want. We recall that Filipinos flowed into World War II Manila despite the risks associated with closer proximity to the occupiers. Rural-to-urban flight continues to be the order of the day in times of disaster, in part as relief efforts tend to focus first on where the most people live. It should therefore not surprise that up to 95 per cent of internally displaced persons (IDPs) in Iraq, Syria, Jordan, Lebanon, Pakistan, Sudan and Somalia remain in or make their way to urban areas.[26] Common sense dictates the choice. Unless one lives in a paradise where a variety of food literally grows on trees and the climate coddles rather than mistreats, the volume of waste discarded by the well-to-do and the availability of shelter even 'on the street' mean most urban-dwellers can at least survive and perhaps do much better than that, as the poorest cull garbage, hawk their findings and shelter in abandoned buildings or vehicles; beneath bridges or awnings; or within doorways, parking garages or parks. Man, woman and child constantly wrestle with Mother Nature in the countryside. In urban areas, she is kept at bay other than when she throws a tantrum.

24   Manuel De Landa, *A Thousand Years of Nonlinear History*, New York, NY: Swerve, 2014, 205–6.
25   Elizabeth Ferris, 'Urban disasters, conflict and violence: Implications for humanitarian work', *On the Record*, Washington, DC: The Brookings Institution, 28 February 2012, available from: www.brookings.edu/on-the-record/urban-disasters-conflict-and-violence-implications-for-humanitarian-work/.
26   de Boar, 'Resilience and the fragile city'.

Then there are the additional opportunities available should a poor urban migrant seek to shed poverty's fetters. The best predictor of whether a sub-Saharan African child completes a basic education is his or her parents' level of education. But where that boy or girl lives also influences the opportunities to learn. Those finding themselves in larger urban areas are better positioned than peers elsewhere, other conditions being equal.[27] It shouldn't surprise that breaking free of poverty and the chance to get an education complement each other. In Brazil's *favelas*, for example, education level has been the best predictor of whether someone born in those slums escapes.[28] Urban areas have long been fertile ground for upward mobility and other forms of social evolution.[29] For better or worse, urbanisation in China has done much to change the expectation that children will provide for their parents in old age; a new freedom releases financial, time and social intercourse resources previously bound up in familial obligations. Many of today's urban Chinese live in households akin to those in the West with only two generations under one roof: parents and children (if any). The change obviously comes with downsides, especially in a social system in which the government depends on such traditional providers in lieu of ponying up support itself. The evolutionary 'neglect' to provide sufficient support to parents became a crime in Shanghai at the end of the previous century.[30] China is not alone; a similar transformation has occurred in African urban areas.[31]

That 'if any' of a couple of sentences ago is another trait that distinguishes urban from rural environments. The mean number of children in a family dropped from seven to two in the West over some 200 years in no small part due to urbanisation and the related waning need for children to assist with farming. Unsurprisingly, given how quickly some developing nations have urbanised, a similar decrease in birthrates can now take place

---

27   'Geography lessons', *The Economist*, [London], 23 February 2019, 50.

28   'Onward and upward: Shanty life in Brazil', *The Economist*, [London], 24 July 2010, 81.

29   It would be wrong to believe, however, that moving from rural to urban living is a guarantee of bettering one's life or further onward movement to more pleasant environs. Up to 80 per cent of India's urban-dwellers live below the poverty line. In Kolkata, where 35 per cent of the megacity's population resides in its slums, more than 70 per cent of those residents have been there for over 15 years and over 40 per cent for more than 30 years. World Vision, *Cities Prepare! Reducing Vulnerabilities for the Urban Poor*, Asia Pacific Disaster Report, Bangkok: World Vision Asia Pacific, 2013, 55, available from: www.worldvision.jp/about/item_img/13_12_en.pdf.

30   Anthony M. Townsend, *Smart Cities: Big Data, Civic Hackers, and the Quest for a New Utopia*, New York, NY: W.W. Norton, 2013, 48; and Richard Sennett, *Building and Dwelling: Ethics for the City*, New York, NY: Farrar, Straus & Giroux, 2018, 112.

31   Carole Rakodi, 'Religion and Social Life in African Cities', in *Africa's Urban Revolution*, Susan Parnell and Edgar Pieterse (eds), New York, NY: Bloomsbury Academic, 2014, 82–109, at 87, doi.org/10.5040/9781350218246.ch-005.

in a generation or two. The fertility rate in Kenya's cities is 3.1 births per woman versus 4.5 in rural areas.[32] London's East End—home to many of the megacity's immigrants—had birthrates exceeding the national average in the dawning years of this century. Less than 20 years later, the proportion of immigrant mothers' births is falling; the fertility rate in East End boroughs lags that for the United Kingdom at large.[33] Urbanisation partners with globalisation to influence cultural evolutions in other, admittedly less impactful, ways as well. Hong Kong customers originally shoved their way forward for service as they shouted food orders and thrust payment over the heads of others when McDonald's first opened in 1975. The introduction of restaurant-hired 'queue monitors' saw turmoil give way to polite lines.[34]

While urban areas undoubtedly introduce challenges for those responsible for security, they also offer opportunities less common in other environments. Whereas we in the West might think of cities as the more dangerous environment, escaping rural violence for the better policed and more ordered city has been a driver of rural-to-urban migration in Latin America and elsewhere.[35] Further—and somewhat surprisingly—at least one student of rural-to-urban movements found the percentage of income spent on both food and housing in Egypt was less for urban-dwellers. This freed up money for nice-to-haves such as furniture, nonessential food and entertainment, as well as the very desirable education and medical care on which city types spend more of their wealth.[36]

Whether major or minor, revolutionary or ordinary, these benefits seem to pile on one another.[37] One study looking at urbanisation in 90 developing countries linked living in urban areas to a reduction in poverty in every

---

32   'A school for small families: Demography', *The Economist*, [London], 2 February 2019, 52.

33   'Hold on: Life on furlough', *The Economist*, [London], 25 July 2020, 38.

34   Donald A. Norman, *Living with Complexity*, Cambridge, MA: MIT Press, 2011, 195.

35   Nina van Rijn, Urbanization in sub-Saharan Africa, Bachelor's thesis, University of Amsterdam, 16 December 2014, 24.

36   Mohamed Asar, 'Going Formal in Egypt: A Way Out for the Urban Poor—Land Titling versus Upgrading in Informal Settlements', in *Shelter for the Urban Poor: Proposals for Improvements— Inspired by World Urban Forum III*, Karin Gundström and Annette Wong Jere (eds), Lund, Sweden: Grahns Tryckeri AB, 2007, 95–110, at 97.

37   Statistics and characteristics of urbanisation in this and the following paragraph, other than those regarding Kenya, come from Peter Engelke, *The Security of Cities: Ecology and Conflict On an Urbanizing Planet*, Report, Washington, DC: Atlantic Council, 18 November 2013, 13, available from: www.atlanticcouncil.org/in-depth-research-reports/report/the-security-of-cities-ecology-and-conflict-on-an-urbanizing-planet/; Ivan Turoc, 'Linking Urbanisation and Development to Africa's Economic Revival', in *Africa's Urban Revolution*, Susan Parnell and Edgar Pieterse (eds), New York, NY: Bloomsbury Academic, 2014, 60–81, at 75, doi.org/10.5040/9781350218246.ch-004; and UN-Habitat, *Urbanization and Development*, 7.

region of the world bar one: sub-Saharan Africa. Yet, there are exceptions even south of the Sahara. Nairobi, Kenya, has among the largest slums in the world. Yet, those who have moved from rural communities conceal the fact they are better off financially for fear of being asked to send funds home. A researcher conducting a recent experiment told select rural-dwellers how much those in the capital made, what the cost of food was and the wages for specific jobs. Two years later, migration from those households was one-third higher than from those not so informed. The same researcher found more than half the capital's slum residents believed their living conditions were better in Nairobi than in rural communities.[38]

The complexity of megacities and the fallacy of the organism metaphor

> Cities are not organisms any more than they are machines … They do not grow or change of themselves, or reproduce or repair themselves. They are not autonomous entities, nor do they run through life cycles, or become infected … But it is more difficult, and more important, to see the fundamental ineptness of the metaphor and how it leads us unthinkingly to cut out slums to prevent their 'infectious' spread, to search for an optimum size, to block continuous growth, to separate uses, to struggle to maintain greenbelts, to suppress competing centers, to prevent 'shapeless sprawl,' and so on.[39]
>
> —Kevin A. Lynch, *Good City Form*

> Although cities have been destroyed throughout history—sacked, shaken, burned, bombed, flooded, starved, irradiated, and poisoned—they have, in almost every case, risen again.[40]
>
> —Lawrence J. Vale and Thomas I. Campanella, 'Introduction: The Cities Rise Again'

---

38   'Tall tales of the city: Kenya', *The Economist*, [London], 11 April 2020, 39.

39   Kevin A. Lynch (*Good City Form*, Boston, MA: MIT Press, 1984, 95), as quoted in Luís M.A. Bettencourt, *The kind of problem a city is: New perspectives on the nature of cities from complex systems theory*, SFI Working Paper 2013-03-008, Santa Fe, NM: Santa Fe Institute, 2013, available from: studylib.net/doc/8927135/the-kind-of-problem-a-city-is.

40   Lawrence J. Vale and Thomas I. Campanella, 'Introduction: The Cities Rise Again', in *The Resilient City: How Modern Cities Recover from Disaster*, Lawrence J. Vale and Thomas I. Campanella (eds), New York, NY: Oxford University Press, 2005, 3–23, at 3, doi.org/10.1093/oso/9780195175844.003.0004.

The more one looks at our population's densest concentrations, the more it becomes evident that urban areas are complex in character, tough to comprehend and difficult to govern. Many have turned to simplifying models as a result, with one of the most popular being to liken cities to organisms—most often *Homo sapiens*. 'It was common to describe the city as a body' and equate a 'blockage of [traffic] circulation with a seizure or heart attack' as early as the eighteenth century.[41] The metaphor has some value in understanding urban areas at the most simplistic level: roads are veins and arteries. Traffic flows into and out of the 'heart' (central business district, or CBD). Industrial zones, airports and financial centres are 'organs', each with a specialised function. Government is the 'brain' (despite ample examples to the contrary). Garbage, sewage and pollution are, well, you can figure it out. A particularly striking metaphor is Ryuji Takemoto's observation that Tokyo's massive daily flows of commuters going to and returning from work are the megacity's inhalations and exhalations.[42] Cities have relations with each other—some providing specific services (banking, for example), others producing goods not available elsewhere. And there are those 'cancers' that some view as needing excising: slums, gangs, insurgents and corruption, to name a few.

The metaphor quickly breaks down when we look beyond the superficial. Much—likely most—of the flow into and out of an urban area does not pour through the CBD or any other single point. Most instead moves between points offering a function specific to an individual or group rather than the whole.[43] No single force (heart) drives all. Few urban governments are consistently 'of a mind'; the best would be lucky if they were only bipolar. Residents and workers refuse to travel at the same speed, in contrast to blood cells. Nor do those cells kick up their non-existent feet for drinks after a day in the heart, later staggering out to cause a wreck at the intersection of Capillary and Vein. Few would consider it a good thing when a stream of blood cells squirts off for a week's vacation. Interactions between cities will play a significant part in our discussions

---

41   Jonathan Conlin, *Tales of Two Cities: Paris, London, and the Birth of the Modern City*, Berkeley, CA: Counterpoint, 2013, 15.
42   Ryuji Takemoto [Lieutenant-General, Japan Ground Self-Defense Force], 'The JGSDF role in megacity security operations', Presentation to Achieving Convergence during Humanitarian Assistance and Disaster Relief Operations in the World's Largest Urban Areas Conference, Tokyo, 16–18 July 2019.
43   Horacio Samaniego and Melanie E. Moses, 'Cities as organisms: Allometric scaling of urban road networks', *Journal of Transport and Land Use* 1(1) (2008): 21–39, at 24, doi.org/10.5198/jtlu.v1i1.29.

to come, but urban areas have yet to link up for procreation. Unlike those pre-twentieth-century cities that saw death rates exceed births, humans cannot look to outside sources for regular replacement of demised cells (organ transplants and blood transfusions notwithstanding).[44]

Perhaps the greatest argument against relying too greatly on the metaphor of urban area as organism is each urban area's uniqueness—a uniqueness even more evident when we compare megacities. Cities might voluntarily twin with one another, but no-one will mistake them for siblings, much less doppelgangers. Different as each human is from another, we are far more alike. Head, torso and limbs are in the same general location. Organs are by and large uniform in function. The body and brain age or fall foul of disease, but there is no dramatic physiological evolution within a single organism's lifespan that compares to what Rome, Paris, London, Shanghai or Seoul once was and now is.

If we need a metaphor to help us understand cities' complexity, we can find a reasonable if imperfect one in ecosystems (which one author describes as 'populations in continuously changing environments' and another as 'a community of organisms together with their nonliving environment').[45] As complex dynamic systems, ecosystems are 'able to adapt in and evolve with a changing environment … in terms of co-evolution with all other related systems'. A few other relevant ecosystem characteristics include:

- Distributed control: 'There is no single centralized control mechanism that governs system behavior … Overall behavior usually cannot be explained merely as the sum of individual parts … This implies that a decision or action by one part within a system will influence all other related parts but not in any uniform manner.'

---

44 Comparisons between cities and machines is another popular, although less common, metaphor, and is even less convincing. Such greatly oversimplified comparisons are fine if we need only a very superficial understanding that ignores human emotions and will, constant changes in daily activities and the development (and vagaries) of relationships with others, to mention just a few exceptions (setting aside *Ex Machina* and *Westworld*).

45   The descriptions are, respectively, H.A. Gleason's, as appears in R.V. O'Neill, Donald Lee Deangelis, J.B. Waide and Timothy F.H. Allen, *A Hierarchical Concept of Ecosystems*, Monographs in Population Biology Vol. 23, Princeton, NJ: Princeton University Press, 1986, 26; and James H. Brown, 'Complex Ecological Systems', in *Complexity: Metaphors, Models, and Reality*, George A. Cowan, David Pines and David Meltzer (eds), SFI Studies in the Sciences of Complexity, Proc. Vol. XIX, Boston, MA: Addison-Wesley, 1994, 419–49, at 422.

- Sensitive dependence: 'Small changes can have a surprisingly profound impact on overall behavior ... Long-term prediction and control are therefore believed to not be possible.'[46]

Both these characteristics obviously complicate efforts at urban planning. This is especially true for organisations employing a backward planning approach in which one starts by identifying the ultimate goal (military types call this the 'desired end state') and works backward to the present, determining along the way what activities will result in achieving the desired goal. Military or otherwise, the lack of predictability in a city's daily happenings demands flexibility in responding to and successfully influencing events. Maintaining that flexibility while making good decisions requires what leaders in the armed forces call 'mission command', though it is a concept practised in various forms and under various names by both civilian and military organisations. We will look at mission command and how it applies to megacity disasters in coming chapters.

Megacities as ecosystems are particularly rich not only in terms of the organisms that occupy them but also from the perspective of the groups formed by the individuals within them. Each resident is part of ethnic, cultural, economic, functional, social and other collectives that together provide those living in urban areas with a variety of exposures and experiences impossible to replicate elsewhere. Just as individuals interact with others intimately, occasionally or not at all, group connections span a similarly broad and complex spectrum in which members occupy several if not many assemblies and thereby are always initiating relationships unlike anything found within the body of a single organism. These relationships range across a vast spectrum. The metaphor of ecosystems accounts for an urban area's many parts cooperating, competing or adapting as one 'species' is lost and another arrives or evolves to fill vacated or newly discovered niches. Unlike with a single organism, resulting evolutions can take place in very short periods (think of a city rebuilding after a disastrous fire or war) and be dramatic in character. As one writer observed:

> Complexity tends to grow as systems evolve ... It may grow by increases in 'species' diversity: under certain circumstances new species may provide further niches that call forth further new species in a steady upward spiral. [In other cases] it may grow by

46   Serena Chan, *Complex adaptive systems*, ESD.83 Research Seminar in Engineering Systems Paper, Cambridge, MA: Massachusetts Institute of Technology, 31 October – 6 November 2001, 2–5, available from: web.mit.edu/esd.83/www/notebook/Complex%20Adaptive%20Systems.pdf.

> increases in structural sophistication: the system steadily cumulates increasing numbers of subsystems or subfunctions or subparts [involving the same 'species' but in evolved relationships].[47]

The 'species' in the case of megacity ecosystems could be new entries into the urban economy that fill a previously unfilled niche—companies offering to change tyres at customers' homes, for example—or ones that meet a demand created by changes in the urban area's makeup, such as vegan restaurants as diet preferences move in that direction. A straightforward example from a notional village helps get the point across. Let's say our very small village has only two residents: a worker and a cab driver who drives him to work in a nearby town. An entrepreneur spots an opportunity and enters the scene, adding a store with a petrol station. Now the cab driver also sees new opportunities. He can increase his offerings to include goods delivery to and from the store to people near or far. Should worker or storeowner add a pet dog, there could be an opening for a veterinary office, the storeowner adding pet supplies and dog wash or the cab driver augmenting his services with pet walking during his driving downtime. We multiply such additions and evolutions by thousands, even millions, in a megacity. The interconnectedness between one urban area and others spurs similar increases in both cities' complexity. (Ironically, though, at some point in our megacity as ecosystem model, individual behaviour may become simpler as complexity increases.[48] Eventually, our cab driver cum deliveryman cum pet walker goes back to focusing on his cab driving as others fill the pet-walking business and delivery services on a permanent basis.)

As the quotations opening this section make clear, cities seem to have found the secret of (nearly) eternal life. With rare exception, they do not die. Today's London, Paris, Mexico City, Istanbul, Cairo and Delhi are among the megacities whose depths include ancient predecessors.[49] They are like good-guy zombies in that sense (if zombies can be good. It's not an area of personal expertise). Cities, especially large cities, survive even the most devastating of tragedies, rising again and often becoming stronger in the years to follow. Empires, countries, governments, even civilisations—cities outlive them all (think Rome, Byzantium/Constantinople/Istanbul, Athens

---

47   A. Brian Arthur, 'On the Evolution of Complexity', in *Complexity: Metaphors, Models, and Reality*, George A. Cowan, David Pines and David Meltzer (eds), SFI Studies in the Sciences of Complexity, Proc. Vol. XIX, Boston, MA: Addison-Wesley, 1994, 65–78, at 65, available from: sites. santafe.edu/~wbarthur/Papers/Evol%20of%20Complexity.pdf.

48   O'Neill et al., *A Hierarchical Concept of Ecosystems*, 115.

49   Monica L. Smith, *Cities: The First 6,000 Years*, New York, NY: Viking, 2019, 4–5.

and the much-punished Jerusalem). They are far more robust than any human could hope to be. Crank the internal temperature of a human up 10 or 15 degrees above 98.6 Fahrenheit (37°C) and that individual has breathed their last. Some urban areas experience annual swings of 60, 70 or more than 100 degrees (Fahrenheit, that is). Many have literally risen from the ashes, though only a few are named 'Phoenix'. London survived its Great Fire of 1666 despite five-sixths of the city being destroyed, including almost all its major public buildings and many of its businesses—just another in a series of disasters that could not prevent resurrection. It had been destroyed in earliest form during Boudicca's uprising in 60 CE less than 20 years after being founded, and again 70 years after that event. It then survived the Roman departure.[50] Almost half its residents died during the Black Death in the mid-fourteenth century. London slowly recovered over the following two centuries—just in time for the 1563 plague that removed one-fifth of its population. Plague returned frequently, with especially savage visits in 1593, 1603 and 1625.[51] Then there was the bombing during World War II that killed more than 20,000 civilians and badly damaged or destroyed 300,000 houses.[52] Chicago's 1871 fire devastated the city. Like the Phoenix, it rose again. Unlike the Phoenix, it transformed itself by becoming the world's first skyscraper city. Anthropologist Monica L. Smith concludes that the only way to kill a modern city of reasonable size is 'through a nuclear catastrophe', citing Ukraine's Chernobyl as the only city in the past thousand years to effectively disappear.[53] Perhaps, though disease, biological weapons, chemical agents wielded to kill or other potential causes might someday prove her optimistic. (She perhaps intended her readers to include Pripyat within her construct of 'Chernobyl'. Pripyat once hosted a population of some 50,000. Now devoid of human habitation, it was closer to the nuclear plant than the smaller city of Chernobyl that gave the facility its name.)

Exceptions to this cities-do-not-die assertion include many from the ancient world, but most of their populations numbered in the few thousands—what we would call towns today. Historian Greg Woolf notes that now we live in a world 'where a small city has less than 500,000 inhabitants … A small city in the ancient world had fewer than 5,000

---

50   Stephen Alford, *London's Triumph: Merchants, Adventurers, and Money in Shakespeare's City*, New York, NY: Bloomsbury, 2017, 26–27; and John Reader, *Cities*, New York, NY: Atlantic Monthly, 2004, 262.

51   Alford, *London's Triumph*, 13, 21.

52   Philip Ziegler, *London at War: 1939–1945*, New York, NY: Alfred A. Knopf, 1995, 161.

53   Smith, *Cities*, 259.

inhabitants'.[54] The chances of a town dying today are far greater than for a city of any reasonable size. The chances are virtually nil if the urban area is a megacity. The past can also be deceptive. Looking back at some of those 'cities' that seemed to disappear, we find they were simply waiting to rise again, as with London, Cairo, Jerusalem and others that today sit atop their ancestors. More importantly in terms of survival, these earlier cities were simple ecosystems compared with their evolved forms, limited in their number of functions and interdependencies. They lacked the robustness of today's larger urban areas in which the removal or 'death' of some economic or other sector sees another stepping in. Alternatively, the remainder of the city might carry on without what proves to be a nonvital part of its environment. Pittsburgh provides an example—flourishing despite the departure of the steel industry.

Evolution helps to explain urban survival. Tokyo was once Edo—little more than a village seat of government terribly prone to fire. It suffered blazes so frequently and destructively they became known as *Edo no hana* (the 'flowers of Edo').[55] Its massive fires burned more than 1,000 homes nearly every winter as village became city. More than 100,000 of its residents died and most of its structures were consumed in the 1657 Great Fire of Meireki. We read of the same happening in 1923, yet Tokyo housed more than 7 million people by the late 1930s. The population dropped sharply during World War II. After the conflict, the remaining 3 million sought refuge in what remained after Allied bombing destroyed 750,000 houses.[56] Today, Tokyo is not only the world's most populous urban area; it is also one of its greatest financial centres. Venice was the hub of Mediterranean maritime commerce six centuries ago. No longer, but it has evolved to become a centre of art, architecture and tourism. Jerusalem was ravaged by Babylonians (in 604 BCE), Romans (repeatedly, including 70 CE), Persians (614 CE) and Christians (1099 CE), with slaughter and expulsion accompanied by

---

54 Greg Woolf, *The Life and Death of Ancient Cities: A Natural History*, New York, NY: Oxford University Press, 2020, 358.

55 Material in this paragraph comes from the following sources: Carola Hein, 'Resilient Tokyo: Disaster and Transformation in the Japanese City', in *The Resilient City: How Modern Cities Recover from Disaster*, Lawrence J. Vale and Thomas I. Campanella (eds), New York, NY: Oxford University Press, 2005, 213–34, at 216, doi.org/10.1093/oso/9780195175844.003.0016; Max Page, 'The City's End: Past and Present Narratives of New York's Destruction', in *The Resilient City: How Modern Cities Recover from Disaster*, Lawrence J. Vale and Thomas I. Campanella (eds), New York, NY: Oxford University Press, 2005, 75–93, at 77, doi.org/10.1093/oso/9780195175844.003.0008; Mark Twain, *The Innocents Abroad*, Ware, UK: Wordsworth, 2010, 138; and Julian Beinart, 'Resurrecting Jerusalem', in *The Resilient City: How Modern Cities Recover from Disaster*, Lawrence J. Vale and Thomas I. Campanella (eds), New York, NY: Oxford University Press, 2005, 181–210, at 182, doi.org/10.1093/oso/9780195175844.003.0014.

56 Kumagai and Nojima, 'Urbanization and Disaster Mitigation in Tokyo', 58, 61.

deliberate wasting of its buildings. Speaking (or rather writing) of Rome, the city of an estimated 1 million people during the height of empire saw its population fall to about 30,000 during the sixth century CE when Justinian ruled in Constantinople; it is home to nearly 4 million people today and is Italy's capital.[57] Even what passed for large cities in ancient times—Ur and Hierakonpolis (or Nekhen) among them—in most cases had miniscule populations by today's standards. Ur is thought to have had 65,000; Hierakonpolis maybe 10,000 people. Hamburg, Germany, lost 42,600 killed during a single week of Allied bombing in World War II.[58] The pile would have been 12.3 kilometres high if the rubble of 1945 Berlin had been stacked on a US football field after months of bombing and the Soviet invasion in the same conflict;[59] it is thought 35,000 of its citizens died during the war. Few of the no-longer-remaining ancient cities reached a population of 100,000 or more. Central America's Teotihuacan was one. Tenochtitlan, on the site of what is now Mexico City, is another. Only 40,000 of Cologne's pre–World War II population of 700,000 citizens remained before fighting ceased in Germany with the others having lost their lives or fled.[60] Cologne flourishes today.

Adapt or don't date

> The Philadelphia yellow-fever epidemic of 1793 had been as savage as an attack of bubonic plague and doomed the supremacy of Philadelphia among the cities of North America.[61]
>
> —David McCullough, *The Path between the Seas*

> Dense urban conglomerations of humans have the power to exert, on wild animals and plants, novel and unusually strong selection pressures.[62]
>
> —Menno Schilthuizen, *Darwin Comes to Town*

57   Elizabeth Kolbert, 'The spread: How pandemics shape human history', *The New Yorker*, 6 April 2020, 58–61, at 58.

58   Adrian Mourby, 'Where are the world's most war-damaged cities?', *The Guardian*, 17 December 2015, available from: www.theguardian.com/cities/2015/dec/17/where-world-most-war-damaged-city; and Jeffry M. Diefendorf, *In the Wake of War: The Reconstruction of German Cities after World War II*, New York, NY: Oxford University Press, 1993, 10–11.

59   Calculated from statistics provided in Diefendorf, *In the Wake of War*, 15.

60   ibid., 16. A very few ancient cities may have hit the 1 million mark. Angkor Wat, in what is now Cambodia, is thought to have reached that number, in addition to Rome.

61   David McCullough, *The Path between the Seas: The Creation of the Panama Canal, 1870–1914*, New York, NY: Touchstone, 1977, 141.

62   Menno Schilthuizen, *Darwin Comes to Town: How the Urban Jungle Drives Evolution*, New York, NY: Picador, 2018, 94.

No less impressive minds than those of Charles Darwin and Plato hint at Schilthuizen's conclusion above. Darwin observed that the more varied the plants in a plot of land, the greater is the vegetation's cumulative weight of life.[63] Plato believed diversity was the key to a city prospering. Urban areas' variety gives rise to strengths, allowing them to adapt to changing conditions and pull through hard times. Cities are definitive examples of synergy, each being far more than the sum of very different yet complementary parts. New York City today is much different than it was 100 years ago. Less a port of call for ships than in decades past, it is a provider of financial and other services as never before. Its internal and ever-changing variety go a long way towards explaining its successful transformations.

Ecosystems are an effective way of thinking about urban areas because cities are, as we have noted, themselves systems—very complex systems, with megacities the most complex of all. That's why any attempt to simplify by comparing urban areas to simpler systems such as ant colonies or beehives (or the human body) quickly reaches a limit in its value as a model. (If you do buy into the 'a city is like a beehive or ant colony', do you consider yourself a drone, a worker or the queen? No options for manager, executive or professional athlete.) As we saw above, and unlike most organisms, urban areas—and often their components and sub-systems—can adapt quickly to change not only socially but also physically. Those evolutions can see buildings, businesses, communities or select species altered or entirely replaced, as often occurs in nature's ecosystems when climate change or other system-altering events assert themselves. The American cliff swallow, a type of bird, underwent human-inspired, construction-induced evolution in the space of a single generation (admittedly, a single human generation and lots of swallow generations). These birds started nesting in Nebraska's highway bridges and culverts in the early 1980s. At the time, the birds nesting in these humanmade structures had wings about the same length as those choosing to nest in natural features. Researchers studying multiple generations found that, by the 2010s, roadkill carcasses had wings half a centimetre longer than survivors along what is a most dangerous environment for birds (roads, urban or otherwise). The pretty obvious conclusion: long wings kill. Shorter wings provide quicker lift and more agile turning than those on their 767 colleagues (think fighter jets).[64] (This would seem to open a PhD topic for some aspiring biologist willing to do a similar study of metropolitan pigeons and their country cousins. There would be no lack of subjects.)

---

63 Reader, *Cities*, 141–42.
64 Schilthuizen, *Darwin Comes to Town*, 99–100.

Swallows (those with shorter wings anyway) are not alone as quick adapters thanks to humans influencing their habitats. Recent studies found urban field mice performed on par with their country cousins on a simple control task of digging through debris to find a treat. Make the task more difficult, however, and the urban-born were successful 77 per cent of the time while the rural mice were so on only 52 per cent of occasions. Nature (heredity) or nurture ('learned' cleverness)? The mice tested had been acclimatised in a laboratory for a year after being captured, but mouse memory could explain the difference if nurture is the reason. Future experiments will raise youngsters born to each group for future testing.[65]

European researchers collected eggs of the triangulate cobweb spider (*Steatoda triangulosa*) from both the Italian countryside and the cities of Milan, Nice and Munich. They put the resultant eight-legged youngsters into boxes with a divider down the middle. One half of the box was lit, the other kept dark, but the arachnids could move to either side with no problem. Two out of three from rural environments built their webs on the Dark Side while half the city types instead chose the Rebel Alliance option. Researchers concluded that urban spiders had evolved to be less afraid of light (and, I venture, further genetic or epigenetic mechanisms could be at play that encourage building webs where lights would attract prey).[66] Reflecting the fact there are plenty of doctoral topics out there for those interested in urban biological studies, another group found that city-bred Túngara frogs (*Engystomops pustulosus*) sing more often and have more complex tunes than their rural cousins. They also stopped vocalising more quickly when a human approached. Rural frogs put in the big city retained their old ways, putting them at the double disadvantage of missing out on dates and being in greater risk of human contact.[67] Urban-dwelling members of a fourth species, *Homo sapiens*, are more likely to have tuberculosis-resistant genes than those from rural communities, demonstrating that while humans might not be able to evolve as quickly as their city, they might—given time—improve their chances of surviving in its environs.[68] Perhaps less exciting than these physiological evolutions,

---

65   'Country bumpkins and city slickers', *The Economist*, [London], 23 January 2021, 65.
66   'Underneath the lamplight: Evolution', *The Economist*, [London], 10 November 2018, 77–78.
67   'Brekekekex koax koax: Animal behavior', *The Economist*, [London], 15 December 2018, 17. Other species that have adapted to urban living include mosquitoes (in London's subway) and lizards in Los Angeles. The latter have fewer dorsal scales—an apparent adjustment to the megacity's hotter environment. For both, see Brendan I. Koerner, 'Street life', *WIRED*, 27 October 2019, 72–85, at 78, 79.
68   Schilthuizen, *Darwin Comes to Town*, 228.

social changes can also occur over very short timespans. The example of McDonald's gentrifying Hong Kong customers' behaviour has something of a match in the marital arena. Urban folk seek different characteristics in their mates than their rural cousins and are quicker to find those with common backgrounds or qualities—a matter of a bigger selection pool thanks to density and sheer numbers.[69] Jolts to a major urban area can fundamentally spur evolution in its relationship with the country of which it is a part. Before the devastation of Tokyo's 1923 earthquake, Osaka was Japan's centre of railway development. Thereafter, reconstruction of the Japanese capital saw it become a commuter city served by a dramatically expanded rail service, promoting its national primacy.[70]

Defining urban areas and megacities

Spartans would never have had cities as 'Spartans despised city walls, bragging that "our young men are our walls and our battlements the tips of their spears".'[71]

—Bettany Hughes, *Istanbul*

For archaeologists and historians the most meaningful difference between a village and a city has nothing to do with size; it is instead a measure of social and economic differentiation … A place occupied exclusively by people who had left the land to become full-time craftsmen, merchants, priests and civil servants was a city, while anywhere occupied principally by farmers was a village. By and large, only farmers lived in villages, while 'a key defining feature of a town or city is that farmers don't live in them'.[72]

—John Reader, *Cities*

As one distinguished professor remarked, 'a scientist would rather use someone else's toothbrush than another scientist's terminology'.[73]

—Murray Gell-Mann, 'Complex Adaptive Systems'

---

69   Jeb Brugmann, *Welcome to the Urban Revolution: How Cities Are Changing the World*, New York, NY: Bloomsburg, 2009, 188.
70   Michael Fisch, *An Anthropology of the Machine: Tokyo's Commuter Train Network*, Chicago, IL: University of Chicago Press, 2018, 32, doi.org/10.7208/chicago/9780226558691.001.0001.
71   Hughes, *Istanbul*, 36.
72   Reader, *Cities*, 16.
73   Murray Gell-Mann, 'Complex Adaptive Systems', in *Complexity: Metaphors, Models, and Reality*, George A. Cowan, David Pines and David Meltzer (eds), SFI Studies in the Sciences of Complexity, Proc. Vol. XIX, Boston, MA: Addison-Wesley, 1994, 17–45, at 17.

Spartans aside, walls were among the defining characteristics present in many early urban areas. The Chinese character for 'city' is also that for 'wall'. Other physical structures were key to ancient Greek understandings of what separated a city from a mere village or town. The writer Pausanias turned his nose up at Phoenicians' claims of city status for a small town 'because it had no government offices, no gymnasium, no theater, no market, no piped water supply … It was these buildings and utilities that distinguished a city from a mere huddle of village houses.'[74] Aristotle had his own discriminators. He:

> thought that the ideal city should contain no more than 5,000 citizens which he considered was the largest number of people who could conveniently meet together to govern themselves, and that the ideal size of a city should be one in which a shout at one end could be heard at the other.[75]

(He did not count women, freemen or slaves; obviously, the '#MeToo' movement had a few millennia to go before making itself evident.) Aristotle also recognised the need for a diverse population—one comprising 'different kinds of men; similar people cannot bring a city into existence'.[76] Other definitions require the presence of a cathedral, though author Brenna Hassett pointed to the absurdity of requiring a cathedral as a necessary condition, noting that Chinese urban areas of 15 million people lack both building and bishop. Witold Rybczynski similarly observed that the existence of a cathedral required no minimum population, meaning cities by this definition might otherwise qualify as a mere town.[77]

Aristotle notwithstanding, the definitions above require buildings or other structures of some sort, often ignoring the vital characteristic: the presence of people. People not only build and populate the walls, offices, theatres and cathedrals, but also link cities to the countryside on which they rely at least in part for food, water and other needs and which in turn seeks the goods and services only a city can provide. That did not mean—and does not mean—the urban goods and services provided necessarily originated in the

74   Lewis Mumford, *The City in History: Its Origins, Its Transformations, and Its Prospects*, New York, NY: MJF, 1961, 133–34. Also see Robin Osborne and Andrew Wallace-Hadrill, 'Cities of the Ancient Mediterranean', in *The Oxford Handbook of Cities in World History*, Peter Clark (ed.), Oxford, UK: Oxford University Press, 2016, 49–65, at 49.
75   Rybczynski, *City Life*, 36; and Sennett, *Building and Dwelling*, 82.
76   As quoted in Sennett, *Building and Dwelling*, 6–7.
77   Brenna Hassett, *Built on Bones: 15,000 Years of Urban Life and Death*, New York, NY: Bloomsbury Sigma, 2017, 94, doi.org/10.5040/9781472948311; and Rybczynski, *City Life*, 38.

urban area. Cities have since their earliest existence tended to connect not only with their immediate surroundings but also with other, often distant, population centres. Coastal European, Asian and African Mediterranean cities were less separated by the sea than brought together by the trade its waters allowed.[78] Urban ties represented mutual dependence between the Roman Empire's urban areas. Gaul's wealthy Lyon sent large amounts of financial aid when fire devastated Rome in 64 CE.[79]

It would be nice to think we have cast aside such seemingly random attempts to define urban areas and settled on a uniform understanding of these phenomena in which more than half of humankind now resides. No such luck. Various countries define 'urban areas' as concentrations of anything from 200 people up to 50,000 or more. For the United States, it's 2,500 people.[80] India chooses to be a bit more on the upside with a mark of 5,000; Egypt decided 20 times that is a better choice, its requirement being 100,000, as is China's. India's definition of a city requires 75 per cent or more of the male population to be working in other than the agricultural sector (again, where's the #MeToo movement?).[81] Other definitions simply make the head hurt. The European Commission will tell you that an urban centre is a contiguous stretch with a minimum of 50,000 people and a population density of 300 people per square kilometre or more, which must be interesting to hear in each of the commission's many languages.[82]

But there is much more to urban areas than populations and buildings, as Pausanias, Aristotle and many others realised. A Middle Ages German saying, *Stadtluft macht Frei* ('City air makes you free'), had both social and legal meanings. Larger urban areas were places where society's rigid feudal hierarchy held less sway. A person could advance in social or economic status in ways not possible in rural communities where serfs were bound to the

---

78 Osborne and Wallace-Hadrill, 'Cities of the Ancient Mediterranean', 49.

79 Susan Ford Wiltshire, *Greece, Rome, and the Bill of Rights*, Norman, OK: University of Oklahoma Press, 1992, 180.

80 Hannah Ritchie and Max Roser, 'Urbanization', *Our World in Data*, 2018, [Updated 2019], available from: ourworldindata.org/urbanization; and Lewis Dijkstra, Ellen Hamilton, Somik Lall and Sameh Wahba, 'How do we define cities, towns, and rural areas?', *Sustainable Cities Blog*, Washington, DC: The World Bank, 10 March 2020, available from: blogs.worldbank.org/sustainablecities/how-do-we-define-cities-towns-and-rural-areas.

81 Gregory Scruggs, 'How much public space does a city need?', *Next City*, [Philadelphia, PA], 7 January 2015, available from: nextcity.org/daily/entry/how-much-public-space-does-a-city-need-UN-Habitat-joan-clos-50-percent; and William H. Frey and Zachary Zimmer, 'Defining the City', in *Handbook of Urban Studies*, Ronan Paddison (ed.), London: Sage, 2001, 15–35, at 26, doi.org/10.4135/9781848608375.n2.

82 ibid.

land and its owner. Economic success in a medieval town or city could raise one's place in the social hierarchy in ways unheard of in rural environments, as could assuming responsibilities in support of the local government. A serf who fled to such a built-up feature and managed to remain free of his or her master for the magic period of one year and a day legally became a part of the town or city and was no longer responsible to their rural master. Thereafter, they were largely free of bonds (unless they entered another subordination such as apprenticeship). Women, in particular, found their lives opened to new opportunities unavailable in rural communities.[83]

Several recent attempts to define urban areas draw on more-than-population or more-than-buildings features. In so doing, they have added a deluge of descriptions—ones pertaining to the world's largest and most interconnected cities. 'Global cities' are principal points in the world's economic system, some of which are less competitors than complements to one another as urban areas specialise in functions necessary to others' products or services.[84] (Others prefer the term 'alpha cities' to global cities. Perhaps urbanists are sometimes like those scientists who 'would rather use someone else's toothbrush than another's terminology'.)[85] As one author put it, global cities collectively offer 'a set of financial, legal, and other specialized service tasks which the global economy performs; these "global functions" are parcelled out to different cities in a network in which each city plays a particular role'.[86] Global cities contrast with those known by another term: 'world cities'. Whereas 'global cities are commanding nodes of the global economic system, world cities articulate large national economies into the global system'[87] (I'm not sure I fully grasp the difference either). Others are 'gateway cities'—distinguished by being thoroughfares for migrants to other countries.[88] Then there are

---

83   Sennett, *Building and Dwelling*, 120–21.

84   Aaron M. Renn, 'What is a global city?', *New Geography*, 6 December 2012, available from: www.newgeography.com/content/003292-what-is-a-global-city.

85   Gell-Mann, 'Complex Adaptive Systems', 17.

86   Sennett, *Building and Dwelling*, 101.

87   James K. Mitchell, 'Introduction', in *Crucibles of Hazard: Mega-Cities and Disasters in Transition*, James K. Mitchell (ed.), New York, NY: United Nations University, 1999, Note b to Table 1.2, p. 5. See also Saskia Sassen, *The Global City: New York, London, Tokyo*, Princeton, NJ: Princeton University Press, 2001, 349, doi.org/10.2307/j.ctt2jc93q.

88   For discussions of these various city types and even variations on some of these definitions, see Sassen, *The Global City*, 27–43; Parag Khanna, 'When cities rule the world', *Featured Insights*, McKinsey & Company, 1 February 2011, available from: www.mckinsey.com/featured-insights/urbanization/when-cities-rule-the-world; and International Organization for Migration (IOM), *Migrants and Cities: New Partnerships to Manage Mobility*, World Migration Report 2015, Geneva: IOM, 2015, available from: www.iom.int/world-migration-report-2015.

'critical cities', so labelled because of their security importance either to a foreign power (Cairo is cited as an example for the United States) or to their own national government (as instability, financial troubles or some other problem in these cities could undermine the viability of national authorities).[89] Still other definitions seek to discriminate between a physical expanse of built-up and densely populated terrain (an 'urban area') and a 'metropolitan area' that includes a built-up/densely populated area and all the surrounding territory linked to it economically. A metropolitan area therefore can be—and generally is—much larger than the urban area that is a part of it. Paris, the urban area, for example, is only one-fifth the size of Paris, the metropolitan area.[90] Adding to the potential confusion (and that potential is considerable), the United States uses the term 'urbanised areas', Australia uses 'urban centres', Canada 'population centres' and the United Kingdom 'built-up urban areas' (as somehow contrasted with built-up nonurban areas or non-built-up urban areas?). Adding to our enjoyment: what is meant by identical or nearly identical terms can differ depending on who is speaking. New Zealand's 'urban areas' include rural terrain—as do many areas of what China refers to as urban, with their claims of having massive urban agglomerations that exceed Tokyo or Jakarta in population incompatible with most usage and our definition to come.[91] Some claim Chongqing, China, has the largest population of any city in the world given an administrative area that is roughly equivalent in size to Austria. Much of what falls within those boundaries, however, is rural and thus does not qualify as an urban area by most definitions. For any still not convinced that one could drown in this sea of descriptions, a Strategic Studies Group on Megacities convened by the chief of staff of the US Army chose 'context, scale, density, connectedness, and flow' to describe a megacity, further muddying the waters by concluding that 'one of the hallmarks of megacities is rapid hetero and homogeneous

89   P.H. Liotta and James F. Miskel (*The Real Population Bomb: Megacities, Global Security and the Map of the Future*, Kindle edn, Dulles, VA: Potomac Books Inc., 2012, 48), as quoted in Phil Williams and Werner Selle, *Military Contingencies in Megacities and Sub-Megacities*, Carlisle, PA: Strategic Studies Institute and US Army War College Press, December 2016, 28.

90   Wendell Cox, 'Largest 1,000 cities on Earth: World urban areas—2015 edition', *New Geography*, 2 February 2015, available from: www.newgeography.com/content/004841-largest-1000-cities-earth-world-urban-areas-2015-edition. China's broad definition of urban area—one that allows considerable interspersion of expanses of rural terrain—may in some cases be better understood in terms of metropolitan areas. That is particularly true as commuters take fast trains, allowing them to travel to and from work from distant locations that are noncontiguous with those places of employment. For more on the increasing number of Chinese commuters choosing to rely on this mode of transport, see 'Build it and they will go', *The Economist*, [London], 27 February 2021, 35.

91   Cox, 'Largest 1,000 cities on Earth'; and *Demographia World Urban Areas*, 15th edn, 5n.9.

population growth that outstrips city governance capability'.[92] Then there are definitions that ignore the reality on the ground as well as trouble the mind. A contiguous built-up area otherwise meeting a population threshold might not qualify as an urban area if it spills across a state, provincial or some other administrative boundary. The Philippine Government grossly underestimates what constitutes the megacity of Manila as an urban area. Indistinguishably blended though they are with the greater mass of urbanisation, contiguous spaces that would otherwise be considered urban are not because they lie in Rizal, Bulacan, Laguna or Cavite provinces rather than the National Capital Region.[93]

So, it appears safe to conclude that definitions and terms for 'urban area' or 'city' are anything but consistent. Some seem not to survive beyond the single article that proposes them. 'Dragon kings' are built-up areas described as extraordinarily large, wealthy or otherwise exceptional[94]— 'dragon' because they are exceptional beasts even though they share some characteristics with other cities and 'king' as they possess disproportionate wealth compared with other of a country's urban areas. Numerous and unnecessarily convoluted as these and other labels seem to be, they can help us understand just how varied, influential, complex and powerful are urban areas.

Seeking a practical and easy-to-envision definition rather than inventing yet another one, for the purposes of this book, an urban area is 'a continuously built-up landmass of urban development containing no rural land—one best thought of as the lighted area that can be observed from an airplane (or satellite) on a clear night'.[95] It is a definition whose character is not new. The Romans used the term *extrema tectorum* to define a city, which meant the expanse of a contiguous built-up area.[96]

---

92   Marc Harris, Robert Dixon, Nicholas Melin, Daniel Hendrex, Richard Russo and Michael Bailey, *Megacities and the United States Army: Preparing for a Complex and Uncertain Future*, Chief of Staff of the Army Strategic Studies Group, June 2014, 11, 12, available from: www.army.mil/e2/c/downloads/351235.pdf.

93   Cox, 'Largest 1,000 cities on Earth'.

94   V.I. Yukalov and D. Sornette, 'Statistical outliers and dragon-kings as Bose-condensed droplets', *Physics and Society*, 7 May 2012, available from: arxiv.org/abs/1205.1364.

95   Adapted from *Demographia World Urban Areas*, 15th edn, 5.

96   *Atlas of Urban Expansion: Monitoring Global Urban Expansion Program*, [Online], Paris: Sciences Po Urban School, n.d., available from: www.sciencespo.fr/ecole-urbaine/en/actualites/atlas-urban-expansion.html.

What, then, is a megacity and what makes it stand out among other urban areas? Extraordinary complexity is part (but not all) of it—complexity such as that found in Chicago a little more than a century ago:

> Let us take a tour down Halstead Street, the center of Chicago's great immigrant ghetto, around 1910. The street was twenty-two miles [35 km] long, and for the most of it filled with a teeming population. Were we to start at its northern end and move south, we would be conscious that it was filled with 'foreigners,' but at every place with different kinds of foreigners, all mixed together. A native might tell us that a certain few blocks were Greek or Polish or Irish, but were one actually to look at particular houses or apartment building[s], one would find the ethnic groups jumbled together.[97]

Heterogeneity of population might be—and in most cases is—characteristic of a megacity. But it, too, is not on its own sufficient to make an urban area a megacity. The many different authorities immersed in those oceans of people add additional complexity that moves us nearer to an understanding of these phenomena. The megacity/urban area of Manila encompasses at least 85 municipalities spread over seven provinces (the Philippine Government's definition of Manila notwithstanding). (The National Capital Region includes only 17 local governments.)[98] This is impressive, but it pales in comparison with Tokyo's 2,400 separate governments of one kind or another distributed over seven prefectures.[99] The megacities of Jakarta and Mexico City are among those that formally changed their names to recognise the multiplicity of governments that combine to make up the whole. 'Jabodetabek' calls on the quintet of primary cities that are among its parts for this moniker (Jakarta, Bogor, Depok, Tangerang and Bekasi).[100] Mexico City has officially become Zona Metropolitana del Valle de México or Valley of Mexico. The megacity of

---

97   Richard Sennett, *The Uses of Disorder: Personal Identity & City Life*, New York, NY: Alfred A. Knopf, 1970, 53–54.
98   Brian H. Roberts, 'Risk and resilience in Asian cities: Case study of Manila', n.d., available from: www.academia.edu/9265596/Risk_and_Resilience_in_Asian_Cities_Case_Study_of_Manila.
99   The World Bank, *East Asia's Changing Urban Landscape: Measuring a Decade of Spatial Growth*, Urban Development Series, Washington, DC: The World Bank, 2015, 33, 56, 57, available from: www.worldbank.org/content/dam/Worldbank/Publications/Urban%20Development/EAP_Urban_Expansion_full_report_web.pdf, doi.org/10.1596/978-1-4648-0363-5.
100   Deden Rukmana, 'The megacity of Jakarta: Problems, challenges and planning efforts', *Indonesia's Urban Studies Blog*, 29 March 2014, available from: indonesiaurbanstudies.blogspot. com/2014/03/the-megacity-of-jakarta-problems.html; and Wendell Cox, 'The evolving urban form: Jakarta (Jabotabek)', *New Geography*, 30 May 2011, available from: www.newgeography.com/content/002255-the-evolving-urban-form-jakarta-jabotabek.

Tokyo is likewise technically Tokyo–Yokohama, just as Japan's second-largest urban area is Osaka–Kobe–Kyoto.[101] The City of Los Angeles—the political entity at the core of the megacity that draws on its name—is home to but 4 million or so residents. The megacity of Los Angeles includes a much larger collection of smaller cities such as Santa Monica, Pacific Palisades, Hermosa Beach, Burbank, Port of Los Angeles, Beverly Hills, Simi Valley, Moorpark, Calabasas, Anaheim, Hollywood, and many more. Together, they are home to more than 15 million people. Most of those somewhat smaller administrative entities have their own mayors, city councils, police, fire and recreation departments, and many other elements of government.[102] Some instead choose to share capabilities in the interests of cost and practicality. Virtually all have some form of cooperative agreement in place so their collective resources can come together should a situation overwhelm one or more of those many parts.

Whether because of a natural disaster, insurgency or combat operations, those leading and managing the various organisations lending a hand can be the difference between anarchy or order and survival for members of a population. General Charles Krulak, former commandant of the US Marine Corps, described how a military force in a city might find itself providing relief to suffering citizens on one block, dealing with demonstrations on an adjacent block and fighting with an enemy force on yet another—what he called the 'three-block war'. Given the presence of both formal and social media representatives in the largest and most influential of the planet's cities, decisions made by even the most junior leader can have consequences that reverberate around the world and impact on an undertaking's ultimate success, leading Krulak to also coin the term 'strategic corporal'.[103]

Massive populations spread between multiple authorities; vast geographic spread (Tokyo covers more than eight times the land area of Hawai`i's island of Oahu); complexity born of those many administrative officialdoms, mixes of ethnicities and many languages; myriad internal and external

---

101 Cox, 'The evolving urban form: Jakarta'.

102 Russell W. Glenn, 'Megacities: The good, the bad, and the ugly', *Small Wars Journal*, 17 February 2016, available from: smallwarsjournal.com/jrnl/art/megacities-the-good-the-bad-and-the-ugly.

103 Charles C. Krulak, 'The strategic corporal: Leadership in the three block war', *Marines Magazine*, January 1999, available from: apps.dtic.mil/sti/pdfs/ADA399413.pdf; and George F. Will, 'Winning the "three-block war"', *The Washington Post*, 14 April 2004, available from: www.washingtonpost.com/archive/opinions/2004/04/14/winning-the-three-block-war/f72ecf07-870b-4d5c-8ce1-a54562d1546c/?noredirect=on&utm_term=.8a82c56fb9bb.

economic, political, social and diplomatic connections; and a related influence that reaches far beyond local rural areas and very likely beyond national borders and nearby countries to extend to locations worldwide— all these are features found in many of the planet's largest urban areas. One must take all into account when planning for or responding to a disaster. Relying on longstanding definitions of a megacity based on population alone (at one time, any urban area with more than 1 million; later, any with more than 5, 8, then 9 and now 10 million, although at least one organisation still goes with 8 million) fails to take these other vital considerations into account.[104]

Avoiding the temptation to add another urban term to the already too many, we will, as said, instead retain a definition for 'urban area' already in use but recognise that a megacity is much more than merely a large population, defining it as *an urban area of extraordinary population size, geographic spread, physical and social complexity, interconnectedness, and similarly exceptional characteristics, to include influence with at least national and broader regional scope*.[105] More wordy than desirable, perhaps, but this is a definition that captures the varied aspects that make megacities stand out from less exceptional cities.

Some cities of more than 10 million do not qualify for megacity status using this definition. Though China's Tianjin and Chengdu have populations of more than 13 and 12 million, respectively, their broader regional and worldwide influence are limited. Tianjin's primary role is to act as Beijing's port; Chengdu's claims to fame are its popularity as a tourist destination and related status as home to giant pandas. The same might be argued for Dhaka, Bangladesh, which, with its 14.6 million residents within 324 square kilometres, is the most densely populated large city in the world.[106] Its influence beyond Bangladesh's national boundaries and other countries in the immediate vicinity, however, is rather limited.

---

104 Mitchell, 'Introduction', 14n.7. TomTom still considered a city of 8 million or more to be a megacity as of 2019. TomTom International BV, 'TomTom Traffic Index: Ranking 2019', [Online], Amsterdam: TomTom, 2019, [Updated 2021], available from: www.tomtom.com/en_gb/traffic-index/ranking/.

105 Definition from Russell W. Glenn, 'Ten million is not enough: Coming to grips with megacities' challenges and opportunities', *Small Wars Journal*, 25 January 2017, available from: smallwarsjournal.com/jrnl/art/ten-million-is-not-enough-coming-to-grips-with-megacities%E2%80%99-challenges-and-opportunities. [Emphasis added.]

106 A.M., Jacob, A. Allen and Larry P. Graham, Megacities and the proposed urban intervention model, Thesis, Monterey, CA: Naval Postgraduate School, June 2016, 8, available from: apps.dtic.mil/sti/pdfs/AD1026697.pdf.

In stark contrast, Singapore's population is just under 6 million. The populations of nearby Malaysian and Indonesian urban areas geographically, economically, socially and otherwise intertwined with Singapore are insufficient to take the total for the whole anywhere near 10 million. Yet, the city-state is the world's largest bunkering (ship refuelling) port, second-largest port in terms of volume and numbers of shipping containers, a port of call for 130,000 vessels annually, a significant economic power and a vital player in maintaining order in the Strait of Malacca—one of the world's busiest waterways through which almost one-third of the planet's sea trade transits annually (including 80 per cent of China's energy imports).[107] Singapore's interconnectedness, influence and other features qualify the island nation and its immediate urban surrounds in Malaysia and Indonesia as a megacity. While its population does not exceed 10 million, its numbers in that regard are nevertheless significant (it is, interestingly, an urban area that can by no means take its security for granted, dependent as it is on external sources for water, food and energy.[108] The systems approach to planning practised by the

---

107 'The long game: The road', *The Economist*, [London], 8 February 2020, 9; Demographia, *Demographia World Urban Areas*, 13th annual edition, Belleville, IL: Wendell Cox Consultancy, April 2017; *Demographia World Urban Areas*, 15th edn; Maritime and Port Authority of Singapore, 'Port statistics', [Online], Singapore: MPA, 2021, available from: www.mpa.gov.sg/who-we-are/newsroom-resources/research-and-statistics; Ship & Bunker News Team, '6 countries are responsible for almost 60% of all bunker sales', *Ship & Bunker*, [Vancouver, BC], 5 January 2016, available from: shipand bunker.com/news/world/608701-6-countries-are-responsible-for-almost-60-of-all-bunker-sales; World Shipping Council, 'About Liner Shipping', [Online], Washington, DC: World Shipping Council, 2018, available from: www.worldshipping.org/about-liner-shipping; and Marcus Hand, 'Malacca and S'pore Straits traffic hits new high in 2016, VLCCs fastest growing segment', *Seatrade Maritime News*, 13 February 2017, available from: www.seatrade-maritime.com/news/asia/malacca-and-s-pore-strait-traffic-hits-new-high-in-2016-vlccs-fastest-growing-segment.html. *Demographia World Urban Areas* (15th edn), from which we adapted our definition of 'urban area', confines urban areas to single nations except when 'there is virtual freedom of movement (principally labor) between the adjacent nations'. Including nearby Malaysian and Indonesian urban areas in the Singapore urban area thus breaks with the publication's definition twice over: once because movement between the pair of close countries does not qualify as sufficiently free and, second, as water separates them from Singapore and thus they are not strictly contiguous (there would be breaks in the illumination as viewed from above). Two points: first, I would argue that Singapore and those nearby Malaysian and Indonesian urban entities are so closely intertwined that we need to give a little slack here and recognise the inclusive Singapore urban area. Second, if the question is whether Singapore is a megacity, there is a strong argument that it so qualifies even if we deny membership to those two countries' urban parcels. For more, see discussion of 'International urban areas' in *Demographia World Urban Areas*, 16th edn, 6. For discussion of why movement within the so-called growth triangle of Singapore and nearby Malaysian and Indonesian urban areas is not free, see Philippe Revelli, 'Singapore, Malaysia, and Indonesia: A triangle of growth or a triangle of inequality?', *Equal Times*, [Brussels], 4 October 2016, available from: www.equaltimes.org/singapore-malaysia-and-indonesia-a?lang=en#.Xzq7xkl7kyk. Singapore material from the sources cited just above and Barber, *If Mayors Ruled the World*, 142.
108 Kent E. Calder, *Singapore: Smart City, Smart State*, Washington, DC: Brookings Institution Press, 2016, 123.

city-state's leaders makes sense given the interwoven dependencies in so many realms).[109] Whether or not one agrees that our more demanding definition of 'megacity' is appropriate, the following pages should make it clear that those urban areas so qualifying are fundamentally different to other cities in ways aside from the number of residents alone.

Understanding these exceptional urban areas requires understanding the systems of which they are a part and the many systems of which each of them is made. There may be no better example of a whole being more than the sum of its parts than a megacity. They are synergy at its finest.

More on megacity exceptionality

Size begets complexity.[110]

—Richard Sennett, *Building and Dwelling*

London also attracted incomers on a conspicuous scale because it possessed a set of attributes that individually were not unique, but that were combined within this vast metropolis to an exceptional degree ... London was also a financial centre, *the* financial centre ... incontestably still the world's richest and most tentacular metropolis.[111]

—Linda Colley, *The Gun, the Ship, and the Pen*

A study of London during the Second World War sets some particularly complex challenges. First, what is London? Before the war the Greater London or Metropolitan Police area covered 700 square miles [1,800 sq km]; the Greater London Town Planning or London Transport area 2000 square miles [5,200 sq km]; the County of London 116 [300]; the City of London 1; the London Telephone area 1200 [3,100]; the London Postal area 232 [600]; the London Electricity District 1840 [4,800]; the Metropolitan Water Board area 573 [1,500]; the London Main Drainage area 159 [410].[112]

—Philip Ziegler, *London at War*

---

109 ibid., 111.
110 Sennett, *Building and Dwelling*, 101.
111 Linda Colley, *The Gun, the Ship, and the Pen: Warfare, Constitutions, and the Making of the Modern World*, New York, NY: Liveright, 2021, 221, 370. [Emphasis in original.]
112 Ziegler, *London at War*, 2.

Why do megacity disasters merit a book? We've already partly crossed the bridge to an answer. Just as a town has a greater variety of worker types, commercial enterprises and buildings than a village, our definition tells us that megacities have many more such parts, relationships and interdependencies, greater complexity and broader variety than cities not qualifying for the label. Just as it is easier for the rich to get richer faster than the rest of us due to their existing wealth, with a megacity's diversity, interconnectedness and resultant influence come opportunities not accessible to other urban areas. Where have major corporations tended to choose to locate their research facilities and headquarters (and subordinate offices for that matter)? A cosy city populated by those representing a limited set of skills or a labour magnet that has attracted many of the talents it needs to perform at its peak? It is no coincidence that the top eight urban areas in terms of global company headquarters locations are megacities.[113] Where, in turn, are the most talented in a field likely to seek work? Where but in a city that offers frequent contact with those of similar interests, abilities and education—characteristics important in both professional and personal partnerships? There are simply fewer chances for opportunity to knock on your door when there are fewer people who need your skills.

This is no revelation. It was the larger urban areas that made possible what would have been impossible in villages or towns even in America's pre-revolutionary times. Sara Rogers of Boston asked to be freed from her membership of the city's First Baptist Church so she could join another of the same denomination.[114] Her request was granted—something a good deal less likely in a rural environment or smaller urban area where social strictures tended to be tighter and where finding a second church of her chosen faith could entail lengthy travel. Megacities are in a class of their own—like but in important ways unlike others. And, yes, while size is only one of the characteristics that makes a megacity stand out, it is a significant one as the first pair of quotations opening this section makes clear. Activities taking place in them will draw more attention—be it praise or condemnation—regardless of the undertaking at hand. The punishment dealt to Puerto Rico by one of 2017's major hurricanes was in many ways more devastating and longer felt than that dished out by those

113 Dobbs et al., *Urban World*, 9, 37.
114 Benjamin Carp, *Rebels Rising: Cities and the American Revolution*, Oxford, UK: Oxford University Press, 2007, 114, doi.org/10.1093/acprof:oso/9780195304022.001.0001.

storms in Houston, Miami and Tampa–St Petersburg, but it was the last three that received the bulk of US federal government attention.[115] Bigger urban areas draw more consideration and resources when disaster strikes.

Megacities are also a relatively new phenomenon—exceptional but no longer unusual given the existence of 35 in 2020. Babylon—perhaps humankind's first great city—had a population of between 200,000 and 300,000 people. The tremendously influential Athens batted way above its numbers of approximately 100,000 people. We know Rome achieved the 1 million mark; it did so just before the birth of Christ and that number does not include the many smaller cities in its nearby environs.[116] It wouldn't be until the first half of the twentieth century that a city reached a population of 10 million (New York City).

There are towns, perhaps even the occasional city, that are largely self-sufficient. Not so megacities. A megacity is both feeder and fed. It has far greater reach, requirements and relationships than other urban areas. Feeder because it offers more opportunities for the talented. Fed because it benefits from those talents. Feeder because it is more willing to accept individuals of differing demography than populations in more conservative environments. Fed because it provides acceptance and jobs elsewhere less likely to be at hand. Prejudice unquestionably raises its ignorant head in these exceptional urban areas, but those demonstrating the backward practices within tend to be a marginalised minority; their proportions skew towards larger values when raw population numbers are smaller. Feeder, too, as the outputs of megacities in terms of goods and services find their way to consumers elsewhere even as the urban folk are fed on what those outside locations offer in the way of food, water and other essentials.[117] There are many more of these symbiotic relationships when a megacity is involved. Understanding this will help us better appreciate megacities and their challenges when it comes to handling catastrophes.

---

115 Smith, *Cities*, 258–59.
116 Bollyky, *Plagues and the Paradox of Progress*, 22.
117 'Heterogeneous' can be a relative term. China, Japan, Republic of Korea and other countries with megacities are shockingly homogeneous in terms of countrywide population ethnicity. Their megacities reflect the lack of diversity, which pales in comparison with Los Angeles, London, Paris and several others, but Shanghai, Tokyo, Seoul and other megacities in the less-diverse countries are nevertheless more socially disparate than their national demographics generally.

Even if we ignore the international ties, we cannot escape being impressed by the vastness of megacities' supremacy, some aspects of which hold surprises. The world's largest urban footprint in terms of physical spread? New York City, with Boston–Providence and Tokyo–Yokohama next in line.[118] The world's least-dense megacity? Also New York City (followed by Los Angeles, which in turn significantly leads third place, Moscow).[119] New York City's primacy in terms of density is unsurprising given it is also the most spread out. And while we might envision Manhattan's shoulder-to-shoulder sidewalk congestion or Times Square on New Year's Eve, we recall that its suburbs are a good deal less dense than its cross-country sports rival and economic partner despite Los Angeles being spread over five counties, 160 municipalities and having nearly 40 per cent of California's population (California being the United States' most populous state by a good measure).[120] Demographers like to tell us that megacities are not the fastest-growing urban areas in the world. That statistic belongs to cities with populations between 100,000 and 500,000 people. What they are less likely to pass on is that the statistic does not mean smaller cities are catching up to the largest. We might find that the city of Mediumburg is growing at a rate of 10 per cent a year. With a population of half a million, that means it picks up another 50,000 next year. In the meantime, a megacity of a modest 15 million picks up a mere 1 per cent—which translates to 150,000 people. Several of the world's 35 megacities are growing at rates faster than a single percentage point—one reason that helps to explain why we can easily find writers claiming Lagos, Cairo, Dhaka, Jakarta or some other developing-world megacity is on the razor's edge of collapse. All those cities have their challenges, but it would be a sucker's bet to expect any to implode in coming months.

That should not be taken to mean that megacity status is permanent. A good argument can be made for Hong Kong being in the ranks of megacities as this book goes to print thanks to its role as a financial and trade bridge between the relatively free economies of the developed world and that of China. That status is increasingly under siege due to the heavy-handedness of the mainland government. According to *Bloomberg*, 2017's top-five financial centres were London, New York, Hong Kong, Singapore and Tokyo. *The Economist* notes Hong Kong 'is disproportionately useful to China [and] has a status within a body of international law and rules that

---

118 *Demographia World Urban Areas*, 16th edn, 40.
119 ibid.
120 Cox, 'Largest 1,000 cities on Earth', 376–77.

gives it seamless access to Western markets'.[121] As of 2019, its stockmarket was the fourth most highly valued in the world, behind only those in the United States, mainland China and Japan. The number of firms with regional headquarters grew from 744 when Hong Kong was still a British colony to 1,333 in 2019. The same *Economist* article reports growing concerns among international firms about China's influence in the city, with Singapore an attractive regional alternative. The tale of killing the goose that lays the golden eggs comes to mind. We will consider the oft-cited fragility of today's megacities further in later pages using Lagos as an example, looking at how it avoided medical disaster after a passenger with Ebola collapsed on entering a city airport terminal in 2014.

Imagine trying to coordinate with even a fraction of the 160 governments in Los Angeles in the aftermath of a massive earthquake much less with individual subauthorities within those governments such as police, fire, human services, parks offices, city engineers or community groups. NGO, IGO or assisting military leaders might consider themselves lucky to find their destination is Mexico City, Buenos Aires, London or São Paulo, where the number of jurisdictions is measured in the dozens. A phone call dispatching their organisations to Abidjan, Côte d'Ivoire, could be looked on with less joy once the leaders realise the number there is in the hundreds despite its population being only 5 million.[122] Areas administered by informal authorities (addressed later as 'other-governed areas') also make megacities exceptional. While a single criminal, dubiously legitimate political or other informal group might dominate a town or small city, no one such organisation is likely to rule a megacity. As in Karachi, Pakistan, the situation will tend to be multiple such enterprises dominating select slums, neighbourhoods or public and private sectors to extents varying over time and space.[123]

---

121 Gavin Finch, 'London retains its crown as world's top financial center', *Bloomberg*, 11 September 2017, available from: www.bloomberg.com/news/articles/2017-09-11/london-still-tops-financial-centers-despite-brexit-survey-says; and 'Seeing red: Turmoil in Hong Kong', *The Economist*, [London], 10 August 2019, 17–18.

122 Intergovernmental Panel on Climate Change (IPCC), 'Urban Areas', in *Climate Change 2014: Impacts, Adaptation, and Vulnerability. Part A: Global and Sectoral Aspects. Working Group II Contribution to the IPCC Fifth Assessment Report*, Cambridge, UK: Cambridge University Press, 2014, 535–612, at 577.

123 Laurent Gayer, *Karachi: Ordered Disorder and the Struggle for the City*, Noida, India: HarperCollins, 2014, 205. Examples throughout this book make it apparent just how dynamically the struggle for control of population sectors, physical terrain or functions such as water delivery evolved as groups competed for influence.

Jane Jacobs took on New York City's most powerful when authorities tried to route roads through neighbourhoods and parks, coming to the rescue of the city's underrepresented communities by arguing that progress should not spew communities aside like slush cast right and left by a snowplough's blade. She was not oblivious to the possible irony in her arguments, recognising that:

> great cities are not like towns, only larger. They are not like suburbs, only denser. They differ from towns and suburbs in basic ways, and one of these is that cities are, by definition, full of strangers … Strangers are far more common in big cities than acquaintances.[124]

What is a stranger? Certainly, it is the London visitor in Tokyo or Manila, but it is also the Manhattanite in Brooklyn's Red Hook or even another Manhattanite living but two blocks distant seen only through a Lyft driver's window during the daily commute to work.

Megacities' national, regional and global links reduce vulnerability to economic downturns. Downturns in one economic sector do not sink the whole as they might in smaller urban areas. New York, Tokyo and London weathered the recession of this century's first decade without undue long-term consequences. They will likely do so again as the world comes out of the Covid-19 crisis. And, for all the pollution urban areas put out and all their residents consume, there are environmental efficiencies inherent in city living, with larger cities offering more in this regard. The carbon footprint of residents in New York City is 71 per cent smaller than the average American's thanks to reliance on public transportation, the proximity of goods and services that means there are fewer reasons to drive, shorter distances to workplaces (10 per cent of workers walk to their jobs) and the efficiencies of vertical living.[125]

Breadth in the sources of residents' incomes means shoppers from a segment less affected by a downturn still have the financial means to provide enough custom to keep afloat merchants who would go under in smaller urban areas. An *Economist* article recognised this value in larger (and, importantly, more diverse) customer bases, noting that London's New Bond Street continued to flourish in 2017 while stores in smaller British

---

124 Jane Jacobs, *The Death and Life of Great American Cities*, New York, NY: Vintage, 1992, 30.
125 Sadik-Khan, *Street Fight*, 23–24.

cities and towns struggled.[126] Interestingly, there is a physical robustness to accompany the economic one. I recall being in Tel Aviv during the Second Intifada. Although Tel Aviv falls well short of megacity status (the urban area's population was somewhere between 3 and 4 million at the time), a bombing in one part of the city had no effect on the welfare of other parts. It more likely than not went unnoticed until the evening news broadcast or the next morning's papers arrived. Life moved on much as it would for a rainforest after a lightning strike caused a few acres of trees and their related ecosystem partners to perish. Megacities are sponges. They absorb any but the most violent of blows, quickly rebounding to form. New York City's recoveries from 9/11 and Hurricane Sandy come to mind while now, years later, Mosul, Iraq, labours to recover from the fighting in 2016–17, as does Marawi in the Philippines from its similar tragedy.

There is incongruity in this robustness. Megacity authorities will be less intimately familiar with their population than those in smaller urban areas. The mayor of a town or small city will not know each of their citizens by name, but they will be sufficiently in touch with representatives of its several communities and business interests to have a sense of their needs and demands. Not so for leaders in a megacity. First, as we have already noted, there will be no mayor whose duties span the entire metropolis. There will instead be tens or hundreds of mayors or their equivalents, each more or less familiar with their city while no-one knows the whole. In contrast, police leaders in urban areas of more limited size can less afford to assign officers to a single beat, instead giving them citywide or ever-changing responsibilities while a megacity counterpart might spend years in the same neighbourhood getting to know its residents, habits and quirks. Wise assignments will keep that officer's long-time beat in their jurisdiction even as promotions increase the expanse of the population looking to that officer for support. The same can be true of 'outsiders' whose jobs take them from city to city. An agent in the San Francisco Federal Bureau of Investigation (FBI) office recalled that while he was a street agent in New York City for 12 years, he tended to 'deal with local, lower-level authorities' whom he therefore grew to know well.[127] His position in the smaller Bay City and also during his time in Seattle

126 'Vacant spaces: Retail property', *The Economist*, [London], 16 December 2017, 58.
127 Bertram Fairries, Interview with Dr Russell W. Glenn, San Francisco, CA, 12 April 2016.

did not allow him the same intimacy of understanding as he often found himself coordinating with high-ranking urban officials in lieu of those on the street.

Urban urban legends: Myths of the megacity

> Meliboeus, stupidly I used to think that the City they call Rome was just like this town of ours here, the place we shepherds often bring the tender young lambs of our flocks.
> Just as puppies are like dogs, and kids are like mother goats, so I used to compare the great with the small.
> But Rome has lifted her head as high among other cities, as cypress trees tower among the weeping willows.[128]
>
> —Virgil, *Eclogue II*, 19–25

> Mega-cities may appear chaotic but most have life expectancies and provision for piped water, sanitation, schools and healthcare that are well above their national average—even if the aggregate statistics for each megacity can hide a significant proportion of their population living in very poor conditions. Some of world's fastest-growing cities over the last 50 years also have the best standards of living within their nation … City life can bring significant health benefits. Cities where environmental health hazards are reduced through provision of a safe water supply, sanitation, waste management and adequate shelter, and in which pollution is monitored and controlled, have lower mortality and morbidity rates.[129]
>
> —International Federation of Red Cross and Red Crescent Societies, *World Disasters Report 2010*

Imagine a pool table. It's a good metaphor for explaining megacity relationships given their complexity. Let's say that three numbered balls on the table represent the population in a rural environment, or maybe a few market towns tied to each other economically. We might hit one, two or maybe all three of that trio after striking the cue ball. Each could in turn impact others. Regardless, the consequences of our strike are

---

128 Virgil, *Eclogue II*, 19–25, as appears in Woolf, *The Life and Death of Ancient Cities*, 379.
129 International Federation of Red Cross and Red Crescent Societies (IFRC), *World Disasters Report 2010: Focus on Urban Risk*, Geneva: IFRC, 2010, 34, 95, available from: www.theisrm.org/public-library/IFRC%20(2010)%20World%20Disaster%20Report%20-%20Urban%20Risk.pdf.

easy to guess beforehand. Now let one rack of numbered balls represent 1 million people in a population. Tokyo's population becomes 38 racks of balls dispersed across the table's felt surface (that's 15 x 38 = 570 balls, for those wondering). Manila is 25 racks (375 balls), Los Angeles 15 (225). Strike that cue ball now. Determining just the second-order effects (the secondary collisions of any initial balls impacted by the cue ball) begins to boggle the mind. Figuring out third, fourth or higher-order effects would send you (or those on your staff, to which you wisely assign the task before going to lunch) fleeing the room. But while the effects of an event can be thought of as those pool balls knocking against each other, a lot of those balls are never jostled or even touched unless the strike of the cue ball is truly colossal, as would be the effects of a mammoth earthquake or attack with a weapon of mass destruction. The density of balls means they absorb the impact of any but these massive-effect events, containing the consequences to a limited space and portion of the population. Unless you are within hearing or sight of an explosion (which means being close, as buildings shield sound, sight and concussion waves, in addition to a city's near-constant ambient noise drowning out all but close or hugely loud events), chances are you will remain as unaware of the event as I was in Tel Aviv. You might hear the sirens or see the police, ambulance or fire vehicle race by, but you are unlikely to know what emergency it is responding to. The residents of a village or small town are far more prone to be aware of an event involving their population than those in a megacity. We might call the belief that everyone is quickly in the know regarding a disaster in larger urban areas the myth of instant knowledge. It is far from the only urban 'urban legend' misunderstanding of life in a megacity. The misleading models of urban areas as humans and slums as cancers could be considered others.

On the other hand, while instant knowledge is a myth, we must account for what complexity theory calls the 'butterfly effect'. Keeping it short and simple, experts tell us that some complex systems are vulnerable to even the tiniest of disturbances. The butterfly effect uses the example of one of those insects flapping its wings in Brazil later influencing the timing, size and even the creation or absence of a tornado in the United States through the many connections between the two events. It was the brainchild of a theorist whose research demonstrated that seemingly inconsequential actions in one location could influence gigantic results distant in time and place.[130] Unsurprisingly, it would be all but impossible to trace the connection between trigger and outcome, especially given the event involved is only one of many influencing the eventual result. But it does help us understand megacity complexity in terms of second, third and higher-order effects, even when the original trigger is more significant than insect wing–flapping. The 1923 earthquake that so devastated Tokyo resulted in violence against Koreans whom local Japanese blamed for the event. The quake also accelerated movement of the more well-to-do out of central Tokyo to the city's periphery. That movement in turn motivated the building of new roads and rail lines to these outskirts (second-order effects), to include new stations in places like Shibuya and Shinjuku that became major commercial hubs away from the city core. Their development was a third or higher-order effect influenced by or influencing many other intermediate events, decisions, motivations and ambitions.[131]

(Let's take a short break for a few seemingly random effects far removed from the initial cue-ball strike represented by the 1923 earthquake. Shibuya Crossing, the intersection outside the community's main railway station, is today said to be the busiest pedestrian intersection in the world, with some 2,500 people crossing from all directions at the same time. [Lights stop traffic so that pedestrians can cross in any direction they like. There is a coffee shop in a nearby shopping mall where you can sit and watch from above; it does a booming business.] That comes to about 1 million people a day. Shibuya Station is also where Tokyo's famous dog, Hachiko, waited every day for years to greet his master after the man died at work, never to return. His statue depicts a healthy-looking animal; kind locals must have made sure he did not lack for daily sustenance.

---

130 Edward N. Lorenz, 'Predictability: Does the flap of a butterfly's wings in Brazil set off a tornado in Texas?', Paper presented to American Association for the Advancement of Science 139th Meeting, Washington, DC, 29 December 1972, available from: eapsweb.mit.edu/sites/default/files/Butterfly_1972.pdf. The underlying concept for the butterfly effect came from Professor Edward Lorenz's 1961 runs on an early computer involving fluid flow in conjunction with weather forecasting. Wanting to analyse a particular run's solution in greater detail, he inserted the variable values into a subsequent run at an intermediate point, entering them with only three digits after the decimal instead of the six-digit accuracy used previously. This meant the variables were still accurate to the closest thousandth. For example, using a notional example regarding the probability of a given wind speed, initial runs used a probability of 46.909045, which in the later run was entered as 46.909. To his surprise, when the model was run with the truncated numbers versus the originals, the results were so different Lorenz thought it must have been a mistake. It was not. Instead, it was apparent that even very slight changes in initial conditions can have major effects in certain system types. Kerry Emanuel, 'Edward Norton Lorenz, 1917–2008', *Science* 320(5879) (23 May 2008): 1025, doi.org/10.1126/science.1159438; and Robert W. Reeves, 'Edward Lorenz revisiting the limits of predictability and their implications: An interview from 2007', *Bulletin of the American Meteorological Society* 95(5) (2014): 681–87, doi.org/10.1175/BAMS-D-13-00096.1.
131 Hein, 'Resilient Tokyo', 223; and Reid, *Confucius Lives Next Door*, 236.

Hachiko might be less happy with the situation today; two cats sheltered on the statue when I last passed by. All these and many, many more are effects countless orders removed of the 1923 quake—an event now nearly a century past.)[132]

Another misbelief—one sometimes innocently but mistakenly taken as true and other times deliberately used as a scare tactic by demagogues or corrupt others—is that of the urban immigrant as criminal. Those who have studied the situation find that crime rates are *lower* among this group than an urban area's long-time residents.[133] A look at a specific type of immigration being the major source of population growth in world megacities—that of individuals coming from other countries—falls by the wayside as well. While some large urban areas have foreign-born populations exceeding one-quarter of their total (Los Angeles, New York City and London among them), others are surprisingly sparse in this regard. Only 2.4 per cent of Tokyo's residents were born outside Japan. Seoul, Jakarta and São Paulo have even smaller percentages, with Mexico City falling below all these as recently as 2005. Less than 0.5 per cent of those living in Mexico's capital could stake claim to recent foreign origins.[134] Meanwhile, Sydney, Australia, alone reportedly had more foreign-born residents than did all of mainland China, as of 2019.[135]

The largest things in life attract mythmaking. One more among the small sample provided here deals with the belief that slums are just transition points that their residents seek to escape when opportunities or resources allow. Some residents certainly do want to move, but believing that slums are inherently unattractive places to live, to be fled at the first opportunity, is simply untrue. Slum living has attractions for many. Criminals find their densely packed living spaces and twisting passageways amenable to hiding from or escaping law enforcement. Informal forms of government often deliver services 'real' officials do not. These other-governments may protect slum residents from the worst of police abuses or other outsider incursions—

132 Makita Brottman, 'Richard Gere and Hachiko, the most faithful dog in history', *The Telegraph*, [London], 25 October 2014, available from: www.telegraph.co.uk/lifestyle/pets/11183010/Richard-Gere-and-Hachiko-the-most-faithful-dog-in-history.html.

133 Christopher Dickey, *Securing the City: Inside America's Best Counterterror Force—The NYPD*, New York, NY: Simon & Schuster, 2009, 254.

134 Lisa Benton-Short, Marie D. Price and Samantha Friedman, 'Globalization from below: The ranking of global immigrant cities', *International Journal of Urban and Regional Research* 29(4) (2005): 945–59, at 952, doi.org/10.1111/j.1468-2427.2005.00630.x.

135 Robert Guest, 'The Anglosphere and the Sinosphere drift apart', [*The World in 2020*], *The Economist*, [London], December 2019, 19, available from: worldin.economist.com/article/17310/edition2020anglosphere-and-sinosphere-drift-apart.

admittedly at a price. There are those in Egypt who remain in slums at least in part to evade paying taxes.[136] Others run successful businesses, earning a living without what would otherwise be hours-long commutes to work. Better to live comfortably poor in a slum than elsewhere impoverished.

The myth of fragility

> The microbe that felled one child in a distant continent yesterday can reach yours today and seed a global pandemic tomorrow.[137]
>
> —Joshua Lederberg, 1958 Nobel Prize winner in physiology or medicine

> Had the index case gotten the opportunity to contact persons in Lagos or Calabar—[another Nigerian city] where he was to deliver a lecture—it may have been a complete disaster.[138]
>
> —Folorunso Oludayo Fasina, senior lecturer, University of Pretoria, South Africa

It does not take long to find declarations of impending doom for developing-world megacities. Nearly two-thirds of Lagos's residents occupy slum dwellings,[139] as do about 72 per cent of all African city and town residents.[140] Some one-third of the population of Dhaka, Bangladesh, lives in slums, many in areas highly exposed to floods. It is true that many slum residents live a precarious existence, but the communities and cities of which they are a part tend to be far more robust than Chicken Littles would have us believe.[141]

---

136 Asar, 'Going Formal in Egypt', 101.

137 As quoted in Bollyky, *Plagues and the Paradox of Progress*, 7.

138 As quoted in Katherine Harmon Courage, 'How did Nigeria quash its Ebola outbreak so quickly?', *Scientific American*, 18 October 2014, available from: www.scientificamerican.com/article/how-did-nigeria-quash-its-ebola-outbreak-so-quickly/.

139 Shagun Mehrota, Claudia E. Natenzon, Ademola Omojola, Regina Folorunsho, Joseph Gilbride and Cynthia Rosenzweig, 'Framework for City Climate Risk Assessment', in *Cities and Climate Change: Responding to an Urgent Agenda. Volume 2*, Daniel Freire Hoornweg, Mila Lee, Marcus J. Bhada-Tata and Belinda Perinaz Yuen (eds), Washington, DC: The World Bank, February 2013, 182–241, at 193, available from: documents1.worldbank.org/curated/en/321111468182335037/pdf/626960PUB0v20B0iesClimateChangeVol2.pdf.

140 ActionAid International, *Unjust Waters: Climate Change, Flooding and the Protection of Poor Urban Communities*, Report, 5 March 2007, Johannesburg, South Africa: ActionAid International, 5, available from: actionaid.org/publications/2007/unjust-waters-climate-change-flooding-and-protection-poor-urban-communities.

141 Clare Stott and Mohammed Nadiruzzaman, *Disaster Risk Reduction in Dhaka City: From Urban Landscape Analysis to Opportunities for DRR Integration*, Uxbridge, UK: World Vision, 2014, 11; and Asif Ishtiaque and Md. Sofi Ullah, 'The influence of factors of migration on the migration status of rural–urban migrants in Dhaka, Bangladesh', *Human Geographies* 7(2) (2013): 45–52, at 50, doi.org/10.5719/hgeo.2013.72.45.

Roughly 60 per cent of Mumbai's population (known as Mumbaikars) lives in slums. The megacity is in fact home to Asia's largest slum, Dharavi, which has between 600,000 and 1 million residents and an estimated one toilet for every 1,000 people living there. Do not expect Mumbai officials to fess up to this, however. A Mumbai slum residence isn't officially recognised unless the house is 'jury-rigged by the inhabitants. No formally built structures, no matter how run down' can qualify—this in a city that has done little to upgrade much of its infrastructure since the Raj period of British rule.[142] The number of slum residents combined with official neglect help explain why the megacity fails to have superior life expectancies compared with the rest of the country. As of 2007, the average Mumbaikar could expect to live 56.8 years while others in India had an average life expectancy of 63.7 years.[143]

Lagos is another city frequently cited as circling the drain. Our earlier walk through history's examples of urban areas surviving the worst that humans or Mother Nature has thrown at them suggests such alarmists need to look beyond initial impressions. Lagos proved its toughness when Liberian-American lawyer Patrick Sawyer collapsed in its Murtala Mohammed Airport during West Africa's 2014 Ebola crisis.[144] Taken to

---

142 Daniel Brook, *A History of Future Cities*, New York, NY: Norton, 340–42.

143 Mahesh Narvekar and Gita Kewalramani, *City Profile: Greater Mumbai*, Mumbai, India: Municipal Corporation of Greater Mumbai Disaster Risk Management Master Plan, 2010, Executive summary, 1, 91.

144 Overview of Lagos's response to the arrival of the infected patient adapted from Russell W. Glenn, Eric L. Berry, Colin C. Christopher, Thomas A. Kruegler and Nicholas R. Marsella, *Where None Have Gone Before: Operational and Strategic Perspectives on Multi-Domain Operations in Megacities. Proceedings of the 'Multi-Domain Battle in Megacities' Conference, April 3–4, 2018, Fort Hamilton, New York*, Fort Eustis, VA: US Army Training and Doctrine Command, 20 July 2018, 13–15, available from: community.apan.org/wg/tradoc-g2/mad-scientist/m/multi-domain-battle-mdb-in-megacities/244661. Additional information from F.O. Fasina, A. Shittu, D. Lazarus, O. Tomori, L. Simonsen, C. Viboud and G. Chowell, 'Transmission dynamics and control of Ebola virus disease outbreak in Nigeria, July to September 2014', *Euro Surveillance* 19(40) (9 October 2014), doi.org/10.2807/1560-7917. ES2014.19.40.20920; Centers for Disease Control and Prevention (CDC), *2014–2016 Ebola Outbreak in West Africa*, Washington, DC: US Department of Health and Human Services, 8 March 2019, www. cdc.gov/vhf/ebola/history/2014-2016-outbreak/index.html; and International Federation of the Red Cross and Red Crescent Societies (IFRC), *Emergency Plan of Action Final Report: Nigeria—Ebola Virus Disease*, Geneva: IFRC, 2 September 2014, available from: reliefweb.int/sites/reliefweb.int/files/resources/ MDRNG017FR.pdf. Another source states that 894 people were exposed and 19 infected, with one additional possibly affected. See Faisal Shuaib, Rajni Gunnala, Emmanuel O. Musa, Frank J. Mahoney, Olukayode Oguntimehin, Patrick M. Nguku, Sara Beysolow Nyanti, Nancy Knight, Nasir Sani Gwarzo, Oni Idigbe, Abdulsalam Nasidi and John F. Vertefeuille, 'Ebola virus disease outbreak—Nigeria, July–September 2014', *Morbidity and Mortality Weekly Report* 63(39) (3 October 2014): 867–72, Atlanta, GA: Centers for Disease Control and Prevention, available from: www.cdc.gov/mmwr/preview/mmwrhtml/ mm6339a5.htm. A third author wrote that officials made 18,500 in-person follow-up visits 'to find any new cases of Ebola among a total of 989 identified contacts'—no easy task in a city where many residences lack street numbers. Courage, 'How did Nigeria quash its Ebola outbreak so quickly?'.

hospital at a time when many of the city's medical personnel were on strike, Sawyer stated he had not had contact with any Ebola patients or medical personnel—even though Sawyer's travel had originated in virus-infested Liberia. (At the time of Sawyer's collapse in Lagos's airport, the 2014 Ebola crisis was killing thousands in the West African countries of Sierra Leone and Liberia, which together have a population several million fewer than Lagos.)[145] Doctors immediately began treating him for malaria—a disease with many symptoms similar to those of Ebola.[146] One doctor, Stella Ameyo Adadevoh, nonetheless concluded Sawyer was instead suffering from the infectious haemorrhagic disease.[147] She refused to allow his departure from quarantine, directing that, for public safety reasons, he remain isolated despite the patient's efforts to leave the hospital and 'immense pressure' from Liberian Government officials. She insisted a barrier be put on his door to ensure compliance. Investigators would later find Sawyer had lied. Not only had he been exposed to Ebola; he had also left Liberia against doctors' orders after being in proximity to a relative with the disease who had died on 8 July. Sawyer had therefore carried the deadly virus to Africa's second most populous urban area (Cairo is first). Thanks in part to his poor judgement and deceit, 891 people were exposed to the disease, a good number of them having travelled to areas well beyond Lagos as several passengers on his flight continued their journeys beyond the megacity.

Fortunately—we might even say miraculously—despite nearly 900 individuals being directly exposed or determined to have had contact with others exposed, the combined efforts of Lagos and broader Nigerian medical personnel, rapid action by public officials, diligent identification and testing of those with first-order or later contacts, participation by key elements of the country's private sector and IGOs such as the United Nations and the US Centers for Disease Control, and no little luck in the initial victim collapsing in the airport before he could enter the city's

---

145 Worldwide, the outbreak would see more than 28,000 people infected, of whom more than 11,300 died. Akaninyene Otu, Soter Ameh, Egbe Osifo-Dawodu, Enoma Alade, Susan Ekuri and Jide Idris, 'An account of the Ebola virus disease outbreak in Nigeria: Implications and lessons learnt', *BMC Public Health* 18(3) (2018), doi.org/10.1186/s12889-017-4535-x.

146 Early symptoms of Ebola virus disease appear from two to 21 days after exposure, with an average of eight to 10 days. Centers for Disease Control and Prevention (CDC), 'Signs and symptoms', *Ebola Virus Disease*, [Online], Washington, DC: US Department of Health and Human Services, 22 May 2018, available from: www.cdc.gov/vhf/ebola/symptoms/index.html; and Otu et. al, 'An account of the Ebola virus disease outbreak in Nigeria'.

147 Will Ross, 'Ebola crisis: How Nigeria's Dr Adadevoh fought the virus', *BBC News*, 20 October 2014, available from: www.bbc.com/news/world-africa-29696011.

general population helped to reduce the number endangered. In addition, authorities had to contact embassies and travel agents to determine the complete manifest as the plane on which Sawyer arrived had an incomplete passenger list. A researcher would later observe:

> [T]he involvement of the private sector and spirited individuals in the health education awareness campaign and screening/scanning of the temperature of every customer that enter[ed] into their business premises was very helpful. Even banks, public eatery places and supermarkets in Nigeria were involved in scanning the temperature of their customer[s] before they were allowed in after due consent was obtained. Those that had a temperature more than the normal temperature of 37°C were booked and subsequently referred to Ebola operation centres for further detailed diagnosis and investigation.[148]

Educating the population of the city and countryside alike was critical, but that education could not begin until audiences were listening. This became evident to officials in Liberia's capital of Monrovia when the country sought to contain Ebola's spread when:

> clashes erupted Wednesday [20 August 2014] as security forces sealed off a sprawling seaside slum in the Liberian capital in a bid to prevent the spread of the deadly Ebola virus … Over the weekend, residents angry about the placement of an Ebola screening center in Monrovia's West Point slum attacked the facility, chasing away sick patients and carrying off bloody sheets and other possibly contaminated items … It is unclear how many more people may have been exposed to the disease.[149]

Lagos brought multiple public information services to bear, including 'social media, bulk Short Messaging Service (SMS), Ebola Alert, mainstream media' (including creation and use of a television jingle) and the establishment of an Ebola hotline.[150] Residents near the hospital where Sawyer was quarantined expressed concerns that they might be in danger

---

148 Obioma Azuonwu, 'Emergence and re-emergence of 2014 Ebola outbreak in sub-Sahara Africa: "Challenges and lessons learned" from Nigerian epidemic outbreak', *Scholars Journal of Applied Medical Sciences* 3(8A) (2015): 2802–14, at 2807–8, available from: www.researchgate. net/publication/326381400_Emergence_and_Re-emergence_of_2014_Ebola_outbreak_in_Sub-_ Sahara_Africa_%27Challenges_and_lessons_learned%27_from_Nigerian_epidemic_outbreak.
149 Alexandra Zavis and Christine Mai-Duc, 'Clashes erupt as Liberia seals off slum to prevent spread of Ebola', *Los Angeles Times*, 20 August 2014, available from: www.latimes.com/world/africa/ la-fg-africa-liberia-ebola-quarantine-curfew-20140820-story.html.
150 Otu et al., 'An account of the Ebola virus disease outbreak in Nigeria'.

of contacting the disease; officials provided 'community enlightenment activities' addressing their worries.[151] Nigeria's popular *Story Story* soap opera became another effective education initiative:

> Unlike many Nigerian soaps, however, *Story Story* has never been available on TV. It's proudly and exclusively a radio show, funded by the BBC's development charity, BBC Media Action, and listened to by about 13 million people ... Most recently, one character returned from Liberia and fell ill with a mystery disease. A false rumor spread in the market that he was an Ebola carrier, based on a flawed understanding of how the disease is spread. As the series develops, the truth emerges and the real facts about Ebola are revealed.[152]

Pop music was likewise recruited in the information campaign, letting listeners know they were not alone in their concern.

It is thought the 891 individuals identified represented 95 per cent of those possibly exposed.[153] Only 20 became infected, 11 of whom were healthcare personnel. Nine of these were exposed to Sawyer before identification of the disease. A bit of luck, perhaps, but the response drew on Lagos's status as a hub for the country's most expert, capable, responsive and well-equipped professionals to stay what could have been a blossoming of the disease in Africa and beyond.[154] Despite the ongoing strike, Lagos's medical community, city officials and others responded effectively, containing the spread such that the resultant deaths numbered but eight. One, unfortunately, was the tenacious Dr Adadevoh; Sawyer also died.[155]

Lagos's robustness in the face of what could have been an Ebola crisis of mega-proportions puts the lie to those suggesting developing-world megacities are inherently on the cusp of collapse. Apocalyptic quotes such as the following overlook the well-functioning systems within these urban areas:

---

151 ibid.; and Azuonwu, 'Emergence and re-emergence of 2014 Ebola outbreak in sub-Sahara Africa'.

152 Leo Hornak, 'It's not just a soap opera, it's a "radio movie"', *The World*, [Boston, MA], 8 September 2014, available from: www.pri.org/stories/2014-09-08/its-not-just-soap-opera-its-radio-movie.

153 Sarah Dwyer, 'Why Nigeria's response to Ebola succeeded', *CapacityPlus Blog*, October 2014, available from: www.capacityplus.org/why-nigerias-response-to-ebola-succeeded.html.

154 Glenn, 'Megacities'.

155 Shuaib et al., 'Ebola virus disease outbreak'.

> [T]he half-abandoned skyscrapers of downtown Lagos Island loom under a low, dirty sky. Around the city, garbage dumps steam with the combustion of natural gases, and auto yards glow with fires from fuel spills. All of Lagos seems to be burning … Lagos was a prospect of millions of 'people squeezed together and trying to survive like creatures in a mad demographer's experiment gone badly wrong'.[156]

So, too, do comments by those who suggest large slum populations and poverty intrinsically imply a city on the precipice, as did one author who found Lagos 'barely managed or manageable. It has great wealth and great poverty. Two out of three Lagos residents live in slums with no reliable access to clean drinking water, electricity, waste disposal—even roads.'[157] Yet, sub-Saharan Africa's most populous urban area manages to absorb 6,000 new arrivals every day. Many—likely most—of them find their quality of life a step up from that in rural Nigeria or other cities from which the country's urban-to-urban migrants come. An urban area of 16-plus million residents, Lagos has considerable economic, social, political and other influence nationally, being described as 'the commercial nerve centre of West Africa with two domestic airports, an international airport and two seaports which have been adjudged to be the largest and busiest in the continent'.[158]

Other megacities are similarly likely to have in place emergency response procedures and other resources key to effective crisis response when compared with smaller urban areas or rural surrounds. Expanding on our theme that disaster preparations of any type hold value regardless of the eventual calamity, a good number of those manning Lagos's emergency operations centre during the Ebola crisis had demonstrated talent and gained valuable experience two years earlier as part of Nigeria's response to the World Health Organization Nigeria's call to redouble efforts to eradicate polio.[159] Access to information of better quality than is often available

---

156 George Packer ('The megacity: Decoding the chaos of Lagos', *The New Yorker*, 13 November 2006, 62–75), as quoted in Dayton McCarthy, *The worst of both worlds: An analysis of urban littoral combat*, Australian Army Occasional Paper: Conflict Theory and Strategy 002, Canberra: Australian Army Research Centre, April 2018, 9, available from: researchcentre.army.gov.au/sites/default/files/the_worst_of_both_worlds.pdf.

157 James Canton, 'The extreme future of megacities', *Significance* 8(2)[SI: Megacities] (June 2011): 53–56, at 54, doi.org/10.1111/j.1740-9713.2011.00485.x.

158 Otu et al., 'An account of the Ebola virus disease outbreak in Nigeria'. The estimates of Lagos's population vary widely, with some stating more than 30 million. That used here is from *Demographia World Urban Areas*, 15th edn, 23.

159 Courage, 'How did Nigeria quash its Ebola outbreak so quickly?'.

elsewhere, experienced authorities and supporting bureaucracies and other key resources will assist megacity planning and response regardless of the crisis. Knowing likely hotspots for problems and identifying the resources essential for effective action do much to make manageable the apparently overwhelming.[160] In the future, identifying such hotspots might benefit from analysing census information, marketing survey results and property records. Call data specifying users' phone numbers, times of calls and mobile tower locations have already been used to track malaria outbreaks in Africa. Captured in a timely fashion, they could similarly help trace the flow of commuters who are later found to have been contaminated in the aftermath of a biological-agent attack or disease outbreaks similar to Covid-19 in 2020.[161] The last tells us that concerns about privacy will be an issue for which officials need to better prepare. Possible solutions include pre-event agreement by residents to have select data made available during times of crisis, passing laws akin to 'information eminent domain' when the welfare of the whole requires use of specific data types or other approaches that could be developed in cooperation with citizen groups.

The outcome in Lagos was by no means assured. Many among the Nigerian public did not originally understand how to protect themselves from Ebola. Like the distribution of misinformation during Tokyo's Fukushima Daiichi threat (on which more to follow), early word provided by the Nigerian media in advance of official information from health authorities was sometimes inaccurate, creating a nationwide scare. As a result, several people resorted to extreme, ineffective and sometimes harmful measures to protect themselves, such as consuming large quantities of saltwater.[162] Similar misinformation plagued US health guidance during the Covid-19 crisis—again demonstrating that rumour, ignorance or misunderstanding can be no less damaging than deliberate manipulation of communications. Such missteps make Lagos's handling of the Ebola threat even more impressive. Perhaps naysayers predicting the doom of developing-world megacities confuse urban areas with the sometimes excessively corrupt and poorly run countries of which they are a part. As one author noted:

> Nigeria's hopelessly corrupt federal government simply can't handle the tribal and religious rivalries that are tearing the country apart. But Lagos is a different story. A succession of efficient regional

160 Glenn, 'Megacities'.
161 ibid.
162 Shuaib et al., 'Ebola virus disease outbreak'.

governments, major Chinese investments, and corporate interest in the city's low-wage workforce and its emerging middleclass are transforming the city and the region.[163]

There is no doubt that some megacities operate at the edge of chaos in one manner or another. Yet, perhaps those seeing this as evidence of imminent collapse should re-evaluate their looking at the glass as half-full. Others view the edge of chaos as the optimal point for dynamism in a system.[164] Megacities' performance as fonts of innovation and growth lends credence to this less pessimistic perspective.

It is worth noting one more myth before moving on (or perhaps it is more an assumption than a myth): disaster responders speak the same language when the language they speak is the same. General James Delk, who was the California Army National Guard field commander during the 1992 riots in Los Angeles, recalled:

> [I]n Compton [part of the Los Angeles megacity], which was marine territory, two Compton police officers took a squad of marines with them and headed out to a domestic dispute. The cops walked up to the door, knocked, and the next thing you know someone fired bird shot through the door. One policeman was hit, but not hurt. His partner grabbed him and as he pulled him back he hollered to the marines 'Cover me!' Now to a cop, that was a very simple command. That means aim your rifle and use it if necessary. To a marine, and there were some well-trained young patriots in that squad, it meant something entirely different. They instantly opened up. A mom, a dad, and three children occupied that house. I later asked the Compton police department to count the bullet holes for me because there was a rumor going around there were 50 or so rounds fired. The police told me there were over 200 bullet holes. In some cases you couldn't tell how many bullets had gone through. They didn't hit anyone, but the point is, those great young marines did exactly what they're trained to do, but not what the police thought they requested. You need to understand the differences in language.[165]

163 Darrell Bricker and John Ibbitson, *Empty Planet: The Shock of Global Population Decline*, New York, NY: Crown, 2019, 155.

164 Fisch, *An Anthropology of the Machine*, 106.

165 James Delk, 'MOUT: A Domestic Case Study—The 1992 Los Angeles Riots', in Russell W. Glenn (ed.), *The City's Many Faces: Proceedings of the RAND Arroyo-MCWL-J8 UWG Urban Operations Conference, April 13–14, 1999*, Santa Monica, CA: RAND Corporation, 2000, 79–156, at 135.

Back to reality

> Workers in big cities are more productive than those in small places.[166]
>
> —'An outsized punch', *The Economist*

> You need to know who's halal or vegetarian and who wants turkey wings.[167]
>
> —Paul Ford, 'Tech support'

Whether developing or developed world, megacities are hubs of talent, economic vibrancy and influence. They also attract the fertile seeds of growth: youth. More than one-quarter of Japan's population are seniors; it is the most aged society in the world.[168] As in many other developed nations (and, increasingly, developing nations), in Japan, birthrates are below replenishment levels and people are living longer. Unlike the United States, Japan has very little immigration to keep its blood young. Ageing it might be, but Tokyo suffers the consequences less than the rest of the country. More of those living in the capital are aged between 15 and 55 than in Japan as a whole; many of those megacity residents are in their twenties or thirties.[169] That means a larger pool of individuals is available for employers to hire, there is more innovation and more income to support local commerce, the arts and other of life's amenities that in turn continue to make the capital attractive to Japanese of working age.

Money moulders without vibrancy. Vibrant money seeks new spaces and creates niches where it can multiply more quickly while promising to multiply yet further. Megacity shoppers looking for produce can choose from tens of nearby markets, meaning those markets reach out to a greater range of suppliers to meet the needs of their diverse population (diverse in tastes even if largely homogeneous ethnically, as is sometimes the case). These large urban areas therefore not only have a greater number (quantity) of commercial offerings, but also those offerings differ in type (quality). Generic markets compete with the more upscale and others focusing on organic produce, locally grown goods or ones specialising in a particular ethnic cuisine. Larger cities have more media companies

---

166 'An outsized punch', *The Economist*, [London], 25 July 2020, 3.
167 Paul Ford, 'Tech support', *WIRED*, September 2020, 14–15, at 15.
168 Bricker and Ibbitson, *Empty Planet*, 80.
169 Seidensticker, *Tokyo from Edo to Showa*, 575.

of a type and more types of media companies. Increasingly, megacities become home to more eclectic populations attracted by this variety of offerings that in turn promote further increases in quantity and niche providers. Visitors in a megacity at any point tend to represent a wider spectrum of geography, functions and professions than found elsewhere, just as do its residents. A further irony touched on above: where more is a characteristic of an urban area, it means less consumption of many goods and services per resident, and therefore greater efficiency. The costs of urban water treatment, streetlights or policing are spread over many instead of fewer. Scale favours urban and though at some point increases in population mean increases in the number of amenities (eventually an increasing population will need two water treatment plants instead of one, for example), it still holds that costs per resident tend to be lower. The density of urban areas means a kilometre of street serves more people, the streetlight illuminates more walkers and the bus carries more passengers. Though megacities consume huge amounts of energy, more people and enterprises benefit for each unit of energy generated.[170]

No wonder youth are attracted to megacity life, where they find an exotic mix of work and play featuring more individuals like themselves in addition to many others unalike. Seoul is a good example. More than 40 per cent of South Korea's population lives in the megacity thanks in part to the capital also being home to 'the vast majority of attractive jobs, schools, and entertainment options. Few people with any ambition can afford not to move there' despite high property prices for both rentals and purchases.[171]

That megacities are a wonder has consequences for those tasked with their security. There are more people who might be a source of willing or coerced supplies, shelter or information for criminals, terrorists or other miscreants. There are also more routes adversaries can use; more buildings and subterranean passageways offering the prospect of undetected movement; more locations from which they can engage with their weapons, locate explosive devices or hide themselves or illicit resources; and more types and sizes of and ways to use those resources. Perhaps the biggest difference is one challenging leaders at higher echelons: determining the

170 Geoffrey West concludes that benefits and negative elements (for example, crime) do not double in an urban area as population does, but rather increase by a factor of 2.15; however, West fails to address reasonable challenges to these findings in his scale despite them being published well before the book's release. For one discussion of these challenges, see Townsend, *Smart Cities*, 312–14.
171 'The high-rise life: Housing in Seoul', *The Economist*, [London], 29 August 2020, 60.

details of a megalopolis's expansive interconnectedness and vast influence knowing that even the seemingly inconsequential decision or most minor of actions can have unforeseen and dramatic implications. Barring the salting of the earth as in 146 BCE Carthage, the devastation imposed on rural features can generally be rectified with the harvest of the following year's crops. A developed-world megacity government cannot focus only on challenges within its own space of contiguous light at night. It must do what it can to ensure that the effects of its actions do not unduly damage the urban area's far-reaching relationships and responsibilities. A megacity disaster is inherently also a catastrophe for many beyond.

3

Disasters' challenges and opportunities

A single blast in Colombo has more value psychologically than full-scale conflict in the north and northeast … The war had always been 'invisible' to most Sri Lankans.[1]

—C. Christine Fair, *Urban Battle Fields of South Asia*

Cities are the crucible of civilization, the hubs of innovation, the engines of wealth creation and centers of power, the magnets that attract creative individuals, and the stimulant for ideas, growth, and innovation. But they also have a dark side: they are the prime loci of crime, pollution, poverty, disease, and the consumption of energy and resources.[2]

—Geoffrey West, *Scale*

Tragedy always teaches us something.[3]

—Yuguo Li, University of Hong Kong

All urban areas—megacities in particular—can be daunting beasts. Mayor, police officer, soldier, awestruck visitor—all can be forgiven for feeling overwhelmed as they look down on a city from atop its tallest building or nearby peak, as in Seoul and Rio de Janeiro. Where to start planning for the devastating earthquake or cyclone that is only a matter of 'when'?

---

1   C. Christine Fair, *Urban Battle Fields of South Asia: Lessons Learned from Sri Lanka, India, and Pakistan*, Santa Monica, CA: RAND Corporation, 2004, 47–48, doi.org/10.7249/MG210.
2   West, *Scale*, 214–15.
3   Quoted in Megan Molteni, 'Fatal flaw', *WIRED*, July–August 2021, 62–73, at 72.

How to find the lurking terrorist hidden among a (mostly) unwitting population? What can be done to oust an enemy imposing its horrors on those living in the city without further adding to their suffering?

How do we account for the extraordinary social, physical or economic complexity that is part and parcel of any megacity in those plans? Density is one way—a way that can be surprisingly helpful in getting a grip on the seemingly ungrippable. Understanding the megacity as a system and subsystems is another. Recognising the character of the connections within and between these systems is a third.

Urban density

Five days later, on October 22, second platoon rolled out of the gate of Loyalty to again patrol Adhamiya [Iraq]. Immediately, they sensed that something was wrong. No one walked the street or gathered at the corner to chat. No children played. Dead quiet. And then, too much noise … [Company commander Captain Mike] Baka wanted to better the odds of survival, and decided to start putting soldiers used to living in the city—the kids who grew up with street smarts—in the first vehicles out on patrol. They picked up on unusual activity the others had missed— a shifty glance, an odd posture, out-of-place clothing—but didn't necessarily know why someone was suspicious. Baka learned to trust it when someone said, 'That guy's just bad. Let's stop him.' Inevitably, they'd be right.[4]

—Kelly Kennedy, *They Fought for Each Other*

They forget that sometimes a cop on a beat likes it that way. The street is his. He knowns everyone on it. He knows who and what they are and where they spend their time.[5]

—Private eye Mike Hammer in Mickey Spillane, *My Gun is Quick*

Density has special meaning for those who must live, protect, govern, assist or fight in an urban area. An aid organisation that might provide relief to several villages and towns in an otherwise rural area can find its resources fully committed to merely a single city block. A company

4   Kelly Kennedy, *They Fought for Each Other: The Triumph and Tragedy of the Hardest Hit Unit in Iraq*, New York, NY: St Martin's Press, 2010, 59, 132.
5   In Mickey Spillane, *The Mike Hammer Collection. Volume 1*, New York, NY: New American Library, 2001, 285.

of a hundred soldiers could expect to defend several hundred metres of frontage in rolling plains or farmland, and a good deal more in the vacuum of the desert or the Arctic. That same company might be responsible for no more than a modest apartment or office building of which every room requires clearing of enemy, and it must secure each passageway to guard against infiltrators attempting to sneak behind its soldiers. The density of rooms and walls, windows and doorways, poses problems of visibility and vulnerability. A barrier between oneself and the foe is no guarantee the latter's fire will not be lethal. Today's bullets can travel through two or more rooms of modern construction. That same projectile might hardly betray its passage through the flimsy materials making up some slum dwellings before inadvertently striking a man, woman or child unfortunate enough to be its final resting place. Ceilings or floors are likewise dubious shields. Knocking a small hole in a building's exterior and a yet smaller one in the wall where a sharpshooter awaits across a street means an ambusher can remain virtually undetectable as they lie in wait for a victim's entry into their site picture. A terrorist, insurgent, gang member or enemy soldier might instead choose to avoid exposing themselves at all, relying on booby traps or readying an entire building for demolition. The dangers are magnified for police, soldiers or other security officials constrained by concerns about the safety of the innocent. These densities in space have company in greater densities of activity per unit time. More infrastructure, people and action in less space mean situations change more rapidly than in other environments.[6]

The densities of humanmade structures and human populations are the two most obvious traits of urbanisation. Unfortunately, more buildings and more people in less space translate to more damage and more injuries when disaster visits. Urban space is better measured in volume than area. Megacity folk often live and work less at ground level than in storeys above or levels below. More floors mean more windows, balconies or other features from which an ambusher can shoot and more rooms that need to be cleared of a foe or searched for someone in need post disaster. Hallways, streets, subway tracks, utility conduits or shopping mall passageways mean more directions from which an adversary can attack. Concern for innocent life and preserving that of fellow police or soldiers can become a zero-sum game. US Marines put their lives at additional

---

6   Russell W. Glenn, *Heavy Matter: Urban Operations' Density of Challenges*, Santa Monica, CA: RAND Corporation, 2000, 2, 5.

risk when clearing rooms in Iraq, opting to not rely on fragmentation grenades—'frags', which disperse hundreds of lethal metal shards on exploding and would kill innocents within—after their supply of nonlethal stun grenades ran out. They instead had to risk fire from a waiting and unsuppressed enemy when entering each room. Room-clearing means contacts with those trying to kill you are sudden and close. Quickness as much as marksmanship determines who survives. It is not by accident that shorter-barrelled rifles are the order of the day for a special weapons and tactics (SWAT) team member or urban warrior. Reduced length means less chance of catching the muzzle on debris or doorsill. The rifles are also just that discriminating millisecond faster to bring to bear on a target.

More buildings and people mean more streets, tunnels, tracks, bridges and vehicles to get residents and workers to and from their destinations. The same is true for police, soldier or another responsible for protecting, defending or providing aid to a city. Pro-Russian forces and the Russian Army learned this to their regret when Chechen forces entered Grozny in March 1996. Russian commanders set up blocking positions along only 22 of the nearly 100 streets leading into the Chechen capital. Their insurgent enemy was only too happy to take advantage of the unguarded routes as they moved to attack.[7]

Fortunately for those rendering aid, what can be challenges for the SWAT team and soldier instead offer benefits. Urban density means more medical professionals, hospitals, rescue personnel and others with needed expertise within reasonable proximity. The role of cities as shipping nodes and transportation hubs suggests warehouses or docks containing essential needs beyond those hospitals, food banks or other critical aid providers have on hand. That the introduction of Ebola into Lagos in 2014 was interdicted so quickly and had so limited an effect was in considerable part thanks to the density of presence in the region's largest urban area of those with essential talents (this, we will recall, even though many doctors were on strike when Lagos's patient zero collapsed in the city's primary airport). The concentration of upper-tier economic jobs also provides opportunities for those less educated or talented. One economist concludes that two additional professional positions and three nonprofessional job opportunities follow every new high-tech job into an urban area.[8]

7   Stasys Knezys and Romanas Sedlickas, *The War in Chechnya*, College Station, TX: Texas A&M Press, 1999, 258.
8   Bruce Katz and Jennifer Bradley, *The Metropolitan Revolution: How Cities and Metros Are Fixing Our Broken Politics and Fragile Economy*, Washington, DC: Brookings Institution Press, 2013, 33.

Less fortunately, a greater density of users of social media, radio and other bandwidth or frequency in less space means communications can be inconsistent during times of crisis. In addition, a megacity's many providers of information make separating truth from rumour more difficult. A routine downside can occasionally offer a crisis upside; rush-hour traffic hinders movement and frustrates drivers, but vehicle availability is a benefit when emergency responders need to augment their own sources of transportation.

A different kind of density burdens disaster response managers: the assortment of authorities that together manage a megacity. Working with even the many parts of a single city's officialdom—the mayor's office, city council, police, fire, health inspectors, courts and so many others—can keep those lending assistance up at night. We have noted that a megacity is an urban area of many smaller cities, towns and other incorporated (and often unincorporated) authorities. Los Angeles County is home to 88 incorporated urban governments, ranging from the City of Los Angeles (population 3.9 million) to the collection of buildings and land making up Vernon, population 76. One can find 42 police departments (not including school police and other purpose-specific forces), 30 fire departments and 80 school districts in that county alone (the county has its own sheriff's department to boot).[9] That is daunting enough for an organisation trying to assist in the aftermath of the 'Big One'—the promised earthquake yet to come. But the megacity long ago cast aside any thought of restricting itself to Los Angeles County. Today, it also embraces all or parts of Ventura, Orange, San Bernardino and Riverside counties. Tokyo is no different with its 23 wards and 26 recognised cities, seven towns and eight villages within just the city 'core' that was Tokyo Prefecture in 1943.[10]

The United Nations acknowledges that density makes urban areas more productive, innovative and greener as people can cycle, walk or use public transportation in lieu of relying on automobiles to cover the greater distances inherent in less-dense community living.[11] Those same civilians whom police, soldiers and other authorities struggle to protect

9   'Less than the sum of their parts: Municipal limits', *The Economist*, [London], 22 December 2018, 41; and John Sullivan (Los Angeles County Sheriff's Department, retired), Discussion with Russell W. Glenn, Los Angeles, CA, 20 October 2021; 'Municipal Police Departments Los Angeles County', *Los Angeles Almanac*, 2022, available from: www.laalmanac.com/crime/cr69.php.
10   Kumagai and Nojima, 'Urbanization and Disaster Mitigation in Tokyo', 57, 88.
11   UN-Habitat, *Urbanization and Development*, 38.

each possess two eyes and two ears—invaluable assets when residents are willing to provide information. The same is true for day-to-day routine security that can prevent a disaster from occurring. Urban terrorists may live close to their targets for fear that ranging too widely while purchasing food, other necessities and the materials needed for their nefarious actions will increase the chances of detection. Citizens reporting 'the absence of the normal or presence of the abnormal' have prevented terrorist attacks. Failing to do so has had the opposite effect. Shouldn't the doctor treating a patient who is missing fingers after what seems to be an explosive-related traumatic amputation report the case to authorities—a responsibility that aces any concerns about the Hippocratic Oath? Might seeing men hauling three or four refrigerators into a small neighbouring apartment be worth mentioning to the police (for reasons we will cover later)? Does the reduced number of children approaching relief agency vehicles mean kids have found better things to do or might cholera be infiltrating the community? Virtually every individual in a city is a potential source of information, a two-eyed, two-eared 'sensor' in military-speak, albeit one who needs to be convinced (and regularly reminded) of the value their reporting of suspicious activities could offer to fellow urban residents and themselves.

Several of the world's largest urban areas are decreasing in density even as their populations grow thanks to construction spreading outward from more expensive and congested inner-city environs. A UN report estimates that the area consumed by urbanisation in developing countries will, by 2050, be four times what it was in 2000.[12] Military leaders in Seoul were shocked to find previously open terrain on the megacity's outskirts—land that had serviced training and other important roles in the past—occupied by highrise apartment buildings after only a few years.[13] Istanbul's government designated 470 parks and other open spaces as assembly areas after a 1999 earthquake killed 17,000 people; only 77 of these had not been consumed by new construction two decades later—construction that often failed to meet tremor-resistant standards.[14]

12   ibid., 28.
13   Remarks by US Army Lieutenant General Michael A. Bills at US Army Pacific LANPAC Conference Panel 5, Honolulu, May 2018.
14   'Picking up the pieces: Turkey', *The Economist*, [London], 5 December 2020, 52.

The megacity as system and subsystem

The economy and population of medieval Europe were rapidly expanding after Dark Age centuries, with unprecedented growth in travel and trade between cities and regions. For all these reasons, the disease was able to spread rapidly—two kilometers a day along major routes, with ships allowing the fleas to hopscotch into northern Europe almost immediately.[15]

—Darrell Bricker and John Ibbitson, *Empty Planet*

Kings and emperors dressed up in armour, led armies and made treaties—but it was banking houses … that in effect paid those armies and kept kings and emperors in the business of looking and sounding magnificent.[16]

—Stephen Alford, *London's Triumph*

Delhi is drying out the country for hundreds of kilometres around which creates more refugees from the land, who come to Delhi, who require more water, so Delhi takes even more—and so it goes on. Not only this, but we do not have the capacity to treat such large quantities of sewage.[17]

—Rana Dasgupta, *Capital*

Just as kings, emperors and armies relied on bankers to wage their wars (or look good on parade), banks relied largely on urban income-generating systems for the money they loaned. Cities ran the world then much as they do today. Additional urban systems provided—and continue to provide—water, power, streets, trains and other essentials of city life while also removing the many forms of waste both enterprises and humans constantly generate. Just as Venice was one of various nodes in the Mediterranean commerce system, urban areas today rely on resources beyond their boundaries to feed operations and operators. The greater the city, the more extensive and complex are its internal systems and those of which it is a part.

Baghdad during the 1991 Persian Gulf War provides an example of this tangled complexity. Coalition commanders conducting the pre-invasion bombing of Iraqi targets ensured hospitals were spared. Medical facilities

---

15   Bricker and Ibbitson, *Empty Planet*, 11.
16   Alford, *London's Triumph*, 45.
17   Rana Dasgupta, *Capital: The Eruption of Delhi*, New York, NY: Penguin, 2014, 430.

were left undamaged for reasons of decency and adherence to international law—decency in the form of concern for noncombatants who relied on those facilities. There was no such relief for features with possible military roles: fuel supplies, power generation plants, bridges and other key transportation nodes suffered damage or destruction while hospitals stood uninjured. Yet, gone was the power essential for the medical facilities' lighting, equipment, airconditioning, heating and other functions. The fuel necessary to power backup generators quickly ran out. Doctors, nurses and cleaners found streets leading to their places of work blocked[18] (similar problems hindered civilians attempting to flee cities in World War II; refugees made homeless during German bombing of London, for example, found much of the city's public transport destroyed, making escape all but impossible).[19] These and other second and higher-order effects of striking other-than-medical targets were fully obvious only in retrospect. The same facilities surely lacked water given the pumps necessary for its distribution would also have had no power—nor would those needed to remove human waste. It takes little imagination to recognise possible additional after-effects were the situation to last long: diseases caused by drinking unpurified water, embryos' growth hindered by diseases contracted by their mothers and the long-term effects of underdevelopment when those babies were born.

Some higher-order effects are straightforward regardless of a disaster's underlying cause. An enemy will be delayed if denied a river crossing when a defender destroys a bridge. Secondary effects for soldier and citizen alike are easy to imagine if that bridge has water, power, sewerage or other lines running under it. This tension between two considerations—denying an adversary opportunity and protecting the civilian population's welfare— spurred arguments as Soviet forces entered Berlin in 1945. German defenders readied bridges and highway overpasses for demolition with the goal of stopping the attackers. However:

> [B]itter quarrels subsequently arose between those who, like the Commander of the Defense Area, advocated military necessity, and those who wished to prevent the demolitions in the interest of the population. Reich Minister Speer, especially, did his

---

18   The author thanks Yuna Huh for the example of Baghdad's medical facilities being handicapped by the coalition bombing strategy in 1991.
19   Aaron William Moore, *Bombing the City: Civilian Accounts of the Air War in Britain and Japan, 1939–1945*, Cambridge, UK: Cambridge University Press, 2018, 121, doi.org/10.1017/9781108552479.

utmost to moderate the extent of the destruction. The question was vitally significant not only because of the need for traffic routes, but above all because the water and sewerage mains lay under the bridges. Speer succeeded in obtaining from Hitler an order whereby a number of particularly important bridges were to be saved.[20]

Urban complexity can also result in greater bang for the buck, providing the opportunity for multiple benefits from single actions. Many reading these pages are sure to be familiar with Baron Georges-Eugène Haussmann's charter from Emperor Napoleon III (Louis-Napoléon Bonaparte) to beautify Paris during the later decades of the nineteenth century—a task he pursued with both vigour and more than one objective. In turning narrow streets into wide boulevards, replacing the dwellings of the impoverished with more visually attractive public and private structures and paving the capital's streets with asphalt-like surfaces instead of cobblestones, Haussmann made Paris more secure for its political authorities. Marching infantry, cavalry with horses abreast and cannon requiring long ranges for their fire found the new avenues more amenable to fast movement and the disruption of demonstrations thanks to both the width of those streets and the absence of stones that could be worked loose and cast at the government's protectors. The new routes fragmented notorious hotbeds of militancy. Haussmann additionally had aqueducts and pump stations built, overhauled the sewerage system, straightened crooked passageways and opened deadends so that a walk that took 90 minutes in 1840 could be made in one-third the time a decade or so later. It is said that pre-Haussmann carriage travel was even slower than walking. So convoluted were those streets that the well-to-do might need two hours for a trip the less wealthy could walk in far shorter time.[21] Were the changes for the good of all? Certainly not for those ousted from their homes or who suffered the military's greater efficiencies. They also led to a phenomenon new to the age—one Parisians continue to suffer today. In another of those hard to determine higher-order effects, travellers used to the capital's twisted streets and jammed alleyways had learned to tolerate

20   Wilhelm Willemer, *The German Defense of Berlin*, trans. R.D. Young, Historical Division, Headquarters, United States Army, Europe MS No. P-136, 1953, 33–34.

21   Twain, *The Innocents Abroad*, 101; Sennett, *Building and Dwelling*, 31–32, 89; Adrian Tinniswood, *Visions of Power: Ambition and Architecture from Ancient Times to the Present*, New York, NY: Steward, Tabori & Chang, 1998, 144–45; and Colin Jones, *Paris: The Biography of a City*, New York, NY: Penguin, 2006, 319.

a journey's inevitable delays. The baron's improvements bred impatience. Parisians discovered road rage thanks to newly born expectations of rapid movement between points.[22]

An excellent pair of briefings given during a 2019 conference in Tokyo provides a more recent example of the complexity of megacity systems and subsystems.[23] Analysing the consequences of a notional 7.3 Richter scale earthquake during what would have been the 2020 Summer Olympics (later postponed a year due to Covid-19), the presenters described Tokyo in terms of flows into, within and out of the megacity. Seeking to keep their discussions manageable, those at the podium limited consideration of those flows to five types: power, water, people, goods and services, and waste. They took on the task in two parts. The first described how those five flows influenced daily city functions and one another. A second turned to the specific challenge of how such a disaster might rend Tokyo's fabric during the Olympics. Even limiting the consideration to five factors quickly showed the far-reaching character of the megacity's interconnecting tentacles. Pondering only power, for example, if Tokyo loses electricity supply: elevators stop, traffic lights go out and subways cease operating. Pumps that deliver water to upper floors of the capital's many tall buildings no longer accomplish that vital task—a first-order effect with second-tier consequences such as toilets no longer flushing and taps failing to provide drinking, washing and bathing water. Pursuing those higher-order effects further reveals just how complex are a megacity's relationships. Even those living at ground level soon find they, too, have access only to unclean water as treatment plants cease operating and stocks of bottled water are exhausted. As would have been the case in Baghdad had the consequences of bombing been long term, going without power for long sees the risk of disease spike dramatically as residents consume, bathe in or clean with unsanitary water. Literally millions who rely on subways are stranded—no small problem when we remember that Tokyo's workday commuters using public transport outnumber the total across the entire United States. Airconditioners stop functioning, which is more than an issue of comfort in those same highrises during Tokyo's

---

22   Sennett, *Building and Dwelling*, 36.
23   To see the briefing slides and video recordings of presentations about Tokyo's systems and subsystems, access the virtual terrain walk files (numbered 1.02, 1.021, 1.022, 1.03, 1.031 and 1.032) from the 16–18 July 2019 Current and Future Operations in Megacities Conference, available from: community.apan.org/wg/tradoc-g2/mad-scientist/m/tokyo-megacities-conference-2019. The author thanks Caleb Dexter, Jesse Geyer and Jheaniell Moncrieffe for their excellent work in preparing and presenting the material underpinning the discussion here.

infamously hot and humid summers, particularly if windows cannot be opened. Other higher-order effects of a power loss include deaths among those chronically reliant on medical equipment or moderate temperatures to survive—an increasing risk as populations age.

A step away from exclusively urban examples reveals that social connections within systems are just as complex as the physical. Efforts to establish effective law enforcement often fail to view systems as a whole rather than merely in terms of their component parts. Leaders in Malaya (now Malaysia) just after World War II, those in East Timor in the late 1990s and others in Iraq and Afghanistan during the first decades of this millennium recognised that their fledgling governments were simply not viable without the rule of law. But the rule of law cannot exist without a functioning legal system. Police—the most obvious component of the whole—received the bulk of attention while other components were sometimes given short shrift. Even an ideal police force cannot protect its community if the evidence it collects is mishandled; if citizens view judges, lawyers and trials as illegitimate; if the corrupt manage the prisons, allowing the convicted to bribe their way out; or the laws, policies and training guiding these and other components of the legal system are flawed. Failure to address the legal system as a whole means good police delivering those arrested to courts become frustrated when the guilty go free as lawyers and judges are found to be in the pockets of gangs, local officials or the wealthy. Laws themselves may be legacies of previous regimes now deemed illegitimate. Even if convicted, the sentenced soon return to the streets thanks to bribes or orders from corrupt politicians. Residents refuse to support legal authorities when those criminals seek revenge on their accusers after avoiding conviction or gaining early release. The young buck (or doe) fresh from the academy cannot save a system rotten at its core; like a child's sandcastle that disappears with the high tide, the sea of corruption quickly erodes its integrity.

Systems are akin to chains: they are only as strong as their weakest links, and the links in a megacity system are many. Understanding those links extending outside the urban area is as important as determining the connections within the city. Aid providers delivering free food to Mogadishu, Somalia, discovered their actions had twofold negative consequences. First, free food drove down the prices of that sold in the capital's markets, undermining locals' earnings and economic stability. Second, people in the surrounding countryside flooded into the city to take advantage of the availability and zero cost.[24]

Urban complexity means even those best at governing cannot completely escape the lurking spectre of hidden effects. As megacities grow, so does the pressure to expand the area from which they draw water. This is acceptable when the resource is plentiful, perhaps, but what will be the reaction in times of drought or when demand routinely exceeds capacity? The megacity of Los Angeles has long been able to provide itself with water thanks to sufficient funds and political influence allowing it to purchase rights in the Owens Valley and more remote northern and central portions of California. The robbing-Peter-to-pay-Paul approach is one reason talk of separating the state's north from the water-hungry south refuses to die.

Water is only one controversial resource sucked from the seemingly ever-increasing expanse of megacities' reach. Recall that the United Nations and the International Energy Agency estimate that urban areas account for between 60 and 80 per cent of the planet's energy use while being responsible for similar proportions of greenhouse gas emissions.[25] Attacks by locals on the south-eastern Iraqi powerlines supplying electricity to distant Baghdad in the aftermath of coalition operations in 2003 provide an example of what can happen when some become fed up when their needs go wanting as city folks benefit. Such tensions will intensify as urban areas grow larger in population, wider in territory and extend the area influenced by their self-induced climates—the last being one of many effects we are only beginning to fully appreciate. Building materials such as asphalt and concrete absorb heat, later radiating it outward (think of trying to walk barefoot on your summer driveway as a kid before you fled to the much cooler grass). On top of that, refrigerators, airconditioners, cars and human body heat add to the mercury's rise.[26] Larger urban areas have their own climates—hotter and wetter than adjacent rural terrain.[27] Models of rainfall and airflow in and around New York City and Tokyo suggest this heat island effect influences cloud formation, fog events and

---

24   Ben Rawlence, *City of Thorns: Nine Lives in the World's Largest Refugee Camp*, New York, NY: Picador, 2017, 59.
25   UN-Habitat, *Urbanization and Development*, 8; and Engelke, *The Security of Cities*, 27, 38.
26   Manuel De Landa, 'The Nonlinear Development Cities', in *ECO-TEC: Architecture of the In-Between*, Amerigo Marras (ed.), New York, NY: Princeton Architectural Press, 1999, 23.
27   Schilthuizen, *Darwin Comes to Town*, 36.

precipitation while raising internal urban temperatures by 10°C or more[28] (that's 18°F—the difference between a comfortable 72°F summer day and a sweltering 90°F). The effects can be almost immediate and devastating. Studies of Europe's 2003 heatwave unsurprisingly found that temperature increases in urban microclimates were strongly associated with increased numbers of deaths. Fatalities went up by 21 per cent for each 1°C rise (about 1.8°F). Shelters with fans or airconditioners should help reduce the number of deaths. Experts believe planting more trees could also help. The temperature of shaded asphalt or concrete is 11–25°C (20–45°F) cooler than unshaded areas, where the surface can be 28–50°C (50–90°F) hotter than the surrounding air.[29] As for precipitation, while increases of up to 25 per cent are most common, communities downwind of a major urban area can experience rainfall more than twice that of those upwind.[30]

A natural response to complexity is to break the seemingly incomprehensible into parts so the brain can—as I corrupt the metaphor—digest the elephant one bite at a time. The challenge is by no means a trivial one: maintain sight of the whole, of the system and of how its parts not only fit together but also complement one another for good or otherwise. Turning once again to Baghdad for an example, US military commanders and city residents were often well served by Commander's Emergency Relief Program funds during the opening decade of the twenty-first century. The US-funded program provided money for smallish local projects. It worked well for wisely considered standalone undertakings but less well when there was no overarching coordination of how the dollars were spent. In at least one instance, a well-intentioned commander invested in providing sewerage services to a neighbourhood (sewerage being the pipes and other parts of a system through which sewage flows). The system of pipes and intermediate pumps unfortunately ended at the boundary that marked the unit's extent of responsibility. The sewage treatment facility was in another organisation's area, leaving the newly installed pipes unconnected to the capital's wastewater treatment system. There could have been many reasons behind the failure. Perhaps it was simply a lack of one unit talking to another. Perhaps it was a joint plan involving the

---

28 IPCC, 'Urban Areas', 551; and J. Marshall Shepherd, Harold Pierce and Andrew J. Negri, 'Rainfall modification by major urban areas: Observations from spaceborne rain radar on the TRMM satellite', *Journal of Applied Meteorology and Climatology* 41(7) (2002): 689–701, at 689, doi.org/10.1175/1520-0450(2002)041<0689:RMBMUA>2.0.CO;2.

29 Robert McDonald, *Conservation for Cities: How to Plan & Build Natural Infrastructure*, Washington, DC: Island Press, 2015, 126–27, doi.org/10.5822/978-1-61091-523-6.

30 Shepherd et al., 'Rainfall modification by major urban areas', 689.

two units but one rotated out of the country before the other and the new commander chose to spend their funds differently. Perhaps they were unaware of their predecessor's commitments. Lest we judge too harshly, the numerous demands on a commander and staff combined with tours of duty of rarely more than a year often saw projects span two or more leaders' tenures. Constant concerns about securing the safety of both soldiers and residents in addition to monitoring such projects meant some oversights were inevitable. The complexity of an urban area increases the risk of such lapses.

A megacity's interconnectedness tends to magnify the consequences of bad decisions. First, there are the immediate consequences of the error itself. Then there are those related to any actions taken to correct the misstep. Both send first and higher-order ripples throughout the system. Some will be minor in consequence, such as a fire department from a jurisdiction distant from New York City responding to a disaster in the Big Apple only to find that while the threads on its engine hoses meet National Standard Thread dictates, the city's do not. In that case, the result might be no more than a few more buildings lost as the visitors await delivery of adapters or another pump truck. Hose connection size and thread incompatibility are a more common problem in the United States than one might think. The problem plagued San Diego firefighters arriving in Oakland during a major fire several years ago—this in addition to the language terms being used by the receiving city's firefighters being different to those from San Diego[31]— with echoes of police and Marines during the 1992 Los Angeles riots. Even just across the bay from Oakland, San Francisco's 3-inch (8-centimetre) hose connections differ from almost all other departments in California—not a good situation should a major earthquake or other fire-inducing disaster strike.[32] Fortunately, 9/11 spurred jurisdictions to identify problems before future events revealed such shortcomings. Key to these early discoveries are exercises in keeping with the Federal Emergency Management Agency (FEMA) Incident Command System that address how to mould personnel, communications, command procedures, equipment and other parts of disaster response systems into a cooperative whole.[33]

31 Janell Myhre (Regional Program Manager, Bay Area Urban Areas Security Initiative), Interview with Dr Russell W. Glenn, San Francisco, CA, 13 April 2016.

32 Stacy Finz, 'HOSED/S.F. hydrants don't fit equipment from other fire departments. In a disaster, the city could be …', *STGate*, [San Francisco, CA], 21 September 2005, available from: www.sfgate.com/news/article/HOSED-S-F-hydrants-don-t-fit-equipment-from-2568046.php.

33 Federal Emergency Management Agency (FEMA), *National Incident Management System, Third Edition*, Washington, DC: Department of Homeland Security, October 2017, available from: www.fema.gov/sites/default/files/2020-07/fema_nims_doctrine-2017.pdf.

Other shortcomings can have greater impact. Coalition planners were aware of this when providing guidance for bombing strikes on Baghdad's power facilities during the 1991 Persian Gulf War. Air units used chaff—strips of metal that shorted out power facility equipment without long-term damage—to reduce the time and cost of post-fighting recovery. Alternative bombing methods such as striking generators would have meant months, perhaps years, of delay before electricity generation could restart. The higher-order effects on Baghdad's economy, healthcare, disease control and other physical and social infrastructure are obvious. The same would be true for a megacity. Consider the financial links between London, Tokyo, New York and Singapore. Returning to our imperfect but hopefully still helpful pool table metaphor, several of those numbered balls leap off the table that represents Tokyo. Some drop to the floor without consequences. Some crash on to other pool tables where numbered balls were already colliding in more ways than the human mind can grasp. The extent and character of the disruption these airborne arrivals deliver depends on the nature of the connections linking the megacities (the several pool tables). Decisions made in the aftermath of an earthquake of magnitude 7.0 or greater striking Tokyo will influence not only that city's and Japan's recoveries, they also will favourably or otherwise impact distant nodes in the world's economic system. The extent of disruption will also affect individual shopowners, impact supply lines, influence whether an interconnected city's government officials or company executives hold on to their positions and have other consequences for the countries of which those urban areas are a part.[34] Supply chain challenges during the ongoing Covid-19 pandemic as I write reflect the fact that earthquakes are not the only possible culprits of concern for megacity leaders.

This widespread systems complexity means that even seemingly positive initiatives can have a dark side that is hard to foresee. In October 2002, Colombian president Álvaro Uribe Vélez sent his country's army into the drug and crime-ridden city of Medellín to rein in the country's most

---

34 The 2011 trifecta of 9.0 earthquake, tsunami and Fukushima Daiichi nuclear reactor failures revealed mismanagement in Japan's largest power provider, Tokyo Electric Power Company Holdings (TEPCO), and motivated questions about Japan's prime minister at the time. The consequences of lost trust, prestige and position paled in comparison with the thousands of lives and billions of yen lost. While not insignificant, the disaster's direct impact on Tokyo was far less than on communities to its north. The local, national and international implications when Tokyo or Los Angeles suffers the 'Big One' are difficult to comprehend and nearly impossible to forecast beyond generalities, as is the case with any megacity regardless of a disaster's cause.

notorious criminal and insurgent group, the Revolutionary Armed Forces of Colombia (FARC). The suppression of the FARC left a vacuum that paramilitary crime lord Diego Fernando Murillo Bejarano (aka Don Berna) was only too happy to fill as he successfully sought to expand his influence. The immediate consequences included positives: Berna's control of the city's poorest areas brought a drop in murders that in turn allowed the mayor's office to expand public services into communities previously not receiving official attention. Berna was arrested later in the same decade. His departure created new voids that were filled by not one but 'tens of criminal groups' fighting for the spoils of extortion, prostitution, drug dealing and other crimes.[35]

The provision of disaster aid can similarly have negative consequences despite good intentions. Relief aid is big business. Drawing on another example with potential application to future megacity disasters, Sierra Leone's leader during its late twentieth-century civil war declined aid when its Canadian providers refused to funnel the money and goods through corrupt government officials because the donors recognised that it would never reach those for whom it was intended. Similar concerns caused Lise Grande, UN Resident and Humanitarian Coordinator for Yemen late in the second decade of this century, to cut off aid to areas controlled by Houthi fighting factions after repeated warnings failed to halt the group's misappropriation. There will always be those willing to see suffering continue as long as outside support lines their pockets or otherwise serves their interests. Poor aid management fuels rather than relieves residents' misery. On the other hand, effective aid orchestration has the potential to swell collective benefits. Too often, however, that orchestration falls victim to participating organisations wanting to play their own tunes rather than creating collective harmony.[36]

---

35   Vanda Felbab-Brown, *Bringing the State to the Slum: Confronting Organized Crime and Urban Violence in Latin America—Lessons for Law Enforcement and Policymakers*, Latin America Initiative at Brookings, Washington, DC: Brookings Institution, December 2011, 3, available from: www. brookings.edu/wp-content/uploads/2016/06/1205_latin_america_slums_felbabbrown.pdf.

36   Such management, if attained, would ideally not limit itself to coordination in the service of avoiding redundancy and misuse. It would also provide some manner of central oversight to reduce secondary but no less popular (among the corrupt reaping the economic benefits) practices of paying premium rates for housing, vehicles, food or other resources, the results of which are local population members being ousted from their homes and disruption of an economy already suffering due to whatever disaster plagues the city (and country) in question. NGOs and IGOs are not the only culprits here; governmental organisations external to the affected region are often equally guilty of these practices.

Benefits of cooperation

> When city leaders cooperate, rather than compete, in a number of areas (crime, poverty, social inequalities, transport systems, infrastructure), a more effective type of regional governance emerges that has direct implications on the quality of life both inside and outside the large urban configuration.[37]
>
> —UN-Habitat, *State of the World's Cities 2012/2013*

> We inhabit a city size XXL that contains cities size S.[38]
>
> —Juan Villoro, *Horizontal Vertigo*

There is no guarantee that the many authorities whose cities, towns, departments, legislatures or councils are part of a megacity will see the benefits of working together. Minneapolis–St Paul provides an example, albeit from a smaller urban area. During the 1960s, many of its municipalities competed against one another to attract businesses and the revenue that followed. Minnesota finally legislated that a portion of all commercial tax income must go into a common account. This (admittedly coerced) cooperation stood the Minneapolis–St Paul region in good stead. Today, residents benefit from increased wealth and home prices that have remained affordable.[39] The many jurisdictions now cooperating suffer less from dog-eat-dog tactics. Municipalities in effect expanded their boundaries by joining forces as all profited (literally) from the arrival of new enterprises. A subsequent study unsurprisingly found that such cooperation made these municipalities less vulnerable to commercial organisations' manipulation. The effect of this urban growth without physically expanding boundaries put a new twist on findings from other studies: urban areas unable to expand beyond fixed boundaries tend to remain poorer and more segregated. They experience less growth, suffer lower municipal bond ratings and have less-educated workforces.[40] Cooperation such as that in Minneapolis–St Paul provides virtual growth—a possible remedy when physical expansion is infeasible.

---

37   United Nations Human Settlement Programme (UN-Habitat), *State of the World's Cities 2012/2013: Prosperity of Cities*, World Urban Forum edn, Nairobi: UN-Habitat, 2012, 32–33, available from: sustainabledevelopment.un.org/content/documents/745habitat.pdf.

38   Juan Villoro, *Horizontal Vertigo: A City Called Mexico*, New York, NY: Pantheon, 2021, 32.

39   *The Economist*, 'Less than the sum of their parts'.

40   ibid.

Minneapolis–St Paul is not alone in its history of regional competition. The Denver Water Board for years wore a black hat in this regard. Its post–World War II policies made Denver's growth a matter of intimidation at the expense of nearby communities needing access to water the board controlled. Being outside the water board's self-defined boundary beyond which it would not serve customers meant the requestor either agreed to be annexed by Denver or found an alternative water source. Resulting fights to deny the bully soured relationships and undermined cooperative growth. A similar temptation is there for the dominant government in a megacity, which can blind it to long-term harms to both it and the communities on which it depends. It may be that the smartest aspect of today's and tomorrow's smart cities will prove to be more the result of interjurisdictional collaboration than new technologies. Somewhat but not too centralised cooperation should avoid the worst effects of harmful competition, especially when it is combined with decentralised management of day-to-day activities tailored to each city's or community's unique requirements.

A revealing example comes in comparing Mumbai's more successful handling of Covid-19 than Delhi's. Both are megacities. Accounting for the population difference, Mumbai's Covid deaths were only one-fifth of Delhi's. The relative success is in part attributed to Mumbai's centralised municipal corporation, while Delhi 'is a morass of overlapping authorities'. The problem is worsened because Delhi overlaps two states while Mumbai remains in and is the capital of Maharashtra State. Finally, Delhi contains the national capital—a status that can bring benefits but can also reap interference and incompetence and exacerbate corruption.[41]

Economic benefits aside, cooperation will also show value in readying for disaster. The US Government's early failure to provide the leadership needed during the Covid-19 crisis reflects the fact that the same is true not only within a single urban area, but also across several areas. Not having overarching guidance or effective management created polarising struggles, needlessly inflated prices and resulted in locations most in need going without in lieu of an equitable parsing of goods that kept a lid on costs. Officials in post-9/11 New York recognised that their security relied on others. They dispatched undercover teams to stores hundreds of miles distant from the five boroughs to figure out how hard it would be for

---

41 'Urbs prima in Indis: City administration in India', *The Economist*, [London], 8 May 2021, 38–39.

a terrorist to buy bombmaking ingredients such as nitrate fertilisers or hydrogen peroxide and the means to detonate a resulting weapon. Alert to the danger and aware of whom to call, officers found most store managers and shopkeepers reported suspicious purchases. Nevertheless, members of city law enforcement recognised the importance of developing programs for sharing such information and training with police departments throughout the region.[42] They are among megacities' officials who recognise international connections are also vital to disaster readiness. New York and Los Angeles count themselves among US urban areas with international engagement offices linking them to distant cities and countries.[43] Both also join other megacities and urban areas as members of the C40 collective of cities that banded together to share information, ideas and initiatives in the face of climate change—even when some of their national governments are less enlightened. Ironically, it may be easier for US cities to share with international partners than with each other. Janell Myhre of San Francisco's Bay Area Urban Area Security Initiative noted that city-to-city cooperation in setting standards (those thread counts on fire hydrants, for example) can look to California's Standardized Emergency Management Systems guidance if they are in the same county. If not, urban leadership must work through state authorities.[44] When Bay Area officials wanted to assist New York City after Hurricane Sandy, for example, requests had to go through the state capitals of Sacramento and Albany, respectively, 'instead of local to local, which really overcomplicated things'.[45]

New York City officials also realised that social systems within and beyond their megacity are just as complex and connected as the physical systems. That the social and the physical are intimately intertwined only enhances the complexity of preparing for disaster (as our example of Baghdad's hospitals demonstrated). There is a further quality of complexity when dealing with the social part of systems that is largely lacking in the physical: the tempo of change in social systems is faster. Economic relationships,

---

42 Chris McNickle, *Bloomberg: A Billionaire's Ambition*, New York, NY: Skyhorse, 2017, 81.

43 Joseph Bogan and Aimee Feeney, *Future Cities: Trends and Implications*, Fareham, UK: Defence and Security Analysis, Defence Science and Technology Laboratory, 17 February 2020, 129, available from: assets.publishing.service.gov.uk/government/uploads/system/uploads/attachment_data/file/875528/Dstl_Future_Cities_Trends___Implications_OFFICIAL.pdf.

44 Myhre, Interview.

45 Cory Reynolds (Regional Project Manager, Whole of Community and Communications, Bay Area Urban Area Security Initiative), Interview with Russell W. Glenn, San Francisco, CA, 13 April 2016.

political alliances and fissures between criminal groups change week to week, day to day or even hour to hour. Community, ethnic, gender, age, religious and financial characteristics are slower to change but still do so more rapidly than the houses in which their residents live or the buildings in which they work. Understanding the nature of social systems is therefore a vital underpinning of security planning and crisis response.

Brooklyn's Red Hook neighbourhood and others nearby house both wealthy and poor. Loss of power and water that would last for more than two weeks after Hurricane Sandy began on 29 October 2013, putting some of those residents at greater disadvantage than others. Some 9 per cent of the residents of the City of New York's five boroughs were diabetic at the time. Only 6 per cent were so afflicted in that part of the Brooklyn 11231 zip code area just north of Red Hook. Red Hook itself had three times that percentage. The difference in asthma sufferers was even starker: 8 per cent for those in the wealthier zip code neighbourhood and 28 per cent in Red Hook. While the wealthier could afford to leave their homes until some sense of normalcy returned or pay for services to compensate for the storm's damage, Red Hook had residents unable to obtain essential medicines (pharmacies were closed), living without water (given no electricity to pump it to upper-floor apartments) and risking hypothermia during a time when temperatures averaged in the mid-40s Fahrenheit (approximately 7°C).[46]

Understanding the state of play in a megacity's communities before a crisis allows for faster and more effective responses. Knowing where vulnerable residents live and the nature of their challenges can mean the difference between demise or survival. Hospitals, clinics, pharmacists, family members, building superintendents and others have bits and pieces of the essential information. Tax records, drivers licence databases and further sources containing age, health, next of kin, religious and other information could be filtered to quickly identify those in the over-65 age group who proved especially vulnerable both in the aftermath of Sandy and during the Covid-19 crisis. This was the same demographic among whom four of every five deaths occurred during France's 2003 heatwave and which the US Centers for Disease Control (CDC) reports account for 40 per cent of heat-related deaths in the United States. (This seems a good time to remind ourselves of the increased temperatures in many

---

46   Schmeltz et al., 'Lessons from Hurricane Sandy', 800–1, 803.

US cities due to climate change, in addition to large cities' heat island effects.)[47] What is too often lacking is a medical information system (yes, another system) that compiles, maintains, protects and can make available essential data when required by those assisting residents in need.

Israel's 2014 Operation Protective Edge saw that country's armed forces battling with Hamas and other groups in densely packed Gaza. The initial weeks of fighting disproportionately affected the poor while leaving portions of the Gaza Strip's middle and upper classes largely unaffected. Israeli officials contacted wealthier residents living in a complex of apartment buildings, warning them to depart. Planes then levelled the structures. Within days, the conflict ceased. Some of the occupants had made it known to Hamas leaders that the costs of the struggle had become unacceptable. *One* factor in bringing the fighting to an end? Likely. *The* factor in doing so? Perhaps. Understanding an urban area's social connections reveals relationships of influence, including who can bring pressure to bear on whom.[48] Knowing who key influencers were and how to communicate with them required an understanding of Gaza's intermingled physical and social infrastructures.

The special case of primate (or primary) cities

> Istanbul is so vast a city that if a thousand die in it, the want of them is not felt in such an ocean of men.[49]
>
> —Bettany Hughes, *Istanbul*

> Metropolitan London is not merely the largest city in the world; it is more than seven times as large as Britain's second city, Liverpool, and thereby stands out alone in a different order of magnitude and significance from those of all other cities in its country. The finest wares are always to be found there, the rarest articles, the greatest talents, the most skilled workers in every science and art. Thither flows an unending stream of the young and ambitious in search of

---

47   Rodin, *The Resilience Dividend*, 77.

48   Russell W. Glenn, *Short war in a perpetual conflict: Implications of Israel's 2014 Operation Protective Edge for the Australian Army*, Army Research Paper No. 9, Canberra: Australian Army, 2016, 53–54, 61–62, available from: researchcentre.army.gov.au/sites/default/files/arp9_glen_short_war_in_a_perpetual_conflict.pdf.

49   Hughes, *Istanbul*, 524.

fame and fortune, and there fame and fortune are found. London is the kingdom's market for all that is superlative in intellectual and material productions. Its supereminence as a market runs parallel to its supereminence in size. It is the primate city of the United Kingdom. In Denmark the less-than-a-million capital, Copenhagen, has won greater relative primacy. It is nine times as large as Denmark's second town.[50]

—Mark Jefferson, 'The law of the primate city'

In 1939, Mark Jefferson defined a 'primate' city as 'a country's city that is at least twice as large as the next largest city and more than twice as significant'.[51] It is an interesting concept—a combination of the objective (either a city has at least twice the population of a country's second city or it does not) and the subjective (just what constitutes 'twice as significant'?). Many megacities dominate their countries in terms of Jefferson's dual factors. The megacity of Bangkok, for example, has 14 times the population of Thailand's next in line. It is no less dominant in economic, political and other influences. Disasters there have disproportionate impacts nationwide; city floods in 2012 were one of the country's worst disasters given the US$45.7 billion cost to Thailand's economy.[52] Nor is this overwhelming dominance limited to Bangkok. Manila is 15 times larger than the Philippines's second most populous urban area and similarly influential. London is now much as it was when Jefferson wrote in terms of its relative importance to the United Kingdom (the megacity's population today exceeds that of Scotland and Wales combined).[53] Paris has primate position in France as do Lagos in Nigeria, Cairo in Egypt, Moscow in Russia and Tokyo in Japan (despite Japan having urban areas with populations close to or exceeding 10 million). Yet, just as not all primate cities are megacities (note Jefferson's citing of Copenhagen), not all megacities qualify as primate. Shanghai and Beijing are arguably megacities—the first given its economic influence, the latter its political and diplomatic impact. Shanghai is China's most populous urban area (given our definition of urban area rather than China's), but at 22 million, it has only 2 million more than China's next in line (Guangzhou–Foshan) and 3 million more than Beijing.

---

50   Mark Jefferson, 'The law of the primate city', *Geographical Review* 29(2) (April 1939): 226–32, at 226, doi.org/10.2307/209944.
51   ibid., 227.
52   World Vision, *Cities Prepare!*, 49.
53   Bagehot, 'England speaks up: A radical new force is reshaping the country', *The Economist*, [London], 20 March 2021, 52.

This lack of perfect overlap between the definitions of megacity and primate city merits a deeper look. Jefferson's primate cities require only *national* impact. Our megacity definition demands broader regional or even global *wasta* (an Arabic term for the sway or influence a leader commands, often due to control of resources). The wealth of urban areas—particularly megacities—means they are also affluent in their relevance to the daily lives of those local, national, superregional and planet-wide populations. The disaster implications are even more obvious. Urban events are far more likely to have local, regional, national and international impacts than is the case in any but the most exceptional rural incidents. Terrorists find megacities attractive targets because of the attention attacks there receive. The 11 September 2001 attack on the World Trade Center had financial and commercial after-effects that permeated distant economies, kept people from flying and touched emotions in even the planet's most remote regions. While there is some redundancy in world financial and commercial systems, there is also great interdependence (the 'interconnectedness' in our megacity definition)—relationships that ensure a blow against one point crosses borders to be felt throughout these broader systems. By comparison, the redundancy and relative isolation of rural systems come with a lesser degree of interdependence; chances are a disaster has only local consequences. Less-prominent cities attract less attention. The horrors of 9/11 touched rural Pennsylvania and the US capital, but the Twin Towers of New York from moment one became the symbol of the tragedy. Author Laurent Gayer concluded his in-depth study of Karachi and its seemingly endless struggles with violence and competitions for power with an observation revealing how greatly a single megacity can impact the welfare of the country of which it is a part. That megacity accounts for 70 per cent of Pakistan's income tax revenue, is responsible for 95 per cent of the country's international trade, 30 per cent of its manufacturing, 50 per cent of its bank deposits and approximately 25 per cent of its GDP.[54] Little wonder that Gayer concludes:

> Because of Karachi's enduring centrality in the national economy but also because of the city's increasingly complex ethic mix, the country will not pull itself back from the brink without bringing Karachi on board. Among many others, Karachi bears the nickname 'mini-Pakistan' for its ethnic, linguistic, and religious diversity. [It has] become a microcosm of the multiple fault lines running across the country.[55]

---

54   Gayer, *Karachi*, 5.
55   ibid., 282.

The very size and heterogeneity of a megacity's population provide social concealment: one hides merely by being among others and not drawing attention. The many resources found in megacities—sustenance, sympathetic population segments, concealment in plain sight, ubiquitous transportation, difference being commonplace and those seemingly innumerable interconnections beyond the urban area—ensure that megacities will continue to attract the attention of those with malevolent intentions. Preparation is crucial to prevention.[56]

Slums

UN HABITAT estimates that by 2050, over 5 billion people will be living in cities, with an average of 30% living in slums.[57]

—Karen Hudson-Edwards and Noah Raford, *Humanitarian Crisis Drivers of the Future*

Cairo's population has nearly doubled since 1996, to 23m … Almost 1m Cairenes live in slums the government considers unsafe, without basic amenities like sewerage and water. Thousands of people live in cemeteries … Others were moved to al-Asmarat, a new public-housing complex 15km south-east of Boulaq. They received two-bedroom flats and a year of free rent. After that they will pay a 30-year mortgage at 300 pounds per month. But the neighbourhood has almost no entertainment or retail, except for a few army-run shops. The commute to downtown Cairo can take an hour or more. It might be affordable, but it is not a place many Egyptians want to call home.[58]

—'Villas and slums', *The Economist*

Slums are another way megacities tend to differ from other urban areas. That is not to say other cities don't have slums. The largest in the world might be Kibera, part of Nairobi, Kenya, a city of about 6 million people

56 Russell W. Glenn, 'Terrorism and Cities: A Target Rich Environment', in *Blood and Concrete: 21st Century Conflict in Urban Centers and Megacities*, Dave Dilegge, Robert J. Bunker, John P. Sullivan and Alma Keshavarz (eds), A Small Wars Journal Book, Washington, DC: Xlibris, 2019, 2–3. Also appears in Russell W. Glenn, 'Terrorism and cities: A target rich environment', *Small Wars Journal*, 1 April 2005, 8–12, available from: smallwarsjournal.com/documents/swjmag/v1/glenn.htm.
57 Karen Hudson-Edwards and Noah Raford, *Humanitarian Crisis Drivers of the Future: Urban Catastrophes—The Wat/San Dimension*, Humanitarian Futures Programme, Report, London: King's College London, 2009, 2, available from: www.humanitarianfutures.org/wp-content/uploads/2013/06/Humanitarian-Crisis-Drivers-of-the-Future-Urban-Catastrophes-the-WatSan-Dimension.pdf.
58 'Villas and slums: Housing in the Middle East', *The Economist*, [London], 16 June 2018, 37–38.

with some regional but little global influence ('might' is the operative term. Determining the number of a slum's residents is notoriously difficult, particularly when those communities are officially ignored by city or national governments, as we noted is often the case in India).

Slum living is frequently difficult. Many residents do not own their homes. Even renting is tenuous as tenant–landlord agreements are often verbal and can end in forced evictions with property owners turning to heavies to oust the unwanted. There have been reports of fires that destroy entire blocks being deliberately set when dwelling-by-dwelling evictions were not thought expedient enough to clear land wanted for other purposes.[59] Though slum residents tend to suffer tenuous water supply and live without adequate sanitation and where crime is commonplace if not ubiquitous, such unexpected displacements nevertheless disrupt economic status and lives more generally. Loss of dwelling terminates what little support residents have available to them. City and state governments frequently do not service slums (a reason they are prone to being 'other-governed'—something we will address in the next section). Any newly homeless are separated from charities or other forms of private support that might be their only recourse should medical attention be needed or children's education desired.[60]

Nor does Mother Nature grant her favours to those exposed to these humanmade risks. Slums tend to form on land no-one else wants because it is prone to flooding, landslides or other hazards. They are often on urban fringes, meaning the trip to and from places of work can take hours. Yet, despite the potential for ouster, vile sanitary conditions, exposure to violence and other disbenefits, there are reasons so many people choose the megacity and its slums over available alternatives.[61] As one observer noted:

---

59   Simone Haysom, *Sanctuary in the City? Urban Displacement and Vulnerability: Final Report*, HPG Report 33, London: Humanitarian Policy Group, Overseas Development Institute, June 2013, 15, available from: cdn.odi.org/media/documents/8444.pdf.

60   'The great urban racket: Africa's slums', *The Economist*, [London], 22 April 2017, 39–40.

61   See Robert Neuwirth, *Shadow Cities: A Billion Squatters, A New Urban World*, New York, NY: Routledge, 2005, 81: 'At 3 shillings per jerry can, Kibera residents pay 10 times more for water than the average person in a wealthy neighborhood with municipally supplied, metered water service. And that's when water is plentiful. When there's a shortage, metered rates don't go up, but the prices in Kibera do. So at those times people in Kibera pay 30 or 40 times the official price of water.'

> [D]espite the excess rain that kept sousing and rotting its foundations … for the people on the streets it was a haven. They were in Calcutta by choice, victims of starvation or persecution elsewhere, and would rather be here, living rough, than in the places from which they had fled.[62]

Estimates of more than 50 per cent of a city's residents living in slum conditions are not unusual. Ethiopia and Republic of Congo are thought to have three-quarters of their countries' city-dwellers living in slums; for Kenya, Tanzania, Nigeria and Bangladesh, the value is half. The estimate for sub-Saharan Africa is nearly two-thirds (62 per cent). For Pakistan, it is roughly 40 per cent.[63] Some 700 million urban residents worldwide do not have adequate sanitation facilities.[64] That's roughly twice the population of the United States.

Why do these people come? Some of the reasons are not that different to why others of nature's creatures leave one habitat for another: escaping drought or other disasters, to improve access to food or because they are forced out of their previous living places. These basic Maslowian causes are not the only reasons. Other animals migrate to survive. They are less likely to consider doing so to improve their quality of life or self-actualise. Rarer yet would be bird or beast choosing to move so it can send resources back to family members remaining in the old ecosystem (the hesitancy of some urban-dwellers notwithstanding). Regardless of the reason, we need to remember that much of the inflow to megacities is not rural-to-urban but rather urban-to-urban as the 'big city' appeals in ways smaller

---

62 James K. Mitchell, 'Natural Disaster in the Context of Mega-Cities', in *Crucibles of Hazard: Mega-Cities and Disasters in Transition*, James K. Mitchell (ed.), New York, NY: United Nations University, 1999, 24. The quotation is from Alexander Frater, *Chasing the Monsoon*, New York, NY: Alfred A. Knopf, 1991.

63 *The Economist*, 'The great urban racket', 39.

64 World Economic Forum (WEF), *Global Risks 2015: 10th Edition*, Insight Report, Geneva: World Economic Forum, 2015, available from: www3.weforum.org/docs/WEF_Global_Risks_2015_Report15.pdf. As with many urban statistics, particularly those involving slums and the poor, the values in this paragraph differ depending on the source or are presented in ways that make comparisons between them virtually impossible. Like definitions of 'urban', what constitutes a slum differs from city to city and writer to writer. That said, those sources generally agree that the number of urban-dwellers living in tenuous conditions lacking many basic services is in the hundreds of millions worldwide. For a small sample of relevant sources, see Ferris, 'Urban disasters, conflict and violence'; Barber, *If Mayors Ruled the World*; Teng et al., 'Urban food security'; Christopher O. Bowers, 'Future megacity operations: Lessons from Sadr City', *Military Review* (May–June 2015): 8–16, at 10, available from: www.armyupress.army.mil/Portals/7/Primer-on-Urban-Operation/Documents/Military Review_20150630_art006.pdf; and Hudson-Edwards and Raford, *Humanitarian Crisis Drivers of the Future*.

cities do not. The source of migrants differs depending on the region in question. While those moving to Dhaka from rural areas account for just under three-quarters of that megacity's growth, urban-to-urban movement is the more likely cause in South America, where rates of urbanisation are already among the highest on the planet. (Not all this in-migration goes to slums—though a fair amount certainly does when the megacity is in the developing world.)

Claims that today's developing-world megacities grew at previously unseen rates do not pass muster. Yes, Democratic Republic of Congo's Kinshasa grew fiftyfold between 1950 and 2015.[65] Estimates are that Lagos saw its population increase by 45 times between that mid-twentieth-century mark and 2019. But Chicago, long the United States' second city, swelled almost sixtyfold between 1850 and 1900.[66] London lags these numbers, its population expanding 'only' sevenfold in the nineteenth century—still impressive, until one considers New York City's population increasing more than 100 times in roughly the same period.[67] But the numbers within the numbers hint at an obvious difference between Western cities' population expansion and that of more recently emerged megacities: rates of growth alone cannot tell the story. The number of individuals constituting the growth reveals where the real difference lies. Chicago's unprecedented growth totalled a mere 1.7 million during the period above, starting from 30,000 people. New York City's impressive leap saw an increase from 30,000 to 3.5 million between 1790 and 1900. Lagos, home to 325,000 in 1950, had a population of 14,630,000 in 2019.[68] Unlike the explosive growth of Chicago, London and New York City that encompassed the Industrial Revolution and its aftermath, Lagos's growth differs not only in population numbers. Its formal economy lacks the ability to absorb anything close to its number of migrants. That alone does not explain the presence of slums. Chicago, London and New York City had theirs. It does, however, explain the size and number of these features in many twenty-first-century developing-world megacities.

65   Statistic for Kinshasa from Williams and Selle, *Military Contingencies in Megacities and Sub-Megacities*, 13.

66   Stephen Malpezzi, Urban growth and development at six scales, Second draft, University of Wisconsin James A. Graaskamp Center for Real Estate, 29 January 2008, 10.

67   'Cleanliness is next to growth: Hygiene', *The Economist*, [London], 1 August 2020, 69–71, at 70.

68   Lagos's 2019 population from *Demographia World Urban Areas*, 15th edn, 23; 1950 population from 'Lagos Population 2020', [Online], Walnut, CA: World Population Review, 2020, [Updated 2023], available from: worldpopulationreview.com/world-cities/lagos-population/; and other sources.

Rio de Janeiro's slums posed a special concern during the 2016 Summer Olympic Games. Concerns about crime meant US athletes were told entering those areas would cause them to be sent home. Some unsuspecting tourists were shocked to find that a bed-and-breakfast that looked so attractive online was in one of the many Rio *favelas*. The US Department of State diplomatic security special agent for the event, Peter Ford (and author of this book's foreword), recalled how the location for the Olympic archery competition was between two slums that routinely exchanged gunfire at night. Expended rounds could be found on the turf in the days after such exchanges.[69]

Not all security risks associated with slums are so dramatic. The more frequently seen have their roots in a combination of living conditions and lack of services. An estimated one in six of Kenya's slum-dwellers suffers from either hypertension or diabetes but is unable to access screening services or medications.[70] It is part of a wicked cycle: many slum residents work in the informal economy. They therefore do not pay taxes, so the government sees little reason to provide services—or recognise their existence. No funding was allocated for those living in slums after the 26 July 2005 flooding in Mumbai, India,[71] which killed more than 1,000 and displaced hundreds of thousands from low-lying ground.

Yet, not all is darkness. Slum residents may find informal authorities provide them with essential services when the officially recognised government cannot or will not. These areas, and at times other parts of a megacity as well, are what we will refer to as 'other-governed' areas.

69   Peter Ford, 'Best practices for securing a megacity during a major world event 2: The 2016 Rio de Janeiro Summer Olympics', Presentation to Current and Future Operations in Megacities Conference, Tokyo, 18 July 2016.

70   D. Sanderson, P. Knox Clarke and L. Campbell, *Responding to urban disasters: Learning from previous relief and recovery operations*, ALNAP Lessons Paper, London: ALNAP, 2012, available from: www.alnap.org/help-library/responding-to-urban-disasters-learning-from-previous-relief-and-recovery-operations.

71   Emily Boyd, Aditya Ghosh and Maxwell T. Boykoff, 'Climate Change Adaptation in Mumbai, India', in *The Urban Climate Challenge: Rethinking the Role of Cities in the Global Climate Regime*, Craig Johnson, Noah Toly and Heike Schroeder (eds), Abingdon, UK: Routledge, 2015, 221.

Alternative authorities in megacities

Most telling was an American request in August 2009 for the extradition of a leading drug 'don,' Christopher 'Dudus' Coke. For months, the prime minister [Bruce Golding] stalled, reluctant to take on a gang leader who ruled the streets in Mr Golding's own Kingston Westerns constituency, handing out schoolbooks and hosting Christmas parties. When the government finally moved against Mr Coke in May 2010, arresting and extraditing him, the confrontation left 83 dead. But it has been followed by a fall of more than 40% in the murder rate.[72]

—'Golding goes', *The Economist*

After [police] confiscate the weapons in one favela, they keep some and sell the rest to a gang in another favela … Some are swapped at the border of Paraguay for drugs.[73]

—Janice Perlman, *Favela*

It is more likely that the emerging places of the world will follow quite different paths and produce different realities. It is probable, in such places, that the formal will never defeat or even rival the informal. Large portions of their cities will continue to be self-administered by communities who are little known to authorities or to each other.[74]

—Rana Dasgupta, *Capital*

Dudus Coke's de facto governing of a Kingston, Jamaica, slum has plenty of company. Rio de Janeiro's Rocinha *favela* is the only one of the megacity's some 1,000 slums with a public road running through it. Even so, it is like others there: a city unto itself where security forces enter at personal risk. Yet commercial enterprises, legitimate and otherwise, go where others fear to tread when money can be made. State security might hesitate to enter, but the state-run Caixa Econômica Federal bank established a branch in Rocinha and offered residents credit cards.[75] The bank is by no means the only business venture known to residents.

---

72 'Golding goes: Jamaica's prime minister', *The Economist*, [London], 1 October 2011, 40.
73 Janice Perlman, *Favela: Four Decades of Living on the Edge in Rio de Janeiro*, New York, NY: Oxford University Press, 2010, 180.
74 Dasgupta, *Capital*, 435.
75 Neuwirth, *Shadow Cities*, 42, 44.

Until his arrest in 2011, Antônio Francisco Bonfim 'Nem' Lopes commanded 120 thugs who helped run an organisation responsible for more than 60 per cent of Rio's cocaine.

Rocinha's government was government by Nem. As was the case with Coke in Kingston and Pablo Escobar in Medellín, Colombia, Nem's enterprise was not only tolerated but also assisted by community members. The number of murders and other acts of violence declined during Nem's rule, with homicide rates dropping from 60 per 100,000 before he took over to about 20 per 100,000 once his regime was firmly in place. There was still violence, but it was by and large related to Nem's men conducting the business of trafficking or maintaining peace. Thefts also fell.[76]

Again, like Coke and Escobar, Nem provided a range of public services, including support for sporting, medical and other amenities the formal city authorities failed to bring to the slum (though, admittedly, electricity, television and other services were often pirated). (This aid by criminals can also be found in the developed world. Organised crime groups known as *yakuza* established soup kitchens when Japanese government authorities took too long to provide relief after the 1995 Kobe earthquake.)[77] Though there is no universal formula for other-governed success, alternative authorities in Brazil's largest cities provide services also found in slums elsewhere: handing out food and other goods, sponsoring NGOs doing the same and offering upward mobility to youths via gang membership—this where other employment opportunities are rare.[78] There may be a degree of benevolence in this provision of goods and services, but gang or other leaders understand that their benevolence garners early warning protection just as their thugs keep outsiders who seek to take advantage of slum-dwellers at arm's length. Services provided to residents are often a source of revenue. Those living in Nairobi slums pay for the 'privilege' of using shared toilets. Taxes ensure property is not stolen and the streets and alleys are 'policed'. Residents pay for water and

---

76   Misha Glenny, 'Cocaine, sex and social media: The untold story of Rio's most notorious cartel boss', *WIRED*, 26 October 2015, available from: www.wired.co.uk/article/rocinha-brazil-drug-cartel-antonio-lopes-nem.
77   'Flu jabs: Japan may have to cancel the Olympics', *The Economist*, [London], 7 March 2020, 36.
78   David C. Becker, 'Gangs, netwar, and "community counterinsurgency" in Haiti', *PRISM: The Journal of Complex Operations* 2(3) (June 2011): 137–54, [Washington, DC: National Defence University], available from: cco.ndu.edu/Portals/96/Documents/prism/prism_2-3/Prism_137-154_Becker.pdf.

electricity, the latter charged by the bulb, whether it is pirated or not.[79] Provision of goods and services is also a means of recruitment. Lopes, who became lord of Rocinha and its estimated 200,000 residents under the street name Nem, joined the *favela*'s other-governed establishment because he needed money to treat his daughter's illness, becoming one of the hundreds who acted as lookouts to warn of approaching police or opposing gangs, transported drugs, provided armed security or performed other tasks essential to the other-government ensuring control. The services provided in such cases are selective, however, with leaders making the choices about what is on offer. Those services provided by the frequently changing Rocinha leadership (thanks to murders and imprisonment) do not include addressing Rocinha's status as a community with one of Brazil's highest tuberculosis rates.[80]

Urban areas tend to have higher rates of tuberculosis than rural areas. Karachi, Pakistan, for example, has nearly twice the prevalence of the disease as the rest of the country. Mumbai and Dhaka are also among the megacities with high rates of tuberculosis. That newly emerging diseases tend to originate in or quickly become urban phenomena is apparent in recent outbreaks of severe acute respiratory syndrome (SARS), H1N1 influenza epidemics and, of course, Covid-19. High population densities ensure exposure. Tests conducted between June and July 2020 found 54 per cent of Mumbai's slum residents had Covid-19 antibodies; the rate in the city's formal housing was reportedly 16 per cent.[81] Some urban populations have better immunity to specific diseases given their greater exposure. The population of Afghanistan's capital, Kabul, tends to become infected with cutaneous leishmaniasis early in life as the disease is endemic to the city. Older rural Afghans are vulnerable, however, having not been exposed. Migrations promoted by the recent years of war have seen the disease achieve epidemic status in the capital as a result. Knowing which segments of a megacity population are at greater risk of exposure to maladies could be vital to aid providers. The greater vulnerability to Covid-19 of the aged, certain ethnic or labour groups and those with pre-

79   Antonio Sampaio and Eleanor Beevor, *Urban Drivers of Political Violence: Declining State Authority and Armed Groups in Mogadishu, Nairobi, Kabul and Karachi*, IISS Research Report, London: International Institute for Strategic Studies, May 2020, 13, available from: www.urban-response.org/system/files/content/resource/files/main/Urban%20drivers%20of%20political%20violence%20-%20IISS%20Research%20Report.pdf.
80   Misha Glenny, *Nemesis: One Man and the Battle for Rio*, New York, NY: Alfred A. Knopf, 2016, 15, 65–66.
81   'Rich slum, poor slum: Poverty', *The Economist*, [London], 19 June 2021, 57–58.

existing conditions is another example. Being aware of second and higher-order effects helps here, too. Though an obvious case, lack of access to potable water would forewarn of those urban residents likely to have higher rates of intestinal parasites, diarrhoea and cholera. On the upside, urban types are generally more exposed to education campaigns and act accordingly. City folk trend lower than their rural cousins in rates of AIDS and HIV due to greater condom use. Slums, which tend to have lower literacy rates than even rural regions of a country, can be an exception.[82] On a positive note: cities may provide a means of quickly detecting the origin of a disease or biological agent as well as its spread. Each year, 21 June is the day representatives of the International Metagenomics and Metadesign of the Subways and Urban Biomes (MetaSUB) International Consortium collect samples of local microbes. Though MetaSUB is far from being able to identify all collected bacteria, much less parse samples that are threatening, the 'vast majority' of identifiable species are narrowly distributed geographically, suggesting a possible future in which swabbing public areas might be a powerful tool in combating diseases before they reach pandemic status.[83]

Other-governed slums and their recruiting methods take on a different character in Nairobi than is the case in Rocinha. Fundamentalist religious leaders are among those who provide what the state will not. Among these extremists was Ahmed Iman Ali, whose links included the Somali insurgent group al-Shabaab, the crimes of which include terrorist attacks in the Kenyan capital. The Pakistani Taliban is among the several other-governing authorities in Karachi. Services provided by these informal governors include electricity (again, stolen), internet and water. Maintaining exclusive control over supply sometimes involves violence and coercion. Residents in one community were forced to drink only one brand of bottled water—presumably, a means of protecting the other-governing authority's monopoly.[84]

Interfering with these other-governors could be risky for outsiders unaware of the complex relationships that involve contacts external as well as internal to the communities in question. São Paulo's and Rio's slum

---

82   Emilie Alirol, Laurent Getaz, Beat Stoll, François Chappius and Louis Loutan, 'Urbanisation and infectious diseases in a globalized world', *The Lancet* 11(2) (1 February 2011): 131–41, at 132–34, doi.org/10.1016/S1473-3099(10)70223-1.
83   'A midsummer bug hunt: Microecology', *The Economist*, [London], 19 June 2021, 76.
84   Sampaio and Beevor, *Urban Drivers of Political Violence*, 15, 20–21.

governors include retired or off-duty police and fire department officers.[85] In other cases, outside businesses and elected politicians both capitalise on and legitimise other-governed authorities for financial gain or as a means of securing large blocks of votes assured by deals with slum governors.[86] Police, politicians and other officials are often complicit even when not integrated with slum management. Bribes or coercion buy complacency and, when necessary, direct support. Imprisonment is no guarantee of separating other-governors from their constituency. Though in prison, leaders of the First Capital Command gang ordered members to attack police and other public targets in 2006 in São Paulo, Brazil. They struck more than 100 police stations and additional government installations, burned over 50 buses and all but shut down the megacity's transportation system. More than 40 police officers were killed in the seven-day 'war' while gang safe havens in the city's *favelas* remained undisturbed.[87]

The situation was similar in the opening years of the twenty-first century across the Atlantic, though the businesses controlled by criminals and corrupt officials again differed in type and scope. Nairobi's *Mungiki*— essentially a banned cult—stepped into areas lacking sufficient police or other formal authorities, as was the case in Brazil, but the organisation also took over key functions throughout the city. Drivers of the Kenyan capital's many *matatu* minibuses are forced to pay *Mungiki* members protection money or risk physical violence—violence that includes beheadings, skinning and removing other body parts. Outlawed in 2002, the organisation remains as an undercurrent in Nairobi and elsewhere in Kenya, with members and supporters including security officials and politicians.[88] In the case of the *Mungiki*, 'other-governed' refers less to a place than to an alternative authority that permeates sectors of the economy or aspects of Kenyan social life much as organised crime has in other major cities' dock operations, refuse removal and other economic

---

85   Or at least such was the case less than a decade ago. See 'Conquering Complexo do Alemão: Organised crime in Brazil', *The Economist*, [London], 4 December 2010, 49.

86   Glenny, *Nemesis*, 15, 46.

87   Richard J. Norton, 'Feral cities: Problems today, battlefields tomorrow', *Marine Corps University Journal* 1 (Spring 2010): 50–77, at 67; and 'A magic moment for the city of God: Security in Brazil', *The Economist*, [London], 12 June 2010, 42–43.

88   Jacob Rasmussen, '"We Are the True Blood of the Mau Mau": The Mungiki Movement in Kenya', in *Global Gangs: Street Violence Across the World*, Jennifer M. Hazen and Dennis Rodgers (eds), Minneapolis, MN: University of Minnesota Press, 2014, 213–35, at 226, doi.org/10.5749/minnesota/9780816691470.003.0011; and Immigration and Refugee Board of Canada, 'Responses to Information Requests (RIRs)', Document KEN103225.E, Toronto: IRB, 16 November 2009, available from: www.refworld.org/docid/4b20f048c.html.

sectors. The *Mungiki* offers several lessons to those who might find themselves responding to a megacity disaster. Among them is the point that 'other-governed' need not be space-constrained. Like the insurgent, the cooperative official or friendly citizen by day can be a coercive other-governor at night (though in this context, 'day' and 'night' have little to do with time and much to do with intentions). History can help us in understanding these forces, but any outsider planning to conduct relief or recovery operations in a megacity would be wise to update what they know about the environment. Criminal enterprises evolve over time, adapting to changed conditions and new opportunities as does any beast of prey. *Mungiki* started out in the 1980s as an ethnically based group seeking to raise the economic status of the Kikuyu people, Kenya's largest tribe.[89] Over time, its members filled or created criminal niches in Nairobi and elsewhere—an unfortunate evolution in the capital's and the country's ecosystems—one fed by what an outsider will very likely find is among the greatest obstacles to their organisation's efforts to support those in need after a disaster: corruption.

The eternal virus: Corruption

> They who give straight judgements to strangers and to the men of the land, and go not aside from what is just, their city flourishes, and the people prosper in it … But for those who practice violence and cruel deeds far-seeing Zeus, the son of Cronos, ordains a punishment. Often even a whole city suffers for a bad man who sins and devises presumptuous deeds, and the son of Cronos lays great trouble upon the people, famine and plague together, so that the men perish away, and their women do not bear children, and their houses become few.[90]
>
> —Hesiod, *Works and Days*

> For the poor of a country where corruption thieved a great deal of opportunity, corruption was one of the genuine opportunities that remained.[91]
>
> —Katherine Boo, *Behind the Beautiful Forevers*

---

89 Rasmussen, 'We Are the True Blood of the Mau Mau', 215.
90 Hesiod, *Works and Days*, trans. Hugh G. Evelyn-White, 1914, lines 225–26, 238–45 [line numbers are approximate], available from: people.sc.fsu.edu/~dduke/lectures/hesiod1.pdf.
91 Boo, *Behind the Beautiful Forevers*, 28.

At this point, we understand that 'other-governed areas' refers not to locations alone, but includes segments of a population or economic sectors controlled by illegitimate authorities. What is legitimately governed and other-governed rarely lends itself to crisp delineation; the line between legitimate and otherwise is often hard to discern when police, politicians and others have a foot in both camps. The two can and frequently do coexist. We have also noted that those seemingly being imposed on are often strong supporters of the other-governors. No few of Kingston's residents killed during the seizure of Dudus Coke were defending his realm at the time.

Megacities feature varieties of unofficial or semi-official parties in addition to those identified above. Neighbourhood associations, service groups and unions or other work-associated organisations are among those who wield considerable influence both day-to-day and in extremis. These groups can be permanent in nature, spontaneous, periodic or ad hoc. Adding to the possibilities are single individuals who come forward in the aftermath of a disaster to help organise volunteers, collect and disperse scarce resources and emergency supplies or otherwise step up when formal government representatives prove incapable or overwhelmed. In short, 'other-governed' need not imply bad. Nor is the situation a case of either/ or; a sector might not be completely governed by formal authorities or those otherwise. Many are legitimately committed to the welfare of residents; others—like the *yakuza* in post-earthquake Kobe—not so much. Political organisations in Dhaka, Bangladesh, are better managed than is the formal city government. Patronage in Dhaka determines who gets which job, who and which communities receive public benefits, which companies win construction and other contracts and who has access to lucrative functions such as licensing rickshaw pullers or receipt of electricity.[92] Corruption seemingly has no limit in the number of forms it can take. Elsewhere around the world, the hyper-influential include the overly rich who buy exemptions from burdens suffered by common folk and use their money to ensure legislation favourable to their interests.[93]

---

92   Institute of Governance Studies, *State of Cities: Urban Governance in Dhaka*, Report, Dhaka: BRAC University, May 2012, 7, available from: www.academia.edu/35811593/STATE_OF_CITIES _Urban_Governance_in_Dhaka.
93   For more on this phenomenon, see Robert J. Bunker and Pamela Ligouri Bunker (eds), *Plutocratic Insurgency Reader*, A Small Wars Journal Book, Bloomington, IN: Xlibris, 2019.

Regardless of their character, identifying other-governed or less-formal authorities will be helpful when seeking to ensure a megacity's successful recovery from a catastrophe. It could be so in preventing one as well. The US Office of Naval Intelligence (ONI) worked with the Manhattan District Attorney's Office to establish relationships with organised crime leaders controlling New York City dock workers during World War II. Those leaders' firm guidance ensured union members reported any suspicious activity while keeping their own tongues tied so as not to release information beneficial to the enemy. ONI expanded these ties, reaching into Sicily with the assistance of mafia leader Lucky Luciano, who arranged for criminal elements on the island to cooperate with Allied forces when they later invaded.[94] Such Dark Side links exist in many megacities today, and could have significant implications for organisations providing crisis relief. Leaders seeking to influence the behaviour of one or more of an urban population's ethnic, religious, labour, social, youth or other groups may find other-than-elected or formally appointed officials more effective conduits of influence than politicians. Less-formal leaders can also provide important information about the resources a community can offer in the aftermath of a calamity. Resources could range from the provision of food, building supplies or other goods to volunteer or paid labour, with these leaders assisting by organising workers, setting wages and—if deemed sufficiently noncorrupt—dispersing pay for work done.

If deemed sufficiently noncorrupt. 'Corruption is the single largest obstacle to [urban] development. [It] acts as a deterrent to direct (and even indirect) foreign investment, as it will influence foreign firms' decisions to locate in a particular country or city.'[95] So wrote UN authors in the opening years of the twenty-first century. Not long after, I was part of a multinational team analysing the effectiveness of the US Agency for International Development (USAID) Community Stabilization Program in Iraq. Corruption was so rife that the initiative was terminated roughly $100 million short of its planned spending limit largely thanks to inadequate supervision of expenditures. The inadequacy was not entirely the fault of USAID inspectors but rather due in part to absurd constraints precluding the organisation's inspectors from visiting construction sites. US State Department dictates prohibited USAID personnel riding in military vehicles. Senior coalition leaders feared any

94   John Strausbaugh, *Victory City: A History of New York and New Yorkers during World War II*, New York, NY: Hachette, 2018, 274–75.
95   UN-Habitat, *State of the World's Cities 2012/2013*, 98.

hint of coalition military presence would undermine efforts to portray the Iraqi Government as the agent responsible for a project—this even though local Iraqis were aware of who was providing the funding. Inspectors were also prohibited from riding in contractors' vehicles. As USAID had insufficient vehicles of its own, there was no practical way to inspect sites given the high-risk security environment. One enterprising Irish USAID contractor arranged for US military representatives to fly unmanned aerial vehicles (UAVs) over construction sites for which he was responsible—an innovative but exceptional solution dependent on the fortuitous proximity of UAV-equipped units.[96]

Karachi public officials deluded themselves into thinking their formal positions allowed them to control their criminal partners. Those believing themselves the puppet masters soon found the puppets free of their strings. Criminal enterprises are thought to have been behind the burning of the megacity's Bolton Market in 2009—an effective way of removing long-time shopkeepers paying low rents. Elsewhere, city land barons seized control of Karachi's edge land for their own profit thanks to political connections. At times, the corrupt authorities and criminal enterprises were one and the same. One aid provider—later murdered—railed against the 'mafias', accusing them of the megacity's rampant land theft and exorbitant water prices, declaring 'there's no land mafia. The land mafia is the government itself.'[97] Whether criminals, politicians, city authorities or some combination of the three, real estate manipulators provided another twist on corruption by creating their own other-governed areas. Residents found themselves virtual captives of those controlling the land. The property masters exercised virtually unrestricted command over homes and commercial enterprises, including access to amenities such as roads, water, sewerage and power that the formal city government failed to provide.[98] The European Union–funded research organisation ENACT found the same was true in Kenya, where:

---

96 For more on the problems with the Community Stabilization Program (many of which were later replicated in Afghanistan), see Russell W. Glenn, Colin Holland, Alasdair W.G. Mackie, Brenda Oppermann, Deborah Zubow Prindle and Myra Speelmans, *Evaluation of USAID's Community Stabilization Program (CSP) in Iraq: Effectiveness of the CSP Model as a Non-Lethal Tool for Counterinsurgency*, Washington, DC: United States Agency for International Development, 2009, available from: pdf.usaid.gov/pdf_docs/PDACN461.pdf. Regarding corruption in Afghanistan, see Special Inspector General for Afghanistan Reconstruction, *Corruption in Conflict: Lessons from the US Experiences in Afghanistan*, Arlington, VA: SIGAR, September 2016, available from: www.sigar.mil/pdf/lessonslearned/SIGAR-16-58-LL-Executive-Summary.pdf.
97 Samira Shackle, *Karachi Vice: Life and Death in a Contest City*, London: Granta, 2001, 167.
98 Inskeep, *Instant City*, 29–36, 108.

drug-traffickers are small fry compared with criminal landlords. 'Land allocation, real estate and property development ... may be the largest type of organized criminal activity in Africa.' In Kibera, a slum in Nairobi, more than 90% of residents rent their homes from absentee landlords [of whom, reportedly, 42 per cent] 'had associations with state and political actors' while 41% were government officials and 16% were politicians.[99]

There are less obvious but no less damaging consequences of corruption that potentially interfere with preparations for and responses to disaster. That corruption undermines trust in formal authorities is obvious. Any outsider naive or foolish enough to associate themselves with such officials is delegitimised. These misguided associations close the mouths of city residents who would otherwise provide valuable information. The Iraqi Security Forces found themselves tainted in this manner as they sought to retake Mosul from the Islamic State of Iraq and Syria (ISIS) in 2016–17:

> Even if you had the courage to report to the police or the governor's office that you were being threatened by ISI [the Islamic State of Iraq, one of several monikers used when referring to ISIS] into say, handing over the details of a government contract, there was no way to know whether the administrator or cop you went to wasn't himself compromised ... For Moslawis, the [formal] government became morally indistinguishable from the insurgency, and then worse than the insurgency.[100]

Humans as bringers of disaster: War and terrorism in megacities

City centers and residential areas are now the battlefields and frontlines of our century.[101]

—Willem Oosterveld et al., *Resilient Cities, Safe Societies*

---

99 'Parcels, plots and power: Property rights', *The Economist*, [London], 12 September 2020, 37–39, at 39.

100 James Verini, *They Will Have to Die Now: Mosul and the Fall of the Caliphate*, New York, NY: W.W. Norton, 2019, 69–70, 71.

101 Willem Oosterveld et al., *Resilient Cities, Safe Societies: How Cities and States Can Cooperate to Combat the Violence Nexus and Promote Human Security*, The Hague, Netherlands: Centre for Strategic Studies, 2018, 3.

LTG Harold G. Moore, commander at LZ (Landing Zone) X-Ray in November 1965 and co-author of the Vietnam [War] classic *We Were Soldiers Once ... and Young*, writes that 'a commander in battle has three means of influencing the action: fire support ... his personal presence on the battlefield, and the use of his reserve.' Urban areas conspire against all three of these.[102]

—Russell W. Glenn and Gina Kingston, *Urban Battle Command in the 21st Century*

Humankind is often crueller than Mother Nature. While the latter's punishments can be catastrophic, the duration of her violence tends to be quick in comparison with that wrought when humans choose to fight their fellows on city streets. War leaves physical devastation no less severe and often far worse than disasters due to natural events. The social damage can be much worse. The upside is that a city readying itself for natural disaster can also take steps helpful in preparing for humankind's brutality.

Pause a moment to remember what makes targeting urban areas attractive. Bigger, better connected, more influential urban areas—megacities— garner even more attention. This goes a long way towards explaining why city-dwellers make up some four-fifths of terrorism's deaths.[103] Urban density means not only more targets to attack but also more places to secrete bombs, less chance of terrorists' detection before their attack and a multitude of ways to escape after perpetration. The 2008 Lashkar-e-Taiba strikes in Mumbai included two massive hotels among other targets. Such structures are more common in larger cities than elsewhere. Such is also the case in terms of the numbers and types of media representatives on hand to cover the act. Lucrative targets tend to be close to others (think of CBDs) and along routes where individuals fleeing one explosion can be caught with a second or third well-placed bomb or ambush. Emergency responders have proved particularly popular targets as they come to assist those injured in an initial attack.

The Irish Republican Army recognised the value of London in this regard. Attacks in Belfast and Londonderry/Derry were not getting the attention the organisation sought. Bombing London's financial district and attempting to mortar the prime minister's residence at 10 Downing Street were among several attacks that succeeded in achieving notoriety

---

102 Russell W. Glenn and Gina Kingston, *Urban Battle Command in the 21st Century*, Santa Monica, CA: RAND Corporation, 2005, available from: www.rand.org/content/dam/rand/pubs/monographs/2005/RAND_MG181.pdf, 23.
103 Oosterveld et al., *Resilient Cities, Safe Societies*, 17.

well beyond the physical damage produced (which in the former case was considerable). That London is the United Kingdom's capital gave the events more *political* impact than would have been the case in any other city in the country. That the megacity is an economic and banking centre for Europe and the world meant there was potential to cause planet-wide *financial* distress. London's attractiveness as a tourist city offered potential to undermine *local economic* wellbeing. That it is the United Kingdom's primate city provided a magnifying glass, further inflating the *domestic social* drama associated with the performance. It is also home to major media headquarters and offices, ensuring attention for days and weeks after an event. The same size stone thrown into Liverpool, Chicago, Perth or Marseilles strikes a semi-large pond in which other-than-local ripples quickly disappear.

The media offers terrorists treasure in addition to broadcasting their performances: information. Live television provides otherwise blind perpetrators with real-time insights into the impact of their attacks and authorities' responses. Such was the case for the remote handlers guiding terrorist actions in 2008 in Mumbai. Mobile phones are obviously another source of information if terrorist managers assign reporting duties to some of their agents. Testifying before the US Congress about the lessons from those dark hours in India, former New York City police commissioner Raymond W. Kelly observed:

> [T]he other issue that we examined in our exercises last month … is the ability of the terrorist handlers to direct operations from outside the attack zone using cell phones and other portable communications devices. With this comes a formidable capacity to adjust tactics while attacks are underway. We also discussed the complications of media coverage that could disclose law enforcement tactics in real time. This phenomenon is not new. In the past, police were able to defeat any advantage it might give hostage takers by cutting off power to the location they were in. However, the proliferation of hand-held devices would appear to trump that solution. When lives are at stake, law enforcement needs to find ways to disrupt cell phones and other communications in a pinpointed way against terrorists who are using them.[104]

---

104 Raymond W. Kelly, 'Testimony by Raymond W. Kelly, Police Commissioner, City of New York', in *Lessons from the Mumbai Terrorist Attacks: Parts I and II*, Hearings before the Committee on Homeland Security and Governmental Affairs, United States Senate, 111th Congress, 1st Session, 8 and 28 January 2009, Washington, DC: US Government Printing Office, available from: www. govinfo.gov/content/pkg/CHRG-111shrg49484/html/CHRG-111shrg49484.htm.

Bringing media representatives into planning sessions and exercises held in preparation for future crises will not prevent all irresponsible reporting. It could reduce its frequency by making the consequences of reporting clear and establishing guidelines for the timing of releases as has long been common when reporters accompany units in combat.

In addition to megacities' political and cultural symbolism, concentrations of attractive targets and shelter from prying eyes, their extensive interconnectedness means attacking well-chosen targets can achieve ends far beyond the urban area in which terrorists operate. A perpetrator could conceivably influence their ultimate target by striking one many miles and nations distant, thus taking advantage of international second and higher-order effects. Recalling our pool table metaphor, the effect in the initial city could be minimal—even unnoticeable—while the objective urban area suffers the desired consequence.

It pays to play the biggest venues if a terrorist, insurgent or other armed group seeks rockstar impact. The populations, structures and functions of the world's largest and most influential cities have been and will continue to be the favourites of those with malicious intentions. These groups may turn to the biggest urban area a local environment offers when no megacity lies within reasonable reach. Baghdad's residents suffered nearly half of all deaths during this century's first decade of fighting in Iraq.[105]

---

105 David Kilcullen, *Out of the Mountains: The Coming Age of the Urban Guerrilla*, Oxford, UK: Oxford University Press, 2013, 26.

4

The key to a megacity: Information

A recent addition to aggregating mobile, social, and location is Ushahidi, a platform that unifies data gathered from multiple sources (SMS, email, web) and distributes it onto a visual map or timeline. This technology was used to track the 'Snowmaggedon' storm in Washington D.C. last winter as well as tracking the progress of voting in India and the movement of swine flu across a map area. Most notably, this technology is being used for post-crisis information in Haiti. It is an open-source platform, which allows developers to see behind the technology and build additional features upon it. The site is rich in documentation to allow users to customize it for specific tasks.[1]

—American Red Cross, *The case for integrating crisis response with social media*

Rescue personnel will need to have information beyond what a two-dimensional grid coordinate can provide. Otherwise time will be lost in trying to determine where in a multi-story building individuals in need are located.[2]

—Russell W. Glenn et al., *Achieving Convergence during Humanitarian Assistance and Disaster Relief Operations*

---

1   American Red Cross, *The case for integrating crisis response with social media*, Paper, Washington, DC: American Red Cross, August 2010.
2   Russell W. Glenn, Colin Christopher, Caleb Dexter, David Norton and Robert Nussbaumer (eds), *Achieving Convergence during Humanitarian Assistance and Disaster Relief Operations in the World's Largest Urban Areas: Proceedings of the 'Current and Future Operations in Megacities' Conference, Tokyo, Japan, July 16–18, 2019*, Fort Eustis, VA: US Army Training and Doctrine Command, 1 October 2019, available from: community.apan.org/wg/tradoc-g2/mad-scientist/m/tokyo-megacities-conference-2019/294569.

Doctors and citizens came together, convincing reporters to warn that the 28 September Liberty Loan parade should be cancelled lest the highly contagious malady infect the thousands who would be packed in close company.[3] Editors refused to publish articles passing on the message. The parade went on as scheduled. At its peak proficiency, the disease would claim the lives of 759 people in a single day. Nearly all the city's eventual total of more than 12,000 dead fell in just six weeks. Few came forward when the city's Bureau of Child Hygiene begged for volunteers to take in the children of the perished or perishing. A medical student working in an emergency medical hospital saw not a single car as he drove the 20 kilometres home one night during the epidemic. He wrote of Philadelphia: 'The life of the city had almost stopped.' To the southwest, 51 per cent of San Antonians became sick, blood flowing from ears, noses, eyes and mouths—the last in a foamy mixture coughed up from deep within the lungs. Cities throughout the country ran short of coffins. Health officials started lying, desperate to contain the panic. The surgeon general assured Americans that all they had to do was follow precautionary guidelines to avoid becoming sick. The head of Los Angeles' public health department reinforced such dispatches. The public quickly came to recognise them as falsehoods. New York City's public health director blamed 'other bronchial diseases', not the real threat of Spanish flu. A British medical journal reassured readers that the influenza was gone when the disease paused to take a breath. Instead, as one author later put it: 'It was more like a great tsunami that initially pulls water away from the shore—only to return in a towering, overwhelming surge.' It was 1918. Trust was as much a victim as were the sick. People fled from their neighbours and neighbourhoods. Hundreds reportedly starved when the ill were left alone and none risked coming near. Almost exactly a century later US citizens would again be victimised by some political leaders' wilful ignorance or deliberate deception as Covid-19 stalked the streets.

It is not melodramatic to say that several of the world's megacities constantly flirt with disaster. That does not equate to pending devastation. We know Manila, Tokyo, Berlin, Paris and London survived World War II. New York City endured Hurricane Sandy and Covid-19. Mexico City, Tokyo (again), Los Angeles, Mumbai and what is now Istanbul exist

---

3   Material and quotations from the description of the 1918 influenza pandemic are adapted John M. Barry, 'How the horrific 1918 flu spread across America', *Smithsonian Magazine*, November 2017, available from: www.smithsonianmag.com/history/journal-plague-year-180965222/.

despite substantial and repeated earthquakes.[4] Manila was 80 per cent flooded in 2009 when Typhoon Ketsana (known as Tropical Storm Ondoy in the Philippines) dropped an average month's rain on the city in six hours. The region has experienced six severe earthquakes during the past century. Authorities admit the urban area is not sufficiently prepared for another despite parts of the megacity spanning two major fault lines.[5] Some of these urban areas are sure to suffer and survive again. Accurate information-sharing before, during and after disasters will underpin the best plans and responses.

Help thy neighbour

A woman rushed up to us in a state of frenzy in her night attire covered in grime and dust, blood streaming from her face and pleading with us to save her child trapped in the wreckage of her home. We tried to grope our way beneath the wreckage in a vain search for the child when we heard a groaning sound and a feeble voice saying, 'Oh please somebody help me.' [It] was that of an elderly woman, pinned down by the weight of the debris and ceiling, and after a struggle [we] managed to extricate her ... What happened to the poor child for whom we began the search I never knew.[6]

—Kenneth Holmes, quoted in Aaron William Moore, *Bombing the City*

We looked around and saw a drab collection of small cement houses lining narrow, busy streets. When Matsuda-san described the neighborhood to us, however, it was clear he saw something different. He saw a community. He saw a few thousand people— the residents, the merchants, the students and teachers at our

---

4   Regarding Mumbai and earthquakes, see Mazhuvanchery Avarachen Sherly, Subhankar Karmakar, Devanathan Parthasarathy, Terence Chan and Christian Rau, 'Disaster vulnerability mapping for a densely populated coastal urban area: An application to Mumbai, India', *Annals of the Association of American Geographers* 105(6) (2015): 1198–220, at 1201, doi.org/10.1080/00045608. 2015.1072792.

5   Sara Meerow, 'Double exposure, infrastructure planning, and urban climate resilience in coastal megacities: A case study of Manila', *Environment and Planning A: Economy and Space* 49(11) (2017): 2649–72, at 2651, doi.org/10.1177/0308518X17723630; and Roberts, 'Risk and resilience in Asian cities'. Roberts notes that though the disaster risk-management plans for Quezon and Makati cities within the Manila megacity lacked institutional capacity, technical capabilities and financing to make them effective, their existence and implementation in the aftermath of this storm made their response 'far more effective' than that for other parts of Manila lacking such plans.

6   Moore, *Bombing the City*, 147–48.

> local schools, the mailman, the two cops who watched over our neighborhood and the adjacent Subsection 2 from their little booth a few blocks down the street—who worked together to make a community. To him, Subsection 3 was a group of people.[7]
>
> —T.R. Reid, *Confucius Lives Next Door*

The survival rate for those rescued by neighbours or a passer-by from beneath debris after Kobe's January 1995 Great Hanshin Earthquake was 80 per cent. The rate for those recovered by emergency response personnel was 50 per cent. That is not a reflection on the competence of the professionals. Blocked roads, scarcity of earthmoving equipment and the fact that individuals found by professionals were likely buried under amounts of rubble immovable except by special equipment meant more of those recovered were killed outright, suffered greater injuries or could not be rescued in a timely fashion. But that does not in any way diminish the importance of *first* first responders: the community members without whom many more of their neighbours would have breathed their last.[8]

Citing lessons from New Orleans and Hurricane Katrina, one author concluded: '[P]robably the biggest change in recent years [is] the realization that disaster response is not just government response. It is a societal response. The federal government has a role, and so does everyone else.'[9] Others writing in 1995 concluded that:

> residents themselves are not only *capable* of contributing considerably to [citizen rescues], but in many cases *they are the primary actors by default*. For example, after the major earthquakes of the past decade (Armenia, Mexico City, etc.), 90 per cent of those rescued have been dug out by their neighbors and not by technical experts.[10]

We recall that most of those who made it to hospitals during the nerve agent attack on Tokyo's subways did not do so in emergency vehicles; more than one-third (34.9 per cent) walked. Another 37.6 per cent

---

7   Reid, *Confucius Lives Next Door*, 74.
8   Perry et al., *The Shakeout Earthquake Scenario*.
9   William Carwile, FEMA associate administrator for response and recovery, quoted in Dave Philipps, 'Seven hard lessons federal responders to Harvey learned from Katrina', *The New York Times*, 7 September 2017, available from: www.nytimes.com/2017/09/07/us/hurricane-harvey-katrina-federal-responders.html.
10   Ben Wisner and Henry R. Luce, 'Bridging "expert" and "local" knowledge for counter-disaster planning in urban South Africa', *GeoJournal* 37 (1995): 335–48, at 344, doi.org/10.1007/BF00814014. [Emphasis in original.]

arrived by taxi or thanks to good Samaritan private vehicle owners. Only 7 per cent arrived by ambulance, with firefighters and police lending transport support in lesser percentages (the numbers do not total 100 per cent, presumably because the means by which some patients reached the hospital remains unknown).

The role of the person next-door is all the more vital when the official capacity to respond falls short. The citizenry of Mexico City stepped forward when their political and bureaucratic leaders did not after tremors shook the region in September 1985. Mexico City, like Tokyo, Los Angeles and many other megacities, is 'blessed' with a seeming perfect storm of vulnerabilities. Some are nature's doing. Others have their roots in either unfortunate ignorance or humankind's lack of care. Mexico City lies atop many fault lines, including those underlying some of its most densely populated communities. Humankind helped nature's violent side by building on what were until the beginning of the twentieth century several lakes. Many of the megacity's structures consequently sit atop soils saturated with water—soils that can turn into thick soup when violently shaken. These soils also amplify the effects of seismic waves up to 30 times more than do firmer soils found on the megacity's higher ground.[11]

Less obvious is the significance of neighbours and community members in the day-to-day welfare of megacity residents. Unexceptional in the seeming randomness of its growth, Lagos's edge communities often have roads lacking signage, pavement or an appreciation for straight lines. Houses are in various stages of building for weeks or months as residents cannot afford to buy building materials other than bit by bit when cash is at hand as they lack land titles and thus cannot secure loans. Some Lagos slum residents see little reason to invest their wealth in significant housing improvements when the inability to secure a title means they might be swept away without compensation. Redemption City is an exception. Established by a church group in the later years of the twentieth century, Redemption City's:

> streets form a grid. The roads are signed ... Some have speed bumps—things that would be wholly redundant on a normal African road ... There are few half-built houses, because the church checks that families have enough money to complete

---

11   Sergio Puente, 'Social Vulnerability to Disasters in Mexico City: An Assessment Method', in *Crucibles of Hazard: Mega-Cities and Disasters in Transition*, James K. Mitchell (ed.), New York, NY: United Nations University, 1999, 305.

them and sets a strict time limit. All the homes are in gated communities, numbering 15 so far. Everything tends to work. Whereas Lagos hums with diesel generators, Redemption City has a steady electricity supply from a small gas-fired power station. It also has its own water supply.[12]

Other religious groups are following suit.

When government falters

The first earthquake, registering 8.1 on the Richter scale, hit Mexico City at 7:19 a.m. on Thursday, September 19, 1985. The second quake followed the next afternoon, registering 7.5 on the Richter scale ... President Miguel de la Madrid admitted that the administration had failed to coordinate rescue efforts adequately. Instead, self-organized groups in affected communities took the initiative. Non-governmental organizations, such as the Red Cross, the Salvation Army, Catholic Relief Services, and numerous rescue teams from other countries such as France, West Germany, and Switzerland also provided assistance ... Public institutional actors jockeyed for power, and struggles ensued between the Ministry of Interior, the Department of the Federal District, the military, and the president's office.[13]

—Aseem Inam, *Planning for the Unplanned*

In 2012, the North Carolina state legislature passed a law that bans the state from using scientific predictions about sea level rise to develop its coastal policies ... During an episode of *The Colbert Report* shortly thereafter, comedian and host Stephen Colbert satirized the law quite appropriately: 'If your science gives you a result you don't like, pass a law saying the result is illegal. Problem solved.'[14]

—David J. Helfand, *A Survival Guide to the Misinformation Age*

Tokyo's community governments are required to prepare disaster preparedness maps. Sometimes with one map per hazard type, other times with the data combined, these resources (at times in English as well as

---

12   The quotation and introductory material are from 'The anti-Lagos: Nigerian cities', *The Economist*, [London], 20 October 2018, 47.

13   Aseem Inam, *Planning for the Unplanned: Recovering from Crises in Megacities*, London: Routledge, 2005, 62–63.

14   David J. Helfand, *A Survival Guide to the Misinformation Age: Scientific Habits of Mind*, New York, NY: Columbia University Press, 2016, 206, doi.org/10.7312/helf16872.

Japanese given the capital's cosmopolitan nature) inform the user of those areas worst exposed to seismic activity, fire, flooding, landslides, tsunamis or other hazards. They also identify emergency centres and facilities offering refuge or other support in a catastrophe's aftermath. Government exercises require officials to practise responses, confirm communications systems work and otherwise validate readiness or identify shortfalls. As we have seen, in Mexico City ... not so much. Occupants of private apartment buildings in the Latin American capital serve as safety marshals and participate in earthquake rehearsals, but as the quotation above makes clear, official preparations and interdepartmental cooperation can be ineffective. This is not a great situation for a megacity with seismic threats slumbering beneath its streets.

The 1985 earthquake killed 5,000 people, injured another 14,000 and left 2 million without homes. Water supplies ceased for many, as did telephone operations, power distribution and medical care. The collapse of telephone services—local, national and international—resulted from damage inflicted on a single downtown building. Tremors wreaked particular havoc on the city centre, meaning many government and commercial headquarters stopped functioning. Overcentralisation—of physical capabilities like those of telephone operations and human management—crippled where the dispersal of key capabilities could have provided redundancy.[15] Mexico City, the country's primate urban centre with more than four times the population of the second city of Guadalajara and home to many of the services on which the rest of Mexico relies, failed to ready itself for the inevitable visits of earthquakes.

Poor judgement in locating so many of the city's medical, governmental and higher-level educational institutions and other critical resources in the same area had egregious company in corrupt, uncaring and criminal authorities. The military distributed aid supplies—but to its own soldiers rather than earthquake victims. Various officials sold rescue material, pocketed aid money and delivered rescue equipment only after demanding bribes. Police rifled through abandoned structures and the clothing of the dead. Authorities directed that residents' neighbourhood organisations had no right to assist with recovery—saying this was a duty only their own

---

15   Diane E. Davis, 'Reverberations: Mexico City's 1985 Earthquake and the Transformation of the Capital', in *The Resilient City: How Modern Cities Recover from Disaster*, Lawrence J. Vale and Thomas I. Campanella (eds), New York, NY: Oxford University Press, 2005, 255–80, at 261–62, doi.org/10.1093/oso/9780195175844.003.0018.

people were to take on for fear that self-reliance outperforming officialdom might precipitate unrest. Citizens ignored the dictate.[16] The city's ruling Partido Revolucionario Institucional (PRI, Institutional Revolutionary Party) had good reason to be concerned; it lost city elections in 2000.[17]

Mexico City's is a particularly ugly story, but responses to the 1995 Great Hanshin Earthquake (Osaka–Kobe), the Tokyo sarin nerve agent attack the same year, the 2011 Fukushima Daiichi disaster (Tokyo) and Hurricane Sandy (New York) are among other examples where better-run and better-prepared urban governments struggled. Much of central Kobe burned.[18] New York City was hamstrung in part by its mayor failing to adequately ready his trusts for the hurricane's landfall yet helped in bouncing back not only by the state's national guard but also by its State Defense Forces, an organisation comprising mostly retired armed forces members, reservists and those from professions such as engineering, medicine and law, in addition to local police, fire and other organisations.[19] Plans and other preparations cannot guarantee a megacity's successful handling of and recovery from disaster, but they go a long way towards doing so even when initial decisions prove to be missteps.

Mobilising for good or ill: Information and influence

> In *The Matrix*, every person has a choice. You can pick a red pill
> … that offers the truth. Or you can pick a blue pill, which allows
> you to 'believe whatever you want to believe.'[20]
>
> —P.W. Singer and Emerson T. Brooking, *Like War*

We differentiate between two types of informative messages: direct, i.e., written by a person who is a direct eyewitness of what is taking place, or indirect, when the message repeats information

---

16   ibid., 273–74.
17   ibid., 270–71.
18   Hein, 'Resilient Tokyo', 228.
19   Steven Bucci, David Inserra, Jonathan Lesser, Matt Mayer, Jack Spencer, Brian Slattery and Katie Tubb, *After Hurricane Sandy: Time to Learn and Implement the Lessons in Preparedness, Response, and Resilience*, Homeland Security Report, Washington, DC: The Heritage Foundation, 24 October 2013, available from: www.heritage.org/homeland-security/report/after-hurricane-sandy-time-learn-and-implement-the-lessons-preparedness.
20   P.W. Singer and Emerson T. Brooking, *Like War: The Weaponization of Social Media*, Boston, MA: Houghton Mifflin, 2018, 273.

reported by other sources. Once we detect informative tweets, we classify them into the following classes … Caution and Advice … Casualties and Damage … Donations … People missing, found, or seen … Information sources if a message points to information sources, photos, videos, or mentions a website, TV or radio stations providing extensive coverage.[21]

—Muhammad Imran et al., 'Practical Extraction of Disaster-Relevant Information from Social Media'

Were it only as easy as providing a pill to influence the dispositions of a megacity population. As any police officer on the beat or soldier in battle knows, a gang member on their own turf or enemy fighting in their own city has the homefield advantage of being familiar with the lie of the land, the local population, social connections, local vulnerabilities, government officials' usefulness and much more. Having the support of a megacity's population can go a long way towards overcoming a visitor's disadvantage when outsiders seek to deliver succour in times of disaster. Police, firefighters, religious leaders and city government leaders are those who, like the person on the street, might be able to provide information regarding where the vulnerable (such as the elderly and disabled) live, what medicines or special care they need, which gangs control which neighbourhoods, who the local powerbrokers really are and other information vital to planning and responding effectively. Securing such information is no easy task in an era of social media and its unavoidable companions of misinformation and disinformation. If the pen really is mightier than the sword, a printing press is more powerful than an army. Social media is the equivalent of nuclear weapons.

For too long, analysts settled for the simple categories of bad guys, good guys and neutrals when considering a population (bad guys = gangs, organised crime syndicates and other evildoers; good guys = police, other government types and those locals or outsiders lending government types a hand; neutrals = everybody else). Leaders and planners used this breakdown whether readying for a crisis or fighting a war. My colleague Jamison Jo Medby offered a seemingly minor but very helpful revision to

---

21   Muhammad Imran, Shady Elbassuoni, Carlos Castillo, Fernando Diaz and Patrick Meier, 'Practical Extraction of Disaster-Relevant Information from Social Media', in *WWW '13 Companion: Proceedings of the 22nd International World Wide Web Conference*, New York, NY: Association for Computing Machinery, 2013, 1021–24, doi.org/10.1145/2487788.2488109.

this model with her 'continuum of relative interests'.[22] Imagine a flat line running from left to right across this page (or look at Figure 4.1. Your call). At the line's far left are the bad guys. Tag them as 'adversary'. Moving along to the right we find 'obstacle', individuals and groups that favour and willingly lend some degree of support to the adversaries. Smack in the middle of the line are those not wanting to favour either extreme ('neutral'). Continuing our trek along the line, we leave those neutrals and arrive at 'accomplice', which designates that part of the population willing to lend our side a hand in some way but stopping short of going whole-hog with that support. At the far right is us, the good guys, whom we label 'ally', and those willing to back us. A little contemplation reveals just how much richness the simple addition of 'obstacle' and 'accomplice' adds to the depth of our understanding of urban populations. First, considering noncombatants as uniformly neutral—once the default—is, to put it mildly, a gross oversimplification. The preferences, prejudices and predispositions of a megacity's noncombatant population and their many associations, communities and other relationships touch just about every point along that horizontal line. Some individuals and groups will be diehard supporters of the adversary (or, more accurately, *adversaries*, for neither the bad guys nor the good guys are any more homogeneous than the rest of the human mass that is a megacity population. Put differently, there are likely way more than just one group at the left and right extremes of the line as well as between the two). A disproportionate number of noncombatants are likely to remain near the 'neutral' centre, hoping to carry on with their lives and not be forced to make a choice between the competing parties. We might call this great mass the 'just leave me alone and let me make a living' segment.

Adversary-Obstacle-Neutral-Accomplice-Ally

Figure 4.1 The continuum of relative interests

Source: Image adapted from Medby and Glenn, *Street Smart*, 99.

Of course, Medby's continuum does not imply a population has only five rather than three categories into which everyone or every organisation fits. A little more thought makes it clear that there is an infinite number of dispositions along that line. A bit more mind work and we realise that even this important observation is only a first step towards better

---

22   Jamison Jo Medby and Russell W. Glenn, *Street Smart: Intelligence Preparation of the Battlefield*, Santa Monica, CA: RAND Corporation, 2002, 94–102.

understanding just how complex is a megacity's population. A group's members are not uniform in their biases. An organisation's leaders might claim their members favour one side or the other while individuals or clusters of people in the assemblage feel otherwise. Nor is a group's or an individual's leaning fixed over time. An adversary's or ally's change of policy or a bit of money pushed in the right direction might convince a religious leader to come off the neutrality fence and preach favouring one opponent over another. Insulting or roughing up an elderly couple at a traffic checkpoint could result in their son or daughter no longer supporting the army or police whose members acted foolishly—or any security force that associates itself with those mistreaters (as US soldiers found in Iraq and Afghanistan when dealing with corrupt or inept local security personnel). Adversary representatives will try to convince neutrals and individuals leaning towards the allies to see a new light, maybe with that bit of cash, some other form of assistance or a bullet in the mailbox that makes clear the risk of not rethinking who gets their support (this was a technique used by militias in Baghdad who wanted to purge a community of those with the 'wrong' religious bent). On the flipside, parties occupying the 'ally' end of the continuum will try to motivate organisations and individuals to shift to the right and be more partial in their efforts. Resources brought to bear in this tug of war include psychological operations messages, community projects and promises of other improvements in the potential favour-shifters' lives. Less ethical parties use threats (that bullet in the mailbox) or the application of violence to convince—something that is well known to many storeowners forced to pay protection money even when there is no threat other than that from the coercing thugs. And, while on the issue of lowlife ethics, the continuum of relative interests applies to children as well as adults. Though they might or might not be conscious of the motivations behind adults who direct their behaviour, the very young have long been tools wielded by adversary elders who recognise Westerners' tendency to consider youths a lesser threat and hesitate to use force even when a threat from that quarter is obvious. It is a dangerous predisposition when youngsters are tasked to collect information, act as couriers, carry supplies, engage with a rifle or bear a bomb.

There are only so many resources available for garnering favour. Choosing to spread those limited resources across an entire urban population makes no more sense than it would for a political candidate to spend significant funds trying to get an opponent's fully committed backers to change their votes. Far better to concentrate on the possibly mouldable. Easier said than done. First, determining just who or which organisations belong where along the continuum demands much in the way of information, and not only in terms of the whos and wheres of these population segments. It is also essential to know how to best reach out to them and what types of messaging and other forms of influence hold most promise of succeeding. Second, figuring out a group's key influencers provides even more bang for the too few available bucks. Marketers hiring actors or sports figures are capitalising on this approach. Confronted with trying to stop the many religious and ethnic groups in 2005 in Mosul, Iraq, from competing instead of cooperating during rebuilding, US Army Colonel (later General) Robert B. Brown asked for assistance from a Kurdish leader who had been imprisoned by Saddam Hussein for 20 years. The leader's legitimacy thanks to those years of suffering acted as a neutral force to bring the competing parties to the table.[23] A further nuance inherent on the continuum of relative interests: those seeking to shape opinions or support must commit resources to keeping those already supporting them from falling prey to efforts by others to lure them away. Parties on the neutral, accomplice and ally portions of the continuum can become frustrated as they watch benefits go to parties less supportive of your objectives than they have been. 'Well,' they might conclude, 'obviously we need to show we can't be taken for granted.' Gaining and keeping support, or at least denying it to adversaries, will be a never-ending task— one that will reward those better able to 'walk around the table' and view a megacity's social situation from all relevant perspectives.

That table is a big one. The most influential perspective might be distant from the city. To draw on a telling nonurban example, the efforts by France, the United Kingdom and Israel in 1956 to stop Egypt's attempt to control the Suez Canal failed in great part because none in that trio recognised the importance of obtaining US acceptance for the incursion into Egypt. Pressure from the United States turned out to be decisive in the three nations eventually withdrawing their forces. Remembering megacities' interconnectedness, the parties interested in goings-on will include many distant from the city itself. The greatest influencers and the parties they bring onside will inevitably include surprises, as the Israel Defense Forces (IDF) found during another operation, this time nearly six decades after Suez. While the IDF maintained a 24/7 presence on six platforms (Twitter and Facebook, for example) in six different languages during its 2014 Operation Protective Edge, it was 16-year-old Palestinian Farah Baker who stole both local and international social media attention.

---

23 Glenn, *Achieving Convergence*.

Virtually an unknown outside Gaza before the conflict, her tweets such as 'I can't stop crying. I might die tonight' saw her worldwide followers skyrocket reportedly to more than 200,000 before the end of the 50-day contest. Israel was forced to fend off condemnation from Europe, the United States and other audiences it had hoped to move rightward along the continuum of relative interests (or lock in place if already occupying positions favourable to Israel). Baker's influence demonstrated how difficult it can be for a state actor to compete in the social media arena. While it is impossible to know just how much messaging such as Baker's influenced calls from the United States or European and Arab nations for Israel to cease military operations, that she added to the diplomatic calculus is a given.[24]

Social media and other forms of communication have proven valuable beyond this ability to persuade. Firefighters in Los Angeles in 2007 benefited from Twitter updates sent by those near the city's Griffith Park conflagration. The inputs allowed managers to guide emergency responders using real-time information.[25] When water supplies were interrupted during fighting in Aleppo, Syria, in 2015, NGOs worked with local authorities to restore access to old wells. However, there remained the challenge of informing the population of the wells' locations. Maps were handed out person-to-person in some areas, but creation of a GPS-enabled map that was shared via social media proved a better alternative for many. That was particularly true in those parts of Aleppo that had suffered so badly that identifying specific buildings, streets or other features was virtually impossible.[26]

Just as there seems to be a yang of opportunity for every yin of challenge during a megacity crisis, the opposite is also true. That is nowhere more the case than with social media. That Farah Baker was really a 16-year-old woman in no way means that future Farahs won't be fabrications by those trying to bend disasters to their own benefit. Faking identities to sway opinion has a history preceding by centuries mobile phones and Facebook accounts. The *New England Courant* was one of the United States' first newspapers. Its pages notably featured entertaining letters by 'Mrs Silence Dogood', better known as Benjamin Franklin. In 2017,

---

24   Glenn, *Short war in a perpetual conflict*, 78–79.
25   American Red Cross, *The case for integrating crisis response with social media*.
26   International Committee of the Red Cross (ICRC), 'Syria: ICRC works to avoid massive water crisis in Aleppo', *News*, Geneva: ICRC, 10 November 2015, available from: www.icrc.org/en/document/syria-icrc-water-crisis-aleppo.

Jenn Abrams drew on *BBC News* and other legitimate sources to push a political agenda on Twitter that included support for Donald Trump— before those managing their platforms identified Jenn as the creation of Russia's Internet Research Agency.[27] Those naively retweeting such disinformation magnified its influence. Civilians used their mobile phones to send the location of Libyan leader Muammar Gaddafi's military force to the North Atlantic Treaty Organization (NATO) during operations in May 2011—assistance at once helpful but vulnerable to misuse by senders wanting to settle old scores or embarrass NATO by directing bombs on to innocent civilians.[28] Nor is potentially valuable information provided to emergency responders or soldiers by well-intentioned social media users always correct. The old saw that 'the first report is always wrong' too often proves true, meaning that those firefighters, paramedics, NGO members or military members could be unintentionally or intentionally misrouted to ill effect.

Parsing true from false requires careful sifting and no little guesswork. The grasp of artificial intelligence (AI) on history, physics and weather will someday be better than humans', meaning that determining the likely path of an urban fire or a message's truthfulness should be less challenging. Crowdsourcing will still be important, but AI will help to determine whether reports are accurate or mistaken. Hopefully, we'll never get to the point of the movie *Minority Report* in which three psychics with dubious quality of life predict future crimes (and what's up with the authorities not listening to the female in the trio?), although clever algorithms fed with years of updated statistics already show Los Angeles and other police the likeliest locations of future crimes. Combined with additional information (for example, that a member of Gang A shot a Gang B member and retribution is likely), AI-assisted use of such data should help law enforcement prevent undesirable events via what military types call 'left of bang' initiatives. The term means stopping detonation of an IED before the good guys' vehicle reaches the point of attack by capturing the bombmaker, interrupting delivery of the materials needed to make the bomb or in some other way disrupting the enemy's system before the attack's execution.

---

27   Singer and Brooking, *Like War*, 113–14.
28   David Kilcullen, *The Australian Army in the urban, networked littoral*, Australian Army Research Paper No. 2, Canberra: Australian Army Research Centre, 2014, 16, available from: researchcentre. army.gov.au/sites/default/files/kilcullen_b5_web_11august_0.pdf.

Essential ingredients: Accurate information, shrewd analysis

Snipers are great to have, but good intel [is even more important].[29]

—Lieutenant Colonel Michael J. Paulovich, US Marine Corps

Nothing helps a fighting force more than correct information.[30]

—Ernesto 'Che' Guevara

Among the 2,753 people killed at the World Trade Center site on 9/11, 343 were FDNY [Fire Department of the City of New York] fatalities … Radio communication became difficult as they ascended higher inside the buildings, whose steel frames and steel-reinforced concrete interfered with the signals. 'When attempting to reach a particular unit, chiefs in the lobby often heard nothing in response,' the 9/11 commission report noted.[31]

—Patrick J. Kiger, 'How 9/11 became the deadliest day in history for US firefighters'

Men, women and children awoke from a peaceful night's rest and began their day with no thought that it might be their last.[32] Or so it was for the first of the many to suffer the disease. Seemingly perfectly healthy at dawn, within hours, a victim's eyes and cheeks sank into their faces. Pinching the skin left flesh malformed. Diarrhoea came suddenly—so severe that the body could lose one-fifth of its weight in a single day. Within 12 hours, the disease could kill what a half-day before was a carefree child, a loving mother or the father on whose wages a family depended.

---

29   Michael J. Paulovich (Lieutenant-Colonel, US Marine Corps), Email to Russell W. Glenn, Subject: Force recon and STA [surveillance and target acquisition] teams, 13 November 2001, as quoted in Russell W. Glenn, *Honing the Keys to the City: Refining the United States Marine Corps Reconnaissance Force for Urban Ground Combat Operations*, Santa Monica, CA: RAND Corporation, 2003, 68.
30   Glenn, *Honing the Keys to the City*, 76.
31   Patrick J. Kiger, 'How 9/11 became the deadliest day in history for US firefighters', *History Channel*, 20 May 2019, available from: www.history.com/news/9-11-world-trade-center-firefighters.
32   The description of the 1854 cholera epidemic in London is adapted from Russell W. Glenn, *Managing complexity during military urban operations: Visualizing the elephant*, Documented Briefing No. DB-430-A, Santa Monica, CA: RAND Corporation, 2004, available from: www.rand.org/pubs/documented_briefings/DB430.readonline.html; and Medby and Glenn, *Street Smart*, 1–3. These in turn drew on material from the UCLA John Snow website—in particular, Ralph R. Frerichs, John Snow Site, [Online], Los Angeles, CA: UCLA Department of Epidemiology, n.d.[b], available from: www.ph.ucla.edu/epi/snow.html. Sandra Hempel's *The Medical Detective: John Snow and the Mystery of Cholera* (London: Granta, 2006) provides an informative and enjoyable read regarding the 1854 outbreak and health conditions in London at the time.

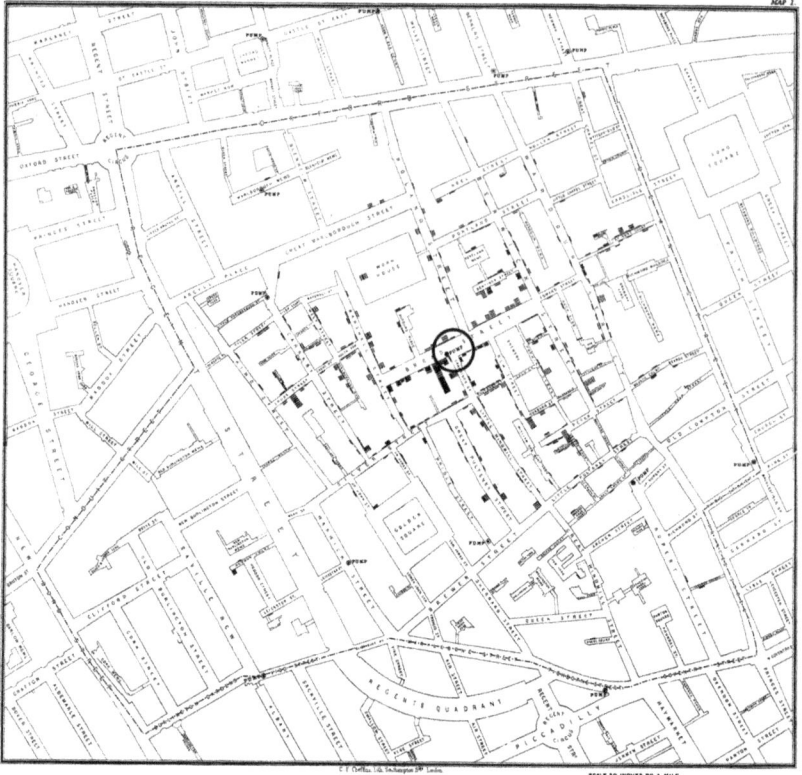

Map 4.1 John Snow's 1854 map of deaths near London's Broad Street pump (circled)

Source: Wikimedia, 'Snow Cholera Map 1' [from Snow, John, *On the Mode of Communication of Cholera*, C.F. Cheffins, London, 1854], available from: upload. wikimedia.org/wikipedia/commons/2/27/Snow-cholera-map-1.jpg.

It was 1854. Asiatic cholera ravaged London. Living to see the evening was no longer taken for granted. Many believed the disease was borne by miasma—gases from swamps or decayed organic matter. Others, Dr John Snow included, thought an infectious microbe was to blame. Snow lived in Soho, an area particularly hard hit by the outbreak. He wrote:

> [W]ithin two hundred and fifty yards [230 metres] of the spot where Cambridge Street joins Broad Street, there were upwards of five hundred fatal attacks of cholera in ten days ... The mortality in this limited area probably equals any that was ever caused in this country, even by the plague, and it was more sudden, as the greater

number of cases terminated in a few hours. The mortality would undoubtedly have been much greater had it not been for the flight of the population.[33]

Snow realised that most of the Soho cases were people living or working within a part of the neighbourhood whose residents used the Broad Street water pump. Of the 89 people who died in the first week of the local outbreak, 79 lived near or regularly acquired water from this source. Snow determined that at least eight of the remaining 10 had consumed water from it shortly before they died. Cholera rates were lower in a nearby workhouse that had its own pump and in a local brewery where a considerable number of employees chose to imbibe other liquid refreshment. Snow revealed his findings to the St James's parish Board of Guardians, the organisation responsible for the area's welfare. The board directed the removal of the Broad Street pump handle the following day, rendering it inoperable. Map 4.1 is Snow's own depiction of his analysis. Each dash represents a single cholera death; there are several when an address suffered more than one. The clustering around the Broad Street pump is obvious. It is not possible to definitively credit Dr Snow's efforts with the subsequent reduction of deaths in Soho. The number of fatalities began to fall even before the removal of the handle. Three-quarters of the area's residents had by that time fled the area. The evidence nonetheless supports a conclusion that Snow had determined the source of the problem and his information played a role in mitigating the disaster's effects—and those of disasters to come.

It does not take a lot of imagination to see how data could be used similarly to detect a disease outbreak or identify a biological, radiological or chemical agent terrorist attack on a megacity. Several cities in the United States already have programs where doctors, clinics and pharmacists feed databases with disease, symptom, prescription and other material so that it can be analysed to detect unusual trends and, hopefully, provide early warning, thereby providing authorities with the information they need to quickly address rising problems (we'll talk more about one of these, ESSENCE II, later). It's helpful to know a neighbourhood has more flu victims than a week ago and that the number a week ago was more than the one before. But are the numbers anything unusual for the time of

---

33 John Snow, 'Instances of the Communications of Cholera through the Medium of Polluted Water in the Neighborhood of Broad Street, Golden Square', in *On the Mode of Communication of Cholera*, London: John Churchill, 1855, available from: www.ph.ucla.edu/epi/snow/snowbook_a2.html.

year? Based on years past, should we be particularly worried or is what we see the normal pace of spread? Are the time of year and number of cases on track for a 'normal' flu season or an exceptional one? Is the fatality rate exceptional? Answering questions like these makes the information much more valuable. (In security terms, once data undergo analysis and processing, they become intelligence. Knowing there were 45 cases of flu last week is information. Putting that datapoint in context and addressing relevant questions such as those above provide intelligence.) Once analysed, information becomes the basis for educated decisions instead of guesswork. One of the reasons Covid-19 was so difficult for New York City to deal with during the spring of 2020 was the lack of a disease history (context) on which to base responses. Early cases triggered a near-frantic search for information. How long was the incubation period? Did everyone show the same symptoms? Could someone have the virus and not show any—or only some—symptoms? If so, could these lesser cases still spread the disease to others? Recommendations to limit testing once test kits became widely available were especially damaging (as was Chinese authorities' refusal to provide information on the disease's communicability). Not only did victims not receive appropriate care as soon as they might have; the resulting delay in gathering data meant there was insufficient information to create intelligence on which to base decisions impacting the lives, employment and survival of thousands.

The lack of insight when such information is not at hand is evident in another historical droplet—this time, from Israel's 1973 attack on Egypt's Suez City. Drawing on interviews with Colonel Nachum Zaken and Colonel Yaakov Hisdai, two of the IDF's battalion commanders making the attack:

> [Colonel Zaken] had only a 1:50,000-scale map of the city [on which 1 inch covers what is 50,000 inches on the ground; 0.8 miles or 1.3 kilometres] … The adversary was known to have forces in the city, but they were thought to be scattered, lacking in cohesion, challenged in leadership, and suffering the same collapse of morale as had much of the already defeated army. 'But,' Colonel Zaken recalled, 'there was a mistake.' The Egyptian leader had arrayed many of his defenders along the avenue that Zaken's force would use to conduct its attack. Concrete walls 80 centimetres high lined both the sides of the road … Tankers and their trailing infantry would find that it took several efforts and five to ten minutes to breach the walls and bypass immobile vehicles, the men forcing the breach suffering incoming enemy fire for the duration of the

frantic efforts. A lack of appropriate maps, overhead imagery, and ground reconnaissance denied the attackers information regarding the foe's dispositions, conditions along the attack route, and other intelligence that would have had a fundamental influence on the planning and execution of the mission.

The armored battalion moved out between 0830 and 0900 [8.30 and 9 am], October 23, 1973, with roughly 40 vehicles … The tankers' mission was to seize the main street of Suez as far as the port after which the two trailing infantry battalions would clear the remainder of the built-up area … The lead elements of the armor battalion reached their destination by early afternoon. The battalion headquarters set up in the city square some four kilometers into the built-up area. Remaining armored vehicles and trailing infantry units were spread out on both sides of the road for nearly the entirety of that distance … Egyptian units [attacked]; complete destruction threatened the three Israeli battalions. There were no surviving medics and no medical supplies beyond those in vehicle aid boxes (which many soldiers did not know how to use effectively). Few men were unwounded. Some tanks had completely exhausted their ammunition. Many knocked out earlier were virtually full, but cross loading was impossible with the continuing incoming fire. Surviving tanks with rounds remaining defended each other by engaging targets on the side of the road opposite themselves, thus taking advantage of the relative standoff distance to achieve greater effect from the elevation of their gun tubes. As most buildings were from four to eight stories high, tanks immediately next to a structure could not raise their main gun barrels sufficiently to engage targets on the upper floors and roofs. There was still little understanding of the enemy's strength or capabilities. The Egyptian soldiers employed hand grenades, rocket-propelled grenades (RPGs), and machine guns to continued telling effect … By 1800 [6 pm] the battalion commander's only means of collecting coherent situation reports was to send a runner north and west along the main streets to assess the situation. The unit eventually moved out of Suez to the southwest. The survivors of the two supporting infantry battalions exfiltrated on foot, leaving their vehicles behind and returning to Israeli lines north of Suez under the cover of darkness. Attacking Suez City without conducting a preliminary reconnaissance had 'proved to be a very grave error'.[34]

---

34 Glenn, *Honing the Keys to the City*, 2–5. Much of this material came from the author's interviews with Nachum Zaken (Brigadier General, IDF, ret.) and Yaakov Hisdai (Colonel, IDF, ret.), Latrun, Israel, 10 April 2000.

The above provides two convincing examples—one involving an epidemic in London, the other a combat situation—of why it is critical to have accurate information when dealing with an urban disaster. Understanding relevant parties' locations along the continuum of relative interests means an outsider is less likely to be at the mercy of local players who might seek to misguide them. So informed, aid providers also have some idea regarding who might seek to disrupt their operations. These could include groups as varied as state militaries, militias of various sorts (some perhaps acting as surrogates for the military), private armies, gangs, other criminals, local political factions more interested in power grabs than aiding a suffering population, insurgents or those seeking to promote personal or business interests. Such knowledge can also point to who has access to valuable skills, equipment or goods and is able to assist in navigating local social byways even more convoluted than the megacity's twisted streets and alleys. The two examples also tell us that understanding the physical world is crucial.

Accurate information tells NGO leaders whether those distributing aid require security before entering a community. Solid intelligence tells a military commander whether his or her soldiers should enter rooms only after a polite knock, following a flashbang grenade meant to preserve noncombatant lives, or only once they have led with a lethal fragmentation grenade or called for a tank main gun round given the expectation that no noncombatants shelter within. Information means not hiring a local gang to protect food stores its members are as likely to plunder as protect. Knowing the layout of a building means not heaving a grenade through a door only to find it rebounds off what is a closet wall. Intelligence means knowing whether the locals trust the police or prefer protection provided by the community's drug kingpin. Understanding a building, inside and out, means having knowledge of the possible larger role of the structure as a cultural (church, mosque or temple), diplomatic (embassy, consulate), communications, power, water or other utility hub, or other vital node in local or even worldwide systems—something not always evident in its external appearance. Old information should cause a leader to call for confirmation or update. Coalition forces relearned that lesson only after two perfectly aimed 900-kilogram bombs punched through the reinforced concrete roof of the Al Firdos command bunker in Baghdad on 13 February 1991. The facility had become a refuge for noncombatants. Some 400 died. Another 200 were severely wounded. Most of the casualties were women and children. Little matter that they were the families of senior armed forces, intelligence or other government leaders.[35]

Were a megacity's multitude of three-dimensional challenges not enough—four, if we add the social dimension—our previous discussions make it clear that considering only the urban area itself is insufficient. Megacities rely on water, fuel, food and much else that comes from outside their boundaries. Identifying where these necessities come from and how disaster will influence their availability means plans can be made for meeting shortfalls. No single organisation will be able to collect, analyse and distribute all the required data any more than one group can meet the total of a megacity's resource shortfalls. Recovery from whatever punishments a disaster inflicts will demand the cooperation of authorities both within and remote from the urban limits.

How to go about collecting this vital information? Methods range from those ancient to others beyond the currently possible. Reminiscent of scouts climbing trees to gaze ahead of their marching army, British Army forces in Northern Ireland's urban areas built towers to observe any goings on that registered the 'absence of the normal or presence of the abnormal'. Highrise buildings have always offered the same advantages; snipers and reconnaissance soldiers have long favoured church steeples, water towers or other perches that dominate surrounding terrain. The overhead perspectives of UAVs make them popular information collectors today. In the short term, such bird's-eye observations can provide the location of residents' suffering, where police need help in managing a demonstration or early detection of an approaching enemy. Long-term observation allows watchers to determine patterns of routine community behaviour ('the normal') and detect variations from those patterns ('the presence of the abnormal'). Police and soldiers gain the same by regularly patrolling the streets of an urban area.

City authorities and experienced aid providers have long recognised that good relations with residents magnify their vision and hearing hundreds or thousands of times over. That means they do not have to see everything themselves to gain knowledge. They do not have to hear first hand to know of a population's grievances or an enemy's movements. A helpful population offers insights impossible to otherwise possess. Drawing

---

35 'The battle for hearts and minds', *The Washington Post*, Fog of War Vignette No. 8, 1998, available from: www.washingtonpost.com/wp-srv/inatl/longterm/fogofwar/vignettes/v8.htm?noredirect=on.

on local knowledge means an outsider knows who those valuable key influencers are, what tensions exist between community groups and many other factors significant to achieving desired ends.

Like money in a bank accruing interest, information creates more information as knowledge breeds additional questions and contacts. Quality information, like a good investment, leads to not only more but also more valuable material. The greater the number of individuals at the 'accomplice' or 'ally' end of the continuum of relative interests, the greater is the flow of information and the better able is a recipient to confirm it as valid. Having mechanisms in place to filter incoming information prevents squandering of resources and loss of legitimacy in the eyes of locals. British Army Lieutenant Ross Kennedy was clever in this regard during his tour as a platoon leader in Iraq in 2003. He hired a local Iraqi to act as his interpreter but had his regular Kuwaiti interpreter—who was wearing a British Army uniform and whose role was unknown to the local hire—stand by during a meeting with a community reconstruction committee:

> I asked the town engineer what I could do for them. What did they most need money for? The engineer [replied], and the interpreter, who was a schoolteacher, [translated] 'We need books' … My Kuwaiti interpreter said 'That's not what he said. He said he wants a water-pumping station.' They all had their own agenda … It was frustrating.[36]

Getting word to members of the public regarding what information outsiders need is all the harder in the immediate aftermath of a disaster or during combat operations. Power could be out for days, weeks or longer. Mobile phone towers might be damaged or overwhelmed. Phone lines, radio and television stations, newspaper printing offices and other normally available means of communicating may be offline even if power is still available. Innovation will help close the gaps. Posting flyers, broadcasting via loudspeaker, having messages affixed to vehicles, passing messages to local residents at aid distribution points or while patrolling or—as worked recently in the Philippines and Iraq—creating a comic book popular with targeted age groups light fuses that burst into widespread sharing of messages via word of mouth. These means of getting in touch inform audiences both regarding megacity government or NGO information needs and of how to pass that information to these

---

36   Ross Kennedy (1st Lieutenant, British Army), Interview with Russell W. Glenn and Todd Helmus, Upavon, UK, 8 December 2003.

resource providers. Soldiers in Iraq painted their information line phone numbers on coalition vehicles and soccer balls given to neighbourhood children. While potentially effective, any such means need to be viewed in terms of the potential risks. Insurgents in Iraq were known to have beaten or killed those whose houses contained items affiliated with the coalition.

Technology might offer additional solutions. Commercial companies providing mobile phone service can step in when disaster knocks out or overwhelms standard capabilities. Depending on the system and type of vehicle transporting it, New York City has vendors who provide a veritable communications zoo via Cells on Wheels (COWs), Cells on Light Trucks (COLTs) or Generators on a Trailer (GOATs). The Jangala briefcase-sized cellular system in Lagos can serve up to 1,000 users. That will be a drop in the bucket during a megacity outage, but such capabilities could address emergency services' needs or niche mobile phone voids. Stretching mobile phone capacity by blocking ads, capping video pixilation and encouraging users to avoid streaming or other high-bandwidth use also helps.[37] (Some urban authorities shut off mobile phone access entirely in parts or throughout their jurisdictions. Those in Karachi, Pakistan, for example, reportedly do so on some religious holidays to deny potential bombers use of mobile phones to detonate explosive devices).[38]

These resources have become particularly important in recent years given the proliferation of mobile phones as virtual necessities. The most effective way of touching chosen audiences can be via targeted mobile messaging, thereby solving the challenge of not only getting word out to specific recipients but also doing so with a system they can use to provide information in return. Disaster planners ideally arrange for backup ways of communicating; Japanese soldiers used bicycles to transport floppy disks in the aftermath of the 2018 great Hokkaido earthquake. Early Tokyo residents received warning of approaching fires thanks to fire towers. Aside from:

> castle towers and a few pagodas, the only noticeable feature of the Edo skyline was for many years the fire tower in each district which contained a bell that was rung with an increasing number of strikes to the minute in ratio of nearness to the fire.[39]

---

37 'Internet providers to the dispossessed', *WIRED Business Special*, [UK edn], November–December 2018, 28–29.
38 Shackle, *Karachi Vice*, 156.
39 A.L. Sadler, *Japanese Architecture: A Short History*, Tokyo: Tuttle Publishing, 2009, 104.

Information is also key to constraining runaway good intentions. Ignorance can mean wasting resources when outsiders introduce technologies beyond an urban area's capacity to sustain them. Recovery efforts in Iraq and Afghanistan provide some notorious examples. They include installing sophisticated medical equipment without confirming whether sufficiently qualified operators lived nearby (Iraq), providing porcelain sinks that broke when users hoisted themselves on to them while performing pre-prayer ablutions (Afghanistan), installing gas ovens when far cheaper and more readily available wood was the normal fuel (Afghanistan again) and introducing airconditioning that immediately caused windows to sheen with condensation in lieu of cheaper to buy, cheaper to run and easier to maintain ceiling fans (Afghanistan a third time). Introducing such uninformed technological 'progress' proved wasteful, harmed benefactors' reputations for good judgement and burdened government officials with popular expectations that they couldn't meet once the rich outsiders departed.

This does not mean those providing relief should pass up opportunities to improve residents' quality of life. Whether replacing slums with improved housing or strengthening damaged buildings during post-earthquake repairs, improvements can be the wiser choice when well informed. Determining how much is enough can be particularly difficult given pre-existing needs. Routine rates of infant mortality in 2012 Manila's slums were tragically high due to malnutrition and disease.[40] The challenge in such circumstances is one of determining how far to go without going too far. Decisions are best made in partnership with the local leaders who will have to maintain any new programs when they are once again on their own.

Savvy megacity governments better their chances of effective response if they collect vital information before an event, thereby avoiding a game of catchup. We have noted more than once that much of the information needed during disaster response will prove valuable regardless of what form the calamity takes. Maintaining the addresses of homebound residents sets the stage for timely delivery of food, medicines and other aid regardless of whether it was a tsunami, tropical storm, earthquake or act of terror that made the assistance necessary. Knowledge of key dates such as those for delivery of social security cheques means officials can make

---

40 Ferris, 'Urban disasters, conflict and violence'.

informed decisions when setting evacuation dates. Receipt of cheques before departure is especially important given it may take several months for subsequent payments to reach displaced recipients.

The kinds of information needed include the obvious and the 'who would have thought'. Well-designed exercises inform new and test existing plans in terms of what information officials need. Helicopter pilots will want to know which air routes put buildings between them and neighbourhoods likely to be the source of potshots. Humanitarian assistance providers need to know how they can access water, food, power and shelter for both their own people and those rendered homeless. The combat soldier knowing what materials dominate in local dwelling construction can choose weapons less likely to injure or kill the innocent. A unit might opt for shotguns, stun grenades or other weapons with less penetrating power when homes are primarily made of wood or corrugated metal. The same soldier might know chosen materials have value in surviving earthquakes and thus are more appropriate when rebuilding post disaster than 'better' technologies imported from elsewhere. Detailed understanding of what lies ahead means knowing which buildings are off-limits and when that 'off' becomes 'on'. In some cases, the restriction will be a matter of social mores: asking permission to enter all or part of a religious structure, perhaps, or limiting entry due to gender norms or quarantine dictates. How a building is being used often determines its standing. The British Army's *Urban Operations* field manual informs its soldiers:

> Like civilian personnel, civilian buildings and towns normally have a protected status—for example, they are not legitimate targets. Buildings and towns lose their protected status if the appropriate authorities determine that the enemy is using them for military purposes.[41]

Sometimes what is not present reveals what is. The absence of mobile phone or other electronic signals in a neighbourhood might suggest the presence of an off-limits intelligence installation—a rock around which the stream of cyber traffic flows. Hyper mobile phone activity, on the other hand, indicates a train, subway or bus station, shopping market or other hub of human activity where the risk of spreading biological or chemical contamination would be extraordinarily high.

---

41   Glenn, *Honing the Keys to the City*, 1.

Subterranean features pose special challenges and opportunities. For soldiers, they are a way to move between points without the enemy detecting or firing on them. The other side of that coin is that the enemy might use such passages to move their attackers into areas previously cleared of a threat, as Israeli soldiers found during fighting in 2014 in Gaza:

> On 20 July, an Israeli APC [armoured personnel carrier] driving with other forces into Shujayia suffered a mechanical malfunction and stopped on the side of the road between two small buildings. As the Israeli soldiers waited for a repair team to come, they were sighted by a Hamas spotter hiding in some buildings down the road. A Hamas team used a tunnel to enter one of the buildings adjacent to the Israeli APC. They then surprised the Israeli soldiers by firing RPG rockets and small-arms fire at the APC and the soldiers around it. Seven Israeli soldiers were killed.[42]

Hamas's use of tunnels and other subterranean features represents an adaptation to Israel's improved detection of aboveground activities. The results were the infiltrations and attacks on IDF soldiers described above and assaults targeting Israeli civilians near the Gaza border. Tunnels—some large enough to support motorbike movement—also provided storage facilities difficult to detect and hard to destroy even when they were discovered. Knowing that finding entrances to the subterranean passageways would be an Israeli priority, Palestinian factions sometimes used children and other civilians to lure soldiers into ambushes with promises of revealing those locations.[43]

Knowing the location and character of underground passageways also offers opportunities for those with more humanitarian objectives. An ability to move beneath the surface provides a safer way to evacuate wounded when combat rages above. Subway stations, subterranean levels of parking garages, below-ground floors in shopping malls and similarly large and accessible spaces are potential hospitals, storage facilities or places where aid providers and those they are helping can shelter when being aboveground proves too risky. All these benefits may have to be forgone if the threat of the use of heavier-than-air chemical weapons exists or sewer gas poses a danger. Fortunately, neither was a significant threat in 1993 in Sarajevo. A tunnel beneath the city's airport took on vital importance when it became the protected link between two Bosnian communities.

---

42 Glenn, *Short war in a perpetual conflict*, 29, 71.
43 ibid., 103.

An average of 20 tonnes of supplies and other materiel and 4,000 people moved through it daily, avoiding Serbian snipers seeking to multiply the number of red-painted 'Sarajevo roses' that marred the capital's streets, marking where someone had fallen to rifle or mortar fire.[44]

While navigating underground complexes can be difficult, moving at surface level is no guarantee of improved understanding of one's location. On the other hand, being aware of local signage can aid navigation even if the local language is a mystery. Eighteenth-century London and Paris featured:

> signs shaped to look like massive animals or objects began as a means of advertising that was intelligible to the illiterate and the literate alike … These boards had an additional function: to help outsiders and residents establish where they were … In the absence of street numbers, packages and visitors to eighteenth-century London and Paris were addressed or directed to a house 'at the sign of X,' or 'by the sign of the Y.'[45]

Relying on other than traditional signage might be the only way to navigate when damage is so extensive that streets and neighbourhoods are unrecognisable even to those who live or work there. This is all well and good if global positioning systems are operating. Innovation will otherwise be the way to proceed. US Marine Corps snipers in 1992–93 in Mogadishu, Somalia, designated locations in terms of where they were in relation to 'Dead Cow Road'—a byway featuring what must have been a reference of decaying value. Features such as those subways, underground shopping malls and subterranean parking garages mentioned above will—the extent of damage allowing—generally be evident thanks to a megacity's signage or their signature characteristics. Consider the 'M' signs denoting Washington, DC, Metro (subway) entrances or the red circles filled with white and overlaid with a blue horizontal bar for London's Underground. The same may not be true with house addresses in residential neighbourhoods, particularly in the case of slums where house numbers might be non-existent. The cosmopolitan character of urban areas—and megacities in particular—means signs might be in English, or at least English script, even when that is not the local language. This is helpful, but the English may not be of a form recognisable even to native speakers of that language. It would

---

44   Williams and Selle, *Military Contingencies in Megacities and Sub-Megacities*, 44.
45   Conlin, *Tales of Two Cities*, 79–80.

take a minute's thought to figure out that 'Satay-Wan' on a Tokyo shop represented a valiant effort to translate '31'—the number of flavours of the Baskin-Robbins ice-cream offered within.[46] Megacities can also have an unspoken language that only those in the know comprehend. London's Underground stations might be easy to identify, but once a rescue team leaves a station for its tunnels, they would confront a maze where 'tangles of wrist-thick electric cables are blackened by dust from the trains' brake shoes, and where the only place indicators are mysterious codes in chalk, spray paint, and ancient enamelled plates'.[47] New York City similarly has its own technical codes below, above and at ground level. Its special tongue reveals to the knowledgeable what lies beneath the manhole cover, utility plate or on the adjacent wall's spaghetti knot of wires. Having someone who can translate this lingua franca reveals where access to electricity, mobile phone systems, water lines and other infrastructure lies hidden. The difference between knowing and not knowing could mean saving an aid organisation or other outsider the need to rely on portable generators or imported water while at the same time those in the know could deny access to undesirable or noncompliant parties. This might include cutting off resources to an uncooperative neighbourhood to coerce more favourable behaviour, encouraging civilians to leave for any one of many reasons or preventing contamination or disease from spreading. Some of an urban area's signs, symbols and codes are so commonplace that their meaning ought to be made known to every member of a coalition. Being aware that a blue background with white arrow and the lettering 'Senso Unico' on a sign in Rome means one-way street and not the direction to the US Embassy can be the difference between mistakenly wandering into danger or getting aid to the needy in time.

Getting smarter faster

> The IRA [Irish Republican Army] were getting better because, don't forget, they had their own intelligence—but the British Army was getting better quicker.[48]
>
> —Charles Allen, *The Savage Wars of Peace*

---

46 Reid, *Confucius Lives Next Door*, 33–34.
47 Schilthuizen, *Darwin Comes to Town*, 3.
48 Charles Allen, *The Savage Wars of Peace*, as quoted in Russell W. Glenn, Steven L. Hartman and Scott Gerwehr, *Urban Combat Service Support Operations: The Shoulders of Atlas*, Santa Monica, CA: RAND Corporation, 2003, 75, available from: www.rand.org/content/dam/rand/pubs/monograph_reports/2005/MR1717.pdf.

Training and intelligence need to identify what's [notable] in the infrastructure. What are the important parts of the power plant? Given two plants, which should I take out?[49]

—Master Chief Robert B. Fitzgerald, US Navy, 1st Force Reconnaissance Company, 1st Reconnaissance Battalion, 1st Marine Division

We earlier noted that homefield advantage applies no less to urban undertakings than it does to sport. The British Army in Northern Ireland was at something of a disadvantage; most of its soldiers were visitors to the six provinces. Lieutenant Kennedy's experience in south-western Iraq tells us that acquiring the information needed to overcome challenges during 'away games' can be daunting.

Soliciting multiple views from a population regarding who should represent their interests (and, conversely, who is suspect) and carefully screening all associations to avoid undermining one's legitimacy via ill-chosen associations are both steps in the right direction. One could do worse than perform an occasional sleight of hand such as employing multiple translators as did our mature-before-his-time Lieutenant Kennedy.

Commonsense precautions when soliciting information also make sense from a security perspective. A relief provider asking a city engineer what load a bridge can handle, for example, might expose supply trucks to ambush and robbery. Why would an organisation ask for such information if it was not preparing to use the crossing? Asking for information on several spans increases the odds of getting the convoy through unmolested. Confirming information via the internet or interviewing multiple neighbourhood individuals when needing to speak to only one reduces risk of compromising plans or exposing an information source to retribution.

The Irish USAID representative's clever use of UAVs to inspect worksite progress reminds us that the ways of remotely collecting information are ever increasing. Tracking population movements by monitoring mobile phone usage can help aid providers more effectively position their resources. Failing to confirm data reliability exposes users to outdated information or data designed less for accuracy than to impress investors

---

49   Robert B. Fitzgerald (Master Chief USN, 1st Force Reconnaissance Company, 1st Reconnaissance Battalion, 1st Marine Division), Interview with Russell W. Glenn, Camp Pendleton, CA, 12 July 2001, as quoted in Glenn, *Honing the Keys to the City*, 80.

or voters.[50] The problem can be worse still in megacities given their rate of growth and authorities' related inability to keep pace with data collection.[51] Maintaining accurate statistics in even developed-world megacities is far from easy. Urban-dwellers tend to be more mobile than rural types. Introduce a devastating storm, tsunami or brush with war and the difficult becomes yet harder. Those with special needs among the recently arrived, in transit or working in the informal sector are especially at risk given they often live close to survival's edge.[52] Even the best disaster planning and accountability endeavours will unavoidably leave large numbers of those in need unaccounted for.[53] Flexible plans and sufficient resources to deal with the unknown but expected will go a long way towards addressing gaps.

Even less good news: keeping up with changes in the physical environment and having a reasonable handle on who lives where could be the easy part. Groups seeking to undermine an effective response deliberately hinder the operations of aid providers. Identifying the various culprits and their motivations will require aggressive intelligence collection and analysis. Israel found this to be true when it chose to divide intelligence responsibilities for Iran, Syria and Hezbollah among separate organisations in the years leading up to the 2006 Second Lebanon War. The nature and extent of ties between Hezbollah and Iran remained opaque until well into the conflict, much to the detriment of Israeli operations.[54] The situation will be considerably more complex given megacities' many formal and informal authorities, each with priorities as likely to differ as agree with those of an outsider. That the locations of these government organisations may be scattered across the megacity further complicates information exchange and coordination. Consider the City of Los Angeles and the many other urban governments mentioned above that together make up the megacity of that name. Add to those the federal military installations at Port Hueneme and Los Angeles Air Force Base, FBI, Border Patrol and customs officials, private universities, major commercial properties, and the list goes on and on. The most 'interesting' cases throw multiple

---

50   Charles Kelly, 'Assessing disaster needs in megacities: Perspectives from developing countries', *GeoJournal* 37 (November 1995): 381–85, at 384, doi.org/10.1007/BF00814020.

51   ibid., 384.

52   D.K. Chester, M. Degg, A.M Duncan and J.E. Guest, 'The increasing exposure of cities to the effects of volcanic eruptions: A global survey', *Environmental Hazards* 2(3) (2001): 89–103, at 100, doi.org/10.3763/ehaz.2000.0214.

53   ibid., 100.

54   Russell W. Glenn, *All Glory is Fleeting: Insights from the Second Lebanon War*, Santa Monica, CA: RAND Corporation, February 2008, 66.

national governments into the mix, as with Singapore spanning the eponymous city-state and parts of Indonesia and Malaysia. Just trying to identify the relevant players is task enough, much less attempting to fathom the relationships between them—relationships possibly evolving in the aftermath of a catastrophe. Information management becomes not science but the art of the possible—a possibility best measured in terms of 'good enough' rather than perfect.

The role of pre-disaster cooperative organisations such as the former Los Angeles Terrorism Early Warning Group (TEWG) and coordinating mechanisms like Los Angeles County's emergency operations centre offer effective foundations for arranging mutual support in times of crisis. Ideally, such organisations would share relevant (and mutually accessible) databases from which any could pull or provide information when preparing for and responding to crises. New York City and London set examples with their liaison exchanges and intelligence-sharing relationships with each other and additional urban areas.[55] Establishing relationships before a disaster will be the difference between getting a leg up on recovery or playing catchup. US Government reconnaissance operations in the immediate aftermath of 2003's Operation Iraqi Freedom focused more on petroleum concerns in Iraq's south-east than those related to electricity provision. Both fed Baghdad's power grid. Only too late did it become apparent that it was the electrical system that was more in need of rehabilitation. By then, the misdirection of personnel and equipment had set back recovery efforts. Lest we think the problem could only occur in distant lands, a White House study in the aftermath of Hurricane Katrina's ravaging of New Orleans concluded that the Federal Emergency Management Agency (FEMA) 'teams that were deployed to assess … damage to the region did not focus on critical infrastructure and did not have the expertise necessary to evaluate protection and restoration needs'.[56] Both these cases make it clear that collecting information is not enough. People with knowledge of an urban area and how it fits into the broader system of which it is a part should be known to authorities before a calamity, thereby speeding effective response once a need arises.

---

55   For more detail on the nature of these relationships, see Brian Nussbaum, 'Protecting global cities: New York, London and the internationalization of municipal policing for counter terrorism', *Global Crime* 8(3) (2007): 213–32, doi.org/10.1080/17440570701507745.
56   The White House, 'Chapter Five: Lessons Learned', in *The Federal Response to Hurricane Katrina: Lessons Learned*, Washington, DC: The White House, 2006, available from: georgewbush-whitehouse.archives.gov/reports/katrina-lessons-learned/chapter5.html.

Today is different than yesterday. The same will be true tomorrow

> Sometimes the city is worse than the jungle. You can get lost in it with a million people within arm's length … A guy could roam the streets for a week without being recognized if he were careful not to do anything to attract attention.[57]
>
> —Private eye Mike Hammer, in Mickey Spillane, *My Gun is Quick*

> The Greeks sometimes imagined that we travel backwards into the future, watching the past recede but blind as to what lies ahead.[58]
>
> —Greg Woolf, *The Life and Death of Ancient Cities*

California's Electronic Surveillance System for the Early Notification of Community-Based Epidemics II (ESSENCE II) was a clever way of making data serve its human masters. ESSENCE II drew on military and civilian healthcare information to detect possible epidemic outbreaks (and, conceivably, a chemical or biological agent attack). This and similar systems rely on hospital emergency room, private medical practice and veterinarian reports along with data on pharmacy prescriptions, school and work absences, nurses' notes and over-the-counter purchases to potentially provide early warning of unusual medical trends.[59] We're not there yet. Early results show promise, but experienced medical personnel thus far tend to prove quicker at detecting such anomalies or routine events such as the arrival of the flu season. The situation might be different when the symptoms are less familiar, as was the case with the sarin nerve agent attack in 1995 in Tokyo. Early detection of problems with water and power distribution or transportation systems has long existed without the aid of a human in the loop. Knowing which such capabilities exist and how to access them would be a boon to any party responding to a megacity crisis. Being aware of which do not exist would mean knowing which experts need contacting to close the knowledge void. Overreliance on classified computer networks handicapped US Government representatives coming to the aid of Ebola-stricken West African countries in 2014. Information

---

57   In Spillane, *The Mike Hammer Collection*, 283.
58   Woolf, *The Life and Death of Ancient Cities*, xvi.
59   Joseph Lombardo, Howard Burkom, Eugene Elbert, Steven Magruder, Sheryl Happel Lewis, Wayne Loschen, James Sari, Carol Sniegoski, Richard Wojcik and Julie Pavlin, 'A systems overview of the Electronic Surveillance System for the Early Notification of Community-Based Epidemics (ESSENCE II)', *Journal of Urban Health: Bulletin of the New York Academy of Medicine* 80(Supp. 1) (2003): i32–i42, doi.org/10.1007/PL00022313.

stored on those networks, classified or otherwise, was not available even to members of the owner organisation, the US Department of Defense, when special equipment was not at hand. NGO, IGO and other partners whose aid would have made soldiers' jobs easier lacked security clearances and were likewise shut out.[60]

Most recruits joining ISIS and supporting its five-month battle in Marawi, Philippines, during 2017 reportedly came not from the city itself but from the surrounding countryside.[61] However, leaders, funding and propaganda from the Middle East were behind the recruitment and sustainment of the local hires. Just as those responding to crises in a megacity need to know how the city's *physical* infrastructure links to external resources, much of the *social* infrastructure will have ties that reach beyond urban boundaries—sometimes thousands of kilometres beyond.

Knowing what information is important will not be the preserve of leaders on high. The men and women daily patrolling the streets, rendering face-to-face aid or monitoring hours of CCTV and other sensor feeds will be the ones best able to sense the absence of the normal or presence of the abnormal. Is the never before seen car on a side street a vehicle-borne explosive weapon or a visitor to one of the residents? Does it sit low on its axles because it contains hundreds of kilos of explosives or due to exhausted shock absorbers? Why is the falafel cart that is normally on the corner not there today? Does the failure to show up mean the owner knows the enemy is up to no good or is it a local holiday and sales are better elsewhere? The daily hum of a megacity's normal routine consists of uncountable dynamic activities. A terrorist, criminal or other hostile group is difficult to detect if it operates as part of this ever-present vibration of activity, remaining below the threshold that would bring it to the attention of authorities. As we will see when looking at the 1995 nerve agent attack on the Tokyo subway in greater detail, all five men who punctured their chemical-filled balloons managed to escape detection. They remained 'concealed' by ensuring they seemed to be just part of the commuter flow on an otherwise typical Tokyo workday morning.

---

60   United States Army Center for Army Lessons Learned (CALL), 'Operation United Assistance: Report for follow-on forces', *Bulletin: Lessons and Best Practices*, No. 15-16, Fort Leavenworth, KS: US Army Center for Army Lessons Learned, September 2015, 7, available from: usacac.army.mil/sites/default/files/publications/15-16.pdf.

61   Kiriloi M. Ingram, 'Revisiting Marawi: Women and the struggle against the Islamic State in the Philippines', *Lawfare*, 4 August 2019, available from: www.lawfareblog.com/revisiting-marawi-women-and-struggle-against-islamic-state-philippines.

Information: The new opiate of the masses

> Our brains have evolved to become highly adept at finding
> patterns but not at gathering comprehensive and scrupulously
> unbiased data.[62]
>
> —David J. Helfand, *A Survival Guide to the Misinformation Age*

> In wartime, truth is inseparable from rumor.[63]
>
> —James Verini, *They Will Have to Die Now*

An IBM study conducted not too many years ago reported that information provided via smartphones, social media sites and other sources every day provides the equivalent of five trillion books.[64] Much of that information is wrong. The reasons range from ignorance, misplaced faith in sources, simple mistakes and misguided good intentions to more malicious causes such as fraud, deliberate manipulation or reinforcement of authoritarian messaging. Disasters provide rich soil for anyone wanting to plant untruths. Think of how frequently you hear of society's weeds fraudulently soliciting donations after a calamity. The city's mayor held two press conferences the day after the 2013 Boston Marathon bombing. He had an equal number of goals. He first sought to keep his constituents informed. Second, he wanted to encourage public unity in the face of any attempts to breed hatred that might be directed at specific demographic groups once the ethnicity of the bombers was known.[65] Both are commendable objectives that have elsewhere proven difficult to accomplish in times of crisis.

Recognition of the need to take control of messaging is noteworthy. Russia, China and other competitors are demonstrating that they would rather outmanoeuvre the United States with propaganda, disinformation, misinformation or mal-information to undermine the foundations of its government than confront US forces in combat. There is no reason to believe anyone seeking to sow chaos or forward their agendas during and in the aftermath of an urban disaster will not use the same tools in increasingly sophisticated ways. Perhaps it is time to adapt those lessons from Boston by offering the option of service in a social media corps in

---

62 Helfand, *A Survival Guide to the Misinformation Age*, 192.
63 Verini, *They Will Have to Die Now*, 147.
64 Helfand, *A Survival Guide to the Misinformation Age*, 2.
65 Rodin, *The Resilience Dividend*, 211.

lieu of more traditional military specialties. Such an organisation would offer the benefits of messaging consistency during day-to-day interfaces with groups along the continuum of relative interests while providing a shield to counter criminal and other adversary misuse of information during a crisis. If historian Daniel Headrick is correct in considering the telegraph as the invisible weapon of empire, information is the battlefield on which millions wage a struggle for truth.[66]

---

66 Daniel Headrick, *The Invisible Weapon: Telecommunications and International Politics, 1851– 1945* (New York, NY: Oxford University Press, 1991), as cited in Paul Farmer, *Fevers, Feuds, and Diamonds: Ebola and the Ravages of History*, New York, NY: Farrar, Straus & Giroux, 2020, 239.

5

Foundation stones for disaster readiness

Subordinate yourself (as appropriate) to the US embassy leadership whenever possible. This practice should also be communicated visually, audibly, and in all business practices and daily routines … Take time to nurture this relationship … Recognize the capacity of numerous other organizations and 'actors' operating or located in the joint operations area. Coordinate and synchronize your efforts with them.[1]

—US Army Center for Army Lessons Learned, 'Operation United Assistance'

The tragedy of [Hurricane] Sandy is not that it was unprecedented; the tragedy is that it was entirely predictable, yet New York City was still not fully prepared for the flooding that came.[2]

—Robert I. McDonald, *Conservation for Cities*

The US Centers for Disease Control (CDC), military epidemiologists and a USAID disaster response team were among the internationals lending expertise as the Ebola virus threatened West Africa in 2014. NGOs, IGOs and other aid providers likewise provided resources as West African governments struggled to contain the outbreak and educate their publics. The US military's senior representative early on was Major General Darryl Williams, commander of US Army Africa at the time. The US ambassador to Liberia, Deborah R. Malac, described how Williams's

---

1   CALL, 'Operation United Assistance', 6.
2   McDonald, *Conservation for Cities*, 106.

first steps included having lunch with not only her embassy staff and others from the disaster response team, but also Médicins Sans Frontières (MSF; aka Doctors without Borders), an organisation with a reputation for not wanting to work with military personnel. Effective response was Williams's goal, as was coordinating his military public affairs messages with other US organisations and local governments. For Ambassador Malac, the general's efforts were simply 'extraordinary'.[3] It was a rare demonstration of a government attempt at a 'comprehensive approach' to an operation—an approach that ensured cooperation between not only the multiple services in the US armed forces (called 'joint' operations), other parts of the federal government ('interagency' or 'whole of government'), those of other countries ('multinational'), but also relevant other-than-government groups, including commercial and volunteer organisations.[4] The fact that the resulting collective effort approximated a comprehensive approach—rarely achieved elsewhere—was notable if all but unheralded. The effort within Lagos was an extension of this success: civilian medical personnel and international organisations working with the governments of Lagos and Nigeria to contain the spread.

It would seem obvious that bringing all relevant partners together is the right step in times of catastrophe. That it is exceptionally attempted and even more rarely accomplished suggest otherwise. It was not too many years ago that my mention of the value of a comprehensive approach brought ridicule from one attendee at a conference in Washington, DC, with the speaker claiming that the sought-after condition was hard to achieve and thus unworthy of pursuit. He was right, but only on the first count. It is hard. Like many megacity endeavours—and undertakings more generally—pursuing the worthy goal potentially brings great benefits even if the efforts fall short of perfection. The costs of not working together can be dramatic. A previous quote relates how leaders in New York City's fire department had problems communicating with their firefighters on the upper floors of the World Trade Center towers on 9/11. Troubling? Yes, especially given the same problems existed during their operations when the complex was first attacked in 1996. Crippling? Absolutely, but more deadly yet was the inability of fire department personnel to communicate by radio with the New York Police Department (NYPD). Many police escaped the buildings before the collapse thanks to those flying overhead

---

3   CALL, 'Operation United Assistance', 6, 37.
4   Bucci et al., *After Hurricane Sandy*, 7.

in department helicopters warning of the second tower's pending fall and relaying that information to their leadership. That police and fire radios were incompatible, that the two departments did not regularly rehearse or conduct exercises together and (related to the second point, presumably) that they reportedly had a history of feuding meant word never reached many fire personnel who could have made it out in time had they been warned. Much has been done to right these wrongs since those horrifying days.[5] The same is not true of many other megacities where tensions or jealousies between fire, law enforcement, military and other authorities continue to undermine disaster readiness.

Reaching for the impossible: Megacity operations, mission command and the comprehensive approach

> President Lincoln preferred to avoid direct interference with his commanders in the field, informing General Banks in Louisiana that while he knew 'what I would be glad for Louisiana to do, it is quite a different thing for me to assume direction of the matter'. [His Chief of Army General Halleck concurred, believing] that the application of … principles should be left to the judgment of commanders, since they had the most local knowledge. General Sherman agreed, believing that it was virtually impossible to 'lay down rules,' and thus he also left 'the whole subject to the local commanders.'[6]
>
> —Nadia Schadlow, *War and the Art of Governance*

> Senior officers should visit units and talk to soldiers in order to understand what is actually happening at that level. But they should not involve themselves with the day-to-day running of units unless something is terribly wrong. If it is, action is probably required at [a] higher level to resolve it.[7]
>
> —Ministry of Defence, *Operation Banner*

---

5   Jim Dwyer and Kevin Flynn, 'Fatal confusion: A troubled emergency response; 9/11 exposed deadly flaws in rescue plan', *The New York Times*, 7 July 2020, available from: www.nytimes.com/2002/07/07/nyregion/fatal-confusion-troubled-emergency-response-9-11-exposed-deadly-flaws-rescue.html.
6   Nadia Schadlow, *War and the Art of Governance: Consolidating Combat Success into Political Victory*, Washington, DC: Georgetown University Press, 2017, 48.
7   Ministry of Defence (MOD), *Operation Banner: An Analysis of Military Operations in Northern Ireland*, Army Code 71842, London: Chief of the General Staff, British Army, July 2006, 4–8, available from: wikileaks.cash/uk-operation-banner-2006.pdf.

The above make great sense—until one considers Abraham Lincoln's additional remark that 'my policy is to have no policy', which demonstrates that even the greatest of us makes mistakes. If there is no policy, leaders have no way of knowing how to fit their decisions into a greater plan— assuming there is a greater plan. Lincoln's was a wise if imperfect application of what we today label 'mission command'. While it is a term used by the US military and many of its English-speaking armed-force partners, other militaries, authorities such as New York City's police and fire departments and additional organisations employ very similar philosophies though the monikers differ. Definitions differ somewhat as well, with that of the Australian Army excelling in both clarity and conciseness, which is what we will use here with the deletion of one word to extend its applicability beyond military organisations alone: 'Mission command is the practice of assigning a subordinate ~~commander~~ a mission without specifying how the mission is to be achieved.'[8]

Savvy leaders understand the necessity of training subordinates to act in the best interests of their organisations—and in trusting them to do so in the aftermath of that training. Former NYPD commissioner James O'Neill recognised that managing operations in large-city environments relies on several truths. Among them: surprise is ubiquitous; the unexpected is the expected. It is impossible for a senior leader to know the details of what's going on at the lowest-leader levels thanks to the dispersed nature of undertakings. The men and women at those lowest echelons are the ones who therefore have the best grasp of a situation thanks to their being closest to the action. For higher-level leaders to have no policy is to accept total chaos, with each lower-level organisation doing its own thing, little if at all coordinated with others. Success demands good information and intelligence, but these are by themselves not enough. Both are squandered without good decisions at the right levels.

Getting mission command right imposes responsibilities on both seniors and subordinates. First and foremost is senior leadership clearly stating: 1) what they expect to accomplish (the 'mission'), and 2) their intent, which provides context for the mission (the military calls it the 'commander's intent'). The mission is an explicit, generally short

---

8   Australian Army, *Land Warfare Doctrine 1: The Fundamentals of Land Power*, Canberra: Commonwealth of Australia, 2014, 45, available from: researchcentre.army.gov.au/sites/default/files/2020-01/lwd-1_b5_190914.pdf. Those interested in reading further on mission command might find value in Russell W. Glenn (ed.), *Trust and Leadership: The Australian Army Approach to Mission Command*, Dahlonega, GA: University of North Georgia Press, 2020.

expression of who, what, where, when and why something is to happen. The 'who' is the organisation or person who is to make that something happen. The 'what' is, obviously, what it is that is to happen. 'Where' and 'when' are clear in meaning. The 'why' gives the who, what, where and when a first cut at context. So, the mission for a medical unit providing support during a pandemic might be: XX Caregivers (the who) move to Blueville (the where) to provide immunisations and lifesaving aid (the what), beginning at noon, 4 July (the when), to reinforce currently overwhelmed mobile medical units (the why). 'How' is left to the leaders of XX Caregivers to figure out. Do they take over a portion of Blueville so other organisations already there can consolidate their overwhelmed resources? Do they instead work side-by-side with them to take advantage of their familiarity with local conditions? For a fire chief, the mission to one of their stations might be 'Station 354 immediately moves to 8521 Main Street, frees survivors trapped beneath rubble, and evacuates casualties to Mercy Hospital'—in this case, the 'why' being understood without overt expression. An example mission for a military unit fighting in a city: A Company attacks to clear Oak Park of enemy forces at 1300 hours to allow 1st Battalion to consolidate and continue the offensive.

Second among senior leaders' mission command responsibilities is accompanying their mission statements with equally clear statements of leader intentions—statements that give subordinates the broader context needed to act appropriately when the unexpected inserts itself into a situation. Statements of intent tend to (but need not) be somewhat longer than mission statements and are less constrained in terms of structure. What if the XX Caregivers team leader finds that reports of the in-place medical unit's personnel being overwhelmed were greatly overstated? What if the leader of Station 354 finds the building adjacent to 8521 Main Street is on fire and no other fire personnel are onsite? What if the A Company commander finds Oak Park already free of enemy but spots an adversary unit waiting in ambush for fellow unit B Company? An intent provides additional insight into what's behind the mission statement so the subordinate can make an advised decision when the mission proves no longer viable or situations change and communications with the senior commander have failed (remembering how difficult it can be to communicate in urban areas). A well-articulated intent provides 'big-picture' context beyond the 'why' in the mission statement such that subordinates' advised decisions support the larger objectives underpinning a mission. The intent cannot cover every possible contingency, but it should do what it can to equip subordinates for dealing with the unforeseen. Drawing on our notional mission examples, an appropriate intent from the senior leader whose responsibilities include Station 354 might simply be: save as many lives as possible. What to do if an adjacent building threatens to collapse on 8521 Main? The Station 354 leader makes the call given the actions he or she judges will best meet the priority of saving lives.

As for an intent for our A Company commander:

> I expect the battalion to secure all ground in our area of operations south of 8th Street (Phase Line Detroit) in preparation for passing the rest of the brigade forward in continuation of the attack. Blunt any enemy attempt to disrupt our momentum and maintain that momentum both during your assault and when passing follow-on forces through your own.

Helpful should Oak Park be found clear of enemy? Yes. Secure Phase Line Detroit and either continue attacking in coordination with flank units or immediately pass follow-on units forward without giving the foe a chance to re-establish its defences. Helpful if a large enemy unit is spotted moving against a neighbouring company? Yes, as continuing A Company's attack and ignoring the enemy would likely cause the whole battalion to fail in its attack.

The value of mission command is hard to overstate. US Army doctrine advises commanders to be aware of the intentions of leaders two levels up in the chain of command to provide even greater understanding of what is to be accomplished from the big-picture perspective than were they to focus only on that from their immediate leadership. Marine General Charles Krulak (who gave us the terms 'three-block war' and 'strategic corporal') realised the importance of mission command: 'The inescapable lesson of Somalia and other recent operations, whether humanitarian assistance, peacekeeping, or traditional warfighting, is that their outcome may hinge on the decisions made by small unit leaders and by actions taken at the *lowest* level.'[9] Nicholas Warr, another US Marine and a veteran of combat in Hue, Vietnam, during the 1968 Tet Offensive, reinforces Krulak while providing another reason a clear mission and commander's intent are not only crucial during urban operations but also fundamental to success should leaders fall in battle. 'Knowledge of the overall plan must

---

9   Glenn and Kingston, *Urban Battle Command in the 21st Century*, 27–28. [Emphasis in original.]

be disseminated down to the rifleman level,' Warr wrote: 'Casualties are so heavy and come so quickly during urban fighting that junior personnel will quickly find themselves leading platoons and companies.'[10] The US Army has long been in the know when it comes to how difficult it can be to conduct operations in urban areas. Drawing on fighting in the early months of World War II, the service's *Attack on a Fortified Position and Combat in Towns* manual related:

> [I]n no other form of warfare except in dense jungle is observation so restricted. This condition makes centralized control difficult. Commanders will be able to get close to their units in contact but will be able to observe only fractions of them at one time. These conditions will mean that most of the fighting will resolve itself into small independent actions and will place a premium upon initiative and aggressiveness of the small unit leader.[11]

The observations apply equally to the police captain responsible for security at a major public event or an NGO leader with food distribution points scattered about a city. Maintaining an understanding of the situation and controlling complex operations during city undertakings are among the most difficult of challenges. Risk assessment and response to a changing situation are no longer in the hands of the chief outside once firefighters enter a building should communications fail. It is the squad leaders' war once soldiers go house to house and room to room. Soldiers, like those firefighters, will inevitably be out of sight and frequently cut off from communications. Understanding of plans and their leader's intent thus must be known not only to those squad or team leaders but also to every man and woman given how busy the reaper can be amid those buildings and rooms, and how great the chances are that small groups and even individuals will find themselves isolated. Mission and intent need to be sufficiently forward-looking and unambiguous to provide subordinates with a basis for good decisions even when guidance is hours or days old. What these often-young men and women confront are 'wicked problems':

---

10 Nicholas Warr and Scott A. Nelson, 'Lessons Learned: Operation "Hue City", 1968', in *Ready for Armageddon: Proceedings of the 2001 RAND Arroyo-Joint ACTD-CETO-USMC Nonlethal and Urban Operations Program Urban Operations Conference*, Russell W. Glenn, Sidney W. Atkinson, Michael Barbero, Frederick J. Gellert, Scott Gerwehr, Steven Hartman, Jamison Jo Medby, Andrew O'Donnell, David Owen and Suzanne Pieklik (eds), Santa Monica, CA: RAND Corporation, 2002, 69, available from: www.rand.org/pubs/conf_proceedings/CF179.html.

11 *Attack on a Fortified Position and Combat in Towns*, Field Manual 31-50, War Department Basic Field Manual, Washington, DC: US Government Printing Office, 31 January 1944, 64.

problems which are ill-formulated, where the information is confusing, where there are many clients and decision makers with conflicting values, and where the ramifications in the whole system are thoroughly confusing.[12]

These problems share a range of characteristics—they go beyond the capacity of any one organisation to understand and respond to, and there is often disagreement about the causes of the problems and the best way to tackle them.[13]

Nothing really bounds the problem solving process—it is experienced as ambiguous, fluid, complex, political, and frustrating as hell.[14]

Similar challenges confront leaders, military or otherwise, when combat is not a part of these goings-on. California Army National Guard Major General Jim Delk found the command challenges equally demanding and potential strategic consequences no less serious during his soldiers' support of civil authorities during rioting in Los Angeles in 1992. Delk recalled:

[A]n E-5, a young sergeant fire team leader with a total of five soldiers, had total responsibility for Gateway Plaza Shopping Center ... We had to trust these young E-5s to do exactly what you would hope they would do without a commissioned officer standing there with his arm around them. And they did.[15]

Mission command requires at least five basic elements if it is to be effective in these toughest of environments. First comes the essential clarity when drawing up mission and intent statements. Muddled wording or—equally bad—failing to provide guidance because the senior leader is afraid to release a grip on control is a disservice to those whose actions most directly affect ultimate success or failure. Mission command is impossible without the second element underlying that release: decentralisation of authority based on trust. It is a both-ways trust. There is the senior leader's trust that their subordinates will do their best to make correct decisions

12   C. West Churchman, 'Wicked problems', *Management Science* 14(4) Application Series (December 1967): B-141–B-142, available from: www.jstor.org/stable/2628678.
13   Australian Public Service Commission, *Tackling Wicked Problems: A Public Service Perspective*, Canberra: Commonwealth of Australia, 2007, available from: www.apsc.gov.au/tackling-wicked-problems-public-policy-perspective [page discontinued].
14   Nancy Roberts, 'Wicked problems and network approaches to resolution', *International Public Management Review* 1(1) (2000), available from: ipmr.net/index.php/ipmr/article/view/175.
15   Delk, 'MOUT', 143.

within the bounds of their mission and intent. Then there is subordinates' trust that should those decisions turn out to be less than perfect, the senior leader will back them as long as the decision was reasonable given the senior's guidance and the junior leader's experience level. The third element: senior commanders must adapt the extent of direction given to individual subordinates. Not all subordinates should receive the same level of supervision, the same degree of detail in the guidance given them or the same freedom of action. These will vary based on: 1) the junior leader's past performance, 2) the subordinate's skill level with regard to mission requirements, 3) a junior leader's experience relevant to the challenges at hand, and 4) the senior leader's familiarity with the subordinate. Thus, a senior leader can afford to provide less-detailed guidance and lesser supervision when a junior leader is familiar to them, of demonstrated ability and familiar with the tasks at hand. Guidance and extent of supervision will be more detailed if: 1) the subordinate's past performance has been less than stellar, 2) the subordinate's mission-related training or skills are limited, 3) the junior leader's past does not include the kind of operation being undertaken, or 4) the subordinate just joined the senior's organisation (and thus is an unknown quantity).

To these three mission command elements we add a fourth: junior leaders must recognise that mission command is not 'fire and forget'. Once they provide a clear mission and intent, the senior retains responsibility to check on subordinates to ensure performance continues to be in line with expectations and to provide any further guidance deemed necessary without defaulting to overly detailed direction. The wise senior will tend to check more often on one with whom they are less familiar or who is less experienced than another in whom they have more trust. The wise subordinate will understand and respect a senior's responsibility to make these checks. Fifth and finally, subordinates also have the responsibility to keep their commander informed of the situation as they see it to the extent feasible. Doing so helps the senior leader gauge whether the subordinate's efforts are indeed within the bounds of mission and intent guidance while also providing information helping the higher-level leader to distribute resources most effectively in the service of accomplishing the mission.[16]

---

16   Readers interested in more on the nature and application of mission command during various types of undertakings might find the following of value: Glenn, *Trust and Leadership*.

Setting the foundation for preparations

A recent documentary film on Istanbul's building boom reflects, 'Everything changes so fast in this city of 15 million that it is impossible to even take a snap-shot for planning. Plans are outdated even as they are being made.'[17]

—Anthony M. Townsend, *Smart Cities*

The single greatest lesson learned from September 11, 2001, was the need for robust local communication channels with emergency response officials. We have made significant progress in achieving this goal in many of the larger cities that we own properties in. New York City has, in my opinion, become the gold standard in this regard.[18]

—Michael L. Norton, managing director, Global Property Management, Tishman Speyer

The formal concept of mission command is relatively new to Western military circles even if its underlying common sense has been long recognised by effective leaders. Those leaders adopted other military procedures that, like mission command, have application beyond the battlefield. Among them: recognition that it is easier to modify an existing plan than to begin from scratch when reacting to a disaster. Having plans 'on the shelf' not only saves time but also serves as the basis for exercises bringing relevant participants together. One author drew on Los Angeles' in-place preparations when looking back on the megacity's 1994 Northridge earthquake to highlight additional advantages:

Los Angeles had a pre-event earthquake recovery plan which specified agency roles and responsibilities and identified relevant programs following a large earthquake. The process of developing this plan had familiarized city staff with earthquake consequences, recovery actions, and the roles of other city agencies.[19]

---

17 Townsend, *Smart Cities*, 308.
18 In United States Senate, *Lessons from the Mumbai Terrorist Attacks: Parts I and II*, Hearings before the Committee on Homeland Security and Governmental Affairs, United States Senate, 111th Congress, 1st Session, 8 and 28 January 2009, Washington, DC: US Government Printing Office, 2009, available from: www.govinfo.gov/content/pkg/CHRG-111shrg49484/html/CHRG-111shrg49484.htm.
19 Robert B. Olshansky, Laurie A. Johnson and Kenneth C. Topping, with Yoshiteru Murosaki, Kazuyoshi Ohnishi, Hisako Koura and Ikuo Kobayashi, *Opportunity in Chaos: Rebuilding After the 1994 Northridge and 1995 Kobe Earthquakes*, Urbana-Champaign, IL, and San Francisco, CA: Department of Urban and Regional Planning, University of Illinois and Laurie Johnson Consulting & Research, 2005 [Online 2011], 11–18, available from: docs.wixstatic.com/ugd/0b4d51_a073dddfe4f0474ba7b91f1d5572dfa6.pdf.

A good plan at the ready helps organisations prepare for, practise, perfect and then execute their response to disaster. Having good metrics to gauge response effectiveness helps further, providing ready means to measure what works, what does not and how even what works might work better, thereby adding a third pillar alongside mission command and preplanning to the foundation for crisis preparation. Identifying metrics before they are needed shares several of the benefits accruing from pre-event planning. Time saved and a chance to refine them during exercises are but two.

Designing good metrics can be tougher than it appears. Leaders lean towards metrics that are easy to understand and allow comparison horizontally across different types of activities at a given echelon and vertically between echelons. Managers at the highest levels can then scan the few similar measures in the belief that they have a good grip on their organisation's performance. Simplification sometimes takes the form of measures appearing in 'stoplight' form. Green represents all is well for a given concern. Yellow (or 'amber', in military-speak) reflects that there are issues interfering with effectiveness. Red shows things aren't going well. The approach is not without its effective applications. For example, it can work well in showing the status of an NGO's vehicle fleet. Green might mean 90 per cent or more vehicles are roadworthy, yellow that 70–89 per cent are operational and red that fewer than 70 per cent are available. It works less well for measuring trends and worse yet if the metric fails to measure what's really important. General David Perkins, who, as a colonel in 2003, led the US Army attacks to seize Saddam Hussein's primary Baghdad palace, recalled a case of the latter from his time as a brigade commander in Fallujah, Iraq.[20] At least one metric was ill-conceived to the point that it reflected failure when in fact success was at hand. His description is a long but worthwhile read:

> I tell people that you have to be very careful regarding the metrics you use because what you measure drives what people do. Everybody wants his or her entry on the status chart to be green. Metrics generate activity and focus ... I would go out and talk to the mayor, sheiks, and other leaders in Fallujah. We were a tank brigade ... We had tanks and Bradleys [a tracked infantry fighting vehicle]. Our patrols through the city at night were keeping people awake and tearing up the roads. Those city leaders told me, 'We don't want you bringing your tanks and Bradleys into

20   David Zucchino, *Thunder Run: The Armored Strike to Capture Baghdad*, New York, NY: Atlantic Monthly, 2004.

the city.' I told them, 'I have to bring them in because I have to conduct patrols. People are getting attacked. We need to secure your markets and protect your residents. You don't want tanks or Bradleys in the city? Then you make sure there are no attacks.' The response was, 'It's not Fallujah people. It's people from outside the city.' I said that I didn't really care who it was. 'I know you know who's doing this stuff and I know you have control over it. Here's the deal: I agree not to bring tanks or Bradleys into the city and you figure out how you are going to keep people from being attacked. We'll start out for a week. If it works, we'll continue not bringing tanks and Bradleys into the city.' So we went for a week. There wasn't a single attack in Fallujah. Not one attack. It was unheard of at that point in time. We go for another week—no attacks. What happens? I get queries from higher: 'Hey, you know we have this chart that tracks the number of patrols units are making. Your unit is the worst of out of [*sic*] all the units we monitor. I said, 'OK, but you understand this is part of the whole dynamic, that we have cut back the patrols because we worked this deal with the sheiks and the mayor and they agreed they are going to keep their city safe. If they keep their city safe and our guys aren't attacked then I don't need to bring tanks and Bradleys into Fallujah.' 'But you don't understand. We measure patrols. We don't measure the number of enemy attacks. You aren't green. You're red. You used to be doing great and now you've dropped off. What happened?' 'But look at the attacks. The number of attacks used to be high and they've dropped off.' We were measuring the wrong thing, and what we were measuring was driving our actions.[21]

A second—and more positive—example is less military than civil government in character, more strategic than down at the tactical level with which Colonel Perkins was dealing. It demonstrates mission command's potential when guidance from above is clear and leaders encourage initiative from junior leaders.

The city is Hong Kong, the year 1945. Japan has just surrendered in Tokyo. World War II is at an end. David MacDougall is dispatched to serve as head of the Hong Kong Civil Affairs Unit to get the city back on its feet. London's guidance to MacDougall directed he was to:

---

21   David G. Perkins (Commanding General, US Division—North), Interview with Dr Russell W. Glenn, Tikrit, Iraq, 28 June 2011, as appears in Russell W. Glenn, *Core Counterinsurgency Asset: Lessons from Iraq and Afghanistan for United States Army Corps of Engineer Leaders*, Study sponsored by the US Army Corps of Engineers, 31 May 2012 [revised 8 December 2016], 261–71, at 262–63.

- Establish a police force and military courts.
- Set up relief camps for the suffering. Provide medical care, public health and adequate sanitation for those individuals.
- Put banking and other financial procedures in place.

… and do all of this using local resources to the extent possible.

Complementing this guidance from the Colonial Office, the War Office offered its input in terms of longer-term ends (the War Office was overseeing Hong Kong during the initial weeks after the Japanese surrender before the Colonial Office could once again assume the reins). We can comfortably equate the War Office guidance to an effective commander's intent:

- Return both public and private physical infrastructure to service with special attention to air and port services.
- Re-establish the colony's education system.
- Prepare for full transition from the current British military colonial administration to civil government.

MacDougall's superior in Hong Kong at the time was Admiral Sir Cecil Harcourt. Harcourt understood the need to grant his senior civilian the authority essential to meeting the guidance dispatched from 10,000 kilometres away in London. He therefore informed the secretary of state for the colonies that 'signals congestion' would limit the sending of civil government dispatches to once a month. London agreed, trusting their man on the ground based on both his previous performance and his considerable experience. (MacDougall's prewar training as a Hong Kong cadet provided some familiarity with the colony. Being in charge of the Hong Kong Planning Unit since September 1944 made him intimately familiar with London's expectations.) The trust paid off. MacDougall took unorthodox but effective steps while acting within his previously received guidance. In his own words:

> We had a whole month, every month, free and then reported what we had done retrospectively. This is why we got so far ahead; everything we did was just click, click, click, and before they knew it things were done, fait accompli. We did things they would never have thought of, things they would never have authorized. We overprinted Japanese notes; I put minimum wages up in half

an hour from fifty cents to two dollars; in a week we paid fifteen thousand people on the streets $2 a day. These things would have taken months to do.[22]

These successes were not merely the result of luck in having the right leaders on the ground at the right time. Plans were put in motion to get the city-colony back on its feet well before the end of the Pacific War. The Hong Kong Planning Unit had been established two years earlier in August 1943. Its staff was militarised in May 1945; each of the 38 staff members was given military rank the better to meld with the armed forces organisation that would rule once the colony returned to British control.[23] The right people were put in charge, given the necessary guidance and permitted to act within its constraints.

Whether reaching halfway around the world as between London and Hong Kong or from one building to that next-door, we might think of mission command as being a little like the driver's navigation app Waze. The app benefits from the same technologies as others but early on had the added benefit of users being able to provide real-time updates as they came across problems. An Israeli friend of mine with a sense of direction Captain Cook would have envied uses it not for getting from here to there in his country's densely populated cities, but to avoid the inevitable traffic jams. Unsurprisingly, densely populated areas offer a breadth and depth of traffic information lacking where drivers are fewer. Waze is therefore of limited value in infrequently travelled rural regions but of notable benefit in densely populated areas.

Okay, Waze is not all that much like mission command. The driver does not have some boss telling them where to go and what to accomplish once they get there (well, depending on the relationship with your significant other perhaps). And the guidance from Waze is far more constant and detailed than effective mission command would dictate thanks to satellites, speed-monitoring algorithms and the like. But the app recognises that its users have a better grasp of detailed road conditions than any central effort at control could ever hope to achieve. Further, individual drivers (equivalent to our junior leaders in mission command) benefit from

---

22 This quote and the previous material regarding British re-establishment of government in Hong Kong after World War II are from Neil Monnery, *Architect of Prosperity: Sir John Cowperthwaite and the Making of Hong Kong*, London: London Publishing Partnership, 2017, 40–42.
23 ibid., 40.

their reporting to 'higher command' via Waze's automatic monitoring of locations; the app can then provide the whereabouts of nearby petrol stations, restaurants and rest stops in addition to traffic delays.

Leaders, regardless of their organisation, are well advised to consider the advice of Molly Phee, former senior Coalition Provisional Authority representative to Maysan, Iraq: 'You will be better served by progressively devolving authority and acting more like a guide than a god.'[24]

24 Molly Phee, senior Coalition Provisional Authority representative to Maysan Province, Iraq, as quoted in Russell W. Glenn, *Band of Brothers or Dysfunctional Family? A Military Perspective on Coalition Challenges during Stability Operations*, Santa Monica, CA: RAND Corporation, 2011, 71.

6

Preparing for hell or high fever to come

Between 1970 and 2014, natural disasters accounted for more than 2 million deaths in the Asia-Pacific, 57 percent of the global total. [Former US Pacific Command commander] Admiral Locklear routinely told his subordinate commanders, 'While you're here you may not have a conflict with another military, but you will have a natural disaster that you have to either assist in or be prepared to manage the consequences on the other side.'[1]

—Timothy McGeehan, 'A war plan orange for climate change'

[Los Angeles was] prepared for the [1994 Northridge] earthquake because we had just gone through a similar disaster (i.e., the 1992 riots) where we had a similar result where we had entire blocks of properties destroyed. So, we had a kind of blueprint on the shelves that we could turn to in our disaster plan … We had a lot of … emergency ordinances after the riots that we just kind of took off the shelf real quick, changed a few little items, and threw it back into the books in response to the earthquake. We waived permitting fees. We waived a lot of requirements to get buildings built again.[2]

—Aseem Inam, *Planning for the Unplanned*

---

1   Timothy McGeehan, 'A war plan orange for climate change', *Proceedings* 143(10) (October 2017): 48–53, [Annapolis, MD: US Naval Institute], available from: www.usni.org/magazines/proceedings/2017/october/war-plan-orange-climate-change.
2   Inam, *Planning for the Unplanned*, 182.

COME HELL OR HIGH FEVER

> I came away with the firm belief that America's medical infrastructure remains extremely vulnerable to natural hazards, and there is an urgent need for disaster planners to involve the larger community in deciding how resources are allocated.[3]
>
> —Sheri Fink, 'Beyond hurricane heroics'

This and the following two chapters turn to history and draw on the hypothetical to offer observations hopefully of value to those responsible for preparing for, responding to or recovering from future urban catastrophes. With the occasional exception, each chapter looks for ways to overcome challenges and seize opportunities by considering the:

- *context* for the disasters drawn on
- wisdom of viewing operations from a *collective* or systems perspective given megacities' extraordinary internal connections and broader interconnections
- importance and ways of maintaining *control* during crises
- need for an effective *comprehensive approach* that includes all relevant parties
- special issues brought about when *combat* underlies a megacity's suffering
- considerations key to maintaining or restoring *capacity*.

Pre-disaster context: The case of Mumbai in 2008

> Chicago pioneered the use of steel and electricity in the construction industry, catalyzed by the great fire of 1871 which destroyed the city's commercial center and literally cleared the way for innovative building techniques to be applied. By the 1890s, Chicago was the world capital of the skyscraper, with New York a close second.[4]
>
> —Manuel De Landa, *A Thousand Years of Nonlinear History*

---

3   Sheri Fink, 'Beyond hurricane heroics: What Sandy should teach us all about preparedness', *Stanford Medicine*, Special Report (Summer 2013), available from: sm.stanford.edu/archive/stanmed/2013summer/article5.html.
4   De Landa, *A Thousand Years of Nonlinear History*, 92.

TEPCO [Tokyo Electric Power Company Holdings] and the Nuclear and Industrial Safety Agency (NISA) were aware of the need for structural reinforcement in order to conform to new guidelines, but rather than demanding their implementation, NISA stated that action should be taken autonomously by the operator. The Commission has discovered that no part of the required reinforcements had been implemented on [Fukushima Daiichi] Units 1 through 3 by the time of the accident. This was the result of tacit consent by NISA for a significant delay by the operators in completing the reinforcement. In addition, although NISA and the operators were aware of the risk of core damage from tsunami, no regulations were created, nor did TEPCO take any protective steps against such an occurrence ... If NISA had passed on to TEPCO measures that were included in the B.5.b subsection of the US security order that followed the 9/11 terrorist action, and if TEPCO had put the measures in place, the accident may have been preventable.[5]

—National Diet of Japan, *The Official Report of the Fukushima Nuclear Accident Independent Investigation Commission*

Hearing gunfire, eight police officers arrived at the Taj Mahal Palace and Tower Hotel (the Taj) just before midnight. They found they were significantly outgunned by terrorists working their way through the massive structure, killing any guests and staff they found. The officers' plastic-lined riot vests could stop a hand-thrown rock but not much more. The assassins weren't throwing rocks. They hunted with automatic weapons, grenades and bombs. The police's vintage .303 bolt-action rifles with only a few rounds of ammunition and their wooden sticks known as *lathis* would have been laughable in comparison with the AK-47 rifles carried by the Lashkar-e-Taiba members were the situation not so tragic. Those in the next level of response, the emergency response police, were little better off. So, the eight men representing law enforcement in India's most populous city backed off to await better-equipped and better-trained commando forces.

The two—later four—terrorists in the Taj were not alone. Companions elsewhere struck the Chhatrapati Shivaji Terminus (CST) railway station. More than 50 people died at the hands of that pair of perpetrators while police—poorly trained in how to use their inadequate weapons—ran

---

5   National Diet of Japan, *The Official Report of the Fukushima Nuclear Accident Independent Investigation Commission*, 16.

from the danger.[6] Law enforcement failure would be the order of the day as the terror dragged on, the perpetrators shocked by how little resistance the so-called public defenders offered. Police only four blocks from a besieged maternity hospital chose to remain in their headquarters. The 2008 siege at the Taj began on a Wednesday. It would not end until the following Saturday. Across the city, some 174 innocents and security force personnel died. Another 300 were wounded. The terrorists numbered 10.[7]

It need not have been this way. Or, at least, it need not have been the tragedy it was. Retrospect is a wonderful perspective, knowing now what those then did not. But that should not forgive the lack of preparedness—a preparedness that would have saved lives and spared others of their wounds. Officials received warnings before the attacks—more than 25 of them. Some came from sources such as the US Central Intelligence Agency.[8] Nor was Mumbai virgin terrain when it came to such criminality. The city had previously experienced 12 prominent acts of terrorism that tallied more than 500 dead and nearly four times that number injured. It had taken less than 11 minutes for 181 people to die in the bombing of seven of the megacity's trains a little over two years earlier. Responses to the scattered attacks that hit the Taj, another hotel, a café, a Jewish centre, the train station, a hospital and several other targets could have benefited from the lessons of these previous events had officials been willing to learn and act—lessons complemented by others from earlier strikes elsewhere such as in London on 7 July 2007. Looking over our shoulder with a critical eye is therefore not without justification. That retrospective offers a striking number of 'what ifs' valuable in terms of preparing for and reacting to future megacity disasters, orchestrating response capabilities, practising mission command, understanding the (sometimes bizarre) behaviour of noncombatants and managing information during a crisis. The Taj Mahal Palace Hotel will be the primary focus from which to draw questions and insights.

6   Sources differ regarding the number of casualties suffered during the 2008 attacks in terms of both individual locations and total. Those used here draw on what are thought to be particularly well-researched sources.

7   Shanthie Mariet D'Souza, 'Mumbai Terrorist Attacks of 2008', *Encyclopedia Britannica*, [Online], n.d., available from: www.britannica.com/event/Mumbai-terrorist-attacks-of-2008.

8   Material in the remainder of this discussion is from the following unless cited otherwise: Cathy Scott-Clark and Adrian Levy, *The Siege: 68 Hours Inside the Taj Hotel*, New York, NY: Penguin, 2013.

The lack of preparation, including of both plans and rehearsals, was evident in the opening minutes of the strikes. Efforts to keep the unknown number of assailants out of the Taj included locking virtually all street entrances to the building. These were, of course, also exits, meaning the effort to deny access trapped hundreds of guests and staff within the building. (The closures failed. Two of those who had first slaughtered diners in the Leopold Café later forced their way into the hotel.) Some threw tables or chairs against lower-floor windows in an effort to get out of the building only to find they bounced off the toughened glass that was designed to reduce injuries should a bomb go off outside the building. Twenty-five minutes after the attacks began, people were still trying to get *into* the Taj, fleeing from gunfire and explosions elsewhere in the vicinity. There was as yet no organised police response or effort to communicate with or control the frantic citizenry.

Confusion would have been inevitable. It was made all the worse by the tactics of the 10 terrorists deliberately seeking that end. Rifle, grenade and bomb attacks struck 13 different locations within two hours during the late evening of 26 November 2008.[9] A taxi was destroyed 5 kilometres north of the Taj, killing the driver and passenger while injuring 19 others nearby. Other bombs were placed at various locations and in vehicles to spread further panic. The police commissioner could not be located. The law enforcement response was either non-existent or scattered in the meantime. When the commissioner did show up, he was concerned more with bureaucratic procedure than decisive action. Further complicating the reaction: the force best equipped to take on the terrorists' weaponry was the National Security Guard (NSG), which was hours away in the capital of New Delhi and requests for help from the military were the responsibility of Maharashtra State (of which Mumbai is the capital), not city authorities. That force waited as Maharashtra State officials refused to admit their own capabilities were overwhelmed. India's central government, the Maharashtra Government and city authorities further delayed effective response by arguing with one another before finally agreeing on how to deploy NSG forces when the state finally asked for assistance. The worst of the slaughter would be over well before they finally arrived.[10] Another specially trained force was stationed within Mumbai:

9   Angel Rabasa, Robert D. Blackwill, Peter Chalk, Kim Cragin, C. Christine Fair, Brian A. Jackson, Brian Michael Jenkins, Seth G. Jones, Nathaniel Shestak and Ashley J. Tellis, *The lessons of Mumbai*, Occasional Paper 249, Santa Monica, CA: RAND Corporation, 2009, 23, available from: www.rand. org/content/dam/rand/pubs/occasional_papers/2009/RAND_OP249.pdf.

10   Boo, *Behind the Beautiful Forevers*, 216–17.

India's Marine Commandos (MARCOS). Akin to US Navy SEALs, their training, it was felt, did not properly prepare them for operating in the city. Again, state authorities refused to request their help.

There was the occasional police officer who had the courage to enter the Taj. One was Vishwas Patil, Mumbai's deputy commander of police for Zone 1, the part of the city containing most of its tourist attractions and major hotels. Patil realised at one point that all four terrorists were in a single room of the building, thereby providing an opportunity to at least isolate if not destroy the threat. Monitoring the situation from the structure's closed-circuit television room, he called for action by the police force's assault teams. Never having rehearsed, exercised in or walked through the massive complex, those teams either could not find their way or simply chose not to respond. The gunmen soon resumed their prowling, operating in pairs, knocking on doors, declaring themselves providers of room service and killing anyone who answered.

The failure to prepare was crippling operations outside the hotel as well. Having determined the mobile phone number used by those managing the attackers from Pakistan, requests to tap the conversations were held up as the only individual who could provide the required written authorisation was trapped within the Taj. Such obstacles were eventually breached only after additional killings and the terrorists set the hotel on fire. MARCOS leaders were finally called into the fight—but only in numbers that totalled less than 20 from a force of more than 1,000. They showed up without helmets or protective vests after travelling from their base less than 2 kilometres from the Taj. They, too, were unfamiliar with the building. Requests for blueprints went unanswered.

Trapped guests included members of India's parliament and influential foreigners. Most conducted themselves as would be expected. They were scared, sought shelter to hide, accepted guidance from employees familiar with the building and remained concealed while awaiting a chance to escape. Many hunkered down in locations the terrorists never realised held more than 100 people. The behaviour of others defied logic. Crouched undetected and silent among many hiding in a restaurant, one held up a camera and took a flash picture as a terrorist walked by in an adjacent hallway. A high-ranking public figure elsewhere spoke on his phone, apparently giving an interview to a television reporter. 'We are in a special part of the hotel on the first floor call the Chambers,' he said. 'There are more than 200 important people: business leaders and foreigners.'

Fortunately, it seems the terrorists and their managers in Pakistan were not tuned into the interview at the time though the latter were monitoring the situation on television.

Hotel staff and guests reassured and assisted one another. In one restaurant, they collectively chose leaders and guides to help them when the time came to attempt an escape. Outside, it was the person on the street who at times stepped forward. Hotel chef Nitin Minocha managed to escape when his group chose to risk running from where they had sheltered for hours. He was wounded by gunfire but managed to get on to the street, where he bandaged his bleeding arm with a piece of cloth. Two riders on a motorbike stopped on seeing him covered in blood. They let Minocha use a phone to notify a relative he was alive, then wedged him between them so he wouldn't topple from the vehicle on the way to hospital. Elsewhere, hotel staff member Amit Peshave took it on himself to remain at a hospital where he found the situation one of chaos. He lobbied for care as injured colleagues arrived, recording their names and the ward to which they were transferred. Without a champion, he feared, those with whom he worked would be ignored or forced to wait while others pushed themselves to the front for treatment.

Security forces eventually killed nine of the 10 terrorists. The tenth was arrested. NSG personnel—the 'Black Cats'—finally overcame officials' hesitation and tore free of bureaucratic red tape to make their way from Delhi to the Taj. There, with the four gunmen trapped, they fabricated two explosive devices, hurling them into the large room and killing all. It had been nearly 58 hours since the first two terrorists' entry into the hotel.

The steps taken by Mumbai and Maharashtra State to improve readiness following what came to be known as '26/11' are a mixed bag.[11] Officials quickly seized on the apparent fix of buying better equipment. They made it known that police and other security forces would receive M4 carbines, sniper rifles, armoured vehicles, speedboats and more, some of which added to preparedness while other purchases seemed based more on their 'cool factor' than legitimate value. Mumbai enhanced its Quick Response Team numbers and upgraded both its training and its equipment. The state government formed a new Force One commando element.

---

11   Details in this concluding paragraph draw on Rhys Machold, 'Militarising Mumbai? The "politics of response"', *Contexto Internacional* 39(03) (September–December 2017): 477–98, doi.org/10.1590/s0102-8529.2017390300002.

The federal government installed an NSG team near the megacity. Less promising was the fact the number of personal protective vests purchased fell short of needs. Expensive M82 .50 calibre antimaterial rifles joined the inventory despite there being no local firing ranges able to support the weapon's maximum range. Perhaps most disturbing was a statement by the head of the Maharashtra Anti-Terror Squad (ATS) that a 'constable does not fight terrorism. We have NSG and Force One to fight terrorism'— a grievous failure to recognise that the cop on the street is a primary source of intelligence, the first echelon who (given sufficient training and commitment) can convert information into actionable form and get it to where it needs to go. Even taken out of context (the ATS chief later said the beat constable 'is the first line of defence, but not the ultimate line'), the remark fails to recognise the essentiality of emphasising how important the police officer, firefighter, city engineer, restaurant inspector and any other official is in preventing acts of terrorism and otherwise acting to protect a megacity's population. This assumes those officials are sufficiently professional to care about that population. When the situation is one in which 'the police continue to be capable of immense repression', as was the evaluation of one writer well after the 2008 attacks, little should be expected from law enforcement or the residents whose help could increase the number of information sources millions of times over.

'What ifs?'

The largest uncertainly in this system is humans.[12]

—Dr Andrea Dutton, University of Florida

Lack of control, caused by decentralization of command, lack of observation for the commander, and the difficulty of maintaining communications, is perhaps the most perplexing problem of the commander … Command and control must be decentralized in view of the possibility that communications might fail at the most critical moment.[13]

—Charles J. Canella, *The defense of small towns and villages by infantry*

---

12   Quoted in Mario Alejandro Ariza, *Disposable City: Miami's Future on the Shores of Climate Catastrophe*, New York, NY: Bold Type, 2020, 34.
13   Charles J. Canella, *The defense of small towns and villages by infantry*, US Army Advanced Infantry Officers Course 1948–1949 Paper, Fort Benning, GA, n.d., 24.

How many innocents would have survived had Mumbai's police rehearsed their response for an attack on their city? It was certainly a logical step after its recent history of terrorism. Well-run exercises would presumably have seen calls for access to blueprints of public and private structures, walk-throughs to familiarise security forces with major buildings and correction of flaws in policies and procedures that proved crippling in 2008. Responsibilities for building familiarisation could have been divided between various law enforcement, local military, fire and other officials with the understanding that each could call on the other when necessary. A common repository of this and other critical information on a limited-access intranet would have put floorplans at the fingertips of organisations with legitimate call for use. Rehearsals—even in so simple a form as talking through challenges—could have detected the need to allow multiple layers of authorities to make critical decisions and grant vital approvals when the first, second or third-tier individual in a hierarchy was unavailable, as was the case with Mumbai's police commissioner.

We remind ourselves that a basic premise of this book is that preparation for *any* urban disaster does much to ready a megacity for catastrophes regardless of cause or type. But making plans is not the same as being prepared. The totality of disaster guidance for Memorial Hospital in New Orleans ran to nearly 300 pages before Hurricane Katrina. Yet, it took only five days for its staff—suffering from lack of information, sleep, medicines and outside assistance—to suffer a downward spiral that saw the facility go from effective patient care to euthanising its trusts. Memorial Hospital was only one of many institutions to suffer unmet needs during those trying days. Failures came at great cost in lives and property but also in trust, the city's reputation and belief that officials who should have led were capable of doing so. The benefits of preparing by bringing together all relevant parties for planning, rehearsing and circulating lessons offered by practising procedures during major urban events such as conventions, sports games and Mardi Gras are obvious when one realises the State of Louisiana's federal recovery funding of some $120 billion was more than three times the size of the state's annual budget.[14] The cost of preparations

---

14   Andre M. Perry, 'New Orleans is still learning from the lessons of Katrina—Houston should too', *The Avenue Blog*, Washington, DC: The Brookings Institution, 29 August 2017, available from: www.brookings.edu/blog/the-avenue/2017/08/29/new-orleans-is-still-learning-from-the-lessons-of-katrina-houston-should-too/.

would have been a fraction of that for recovery. Another benefit of proper preparation: buy-in. Organisations and individuals tend to be more willing to support activities if they play a part in planning.

Planning is vital, but the resulting plans must be executable and kept up to date. They should also be 'red teamed' (of which more below).

Pre-disaster systems considerations

> It was also well known in London that China could effectively ruin the Hong Kong economy by cutting its supply of food or, more importantly, water.[15]
>
> —Neil Monnery, *Architect of Prosperity*

> Stations had no gas to pump. This was due to severe breakdowns in the supply chain serving New York … Flood damage at critical facilities in Southern Manhattan, Red Hook, and the Rockaways disrupted landline and Internet service throughout the neighborhoods they served for up to 11 days … In areas with power outages, the pumping systems in high-rise buildings ceased to function, leaving residents on upper floors with empty taps and no way to flush toilets.[16]
>
> —NYC Special Initiative for Rebuilding and Resiliency, *PlaNYC*

Whether Hong Kong in 1941, Manila in 1945, Mosul in 2016 or Tokyo, New York or Los Angeles today, residents do not drink, bathe, wash or flush a toilet if water cannot make its way from outside the city to its residents. The city becomes a desert packed with humanity that cannot long survive without what deserts by definition lack.

Those suffering will have vastly different abilities to deal with a crisis. We have noted that slums are more likely to occupy low-lying ground prone to floods or landslides. The average poor resident of Bogotá, Colombia, lives on land with twice the seismic risk of that under rich households.[17] Cupboards fat with food are a luxury of which the less well-to-do only dream. Meals are fewer for the poor; hunger a frequent companion. Food is routinely purchased and cooked on the day it is eaten

---

15 Monnery, *Architect of Prosperity*, 282.
16 NYC Special Initiative for Rebuilding and Resiliency, *PlaNYC: A Stronger, More Resilient New York*, City of New York, 2013, 15, 16, 17, available from: www1.nyc.gov/site/sirr/report/report.page.
17 Lall and Deichmann, *Density and disasters*, 19.

either due to lack of money to buy more or for want of a means to keep it from spoiling.[18] Interruption in the supply of drink, food or the fuel to prepare meals quickly turns the destitute into the distressed—and dangerously susceptible to the diseases that prey on the malnourished. The problem is greater when flood, earthquake, war or other calamity forces the poor from their homes. Lacking the funds to pay for food, much less alternative shelter, the chances of megacity internal refugees (or 'internally displaced persons' in aid-speak) avoiding disaster are worsened by ignorance of where they can find sources of essentials once they move. Authorities able and willing to help, when they exist, often do not know where the displaced moved to. The lucky poor will find official shelters or stay with relatives. The less fortunate scatter to abandoned buildings or live rough beneath bridges, in parks and on sidewalks.[19] All are vulnerable. Those with medicine dependencies, limited mobility or chronic conditions requiring treatment soon find themselves at the precipice. Despite the wealth associated with Western countries' largest cities, the Bronx in New York City is home to the poorest urban county in the United States. Nearly 40 per cent of South Bronx residents live below the poverty line (the value for the city as a whole is just under 20 per cent).[20] Neighbouring Queens might be less impoverished, but those wanting to aid its residents during a future crisis will be challenged by the linguistic and cultural variety inherent in half its population being foreign born.[21] Adversity quickly stresses officials responsible for an urban population at risk—a population that can swell as rural residents seek relief in nearby urban centres thought to be hubs for aid distribution.

Addressing social media's potential during crises, public information officer and 25-year veteran of the Los Angeles Fire Department Brian Humphrey recalled: '[P]eople want to help in a crisis and the currency is not dollars. It's information … Every citizen is a communicator or contributor.'[22] Cities are seas of knowledge and information; megacities, it follows, are oceans. We have noted that the greatest knowledge lies

---

18   Acción Contra El Hambre [Action Against Hunger], *Urban Disaster Lessons Learnt*, Paris, n.d., 21, available from: silo.tips/download/urban-disaster-lessons-learnt.
19   Internal Displacement Monitoring Centre, *Global Report on Internal Displacement 2018: Part 1. On the GRID: The Global Displacement Landscape*, Geneva: IDMC, 2018, available from: www.internal-displacement.org/global-report/grid2018/downloads/report/2018-GRID-part-1.pdf.
20   Kevin Baker, 'The death of a once great city: The fall of New York and the urban crisis of affluence', *Harper's Magazine*, 8 July 2018, available from: harpers.org/archive/2018/07/the-death-of-new-york-city-gentrification/.
21   ibid.
22   American Red Cross, *The case for integrating crisis response with social media*.

within the urban area's citizenry, authorities and local aid organisations. Who better knows an apartment building than its manager or long-time doorman; a neighbourhood than its shopkeepers, police or firefighters? These men and women are holders of *individual* information: who resides where, who has particular needs, which families have children or elderly relatives and where they might be should an earthquake or other disaster strike unexpectedly, who goes to which schools and daycare centres or plays what sports where and when. Establishing procedures to mine such knowledge before it is needed is time and money well spent. Preparations also pay off in times of lesser crises.

Crime, medical, transportation, tax and other statistics; data on construction sites, storage locations or warehouse facilities holding construction materials; and information regarding access to trucks, construction equipment, food or other resources provide *collective* information that complements the individual. Knowing how to access these data means police are aware of where looting or gang-on-gang violence is likely to rear its ugly head when the lights go out. Understanding where the worst will make its appearance also helps when demands are many and resources too few. Which areas will be most at risk in times of flood should be common knowledge thanks to flood-zone maps and databases—if they are well kept, as is the case in Tokyo. Less known, perhaps, is what types of buildings (and therefore which occupants) will suffer most as waters rise or tremors strike. Hurricane Sandy's visit to New York City revealed that edifices of 1) one storey, 2) wood construction, 3) built before 1961, and 4) (no surprise here) close to shorelines proved the most vulnerable. These accounted for 18 per cent of the urban area's structures but proved to be 73 per cent of those destroyed or left structurally damaged.[23] Knowledge of needed practices is likewise vital. Based on her study of Hurricane Katrina, Pulitzer Prize–winning author Sheri Fink made clear the need for authorities to triage the truly needy from others who believe themselves physically suffering but who are in fact 'worried well' or 'sympathetic casualties'—individuals whose 'injuries' are psychological in nature (though those psychological beliefs can result in very real physical symptoms similar to those of the actually exposed).[24] Hospitals serving patients during the 1995 Tokyo sarin attack faced the same problem. Doctors found that roughly 70–80

---

23 NYC Special Initiative for Rebuilding and Resiliency, *PlaNYC*, 75.
24 Fink's comments can be found in Glenn et al., *Where None Have Gone Before*.

per cent of those seeking care fell into the worried-well category.[25] These individuals wrongly believed they had been physically affected by the nerve agent. Many demonstrated symptoms like those of the exposed victims, overwhelming medical personnel who were providing treatment for more than 5,500 individuals, of whom some 4,000 were merely worried well.

Though larger urban areas tend to have younger populations than their countries at large, megacity populations will nevertheless reflect national ageing trends, if to a lesser extent. That means more of a megacity's population will suffer from reduced mobility, diminished mental capacity and greater need for medical assistance when catastrophe strikes. More than one in every 14 citizens in Japan's 2019 population was disabled.[26] Other countries—and their cities—are evolving in the same direction. Only those in Africa resist the trend.

Pre-disaster control

> Most people, in fact, will not take trouble in finding out the truth, but are much more inclined to accept the first story they hear.[27]
>
> —Thucydides, *History of the Peloponnesian War*

> In solving a problem of this sort, the grand thing is to be able to reason backwards.[28]
>
> —Arthur Conan Doyle, *A Study in Scarlet*

Mumbai in November 2008 and the Taj Mahal Palace and Tower in particular offer a good starting point for understanding the variety of challenges that include essential decisions, unexpected behaviours and many other aspects when dealing with a catastrophe. Could toughened glass be designed so that it shields against exterior pressures while being breakable from the interior in case of fire or other need to flee? Could those window designs include panes opened manually to achieve the same purpose? Given that panic, confusion or arrogance will cause some who are at risk to behave in ways that endanger others, what steps could be taken to control or cut select communications or media access

---

25   Glenn et al., *Achieving Convergence during Humanitarian Assistance and Disaster Relief Operations.*
26   'Chairbound but seated: Japanese with disabilities', *The Economist*, [London], 3 August 2019, 29.
27   Thucydides, *History of the Peloponnesian War*, trans. Rex Warner, New York, NY: Penguin, 1972, 47.
28   Arthur Conan Doyle, *A Study in Scarlet*, London: Ward Lock & Co.,-1887, Pt II, Ch. 7.

within specified areas? Does the apparent wisdom of these steps bear out during a rehearsal? (Note that 'control' as used in these pages refers to restoring or maintaining a desirable condition of public safety, stability and confidence during or after a catastrophe rather than imposition of unjustified coercion.)

That the forces responding in Mumbai were poorly coordinated is obvious. The responses within medical facilities and for getting injured to those facilities (or treated onsite) were likewise. The striking of numerous targets demonstrated that the Mumbai terrorists recognised the value of assaulting multiple sites to confuse emergency response systems. It was fortunate that the 9/11 attacks in New York City struck only a single target. What responses might an exercise addressing future misfortunes reveal given a scenario that includes bombs going off throughout the urban area and multiple teams of shooters moving between widely dispersed targets? Paris's effective response to its 2015 tragedy is an excellent example of a megacity that internalised lessons from previous terrorist attacks; we will look at that response in pages to come. New York City is another among major urban areas around the world that has done likewise. Its Strategic Home Intervention and Early Leadership Development (SHIELD) program is a way for the NYPD to educate some 3,000 private security managers in the megacity area. It joins another partnership, Operation Nexus, in which detectives visit companies to educate commercial enterprises about how to identify and report suspicious activities at hotels, truck rental companies or companies selling relevant goods, for example.[29]

Dramatic as the 2008 attacks on Mumbai were, nature and humankind possess the power to make even those horrendous losses seem an afterthought. Regardless of a disaster's cause, the punishment suffered must be viewed as the starting point for relief and recovery. Better-led urban leaders will have already put appropriate steps in place before the last raindrops fall, shaking stops or shots are fired.

Effective plans require looking much deeper in time than one might expect. As the renowned philosopher 'Yogi' Berra put it, 'If you don't know where you are going, you'll end up someplace else.' Without a point from which to backward plan, government officials and others joining the effort will each follow their own paths—paths more likely to point in different directions than join in pursuit of a common goal. Given the

---

29   United States Senate, *Lessons from the Mumbai Terrorist Attacks.*

impossibility of predicting when a disaster will strike, planners should define this distant planning point in terms of a situation rather than a point fixed in time. That planning point might be a return to normalcy. More likely, it will be some form of what existed before the disaster and what could be should leaders seize opportunities for improvements presented by the event's destruction (think of Chicago and its post-fire skyscrapers). Once the base plan is in place, other plans can use this foundation to prepare for conditions varying from the original assumptions: greater or lesser magnitude quakes than the base plan assumes, terrorist attacks striking different locations or numbers of locations or a combination of interconnected catastrophes such as the quake, tsunami and nuclear facility disaster experienced in 2011 in Japan. Additional plans founded on a base plan will adapt new courses of action given changed conditions (called 'branch plans' in the military). Plans that extend beyond the base plan are 'sequels'.

Control during and in the aftermath of these events is impossible without effective communications. Language would seem an obvious challenge easily identified before an outsider's arrival. Recall the 800 languages spoken in New York City or the 199 in Los Angeles schools. The problem will be less but not absent in more homogeneous megacities such as Tokyo, Seoul or Jakarta. Knowing which languages are spoken is but a snowball on the tip of an iceberg. Which languages are spoken across the city? Which primarily only in certain communities? Which groups speak a second language but understand the one most used in the urban area, meaning that translation might not be necessary, that demands for translators are therefore reduced or that the pool of potential translators is larger than would otherwise be the case? Little wonder the NYPD in the aftermath of 9/11 could call on 275 certified interviewers able to communicate in 45 languages—in addition to officers fluent in one or more of a variety of languages including Farsi, Pashto and Urdu. NYPD linguists are sometimes shared with federal agencies lacking similar capabilities.[30]

And this addresses only varieties of languages. What medium will best reach the audiences who need to receive the messages ('receive' not merely 'hear' is the appropriate word as some of those on the receiving end will be hearing impaired)? The answer can be less obvious than it

---

30 Nussbaum, 'Protecting global cities', 221.

might seem. Apps purpose-designed for emergencies, blanket mobile phone messages or relying on Twitter, Facebook or other platform users to forward messages all have value—until batteries run low and there is no electricity to recharge or power phones, iPads and computers. Recall that reliance on the internet failed to touch many in the aftermath of the 2011 Fukushima disaster because the population in affected areas included many non-users. Television, radio and other electricity-dependent ways of communicating suffer similar limitations. Dropping leaflets could work, though design, printing, translating into all languages needed and distribution would cause a lag in getting messages to some audiences. A comic book or cartoon format can overcome language and literacy issues if the message can be communicated pictorially (remembering periodic issues of comic books published to spread pro-government messages during ongoing insurgencies in the southern Philippines and Iraq proved effective in reaching targeted teenagers and males in their early twenties. Unfortunately, terrorists also use this method to recruit as was the case with the Pakistani Lashkar-e-Taiba before the Mumbai attacks).[31] Another challenge is that details can be hard to get across without the written word. Clever 'mascots' can help in communicating a message and supporting recall of information; think the Geico gecko, long a spokesperson for that American insurance company (well, spokeslizard actually). (When I was an exchange officer with the British Army, billboard advertisements in our community pictured nothing but a piece of purple cloth being sliced, clipped, snipped or sheared in some way. It turns out that what at first was indecipherable to we Americans was marketing for Silk Cut cigarettes. The visual image was so well established that words were unnecessary … other than the mandatory antismoking warning.)

Newspapers can be an effective means of getting the word out even if literacy is limited. Posting them (or other written messages) in gathering spots such as markets or outside police stations draws crowds where the literate read for the benefit of others. Mixing key messages with other news of interest such as sports scores or the doings of popular personalities can increase the crowds drawn to these sites. Those personalities might help by lending their voices on TV or radio. The *Story Story* radio soap opera that was helpful in teaching listeners facts and debunking the many myths and rumours infiltrating communities during the 2014 Ebola crisis provides an example of how critical messages can reach a public before, during

---

31 Scott-Clark and Levy, *The Siege*, 104.

and after a crisis. These examples only begin to touch on the possible ways of communicating with an urban area's many audiences. Disaster communications are the playground of the innovative and imaginative—given bosses willing to listen to them.

Though tainted in some circles due to their past or present coercive use in the Soviet Union, China, Tanzania and elsewhere, community associations or neighbourhood committees have tremendous potential for helping authorities with messaging and managing the potential of the person on the street. Day-to-day benefits are evident in New York City, for example, where Orthodox Jews' Shomrim neighbourhood watch groups work with local police. It is often to the Shomrim that residents first go when a crime has been committed or a child is missing.[32] Tokyo and Beijing are well known for the benefits of their neighbourhood committees. Those in the latter city were key to containing Covid-19 in the country's capital and elsewhere. They stood guard outside housing complexes, restricting who could leave or enter and monitoring those in self-quarantine, even using alarms and webcams to restrain potential violators of official dictates. They also oversaw delivery of food and kept their neighbourhoods advised of government policies.[33] Extreme by Western standards? Yes, but that should not cause us to overlook the benefits of authorities having a single neighbourhood point of contact if face-to-face communications are among the limited communication means available. Getting word out regarding how to access water, food, medical care or other supplies and services is quicker if those delivering the message can go to one individual who then uses a neighbourhood 'alert roster' to spread the information quickly (for example, the head of the committee notifies five prearranged contacts, each of whom calls five more, and so on). As with the Shomrim, committee representatives can also be the first point of contact for the police when trouble arises. That is particularly important in times of crisis when these representatives might settle issues without causing law enforcement officers to be rerouted from higher-priority calls. And there may be cases where keeping officials informed of behaviour that threatens general welfare is essential, as in the case of those who would, Patrick Sawyer–like, refuse to obey dictates necessary to containing the spread of biological or chemical contamination.

---

32   Patrick Sharkey, *Uneasy Peace: The Great Crime Decline, the Renewal of City Life, and the Next War on Violence*, New York, NY: Norton, 2018, 226n.20.

33   'On every street: Urban society', *The Economist*, [London], 13 June 2020, 31–32.

Recent years have seen a dramatic increase in the risk of cyberattacks. Estonian and Ukrainian urban residents are among those who can attest to cities' vulnerabilities. Interruption of power, water, communications or other resources essential to human survival would dramatically complicate operations and potentially undermine government legitimacy. The number of vulnerable nodes, inexperience in defending against such attacks or their second, third and higher-order consequences and difficulty in determining the perpetrator are problems officials are only beginning to consider much less address effectively. Determining the cause of an outage can be hard; savvy operators might strike ultimate targets by capitalising on second or higher-order effects, meaning the initial attack is distant from the desired end in terms of both time and space. Smart city initiatives complicate the situation further. These capabilities can speed road repairs, reduce flooding and otherwise greatly benefit communities. Ironically, while urban authorities tend to be cautious regarding resident concerns about protection of private information, they are sometimes less mindful of criminal, foreign power or other cyber threats that exploit their city's smart components to ill effect. Hackers have already been successful in manipulating access-control systems to facilitate denial-of-service attacks and open smart software–controlled doors.[34]

Containing the number of those suffering loss of resources is one benefit of decentralisation. Design of infrastructure systems that avoids overcentralisation and provides redundancy means controlling authorities can selectively reduce or deny specific areas of select services. So-called graceful failures[35] allow limiting consumption in some communities to restore interrupted services elsewhere. This control also permits officials to employ infrastructure when influencing behaviour is essential to public safety or security, where riots, enemy action or other activities act counterproductively to the welfare of the whole city, for example. Depending on the sophistication of infrastructure control, authorities could conceivably deny resources to an individual city block, building or even apartment level—all from a remote location. Such partial or total restriction of access also provides ways to protect communities from contaminated water, cyberattacks targeting specific or general software (acting as the equivalent of a cyber circuit-breaker) or contaminated public transportation. Decentralisation comes with costs. A primary

---

34 Alexander Braszko, 'Military implications of smart cities', *Mad Scientist Blog*, 4 June 2020, available from: madsciblog.tradoc.army.mil/242-military-implications-of-smart-cities/.
35 Townsend, *Smart Cities*, 300.

reason fewer, larger, more centralised infrastructure nodes such as power or water treatment plants are attractive is because they offer economies of scale. It's cheaper to build and maintain one large facility than many smaller ones scattered across an urban landscape. Post-disaster and other future designs could nonetheless seek a better balance than currently exists between cost and security. Infrastructure decentralisation receives more attention in later pages.

Providing a bit of early warning when service losses threaten might be the best officials can do under some circumstances. Israeli authorities turned to an innovative solution to warn vulnerable civilians of rocket attacks from Gaza during 2014's Operation Protective Edge:

> The Yo app was thought to be nothing more than a gimmick; all it did was allow an individual to send the one-word greeting of 'Yo' to another. It has come to serve a far more valuable service in Israel. The country developed its Red Alert real-time missile notification system following the 2012 introduction of a siren-based emergency warning system. Fearing that some might not hear the audible signal, Red Alert was an app that provided an additional alert to RedAlertIsrael followers on phones whenever a missile or rocket threatened an entire urban area, e.g., Tel Aviv. By partnering with Yo, an expanded number of individuals— those in the vicinity of Gaza in areas not covered by Red Alert, for example—can now get a 'Yo' signal that gives between 15 and 90 seconds warning of incoming munitions.[36]

How might a similar app serve elsewhere? During New York City's 2003 loss of electricity (part of the larger US East Coast blackout), utility provider ConEd had about 40 seconds between when it detected a problem and the loss of power.[37] Yo! Get out of that elevator on the next floor or be like the hundreds stuck in 2003.

Knowing where to look before you have to look

> The chaos of the immediate aftermath of a disaster is not the best time to be thinking about far-reaching policies.[38]
>
> —Elizabeth Ferris, 'Urban disasters, conflict and violence'

---

36 Glenn, *Short war in a perpetual conflict*, 72–73.
37 Rodin, *The Resilience Dividend*, 19.
38 Ferris, 'Urban disasters, conflict and violence'.

> A difference in scale can at some point become a difference in kind.[39]
>
> —Phil Williams and Werner Selle, *Military Contingencies in Megacities and Sub-Megacities*

It was popular in early twenty-first-century writings on counterinsurgency to consider the population of a country as the 'centre of gravity'—a military term referring to those elements that in and of themselves could in some manner prove decisive to success or failure.[40] This is nonsense. As we observed in the above discussion about the continuum of relative interests, expecting to mould the thoughts or behaviour of an entire city's population is like a politician spending their time and money trying to convince everyone in a constituency to vote for them. It is the same with populations in general. Wiser leaders allocate their always limited resources to winning over key personalities or groups who can then help to sway others who are potentially swayable. But how do we identify and communicate with those who are the mediums for our messages?

The sheer size of megacities means identifying social or physical centres of gravity will take on fundamental, even decisive, importance. We recall that it was only after Gaza's more influential residents complained about the loss of their homes that Hamas agreed to a ceasefire during the 2014 Operation Protective Edge.[41] Savvy megacity authorities often identify similar key social nodes to help them in their day-to-day efforts to protect residents. Los Angeles Police Department officers plotted the locations of gang-related violence and found that the seams along different groups' territories were where frictions sparked conflict. Forty per cent of Chicago's firearm deaths are attributable to just 4 per cent of its population. Two-thirds of Boston's street robberies occur in only 8 per cent of its area.[42] In Seattle, police analysed 14 years of statistics and found that half of all crimes were committed on less than 5 per cent of the city's streets.[43] In large and medium-sized Latin American cities,

---

39   Williams and Selle, *Military Contingencies in Megacities and Sub-Megacities*, 7.
40   This description is admittedly oversimplified. The definition and meaning of centre of gravity—a concept originally introduced by Carl von Clausewitz in *On War*—have long been and continue to be items of vigorous debate in military circles. The United States' interservice (or joint) doctrine defines centre of gravity as 'the source of power that provides moral or physical strength, freedom of action, or will to act'. Department of Defense (DOD), *Department of Defense Dictionary of Military and Associated Terms*, Arlington, VA: US Department of Defense, 1972, 29.
41   Glenn, *Short war in a perpetual conflict*, 77, 84.
42   Sharkey, *Uneasy Peace*, 158–59.
43   'Algorithm blues: Predictive policing and sentencing', *The Economist*, [London], 2 June 2018, [Technology Quarterly] 9–11, at 9, 10.

approximately 80 per cent of homicides occur in only 2 per cent of an urban area. In 2011 in Karachi, 47 per cent of murders took place on 3.5 per cent of land that housed less than 10 per cent of the city's population.[44] New York City and Los Angeles have used such data to prioritise where they focus local law enforcement efforts.[45] In an example from New York City's 2020 Covid-19 crisis, the issue of how to allocate ventilators became a life and death decision for its victims. Presciently, the city had put together a taskforce in 2007 to recommend policies for just that issue should a pandemic such as the Spanish flu recur. A report released in 2015 provided recommendations—for example, that patients with some conditions are not put on a ventilator when availability falls short of demand. These included unresponsive patients or those with severe burns, traumatic brain injury or suffering cardiac arrest. Members of the group involved in the initial taskforce participated in a mid-March 2020 renewed discussion of the problem. Reconsidered issues included tough choices such as which hospitals should receive newly arrived funding or equipment. Recommendations included favouring previously underresourced hospitals. A counterproposal noted that better-funded hospitals tended to receive and treat the most vulnerable patients. Fevers burned and patients died as politicians dithered rather than made the tough decisions. The number of deceased became so great that morgues could not keep pace. Refrigerated trailers parked outside medical facilities served as temporary morgues while the report's recommendations disappeared into the mire of bureaucracy. Doctors, lacking policy guidance, spent resources attempting to save those with little chance of survival.[46] Indecision is a decision in times of crisis.

Time for another brief pause before we move on. Given the below, we might find it helpful to distinguish between 'prediction' and 'forecasting'. The Pacific Northwest Seismic Network provides a pragmatic description that allows us to see the critical difference between the two:

> A prediction of an earthquake needs to state exactly where and when the event will happen with enough specifics to be useful for response planning purposes. For example, the statement 'there will be an earthquake tomorrow at 7:45 AM' is almost certainly going to be correct somewhere in the world, but it has no value as

44   Gayer, *Karachi*, 7.
45   'Shining some light: Latin America's homicide problem is a harbinger for the developing world', *The Economist*, [London], 7 April 2018, 16–18, at 17.
46   Tyler Foggatt, 'Protocols: Who gets a ventilator?', *The New Yorker*, 20 April 2020, 13–14, at 14.

a prediction. Similarly, saying that there will eventually be a large earthquake on a very active fault is useless; while it is true, almost nothing can be done with this information. Without a specific date or location, a statement cannot be a prediction. Currently, no one can predict where or when big earthquakes will occur to meet these criteria. However, seismologists have gotten much better at forecasting earthquakes. On a sunny Monday afternoon, meteorologists may forecast a wet weekend ahead, and can add an estimate of how certain they are that their forecast will be accurate; i.e., 'we forecast a 60% chance of rain on Saturday.'[47]

No-one should expect even the most able of leaders or staff to predict crises, but forecasting might be within the realm of the possible. Accurate forecasting only helps the prepared, however. The better readied a megacity is for disaster, the better are the chances that misfortune falls short of achieving disaster status. Tokyo, with its phenomenal combination of threats—typhoons, the active Mount Fuji volcano, floods, tsunamis and earthquakes, much less missile attacks from North Korea or the failure of another nuclear power facility—has taken steps to ensure its residents are among the best prepared in the world. We have mentioned neighbourhood governments' disaster preparedness maps that highlight areas prone to earthquake, fire, flooding, tsunami, landslide or other dangers. Newly constructed buildings must meet stringent structural standards; older structures once deemed vulnerable can be spotted thanks to their retrofitted earthquake bracing. Open areas are set aside not only for recreation purposes. A bit of searching will reveal a public information map showing what nearby terrain is exposed to natural hazards. Parks have benches that can be converted into grills for cooking by those left homeless. Locations have been fitted with underground receptacles that can be covered by a tent or surrounded by screens while serving as public toilets. The city has contracted with local ferry companies to move people or goods by water should ill fortune isolate communities due to blocked roads or fires. The list goes on.

Los Angeles has some way to go before achieving anything close to Tokyo's accomplishments, but officials have in the past been good about drawing on previous events as opportunities to learn, design rehearsals and develop

---

47   Lauren Burch, 'What's the difference between predicting and forecasting earthquakes?', *Blog*, Seattle, WA: Pacific Northwest Seismic Network, 23 May 2016, available from: pnsn.org/blog/2016/05/23/what-s-the-difference-between-predicting-and-forecasting-earthquakes.

response policies as the megacity readies for the inevitable quakes to come. 'Advanced notice allows citizens to prepare', former Los Angeles County Sheriff's Department commander Sid Heal observed:

> We've had people die trying to save cats … Many have taken steps to find their own shelter, which in turn lightens the logistical burden on us. When we have mass casualty incidents, it has proven far better to move medical personnel to the scene rather than move victims to a medical facility. Victims can be stabilized; the transportation time is not working against the 'golden hour' and we are not wasting time and effort moving people who are going to die enroute or live without the transportation. Linking friends and families to victims allows an informal support system to develop that often takes uninjured or lightly injured victims out of the emergency response logistical systems … Linking the public emergency response system to private enterprises provides and enhances capabilities without requiring a heavy logistical burden. This usually takes the form of retainer contracts so that emergency response has access to heavy equipment, facilities, tools, vehicles, etc. without actually owning them. Moreover, we usually contract with the skilled operators at the same time so that we have a turnkey system. A bulldozer comes with an operator, a helicopter comes with a pilot, etc.[48]

Pehr Lodhammar was senior program manager for the UN Mine Action Service during and in the aftermath of operations in Mosul. His mine-clearing team could not enter Mosul until the fighting stopped, but they distributed water bottles with labels warning recipients of the dangers of IEDs ('If you see this, don't touch it!'). They also conducted safety classes. Lodhammar recommended similar instruction be provided to urban residents before a disaster—perhaps having teachers give brief classes twice a year and including basic first aid and precautions for when an individual comes across a possible explosive device.[49] Obviously, similar training for dealing with hazards other than those with wartime origins would likewise have benefits.

With some notable exceptions, disaster lessons learned by one urban area too rarely reach others. Douglas Brinkley, identifying one of the many failures in preparing for and reacting to Hurricane Katrina in New Orleans, confirmed Sid Heal's observation about the importance of accounting for

---

48   Charles S. Heal, Email to Russell W. Glenn, Subject: Megacities research, 17 March 2016.
49   Pehr Lodhammar, Skype interview with Dr Russell W. Glenn, 7 June 2021.

the importance of pets to many residents. The city did not allow pets on evacuation buses after the city's flooding—a decision that 'caused a lot of grief' and has elsewhere more than once resulted in owners' deaths.[50] Some sense of how many evacuees will have pets and what type they are provides planners with important information when readying housing, food stocks and other support.

Pre-disaster readiness and the comprehensive approach

> In *Democracy in America*, Alexis de Tocqueville marveled at Americans' propensity to solve problems outside the bounds of government … 'Wherever at the head of some new undertaking you see the government in France, or a man of rank in England, in the United States you will be sure to find an association.'[51]
>
> —Anthony M. Townsend, *Smart Cities*

> The unprecedented terrorist attack that France experienced in 2015 marked a major change … After decades that had seen war kept at bay, our population has once again become a target in need of protection. But our population might also be the best weapon to oppose the enemy.[52]
>
> —Jean-Yves Le Drian, *Who Is the Enemy?*

Even the best-prepared megacities cannot take readiness for granted, as Tokyo's experience with the religious cult Aum Shinrikyo's 20 March 1995 sarin nerve agent attack makes clear. Five members of the group grasped their umbrellas and drove the sharpened points home, penetrating the membranes at their feet to free the liquid contained therein amid Tokyo's morning rush-hour commuters. The subway cars were packed; rush hour sometimes sees them carrying up to 200 per cent of their design capacity. Delays in recognising the nature of the threat meant trains continued to run for more than an hour after the first release of sarin. Contamination would ultimately spread to 15 stations. Twelve of the more than 5,500 patients seeking medical attention would die. The deceased included

---

50   Douglas Brinkley, *The Great Deluge: Hurricane Katrina, New Orleans, and the Mississippi Gulf Coast*, New York, NY: William Morrow, 2006, 592.
51   Townsend, *Smart Cities*, 308.
52   Jean-Yves Le Drian, *Who Is the Enemy?*, trans. Sandra Smith, Paris: Les Éditions du Cerf, 2016, 64, 65.

police and maintenance personnel who unwittingly exposed themselves either to vapor or, in the case of those cleaning up the spills, when they mopped up the liquid without protecting their skin or airways. At the time of the attack, Dr Tetsu Okumura was on staff at St Luke's International Hospital, the facility that treated the largest number of patients. Okumura wrote of communications and responder capabilities quickly being overwhelmed.[53] Delays in identifying the toxic agent not only resulted in deaths but also contributed to 10 per cent of medical and other personnel in some facilities suffering contamination. Onsite treatment was limited and often inadequate. City policies did not include moving physicians to disaster sites. Emergency medical technicians were not allowed to intubate patients unless under a doctor's supervision, nor were they equipped with auto-injectors, decontamination lotion or other medications for dealing with chemical exposure.

Firefighters, police and hospitals struggled to communicate in the immediate aftermath of the sarin attack. This hindered coordination, undermined effective responses and delayed identification of the agent involved. The first report mistakenly attributed casualties to an explosion. Not knowing the identity of the contaminant meant medical personnel did not think to don protective equipment (which was in most cases not available anyway). Nor were patients or hospital staff initially decontaminated (and, again, the specialised equipment needed was not on hand). Ventilation in treatment rooms was insufficient. Police and fire representatives sent to hospitals sought information but provided little in return. Centralised crisis management was lacking due to the communications issues. Tokyo's fire department, which was responsible for coordinating patient movements to avoid overwhelming facilities, therefore could not do so. There was no overarching policy regarding responder coordination. Further complicating effective response: recall that between 70 and 80 per cent of those seeking medical attention were the 'worried well' or 'sympathetic casualties'—individuals who had not been exposed to sarin but believed they were victims of contamination. Triage at hospitals attempted to separate such individuals from the contaminated—a task made harder by the delays in identifying sarin as the contaminant and the similarity of worried-well and exposed patients' symptoms.

---

53   Those wanting more detail on the response to this attack should access Dr Tetsu Okumura's excellent article: Okumura et al., 'The Tokyo subway sarin attack', 613–17.

Steps have been taken to address shortfalls identified on that March day more than 25 years ago. Not all are sufficient. Decontamination equipment and procedures are more readily available. The Japanese Poison Information Centre has since been designated national coordinator for information about chemical disaster management. The centre has created a model for incident information flow and coordination of response assets. Japan's government compiled a list of chemical agent–knowledgeable personnel who meet regularly and are linked by mailing lists and other means.[54]

However, though Tokyo police and fire personnel now reportedly have sufficient protective equipment, hospitals remain badly underequipped. Emergency medical technicians in 2019 in Tokyo were still not authorised to intubate or perform some other lifesaving procedures during mass-casualty events barring oversight by a licensed doctor (with exceptions granted for cardiopulmonary arrest patients). Tokyo's doctors do not routinely move to disaster sites—this a quarter-century after the attack and despite the value of doing so being demonstrated during responses to Paris's 2015 terrorist attacks and elsewhere.[55] Officials have yet to develop procedures for situations in which normal communications capabilities are overwhelmed or lack of power renders them inoperable. Cooperation between agencies responsible for disaster response leaves much to be desired.[56]

A small step too rarely taken: Rehearsals

> The FBI had [terrorist suspect] Iyman Faris down at Quantico talking about his plans … 'Oh, I was gonna drive my truck over the Brooklyn Bridge,' remembers one of the frustrated [NYPD] investigators. 'Well, any New York cop knows you can't take a truck over the Brooklyn Bridge. But the FBI agent may not know that, because none of them live in Long Island. They all live in New Jersey.'[57]
>
> —Christopher Dickey, *Securing the City*

---

54 Glenn et al., *Achieving Convergence during Humanitarian Assistance and Disaster Relief Operations*.
55 ibid.
56 ibid.
57 Dickey, *Securing the City*, 154.

Jungle fighting skills and determination couldn't compensate for lack of training in urban operations and special tools such as smoke grenades.[58]

—Charles Knight and Katja Theodorakis, *The Marawi Crisis*

A record 945 millimetres of rain fell on Mumbai within 24 hours on 26 July 2005. Just under 760 millimetres of that amount fell within only five hours during in the same period. At least one-third of the city flooded, the city's airport runways and terminal buildings included. Lower-lying areas were submerged under 3 to 4.6 metres of water. Those living in slums were especially hard hit, with thousands of homes washed away or otherwise destroyed. Lingering floodwaters fed outbreaks of dengue fever, malaria, leptospirosis and diarrhoea.[59] This can in part be explained by the poor condition of human waste facilities in the city. Approximately 9,700 public toilet blocks were in place two years before the floods. A survey found that roughly 80 per cent were inoperable; the number was sufficient to address the needs of only half of Mumbai's more than 18 million residents even had all been functioning.[60] Most of the city lost wired telephone services. It would be weeks before some locations saw it restored. Parts of the city were likewise without mobile phone service. Much of the megacity lost power for days. In some cases, the electricity was deliberately cut to prevent electrocutions. All three of the megacity's suburban rail lines shut for the first time in Mumbai's history. Looking back on the disaster seven years later, city disaster planners noted:

> [T]here was a total collapse of the transport and communication system. The domestic and international airports were closed for two days and the major roads linking the city to other centres in the country were submerged. Intercity train services were cancelled for over a week, while suburban trains, which are the lifeline of the city, could not operate for 36 hours … ATM transactions could not be carried out, not only in the city but in several parts of the country during this period due to failure of connectivity with their central systems located in Mumbai.[61]

---

58   Charles Knight and Katja Theodorakis, *The Marawi Crisis: Urban Conflict and Information Operations*, Special Report, Canberra: Australian Strategic Policy Institute, 31 July 2019, 14, available from: www.aspi.org.au/report/marawi-crisis-urban-conflict-and-information-operations.
59   Conservation Action Trust, *Mumbai Marooned: An Enquiry into Mumbai Floods 2005*, Final Report, Mumbai, India: Conservation Action Trust, 26 July 2006, 4, 57; and Boyd et al., 'Climate Change Adaptation in Mumbai, India', 219.
60   Conservation Action Trust, *Mumbai Marooned*, 30.
61   Narvekar and Kewalramani, *City Profile*, 106.

All India Radio reported that 150,000 people were stranded at various rail stations, some for nearly 24 hours.

Residents stepped forward. Strangers risked their lives to save others—even in areas known for communal violence. There was very little looting or robbery and no reports of rape. At the same time, outrage rose as the consequences of official incompetence and corruption became known. The authors of an independent report wrote that 'it was clear that if any people and their belongings were saved, it was due to the intervention of common people, not because of the government but in spite of it'.[62] Reminiscent of Mexico City after its 1985 earthquake, in Mumbai, examples of mismanagement and corruption included aid showing up on the black market and up to one-fifth of all aid going unaccounted for. Slum areas comprised roughly half of the megacity's population at the time. They received very little assistance. It was alleged that officials feared doing so 'would be an acknowledgement of their illegality'—even as both public and private construction had long been tolerated in areas that experts would later attribute to worsening the flooding's destructiveness. NGOs stepped in to assist. Authorities demanded they disperse their money through government offices instead of going directly to those in need—a step that would have both delayed distribution to the needy and increased graft.[63] At the same time, the central control facility responsible for providing overarching coordination of rescue and recovery was deemed 'completely nonfunctional'.[64] Officials failed to inform residents which parts of Mumbai were flooded, meaning commuters put themselves at risk as they tried to return home. The response was further crippled as key agencies like the Slum Rehabilitation Authority, Maharashtra Housing Area Development Authority, Mumbai Metropolitan Region Development Authority (MMRDA) and Maharashtra State Road Development Corporation (MSTDC) failed to cooperate. It was a situation not helped by each reporting to different government departments (recall that Mumbai is the capital of Maharashtra State). We can add bad planning to this lack of cooperation between organisations that should have been arm-in-arm during preparation and response. The same report concluded that 'the flooding in the city is more the result of bad planning than unprecedented rains or high tides'.[65]

---

62 Conservation Action Trust, *Mumbai Marooned*, 6.
63 ibid., 10.
64 ibid., 11.
65 ibid., 18.

Reflective of both this fragmentation and a lack of good plans were official policies that designated no statutory role for the police. A former Mumbai police commissioner related that the police appeared nowhere in the disaster management plan. Neither the MMRDA nor the MSTDC sent representatives to the regional monsoon preparedness meeting. It was discovered that MMRDA road upgrade projects had hindered storm drainage. This mismanagement—very likely complemented by Mumbai's notorious corruption—existed at higher levels as well. The MMRDA should have been the megacity's premier planning body. It had been studiously ignored by the BJP–Shiv Sena political coalition that ran the Maharashtra State Government in the decade before the flooding. This might help to explain the flaunting of regulations dictating that 15–25 per cent of land in commercial and residential zones be left as recreational open space—space that would have decreased runoff by permitting percolation of rainwater.[66] Were these failures to prepare not enough to anger the megacity's residents, the Maharashtra State Government declared a holiday for the two days after the flooding. Its offices were therefore closed during the worst of the crisis.[67]

An exception to the seemingly near-universal failure among Mumbai and Maharashtra's officials was the Indian Coast Guard, which is part of the country's Department of Defence. While much of the city suffered communications challenges, the Coast Guard relied on satellite phones and thus maintained contact independent of local telephone and mobile systems. While Mumbai's fire department took 15 hours to reach the Saki Naka landslide site where more than 100 slum-dwellers died, the Coast Guard had one-third of its personnel on call. Yet, reminiscent of what would happen three years later during the 2008 terrorist attacks, Maharashtra authorities failed to request use of this valuable capability.[68]

What plans existed before the deluge had been left uncoordinated, untested and unrehearsed. The notorious corruption and lack of commitment underlay the general ineffectiveness. In addition to turning a blind eye to builders creating slum homes on flood and landslide-vulnerable land, officials had likewise done little to stop destruction of the mangrove swamps that were vital to mitigating flood extremes or

66 ibid., 29.
67 ibid., 22, 23, 25.
68 ibid., 61. Other sources put the number of deaths significantly higher. For example, see page 219 of Boyd et al., 'Climate Change Adaptation in Mumbai, India', who state that more than 1,000 were killed.

projects that reduced the width of local rivers. The flood's surging waters thus backed up into areas once at little risk. Maharashtra state employees taking their two-day holiday had company in the failure of some police stations to respond to nearby disaster sites (again, repeated in 2008). Corruption resulting in the misdirection of relief aid paled in comparison with manipulation of flood recovery funds that saw builders illegally upgrade wealthy properties at public expense while slum residents who had lost everything received no support. One can only wonder how many of Mumbai's 447 lives lost would have been saved had relevant Mumbai, state and federal representatives rehearsed and then revised disaster plans based on rehearsal findings.

The failures behind the deaths, injuries and extensive property damage would be inexcusable even without a history of disasters from which to draw lessons. A Mumbai flood almost five years to the day before this one had provided many insights that unfortunately went all but unheeded despite severe devastation. Official reactions during the later event were in some ways worse than during the earlier calamity. The Mithi River flows through Mumbai. Residents on its banks were stranded during the 2005 flooding, with government officials claiming they could not requisition naval boats to help them. Those vessels' quick requisition during the 2000 flooding had allowed an almost immediate rescue of those who stood in the same locations five years later.[69] This lack of effort to improve interorganisational cooperation and coordination was evident in the comment in the post-2005 flood independent report that 'there are too many agencies involved in disaster management, with no clear chain of command'.[70] What is clear is that the residents of one of the world's most populous urban areas were poorly served by administrators more skilled in post-event finger-pointing than effective action. The same report reinforces a conclusion that it was often corruption that was behind these enduring and seemingly wilful failures:

> Corruption has become so much a part of our life that many of us no longer stop to question it or deal with it as a separate issue. Yet corruption is the underlying reason behind the open flouting of development norms; building violations; ecological destruction in the name of development; an ill-equipped fire brigade/police/ BMC [Brihanmumbai Municipal Corporation, Mumbai's civil

---

69   Conservation Action Trust, *Mumbai Marooned*, 63.
70   ibid., 65.

government authority; and] inadequate, badly constructed or maintained roads, sewerage, and sanitation. The roots of almost any problem in Mumbai can be traced back to the twin bedfellows of corruption and politics. The common Mumbaikar has been forced to endure this, with tragic consequences, for too long.[71]

Emily Boyd and fellow researchers separately reinforced these findings:

The cause of inundation needs to be clearly understood. All identified causes—choking of Mithi River, overuse of plastic bags, failure to implement segregation of domestic waste, narrow storm-water drains, programmatic failures in disaster management, and the failure to disseminate weather forecasting— are not climate-induced [crises] but long-pending administrative lacuna [*sic*] ... It also underlines a pronounced two-culture debate, between science and society in India.[72]

Given the above, the inadequate reaction to the 2008 terrorist attacks three years later can be seen as simply a continuation of a well-established trend. Nor has the threat of floods been dealt with effectively. At least 43 people died in flooding in July 2019 in Mumbai, as did another 31 two years later.[73]

The value of rehearsals

It means that we are willing to be quite plugged in with regard to what a coalition is doing, but we would never be a part of a coalition ... We would be willing to share information regarding humanitarian needs ... We will not inform either side of the other's pending military operations ... [T]he military also understands that if we did share with the military, it would be the end of our operations there. There would be no access to prisoners ... The military should not rely on us for their intelligence ... We are the people who will be the neutral intermediary ... We have to preserve that role. What we do in one country reflects on another.[74]

—Michael Khambatta, International Committee of the Red Cross

---

71 ibid., 64.
72 Boyd et al., 'Climate Change Adaptation in Mumbai, India', 226.
73 Rhea Mogul and Swati Gupta, 'At least 31 people killed after Mumbai hit with torrential rain', *CNN*, 19 July 2021, [Updated 20 July 2021], available from: www.cnn.com/2021/07/19/india/mumbai-heavy-rain-landslide-intl-hnk/index.html.
74 Michael Khambatta, Interview with Dr Russell W. Glenn, Washington, DC, 26 February 2008.

No one apparently had thought that an event fierce enough to damage a reactor might also disrupt basic communications.[75]

—David Lochbaum et al., *Fukushima*

Always try for perfection. There's never been a perfect ball player. Willie Mays came closest. But always try.[76]

—Joe DiMaggio

Thinking through, planning for, rehearsing and otherwise readying to deal with megacity disasters before an event and converting the results into policies will pay off whether the episode is overseas or at home. Bringing participating parties together during these preparations—including those from local communities as well as outsiders—gives leaders a chance to work on solutions before challenges show themselves. NGOs in Somali urban areas during the near anarchy of the 1990s paid local armed groups to protect their members and relief stores from violence or theft. The role as defenders came with permission for the hired guards to carry weapons—a privilege denied other locals in an attempt to control the rampant brutality that plagued the country. But international military forces found it hard to determine which groups continued to faithfully serve the NGOs that had hired them and which instead had turned on the organisations for which they worked—until the armed locals fired on international coalition soldiers.

Intramilitary disconnects and disregarding the need to vet and monitor contractors had similar effects during actions in early twenty-first-century Iraq and Afghanistan and—barring change—will do so again when nature or human-induced misfortune touches the world's most influential urban areas. Failure of a special operations forces (SOF) unit to communicate with the US Army commander responsible for a village resulted in the fracturing of carefully constructed relations with local Afghans when SOF soldiers burst into a home and seized a suspected enemy leader. Hearing of the damage left unaddressed by the raiding soldiers, the US unit responsible for the sector sent men to complete needed repairs. They found them already done, complete with an accompanying sign crediting the local Taliban.

---

75   Lochbaum et al., *Fukushima*, 16.
76   Quoted in Louis D. Rubin, Jr (ed.), *The Quotable Baseball Fanatic*, Guilford, CT: Lyons Press, 2000, 262.

Most private security companies operating in Iraq and Afghanistan stayed within the constraints of local law and were appropriately sensitive to how their behaviour impacted on coalition efforts to secure public support. Most. Not all. I recall accompanying a patrol of soldiers from the 2nd Brigade, 1st Infantry Division in September 2007 in Baghdad. The soldiers left their vehicles, patrolling on foot to make themselves more accessible while speaking face-to-face with shopowners and their clientele. It was early dusk. The gentle light was fading, giving the street an atmosphere of calm after a busy and hot day. The sense of peace was brutally shattered by the speeding arrival of four black sports utility vehicles (SUVs), blue lights flashing, a well-known international security company's men protruding from hatches in roofs, guns at the ready. It was a garish demonstration of force ill suited to a becalmed community—one that at best impressed its residents with the vehicle occupants' fears rather than any aura of power. Such events were unfortunately not uncommon.

Never completely avoidable, episodes like these can be reduced by stricter screening and mutual agreement regarding objectives and operational approaches. The earlier-mentioned Los Angeles TEWG was an effort to reach this desirable state. The monthly group meetings of local, state and federal authorities included private sector counterparts' infrastructure liaison officers who would help to ensure the flow of information between government authorities and local for-profit and nonprofit groups when calamity struck.[77] Familiarity born at these meetings and the all-important informal discussions that were inevitably part of each meant members at a minimum understood what would be expected when an event brought them together under more demanding circumstances. TEWG meetings increased mutual understanding, reducing chances that actions by one party would undermine those of another while boosting the likelihood those parties spoke with a consistent voice in times of crisis. Another benefit—one that might easily be overlooked until too late—is that the resultant bonds enhanced the chances the organisations' members would understand one another even if they continued to speak their unique professional languages.[78] (The TEWG was unfortunately suspended after its replacement with the Los Angeles Joint Regional Intelligence Center, or JRIC, in 2010. As its name implies, the JRIC's role is primarily an

77   John P. Sullivan and Alain Bauer, *Terrorism Early Warning: 10 Years of Achievement in Fighting Terrorism and Crime*, Los Angeles, CA: Los Angeles County Sheriff's Office, October 2008, 29.
78   CALL, 'Operation United Assistance', 22.

intelligence/information integration and dissemination one rather than a more general coordinating or orchestrating one, as was the case with the TEWG.)[79]

Such cooperation is all for the good, but how can those authorities ensure their informal relationships translate to effectiveness when disaster visits? New Orleans city government representatives originally turned away small boatowners responding to fellow citizens' needs in the aftermath of Hurricane Katrina. Only later, when it became obvious that official resources fell far short of what was necessary, did the call go out to correct the misjudgement. (Tokyo's standing arrangement with commercial tourist boat services provides a well-considered counterexample.) Later estimates credited this 'ragtag flotilla' with rescuing thousands[80]— an eventual happy ending of sorts, perhaps, but bringing government, commercial, neighbourhood and other relevant organisations together before the event is greatly preferable.

The bottom line: the challenges world megacities confront in times of catastrophe make preliminary planning and rehearsal of plans essential. Participation in pre-disaster gatherings and familiarity with other parties likely to join forces during and after a crisis are only the first steps. Partners will range from those with membership in the tens of thousands to others of only one or two. The quality of their preparations will span an equally vast scope. Establishing relationships before they are put to the test offers the chance for each party to offer to others knowledge of its strengths and limitations. Conducting exercises and rehearsing plans with even a limited number of those who will be part of a response can reveal capability gaps and where orchestration of available capabilities needs fine-tuning, making it easier to incorporate new arrivals when the time comes.

Bringing these groups together offers the additional benefit of providing a chance to test the strength of plans by having designated experts play the role of devil's advocate (the civilian term) or conduct what military types call 'red teaming' (the good guys are generally depicted on maps with blue symbols in the United States, Australia and among their partners;

---

79   For more on the Los Angeles TEWG and JRIC, respectively, see Sullivan and Bauer, *Terrorism Early Warning*; and Robert Fox, Los Angeles Joint Regional Intelligence Center, Los Angeles Police Department Briefing, n.d., available from: docplayer.net/3600423-Los-angeles-joint-regional-intelligence-center-lieutenant-robert-fox-los-angeles-police-department-jric-co-program-manager-562-345-1102.html.
80   CALL, 'Operation United Assistance', 22.

the bad guys with red). The processes seek the same end by challenging assumptions, questioning the viability of plans and otherwise helping those with other than thin skin detect where their readiness merits improvement. Devil's advocacy/red teaming recognises that plans do not equal reality. Prussian General Helmuth von Moltke is famously known to have said, 'No plan survives contact with the enemy', meaning that while plans are essential to preparation, the best are flexible and designed to be moulded to the unpredictable and unexpected. The organisations that execute (and inevitably will have to adapt) those plans similarly need to be agile. Crisis response requires quick and effective adaptation when conditions demand. Yet, designing agile organisations only provides the vehicle. Training and rehearsals prepare the drivers to steer them to success.

In her intriguingly titled *The Resilience Dividend: Being Strong in a World Where Things Go Wrong*, Judith Rodin highlights the US Coast Guard's 'culture of preparedness [that] allowed them to generate rapid situational awareness, make smart assessments, and take immediate action without a specific action plan and without the go-ahead from higher ups'—the last sounding much like the mission command we noted earlier. That does not mean the Coast Guard fails to plan but rather its plans provide an outline for potential actions by units trained to assess a situation effectively and accordingly shape their actions to meet mission command guidance. Rodin contrasts this desirable combination of good planning plus organisational agility with New Orleans' Memorial Hospital during Hurricane Katrina, the facility that was at the centre of Sheri Fink's *Five Days at Memorial*. Rodin relates that the facility had 20 distinct emergency plans, but there was little evidence the separate plans had been coordinated or that staff and facility had been properly readied to react effectually in the event of a major disaster. She uses the example of expectations that the hospital's generators would run for at least 72 hours under emergency conditions—without them ever having been tested to see if they could.[81]

Other organisations share similar shortcomings. It is standard procedure for the best of them to plan, then repeatedly rehearse the plan, before ever having to put it into action. Rehearsal is all the more important when organisations unfamiliar with one another are part of an undertaking. That this did not happen before the tragedy of 3–4 October 1993 in Mogadishu—the event later known as 'Black Hawk Down'—is obvious

---

81   Rodin, *The Resilience Dividend*, 202.

from the comments by one of the young officers from the US Army's 2nd Battalion, 14th Infantry Regiment, 10th Mountain Division. Looking back on his participation in the operation in which two helicopters were shot down, 18 US soldiers died and another 73 were wounded, Lieutenant Mark Hollis said he:

> thought the plan 'was simple: Pakistani tanks would lead Malaysian armored personnel carriers carrying 2d Battalion soldiers ... I had never seen or heard of a German Condor [the Malaysian personnel carrier] until the day of execution. Finding out how to open the door to a vehicle 15 minutes before rolling out the gate is not the way to start a mission. A platoon leader needs to coordinate through his company commander to arrange a time when the allied forces can come over and teach his soldiers about their equipment. This is particularly significant at a time when operations with other United Nations forces are becoming more frequent ... How do we communicate with those who do not speak English in the midst of battle, with no interpreters available?'[82]

Good plans get better when they are rehearsed. They get better yet as more organisations that are part of the plan participate. These rehearsals can take many forms. In their sparsest sense, when time is short, a rehearsal may be little more than various organisations' leaders briefing back to seniors and contemporaries what they understand their tasks to be, how they will approach them and how their actions will impact or depend on other participants. More time improves the chances that a plan is tested and corrections are made when it is found to be in some way wanting. Ideally, time allows for full-blown, deliberate progression through a plan using detailed models of the terrain or computer simulations. These might include creating life-size mockups of key buildings or entire city blocks and repeatedly practising various courses of action for days or weeks while other participants take the roles of population members, terrorist groups, criminals, local officials or an enemy force, any of whom can and should be comfortable in that devil's advocate/red teaming role.

Bringing key personalities together to 'war game' a plan falls between these two extremes. Irreverently referred to as a BOGSAT (Bunch of Guys Sitting around a Table), the value of bringing those with the needed expertise together to identify and solve problems can pay big dividends. Another in-between approach is what the military calls 'sand table exercises' in which

---

82   Glenn and Kingston, *Urban Battle Command in the 21st Century*, 3.

a rough model of the terrain represents the area in which participants will execute their plan. I was once part of a sand table rehearsal where the label was more than a little appropriate. In what was a far cry from readying for an urban operation, it fell to several colleagues and me to prepare a terrain model for the US Army's 3rd Armored Division before it attacked into Iraq during the 1991 Persian Gulf War. Our planning team laid out the various boundaries between units and miniature representations of the geographic features the division would encounter—all on a large patch of Saudi desert sand. We then set about representing each of the division and supporting units on this model. Together these organisations included roughly 20,000 men and women and 12,000 vehicles of one type or another. Unlike wooded or other terrain types, the desert offered little in the way of material to help us represent infantry battalions, medical units, military police and the many other types of organisations that would participate in liberating Kuwait. There were certainly no shops nearby at which we could buy toy tanks, artillery, soldiers or other life-like pieces. Even rocks were in short supply. So, we raided a nearby tent and borrowed a few materials. The small (and flat) packets of toilet paper that come in soldier ration packs became tank battalions. Lip balm containers were artillery pieces, and so on. The result allowed the division's senior leaders to walk step-by-step through the pending attack, making sure each knew his or her role, how they would support each other and what problems might arise due to enemy action, weather or the play of chance. (The rehearsal went well, as did the attack, the only complaint coming from the Apache attack helicopter battalion commander. He was not amused that his units were represented by tampons during the rehearsal. Hey, you work with what you have.)

Another look at the 1995 sarin attack in Tokyo offers us a chance to consider might-have-beens had emergency responders, city government officials, hospital representatives and others regularly conducted detailed rehearsals (regularly being necessary because not only conditions but also individuals in key positions change). Might a rehearsal have revealed the need to create guidelines for police and maintenance personnel when confronting an unknown substance? Might a more effective way of screening the worried well from the exposed been identified? The fact that nearly 25 years after the attack it is still not routine for Tokyo's doctors to leave their hospitals and treat patients at a mass-casualty scene suggests current plans could benefit from both rehearsals and study of other megacities' experiences such as those in 2015 in Paris (of which more later). We recognise that rehearsals offer a chance to identify previously unforeseen problems and that repeated rehearsals can likewise identify new approaches and their tailoring to specific situations. Alternatively, rehearsals provide an opportunity to address issues exposed during previous events. It is very likely that rehearsals of some sort lie behind Tokyo's commendable emergency preparations already in place. Cooperation between world megacity authorities means urban officials do not need to experience a disaster at first hand to learn from it, but each urban area will have to modify lessons to fit its own context. Yet, the case of New York City's leaders sidestepping tough decisions during the Covid-19 pandemic tells us that even the best preparations can be undone by personal shortcomings. Citizen responses to the contagion in that city, in Rio de Janeiro and in too many other cities in the United States and worldwide reflect the fact that ours is not as sophisticated a world as we might like to believe. Poking a bit of fun at itself, *The Economist* recalled a misguided passage from an 1849 issue that sounds all too familiar more than 170 years later:

> The belief in contagion, like the belief in astrology and witchcraft, seems destined to die out; and as we have got rid of all regulations … against feeding evil spirits and punishing witches, so we shall no doubt in time get rid of the quarantine regulations that were established from the old belief in contagion.[83]

Perfection is impossible. Mistakes will be made. But the prepared megacity is eons ahead of those unprepared even if flawed leadership and the wilfully ignorant seek to hamstring effective responses when crisis strikes.

Practising plans further assists in early identification of issues about the span of control (how many organisations a leader or higher-level organisation is to manage) and how participants will coordinate with one another. NGOs, IGOs and faith-based organisations, for example, are likely to number in the hundreds during a megacity disaster response. There are IGOs and NGOs that specialise in coordinating fellow organisations—obviously, excellent candidates for rehearsal participation. It is better to determine effective spans of control and symbiotic partnerships during rehearsals than later when communications are stressed, ports and airfields have become fields of competition and local authorities are overwhelmed by immediate demands. Should anyone think these challenges are overstated, let's remind ourselves of the scope of them when dealing with the number

---

83   *The Economist*, 'Cleanliness is next to growth', 70.

of jurisdictional entities in the San Francisco–Oakland–San Jose urban agglomeration. The number of separate governments exceeds 100 in the extended Bay Area alone. This includes 12 counties in addition to the many town and city authorities—and this is before we even begin to consider organisations formally unaffiliated with governments. The City of Palo Alto itself (neighbour to Stanford University and many associated establishments such as Stanford Health Care medical capabilities and partners that include the local Veterans Administration facility) has an extensive emergency volunteer establishment in addition to connections with various state response institutions.[84]

Rehearsals are also the time to identify what is in the realm of the possible when it comes to the nature of relationships between these many organisations. There is coordination, which in Australian Army parlance is the weakest of the trio (the Australians having provided admirably succinct definitions, of which we will take advantage here). Cooperation, synchronisation and orchestration follow in order—the last at once the strongest and by far the most difficult to accomplish:

- **Coordination (Australian Army definition):** 'An arrangement where parties operating in the theatre communicate their intended actions to one another and will self-synchronise their activities but will not negotiate the manner of their actions.'[85]

- **Cooperation (Australian Army definition):** 'An arrangement where parties operating in the theatre are under no agreement to undertake military actions together but through mutual interest will not only coordinate their actions but negotiate the manner of these actions.'[86]

- **Synchronisation (US multiservice definition):** 'The arrangement of military actions in time, space, and purpose to produce maximum relative combat power at a decisive place and time.'[87]

- **Orchestration (admittedly, my definition):** The arrangement of organisations' actions in time, space and purpose to produce maximum effects in the service of accomplishing objectives.

---

84   Ken Dueker (Director, Emergency Services, City of Palo Alto Office of Emergency Services), Interview with Dr Russell W. Glenn, 14 April 2016.
85   Australian Defence Force (ADF), *ADF Concept for Command and Control of the Future Force*, Version 1.0, Canberra: Commonwealth of Australia, 13 May 2019, 46.
86   ibid., 46.
87   DOD, *Department of Defense Dictionary of Military and Associated Terms*, 210.

The definitions of 'coordination', 'cooperation' and 'orchestration' are applicable to a broad spectrum of operations that include more than military or government undertakings alone (if we strike 'military' from the definition for cooperation). The definition for 'synchronisation', unfortunately and short-sightedly, fails in this regard given it is limited to military and, specifically, combat operations. Regardless, even partially attaining any of the four is a step in the right direction. Coordination is the least demanding and therefore the easiest to accomplish (recognising that 'easiest' need not imply 'easy'). It implies not only informing other alliance, coalition or partnership members but also taking steps to ensure one organisation's actions do not interfere with those of another. Even coordination will pose challenges as some organisations seek to avoid being seen as supporting, being supported by or working with military organisations. Cooperation takes coordination a step further but still falls far short of planning, preparing for and conducting actions with maximum effectiveness and efficiency. Synchronisation we can cast aside due to its definitional limitations. Orchestration is rarely attempted and seldom achieved even when numbers of participants are few and the tasks at hand are straightforward; it tends to be based on personal rather than institutional relationships. That it is hard does not mean it is not worth pursuing, especially when rehearsals give groups a chance to work out issues interfering with accomplishing their ends. Trying to achieve but falling short of orchestration should nonetheless mean better outcomes than merely shooting for the lesser goals of coordination or cooperation. Orchestration might be best viewed as a mark on the wall—one for which leaders and organisations can strive while recognising full realisation will prove elusive.[88]

This is all well and good, but expecting these literally hundreds of organisations to start working together while singing 'We Are the World' isn't going to cut it. The plans and preparations they can help improve are also vehicles for determining not only who does what but also the details of relationships as each plays its part. What will be the basis for cooperation: One organisation in charge? Rule by committee? Oversight by an orchestrating few? Chaos? Who will provide what logistical support to whom (it is helpful to determine this before a disaster or soon thereafter so organisations do not compete for limited resources, thus driving up costs and risking losing more urgently needed capabilities to others)?

---

88 Glenn et al., *Achieving Convergence during Humanitarian Assistance and Disaster Relief Operations*, 29–32.

Who establishes rules of engagement when lethal force might be brought to bear? Longstanding relationships with permanent members would suggest a formal alliance is the best form for laying out responsibilities. Less fixed membership with more flexible ties is far more commonplace, making a coalition the practical answer.[89] Regardless, it is better to work out as many decisions as possible before 'the balloon goes up'— decisions ideally made during rehearsals that test and work to perfect plans. Information and intelligence-sharing are sure to be points of contention. What agreements and procedures can be put in place to allow the exchange of sensitive material without undue risk of compromising participants' safety, security or intelligence-sharing policies? Much of the information needed to support emergency responses is available from open sources readily accessed on the internet, in libraries or otherwise available in unclassified, publicly available form. A well-orchestrated collective effort will have a component that consolidates information needs from members, suggests procedures for collecting that information, then gets the results to appropriate users in exploitable form in a timely manner. A good information-collection plan means every NGO aid provider, UN manager, infantryperson, local government representative, pilot, truck driver and other participant becomes a potential source and recipient if they have been told what material is of value. The quote from International Committee of the Red Cross (ICRC) representative Michael Khambatta at the start of this section makes it clear that not all members will be willing to share equally when it comes to information. For good reason. As in the case of the ICRC, some will not share specific types of information with military or other government organisations if the situation is one in which opposing sides are fighting—rightly recognising that to do so compromises their neutrality and, by extension, their value to all parties in the city or other area in which operations are taking place. Government organisations will be similarly justified in not freely sharing intelligence when it might put sources or sensitive activities at risk. Here again, the value of rehearsals comes into play as steps towards determining who shares what with whom can be addressed before the fact, reducing the likelihood of later flare-ups due to misunderstanding.

---

89   The long-held understanding of a coalition as 'an ad hoc arrangement between two or more nations for common action' merits reconsideration given responses to disasters now involve more than national assets. A better definition would account for the full range of participating organisations. A coalition then becomes 'an ad hoc arrangement between two or more organisations in the interest of common action'. Michael Khambatta's remarks at the top of this section make it clear that a coalition needs to be flexible in its definition of membership and willing to recognise varying degrees of participation or association. Glenn, 'Megacities'.

It will be the rarest of cases when planning and rehearsals manage to include all participants. Some will have no idea they might be dispatched to assist during a disaster. Others will not know what type of role they will be called on to play even if they suspect their talents might be of value when the time comes. Primary among these are community residents. Yet, urban authorities can support the creation of and recruitment for neighbourhood volunteer organisations. Steven Bucci makes clear the importance of recognising the person on the street's vital role in his review of New York City's reaction to the 9/11 attacks and Hurricane Sandy:

> The 'first' first responders on 9/11, as in most catastrophes, were private-sector civilians. Because 85 percent of our nation's critical infrastructure is controlled not by government but by the private sector, private-sector civilians are likely to be the first responders in any future catastrophes. It is the person whose family is safe and secure who is able to volunteer at a disaster relief center. It is a not-for-profit community food bank whose supplies are protected that can resume its delivery of meals to those who cannot leave their homes. It is the big-box retailer whose employees are accounted for and whose stores are assessed for damage that can donate bottled water and clothing to the victims of a disaster and reopen rapidly to serve its battered community.[90]

The importance of wrapping commercial representatives into the planning and rehearsal process is evident in retailer Home Depot's neighbourhood stores supporting the NGO Team Rubicon when disaster strikes a community, whether by providing parking lots to store equipment and supplies or providing goods and expertise. Another of many possible examples: bringing bus companies, school bus managers and others into the fold allows urban authorities to surge volunteers from less-affected neighbourhoods into areas where they can assist others.

As said, orchestrating (even coordinating) alliance members, coalition partners and other parties' actions in the spirit of consistency, efficiency and improved effectiveness will prove no easy task. Partners they might be, but objectives are more likely to be similar or overlapping than identical. Megacities themselves are likewise non-uniform in the sense of the various authorities governing them. City, town and other authorities that collectively are part of the megalopolis will have different motivations. The mayor of the City of Los Angeles has priorities of limited interest to

---

90 Bucci et al., *After Hurricane Sandy.*

the heads of Santa Monica's, Burbank's or Anaheim's governments even though all are part of the urban agglomeration that is the megacity. Even relationships at the lesser end of cooperation can have a short lifespan. This is particularly true as time goes on and success is increasingly within reach—a situation that tends to loosen the ties of shared commitment that once bound participants together. Yet, reaching for but failing to achieve that orchestration 'mark on the wall' still beats not trying at all. In Yoda-speak, hard it will be, but benefit from even limited success all will.

Despite the benefits available in harnessing residents' cooperation during planning and rehearsals, it is ore rarely mined. Politicians may feel threatened by neighbourhood groups as when Mexico City community associations stepped up after formal authorities failed to in the aftermath of the 1985 earthquake.[91] On the other hand, the Homeless People's Federation of the Philippines offers a counterexample demonstrating the benefits when governments partner with local groups. The federation has historically aided those of the established order by gathering community information during a disaster, assessing damage and making victims' needs such as for loans or building materials known, organising neighbourhood groups and acting as a trusted agent. Familiarisation with groups like the federation promotes participation during planning and rehearsals and allows early identification of who fills which niches or which niches remain unfilled.[92] Other examples of successfully mining this valuable ore include the privately owned Rockaway Beach Surf Club, in New York City's borough of Queens, and the surf life saving volunteer organisations in Sydney, Australia. The former saw flooding and some damage to its facility during Hurricane Sandy, as did the on-beach facility for the Coogee Beach life savers Down Under when storms struck. Both organisations stepped forward, continuing to operate despite the setbacks. The Rockaway club was a known location and community gathering spot. The club's leaders had a reputation for community support. It therefore made sense when it assumed the role of a local relief supply distribution centre. Anyone in need could make specific requests via the club's Facebook page—further increasing the value of its services.[93] Participation by such groups during pre-event planning and other preparations magnifies their ultimate value given they are well positioned, effectively organised and

91   Puente, 'Social vulnerability to disasters in Mexico City', 62–63.
92   IPCC, 'Urban Areas', 566.
93   Rodin, *The Resilience Dividend*, 184.

trusted. The extensive first aid and other training received by groups like the Coogee Beach Surf Life Saving Club mean they bring multiple much-needed skills that can be incorporated into plans.

A little imagination on the part of public officials and community-minded private enterprises can help in matching capabilities with sure-to-be needed requirements. Once again, New York City provides a pithy example. While Airbnb does not own the facilities it rents, it does have a potentially valuable database of empty dwellings. This potential was realised after Hurricane Sandy when one of its hosts contacted the company asking to help those rendered homeless. Airbnb employees responded by working all night to list housing for $0 a night when property owners agreed. A page was specially designed to identify owners who stepped forward—one where a click made their volunteerism known. More than 1,400 properties were made available in less than a week.[94]

Creating such a database pre-calamity could be invaluable during planning and again once catastrophe strikes. Megacities, particularly those in countries known to have stable economies and respect for the rule of law, are particularly rich in empty residential properties. It is in these urban areas that the ultrarich invest. Some residences are large enough to house multiple families. In Sydney, for example, a Chinese state-owned developer is constructing a 235-metre tall residential tower in the city's CBD. Mumbai's private Ambani residence is 168 metres high with 37,200 square metres of interior space.[95] Tax and insurance records should help with efforts to identify potential temporary residences. While the willingness of property owners to support the displaced will differ, procedures that facilitate sharing are worthy of pre-calamity consideration. Perhaps there is a need to create an emergency form of eminent domain when volunteerism falls short and suffering demands extraordinary action. In the longer term, building permits or the right to purchase by those who do not self-occupy for much of a year could be contingent on an agreement to permit others' use *in extremis*.

An observation from the 2003 Regional Assistance Mission to Solomon Islands (RAMSI) offers a chance to reconsider for those still questioning how difficult orchestration can be. Before reading, consider that at top

---

94   ibid., 187.
95   Robert J. Bunker and Pamela Ligouri Bunker, 'Plutocratic Insurgency Note No. 5: The Techno-Palaces of the Global Elite', in *Plutocratic Insurgency Reader*, Robert J. Bunker and Pamela Ligouri Bunker (eds), A Small Wars Journal Book, Bloomington, IN: Xlibris, 2019, 128–40, at 131, 133.

strength RAMSI had a total of only 2,000 or so participants representing the military, police, diplomatic corps, relief agencies and other organisations of 10 different countries. Any significant undertaking in a megacity might involve tens of thousands of military, aid and other personnel and their organisations. RAMSI's initial international force commander, Australian Lieutenant General John Frewen said:

> We were still discovering significant misalignment of capabilities and misunderstanding between RAMSI participants though deployment was but days away. Our saving grace was a whole of government rock drill. [This] synchronization rehearsal included all participating and supporting agency leaders along with those from academia who assisted us in better understanding the operating environment … It was to prove one of the most significant activities we conducted as a multi-jurisdictional and multi-disciplinary group. This interagency rehearsal helped all participants gain a common understanding of the plan. It also was invaluable in helping us to synchronize our efforts during the first days of the mission.[96]

Pre-combat preparations

The worst policy is to attack cities. Attack cities only when there is no alternative.[97]

—Sun Tzu, *The Art of War*

The course of the fighting in Berlin showed that a battle for and in a large city is extremely difficult, not only for the defenders, but even for a far superior attacking force … The ability of large cities to defend themselves depended not so much on specially prepared installations, but rather on the extent to which the city is built up. The greater the destruction by fire and explosion in a city, the more suitable it is for defense.[98]

—Wilhelm Willemer, *The German Defense of Berlin*

---

96   John J. Frewen [Lieutenant-General, Australian Army], 'The Solomon Islands Intervention: The Regional Assistance Mission 2003', in *Trust and Leadership: The Australian Army Approach to Mission Command*, Russell W. Glenn (ed.), Dahlonega, GA: University of North Georgia Press, 2020, 206–40.
97   Sun Tzu, *The Art of War*, trans. Samuel B. Griffith, New York, NY: Oxford University Press, 1982, 78.
98   Willemer, *The German Defense of Berlin*, 52.

It might seem odd to start a section on combat in megacities by looking at expanses reaching far beyond the urban area. Los Angeles depends on water sources hundreds of kilometres to the north in California. In Mexico City's case, the distance to its primary water source is almost 300 kilometres. Pumps must raise the water more than 800 metres during its flow to Mexico's capital—a literal case of the old saying that 'water flows uphill to money', for certainly the capital holds centre place as focus for the country's wealth.[99] (As a quick aside, there is solid evidence that cities were the eventual spur for the invention of money—even though cities existed for 3,000 years before someone got around to that invention.)[100] These examples and those of Manila, Hong Kong and Tokyo make it clear that one way to a megacity's heart is through its water supply. That is true whether an army needs to control all or part of an urban population or deny essentials to a defending enemy. Cities are similarly dependent on far-flung energy sources, food supplies, medical provisions (as Covid-19 made only too clear to New York City and others in early 2020) and much else without which they cannot function. Such reliance on remote resources is a vulnerability in cases where a natural disaster might sever the vital connection or when terrorists, insurgents or other malcontents seek to make the innocent suffer. Russia's Black Sea Fleet capitalised on such distant dependencies when it sailed against the Turkish port of Zonguldak on the northern coast of Anatolia during the opening weeks of World War I. It was from there that coal fuelling both Türkiye's naval vessels and the country's largest city of Constantinople came. Russia succeeded in blockading Zonguldak, denying both the Turkish fleet and the city.[101]

Human capital is another invaluable and often distant resource. Deny a city its commuting workers and it will soon cease to function no less than when it is without water, power or food. Such is the tyranny of the megasystem, much of which is not urban at all. The military commander failing to consider a megacity as part of a larger system courts failure, particularly if his competition is savvy. Theorists will tell you the character of war does not change, as it is but an extension—or tool—of politics (or diplomacy, or economics, or ideology). The nature of warfare—how

---

99   David Satterthwaite, 'How urban societies can adapt to resource shortage and climate change', *Philosophical Transactions of the Royal Society A: Mathematical, Physical and Engineering Sciences* 369(1942) (2011): 1762–83, doi.org/10.1098/rsta.2010.0350; and Villoro, *Horizontal Vertigo*, 9.
100 Smith, *Cities*, 153.
101 Mungo Melvin, *Sevastopol's Wars: Crimea from Potemkin to Putin*, New York, NY: Osprey, 2017, 353.

war is conducted—does evolve. Former general and US Secretary of Defense James Mattis observed: '[F]or all the "4th Generation of War" intellectuals running around today saying that the nature of war has fundamentally changed, the tactics are wholly new, etc., I must respectfully say ... "Not really".'[102] And so it is with urban areas in wartime. Their value is not innate but rather dependent on their political, diplomatic, economic, ideological or symbolic role in a conflict's greater purpose.

Soldiers wrote much of and trained repeatedly for 'deep battle' during the Cold War. For the rifleman in the foxhole, this meant aircraft, artillery and other means of engaging the foe tens of kilometres distant to reduce what he would eventually confront at several hundred metres—the range of his weapon. The nature of those far-flung engagements might change dramatically when the focus is not an enemy force but control of some distant part of a resource delivery system. Letting Mexico City serve as a notional example of a megacity unfortunate enough to be involved in a war, the distant parts of the water delivery system let us see how many ways its parts might be used to deny the city—and how hard maintaining that vital flow of water could prove. That nearly 300 kilometres of distance and 800 metres of elevation mean the system includes reservoirs, kilometres of tunnel, stretches of aqueduct and canal and individual pumping stations all begging for a potential denier's attentions.[103] The opportunities for that denier are greater if we instead look to New York City for our notional example. That megacity's watershed of almost 5,200 square kilometres (roughly the size of Delaware), 19 reservoirs and its own system of dams, aqueducts, pumping stations and other components make those opportunities only too clear—even though the flows of the Hudson and East rivers and other smaller waterways bring freshwater directly to much of the world's most widespread megacity.[104] Among the historical sources of water for Los Angeles is Owens Valley, 307 kilometres away. Once rich with agricultural use, parts of the valley are now desert. The valley's Owens Lake has dried up completely. Beijing similarly draws so much water that most rivers in the vicinity are dry for much of the year.

---

102 Glenn, 'Megacities'. The Mattis quote is from Geoffrey Ingersoll, 'General James "Mad Dog" Mattis email about being "too busy to read" is a must-read', *Business Insider*, 10 May 2013, available from: www.businessinsider.com/viral-james-mattis-email-reading-marines-2013-5.
103 Reader, *Cities*, 189.
104 Alice Kenny, 'Ecosystem services in the New York City watershed', *The Ecosystem Marketplace*, 10 February 2006, available from: www.forest-trends.org/ecosystem_marketplace/ecosystem-services-in-the-new-york-city-watershed-1969-12-31/.

Its once primary river, the Yongding, was deprived of its last flow decades ago.[105] Both these urban areas therefore must reach further afield for their liquid sustenance, increasing their vulnerability to interruption.

Such is the situation for the commander having to attack or defend a megacity. Our rifleman in a foxhole must leave worries about those distant vulnerabilities to his seniors. His immediate concern is less one of distance than of density: that density of windows, doors, rooftops and other features from which an enemy can observe movement and bring fire to bear. Other challenges include the obstacles to his movement even when streets are not filled with rubble or other debris, the ease with which defender or attacker can manoeuvre to cut off supplies and many other features that translate what is meant by 'depth' for the soldier on the ground being at most a few blocks on a good day and a few tens of metres on a less favourable one. Should that soldier be tasked to interrupt a neighbourhood's or building's water supply, the opportunity might lie no more distant than a local shutoff valve or the nearest bridge under which pipes flow.

Even this small sample of concerns hints at why the US Army's guidance to leaders as late as 1979 directed 'that urban combat operations are conducted only when required and that built-up areas are *isolated* and *bypassed* rather than risking a costly, time-consuming operation in this difficult environment'.[106] The problem for soldiers fighting along urban streets or hacking passage through interior walls is that the sites set aside for urban combat training come nowhere close to the extent of demands found in a large urban area. That is especially true when the urban area is a megacity. Most megacities feature ocean shores or rivers. Very few urban training locations are on bodies of water, meaning it is hard to provide challenges like those police or soldiers would confront if a Mumbai-like terrorist attack or enemy amphibious landing was on the cards. Structures differ not only within each individual city but also between them—a fact evident in looking at even the small urban areas of Zamboanga and Marawi on the southern Philippine island of Mindanao. Many of the former's buildings had walls no more substantial than low-grade plywood, meaning it was one of those built-up areas where a misdirected or careless rifle shot could fell

---

105 Enjie Li, Joanna Endter-Wada and Shujuan Li, 'Characterizing and contextualizing the water challenges of megacities', *Journal of the American Water Resources Association* 51(3) (2016): 589–613, at 602, 605, doi.org/10.1111/1752-1688.12310.
106 Department of the Army, *Military Operations on Urbanized Terrain (MOUT)*, Field Manual 90-10, Washington, DC: US Government Printing Office, 15 August 1979, 1-1. [Emphasis in original.]

an innocent civilian or fellow soldier several rooms away. Move the soldier's unit to Marawi half the island away (and site of the vicious fighting in 2017 between the Philippine military and ISIS forces) and building materials tend to be more substantial thanks to *rido* ('clan conflicts') that make basements and concrete shelters a wise investment.[107]

Readying those who will have to fight in and around vast expanses of urban areas therefore remains an unmet challenge. Many military installations worldwide have one if not several major clusters of buildings designed to train urban attackers or defenders. Yet few of these sites challenge leaders and led with the types of highrise found in even small cities or large towns around the world today. It's an important shortfall; attacking an enemy in a 12-storey building isn't simply four times as hard as clearing one with three floors. Nor, if we reverse the lens, is the difficulty of defending taller buildings simply a matter of multiplying by the number of levels. Either task is more difficult because highrises rarely occur in isolation. They tend to have similar structures next-door, across the street and for blocks in all directions, especially in the case of megacity CBDs. The same challenges can exist in multiple locations in these largest of urban areas when the smaller cities they comprise have cores of their own. Los Angeles provides an example. The City of Los Angeles' cluster of downtown tall structures has junior companions in Burbank, Santa Monica, Newport Beach, Marina del Rey and a good number of others that are part of the Los Angeles megacity. Few if any of the installations set aside for training city fighters are vast enough to allow even a battalion taskforce (a battalion with all its added attached and other supporting units) to fight, manoeuvre, be resupplied, meet the challenges of thousands of civilian residents or realistically confront combat conditions without artificially leaving the built-up area. It is theoretically possible to cleverly use computer modelling and simulation to exercise leaders and staff at higher levels while smaller units conduct 'live' training on a training site's artificial streets and in its buildings. Unfortunately, modelling and simulation have a considerable way to go before they can accurately replicate urban combat conditions for the many levels, skill sets, responsibilities and other-than-military participants involved.[108]

107 Franco, *The battle for Marawi.*
108 Considerable progress was being made in the urban modelling and simulations arena during the last decade of the twentieth century thanks to the emphasis put on urban training after Operation Just Cause (Panama, 1989) and fighting in Mogadishu, Somalia (1993). That momentum was lost when focus and dollars shifted to commitments in Iraq and Afghanistan in the early years of the following century.

This inability to ready leaders and led for the social, physical, economic and other challenges at the strategic, operational and tactical levels of war has a companion temporal shortfall. Training also fails to prepare these individuals to deal with the need to look deeply in time. History tells us that the second and higher-order effects we have repeatedly mentioned often will not fully reveal themselves until fighting stops. Iraq in 2003 saw government buildings in the country's south stripped by vandals of wire, furniture and plumbing—anything that could be carried away—once US or other coalition soldiers continued their attacks northward. Governance stumbled in Iraq just as it had in post–World War II Germany when de-Nazification purged towns and cities of the individuals most familiar with their urban areas' functions. Those are the officials who know police and other officials capable of securing buildings and limiting wanton destruction of water, power, sanitation and transportation infrastructure. These are actions that if prevented do much to hasten recovery and convert battlefield success into lasting victory. Just as any urban area is a system, waging war in larger cities is a system of actions, people, decisions, immediate effects and longer-term consequences routinely addressed as separate parts and too rarely as part of their collective whole.

This need to grasp the consequences of second and higher-order effects applies to challenges short of combat as well: preparing for or denying acts of terror, and dealing with riots or mass demonstrations and other events nested in the grey area between war and more benign occurrences. Police must train for these much as soldiers must make ready for combat (and, as Charles Krulak's three-block war metaphor tells us, so, too, must those soldiers). This preparation should include equipping and training individuals who will be at the sharp end of contact about how and when to employ nonlethal in lieu of or as complements to lethal means. Both provide valuable arrows in a force's quiver of responses. Being able to draw those arrows provides a capability to render the evildoer inert while protecting innocent lives, thereby separating human chaff from society's wheat. As our long-time member of the Los Angeles County Sheriff's Department Sid Heal observed, security forces can use these less-than-lethal assets to:

- deny or protect logistics sites, gun shops, food and water distribution points and other facilities
- clear areas of demonstrators bent on violence or innocents who may unwittingly be exposed to manipulation or harm

- secure passage for security forces or relief supplies
- quarantine or isolate individuals exposed to a communicable disease or a chemical or biological agent—the latter two via either an accident or a terrorist act
- suppress undesirable behaviour such as looting, rioting or individuals bent on producing mass casualties.

Which facilities or communities to protect, which areas to clear, how to prevent the spread of a contagion and the choices made in containing those bent on disrupting megacity functions will have tactical, operational and strategic consequences locally and more widely no less than decisions made by military leaders in times of war. As is the case with those military leaders and their soldiers, the means available to prepare urban officials for making such tough decisions currently falls short of need. Lessons learned from urban responses to Covid-19 suggest much can be done to better prepare for the next bio-crisis—one unlikely to wait the century that separated the 1918 flu and the virus bursting on the New York City scene just over a hundred years later. Drawing on their years of studying quarantines, authors Geoff Manaugh and Nicola Twilley suggest recognising how public and private facilities might be designed to support infection control so they are 'substantially cheaper and faster to flip in an emergency situation—not to mention much easier to return to their original function once that danger had passed'.[109]

Pre-disaster capacity-building

One very highly successful response to sudden shocks in cities is routine planning.[110]

—Aseem Inam, *Planning of the Unplanned*

Every disaster is a rehearsal if treated appropriately.[111]

—Geoffrey Demarest, 'Urban Land Use by Illegal Armed Groups in Medellin'

---

109 Geoff Manaugh and Nicola Twilley, *Until Proven Safe: The History and Future of Quarantine*, New York, NY: Farrar, Straus & Giroux, 2021, 169.
110 Inam, *Planning for the Unplanned*, xiii.
111 Geoffrey Demarest, 'Urban Land Use by Illegal Armed Groups in Medellin', in *Blood and Concrete: 21st Century Conflict in Urban Centers and Megacities*, Dave Dilegge, Robert J. Bunker, John P. Sullivan and Alma Keshavarz (eds), A Small Wars Journal Book, Washington, DC: Xlibris, 2019, 102–20, at 115.

It is worth pausing to ask how much disaster preparation of a megacity's population is necessary, wise or economically feasible. Certainly, Mexico City's highrise apartment building earthquake drills are worth emulating regardless of whether the natural threat is shaking earth, floodtide, slipping soil, devastating storm or a volcano's ash and fire. The limits on physical interactions and wearing of masks during the 2020 Covid-19 crisis demonstrate that large numbers are comfortable with—even supportive of—inconvenience in the service of others' health, fellow citizens' employment and their own welfare even when the less enlightened are not. There will always be understandable, though not acceptable, efforts to sidestep policies dictated in the interest of the greater good. A grandfather with his grandchild in a megacity subway might seek to escape despite authorities' orders to remain in place to prevent spreading human contamination due to a chemical or biological attack. Those with similar intentions could quickly overwhelm police tasked with containing dissemination—another instance in which nonlethal means of enforcing quarantine or isolation could be valuable.

In the years before the Japanese invasion of the British colony of Hong Kong in World War II, residents successfully resisted the building of pillboxes and other unsightly defensive positions in their neighbourhoods. It would not be the only factor underlying the quick Japanese capture of the colony. It is nonetheless a revealing case of security nimbyism ('Not in My Back Yard')—a phenomenon more common today in the context of low-income housing, power plants, drug rehabilitation accommodation or other facilities thought to be unpleasant when nearby. Confronted with the question of whether to install generators to support flood-control pumps, experienced Miami Beach city engineers waved off the initiative. Experience told them citizens would never allow them because 'they were ugly'.[112]

We find that urban types are in some ways not much different from humans anywhere. There will be those as short-sighted as Hong Kong and Miami residents, sure to later complain that city officials failed to properly prepare them for disaster. As with those unwilling to wear masks and take other precautions in 2020, large numbers will fortunately show they are made of stronger stuff. Londoners, Hamburgers and Tokyoites were among the millions of residents who suffered tremendously yet prevailed

---

112 Ariza, *Disposable City*, 50.

during the bombings of World War II. It was not the first time these cities' populations demonstrated their resilience. London recovered from devastation wrought by the Black Death and the horrific fire of 1666. Hamburg was destroyed by fire in 1284 (apart from, reportedly, a single building) and its economy was devastated during French occupation in the Napoleonic Wars.[113] We know that Tokyo's 1923 fires were but one of many devastations by flame. Our discussion regarding the misnomer of cities being akin to organisms told us that the world's larger urban areas are survivors. It is the human organisms living within who ensure their recovery.

Responses to crisis should be guided by standing plans and procedures known to urban residents. Public education programs meant late twentieth-century Londoners were aware of how to report a parcel left unattended in public as terrorism from Northern Ireland threatened. Rehearsals should include devil's advocate input from residents capable of challenging officials by presenting realistic scenarios or countering false assumptions. Importing veterans of megacity disasters elsewhere brings fresh yet experienced minds to the task. Lessons might include those from 9/11 in New York City when both on-duty and off-duty emergency response personnel rushed to the point of attack. These were commendably good intentions, but one might ask how those living and working elsewhere in Manhattan would have been served had there been additional strikes elsewhere on the island. The conditions as police and firefighters dealt with the ongoing disaster at the Twin Towers lend a clue:

> The city's intricate network of safety coverage showed signs of unraveling that morning because of the headlong rush to Lower Manhattan. Police officers left their posts … At Ladder Company 16 on East 67th Street, four firefighters who were scheduled to go off duty wanted to stay and help. But Lt. Dan Williams told them 'to get the hell off the rig,' he said later. 'Why? I took one look at the TV and I said, 'We're going to lose people here today.' There was no doubt in my mind' … The men got off. Then they went outside and caught rides to the trade center in a police car and a city bus. One was killed in the collapse of the north tower. He was among the 60 off-duty firefighters to die … 'You have to train them,' said the Port Authority police chief, Joseph

---

113 Keith Lowe, *Inferno: The Fiery Destruction of Hamburg, 1943*, New York, NY: Scribner, 2007, 7, 11.

Morris. 'You can't have everybody coming in' ... At one point, the Emergency Medical Service had no ambulances for some 400 backed-up emergency calls.[114]

Multi-location terrorist attacks could become more common in future. We have already covered the example of 2008 in Mumbai and will look in detail at another, including assaults on Paris's Stade de France sports stadium, a restaurant and the Bataclan concert hall in November 2015. Effective response plans require that sufficient capabilities are held in reserve (as was the case with medical teams during the Paris contingency). Casualties need not be the only objective of attackers. Assessment of responses needs to incorporate how leaders can mitigate negative economic, diplomatic and other consequences not only for the city itself but also for the larger system of which the urban area is a part.[115]

Overcoming 'been there, done that' resistance to public guidance will be a particular challenge. Individuals who have survived previous hurricanes or typhoons are more likely to ignore orders to evacuate, the previous event having instilled a belief that they will be able to ride out what is to come. Bureaucracy can also play a hampering role. There are several reasons New York City failed to respond more effectively to Hurricane Sandy. A too-late call for evacuations was among them. So was an unexpected change in the way warnings were passed to city officials. The expected source of information, the National Hurricane Center, could no longer provide advisories or storm forecasts once the storm dropped out of hurricane status before making landfall. The centre's software would not allow for a continuation of those services. New York City authorities' ability to process information was handicapped once they were denied that source and information began arriving from another organisation in a different form.[116] New Orleans confronted a similar bureaucratic seam—theirs involving a post-disaster problem. 'After Katrina left hundreds of bodies to decompose in homes and streets,' one historian reported, 'Louisiana officials looked to the Federal Emergency Management Agency for help in removing them. But since cities and localities had historically recovered bodies from mass casualties, FEMA says, it had made no arrangements.'[117]

---

114 Dwyer and Flynn, 'Fatal confusion'.
115 This paragraph is adapted from Glenn, 'Terrorism and cities', 4–5.
116 Simon Worrall, 'Two years after Hurricane Sandy hit the US, what lessons can we learn from the deadly storm?', *National Geographic*, 19 October 2014, available from: www.nationalgeographic.com/adventure/article/141019-hurricane-sandy-katrina-coast-guard-hunters-ngbooktalk.
117 Brinkley, *The Great Deluge*, 610–11.

Planning and rehearsing before an event offer a chance to both ask and answer the many 'what if' questions sure to arise when knowledgeable citizens and officials gather (a solid reason for ensuring participants at such events are more than token representatives of their organisations).

The quote that 'every disaster is a rehearsal if treated appropriately' offers value for those willing to listen to its lessons. Junichi Hanawa's personal experience while travelling during the 5 September 2018 great Hokkaido earthquake is one such lesson. Used to relying on credit cards, as are most of us, he found himself short of currency when power outages rendered automatic tellers, credit card machines and other sources of cash or means of payment inoperable. Fortunately, the local airport and his hotel provided travellers food and drink free of charge. Realising such services might not always be available, Hanawa now carries a reasonable amount of emergency cash when travelling. His experience again reinforces one of this book's basic premises: lessons from and preparations for one type of disaster offer insights to those of another. The habit of always carrying emergency cash is a bit of insurance regardless of a calamity's cause. Hanawa's experience also tells us that officials or volunteer service providers should plan how they will tell both visitors and locals where necessities can be found when normal ways of communicating are lost.[118]

Concluding thoughts on preparation

> In many cities, there is evidence of what used to be a 'once in a hundred years' event becoming more common than this. In addition, cities are also vulnerable to any damage to the larger systems on which they depend—for instance for water supply and treatment, transport and electricity (and thus everything that depends on electricity, including lighting, pumping and communications).[119]
>
> —David Satterthwaite et al., *Adapting to climate change in urban areas*

> According to the Overseas Development Institute, a British think-tank, and the Global Facility for Disaster Reduction and Recovery … just 12% of disaster-relief funding in the past two decades

---

118 Glenn et al., *Achieving Convergence during Humanitarian Assistance and Disaster Relief Operations*.
119 Satterthwaite et al., *Adapting to climate change in urban areas*, 17.

has gone on reducing risks in advance rather than recovery and reconstruction afterwards. That is despite evidence that a dollar spent on risk-reduction saves at least two on mopping up.[120]

—'Disaster foretold', *The Economist*

Most megacity infrastructure was built when sea levels were lower and our understanding of urban systems' vulnerabilities was less. Backup generators, the circuit-breakers and fuel pumps on which they rely and other emergency features have again and again been proven to be located too low to survive recent events in New York City (Hurricane Sandy), Fukushima, New Orleans (Hurricane Katrina) and elsewhere.[121] Furthermore, accreditation standards for emergency generators tend to focus on short-term outages as would occur if a tree cut powerlines rather than days or weeks as is now not unusual. Even when working, backup power generation is often insufficient to meet all critical needs—for example, not only a hospital's medical equipment, but also its heating, airconditioning and ventilation systems.[122] In a world increasingly threatened by cyberattacks, plans that fail to consider strikes that simultaneously neutralise multiple parts of a system's electrical power, fuel supplies and traffic controls, for example, are inherently flawed. As megacities grow, the penalties for unpreparedness and the costs of recovery do likewise. Storms, earthquakes or other events that in the past might have been only inconveniences would now qualify as crisis-makers given sea-level rise, slum expansion into increasingly vulnerable areas, substandard construction and other factors. Were increased severity not enough, the greater frequency of climate change–related catastrophes will add to the suffering.

New York City's first Covid-19 case was confirmed on 1 March 2020. The number of confirmed or suspected cases by the end of May was 10,437 or more than 113 a day. Nearly one in five of those patients required

---

120 'Disaster foretold: Planning for El Nino', *The Economist*, [London], 7 November 2015, 55–56, at 56.
121 For example, during Hurricane Sandy in New York City, basement flooding overwhelmed fuel pumps in Tisch Hospital. Two blocks to the south, Bellevue Hospital, which also had its backup generators' fuel pumps in the basement while the generators themselves were on the thirteenth floor, had sealed the pumps behind 'submarine doors' made of steel and rubber after Hurricane Irene threatened in 2011. To no avail: Hurricane Sandy's floodwaters drowned the fuel pumps. David Oshinsky, *Bellevue: Three Centuries of Medicine and Mayhem at America's Most Storied Hospital*, New York, NY: Doubleday, 2016, 300–1, 304–5.
122 For example, see Fink, 'Beyond hurricane heroics'.

admittance to an intensive care unit.[123] Writing in his *The Plague Year*, author Lawrence Wright concluded that experience dealing with an epidemic or pandemic and leadership were the two factors most critical to successfully dealing with the onslaught of a major disease. Countries and cities that had dealt with SARS—Taiwan, Hong Kong and Vietnam among them—tended to better handle Covid-19.[124] Better-led countries, states and urban areas also tended to better handle Covid-19 in contrast with places where wavering, pliable or incompetent politicians were unwilling to introduce and enforce restrictions.

Mexico City lacked both pandemic experience and effective leadership when Covid arrived. Policymakers closed restaurants but allowed the city's subway system to continue service for its more than 5 million daily passengers.[125] While Seattle's public health system provided wise council, New York City's mayor urged residents to take advantage of public and private facilities. Another critical element in Seattle's success: while its citizens paid attention and took precautions, those in New York and elsewhere largely failed to do so until it was too late. Dangers unsurprisingly also proved greater when an urban area was a major transportation hub. The period December 2019 to March 2020 saw more than 3,000 direct flights from China to the United States, most of which arrived in New York, Los Angeles or San Francisco.[126] New York's death rate from Covid-19 would be 294 per 100,000, that of Los Angeles 201 while Seattle's was only 64—well below the 135 US average.[127]

Experience is a fickle mentor. Yes, living through a hurricane can cause someone to underestimate the danger even when the one threatening is far more powerful than the previous storm. But time also plays a role. US cities brutalised by influenza in 1918–19 remembered little from their century-old experiences, despite the means available for dealing with a pandemic being surprisingly similar whether in the early twentieth century or the second decade of the twenty-first. Those countries that had dealt with SARS effectively likely benefited from their governments'

123 Syra Madad, Nicholas V. Cagliuso, Sr, Dave A. Chokshi, Machelle Allen, Remle Newton-Dame and Jesse Singer, 'NYC Health + Hospitals' rapid responses to COVID-19 were built on a foundation of emergency management, incident command, and analytics', *Health Affairs*, 11 June 2020, available from: www.healthaffairs.org/do/10.1377/hblog20200609.171463/full/.

124 Lawrence Wright, *The Plague Year: America in the Time of Covid*, New York, NY: Alfred A. Knopf, 2021, 239–40.

125 Villoro, *Horizontal Vertigo*, 249.

126 Wright, *The Plague Year*, 76.

127 ibid., 241.

and populations' experiences being more recent. Masks, physical separation, quarantine, isolation and enforcement of health authority dictates were and remain vital:

> [In 1918, New York's] health commissioner, Dr. Royal S. Copeland, enforced compulsory isolation and staggered business hours. He allowed individual theaters and cinemas to remain open, but only if they were well ventilated and banned coughing, sneezing, and smoking. Sanitary police stood guard to yank anyone out of the audience if they violated the rules. [Meanwhile,] on September 27, about 200,000 Philadelphians crowded along Broad Street to watch the [World War I Liberty Loans] parade ... Infections skyrocketed ... Philadelphia had the second-worst mortality rate in the nation.[128]

Influenza killed roughly 40 million people worldwide during the 1918–19 pandemic, 550,000 of them Americans.[129] Ignorance was another feature common among too many of those dealing with the influenza and Covid-19 pandemics. Refusals to wear masks in 2020 had predecessors a century earlier in San Francisco's 'Anti-Mask League'—an organisation that included doctors and community leaders in its ranks.[130] Its reward: San Francisco's influenza excess death rate would rank among the worst of 43 US cities considered in a study looking back on the pandemic. St Louis ranked among the best thanks largely to early implementation and sustainment of policies that included a layered approach to defeating the disease's spread.[131] ('Layered' here refers to employing multiple policies such as closing schools and cancelling public gatherings. An early twentieth-century official compared it to Swiss cheese: one layer would be full of holes, but by layering the slices, many of the holes are closed.)[132] New Orleans

---

128 ibid., 51–53.

129 Howard Markel, Harvey B. Lipman, J. Alexander Navarro, Alexandra Sloan, Joseph R. Michalsen, Alexandra Minna Stern and Martin S. Cetron, 'Nonpharmaceutical interventions implemented by US cities during the 1918–1919 influenza pandemic', *Journal of the American Medical Association* 298(6) (2007): 644–54, at 644, doi.org/10.1001/jama.298.6.644.

130 Wright, *The Plague Year*, 54–55.

131 Markel et al., 'Nonpharmaceutical interventions implemented by US cities during the 1918–1919 influenza pandemic', 651.

132 Wright, *The Plague Year*, 54–55. Wright later (p. 105) cites Marchionne di Coppo Stefani, who provided a sense of the social devastation resulting from the Black Death in fourteenth-century Europe: 'Child abandoned the father, husband the wife, wife the husband, one brother the other, one sister the other ... Those who were responsible for the dead ... threw them into the ditch.' Cheese metaphors must be particularly popular when describing pandemics, as Stefani went on: 'The next morning, dirt was thrown on the bodies as new corpses were piled on, "layer by layer but like one puts layers of cheese in a lasagna".'

allowed Mardi Gras celebrations during the flu pandemic; Orleans Parish would soon have the country's highest death rate.[133] When city authorities were not quick to adopt effective policies, it was their citizens who paid in dead. New York City's response was early and sustained but not layered; its excess death rate reflected the flawed approach.[134] Pittsburgh, with the worst death rate in the country, was slow to implement interventions, did not sustain them and applied them individually rather than by layering.[135] Among the lessons: effective responses include four characteristics. They are *sustained* in duration, *orchestrated* in the sense of bringing all necessary capabilities to bear, *layered* in approach and *early* in application, which makes for a nice acronym should one be sought: SOLE.

From lessons to plans

> One of the devastating consequences of Sandy was its impact on research. The storm … drowned thousands of animals stacked in basement cages; the power outage … ruined precious cell lines and specimens stored in laboratory freezers. [We] 'lost some of our archives—samples obtained from villages and patients all over the world … They were irreplaceable' … Some of the samples were hazardous if not properly contained … Criticism also came from those who had suffered similar losses in the past. In 2001, Hurricane Allison drowned tens of thousands of caged mice at the Baylor and University of Texas medical research facilities in Houston, along with dozens of monkeys, rabbits, and dogs. Five years later, Katrina killed thousands more living underground at LSU [Louisiana State University] and Tulane. As a result, all four universities had taken steps to prevent a recurrence. 'We will never place animals or critical equipment in the basement again,' UT's [University of Texas] president declared.[136]
>
> —David Oshinsky, *Bellevue*

Every disaster and exercise potentially offers lessons—examples or insights—of value during disaster planning, lessons that might well preclude repeating mistakes made elsewhere, as was the case with the research losses consequent of Hurricane Sandy in New York. To provide but a few additional samples:

---

133 ibid., 79.

134 Markel et al., 'Nonpharmaceutical interventions implemented by US cities during the 1918–1919 influenza pandemic', 651.

135 ibid., 651.

136 Oshinsky, *Bellevue*, 308–10.

- As every disaster offers lessons, planning, exercises and gaming of possible responses should not only draw on similar historical events but also adapt those from others. The effective response of Paris's medical system to the city's 2015 terrorist attacks and problems identified after Tokyo's 1995 sarin experience hold multiple disaster management insights despite their very different forms of threat.

- Disaster responders need to prepare for urban contingencies in our increasingly urbanised world. Pehr Lodhammar's explosives-clearing in Mosul confronted his experts with never-before-seen challenges. Their previous experiences were limited to less urbanised environments. The example provides a warning of just how different urban conditions can be. Many NGOs and IGOs have rarely conducted operations in a major urban area.

- Urban hospitals have learned a tremendous amount during the Covid-19 pandemic. One-on-one and many-on-many exchanges of lessons are hopefully forthcoming. Likewise, articles such as those written by Dr Tetsu Okamura after the 1995 sarin attacks on Tokyo's subway and that by Martin Hirsch describing the response to the 2015 Paris terrorist event are invaluable for advising the catastrophe planning and preparations of other urban areas. Such articles and books on the medical challenges associated with urban disasters can be a starting point for plans or exercise design. Among the many other lessons relevant to medical responses:

  - Design plans and standards for the long haul. New Orleans after Hurricane Katrina and New York after Sandy both saw power outages that lasted for days. Account for such possibilities even if standards dictated by others do not. Machines are not the only resource inadequately studied. Staff of Bellevue Hospital in New York City 'knew instinctively how to click into emergency mode. Before Covid, that might last thirty or forty minutes—say, with a patient who has a heart attack. If there is a bus wreck or a mass casualty event, emergency mode could last all day. But with Covid, it was day after day for weeks on end.'[137]

  - The military calls it 'cross-training'—being able to perform duties not normally one's own. In New York City, nurses had twice as many intensive care unit (ICU) patients to care for during crisis periods in 2020. 'Some departments, like emergency, were

---

137 Wright, *The Plague Year*, 113.

constantly on the verge of being swamped; others were looking for a role to play. Ophthalmologists were helping in the ICU; general surgeons treated non-COVID patients; and orthopaedic surgeons began devoting their entire shifts to turning patients—"proning"— to facilitate breathing.'[138]

– We will find that the Paris medical system managed patient loads well during the megacity's 2015 terrorist attack. Tokyo in 1995 and New York in 2020 did so less effectively. Efficacy is not a matter of management alone. Compatible communications— reporting a hospital's status in terms of not only bed availability but also specialists, general staff, equipment, supplies, human remains storage, power generation, overpressure capacity and other variables—all during periods when power or routine means of communication are limited—requires extensive pre-event planning and practise.

– Personal protective equipment works, yet Tokyo's medical facilities in 1995 and those in New York in 2020 lacked the requisite numbers and types needed.

– As is to be expected during not only pandemics, but also biological, chemical or radiological terrorist attacks, patients will have to be isolated from their families. Procedures for linking families with those receiving care should not be ad hoc as was frequently the case in 2020 when nurses and other staff shared their personal phones for video conferences so family members could say goodbye as death loomed.[139]

– Expect assistance from outside sources. Thirty thousand personnel responded when New York called for help in dealing with Covid-19.[140] How to integrate these individuals into staff rotations, house and feed them and otherwise ease the process of incorporation when billeting is limited and domestic staff are already overburdened is best planned before the need arises.

– Seemingly dissimilar facilities might hold lessons of immediate importance. The spread of Covid-19 in prisons and assisted-living facilities made them potential laboratories for studying the virus's spread and other characteristics.

138 ibid., 114.
139 ibid., 113.
140 ibid., 116.

- Cancelling all elective surgical procedures, centralising supply chain operations, implementing or revising phone hotline and telehealth operations, level-loading patients within as well as between facilities, developing alternative care locations (such as ICU capacity)—all will have application to multiple types of urban disaster response.[141]

- As with any disaster plan and response, keep an eye on near and more distant-term post-calamity demands. Hospitals immediately cancelled elective surgeries as crises in Tokyo, Paris and New York became apparent. Patients with life-threatening conditions put themselves at additional risk by not coming to hospitals as they sought to avoid exposing themselves to Covid-19. Addressing resultant backlogs in such cases might be eased by informed decisions made before and during a disaster. Most backlogs, though unavoidable, can be mitigated. Alternative procedures and the use of pharmaceuticals in lieu of immediate surgery require pre-event study and dissemination to practitioners and policymakers.

- Contemplate the challenges in even the seemingly routine. Patient evacuation, including prioritisation, movement during power outages, sustainment of essential care (for example, breathing assistance), transport down stairwells, handling of grossly obese, mentally ill or incarcerated individuals—these and other procedures proved extremely challenging in the aftermath of both Hurricane Katrina and Hurricane Sandy.

• 'Make the training harder than the game.' Bring in outsiders to challenge organisations' assumptions, including politicians' decisions. Judgements made during non-stressful exercises when doughnuts and coffee are on the table are unlikely to withstand reality when rulings carry job-threatening potential. Devil's advocates should include the play of corruption, criminality and favouritism in their inputs during planning and exercises, as the case of funds distribution in post–Hurricane Sandy New York City made clear: Langone Hospital 'had already received $1.2 billion from the Federal Emergency Management Agency ... Bellevue, meanwhile, had received only $117 million from FEMA ... The report sparked more anger than surprise. Who didn't expect a well-connected private hospital to get preferential treatment?'[142]

---

141 Madad et al., 'NYC Health + Hospitals' rapid responses to COVID-19'.
142 Oshinsky, *Bellevue*, 312–13.

Good plans and exercises can save millions of dollars in addition to lives. Federal stimulus cheques and the Paycheck Protection Program were hastily implemented and inefficient. While some of the deserving benefited, many others were not in need of the programs' help. The latter is thought to have cost taxpayers about $375,000 for every job saved in part because cheques went to companies that were not planning to lay off many workers. Off-the-shelf, preplanned and rehearsed programs developed by urban leaders could do much to preserve fiscal resources. They would also provide guidance for difficult decisions that will have to be made during a disaster. Hospitals will face triage decisions when it is impossible to provide the necessary care to all patients; standards should be in place before those decisions become necessary. Similar guidance should be available in support of economic triage. One estimate expects that perhaps one-third of New York City's small businesses will never recover from Covid-19 closures.[143]

Preparing now saves lives later, lends organisation to what will otherwise be chaos and both speeds recovery and reduces its costs. It won't be easy. Planning, rehearsing, otherwise practising responses, stockpiling essential stores and equipment, designing and conducting training and putting in place the many other components of preparations are demanding and expensive. They also are not one-shot events; repetition and updating are key to avoid backsliding.

Yet, there is good news. Science is already stepping forward in ways that combine forecasting with political awareness and the power of data to decrease if not prevent disaster's effects. Providing money to Bangladeshis who are at risk of flooding has proven valuable when the funds are specified for use in moving out of harm's way.[144] Virginia health officials in the state's populous south-east have demonstrated they can detect Covid-19 in human wastewater even before individuals have symptoms, thus presenting the possibility of early identification and institution of preventative measures before a virus spreads its suffering. Similar approaches have been successful in tracking polio, opioid use and leaking sewage that could contaminate local waterways and spread disease.[145] Another study using sewage testing found reasonable association with

143 Wright, *The Plague Year*, 144, 235.

144 'Missions impossible: Global firefighting', *The Economist*, [London], 20 June 2020, Special report pages 6–9, at 8.

145 Marie Albiges, 'Wastewater could be indicator of where virus will strike: Surges noticed in water prior to spike in cases', *The Virginia Gazette*, [Williamsburg, VA], 12 August 2020, 2A.

Australian census data. Caffeine consumption correlated positively with education levels (especially when coffee is five bucks a pop, presumably). Amphetamine use (unsurprisingly) did likewise with crime. Other associations addressed social life, housing status and income.[146] It does not take a lot of imagination to realise that such information could help in planning for the allocation of resources post disaster. For example, if a megacity's poor are known to suffer specific medical challenges, as is the case in parts of New York's Brooklyn, specialists and medications addressing those could be prepositioned to facilitate treatment even before misfortune visits.

Preparation efforts will have little chance of success unless they build on what was learned (or should have been learned) from previous events. Better-run megacities recognise that their interconnectedness can serve residents' security if they share in drawing on past experiences. We noted that New York City maintains direct connections with other major world cities and routinely shares lessons learned from terrorist and other events. They will surely do the same given their misfortune in being the United States' first major Covid-19 epicentre. Members of the Japan Ground Self-Defense Force readying to support the 2020 Summer Olympic Games benefited from interactions with representatives drawing on experiences with the Los Angeles, Sydney and Rio de Janeiro Olympics and other major sports and security events. Recalling the importance of the citizen as *first* first responder, we remind ourselves that obtaining critical information may be as straightforward as ensuring residents know: 1) what information will help megacity authorities act most effectively, 2) who to contact with that information, and 3) how to do so (including when normally available communications are not available). A fourth step, providing feedback to residents who provide information—notably, publicly praising the action—is also crucial as it encourages them to do so again while prompting others to do the same.[147]

The dramatic expansion of social media and those platforms' capabilities are ripe for innovative ways of sharing information in times of disaster. Plotting locations on app maps or providing photos of victims and sites to aid responders dispatching resources means authorities can facilitate getting the right stuff to the right place, helping to avoid the

---

146 'Class acts: The socioeconomics of sewage', *The Economist*, [London], 18 July 2020, 65–66.
147 Brian Jenkins provided a brief on these four elements during a session attended by the author. While the context at the time was counterterrorism, the quartet applies equally to other situations.

squandering of always limited government, NGO and other resources. Urban catastrophes are also rich in crowdsourcing opportunities, but the payoff will be far less if they are not planned for before a crisis. Identifying these opportunities and including them in rehearsals will reveal shortfalls and ways to make the good even better. Testing new capabilities means less chance of making the mistake Japanese authorities discovered too late when they relied on the internet to notify older victims of the Fukushima nuclear reactor failure who were not internet users. More robust rehearsals that test capabilities such as the sharing of photographs, video, map locations, victim status and location and other information provide insights lost in less bold exercises. A simple example: running an exercise based on a two-dimensional map could fall short of revealing the importance of the third dimension that provides rescuers with crucial information—whether a victim is at ground level, below ground or on an upper floor.[148]

No amount of preparation will ready a megacity for all possible situations. Murphy's Law tells us that preparing for 100 contingencies means fate will pitch number 101; but readying for that 100 makes residents and officials alike better able to adapt to the unexpected, unexperienced and unforeseen so that the actions required are not too distant from the familiar.

---

148 Glenn et al., *Achieving Convergence during Humanitarian Assistance and Disaster Relief Operations.*

7

Meeting challenges and finding opportunities during megacity disasters

Where there is no widespread population displacement, large outbreaks of communicable disease are rare after natural disasters. However, outbreaks are significantly more likely where populations are displaced, where nutritional status is poor, and/or where water and sanitation systems are damaged.[1]

—D. Sanderson et al., *Responding to urban disasters*

I suppose one of the things that we learned very quickly in Hue City was that if a man was wounded, you didn't pull back and call for a corpsman because then you'd have two guys down … We found out that in the city you have to carry on and leave the guy, that the guy had a better chance of surviving if we just kept going and let the guys behind us pick him up. It's a difficult thing to do.[2]

—Lieutenant General (ret.) Ernest C. Cheatham,
US Marine Corps

The fighting in Saigon, Hue and other Vietnamese cities during the 1968 Tet Offensive brought together many of the challenges soldiers and others have since repeatedly confronted when violence visits urban areas. That the enemy attacked five of the country's six autonomous cities and 36 of 44 provincial capitals acknowledged the political and social significance of these centres. The combat was brutal. US and Republic of Vietnam

---

1   Sanderson et al., *Responding to urban disasters*.
2   Quoted in Glenn, *Honing the Keys to the City*, 57.

soldiers fought North Vietnamese regulars and Viet Cong irregulars at intimate quarters. Those taking up arms included mechanics, cooks, clerks and others finding themselves at the sharp end of war for the first time. Infantrymen advancing street by street and block by block had to stay their trigger fingers as civilians unexpectedly appeared from buildings and alleys, fleeing the enemy. Controlling the many refugees was all but impossible. Filtering out enemy infiltrators was likewise. The innocent fled with good reason. The enemy executed thousands in Hue alone; government officials, teachers and others thought to be associated with South Vietnam's government were later found in mass graves.

The attacking North Vietnamese and Viet Cong sought to inspire an urban uprising and thereby cause the collapse of South Vietnam's government. They failed. The fighting left thousands homeless even so. Reconstruction of ruined dwellings was interrupted by a second wave of attacks in May 1968 against fewer urban areas, with the capital, Saigon, the primary focus. The adversary struck again in August.[3] Providing shelter for those made homeless was only one challenge. Distributing food and water, preventing disease among the displaced, caring for the newly orphaned and elderly deprived of caregivers and reuniting those separated during the chaos that inevitably accompanies disaster are only a few of the additional tribulations suffered in excess.

The view through history's lens is far clearer than that of what is yet to come. The view forward tends to be even less sharp when the subject is response to urban disaster because of the unique character of each catastrophe. Inexperience further dims perceptions. Drawing on a military example, the soldier can look back on World War II and find exceptionally detailed statistics on how much fuel was used, ammunition fired and food consumed, which vehicle parts wore out fastest or how many casualties were suffered when fighting occurred in a jungle, on the plains of Europe or in a desert. Not so when the fighting was in an urban area. Such statistics rarely exist.

You are likely among the world's hundreds of millions who were restricted to their homes due to Covid-19. There will surely be books aplenty condemning the misjudgements and misdirection employed as the virus

---

3   For those wanting to read further about the multiple 1968 offensives against Republic of Vietnam urban areas, see Adrian G. Traas, *Turning Point, 1967–1968*, Washington, DC: US Army Center of Military History, 2017.

spread. More important will be the lessons captured and shared regarding which procedures proved better than others, which policies and regulations helped or hindered and how wiser decisions might be adapted next time so the world's megacities are better prepared. Just as was the case with the 1995 nerve agent attack in Tokyo and the lack of changes made in the ensuing 25 years, however, knowing is not doing. The following pages are aimed to assist those who can and will 'do' when urban disasters call.

Systems as context during megacity disasters

> Tokyo has approximately 63,000 underground areas, with underground paths, subway systems and shopping complexes comprising 40 percent of the total … The Tsukiji-Toranomon Tunnel is buried about 2 meters underground, and is separated by just 30 cm—roughly the width of a Japan Times Sunday page— from an underground utility conduit jointly operated by gas, water and telecommunications companies, among others, that runs beneath it. The conduit, meanwhile, is also located 30 cm above the Toei Mita Subway Line … One can walk all the way from Otemachi, cross Tokyo Station and the Yaesu shopping district, past JR Yurakucho Station and make it as far as Kabukiza theater in Higashi-ginza without ever needing to walk on the surface. All in all, that's a walk of 4.05 km.[4]
>
> —Jun Hongo, 'Tokyo underground'

> Tokyo subways carry 10M per day.[5]
>
> —'Walking Tokyo', *National Geographic*

Not all is what it seems in a megacity. A bridge is a bridge but can be so much more. It is a way out for those fleeing disaster, a way in for those bringing help, a comfort for defenders who know they will have to depart should things go wrong and a means of exploiting success for an attacker pursuing a defeated foe. But a bridge is often more than only its travelled way. We noted that powerlines and waterpipes might run beneath and be the difference between neighbourhood residents' keeping cold or sickness

---

4   Jun Hongo, 'Tokyo underground: Taking property development to new depths', *The Japan Times*, [Tokyo], 12 April 2014, available from: www.japantimes.co.jp/life/2014/04/12/lifestyle/tokyo-underground/#.XDp77M9KgWo.
5   'Walking Tokyo', *National Geographic* 235 (April 2019): 38–65, at 53.

at bay and death should the span be destroyed by an earthquake's tremors or military force trying to keep an enemy from crossing. Intact lines and pipes mean urban authorities can turn their attentions to other problems in a time of crisis. A destroyed bridge means those same officials must commit resources to providing lost essentials to the civilian population. In times of war, every successful metre gained in an attack imposes an additional metre of occupier responsibility under international law. Is halting an enemy's escape worth having to find alternative ways of providing power and water to a population for days, weeks or months? The potential occupier needs to prepare for two futures even if they have no intention of dropping the span: one with the bridge intact, and a second with it lying submerged beneath the river's flowing waters—for the enemy always has a vote. The bridge's survival is not dependent on one side's actions alone. While the future occupier might wish to see the bridge stand, a fleeing enemy finds itself in a double-bonus situation: destroying the bridge delays a foe's pursuit. Dropping the span further burdens that enemy with additional occupier responsibilities. Should it be an earthquake or other act of nature that fells the span, the problem is not only losing the vital resources in the lines and pipes but also there is one less way to bring relief to the deprived.

Such are the tortuous decisions for the city councillor or attacking infantry colonel. Take a couple of steps up the ladder of seniority and the decisions change in character and consequences. What is the point at which priority shifts from meeting a megacity population's expectations of a quick return to pre-disaster normalcy to restoring far-flung commercial ties that preserve the urban area's status and infuse funds into its traumatised economy? Though the media and community authorities will favour focusing on the directly affected population, what of the thousands or millions who live beyond the city's limits but depend on its ports, airfields, trains and roads for essentials? Given the megacity consists of multiple governments and hundreds of community groups, who decides who gets what when? Every decision made or not made has repercussions—those ripples in nearby and distant ponds that represent second and higher-order effects being impossible to predict, hard to forecast and sure to have consequences for decision-maker and resident alike in both the immediate and the longer terms.

Control during megacity disasters

> Rescue workers rummaged through wardrobes and drawers in bombed homes … Looters freely roamed the streets stealing fuel, food, and even old ladies' clothing.[6]
>
> —Aaron William Moore, *Bombing the City*

> Major Hassan turned to me with an expression of disbelief. 'I face difficulties with these civilians,' he said … 'They just come here and walk around … Sometimes they ask very stupid things.'[7]
>
> —James Verini, *They Will Have to Die Now*

Failure to quickly gain control during urban disaster response means loss of government legitimacy. Coalition operations in early 2003 in Iraq lacked the manpower to prevent the rampant looting and accompanying wanton destruction of the country's southern towns and cities as forces moved north.[8] True, combat forces needed to maintain their momentum if they were to deny Saddam Hussein's forces the time needed to prepare defences. Yet unchecked looting meant the loss of vital property records and delayed the return of public services before the coming torrid summer months. Perhaps greater priority will be given to increasing the number of units in trailing echelons tasked to secure bypassed urban areas during planning for future military urban operations, that in conjunction with increasing military police and more effective efforts to retain local law enforcement with promises of continued wages. These concerns should be no less a priority in the absence of war. Looting, destruction and assaults on innocents are as much a threat to recovery when the environment is one of rioting, as in 1992 in Los Angeles, or of flooding, as in Dhaka, Jakarta or Shanghai. How much force is justified in stopping such behaviour? Like patient triage, guidance is best created and made known before misfortune visits.

Post-disaster evaluations will always include looking over one's shoulder at why preparations failed to identify decisions, actions or behaviours that would later prove ill advised. The 7 August 1998 truck bombing of the US Embassy in Nairobi, Kenya, is no exception. Shots rang out. A grenade exploded as the attacking terrorists responded to guards halting their

---

6 Moore, *Bombing the City*, 124.
7 Verini, *They Will Have to Die Now*, 256–57.
8 James N. Mattis, Interview with Russell W. Glenn, Palo Alto, CA, 31 August 2014.

vehicle. Curiosity drove embassy workers and those in nearby structures to windows. This understandable reaction was a fatal one. Many died or were maimed when the bomb detonated, shattering window glass that tore into spectators who should have been trained to flee from the sounds of an attack. Seven years later, on 7 July 2005, terrorists struck the megacity of London with three nearly simultaneous bombings. All the explosive devices used hexamethylene triperoxide diamine (HMDT)— a compound that degrades and destabilises when warmed. The NYPD's Michael Sheehan, who is in charge of the department's counterterrorism section, noted lessons that could foretell similar attacks in the future. The terrorists had used commercial-grade refrigerators to keep the materials stable. They had loaded the explosives into coolers for transport before transferring them to the refrigerators. While that may not have been thought suspicious by any but the most security-conscious, the purchase, delivery and movement of the refrigerators into the terrorists' living quarters (described as a 'flophouse') could have triggered lifesaving suspicions, multiplying the opportunities for police to hear of the presence of the abnormal.[9] Public information programs arm potential victims with knowledge. The better the preparation, the better are the choices made that mean the difference between death and survival, disaster and interdiction.

Some of history's lessons might surprise. An estimated one-third of patients hid from contact tracers and would not report to treatment centres as Ebola ravaged Sierra Leone in 2014–15. Others who had tested positive fled treatment centres—at times with the help of family members.[10] Despite pleas from health authorities, families in West Africa also insisted on sharing a last meal with the highly contagious corpse of a recently departed relative during the crisis. The seemingly inexplicable behaviour (until one realises it is a cultural norm) has historical company:

> In 1883, during the fifth cholera pandemic, the German physician Robert Koch established the cause of the disease by isolating the *Vibrio cholerae* bacterium. The following year, the pandemic hit Naples. The city dispatched inspectors to confiscate suspect produce. It also sent out disinfection squads, which arrived at the city's tenements with guns drawn. Neapolitans … responded with an impressive sense of humor, if not necessarily a keen

9   Dickey, *Securing the City*, 212.
10   Manaugh and Twilley, *Until Proven Safe*, 176.

understanding of epidemiology. Demonstrators showed up at city hall with baskets of overripe figs and melons. They proceeded … 'to consume the forbidden fruit in enormous quantities while those who watched applauded and bet on which binger would eat the most.'[11]

Setting priorities: Doing first things first

Fifteen-year-old Ono Kazuo was completely disorientated by the annihilation of his neighbourhood in Takamatsu, trying to navigate theretofore familiar streets that were suddenly covered in destroyed houses, downed power lines, and ruined institutions such as schools, hospitals, train stations, and shops.[12]

—Aaron William Moore, *Bombing the City*

Another put on a blue trilby hat and purple scarf. I asked if he'd found the accessories in the house. He looked almost insulted. 'I wouldn't take another person's clothing,' he said.[13]

—James Verini, *They Will Have to Die Now*

Flexible plans and adaptation in applying them are as close as a megacity's responsible authorities will have to a silver bullet in meeting the challenges rushing at them during a crisis. Getting it perfect will be impossible. Getting it not too wrong, on the other hand, will be a notable accomplishment. Leaders were met with far more challenges than means to meet them when riots broke out in 1992 in Los Angeles. Failing to put a high priority on securing gun shops meant an estimated 3,000 handguns, rifles and shotguns were looted. Only 200 of these had been recovered months later.[14] Decision-making failures at the federal level in the United States during the early 2020 coronavirus outbreak meant the locations most likely to suffer the most rapid spread of the disease—its major urban areas—lacked consistent direction, accurate guidance and policies that ensured rare resources were managed centrally rather than as treasures fought over between states, federal authorities and private interests. The United States' federal response stood out as especially incompetent, but it was not the only subpar performance. Lacking sufficient guidelines from Japan's national leaders, Tokyo Governor Koike Yuriko's more aggressive

---

11   Kolbert, 'The spread', 61.
12   Moore, *Bombing the City*, 41.
13   Verini, *They Will Have to Die Now*, 35.
14   James D. Delk, *Fires & Furies: The L.A. Riots*, Palm Springs, CA: ETC, 1995, 36.

approach upstaged that of then prime minister Abe Shinzo and included the dramatic step of shutting the red-light district for the first time since the fire-bombings in World War II.[15]

Getting the priorities right—or not too wrong—means recognising what is most important amid the chaos. The great war theorist Carl von Clausewitz provided his thoughts on the traits an effective military leader needed to prevail in such times. His nineteenth-century observation applies no less to those struggling during the initial hours, days and weeks of a megacity crisis 200 years on. Clausewitz called his essential character feature *coup d'oeil*—best translated as a mix of strength of mind, drive and resistance to fluster—which the Prussian himself described as 'the quick recognition of truth that the mind would ordinarily miss or would be perceived only after long study and reflection'.[16] One possessing *coup d'oeil* breaks through the sense of being overwhelmed to which others fall victim. He or she should therefore be able to grasp what needs to be done to address the demands of the present without too greatly risking future success. Leaders must not only manage an in-progress crisis. They must also keep an eye on what were routine day-to-day threats before a disaster while also being aware that some people will see catastrophe as an opportunity for gain at others' expense. Japanese leaders in Tokyo realised this during the 2011 Fukushima Daiichi disaster. With Tokyo threatened and much of Honshu's population under siege, a regional enemy chose to test the country's national security preparedness by menacing Japan's airspace.[17] The United States similarly saw China, Russia, North Korea and Iran all seek to take advantage of perceived US vulnerabilities as it sought to keep the worst of the Covid-19 pandemic at bay.[18] China sank a Vietnamese fishing boat in the South China Sea on 2 April 2020 and dispatched an aircraft-carrier to skirt Japanese and Taiwanese territorial waters, testing America's commitment as the virus sickened US Navy crews. Air force jets intercepted two Russian patrol aircraft near Alaska; a week later, a fighter from that country came within 8 metres of a US Navy reconnaissance aircraft. North Korea's missile launches spiked in

---

15 'The drifters', *The Economist*, [London], 4 April 2020, 31.
16 Carl von Clausewitz, *On War*, ed. and trans. by Michael Howard and Peter Paret, Princeton, NJ: Princeton University Press, 1976, 102.
17 Glenn et al., *Achieving Convergence during Humanitarian Assistance and Disaster Relief Operations*.
18 Ellen Mitchell, 'Foreign powers test US defenses amid coronavirus pandemic', *The Hill*, [Washington, DC], 19 April 2020, available from: thehill.com/policy/defense/493490-foreign-powers-test-us-defenses-amid-coronavirus-pandemic.

March 2020 while Iranian Islamic Revolutionary Guard Corps vessels made 'dangerous and harassing approaches' to US Navy and Coast Guard ships.

Coup d'oeil alone cannot ensure success. Getting it not too wrong also requires accurate information no matter how strong the mind and calm the spirit. Acquiring the information needed and getting it to where it needs to go will be notably challenging when the environment is the hypercomplex one found in a megacity. It will be a collective effort that succeeds only if all know how to play their parts. *Coup d'oeil* might take on a collective character when the parties agreeing to support a comprehensive approach work together to strip away the fog that otherwise impedes clear decisions.

Knowing what you don't know

> Nearly 65 per cent of the traffic is composed of non-powered vehicles (e.g., rickshaws, bicycles), which are not physically separated from cars, buses, and other powered vehicles.[19]
>
> —Saleemul Huq, 'Environmental Hazards in Dhaka'

> It took a little time to realise that the best 'chatter-up' was not necessarily the most senior member of a patrol.[20]
>
> —MOD, *Operation Banner*

The above two quotations provide lessons for even those savvy in the ways of gathering information. Having seen donkey carts adding to rush-hour in Basra, Iraq, and the deluge of bicycles in Dutch urban areas at seemingly any time of day would not prepare me for Dhaka's streets. Nor would I, as an inexperienced lieutenant, have been smart enough to realise that several of my platoon members were better able to talk the talk with locals in a city whether at home or abroad. No matter how good the pre-calamity information-gathering, events will demand much in the way of updating, refining, disproving and discovery.

Those same databases that provided overview-type input during planning and rehearsals can be fine-tuned to specific needs once calamity strikes. Census information, tax records, marketing survey results, those hyper-

---

19   Saleemul Huq, 'Environmental Hazards in Dhaka', in *Crucibles of Hazard: Mega-Cities and Disasters in Transition*, James K. Mitchell (ed.), New York, NY: United Nations University, 1999, 128.
20   MOD, *Operation Banner*, 5-1.

important property records—some, all or others can feed the voracious appetite for information depending on the nature of the crisis, location, demographics, gaps in local capabilities and aid provider resources. (The reason property records are so critical—and a reason insurgents or criminals deliberately target them for destruction—is that landownership proves a boon to anyone who can convince a government they own a plot or want to undermine a government by causing it to appear to be the power stealing from rightful owners.) We noted that medical records can tell aid providers who needs which treatments and medications, where they live and which challenges exist (mobility limitations, deafness, asthma, reliance on home respirators and psychiatric problems, for example) if patients have waived release of relevant medical information or local policies permit access regardless. Pharmacy information provides less comprehensive but potentially still valuable insights. The potential to save begs the question of whether policies are in place to make such information available during a catastrophe. Rehearsals and other exercises should point to additional information that healthcare providers could include as data to release in times of emergency. Does the home respirator for a given patient have battery backup? If so, how long will the charge last? If not, does the residence have a backup generator? If so, how much fuel is stored at the location?

While the above can help those hoping to know who lives where and what needs those individuals have, mobile phone data will continue to have notable potential given their 'real-time' character. As we noted earlier, officials have used data records providing call times and mobile tower locations to track malaria outbreaks in Africa and such use could similarly help trace the flow of commuters exposed to biological or chemical contamination. The State of Virginia fielded its COVIDWISE app in July 2020 to track exposures and notify any who downloaded the application that they may have come in contact with individuals testing positive. Geoprofiling shows promise for finding terrorists via analyses of where incidents occur. Recall that attacks might be a shortish distance from perpetrators' dwellings, material storage locations or stores used for purchases to reduce chances of detection. Even knowing where a megacity's sex trade or bar scenes flourish can be helpful if the nature of the terrorist is such that he or she finds such locations unpalatable—or otherwise.[21]

---

21 Glenn, 'Megacities'.

Cultures can throw outside relief providers a curve, however, and while those non-natives are likely working hand-in-hand with locals, the locals may not know which of their customs the visitors find unusual. Oral thermometers requiring sanitisation between uses weren't a practical choice for medical personnel trying to determine who had the highly contagious Ebola in 2014 in West Africa. 'Fever guns' aimed at individuals' foreheads seemed the logical replacement; they proved otherwise. Some locals thought the technology meant the user was reading minds to determine voting intentions in a pending election.[22] Nor should an outsider believe the developed world is devoid of the seemingly nonsensical. Acknowledging superstitions means some (but not all) buildings in urban areas skip one or more floor numbers. We already noted that providing a two-dimensional grid coordinate gives a location on the ground but not how far above or below that point the item or person of interest might be. Adding the floor or level number would in most cases do the job for someone assisting inside a structure (as floor numbers are generally clearly marked). The view from inside and outside can be considerably different in terms of location, however—a potentially vital bit of information for an emergency medical technician, pilot, sniper, firefighter or another viewing the building from its exterior. Many US highrises have no thirteenth floor—a critical factor should a shooter or victim have to be dealt with from the outside of the structure after a report that the person in question resides on a level above that number. In China, it's the fourth floor or any ending in '4' that might be skipped (in some cases, any floor with '4' appearing at all, which also casts out 40–43 and 45–49). Given the city's considerable Chinese population, one apartment building in Vancouver, Canada, has a sixtieth floor—a pretty amazing feat for a building with only 53 levels. The builder passed over not only all floors ending in '4' but also the thirteenth. (If there's a bit of engineer in you and you are checking my maths, Canadian buildings at times call what Americans would label the first floor the 'ground' or 'main' floor. In the case of this building, the floor immediately above the ground floor is the second, not first, floor. There is no first floor! See Footnote 23 for the maths involved.) Some buildings catering to Chinese also have no apartment or room numbers ending with or containing a '4', complicating responders' jobs even further, especially when smoke or lack of power limits visibility during rescue efforts. Fortunately, Vancouver recently changed its policy

22 Laurie Garrett, 'Welcome to the first war zone Ebola crisis', *Foreign Policy*, 18 October 2018, available from: foreignpolicy.com/2018/10/18/welcome-to-the-first-war-zone-ebola-crisis/.

to reduce these risks; floors with fours and the thirteenth are back.[23] Presumably, so too are suite numbers and the like in new construction, meaning there will be some foured and thirteened buildings (good luck, first responders). The way to communicate vertical dimensions needs to be made known to all relevant parties managing and lending assistance in times of need along with such oddball features as these.

Similar challenges sometimes lurk within other urban addresses. The importance of having an address—and that address accurately reflecting a location—has meant the difference between life and death. John Snow—he of cholera maps and the Broad Street pump—could discover the connection between disease and water source because England's Parliament had in 1765 dictated that all houses have a number. Seventy-two years later, in 1837, births and deaths began to be recorded by the country's General Register Office. These two bureaucratic steps meant Snow could get the date and cause of death and the address at which it took place, thus allowing him to plot that famous map and draw his vital conclusions.[24]

Fine, you might think, but buildings having addresses are not a problem today—well, unless the disaster involves a slum where authorities have either deliberately or otherwise not assigned addresses to homes and other structures. Or maybe crisis strikes a country in which accurate mapping remains a challenge. Or one where a single location has several addresses. Author Juan Villoro lives in Mexico City. His neighbourhood has two official names, Villa Coyoacán and Coyoacán Center. Uber refers to it by a third name, Santa Catarina. His street is named after a strongman from the Mexican Revolution—one of 412 streets, avenues or traffic circles

23   JLee, 'No more skipping 4, 13, 14, or 24 in Vancouver floor numbers', *Vancouver Sun*, 14 November 2015, available from: vancouversun.com/news/local-news/no-more-skipping-4-13-14-24-in-vancouver-floor-numbers. The maths: 53 floors. Delete numbers 4, 13, 14, 24, 34, 44, so add six floors = 59, but if you add six to 53 you have to skip 54, so the 53-storey building has 60 floors on the elevator panel. Remember that what would be the first floor in the United States is labelled the ground floor in the apartment building with that immediately above as the second floor (so our floor count calculations are not affected by what is an anomaly for Americans). European buildings and some elsewhere, however, often have a ground floor with what is called the first floor immediately above. Important? It sure would be if Americans providing assistance in, say, London, were unaware of the difference when sent to help someone on the first floor. Once again, it's about the importance of accurate information—'accurate' having to sometimes include more than might be, well, what meets the eye from the outside of a structure.
24   Deirdre Mask, *The Address Book: What Street Addresses Reveal about Identity, Race, Wealth, and Power*, New York, NY: St Martin's Press, 2020, 40–41.

bearing the name 'Carranza'.[25] But in developed-world megacities addresses shouldn't be a problem, you say. Wrong again, I'm afraid. Understanding the tongue being spoken by a local urban resident might not mean resident and aid provider are communicating in the same language. Those living or working in a neighbourhood sometimes have their own names for streets, squares, buildings or other features. Depending on whom the aid provider is speaking with, even neighbours in a community might refer to a location differently. Author Deirdre Mask found that 'immigrants from different regions in China have their own Manhattan [New York City] street names for the same street according to region and dialect'.[26] No problem—just make sure those unfamiliar with an area have the official address (if one exists), right? Not so fast. Mask goes on to write about 'vanity addresses'—those reflecting locations considered posher than others, and thus ones for which real estate developers can charge more. The problem comes when officials sell or allow addresses that do not accurately reflect the real location (another example of corruption having many forms perhaps?). Manhattan again provides an example, though New York is not the only city with the problem. Mask relates that number 520 Park Avenue isn't on Park Avenue at all; the building fronts East 60th Street, 46 metres away. No big deal (other than for those paying 5 to 10 per cent more for the 'fake' address)? Tell that to the family of Nancy Clay, who lost her life in another city because of such mislabelling. Clay died in Chicago because the city's firefighters did not know her office at One Illinois Center was really on the less posh East Wacker Drive.[27] And that was local fire responders; visiting disaster responders wouldn't have a clue. Fortunately, there are efforts under way to come up with universal addresses for any location in the world. Less fortunately, these are still in development and some of the eventual products may require commercial purchase.[28]

Maps, overhead photography and GPS might get an individual or group to where they want to go, but do they tell them anything about conditions on the ground when they get there? Recalling his visit to Medellín, Colombia, author Richard Sennett relied on young guides who routinely provided tours of city *barrios*. 'They knew every alley and byway,' Sennett wrote:

25   Villoro, *Horizontal Vertigo*, 28.
26   Mask, *The Address Book*, 86–87.
27   ibid., 229–31.
28   ibid., 260–68.

> They gave an exhaustive description of dangerous and safe streets which would have done a policeman proud. Holding my eight-year-old guide's hand, I felt his slight, restraining, cautionary gesture whenever we turned a corner. On a later visit at night to the barrio, I noticed that as my protectors rounded corners they would slow down a bit and survey the lights on in the houses lining the street. If the houses of friends whom they'd just seen were in darkness, my protectors would then stop: why wasn't this family at home when they were supposed to be having supper? Once I asked if anything was wrong; 'no' one ten-year-old protector replied, 'but there might be.'[29]

Even at eight and 10 years of age, locals register the absence of the normal and presence of the abnormal—information that could prove invaluable to a new arrival unfamiliar with a city.

Relying on local support is not without its risks, however. Some offering assistance in the past were taking advantage of the naive newly arrived, employing the unwitting outsider to settle old scores by falsely identifying fellow noncombatants' homes as those of the enemy. The benefits for the misinformation providers were twofold. First, a competitor is eliminated or that old score settled. Second, as it is the foreigner who does the deed, the real perpetrator escapes blame and thus the endless chain of retribution is broken as the naive surrogate becomes the culpable party. It is quickly understood that outsiders, especially those from wealthy countries, also have the means to grant power and provide funds or other favours. Recall again the example of British Army First Lieutenant Ross Kennedy and the Iraqi translator deliberately mistranslating to try to obtain funding for school supplies.

There's obviously more to managing information than simply getting more of it. The wise authority will keep an eye out for damaging lies, destructive use of biases and truths wielded to harm in today's world of pervasive attempts to spread misinformation or disinformation. Despite Pope Clement VI's papal bulls noting that Jews were also dying and thus were unlikely to be responsible for Europe's bubonic plague in 1349, Jewish communities suffered obliteration in Cologne, Frankfurt and Mainz. We remember from the pages above that Tokyo's residents attacked Koreans they blamed for the 1923 earthquake that so devastated Japan's capital. Sometimes second or higher-order effects lend credence

---

29 Sennett, *Building and Dwelling*, 173.

to conspiracy theorists looking to believe what they want to believe no matter its viability. Sometimes officials undermine their own credibility. Haitians rioted after cholera bloomed in Port-au-Prince after the 2009 earthquake, blaming the United Nations contingent from Nepal for the outbreak. It was an accusation vehemently denied. Unfortunately, for the United Nations' reputation, revelations years later proved it to be true.[30]

Crime and control

> If he has a drug problem at home, he has a drug problem in the refugee center. If he was a spouse abuser at home, he will be a spouse abuser in the refugee center.[31]
>
> —Commander (ret.) Sid Heal, Los Angeles County Sheriff's Office

> The size of urban populations and the scale of needs in urban disasters limit the contribution that any single actor can make.[32]
>
> —D. Sanderson et al., *Responding to urban disasters*

Perhaps the most well-known policing initiative in the latter half of the twentieth century was New York City's zero tolerance 'broken windows' approach to the crime that had for decades plagued America's largest city. Seemingly small stuff previously thought too petty to consume police time became a focus: graffiti, jumping over subway toll barriers to avoid paying—these were given attention, along with former foci like robberies and other forms of 'bigger' lawbreaking. Crime dropped; New York today is far less a feared environment than during those earlier decades.[33] Fast forward to 2003 in Iraq's urban areas where looting went unchecked due to a lack of sufficient coalition numbers. Very different situation, very different consequences. Yet, one is left wondering how the months and years following the allied invasion of Iraq might have gone differently had law and order been a priority from the moment forces crossed the line of departure.

---

30 Kolbert, 'The spread', 61.
31 Quoted in Glenn et al., *Achieving Convergence during Humanitarian Assistance and Disaster Relief Operations*.
32 Sanderson et al., *Responding to urban disasters*.
33 Sharkey, *Uneasy Peace*, 153.

We touched on alternative approaches. Making it clear to Iraqi police in those urban areas that those staying on the job would be retained and paid might have made a difference. Doing the same with Saddam's military units would have been a greater risk but perhaps one worth taking on a case-by-case basis. (Allied forces in parts of Asia relied on surrendered Japanese Army soldiers to [ironically] keep the peace in the immediate aftermath of World War II until conditions permitted the victors to assume those duties.) Once Saddam's forces were thoroughly beaten, combat units did turn their attention to bypassed cities. By then, unfortunately, much of the looting that stripped property and undermined coalition legitimacy had already set recovery back months, if not years.

There is also the argument that coalition leaders could not have known that looting would be a problem. That explanation does not survive scrutiny, however. The US Army went into Panama less than 14 years earlier, in late 1989, to oust the corrupt president Manuel Noriega. As then battalion commander Lieutenant Colonel Johnny Brooks recalled:

> We authorized the shooting of anyone who had a weapon. A tremendous number of the looters had weapons as they conducted their thievery. Our shooting of the armed ones opened the eyes of the others to the point that it halted the looting ... We were able to control the looting in that one case simply by following our ROE [rules of engagement].[34]

Urban areas in both Panama and Iraq suffered combat damage, but the former rarely suffered the denuding of buildings that occurred in the later operation—damage that set back the recovery of communities and entire cities due to the destruction of those vital property records in addition to other resources. For any who might think 'it can't happen here', reconsider. Douglas Brinkley wrote of New Orleans in the days immediately after Hurricane Katrina's landfall: 'The robberies and marauding were paralyzing the progress, such as it was, of recovery ... Buses that straggled into the city drew anarchist gunfire. In response, bus drivers took evasive action: they just returned home.'[35]

---

34 Johnny W. Brooks, Personal communication, Subject: Looters in Panama, 13 September 2004.
35 Brinkley, *The Great Deluge*, 489, 508. Though some debate the existence of snipers and gunfire in the days after Katrina's passage, the number of sources citing the criminality considerably outnumbers the doubters.

Among the solutions: establish on-the-spot courts and temporary detention facilities if the number of miscreants exceeds the available jail space. Swift, appropriately restrained reaction convinces good and bad alike that a legitimate sheriff is in town. That will prove true both at home and abroad. It is worth mentioning in passing: the sheriff needs to ensure their own forces are on the right side of the law. A World War II manual warned against looting by US troops from the purely pragmatic viewpoint that it 'detracts from alertness, slows initiatives, and may seriously interfere with the progress of the attack'[36] (ignoring how it could impact the perspectives of the occupied population). Nor is it only military forces whose feet need be held to the fire of justice. At least one member of a New York City–based group supporting medical efforts during 2016–17 fighting in Mosul, Iraq, took to Facebook to blatantly show off the jewellery she had appropriated from a resident's home.

Dr Aaron Epstein's experiences during his organisation's provision of medical support to those wounded or otherwise injured during that period of fighting make clear the importance of vetting less well-established NGOs and similar groups:

> Within our organization, we have about 1000 medical personnel. About 200 are physicians, 800 are nurses and the like, but we also have people who were coordinating with DoD [US Department of Defense] reps or the intelligence community to determine where to go. Our group was kind of [angered] because they saw these adventurists, war tourists for lack of a better term, dressed up like special ops guys who threw on the Red Cross badge and were putting chest tubes in though they never had done it before … Some were doing CPR [cardiopulmonary resuscitation] just for the sake of doing CPR for a camera crew. There was a case of someone pulling off a chest bandage for the camera, which would have caused the lung to collapse. There are times when no medicine is better than bad medicine as it is just extending a painful death. That's unethical … There are groups who live off these donations. The unfortunate reality is that upwards of 60–70% of participation is just all-out fraud. That's why [our organisation] has 100% volunteers and no one is making a living off it … I know there were some that were trying to pose as DoD or part of coalition forces … Vetting was absolutely inadequate and bordered on criminal negligence … If it's an area where DoD

---

36 *Attack on a Fortified Position and Combat in Towns*, 66.

isn't there, then the UN should establish a minimum standard ... That way if the military has to hand off a patient to someone, they know that the patient will be getting the care they should.[37]

Dr Epstein was not alone in his observations. Journalist James Verini recalled:

> [T]here were the American volunteer medics, the most flagrant of whom belonged to a group that was led by a wiry, loquacious middle-aged man who said he was a former Special Forces officer and Ranger. He inserted himself into various conflicts around the world, often dragging along his wife and children, and insisted on saying prayers for you at every opportunity whether you wanted him to or not ... He also said prayers over the corpses of Islamic State fighters, some of which he claimed to have shot himself. Unlike the other volunteer medics, his group all carried rifles, and it was clear from their behavior they had only the barest interest in doing medical work. They were there because they wanted to kill jihadis, though, aside from the leader, none of them appeared to know their way around their weapons. He told me ... he had no formal medical training.[38]

Dr Epstein offered his thoughts on ways to improve the provision of goods and services to needy members of urban populations, including the desirability of expanding the responsibilities of NGOs willing to orchestrate the efforts of others when that capability is otherwise absent. Additional functions would include pre-event planning, running exercises to improve the coordinators' understanding of participating groups, organising participants both before and during operations into primary and backup roles and vetting NGOs. These coordinating (or, ideally, orchestrating) organisations would also be the primary points of contact for military forces rendering aid, local governments trying to manage relief providers and—conceivably—media representatives, to avoid the last's sometimes unhelpful influence when it comes to allocating aid. NGO InterAction's Jennifer L. McAvoy astutely noted that while military, other government or intergovernmental organisations often expect NGO representatives to participate in pre-deployment exercises, they too seldom involve those NGOs during the *design* of these events, meaning their participation can be superficial or ad hoc as the complexity of their support is never properly integrated. McAvoy went on

37   Dr Aaron Epstein, Telephone interview with Dr Russell W. Glenn, 25 September 2019.
38   Verini, *They Will Have to Die Now*, 188.

to observe that ongoing relationships rather than ones based exclusively on occasional exercise participation would further enrich understanding and effectiveness. Further, she noted that inefficiencies during operations in and around Mosul were sometimes due to NGOs not knowing what questions to ask because of their unfamiliarity with combat operations generally and urban undertakings specifically. Chances are good that military and other governmental representatives are similarly ignorant when it comes to asking questions about NGOs' and other potential partners' capabilities.[39] (Readers who conduct such exercises might argue that security classifications impede greater coordination with NGOs, IGOs and other organisations during training. McAvoy legitimately asked why hosts could not design exercises that did not require security clearances. Having participated in innumerable such events, I have found the benefits of including classified material generally pale in comparison with those gained by 'uncleared' partners' full integration.)

The steps taken to promote stability and the rule of law on the ground in megacities can include what Peter Ford described as 'soft checks'. At a 2019 conference, he drew on his experiences as a senior US representative to Rio de Janeiro assisting Brazilian authorities with security during the 2016 Summer Olympic Games. These soft checks 'provided layered security for Rio's transportation system. As every rider was required to have a subway ticket, security personnel posted themselves at key points in the system to ensure multiple checks prior to individuals embarking on trains.'[40] Speaking at the same conference, Lieutenant General Ryuji Takemoto of the Japan Ground Self-Defense Force observed that improved technologies can effectively complement these human checks. Used appropriately, near-ubiquitous security or traffic cameras (at least in some urban areas) and voice and image recognition have demonstrated their potential both during day-to-day policing and in times of heightened concern. Enhanced in years to come by AI, these and other technologies should further assist in improving the responsiveness of humanitarian assistance as well as maintaining law and order after a megacity suffers misfortune.

Good judgement properly balanced with restraint will be key to guaranteeing law and order and protecting citizens' rights. The person on the street wants to be treated with the respect and courtesy that should

39   Jennifer L. McAvoy, Telephone interview with Dr Russell W. Glenn, 4 February 2021.
40   Glenn et al., *Achieving Convergence during Humanitarian Assistance and Disaster Relief Operations*.

be forthcoming for any who have not demonstrated they have sacrificed that right. Such is true during times of crisis no less than otherwise. Mark Twain's pen could gently damn officials who, admittedly in far different times, subjected him and his travelling companions to a seemingly unnecessary procedure during an 1867 visit to Europe. After a lunch at Como on the Italian lake of the same name, the group took a ferry to the town of Bellaggio, where police:

> put us into a little stone cell and presently a smoke rose about our feet—a smoke that smelled of all the dead things of earth … We were there five minutes … They fumigated us to guard themselves against the cholera, though we hailed from no infected port.[41]

It couldn't happen here, readers might again think. Sid Heal, formerly with the Los Angeles County Sheriff's Department, recalled a recent case that proves otherwise—this one due to an arguably overly cautious Los Angeles public official:

> Receipt of a letter containing a powdery substance and accompanying threatening letter had resulted in the evacuation of about 400 business and clerical workers from the targeted office building. As the situation unfolded, my partner became convinced that this was another hoax. Weaponized anthrax is tan in color; that in the envelope was white. Likewise, weaponizing anthrax requires a highly sophisticated process usually requiring an advanced education in chemistry, biology, or related subjects. The threatening letter, however, had numerous misspellings; it also identified anthrax as a virus rather than a bacterium, something that is almost inconceivable to anyone with the knowledge needed to perform the weaponization process. We continued acting as if the threat was real even as my partner sought to convince the incident commander that the threat was a hoax. Unconvinced, the incident commander opted to decontaminate all the people being detained.

> The decontamination process was not a pleasant one. We were using 'Kwell lotion' (Lindane), which is sprayed on the naked bodies of inmates to kill lice, crabs, mites, and other parasites. It is often cold and has the viscosity and appearance of mucus. Trusting in our professionalism, these people suffered the indignity of taking their clothes off to be sprayed with this messy substance. They were then wrapped in blankets and filmed by the media as

---

41 Twain, *The Innocents Abroad*, 127.

they were released. After discovering that the incident was a hoax and that the authorities could have recognized this prior to the decontamination procedure, those suffering the decontamination were upset despite the explanation that the incident commander was erring on the side of their safety. The implications of the resultant lack of trust are not trivial. How much public cooperation do you think we can expect during future events? What if the next incident involves an actual threat and people refuse to cooperate because they believe we previously violated their trust? If you carry that to the logical conclusion, we could very well end up having to use force on victims![42]

Mission command during megacity disasters

One of the toughest lessons the US military learned from Operation Tomodachi [to support Japan during the Fukushima Daiichi disaster] is that it sometimes has to fight its natural inclination to take charge.[43]

—Wyatt Olson, 'After 2011 Japan earthquake, US military learned to play supporting role in disaster relief'

The city had reached the bottom of its existence, and it continued to survive only by virtue of its inhabitants' commitment to making it so.[44]

—Aaron William Moore, *Bombing the City*

Orchestrating the efforts of a megacity police force, its city engineers, fire department, health officials and a military force lending assistance during a crisis response is hard enough. Add the variety of other governmental, nongovernmental, intergovernmental, faith-based, private commercial and whatever other groups will more or less join forces during a disaster— many of which are appearing on the scene for the first time and are therefore completely unfamiliar with the terrain or its population—and it's easy to see why some give up trying to orchestrate a comprehensive approach involving the activities of all relevant parties. Though there will be missteps, guidance *within* law enforcement departments, military

---

42   Quoted in Glenn et al., *Achieving Convergence during Humanitarian Assistance and Disaster Relief Operations.*
43   Wyatt Olson, 'After 2011 Japan earthquake, US military learned to play supporting role in disaster relief', *Stars and Stripes*, [Washington, DC], 8 March 2016, available from: www.stripes.com/news/after-2011-japan-earthquake-us-military-learned-to-play-supporting-role-in-disaster-relief-1.396953 [page discontinued].
44   Moore, *Bombing the City*, 144.

and other organisations will generally be consistent. Members of each will be marching to the same drummer even if the drummer for a given group has its own beat. Not so across organisations as their numbers grow. Priorities will differ, as will willingness to work with other groups seen as funding competitors.

We have noted that the chokepoints on which these many organisations rely (airports, seaports and border crossings, for example) and the resources they require to operate (mobile phone bandwidth, electricity and access to buildings, vehicles, water and food) will be constant sources of competition. For an example, one need only look at the behaviour of the US Trump administration in barring the American 3M company from providing protective masks to other than US customers in early April 2020 (which included denying delivery of masks already paid for by habitual US allies and partners).[45] Organisations used to being in charge—the US military primary among them—will find their oversight unappreciated or outright rejected, as did the commanding general of the 101st Airborne Division in West Africa during the 2014 Ebola crisis. There can be benefits to granting a leadership role to that sometimes bull in a china shop that is the armed forces. US military tours tend to be longer than those of many of its interagency and international military partners; they thus provide continuity that is valued despite occasional perceptions of heavy-handedness.[46] In other instances, there may be good reason for the soldier to take a back seat. Others more familiar with the conditions at hand (as in West Africa) or whose skills dominate may be the logical choice to assume the mantle of leadership while the military's is more appropriately a supporting role. This was pointedly recognised by the US Army's Center for Army Lessons Learned as it looked back on that Ebola contingency:

> Being subordinate to a civilian agency while maintaining the freedom to insert ideas and suggestions in a multiagency/ multinational planning, operational, and execution process is an art. This is an art US Army leadership declines to practice sufficiently (if at all).[47]

---

45   Jeanne Whalen, Loveday Morris, Tom Hamburger and Terrence McCoy, 'White House scrambles to scoop up medical supplies worldwide, angering Canada, Germany', *The Washington Post*, 4 April 2020, available from: www.washingtonpost.com/business/2020/04/03/white-house-scrambles-scoop-up-medical-supplies-angering-canada-germany/.

46   CALL, 'Operation United Assistance', 37.

47   ibid.

Not assuming the leadership role may mean military leaders find themselves in unfamiliar territory. Soldiers favour unity of command— a condition in which everyone falls under the jurisdiction of a single commander. When not in charge, the military's leaders and led may have to settle for being part of a less hierarchical but frequently more widely acceptable relationship known as unity of effort in which the various parties agree to work towards a somewhat common set of objectives. It is a situation best described as competitive cooperation, where some will be more competitive even as others give precedence to cooperation.

Smaller organisations may find it feasible to exercise centralised management of their assets, including personnel. Teams may be so small that the boss is virtually always present onsite. Larger ones are more likely to benefit from mission command and its reliance on the good judgement of members strewn over a megacity's landscapes and socialscapes. Their judgement will hopefully be guided by clearly stated and well-understood direction that covers the expected challenges but is broad and flexible enough to account for the ever-present threat of ambush by the play of chance. Putting the right person in charge will be key. Once again, we draw on former Los Angeles County Sheriff's Department commander Sid Heal's 30-plus years of experience. Heal recommends turning to the most qualified individual for leadership rather than defaulting to whomever happens to be on duty when the request for assistance arrives. We recall that the individual best able to communicate with the person on a megacity street is frequently not in charge. The same applies here. Leadership called for in a given situation can demand talents different to the experiences and demonstrated skills that saw a senior leader promoted in the past.[48]

Making sure plans and decision-making include the flexibility necessary to deal with megacity complexity has the added benefit of opening the door to resources that might have previously gone unrecognised. New York City's response to Hurricane Sandy's destruction took advantage of its coastal location. Both the US Navy and the Coast Guard rendered assistance. The latter's medium-endurance cutter *Spencer* stepped (floated?) forward to serve as headquarters for orchestrating the two organisations' efforts.[49] Coalition members in Iraq came up with the idea of using concrete barriers to wall off those parts of the city suffering ethnic-

48   Glenn et al., *Achieving Convergence during Humanitarian Assistance and Disaster Relief Operations*.
49   Bucci et al., *After Hurricane Sandy*.

cleansing by religious extremists. We have already highlighted the benefits of employing a thermostat approach to controlling troublesome megacity districts, neighbourhoods or even specific buildings by influencing access to vital resources such as power, water or communications.[50] Access can be a reward for cooperation when such resources are limited. Colonel David Perkins agreeing to stop patrols in Fallujah was the flipside of that coin; local leaders saw not having his heavy vehicles rumble through the city's night-time streets as a reward for their control of violence.

Redundancy is another advantage of mission command savvy. The events of 9/11 and combat operations highlight the exposure to risk suffered by police, fire, military and other leaders in key positions. Well-informed subordinates supported by good planning mean the disruption caused by loss of leaders is kept to a minimum. The 1/5 Marine Battalion's experiences in Hue during the Tet Offensive provide an example. Its C Company lost two of its three platoon commanders. The A Company's commander, executive officer and many of those in the remaining company headquarters were likewise casualties.[51] Both units continued to fight effectively despite the potentially crippling losses thanks to subordinates familiar with their mission and higher-level expectations. Firefighters and police rendering assistance during 9/11 did likewise even as their leaders died during an unprecedented emergency. Equipped with effective training and guidance, subordinates didn't allow chaos to escape its cage.

Exercises and rehearsals are key to ensuring subordinates understand guidance. Including experts in these sessions reveals what otherwise seems obvious only in retrospect. While such events would ideally cover all relevant questions pre-disaster, conducting follow-on exercises and rehearsals once conditions on the ground are known can better inform decision-making. Where, for example, should organisations locate camps for residents displaced by a catastrophe? On the edge of the affected megacity might seem the obvious choice. Expert insight suggests otherwise, as such 'camps can increase displacement and population movement as surrounding populations move in to take advantage of

---

50   Townsend, *Smart Cities*, 300.
51   Russell W. Glenn, Sidney W. Atkinson, Michael Barbero, Frederick J. Gellert, Scott Gerwehr, Steven Hartman, Jamison Jo Medby, Andrew O'Donnell, David Owen and Suzanne Pieklik, *Ready for Armageddon: Proceedings of the 2001 RAND Arroyo–Joint ACTD-CETO-USMC Nonlethal and Urban Operations Program Urban Operations Conference*, Santa Monica, CA: RAND Corporation, 2002, 63, available from: www.rand.org/pubs/conf_proceedings/CF179.html.

camp services. Alternatively, they can lead to tensions with surrounding populations.' Instead, 'temporary camps should be established as close as possible to neighbourhoods of origin', thereby maintaining community ties, encouraging local recovery and, presumably, easing the quick return of residents to their homes once the immediate crisis passes.[52]

Previous exceptional events offer lessons to those prepared by exercises and rehearsals. Dan Mahoney, a 31-year veteran with the San Francisco Police Department and later a member of the Northern California Regional Intelligence Center, explained how the Bay Area took steps to ensure emergency responders would be able to communicate if a crisis occurred during one of the world's premier sports events:

> The Super Bowl was a nine-day event, not a three-hour game. You had a couple hundred thousand people in a four-block area. Next time you go to a sellout baseball game, tell me how well your cellphone works, because all those cellphones eat up the bandwidth. So police can't talk to fire, etc. because all the bandwidth is eaten up. Technology is not able to keep up with it. So we got cells on wheels (COWS) and cells on light trucks (COLTS). We were thus able to park trailers around the event to grow the bandwidth so that law enforcement/public safety had comms.[53]

The second quotation opening this section again reminds us of the importance of the megacity resident in a catastrophe. Their eyes are allies when it comes to preventing the bad from becoming worse. Experienced organisations know their chances of receiving public support are better if there is a connection between citizen and outsider. The military's default approach when it comes to dividing up responsibilities for an urban area is to do it by organisation. In a coalition with members from multiple countries, that means Americans get some neighbourhoods, Canadians others, and so on. Lieutenant Colonel John Frewen took another tack as commander of the military contingent that went into Solomon Islands' capital of Honiara in 2003. Australia, New Zealand, Papua New Guinea, Tonga and Fiji all sent units to help restore stability in the troubled city. Rather than defaulting to the simplest option of assigning sectors according to national contingent, Frewen wisely chose to create multinational units in which soldiers from the last three countries joined

---

52 Sanderson et al., *Responding to urban disasters*.
53 Dan Mahoney (Northern California Regional Intelligence Center), Interview with Dr Russell W. Glenn, San Francisco, CA, 12 April 2016.

units from Australia and New Zealand. This meant each patrol had one or more representatives from the smaller nations' armed forces—soldiers whose culture was more akin to Solomon Islanders' than was that of those from the bigger countries. Improved citizen communications and greater willingness to share information were the result—an example of the senior-most member of an organisation recognising that he and other leaders might not be the ones best at bonding with locals.

Informing urban residents how they can assist relief providers helps reveal a city's secrets. Locals know the location of vehicles that might be rented or borrowed, where supplies might be purchased, who possesses the keys to local services such as medical care, policing and firefighting, which leaders can aid in getting word to communities or providing critical expertise and much else. Volunteers or local security forces can be valuable in augmenting relief efforts once trained, equipped and supervised, which goes far towards explaining why cities like Tokyo do so much to educate residents prior to crises. The previous example of hiring locals to provide NGO security in Somalia provides a red flag, however. Care must be taken to ensure the legitimate use of violence remains under the control of proper authorities:

> Community-oriented policing should not be confused with vigilantism. Although widely practiced in the slums of many parts of the world, including in Latin America, and although frequently accepted as legitimate by some local populations and tolerated or even encouraged by official police forces, such community militias and 'watch groups' often are the source of much indiscriminate violence, extrajudicial killings, ethnic cleansing, looting, and other forms of crime. They rarely truly reduce crime—often merely replacing one form of criminality with another—while they further undermine the rule of law and sever the bonds between citizens and the state.[54]

---

54 Felbab-Brown, *Bringing the State to the Slum*, 16.

The comprehensive approach during a megacity disaster

The more Moslawis were killed, the more they resented the soldiers, and the more soldiers were killed, the more they resented the Moslawis.[55]

Anne Barnard, 'How a caliphate ends'

[Regarding] the unprecedented terrorist attack that France experienced in 2015 … After decades that had seen war kept at bay, our population has once again become a target in need of protection. But our population might also be the best weapon to oppose the enemy … Material strength is not enough. The moral strength of the nation has an important role to play.[56]

—Jean-Yves Le Drian, *Who Is the Enemy?*

Both blast and sound rolled through the crowd as the first explosion shredded the innocent at Paris's Stade de France. The thunder of three more explosions roiled the air within 50 minutes, each targeting a popular restaurant or public event packed on that Friday night. Reports of the detonations reached the Assistance Publique–Hôpitaux de Paris (APHP), Europe's largest hospital trust, as information told of four further locations where people had been shot. One, the Bataclan concert hall, where a rock band had been playing, was still under siege. Ultimately, 130 people would die across the megacity of 11 million. Hundreds more were wounded, many severely. APHP's director-general quickly activated the 20-year-old but never used 'White Plan' to respond to the 13 November 2015 terrorist attacks. Forty hospitals mobilised. Directors recalled staff to duty. Personnel prepared beds for the surge of incoming wounded so that emergency rooms could be quickly cleared of patients after surgery. The sky above France's capital reverberated as the blades of 10 helicopters thundered overhead, crisscrossing the city, with air evacuation complementing the mass ground movement of the wounded. Additional 'reservoirs' of medical capacity—Paris hospitals not yet receiving patients and university facilities outside the city proper—stood by should the maimed exceed the capacity of the initial 40 facilities.

---

55   Anne Barnard, 'How a caliphate ends: On the frontline of the fight against ISIS', *Foreign Affairs* 98(6) (November–December 2019), available from: www.foreignaffairs.com/reviews/review-essay/2019-10-15/how-caliphate-ends.
56   Le Drian, *Who Is the Enemy?*, 64, 65.

Timely activation 'had a critical effect'.[57] Having the White Plan on the shelf proved key. So, too, did the experience of medical personnel who had treated victims after the attack on the offices of *Charlie Hebdo* magazine the previous January. While helicopters, ambulances and other transport raced the bleeding to hospitals, physicians, nurses and drivers in 45 mobile units sped in the opposite direction to triage patients on the spot and dispatch them to the most appropriate of the 40 waiting facilities. Another 15 teams waited in reserve should there have been additional attacks. Even those inexperienced in terms of previous mass-casualty events were prepared thanks to training in gunshot wound treatment and participation in three recent field exercises focusing on treatment 'in the field'—that is, before wounded reached hospitals. Those preparations had drawn on studies of earlier attacks in Israel, Boston, Spain and the United Kingdom. If a hospital lacked the capacity or expertise needed, authorities transferred victims to other medical facilities. Innovation and decisiveness by doctors, nurses and medical technicians, their hands covered by victims' blood, were commonplace. Patients showed up at hospitals with belts tightened around shredded limbs: mobile medical teams had turned to the expedient when they ran short of tourniquets.

The formal plans, rehearsals, other exercises and initiative meant chaos lapped at the ankles of responders but never overwhelmed. Paris's wounded benefited further from off-duty medical personnel rushing to hospitals without being asked and the good fortune of no second or third bomb attacks deliberately targeting responders.[58] Paris also had an advantage common to all megacities: concentration of the best and brightest minds, large numbers of talented people and the most advanced technologies.

---

57   This paragraph draws on Martin Hirsch, Pierre Carli, Rémy Nizard, Bruno Riou, Barouyr Baroudjian, Thierry Baubet, Vibol Chhor, Charlotte Chollet-Xemard, Nicolas Dantchev, Nadia Fleury, Jean-Paul Fontaine, Youri Yordanov, Maurice Raphael, Catherine Paugam Burtz and Antoine Lafont, 'The medical response to multisite terrorist attacks in Paris', *The Lancet* 386(10012) (19 December 2015): 2535–38, doi.org/10.1016/S0140-6736(15)01063-6; and 'Paris attacks: What happened on the night', *BBC News*, 9 December 2015, available from: www.bbc.com/news/world-europe-34818994.

58   Commendable perhaps, but as our example of 9/11 showed, there are risks incurred when those in off-duty status or others with responsibilities elsewhere rush to the site of a major emergency, no matter how well intentioned. Plans and rehearsals should include guidance on how all members—on duty and the disaster occurs in their jurisdiction, off duty or on duty but their responsibilities are remote from the crisis site—should respond. The example of the APHP in Paris with its standby facilities and medical teams is a worthy one.

Not all cities are Paris. An NGO, IGO or other relief organisation deploying to a post-disaster megacity might know where to find water supplies. What might be less obvious is whether that water is potable. Beijing's chemical pollution has rendered 40 per cent of its water unsuitable for consumption; Shanghai is worse off yet, with 56 per cent unusable.[59] Yet, it is no coincidence that the doctor treating Patrick Sawyer after he collapsed in Lagos's airport had both the medical expertise to see through Sawyer's lies regarding exposure to Ebola and the strength of character to resist diplomatic pressure to release him. Tax, health, demographic and other records helpful to planning and reacting to calamities will tend to be better in a nation's dominant urban area. It is there that a country and a region's various demographics come together. That means any outsiders should be able to find significant numbers willing to provide information even as others might find the new arrivals less popular. Knowing who has what talents, which resources exist and where, which dangers lurk—such as a general dearth of drinkable water—and how those dangers can be overcome will be as important to success as knowing the opposition is to winning a football game (regardless of the ball's shape). San Francisco's Dan Mahoney, quoted above regarding the Bay Area's Super Bowl preparations, went on to say that knowing the players before a disaster means a handshake or a promise made at the other end of a phonecall will suffice when under other circumstances there might be a demand for time-consuming negotiations and a contract.

Mission command can do much to promote the success of not only individual organisations but also coalitions and partnerships. It is impossible to overstate the importance of trust in achieving these successes, but trust does not exist on first acquaintance. Those TEWG meetings and continuity of leadership in participating organisations mean the cop knows the soldier and the fire chief has convinced NGOs he'll be there when they call. While lengthy commitments to assist at international destinations obviously require rotating personnel, unnecessarily switching people or permitting 'tourist tours' so personnel can punch the 'been there, done that' ticket disrupts established relationships and the trust built. Maintaining crucial associations merits more consideration than is sometimes the case when deciding how long people will stay in high-risk or otherwise unpleasant locations. Trust will also have to survive the

---

59   Rahm Emanuel, *The Nation City: Why Mayors are Now Running the World*, New York, NY: Alfred A. Knopf, 2020, 226.

inevitable differences in operational approaches taken by organisations. Not all will agree with the policies proposed in these cooperative ventures. Frewen was justifiably concerned that the sudden influx of 2,000 members of RAMSI would seriously disrupt the capital's—and, by extension—the country's economy. He therefore prohibited his soldiers from spending money in downtown Honiara during the earliest weeks of the deployment and later only gradually loosened that restriction. Not all other RAMSI partners adopted Frewen's policy, but as his soldiers represented 1,800 of the mission's 2,000 personnel, keeping their money in their pockets had the desired effect of holding at bay the potential negative economic effects that could have been inflicted by the new arrivals.

Disaster social messaging and the comprehensive approach

> People want to help in a crisis and the currency is not dollars; it's information. We believe that there can and should be a social media layer of data and we're eager to incorporate those data for our own fact checking. Every citizen is a communicator or contributor and we will benefit greatly from those initiatives.[60]
>
> —American Red Cross, *The case for integrating crisis response with social media*

> It is important to communicate with the population in non-military speak. Likewise, it is better to encourage than to order.[61]
>
> —Brigadier Ian Langford, Australian Army

Both the message and how it is conveyed are critical in efforts to influence popular behaviour. Failing in one renders both ineffective. Liberia's citizens needed something more helpful than its government's message of 'Ebola is real—if you get it, you'll die!', as the disease ravaged West Africa in 2014. A more effective message would have been, 'Ebola is real, but if you seek treatment, you have a 50 per cent chance of recovery'. It turned out the Liberian tune 'Ebola in Town', with the catchy line 'Don't touch your friend/I say it will kill you!', had the right mix of message and method for its audience. Marketing during a crisis is just as necessary for public information campaigns as it is when selling cars, insurance or soft drinks.

---

60 American Red Cross, *The case for integrating crisis response with social media*.
61 Ian Langford [Brigadier, Australian Army], 'Mission command during megacity HADR operations', Presentation to Current and Future Operations in Megacities Conference, Tokyo, 16 July 2019.

The United Nations Children's Fund (UNICEF) incorporated Ebola issues into an American-style radio soap opera to help Sierra Leonean survivors cope.[62]

Social media played a different but similarly beneficial role as China's first Covid-19 hotspot of Wuhan (population 11 million-plus) struggled with the virus. Domestic NGOs included not only the well-established Blue Sky Rescue Team but also new organisations created and mobilised thanks to social media coordination. Services provided included delivery of medical supplies and disinfecting of public spaces.[63]

It's clear that getting a message out effectively is something of an artform— a challenge made all the harder when the artist must deal with power interruptions, an unfamiliar culture and seemingly illogical behaviour. Recall how Miami's and other Florida beaches were packed with spring-breakers in March 2020 while authorities (other than the governor of the state, unfortunately) called for social distancing to hinder the spread of Covid-19. Eight months later, millions more ignored expert advice to stay home for Thanksgiving even as the United States set daily records for new cases and deaths. Parents refused to evacuate their children during the worst of the bombing in Tokyo and London during World War II despite programs offering to take the young to safer locations until the danger passed.[64] Messages must also reach the right audiences. A survey used by Tokyo authorities to gauge residents' reactions after a major earthquake found college and high school students tended to hunker down on campus. Those in their parents' age group were more prone to try to reach relatives who might need assistance. The survey also found that the messages effective with women might be less so for men (ya think?). Further, the latter are more likely to try to get home during a crisis, especially when the fate of families is unknown. This was especially true for men aged in their forties even when obstacles included intimidating distances, walking as the only option, the possibility of raging fires along the route, streets packed with emergency equipment and the fact that recognising even one's own neighbourhood much less unfamiliar ones along the route can be difficult when destruction is sufficiently severe.[65]

62   Sarah Stillman, 'Ebola and the culture makers', *The New Yorker*, 11 November 2014, available from: www.newyorker.com/news/daily-comment/ebola-culture-makers.
63   'Who you gonna call? Civil society', *The Economist*, [London], 11 July 2020), 32–33, at 32.
64   Moore, *Bombing the City*, 30.
65   Toshihiro Osaragi, 'Modeling a spatiotemporal distribution of stranded people returning home on foot in the aftermath of a large-scale earthquake', *Natural Hazards* 68 (2013): 1385–98, at 1385, 1389, 1396, 1397.

Knowing how to tailor messages to specific audiences in terms of understanding which groups are likely to behave in what manner, how those groups receive information (for example, via television, radio, one or more social media apps, word of mouth?) and 'talking the right talk' is a start. Brigadier Langford's caution to avoid military-speak gets at the heart of it, though interestingly his additional observation that 'it is better to encourage than to order' is—depending on the audience— sometimes more effective in the breach. The Danish Government, knowing its citizens prided themselves on being 'the anarchists of the Nordic countries', bypassed the sensitive approach for an in-your-face one as the coronavirus ravaged parts of Europe in early 2020. While Sweden's government encouraged with gentle messaging such as 'Ahead of the breaks and Easter, it is important to consider whether planned travel in Sweden is necessary', Danish authorities opted for 'Cancel Easter lunch' and 'Postpone family visits'.[66] Airline, fire and other personnel know that nice guys (and gals) let people die. Author Amanda Ripley, in her *The Unthinkable: Who Survives When Disaster Strikes—and Why*, describes how people will hesitate to jump on to evacuation slides even when their plane is on fire:

> If a flight attendant stood at the exit and screamed at people to jump, the pause all but disappeared … People moved just as slowly for polite and calm flights attendants as they did when there were no flight attendants present.

Ripley goes on to describe how:

> in river rescues, members of the Kansas City Fire Department rescue squad yell profanity-laced threats at victims before they get to them. If they don't, the victim will grab on to them and push them under the water in a mad scramble to stay afloat.[67]

Being aware of cultural differences isn't a need limited to those deploying to another country or into communities with unfamiliar religious, ethnic or other characteristics. My flippant 'ya think?' above emphasises the seemingly but obviously not obvious if one looks at recent historical examples in which women's perspectives are ignored. Two men speaking at a 2019 megacities security conference—both with extensive experience

---

66 'Corona-speak', *The Economist*, [London], 4 April 2020, 70.
67 Amanda Ripley, *The Unthinkable: Who Survives When Disaster Strikes—and Why*, New York, NY: Crown, 2008, 132, 133.

in dealing with disasters—emphasised the indispensability of including women's insights in the design and running of displaced persons' camps, urban shelters and similar facilities, which is an indispensability often overlooked.[68] Another cultural norm: advice is more likely to be accepted when recipients believe the sender is an expert—the inexplicable behaviour of some ignoring expert guidance on Covid-19 notwithstanding. Social pressure also has its place. The charity BRAC sought to get 5 million of Bangladesh's citizens to support its building of toilets where their absence posed health risks. Being considered as expert helped to get poorer segments of the population to accept the need. Getting resistance from some, BRAC built many latrines for the poor, then shamed wealthier holdouts into following their lead.[69]

Communications allow disaster response managers to orchestrate their instruments. Some emergency responders will be unable to reach their places of work due to disrupted public transportation, destroyed personal vehicles, flooding, debris, fires and many other reasons. And those designated locations will sometimes need their services less than do others elsewhere. Designating second and third alternative reporting locations before an event constitutes good planning. Being able to adjust those designations during the response because conditions render plans no longer applicable reflects the flexibility built into any good plan.

Flexibility of mind to accompany that in plans doubles the value. During the British attack on the Dutch city of Arnhem in World War II, army leaders did not realise the local phone system was functioning. Had they (and had the British brought the Dutch coins needed to operate the equipment, which is no longer a problem thanks to the ubiquitous euro), they could have communicated with those who might have provided much needed support to the ultimately unsuccessful offensive.[70] Nearly 30 years later, in 1983, American military personnel in Grenada during Operation Urgent Fury did realise the island nation's phone system was in working order.[71] A Navy SEAL unable to contact an AC-130 gunship overhead called Fort Bragg, North Carolina, from a telephone booth.

---

68   Comments by Lieutenant General Kobayashi (Japan Ground Self-Defense Force, retired) and Brigadier Langford (Australian Army). See Glenn et al., *Achieving Convergence during Humanitarian Assistance and Disaster Relief Operations*.

69   'Beating the bugs: Sanitation in Bangladesh', *The Economist*, [London], 24 March 2018, 33–34, at 33.

70   Jenkins, 'Some notes on fighting in built-up areas', 32.

71   Mark Adkin, *Urgent Fury: The Battle for Grenada*, London: Leo Cooper, 1989, 221.

He was reportedly patched into the aircraft's radio frequency through which he called down supporting fire that kept an enemy attack from advancing against the governor-general's home where he and others were besieged until US Marines arrived to relieve the exhausted unit.[72]

It pays when the person next to you understands that what you said means the same to them as it does to you. Terminology makes a difference whether talking to other aid providers or members of the population. The British Royal Air Force's Richard William Kelly found that basic terms had different interpretations even when working with fellow members of NATO. The seemingly obvious word 'target' provides an example.[73] Reminiscent of our example from the 1992 Los Angeles riots, for a rifleman, 'target' means something at which to shoot. For a police investigator, it might mean the subject of their investigation. A mayor might speak of a target audience for their public education campaign. British Army Major-General Paul Newton commented on military terms in a way Ian Langford would have appreciated. He noted that 'even the word "campaign" is a military term packed full of implied meaning that others may not get'—including others in the same government that includes the military.[74]

Procedures can be just as foreign to others as language. The United Kingdom's senior political representative in south-east Iraq during the early months of coalition operations found he had fallen down Alice's rabbit-hole when it came to understanding the senior coalition partner's bureaucracy. The United States, as lead nation, dictated that other parties provide spending data so that some idea of who was accomplishing what with how much could be understood. The Americans in Baghdad wanted everyone to follow US accounting practices when reporting. To the savvy Brit Hilary Synnott fell the duty of telling those in the capital that their guidance was a nonstarter. 'I observed that we British unfortunately had no experience of American accounting procedures,' Synnott wrote, 'Hence we were unfamiliar with the various regulations and acronyms … We eventually managed to impress upon Baghdad that we simply could not realistically fulfill US accounting procedures with which our

---

72   Sharon Tosi Lacey, 'How the invasion of Grenada was planned with a tourist map and a copy of "The Economist"', *Military Times*, [Arlington, VA], 26 October 2018, available from: www.militarytimes.com/veterans/military-history/2018/10/25/how-the-invasion-of-grenada-was-planned-with-a-tourist-map-and-a-copy-of-the-economist/.
73   As quoted in Glenn, *Band of Brothers or Dysfunctional Family?*, 55.
74   ibid., 65.

multinational team were completely unfamiliar.'[75] This was hard enough for someone who (sort of) shares a language with the Americans. The short-sightedness of those sitting in Saddam's Baghdad palace must have been more punishing yet when some other coalition member asked to follow the designated procedures did not share English as a first language. A countryman of Synnott, General David Richards, would later look back on the very successful General Gerald Templer and his leadership while heading Malaya's post–World War II counterinsurgency. Speaking on his experiences in Afghanistan, Richards recalled:

> [W]hen General Templer said to his coalition, 'We're all going to focus on that. Turn right. These are my priorities,' the whole institution turned right. When I as a coalition commander said that in Kabul, a large number might say, 'Who are you to tell me anything?'[76]

We've already noted the potential offered by social media apps and the value they can provide in tracking individuals with a disease or identifying those with whom they come into contact, for example. Other instances from the past abound. 'Scraping' social media for general trends (thus, not requiring the association of specific messages with individuals and so avoiding privacy concerns to some extent) has proved effective in early identification of problems. The US National Weather Service's Mt Holly, New Jersey, office reportedly always has at least one of its large computer screens displaying Facebook for just that reason.[77]

Benefits and pitfalls of the comprehensive approach during megacity undertakings

> Médecins Sans Frontières (MSF) did not originally want to work with the US military during Ebola epidemic operations in 2014 West Africa. Fortunately, conditions mandated these parties come together in the service of population welfare and each organization's objectives. The result was recognition of and an appreciation for the benefits of cooperation.[78]

---

75 David Richards (General, British Army), Interview with Russell W. Glenn, Wilton, UK, 2 April 2008. The quote appears in Glenn, *Band of Brothers or Dysfunctional Family?*, 63.
76 As quoted in Glenn, *Band of Brothers or Dysfunctional Family?*, 69.
77 Kathryn Miles, *Super Storm: Nine Days Inside Hurricane Sandy*, New York, NY: Dutton, 2014, 60.
78 Benjamin Espinosa (Commander, US Navy), 'Operation United Assistance: The Department of Defense response to the West African Ebola virus epidemic', Presentation to MDB in Megacities Conference, Fort Hamilton, NY, 4 April 2018.

—Commander Benjamin Espinosa, US Navy, 'Operation United Assistance'

Many Americans had, in the past few years, volunteered to help the militias fighting the jihadis in the rural border regions of Iraq and Syria, and now a few had found their way into Mosul. The volunteers included soldiers of fortune, Evangelical Christians, thrill-seekers, lost souls, even some combat veterans, and very occasionally—the only one of any real use—medics ... A few really knew what they were doing.[79]

—James Verini, *They Will Have to Die Now*

Operations against ISIS in 2016–17 in Mosul, Iraq, make clear how important it is to have a wide range of talents and capabilities during urban operations. As with Manila, Mexico City, Tokyo, New York and any megacity during times of catastrophe, features outside the bounds of the urban area are critical to the welfare of the city itself. North-west of the Iraqi city, Mosul Dam had since 2014 received none of the maintenance necessary to ensure it remained a reliable barrier. The casualties should it fail were estimated at more than 1 million killed in its namesake city downstream.[80] But a greater threat lived among the city's ethnically and religiously diverse residents. ISIS had from the beginning of its occupation shown little concern for the welfare of those who had not fled. It showed even less as time went on, with atrocities including gunning down those who belatedly tried to escape. The insurgents controlled all access and escape routes from December 2016 into February of the next year. Food, medicines and other necessities became scarce. Airdropped and other supplies were first looted by ISIS, thereafter serving as bait when its members fired on residents trying to recover the leftovers. The United Nations considered the humanitarian crisis in Iraq's third most populous city as Level Three—the most catastrophic in their ranking system.

Officials in Baghdad created several committees and assigned them leaders to assist in managing the efforts of Iraqi Security Forces, NGOs, UN representatives and US advisors in Mosul. In an example we will later

---

79 Verini, *They Will Have to Die Now*, 8.
80 Much of the material in this description relies on material from Lise Grande, 'Humanitarian assistance and disaster relief: Lessons from a combat zone', Presentation to Achieving Convergence during Humanitarian Assistance and Disaster Relief Operations in the World's Largest Urban Areas Conference, Tokyo, 18 July 2019; Jesse L. Skates, Interview with Dr Russell W. Glenn, Fort Eustis, VA, 21 January 2020; and Janette L. Kautzman, Managing internally displaced persons (IDP) in an urban fight, Unpublished paper, n.d.

return to in greater detail, UN Resident and Humanitarian Coordinator Lise Grande worked with Government of Iraq representatives and US military civil affairs personnel to minimise redundancy and fill capability gaps as the offensive unfolded. Attacks pulsed: Iraqi Security Forces moved forward, then paused while commanders and staff coordinated with UN High Commissioner for Refugees (UNHCR) leaders who worked with the several organisations building displaced persons camps or providing medical care, seeking to keep both from being overwhelmed by sudden surges. Some NGOs did not hesitate to work with the armed forces. Others did so under the condition the cooperation was not broadcast. Yet others would not work with soldiers but were helpful in separate locations such as the camps. A fourth group was vehement in its refusal to have any restraints that limited freedom of action but offered value nonetheless.

Not so others. James Verini's quote above reinforces earlier observations regarding groups posing as legitimate NGOs that used the cloak of aid provider to engage in combat or otherwise satisfy a thirst for thrill-seeking. The situation in Mosul was made even more complex by Iraq's omnipresent Sunni–Shia and other ethnic divisions. Shia—soldiers and government representatives among them—often suspected that anyone of Sunni persuasion who had remained in Mosul during the years of ISIS occupation had done so voluntarily in sympathy with the invaders. The consequences of this bias were predictable. Then there were Moslawis who refused to wait for security forces to remove IEDs or other explosives once a neighbourhood had been cleared of enemy, forcing Iraqi units to dedicate much needed manpower to preventing these overanxious people from trying to return home and thereby putting themselves at risk— another example of seemingly illogical (and unpredictable) behaviour on the part of urban residents.

Recognising that what one expert, authority or citizen considers significant might seem otherwise to another, Dan Mahoney described how his northern California organisation created a public information program to enlist the expertise of a long list of volunteer addressees. His Northern California Regional Intelligence Center sent out messages twice a week summarising incidents with possible security implications. In Mahoney's words, the messages were valuable for informing:

> everyone who might be involved. The cop doesn't care about malware threatening hospital databases any more than a doctor cares if someone is taking a photo of a bridge. For example, let's

say you are one of the Tsarnaev brothers from Boston who blows his thumb off and goes to the hospital to have it sewn on and says, 'Oh, the rice cooker blew up in my hand.' So now we are trying to have people—ambulance drivers, doctors, etc. [report suspicious activity]. Every station has a terrorism liaison officer, at least one. So if the doctor reports to a local police station, the station knows to go forward.[81]

The goal: that someone on the address list will be suspicious of such an explanation whereas someone else might simply treat the wound and not give a second thought to reporting the incident to the police or the FBI. (Individuals saw the perpetrators of the first attack on New York's World Trade Center in 1993 mixing chemicals and acting suspiciously but failed to report their observations to the authorities.)[82]

During the 1995 chemical attack on Tokyo's subway, it was an off-duty doctor who saw news reports and called the police, telling them sarin was the likely agent involved.[83] It was a case of good luck rather than preparation; the doctor was not part of a group like that of Mahoney's in the San Francisco area. The luck did not hold. No-one forwarded the doctor's message, making clear the need for urban authorities not only to have access to experts who can screen citizen reports but also to make known how to filter and share incoming information. Establishing pre-disaster relationships is a virtually cost-free exercise with potentially huge payoffs. Recent coalition operations in Iraq and Afghanistan provide a good template for forming similar relationships for international contingencies. Major Jesse Skates was serving with the US 101st Airborne Division (Air Assault) during operations in Mosul from 2016 to 2017. Despite successes with what resembled a comprehensive approach involving the UNHCR, NGOs and others, Skates reflected:

> The big thing is to get more experience with NGOs ... There are those that don't want to be associated with the military, but it would be helpful if they trained with us so we could be familiar

81 Mahoney, Interview.

82 Donald N. Van Duyn, 'Testimony by Donald N. Van Duyn, Chief Intelligence Officer, Directorate of Intelligence, National Security Branch, Federal Bureau of Investigation', in *Lessons from the Mumbai Terrorist Attacks: Parts I and II*, Hearings before the Committee on Homeland Security and Governmental Affairs, United States Senate, 111th Congress, 1st Session, 8 and 28 January 2009, Washington, DC: US Government Printing Office, available from: www.govinfo.gov/content/pkg/CHRG-111shrg49484/html/CHRG-111shrg49484.htm.

83 Dustin Harrison (Lieutenant Commander, US Navy), Interview with Dr Russell W. Glenn, Fort Detrick, MD, 30 March 2018.

with each other. Most of our [senior] officers at division level have 32–33 years of experience maneuvering units. Then they get to CAPSTONE and get a two-hour block on these niche capabilities. It's too late.[84]

Cooperation among relevant parties is desirable before a disaster; it should be a minimum condition once disaster strikes. While orchestration is the sought-after mark on the wall, avoiding conflict between participants with varied and potentially incompatible goals means more effective use (and sharing) of resources, consistency of messaging to the affected population and faster recovery. Conflicts and disconnects are inevitable; our previous quote from a Red Cross executive makes it clear that there are legitimate limits to the extent to which some organisations will support requests from the armed forces. Nevertheless, leaders can reduce most obstacles to a level that benefits all parties—including the noncombatant population. Complete noncommunication not only sacrifices these benefits but is also foolhardy, especially if operations find these many organisations in a combat zone. Refusing to inform military forces of where an NGO's personnel will be operating and what route they will take to get there unnecessarily puts those personnel, and those they are helping, at risk. Even as technologies allow extraordinary accuracy of munitions—and similar (if less extraordinary) capabilities to discern the character of a potential target—weather, human error or deliberate malfeasance on the part of parties wanting to cause an incident can all lead to confusion, manipulation and fatal mistakes. Clausewitz may have been writing two centuries ago, but his concepts of friction and the fog of war are as applicable to the twenty-first century as to the nineteenth. Diligence in displaying red crosses on buildings or tents is no assurance of safety when a possible target is distant and rain, dust, fog, smoke or darkness limits visibility. The probability of deadly errors spikes even when the targeting technologies are the best in the world if those providing the fire are supporting less-professional or well-trained armed forces. Now add to some or all these factors the complexity introduced by urban environments such as swirling gusts at intersections, laser reflection off glass or other

---

84   Skates, Interview. CAPSTONE is a course for those promoted to general officer or admiral rank, conducted by the US National Defense University, which describes it as follows: 'The course objective is to make these individuals more effective in planning and employing US forces in joint and combined operations. The CAPSTONE curriculum examines major issues affecting national security decision making, military strategy, joint/combined doctrine, interoperability, and key allied nation issues.' From National Defense University, 'CAPSTONE General and Flag Officer Course', Washington, DC: NDU, n.d., available from: capstone.ndu.edu.

smooth surfaces, lines of sight interrupted by one or more buildings and who knows how many innocents concealed from view. This will be the case even in urban areas that would occupy no more than a pinhead's worth of space in a megacity. That was the case in Calivigny during the 1983 US invasion of Grenada. A soldier passed targeting information to a pilot overhead after spotting enemy fire coming from 'a white house with a red roof on the ridge north of a drive-in movie' theatre, adding the directional bearing from what seemed an easily identifiable landmark. The aircraft made three passes over the target, the ground controller each time confirming when the plane was over the enemy-occupied building. The pilot engaged what he was now sure was the correct structure, firing a stream of 20-millimetre shells into an American command post. Seventeen people were wounded. One would later die.[85] This was an incident involving highly trained and practised military personnel. Taking even the minimum precaution of ensuring those with the capability to inflict harm know of NGO, IGO and other innocents' locations—whether through simply sending a message or coordinating for technologies that identify an organisation's location—adds just that additional datum that could stop a potentially fatal error.

Fratricide has less tragic but nevertheless significant other forms as well. Recall the Western private security contractors poised behind their vehicle-mounted machine-guns, barrels sweeping the crowd, as their small convoy raced past US soldiers conversing with residents of a Baghdad neighbourhood. The fratricide victim that day was the goodwill of those to whom the soldiers had been talking.

Given the importance of community populations, it is surprising that their views are not given more consideration during pre-crisis planning and decision-making when calamity strikes. Several international medical groups working in Democratic Republic of Congo (DRC) provide an example. The organisations understandably sought police escort protection when going into what could be violent neighbourhoods during the 2019 Ebola outbreak. Some citizens were already associating the NGO and the World Health Organization (WHO) with the broadly detested DRC national government. Aligning themselves with similarly unpopular police gave those beliefs further credence despite both groups

---

85   Adkin, *Urgent Fury*, 286.

operating independently of government authorities. As reported in *The Economist*, health organisations working in the vicinity of the country's north-eastern city of Butembo later recognised:

> that they should have done more to involve local people. 'The response started badly,' complains a young motorbike-taxi driver in Katwa, on the edge of Butembo. 'They came here with police escorts to be protected. That wouldn't have been necessary if they had employed people from Katwa to work with them.' Progress has been made … William Perea, the incident manager for the WHO says that some once-hostile villages are now letting his teams in … The key is 'to get as close as possible to the communities.'[86]

The issue of the outsiders being confused with representatives of an unpopular government is one worth remembering. Guilt by association is not uncommon during international operations. Both the well-intentioned US soldiers and the less-enlightened contractors who raced through Baghdad's community with guns threatening were likely viewed as a common 'them' in the eyes of Iraqis witnessing those three black vehicles.

Knowing that many earthquake and other disaster survivors are saved not by emergency responders but by neighbours able to free victims not too deeply buried under debris, telling a megacity population where to take the injured, how to notify authorities of the types of injuries before arrival (thus allowing them to be rerouted to less busy nearby facilities in addition to giving hospitals early warning regarding the medical skills necessary on arrival) and other vital information will save lives. It will also aid in scheduling medical personnel as most rescues take place during the 24 hours immediately following a sudden onset of crisis with a significant drop-off in rescues thereafter.[87]

Most survivors will not need rescuing, but many will require shelter, food, potable water, medical support for injuries, assistance with pets (including food), delivery of medicines due to loss of normal ways of filling prescriptions and additional forms of support. Urban-dwellers tend be more vulnerable than those closer to the land, where basics such as

---

86 'Fighting Ebola, and myths: Congo', *The Economist*, [London], 23 March 2019, 42–43, at 43.
87 Andrea Bartolucci, Darren Walter and Tony Redmond, 'Comparative review on the cost-effectiveness analysis of relief teams' deployment to sudden-onset disasters', *Prehospital and Disaster Medicine* 34(4) (12 July 2019): 415–21 at 417, doi.org/10.1017/S1049023X19004540.

food and water tend to be more accessible. Community support will be key. Two megacities offer different approaches to earthquake recovery, both seeking to serve the best interests of victims suffering loss of their homes, one proving in retrospect to be the more successful in terms of rebuilding policies. It was collective toughness that pulled many megacity-dwellers through despite limited communications, lack of sufficient water and the winter cold in the days and weeks following the January 1995 Great Hanshin Earthquake.[88] Japanese wards in the Osaka–Kobe area formed 'Disaster-Safe Welfare Communities' (*Bosai-Fukushi Komuniti* or BOKOMI in Japanese) immediately after the quake. These were part of an informal assistance initiative—one that in later years spread to urban areas throughout the country. Senior citizens', neighbourhood, women's, school and other associations were behind BOKOMI formation, thereby ensuring community consensus during the formation of block groups and their coordinating bodies.

BOKOMI capabilities can be quite elaborate. They include headquarters, aid distribution, firefighting, water and food supply, information dissemination and evacuation guidance teams.[89] Some communities have Disaster-Reduction Junior Teams comprising elementary and junior high school students who augment adult organisations.[90] In Kobe, neighbourhoods created planning processes involving *machizukuri* ('intercommunity dialogue') consultants who acted as community go-betweens with local urban governments. Neighbourhood planning groups used these and other conduits to inform city authorities about residents' immediate needs and longer-term requirements. One *machizukuri* organised temporary housing and parking for displaced residents and access to currency for local retailers. Major decisions remained at city level, but these consultants reviewed what came from those authorities and provided comments when necessary.

A step in the right direction? Undoubtedly, though at least one author thought the neighbourhood relationships with the city should have been tighter and city authorities could have been more open to community inputs when it came to establishing policies. That was notably the case regarding governmental post-earthquake strategies that favoured tearing

---

88 Acción Contra El Hambre, *Urban Disaster Lessons Learnt*.
89 City of Kobe, *Comprehensive Strategy for Recovery from the Great Hanshin–Awaji Earthquake*, Kobe, Japan, March 2010, 290, 293.
90 ibid.

down damaged structures in lieu of repairing them. Across the Pacific, a different approach benefited residents in Los Angeles after the 1994 Northridge quake. Decision-makers sought to speed the return of the displaced to their properties at reasonable cost while maintaining the community relationships existing before the tremors. Federal recovery funds went into the City of Los Angeles' multifamily housing loan program, which was focused on repairing rather than demolishing and rebuilding even in cases where repairs required stripping a structure down to its frame. Only 500 of more than 36,500 damaged units had to be demolished. Japanese officials looking back at their policy of rebuilding in lieu of repairing in Kobe believe better incentives for the latter should have been on the table after the January 1995 quake. They found that while rebuilding rather than repair improved the speed of rehousing and reduced recovery costs, landlords subsequently tended to charge higher rents once new buildings were in place. Many long-time residents were permanently shut out of their long-time pre-earthquake neighbourhoods as they could not afford the new rates. Both individuals and community cohesion suffered.[91]

Los Angeles has a history of citizen involvement. The Concerned Citizens of South Central Los Angeles formed 57 block clubs to improve community quality of life. Initiatives include preventing dumping in alleys and drug-dealing.[92] The role of *Shomrim* in New York City mentioned previously is another example from the United States' other megacity. In both cases, previously established relations with police mean there exists a means of law enforcement rapidly getting word out to the community and, vice versa, neighbourhood leaders know which authorities to contact when they require assistance. Community leaders can also be conduits of information for an outsider. This can be a valuable means of collection, especially in cases where many urban residents hesitate to reveal their identities or are illiterate—the latter meaning other proven means of obtaining information such as anonymous drop boxes will be less effective. Community representatives can also help when volunteers from neighbourhoods less affected by a calamity are willing to assist elsewhere. Such help can be beneficial but must be managed to preclude interference with other efforts. Here again, working through community leaders can pay dividends.

---

91   Olshansky et al., *Opportunity in Chaos*, 11-2, 11-15.
92   Sharkey, *Uneasy Peace*, 51.

Established community groups' social networks additionally provide means to communicate with large numbers of people when power is out and mobile phone systems are down. This can lend some measure of control over information flows, helping to route messages so they only reach intended audiences—something impossible with mass messaging. A blanket message regarding where those in need can find food, shelter and other services will result in many who are in less dire straits trying to take advantage of the freebies. Going through only those parties representing the worst-hit communities should reduce such abuse. Even sharper focus (and faster dissemination) is possible if neighbourhoods have established the aforementioned alert rosters (chain communications).

Incorporating commercial organisations during disaster response provides capabilities governments alone cannot. With New Orleans flooded and the population in distress, local government 'sputtered', as one author kindly put it. Coca-Cola and Walmart were among the businesses stepping into the breach. Coca-Cola provided water, juice and other drinks—an added advantage being their fleet of trucks able to complement production with delivery. Walmart opened a smaller version of its box stores to address specific needs of hurricane victims in addition to providing cash donations.[93] Home Depot, in its support of NGO Team Rubicon mentioned above, also dispatched employee volunteers to North Carolina during flooding in 2019. The cynical might say this support is merely marketing. They should not begrudge any economic benefits accrued; not all companies that can help do. They are, however, correct in recognising that aid inherently has a marketing role—one that can as easily work against as for a provider. As with the case of NGO and WHO representatives in the DRC, organisations providing goods and services risk alienating rather than gaining the support of urban residents if the providers are seen to be aligned with corrupt, criminal or otherwise despised local entities—governments included.

Concluding observations regarding a comprehensive approach

The United Nations Task Force's (UNITAF) [sic] establishment of a Civil–Military Operations Center (CMOC) helped to ensure that both civilian and military efforts to aid Mogadishu's suffering

---

93   Brinkley, *The Great Deluge*, 252.

were moving in the same general direction despite their not always sharing identical approaches or motivations. US and multinational commanders developed liaison ties that were a significant element in reducing operational conflicts and misunderstandings. Progress beyond these basic levels of cooperation proved too difficult to attain in many circumstances. Various nations refused to allow their forces to support actions in the city of Mogadishu, restricting personnel to areas away from the capital. The situation was much like that in Bosnia, about which a commander commented that 'every troop contributing nation had its own national command structure within the main UN staff, and each nation had its own political agenda as well as a chief of contingent who held the national red card.' In this and many other regards, Mogadishu offers lessons that commanders are well advised to consider now rather than after they are committed to an urban area in a domestic or overseas theater.[94]

—Russell W. Glenn and Gina Kingston, *Urban Battle Command in the 21st Century*

An urban area is different from a municipality (also called a city, city proper, or a local government authority). Municipalities have political boundaries that usually constitute only a part of the urban area. For example, the city of Seoul represents less than one-half of the population (and a declining proportion) of the Seoul–Incheon urban area, which extends well beyond the municipality. On the other hand, a municipality may be considerably larger than an urban area and therefore contain considerable non-urban (or rural) territory. Zaragoza, Spain is an example. A large part of the municipality of Mumbai is rural, composed of the Rajiv Gandhi National Park and thus not included in the urban area.[95]

—*Demographia World Urban Areas*

The extent to which the whole is greater than the sum of its parts during a megacity crisis response depends on how well the pieces of a response work together. The talents available can be unique to the disaster at hand. Having been in West Africa during the 2014 Ebola crisis, author Sheri Fink noted the great value of survivors willing to work with aid providers. Anyone recovering from Ebola was immune to reinfection. They were local treasures. Survivors could assist medical personnel without having to wear protective gear. Not only did they not consume supplies of the valuable personal protective equipment; they were able to work much

---

94 Glenn and Kingston, *Urban Battle Command in the 21st Century*, 11.
95 *Demographia World Urban Areas*, 16th edn.

longer at a stretch than others sealed up and thus vulnerable to overheating, dehydration and exhaustion. Our earlier observation about the value of residents' eyes and ears in providing information takes on even greater relevance when that information need not be acquired face-to-face. Sharp-eyed (and equally quick-witted) Tunisians reporting suspicious activity on a social media site stopped an attack and led to the arrest of 11 potential perpetrators. Those eyes might not be in the urban area itself, or even in the same country. Authors Peter Singer and Emerson Brooking related how several individuals:

> spotted evidence of an impending attack on social media, leading to the arrest of eleven suspected militants. ISIS recruiters in Indonesia, careless in masking their IP address, awoke to a police raid, their identities leaked by hacktivists halfway around the world.[96]

While AI is slowly increasing the breadth and speed of information-processing in many ways, humans will long hold the upper hand in reading between the lines of social media messages.

When war visits: Combat in the megacity

> Within weeks of seizing Baghdad, US soldiers recognized that their inability to address basic human needs and meet fundamental living requirements was turning citizens against them. 'We are dying for help from the NGOs, and we get zero from OCPA [Office of the Coalition Provisional Authority],' said one. 'You can feel it out on the streets; people are frustrated, and we're getting rocks thrown at us in neighborhoods where we never did before.'[97]
>
> —Stephen R. Dalzell, 'Where the Streets Have No Names'

> You're thinking about who's in that house, what's he armed with, how he's gonna kill you, your buddies. You're going block by block, fighting with rifles good to 550 meters, and you're killing people at five in a concrete box.[98]
>
> —Phil Klay, *Redeployment*

---

96 Singer and Brooking, *Like War*, 213.
97 As quoted in Glenn, *Band of Brothers or Dysfunctional Family?*, 41.
98 Phil Klay, *Redeployment*, New York, NY: Penguin, 2015, 1.

Those ISIS fighters who killed noncombatants attempting to flee Mosul in 2016–17 didn't treat those who stayed well either.[99] Should the Government of Iraq have recommended Mosul's residents stay or attempt to escape? It chose to direct that they stay. And so it was that hundreds of thousands did. And suffered. As did those seeking to relieve them of ISIS cruelty. Aircraft supporting Iraqi Security Forces trying to retake the city had to exercise great restraint just as those warriors on the ground could not use the full extent of firepower otherwise available to them given the presence of noncombatants. Was it the right decision? The civilians would have been subjected to harsh conditions in refugee camps, the government explained—refugee camps that would have been overwhelmed had too many tried to reach them early on. Without the stay-behinds, both sides would have caused more destruction to Mosul's homes and other infrastructure, meaning rough living would continue for months, perhaps years, after the purging of the occupiers. Such had previously been the case in Ramadi and Fallujah. Other cities near Mosul already had housing shortages and problems meeting their own healthcare demands given previous surges of refugees. International NGOs and the United Nations were able to help to an extent but recall that the UNHCR was already working with Iraqi military leaders to balance IDP camp capacity and available medical resources with the number of civilians seeking assistance. UN and other officials observed that the order to stay had worked well in East Mosul during the first part of the fighting, which ended in January 2017.

Iraqi soldiers suffered greater numbers of wounded and dead than they would have had they been able to use artillery and air bombardment more freely. Those in the security forces must have looked on older, denser West Mosul's Old City with trepidation once East Mosul was cleared of enemy. The western environs' twisting narrow streets meant more opportunities for ISIS to set up ambushes. About 150,000 civilians did manage to escape during the earliest fighting for the Old City once the attackers renewed operations on 20 February. That still left an estimated 750,000 people unable, unwilling or too scared to attempt flight.

---

99 Material regarding noncombatant care during the 2016–17 battle for Mosul is from Shelly Culbertson and Linda Robinson, *Making Victory Count after Defeating ISIS: Stabilization Challenges in Mosul and Beyond*, Santa Monica, CA: RAND Corporation, 2017, 11–28, doi.org/10.7249/RR2076.

Relief workers followed closely on the heels of the advancing attackers rather than waiting for the rest of Mosul's liberation. The cry for medical care was a desperate one as the city had long been without it, or at least what was available went to ISIS members first. Water, too, was in short supply, as was safety for the aid providers braving the many IEDs, snipers and other ISIS hazards. They knew the risks. A single suicide bomber had killed 23 residents and four aid workers in East Mosul the previous December. Despite three provincial hospitals being set aside for Moslawis, beds, medicine and specialist care such as burn treatment were quickly in short supply. The WHO set up another six hospitals just to deal with the casualties resulting from fighting in the Old City. By July 2017, the number of displaced had already reached 1 million. Some had families elsewhere who took them in, but 85 per cent went into the camps set up in the vicinity of Mosul. Each refugee first went through a checkpoint manned by one of the three major Iraqi fighting forces: the Iraqi Security Forces (army), Popular Mobilisation Forces or Kurdish Peshmerga. Those running the checkpoints took into custody individuals whose names appeared on lists of ISIS members. Others were allowed to climb aboard a bus for movement to one of the IDP camps. The flow was too great for all to be thoroughly screened for weapons, allocated beds or receive the care needed despite UNHCR coordination with the attackers. The camps overflowed; thousands slept on the ground. Bureaucracy (and perhaps corruption?) reared its ugly head as both the government in Baghdad and that controlling Kurdish lands were too slow to set aside territory for the camps—a lack of competence that was all the more unfortunate because funds for establishing them were sufficient. Eventually, only 20 per cent of the displaced were housed in camps with the remainder either in urban locations (schools, host families, rented buildings or others under construction) or in 'non-camp' areas so designated because they failed to meet international standards.

Descriptions of urban combat through the ages are plentiful. Josephus describes the brutality of both sides as Romans sought to subdue the Jewish uprising during the first century CE in what is now Israel—fighting that saw the Temple destroyed in Jerusalem. Sun Tzu warned against fighting in cities if it could be avoided—a half-millennium before Josephus penned his history. Alexander the Great took seven months to besiege Tyre, then turned his attentions to Gaza, 240 kilometres to the south, where the defenders 'fought on until all their fighting men were slain, which can only mean that no quarter was given'. He must have considered the cost worthwhile. Gaza's fall meant Alexander's supply lines were safe. No further major obstacles lay ahead on his trek to Egypt.[100]

World War II witnessed what are among the costliest urban battles of all time—those for Stalingrad, Manila and Berlin among them—while Tokyo, Hamburg, Dresden, London and, of course, Hiroshima and Nagasaki saw thousands upon thousands killed during aerial bombardments and in the fires that followed. Panama in 1989 and Iraq in 2003 remind us that military conquerors should expect looting as the norm when combat comes to a city—a consequence of opportunity and a vacuum of restraint that result when police seek shelter from the violence that accompanies war.

Urban warfare is a particularly brutal teacher, harvesting the inexperienced and unlucky whose deaths are the cost of lessons learned by the more fortunate. Fighting between Chinese Nationalist forces and the Imperial Japanese Army offers both soldiers and future aid providers lessons best recognised before they depart home.

Shanghai, 1937

> Looting soon became widespread. Crowds attacked trucks transporting rice or smashed their way to shop supplies. The authorities were merciless in tackling the problem. On at least one occasion, French police opened fire on a crowd that had attacked a food hawker ... The [Chinese] 87th Infantry Division was given disposal of two armored companies, and it lost everything. Some of the tanks had just arrived from Nanjing, and their crews had not had any time to undertake training in coordinated attack, or even simply to establish rapport with local troops ... Not all officers trusted reports that their own units sent back to them. One regiment of the 87th Division was under specific orders to document any advance it made. Every time it had taken a key objective along its predetermined route of advance, it was to pull down a street sign and send it back as evidence that it indeed was in control of the position.[101]
>
> —Peter Harmsen, *Shanghai 1937*

---

100 J.F.C. Fuller, *The Generalship of Alexander the Great*, New York, NY: Da Capo, 1960, 215–18.
101 Peter Harmsen, *Shanghai 1937: Stalingrad on the Yangtze*, Havertown, PA: Casemate, 2013, 74–75, 80, 83.

History holds no case of major combat in a modern megacity. Fortunately for those who might try to avoid repeating mistakes such as those in Mogadishu and Shanghai, the past does have plentiful examples from which to learn. The unfamiliarity of Chinese armour crews with the infantry they were sent to support would sound familiar to veterans of Mogadishu in 1993, both when US soldiers mounted Malaysian armoured-personnel carriers for the first time during the Black Hawk Down battle and again later in the year when Lieutenant Colonel Bob Clark's tanks arrived from Fort Stewart, Georgia, to find US infantry soldiers in the city had never trained with the vehicles.

Shanghai was the only Chinese city with which many foreigners were familiar in 1937. Chinese Nationalist leader Chiang Kai-shek believed his forces needed to retain the cosmopolitan city with a long history as a port if the eyes of the world were to remain focused on his people's plight at the hands of the Japanese invaders. 'This was not a distant battlefield, reached by adventurous reporters at overwhelming personal hazard,' wrote author Peter Harmsen, 'but one of the great cities of the world. Foreign correspondents were already present in great numbers, or could easily sail in from places like Tokyo and Manila.'[102] Only Tokyo had a larger population among Asia's cities; Shanghai's of 3.5 million was the fifth-largest in the world. When Chiang ordered his forces to attack Japanese invaders during the night of 13 August, he directed they avoid bringing the fight to the International Settlement to preserve relations with the nations represented there. This protection bizarrely included even the Japanese portion of the settlement. The less well-equipped Chinese initially benefited from the city's neutralising of the Japanese military's technological superiority during the close combat that carried on both day and night. As is so often the case—Manila in 1945, Hue in 1968 being but two examples—early instructions to minimise damage to Shanghai were soon cast aside as Chinese army casualties mounted.

The disaster brought by war far surpassed anything the city's ambulance and fire personnel had previously confronted. They adapted quickly, tailoring their practices as thousands of their fellow residents fell, grievously injured or dead. There had already been thousands of civilian casualties when Republic of China aircraft mistakenly bombed Shanghai on 14 August, on what became known as 'Black Saturday'. An artillery shell tore through the side of a department store on Nanjing Road in

---

102 ibid., 171. This description of the battle and the impact on its population draws further on this resource.

the city's busiest shopping district only nine days later. The explosions shredded the building's three lower floors. Water coursed through the store from a shattered waterpipe, running red with the blood of the killed and injured as it flowed into the street. Chinese Boy Scouts worked alongside local members of the Red Swastika (equivalent in mission to the Red Cross) and other civic groups to help wounded survivors or remove bodies despite the almost overwhelming stink of the dead putrefying in the summer heat.

Refugees fled combat zones and ruined neighbourhoods, challenging Shanghai authorities' ability to deal with them, much as would be the case in Mosul 80 years later. Criminal gangs filled the vacuum as city officials abandoned neighbourhoods. A cholera epidemic broke out, punishing the poorest most severely. In late September, Father Robert Jacquinot de Besange, a Jesuit priest from the French Concession, approached a Japanese commander, proposing a safe zone to which noncombatants could go and be free of the ongoing fighting. Permission was finally granted more than a month later when a designated district opened on Shanghai's northern edge on 9 November. What came to be known as the Jacquinot Zone soon housed an estimated 100,000 refugees. It would remain open into 1940.

The megacity combat zone

> Beirut was the birthplace of a new and deadly kind of warfare: an urbanized, shape-shifting mode of combat that combined elements of the tribal feud, patron–client relationships, urban street gang organization, Mafia-style 'hits,' and international intrigue with high-tech weaponry, asymmetrical tactics, organized crime, and politically charged media spectacles such as highjackings and bombings. This was not a war for conventional armed forces … No place was safe. No place was predictable.[103]

—Mounir Elkhamri et al., 'Urban population control in a counterinsurgency'

> Windows split the city's great hell into tiny hellets.[104]

—Vladimir Mayakovsky, 'Great Big Hell of a City'

---

103 Mounir Elkhamri, Lester W. Grau, Laurie King-Irani, Amanda S. Mitchell and Lenny Tasa-Bennett, 'Urban population control in a counterinsurgency', *Small Wars Journal* (n.d.), available from: smallwarsjournal.com/documents/urbanpopulationcontrol.pdf.
104 Vladimir Mayakovsky, 'Great Big Hell of a City', in *Imagining America: Influence and Images in Twentieth-Century Russia*, Alan M. Ball (ed.), Oxford, UK: Rowman & Littlefield, 2003, 46.

Shanghai today has a population of more than 22 million compared with its 3.5 million in 1937. The extent of catastrophe should it or any other twenty-first-century megacity suffer a battle between modern armed forces is difficult to imagine (though ongoing operations in Ukraine as I write provide an unfortunate lens). Recalling that Iraq's security forces could not isolate even so small a city as Mosul during the fighting in 2016–17, it would be delusional to think a military could surround an entire megacity today or operate within every part of it simultaneously. Operations would instead have to focus on select areas chosen for their payoff in attaining whatever objectives a military commander sought. These would be select bites of the megacity elephant. If there is a silver lining, it is that these urban areas are so massive in spread and plentiful in population that no clash of coalitions could threaten all parts simultaneously barring the use of weapons of mass destruction (nuclear, biological, chemical or radiological. There is no silver lining when it comes to those). As retribution for disturbing the urban area's peace, a force choosing to fight in a megacity is likely to find it a voracious beast able to consume whatever quantities of manpower and equipment its generals can bring to bear. Technology will help the combatant, but even technology will struggle. During the summer of 2019, some UAVs flopped to the ground like exhausted dogs, unable to perform during an equipment demonstration in the heat island of New York City.

What does this mean for the soldier other than greater misery while humping weapon, helmet and other gear? We earlier noted that glass is among the surfaces that can reflect lasers meant to guide precision munitions. Dust and smoke impede the ability to see and the strength of those laser signals. Buildings block lines of sight needed to engage targets from both the ground and the air. Any window, door, street gutter opening, rooftop and wall could be concealing a sniper. Some of those marksmen will instead choose to bore their own openings through walls or sloped roofs, making them all the harder to detect before they wreak their damage. Warehouses and parking garages can hide entire tank units. Shadows cast by buildings make vehicles and enemy foot soldiers harder to detect with both the naked eye and other means of surveillance. We recall that tank and other guns can only elevate so far, making them vulnerable to attack from higher floors—something a smart defender will recognise only too quickly. (First-century CE Roman soldiers would have sympathised. Female defenders bombarded them with debris as the Romans fought male town members sword against sword in the streets of Japha in what is now northern Israel.)[105] Then there is the soldier's basic urban combat conundrum: more firepower saves attacking soldiers' lives but the devastation kills far more innocents than enemy, raising the question of whether what those attackers are trying to accomplish is worth the resulting death and destruction. And while that firepower does tend to kill enemy along with innocent, the rubble created reduces the advantages gained as the defenders have new places from which to fire and new obstacles to hinder movement. US Army Major Jesse Skates noted that one can think of an attack in terms of Force = (Mass)(Acceleration), just as in physics. Narrow streets, buildings and other obstacles make it hard to mass combat power in a city. Debris, defender obstacles and incoming fire challenge any unit trying to accelerate. Thus the difficulty in creating sufficient force to overcome defensive positions. It is a challenge more difficult in some urban areas than others. In the United States, a city normally has between 20 and 30 per cent of its area taken up by streets. In India's Delhi, this is 21 per cent. In Kolkata, the number is a meagre 5 per cent. Mumbai's streets take up but 11 per cent—the average for major Asian cities.[106] Those values differ from location to location within an urban area as well as between them. Regardless of how wide or what percentage of space they take, streets are where the defender hopes to see the attackers. If he can see them, he can shoot them. Lieutenant General Ernest C. Cheatham, veteran of combat in 1968 in Hue, recalled: 'You can't stay on the street. If you stay on the street you're dead. You have to go through buildings and walls.'[107] No wonder the US Army's *Infantryman's Guide to Urban Combat* informs soldiers that only 5 per cent of the targets in urban operations appear at over 100 metres range; 90 per cent are confronted at the very short range of 50 metres or less.[108]

Encouraging the departure of noncombatants when it is feasible (as it was not for many in Mosul) raises the possibility of loosening those constraints otherwise frequently put on the use of artillery or bombing from the air. Or perhaps we should replace 'encouraging' with 'allowing', for an attacker has no obligation to allow an urban defender to evacuate a city's population. There is something of the 'no good deed goes unpunished' should an assaulting force encourage civilians to leave. It then falls to the

105 Josephus, *The Jewish War*, London: Penguin, 1959, 213.
106 UN-Habitat, *State of the World's Cities 2012/2013*, 53.
107 As quoted in Glenn, *Honing the Keys to the City*, 56.
108 Department of the Army, *An Infantryman's Guide to Urban Combat*, Field Manual 90-10-1 [Advance copy], Washington, DC: US Government Printing Office, 12 May 1993, 1-1.

ethical attacker to house, water, feed and otherwise care for the thousands, tens of thousands or more displaced persons just created (while relieving one's adversary of the burdens); Mosul once again provides a cautionary example.

An attacker can be sure that a defender will make winning as costly in time, lives, ammunition and reputation as possible. Philippine army and marine units clearing Marawi took more than a month to oust the last 50 ISIS defenders from a 1,000 by 800 metre area of the city[109] (that's less than two-thirds the size of the National Mall in Washington, DC). The defenders, as with those in Mosul, cared little for the dictates of international law or human decency. Mosques, historical buildings, hospitals, schools, apartment buildings and other structures that should normally be spared military use and destruction routinely housed weapons, ammunition or fighting positions and headquarters, making them legitimate targets for the attackers. The Philippine president nonetheless dictated that mosques were not to be engaged with large-calibre weapons such as artillery. Use of tear gas finally broke standoffs after the repulse of repeated assaults by the Armed Forces of the Philippines.[110] (The same approach was ultimately used in Hue 39 years earlier. Though some of the gas drifted across unwarned and none too happy friendly lines, the unprepared enemy withdrew, allowing US Marines to take 12 city blocks in less than three hours without a single casualty. There are good arguments for revisiting international restrictions on the use of chemicals when those agents are nonlethal and can save both noncombatant and combatant lives.)[111] Knowing that Israeli forces would demonstrate restraint rather than kill innocents on the floors above, Hamas put a headquarters in the basement of Gaza's largest hospital during fighting in 2014.[112]

Each urban area is unique. That makes preliminary studies to reduce information requirements once operations begin all the more important. The United Nations tells us that residential properties occupy more than 70 per cent of land in most urban areas.[113] But we have already observed that to focus on urban land surface area alone is to deny oneself understanding of belowground and aboveground features. Los Angeles

---

109 Knight and Theodorakis, *The Marawi Crisis*, 17.
110 ibid., 16.
111 Glenn et al., *Ready for Armageddon*, 67–68.
112 Glenn, 'Megacities'.
113 UN-Habitat, *Urbanization and Development*, 12.

has more than 320 kilometres of underground storm drainage.[114] The behaviour of noncombatants will also differ from location to location, but for whatever reason—and as Mosul recently and Hamburg, Tokyo and London in World War II showed—noncombatants will tend to stay in a contested city until housing stock is so badly ravaged that what remains cannot reasonably be used for shelter.[115] Those conducting peacetime disaster relief operations may experience other surprises. Four hundred people lacking local residence permits were found living in an underground bunker in 2017 in Beijing.[116]

ISIS barbarity in Mosul notwithstanding, civilians are more likely to die as inadvertent victims than deliberate targets during combat. The source of death or wounding ranges beyond the obvious weapons of bomb, bullet or shell. Sabot rounds fired from tanks consist of a thin metal rod approximately 1 metre long that weighs more than 9 kilograms (exact specifications depend on the model used). The munitions are designed to kill either via the spalling of metal once the high-velocity shaft penetrates a target's armour or the overpressure caused when it enters the crew compartment at great speed. The penetrator is far too thin to fire from tank guns without packaging that fills the rest of the gun barrel. Sabots are the parts of this packaging that hold the penetrator in place until it exits the gun tube. At that point, they separate from around the metal rod. Travelling at great speed, these discarded pieces fan out from the muzzle and can kill any unshielded individual up to a kilometre from the firing point.[117] Other less obvious dangers to innocents (and soldiers for that matter) include organ damage due to concussion when large guns are fired within courtyards, on narrow streets or in other enclosed areas and threat of injury from military vehicles navigating streets, with the driver often having far less visibility than is offered in an automobile. The combination of military units moving along streets and soldiers' good intentions in the form of tossing candy or other treats to children has more than once resulted in deaths when the scramble resulted in an intended recipient being struck.

---

114 Williams and Selle, *Military Contingencies in Megacities and Sub-Megacities*, 44, quoting United States Marine Corps, *Urban Operations I: Introduction*, Basic Officer Course Student Handout B4R5359, Camp Barrett, VA: The Basic School, Marine Corps Training Command, 6.
115 Diefendorf, *In the Wake of War*, 10.
116 Bogan and Feeney, *Future Cities*, 54.
117 *Abrams Urban Quick Reference Guide*, Publication Number ST 3-20.12-1, Fort Eustis, VA: US Army Training and Doctrine Command, December 2002.

Urban areas offer opportunities as well as these downsides. Cities are rich with opportunities for the deceptive thinker. Irish Republican Army attacks repeatedly used a primary bomb to set up additional explosive ambushes targeting police, soldiers or other responders. In another instance, it was a tyre lying in the street with wires protruding that caused a patrol to stop, rightly fearing an explosive device. It was a fake, but one that increased the chances of a sniper's successful shot; hitting a stationary explosives expert while they are checking out a threat is far easier than shooting a moving soldier. ISIS used a drone to drop a small bomb on to an Iraqi Security Forces position. The drone attack was merely intended to draw attention away from the suicide bomber who took advantage of the distraction to drive his vehicle towards the compound unmolested and trigger the explosion. Just as the hum of a megacity's daily activities can shield an evildoer from detection if properly exploited (think of trying to move a truck bomb into a city during rush-hour versus in the dead of night or during the Covid-19 lockdowns of early 2020), these many activities also can help clever good guys. Military units wanting to remain undetected when setting up observation posts drive their vehicles through neighbourhoods on a seemingly random route. Those designated to man an observation post jump out at a spot where no-one is likely to notice their entry into a previously identified structure. The vehicle drives on, just another of many.

The nature of challenges and opportunities will differ depending on the type of organisation involved and what it hopes to accomplish. Units depending on vehicles find that urban areas' curbs, building overhangs and constant travel on hard surfaces wear out tyres and tracks faster, snap antennas and fracture parts due to constant vibration. The same hard surfaces jar equipment, making more frequent calibration necessary. Frequent starts and stops increase fuel consumption and brake wear. Supply units must 'best guess' as to fuel, parts and ammunition consumption rates given the lack of historical data for urban combat. Soldiers' sharing of rations with impoverished noncombatants means resupply of foodstuffs (known as Class I in US military parlance) must be more frequent. On the other hand, the megacity's many warehouses and large parking garages that can be used to store supplies offer shelter from the elements and shielding from unfriendly eyes or enemy fire. Those beleaguered suppliers can also take advantage of urban areas' timber yards, car parts stores and other commercial riches, helping to balance the downside of operating in a built-up area. Underground facilities are also attractive because their limited access points make them easy to secure against looters or enemy infiltration. Another example of a megacity's yin and yang of challenges and opportunities: transport times are longer when traffic fills streets, but the availability of vehicles for rent or purchase far surpasses that in rural environs. (Eighteen of the world's 35 urban areas with a population of more than 10 million were among the top-50 on the planet for bad traffic in 2019, and Beijing and New York were numbers 51 and 52, respectively.)[118]

Those yins and yangs are especially numerous for medical personnel. The wounds and injuries sustained in urban environments differ from those found in rural areas. Crush and thoracic (chest) injuries are more common due to building collapse or overpressure. That overpressure can be the result of proximity to large-calibre weapons in tight spaces or enemy use of thermobaric munitions that release fuel in aerosol form then ignite it to squash anything beneath. Crush and overpressure injuries can be particularly hard to detect. The sufferer may feel fine in the immediate aftermath and externally seem to be uninjured. Barring savvy medical types, the resulting injury to internal organs can go unnoticed until it is too late for treatment. Introducing intravenous fluids or transport by helicopter can worsen a patient's condition if they have suffered lung damage (the second due to changing atmospheric pressures as altitude changes). Different skill sets and equipment therefore need to be closer to expected injury sites than would elsewhere be the case, including surgical specialists and ventilation support. Leaders of NGO, military and other medical organisations obviously need to be aware of the potential of such injuries and accordingly train, plan and organise for different mixes of medical specialties when the environment is an urban one. This points to medical personnel needing to rehearse for operations no less than do police, fire, military and others. Combat commanders must make the tough decision of sending the few medics they have assigned to them forward with the units expected to meet the greatest resistance or holding them back and dispatching them when casualties become evident. Moving laterally across urban battlefields is difficult and time-consuming even under the best conditions. In combat, it is also extremely dangerous, meaning getting it right regarding allocating these valuable but limited assets is critical.

---

118 TomTom International BV, 'TomTom Traffic Index'.

It should be apparent by this point that decision-making during urban combat operations is anything but routine. Locating aid stations and field hospitals will be something of an art. Telling those in reconnaissance, logistics or other units which characteristics are needed in this regard increases the chances of finding appropriate locations and having others identified as backups (cover from enemy fire, room to park ambulances, nearby locations where helicopters can land and access to potable water are examples). Accessibility for those segments of the civilian population who are at notable risk might be another factor, with the same being true during flooding, after an earthquake or when another disaster has caused injuries or exposed individuals to disease. In times of combat, policies regarding which treatments can be offered to civilians and where noncombatants should go for care need to be identified early and made known both within a force and to the population. Providing medical care can be a significant first step towards winning or maintaining civilian support for a military when the pace of operations and available resources permit. However, demand for care can expand dramatically beyond what would be expected in rural environs as media members, NGO representatives and others join local civilians in addition to the medical unit's own personnel in seeking services likely to be in short supply during a crisis.

Whether for medical or other purposes, innovation is no less valuable for those seeking to conceal their activities. Use of smoke to conceal recovery of the wounded is effective under some circumstances though the swirling air currents common in cities mean the concealment can suddenly disappear at the most inopportune times. We remember that Armed Forces of the Philippines units in Marawi innovatively used bolts of cloth to block enemy snipers' views of streets. An unlucky soldier (perhaps the fastest in a unit, but still unlucky) would be tabbed to race across the open area holding one end of the fabric, then fasten it to the other side. ISIS used sheets of tarpaulin for the same purpose in Iraq, putting the visual barrier up before coalition forces entered a neighbourhood. The group also suspended sheets of fabric horizontally to conceal movement from manned aircraft or UAV observation.[119] Forces opposing the IDF did the same in Gaza, using corrugated metal or other materials to mask activities in alleyways or on narrow streets.

---

119 Robert Postings, 'A guide to the Islamic State's way of urban warfare', Article, West Point, NY: Modern War Institute, 9 July 2018, available from: mwi.usma.edu/guide-islamic-states-way-urban-warfare/.

The resulting inability to see and the compartmentalised, twisted-street nature of urban areas mean that recovering a wounded soldier can be hard even after an area has been cleared of enemy. In the future, sensors reflecting a wearer's status and location may help. Knowing whether he or she is alive or the nature of wounds or injuries would allow leaders to make more effective use of those limited numbers of medics, physician assistants and doctors. The dead can wait. Those with particular skills would move to a survivor needing their talents. Minor but debilitating wounds could be assigned to combat lifesavers—soldiers with a bit of additional medical training but whose skills fall short of those of trained medics. The US Army sometimes uses the 'buddy system' in which soldiers are paired, meaning a wounded soldier is more likely to have someone nearby who can render immediate first aid or, if equipped with a radio, inform anyone trying to bring further care. Using procedures such as the buddy system could be a good idea even once those sensors become generally available. The many barriers to lines of sight complicate communications, but not all forms of communication are created equal. That means while sensor data might not get through, a buddy's radio might. If both communications fail, then what aid the fellow soldier can provide could be the difference between life and death. Fortunately, recent advances in individual medical treatment have helped when a soldier must be left behind. The 9/11-inspired wars in Afghanistan and Iraq saw men and women equipped with self-applied tourniquet kits and materials for quickly staunching severe bleeding.

Soldiers speak of the psychological stresses experienced during grinding combat in Stalingrad, Fallujah and other cities. Marine leaders in Hue and elsewhere found that rest, hot food and being out of immediate danger helped stave off the worst of these assaults. Fellow soldiers knowing the telltale signs of combat exhaustion will be the first to notice, offering the possibility of getting attention for those in need before they reach breaking points. Training in what to expect in the way of psychological stressors might benefit as well. The guilt associated with noncombatant deaths can be especially burdensome, as reported by Mark Bowden in his urban combat classic *Black Hawk Down*. Specialist Eric Spalding of the 3rd Battalion, 75th Ranger Regiment, was in a truck as it rolled through Mogadishu, rifle rounds pinging off the vehicle's side when:

> A woman in a flowing purple robe darted past on the driver's side of the truck. [Private] Maddox had his pistol resting on his left arm, pretty much shooting at whatever moved.

'Don't shoot,' Spalding shouted. 'She's got a kid!'

> The woman abruptly turned. Holding the baby in one arm, she raised a pistol with her free hand. Spalding shot her where she stood. He shot four more rounds into her before she fell. He hoped he hadn't hit the baby. They were moving and he couldn't see if he had or not. He thought he probably had. She had been carrying the baby on her arm right in front. Why would a mother do something like that with a kid on her arm? What was she thinking? Spalding couldn't get over it.[120]

Like Spalding, soldiers fighting in urban areas will continue to find themselves in situations where their or their buddies' survival demands quick use of lethal force—force that will sometimes unavoidably endanger an innocent. Foes have and will continue to use civilians as shields, making that likelihood all the greater. Drawing on another incident from Mogadishu, Ranger Specialist Shawn Nelson found shelter from enemy fire behind a burned-out car:

> Peering out from underneath toward the north now, Nelson saw a Somali with a gun lying prone on the street between two kneeling women. The shooter had the barrel of his weapon between the women's legs, and there were four children actually sitting on him. He was completely shielded in noncombatants, taking full cynical advantage of the American's decency ...
>
> 'What do you want to do?' [fellow Ranger Specialist John] Waddell asked.
>
> 'I can't get to that guy through those people.'
>
> So Nelson threw a flashbang, and the group fled so fast the man left his gun in the dirt.[121]

Unfortunately, Eric Spalding did not have the option of using a nonlethal flashbang grenade in his situation. Nor did Sergeant Chuck Elliot elsewhere in the city. Seeing a woman approaching Lieutenant Larry Perino and himself, he noticed there was a gunman behind the woman holding a gun under her arm, ready to engage the two men. Perino told Elliot to fire. Elliot, manning an M60 machine-gun, did so, killing both gunman and

---

120 Mark Bowden, *Black Hawk Down: A Story of Modern War*, New York, NY: Atlantic Monthly Press, 1999, 106–7.
121 ibid., 46.

shield.[122] Confronting soldiers with these deplorable situations in training will have the dual benefits of reducing the chances of what could be a fatal hesitation to shoot and letting the soldier know that the decision to fire is the right one despite its attending horror. Knowing such is the case before the incident may not lessen the pain after the act, but it will give greater legitimacy to a leader's or fellow soldiers' comforting comments, hopefully reducing feelings of guilt.

The best training includes the most demanding challenges. While on a callout to a reported hostage situation during research some years ago, a SWAT member revealed to me that their instructions on receiving new team members facing a group of criminals or terrorists was 'Shoot the women first' (a line on to which Hollywood later latched). The guidance had nothing to do with gender issues. Rather, culturally imbued standards regarding how to treat women had in the past caused Americans in law enforcement to hesitate that extra heartbeat before firing on a woman versus a male. Women in terrorist groups had also more than once proved more aggressive than their male counterparts, adding a second element to a potentially deadly combination. The guidance was meant to increase officers' chances of survival.

With megacities well known for being among the toughest of environments in which to fight, there are nevertheless potential benefits in finding one's unit in such a location confronting a well-entrenched enemy that aren't available in smaller urban areas. The expanses of larger urban areas present situations like those Clausewitz described when writing of mountain defences. The limited number of passes and rugged nature of mountainous terrain mean military leaders tend to believe these environments favour a defender. Clausewitz challenges this default thinking. 'Defensive mountain warfare [should be] meant to last only a certain time,' he wrote. 'Mountainous terrain is of no help to the defender; on the contrary ... it favors the attacker.'[123] He posits that a way to flank defensive positions will eventually be found, just as the Persians outflanked Greek defenders at Thermopylae. The many streets, alleys, underground and aboveground passages and related shields from view and enemy fire mean that chances are good that a diligent attacker will eventually find similar ways to bypass a defender.

---

122 ibid., 43.
123 Glenn, 'Megacities'.

Concluding observations on megacity combat

> In Raqqa, more than 90 percent of attacks on SDF [Syrian Defense Forces] by IS were in the form of hidden IEDs.[124]
>
> —Robert Postings, 'A guide to the Islamic State's way of urban warfare'
>
> Wars of the future will not be fighting for cities, but rather fighting within them.[125]
>
> —Levi Maxey, 'Preparing for the urban future of counterinsurgency'

Post–World War II conflicts have unfortunately made it clear that fighting (and conducting terrorist attacks) in urban areas can pay off. The larger the urban area, the bigger is that payoff. Examples include the Al-Qaeda 'public relations' coups rendered by a few misguided individuals on 9/11 and the attention given to the targeting of Paris on a Friday night in 2015. The 2002 takeover of a Moscow theatre by Chechen terrorists initially drew more attention than did thousands of Uyghurs in detention camps in remote western China in 2020 or the hundreds of thousands displaced Rohingya in western Myanmar and eastern Bangladesh during the second decade of this century.

Larger forces are often needed to clear urban areas of an adversary given how manpower-intensive these operations tend to be. The enemy will take advantage where an adversary's strength is less, moving to those locations in what becomes a deadly game of whack-a-mole. A relatively small force can cause even a much larger one disproportionate casualties, embarrassingly extend the duration of fighting and bring loss of legitimacy in the eyes of governing authorities and the population alike.

Urban combat will never be only about the fighting any more than a megacity's recovery from a natural disaster will focus only on repairing buildings. Ultimately, it's about the people. Past urban combat operations tended to handle events sequentially: win the fight and only then worry about what comes after. That is an approach that is both costly and likely to prove disastrous from a humanitarian and a political standpoint

---

124 Postings, 'A guide to the Islamic State's way of urban warfare'.
125 Levi Maxey, 'Preparing for the urban future of counterinsurgency', *Indian Strategic Studies Blog*, 10 March 2018, available from: strategicstudyindia.blogspot.com/2018/03/preparing-for-urban-future-of.html.

should the future include major combat operations in a megacity. As the preceding pages more than once suggest, looking well beyond the end of hostilities, then backward planning, will prove the wiser method, imperfect though it may be given megacity complexity. Knowing what all participating parties and not just the fighting force seek as ultimate objectives should influence actions taken in the days, weeks and months prior to the adversary's defeat. Is the destruction of a religious site being used in violation of the laws of land warfare worth the consequent diplomatic repercussions? Will working with the local government promote or undermine the city's stability in the long run given residents' views of those authorities? The questions are many and the second and higher-order effects of getting the answers wrong difficult to forecast. Yet, even a modest attempt to look beyond the combat will prove valuable and, very likely, serve as the basis for a quicker, more economical and less painful recovery for all involved.

The military language of counterinsurgency speaks of 'white' areas— those cleared of insurgent influence that can then serve as points from which to expand into contested 'grey' or foe-controlled 'black' areas. Counterinsurgency theory compares this expansion from white areas to the spreading of a spot of grease dropped on a piece of paper. The same analogy applies when trying to assert influence over urban populations regardless of whether the threat is insurgent, criminal or of some other form. The concept has application when providing aid as well—for example, referring to a neighbourhood as white when all diabetes sufferers have received a week's supply of insulin, grey when provision of the medication is in progress and black when supplies are inadequate and a community is going without. In the context of combat, however, as difficult as it is to isolate white areas in rural environments, it will be well nigh impossible in cities. Authorities need to recognise that theirs will be a situation where the best they can achieve is shades of grey rather than the purity of white. Those shades will lighten and darken over time and space as individuals or groups move or change attitudes, making control of neighbourhoods and population segments dynamic and more akin to a lava lamp than a fixed state.

We are fortunate that no megacity has yet suffered major ground combat. Recent history tells us we need to be ready for the possibility.

Sustaining megacity capacity during a catastrophe

> One astute student of Mosul politics whom I know puts it differently. He calls Mosul 'the end of the river.' When I ask him how he means that, he says darkly, 'Like Conrad meant it.'[126]
>
> —James Verini, *They Will Have to Die Now*

> We know many of our soldiers are members of gangs ... When those men subsequently put on America's uniform, they were good soldiers. They helped us to understand gang behavior. They were soldiers first and gang members second.[127]
>
> —James Delk, 'MOUT'

Decisions made in support of disaster response will have both immediate effect and lasting consequences whether the cause of catastrophe is combat or otherwise. It is widely accepted that charging even a small amount rather than giving something for free often leads to better use of the resource received; recipients rightly feel they have something invested, giving the good or service value. Poorly thought-out aid can instead have a variety of unintended consequences. Providing funding for all or part of rebuilding even though original locations are in vulnerable areas reinforces views that it is okay to risk repeat events.[128] The form of aid can also influence perceptions favourably or otherwise. When the state of a local economy and availability of essentials allow, some NGOs prefer providing cash or replenishable cash cards rather than delivering food, diapers, medicines and other forms of assistance. The benefits include cash delivery being cheaper and less logistically demanding; a US Government estimate figures transport and other costs consume up to 65 per cent of emergency food assistance funds. The same study concluded that almost 20 per cent more people can receive aid when it comes in the form of cash.[129] As long as a functioning economy remains, cash will tend to go towards purchases needed by the urban resident, who is very likely the individual best able to determine what they most require (like the person

126 Verini, *They Will Have to Die Now*, 59.

127 Delk, 'MOUT', 87.

128 Abbas Jha, Jessica Lamond, Robin Bloch, Namrata Bhattacharya, Ana Lopez, Nikolaos Papachristodoulou, Alan Bird, David Proverbs, John Davies and Robert Barker, *Five feet high and rising: Cities and flooding in the 21st century*, Policy Research Working Paper 5648, Washington, DC: The World Bank, May 2011, 30, doi.org/10.1596/1813-9450-5648.

129 'Free exchange: Hard-nosed compassion', *The Economist*, [London], 26 September 2015, 70.

on the spot best knowing a situation during the application of mission command). Cash distributions will therefore in many circumstances have a better means-meets-needs rate than one-size-fits-all distributions of select foods or services chosen by an outsider. Cash can also be given directly to the individual requiring assistance, helping to hold disaster's close kin of corruption at bay by avoiding one or more middlemen who might skim. If mobile phone towers are working, dispensing aid in the form of electronic cash transfers similarly reduces the dangers of loss from theft as recipients depart distribution points. Given the appropriate conditions and when closely monitored, cash distribution in reasonable amounts further benefits by not feeding inflation.

Another lesson passed on from previous disasters: too many of those in vulnerable urban areas are poor students of history. Electricity components, business computers and other vital infrastructure continue to sit in floodprone areas despite failures in New Orleans, Fukushima and elsewhere. An electrical substation on New York City's East 13th Street sat on the banks of the East River in the middle of a flood zone. The result: three days of blackout for almost all of Manhattan below 34th Street when Hurricane Sandy struck—an area that included two major hospitals whose backup generators also failed because key system parts were in flooded basements. Individual citizens can also be surprisingly uncaring (or too lazy) when it comes to their property. Beekeeper Andrew Coté describes how a man responsible for 20 beehives turned down help to carry his trusts a short distance to higher ground as Sandy threatened to flood the pier on which they sat. Sure enough, the bees were destroyed. Perhaps as predictable as the neglect shown in these several examples is the existence of those willing to capitalise on offers of money following a calamity. In this case, the negligent beekeeper blamed the storm rather than his judgement for the loss, raising more than $22,000 in an online campaign to cover what Coté estimates was $6,000 worth of bees and related equipment.[130] Regardless of the form it takes, corruption is ever the evil twin of disaster.

Catastrophes have a way of bringing shortcomings to light for individuals who fail to do that 'walk around the table' and view their plans, procedures and preparations from all relevant perspectives. The events of 9/11 were a tragedy. Tragic as it was, the situation could have been much worse had

---

130 Andrew Coté, *Honey and Venom: Confessional of an Urban Beekeeper*, New York, NY: Ballantine, 2020, 222–25.

fires reached the 750,000-litre underground tank of freon that supplied the World Trade Center's cooling system. Heated freon can become phosgene, a gas used in chemical weapons. It is encouraging that officials in some megacities are learning from previous events in their own and other urban areas as climate change increases the chances and likely magnitude of catastrophic flooding and other calamities. Both Tokyo and New York, for example, seek to create comprehensive maps identifying all underground facilities. Less encouraging: neither megacity is close to achieving that goal. Meeting it is a gargantuan task—one that would be monstrous even if the responsible party could get its hands on the details of New York City's 800 kilometres of subway tunnels, Con Edison's 160-kilometre steam delivery system or the thousands of subterranean electrical, sewer, natural gas, water and telecommunications lines, much less who knows how many underground garages, shopping malls or other features in the megacity's five boroughs alone.[131] On top of this, knowing what types of soil these features pass through could prove crucial. George Deodatis, a civil engineering professor at Columbia University, observed that 'knowing the type of soil is very important for the behavior of the infrastructure … If you have a gas explosion, certain types of soil will absorb the blast.'[132] In other cases—Mexico City included—knowing whether the soil above is easily saturated or drains well could mean the difference between being prepared for landslides or allowing construction on ground where liquefaction would put lives at risk. Knowing such vulnerabilities exist before an event is the right answer. Knowing what questions to ask and what to check before a disaster beat finding out only after the lights go dim, an apartment complex washes downhill or hundreds in a slum are buried beneath a landslide. The time to identify those vulnerabilities was yesterday. According to at least one estimate, over half of New York City's power-generating capability will be in the once-in-100-year floodplain by the middle of the twenty-first century—but that was last century's 100-year floodplain. By 2050, those same floods could occur on the average of once every four years.[133] Yesterday was preferable. Tomorrow will have to do. Chances are the day after tomorrow will be too late.

---

131 Greg Milner, 'Nobody knows what lies beneath New York City', *Bloomberg Businessweek*, 10 August 2017, available from: www.bloomberg.com/news/features/2017-08-10/nobody-knows-what-lies-beneath-new-york-city.

132 ibid.

133 Miles, *Super Storm*, 246.

The right stuff at the right time

> Practically the whole of the south of England supplied the city with food, and the malt used to brew Londoners' ale came from as far away as Norfolk ... The city government held huge stores of wheat, barley, oats, and malt on London Bridge and at Bridewell hospital just in case of emergencies, and the lord mayor monitored and sometimes fixed the prices of essential foodstuffs.[134]
>
> —Stephen Alford, *London's Triumph*

> In 717, the besieging forces, led by the brother of the Syrian-based Umayyad Caliph Süleyman, attacked [Constantinople] by both land and sea ... That year the city planted wheat in the gaps between her famous walls.[135]
>
> —Bettany Hughes, *Istanbul*

A study done after the 1995 Kobe earthquake:

> found that approximately 77% of those who lost their lives died within an hour [of the quake]. Furthermore, they found that 36% of injured victims who died between three and 12 hours after the earthquake might have been saved if the appropriate initial emergency response had been available ... The published literature suggests three days to be the average time for an EMT [emergency medical technician] to arrive and become operational in the affected country ... The team focusing on immediate trauma care will arrive too late and find that they are caring for relatively minor injuries and for health problems not directly related to the disaster.[136]

Three to four days is the limit cited by experts in disaster recovery operations. Beyond that point the chances of finding someone alive approach the level of miracle. At a minimum, access to air, escaping severe injury and having a source of liquid to drink all need to come together. As the above quote implies, the right type of assistance will be time-dependent. The wrong type does little other than interfere with the arrival of equipment or services in greater demand given limits on how much traffic ports and airports can handle. Less-essential relief workers further burden the city with additional mouths to feed and bodies to shelter when both food and housing are short.

---

134 Alford, *London's Triumph*, 20.
135 Hughes, *Istanbul*, xxiv.
136 Bartolucci et al., 'Comparative review on the cost-effectiveness analysis', 419, 420.

It's comforting to know that sixteenth-century Londoners were in no danger of a beer shortage.[137] Then, as now, the bulk of a megacity's essentials came from beyond its boundaries. Yet, remarkably, much was produced within. The parks of London's Croydon community alone provided vegetables sufficient for 15,000 meals a day during World War II.[138] Today, the city's bees provide 10 per cent of its population's honey, while 16 tonnes of vegetables are homegrown every year. Bangkokians reportedly plant on 60 per cent of the city's land area. Amazingly, given the hundreds of millions of Chinese living in cities, virtually all the vegetables and half the meat and poultry consumed in its 18 largest cities reportedly come from within the urban areas.[139] (Well, not so amazingly, perhaps. We need to remember that China's definition of 'urban' is far more lenient than that used here and contains significant stretches of rural terrain.) It is estimated that the poorest of those living in Harare (Zimbabwe), Kampala (Uganda) and Dar es Salaam (Tanzania) produce between 20 and 60 per cent of what they consume. Backyards support yams, cassava, other vegetables, fruits and poultry. Residents in developed nations' urban areas tend to produce considerably less. North of London, Oxford produces less than 0.5 per cent of the food its residents consume.[140] On the other hand, the city-state of Singapore is nearly self-sufficient in eggs, poultry and pork while supplying one-quarter of its population's demand for vegetables.[141] Megacity shortages may be due less to a lack of foodstuffs than to a lack of knowledge of where supplies are short or an inability to find transport. Showing us that the term 'smart city' can have meaning beyond what the government provides in the way of information technology, Birmingham in the United Kingdom is among the urban areas that use an app that provides catering services with information about which charities are ready to take donations of any excess food.[142] The same

---

137 We recall that if those Londoners had fast-forwarded about 300 years, they would have seen that drinking beer can save lives. See John Snow's own discussion in his 'Instances of the Communications of Cholera through the Medium of Polluted Water in the Neighborhood of Broad Street, Golden Square', in *On the Mode of Communication of Cholera*, London: John Churchill, 1855, available from: www.ph.ucla.edu/epi/snow/snowbook_a2.html; or Hempel, *Medical Detective*.

138 Ziegler, *London at War*, 159.

139 Reader, *Cities*, 166–67. Also see Teng et al., 'Urban food security', 58, 60.

140 Steve Jennings, Julian Cottee, Tom Curtis and Simon Miller, *Food in an Urbanised World: The Role of City Region Food Systems in Resilience and Sustainable Development*, International Sustainability Unit Report, Long Hanborough, UK: 3Keel, April 2015, available from: www.3keel.com/wp-content/uploads/reports/CRFS%20Final%20Draft_0.pdf.

141 Luc J.A. Mougeot, *Urban Food Production: Evolution, Official Support and Significance*, Cities Feeding People Series Report 8, Ottawa: International Development Research Centre, 1994, 21, available from: idl-bnc-idrc.dspacedirect.org/bitstream/handle/10625/14949/103013.pdf?sequence=1.

142 Barber, *If Mayors Ruled the World*, 246–47.

apps could be valuable in times of disaster—power and internet access allowing. Effective distribution information makes for more effective aid. Less-effective control of the information can result in overwhelmed dispersal locations, shortfalls and the possibility of rioting.

Some form of centralised aid distribution oversight is advisable to minimise loss. We earlier alluded to Canada and Sweden refusing to route their aid through the corrupt government of Siaka Stevens in Sierra Leone during the late twentieth-century insurgency plaguing that country and its capital, Freetown.[143] Also worth remembering: UN Resident and Humanitarian Coordinator for Yemen Lise Grande similarly ceased food deliveries to Houthi rebels in that country in 2019 despite the population's desperate needs (and her mother's dismay on being told) after repeated warnings failed to stop misrouting to military or other parties for which it was not intended.[144] These choices are extraordinarily hard ones to make, particularly for NGOs whose donors may not understand the reasons underlying the withholding. But they are essential to the control of corruption and criminality; with them, aid providers support the likelihood of bringing a disaster to a more timely conclusion. Other forms of control include denying funding to unresponsive governments as a way of coercing necessary change. At times, the causes of the need for strong-arming might be less than immediately obvious. Members of Kenya's parliament ensured resources committed to build shelters in the massive Dadaab refugee camp went to favoured contractors. They also dictated that no permanent structures were to be built as these for Somalis would be better than what many Kenyans elsewhere had available to them. The result: 130,000 tents torn asunder in the region's high winds[145]—and perhaps, more money yet for those contractors and their corrupt benefactors.

Lise Grande, Canada and Sweden are not alone in making difficult decisions to halt aid when conditions demand. The United States ceased funding the World Food Programme in Somalia after it became aware that fake NGOs and warlords were taking the majority of that IGO's food and selling it in Mogadishu's Bakaara market. Other organisations were giving over three-quarters of their relief supplies to competing warlords

---

143 Russell W. Glenn, *Rethinking Western Approaches to Counterinsurgency: Lessons from Post-Colonial Conflict*, London: Routledge, 2015, 253, doi.org/10.4324/9781315744650.
144 Grande, 'Humanitarian assistance and disaster relief'.
145 Rawlence, *City of Thorns*, 112–13, 219.

as bribes to get what was left to the truly needy.[146] Governments and other organisations providing aid in urban areas should ready themselves for similar challenges. The scale of aid delivery needed to meet demand for food and other necessities during a megacity crisis will likely only be within the capacity of national governments to meet. NGOs can certainly assist, but they have historically shown they lack the capability to meet requirements of such magnitude.[147]

A megacity won't survive on homegrown food for long, but internal sources might help residents weather the first days of empty shelves. Feeding urban folk is not the only issue. We know some cities rely on nearby rural regions for leafy vegetables and other perishable products. Shortages downtown can therefore deprive local rural populations when wealthier urbanites suck limited supplies from surrounding farms in time of excessive need.[148] This is fine for the rich but rising costs will be an issue for poorer urban and nearby rural-dwellers alike. Local urban–grown food is already sometimes more expensive than internationally imported products.[149] Chances are demand and unscrupulous sellers will cause an increase in prices, making it even harder for the less well-off to find what they need when damaged ports, airfields, roads and railroads restrict supply. The poor in the world's less-developed countries' largest urban areas spend between 40 and 60 per cent of their income on food.[150] Ho Chi Minh City, Lagos, Istanbul, Kinshasa and Kolkata were megacities particularly hard hit in the not too distant past in this regard.[151] Making matters worse: developing-world urban areas may have a significant number of poor individuals already on the knife's edge of survival *before* a disaster strikes given they are able to afford only one meal a day.[152] Diet-related sickness among urban-dwellers could spike even for those able to purchase food due to changes in diet. City folk tend to eat different foods to those in the country, favouring diets richer in fruit and meat, for example.[153]

146 ibid., 70.

147 Charles Kelly, *Acute food insecurity in mega-cities: Issues and assistance options*, Disaster Studies Working Paper 7, London: Benfield Hazard Research Centre, University College London, July 2003, 9, available from: www.ucl.ac.uk/hazard-centre/sites/hazard_centre/files/wp7.pdf.

148 ibid., 3.

149 Mougeot, *Urban Food Production*, 16.

150 Teng et al., 'Urban food security', 58, 60.

151 Mougeot, *Urban Food Production*, 17.

152 ibid., 18.

153 'Into the urban maw: Cities and farming', *The Economist*, [London], 17 February 2018, 53–54, at 53.

Returning our attention to providers rather than product, bureaucratic restrictions can impact what an outsider is allowed to offer in the way of aid. Japan's restrictions on emergency medical technicians intubating patients during the Tokyo sarin attack make it clear that outsiders need to be well advised regarding local regulations and permission requirements. Across the Sea of Japan, only qualified nurses (and presumably doctors) are permitted to employ intravenous lines in South Korea's military. When a North Korean defector was shot five times while crossing the Demilitarised Zone in 2018, a Republic of Korea Army officer turned to a US non-commissioned officer to provide the lifesaving stabilisation procedures needed during the ensuing helicopter evacuation.[154] There may be good reason for such constraints. Knowing them before deploying relief personnel—like understanding that earthquake victims are more likely to require treatment for crush injuries—should mean sending those with the right skills and equipment. Similarly, NGOs and IGOs differ in their willingness to have their personnel go into harm's way, particularly in combat environments. Determining what level of risk each is willing to tolerate is something worth discussing during planning and rehearsal sessions.

Concluding thoughts on megacity crisis response

> Col Irwin Hunt, the officer in charge of civil affairs for the Third Army and American forces in Germany during World War I … observed that it was 'extremely unfortunate that the qualifications necessary for civil administration are not developed among officers in times of peace.'[155]
>
> —Nadia Schadlow, *War and the Art of Governance*

> Cooperation is difficult, especially with other people.[156]
>
> —Gideon Rose, 'The fourth founding'

---

154 James Machado (Major, US Army), Discussion with Russell W. Glenn, Republic of Korea, 7 November 2018.

155 Schadlow, *War and the Art of Governance*, 19.

156 Gideon Rose, 'The fourth founding: The United States and the liberal order', *Foreign Affairs* 98(1) (January–February 2019): 10–21, at 14.

The US Army had learned from its lack of preparation for occupying Germany after World War I. Civil affairs officers were trained early and dispatched to assist with occupier duties even as fighting continued in World War II. A civil affairs branch exists in the army today, but chances are it would be overwhelmed by the number and variety of duties falling to its members given major commitment to a megacity regardless of its underlying cause. Civil affairs personnel should partner with NGO and other organisations in such situations, the goal being to fit civil and military capabilities into the whole of an effective, comprehensive response. The needs of a megacity's residents could quickly overwhelm even these combined efforts. That modern forms of communication might be inoperable would make the tough even harder. The Japan Ground Self-Defense Force's Lieutenant General Yamaguchi cited instances during twenty-first-century post-earthquake operations in which Japan's military leaders had to rely on runners to carry messages or return to mid-twentieth-century means such as walkie-talkies when mobile phones and other forms of communications either were not operating or proved incompatible with systems used by militaries from assisting nations. The military relied on floppy disks transported by bicyclists as recently as the 2018 great Hokkaido quake in the north of Japan.[157]

Water, power and transportation could be offline for months following a major megacity disaster. The higher temperatures found in these urban areas would stress humans and equipment alike during summer months or when the city in question is in the tropics. Those arriving from other countries to render assistance could be at the added disadvantage of not knowing how residents will react to the arrival of strangers and their unfamiliar equipment. Planning and other preparations should not stop when relief organisations arrive. Earlier arrivals will learn important lessons. Barring a system to collect and disseminate those lessons, new arrivals will have to gain those insights at the same cost in wasted time and effort. US Army units in Vietnam set up their own schools to teach newly assigned soldiers what training in the United States had not, including enemy tactics specific to their unit's tactical area, local customs and other vital information. Few are the NGOs or IGOs that have in-country training for their newly arriving representatives, much less more ambitious programs that bring individuals together from multiple organisations. Time spent in such training would also provide a period

---

157 Glenn et al., *Achieving Convergence during Humanitarian Assistance and Disaster Relief Operations.*

of acclimatisation to those high urban temperatures, local weather, food and other conditions unique to the urban area in question. Better yet, predeparture training to complement these post-arrival opportunities to learn and work alongside each other would reduce logistical burdens in the receiving disaster area. The United Nations or NGOs that take it on themselves to coordinate the activities of their peer organisations would be candidates for establishing and conducting these training and education programs. Combined with greater participation during routine planning, rehearsals and exercises conducted before a specific crisis arises, these pre and post-deployment initiatives would bring any undertaking closer to that mark on the wall that is a well-orchestrated comprehensive approach.

8

Post-disaster recovery

When we got to Najaf (about half-way to Baghdad) … I called Lieutenant General (LTG) Wallace, the V Corps Commander, and said, 'Hey boss, there's good news and bad news. The good news is we own Najaf.' And he responded, 'Great, congratulations! … So, what's the bad news?' And I explained, 'The bad news is the same as the good news: we own Najaf.'[1]

—David Petraeus, 'Reflections on wars in Iraq and Afghanistan'

As megacities grow, lesser natural events may cause greater suffering and damage. Jakarta's January 2013 flooding displaced over 40,000 people despite the amount of water flooding the city being less than that in 2007.[2]

—World Vision, *Cities Prepare!*

Most post-disaster recovery undertakings follow some progression along the lines of: 1) immediate relief (during which the focus is on saving the lives of those trapped beneath rubble, urgently in need of medical attention or otherwise at dire risk; 2) initial recovery (including getting food and other needs to residents and the initial cleanup of debris, among other activities; and 3) rebuilding/reconstruction. The three are sequential to an extent but overlap considerably. As with targeting during urban combat, it's important to consider both the short and the longer-term implications of decisions and actions throughout. The previous example of focusing on repairing damaged multi-unit housing structures rather

---

1   David Petraeus, 'Reflections on wars in Iraq and Afghanistan', *PRISM: The Journal of Complex Operations* 7(1) (14 September 2017), [Washington, DC: National Defence University], available from: cco.ndu.edu/News/Article/1299605/reflections-on-wars-in-iraq-and-afghanistan/.
2   World Vision, *Cities Prepare!*, 61.

than tearing them down and rebuilding from scratch is a good one. While rebuilding might be cheaper or more desirable from the landlord's perspective, ways of more quickly bringing residences back into service—perhaps while renters live in less-damaged portions—hasten the return to normalcy, preserve community cohesion and allow the economically disadvantaged to return to previous, affordable housing. No differently than in preparing for or dealing with a disaster in progress, keeping an eye on the big picture and systems effects in its aftermath increases the chances of ultimate success.

The context of recovery

> Hamburg also used rubble to raise the level of one whole bombed-out area, Hammerbrook. [It] had been built originally on marshland and had perpetually suffered from bad drainage and defective sanitation … During the blockade, Berlin trucked its rubble to the airports at Tegel, Tempelhof, and Gatow to build new runways.[3]
>
> —Jeffry M. Diefendorf, *In the Wake of War*

> Urban growth that occurs in wartime is extremely difficult to reverse and is likely to be permanent.[4]
>
> —Jo Beall and Tom Goodfellow, 'Conflict and Post-War Transition in African Cities'

Reversing a city's population growth after rural drought, insurgency or another of nature or humankind's ravages is no less difficult than after a war. Whether aid provider, urban authority or soldier, it is after the event that the toughest challenges present themselves. The city will survive. The question is at what cost to its population.

Common sense is one key to keeping costs low—or at least lower than if it is absent. 'Social distancing' became the phrase of the day (and weeks and months) during the Covid-19 crisis in New York City. Self-isolation of those exposed went hand-in-hand with what should always be routine but became gospel: diligence in handwashing and, once the evidence became clear, wearing masks. But beware the terms 'common sense' and 'routine'.

---

3   Diefendorf, *In the Wake of War*, 27.
4   Jo Beall and Tom Goodfellow, 'Conflict and Post-War Transition in African Cities', in *Africa's Urban Revolution*, Susan Parnell and Edgar Pieterse (eds), New York, NY: Bloomsbury Academic, 2014, 18–34, at 26, doi.org/10.5040/9781350218246.ch-002.

What is common sense for some has difficulty taking root elsewhere. The amount of hand sanitiser used in 2011–12 by Norwegian, Swedish and Danish hospital personnel was more than five times that used in Italian, Bulgarian and Romanian hospitals.[5] In 2014 in Amsterdam, access to pressurised chambers was provided for medical personnel dealing with Ebola patients in contrast with the cross-contamination that characterised the sarin attack in Tokyo (those entering or leaving the 'Ebola room' had to wait until a wall monitor signalled they could enter or depart, the overpressure ensuring the virus could not escape).[6] Conditions in various urban areas are certainly no more uniform today. The same is true of property ownership, recordkeeping, safety regulation, policy wisdom or cultural responses to disaster conditions. At least one New York City religious community demonstrated little social responsibility during even the worst of Covid-19's rampage by ignoring social distancing guidance and policies for group gatherings. The lack of responsibility would later find company in beachgoers, church services and political rallies elsewhere in the country.

Two developed-world megacities offer an interesting comparison in terms of post-earthquake recovery. While our previous discussion of post-quake Los Angeles and Osaka–Kobe focused on the benefits of restoring rather than tearing down and replacing multifamily structures, there are additional factors in play when considering a broader range of property ownership types. Who owns a plot of land in Los Angeles is seldom in question. Such is the case in most of the United States. This clarity meant knowing who was responsible for making recovery-related decisions was straightforward after the 1994 Northridge tremors. The physical nature of lots also simplified recovery. Properties in affected areas tended to be somewhat large with significant space between adjacent structures. Permission to access a property therefore relied only on its owner. The same was less true a year later when Osaka–Kobe was badly shaken. Greater building densities, laws allowing overlapping responsibilities for a given plot of land or structure and competing levels of influence meant healing was more complicated.[7]

Similar trials can arise when multiple authorities share rights to a piece of land or the strata below and above ground (think of an owner or local utility being responsible for water or sewage piping depending on where

---

5   'First, wash your hands: Battling superbugs', *The Economist*, [London], 26 January 2019, 43–44.
6   ibid.
7   Olshansky et al., *Opportunity in Chaos*, 11-3.

a break occurs). Here again, the experiences of war can tell us something of the challenges to come as subterranean features become increasingly common in urban areas. Both Berlin's and Hiroshima's devastation in World War II left subterranean infrastructure less damaged than that aboveground. Buried waterlines throughout the area torn apart by the first atomic bomb attack suffered little damage compared with surface construction.[8] The same was true of Berlin's buildings after its air bombardment. As underground shopping centres, public transportation and even private homes become the norm rather than the exception, who should receive priority in the sequencing of repairs, right of way during construction or for decisions regarding lengthier or more timely reparations? If policies are not in place pre-calamity, decisions or court cases will both delay community recovery and make it more expensive.

Urban systems during recovery

In Manila and Nairobi a cash-transfer delivery system helped ... regain a measure of food security; it was also used by beneficiaries to restart their livelihoods.[9]

—Jean Yves Barcelo et al., *Meeting Humanitarian Challenges in Urban Areas*

Nigeria has a youth population of about 80 million, representing 60 percent of the total population ... A specific form of witchcraft used to evade the police is called ayeta, or 'bulletproof.' Members of the gang consult witchdoctors, who perform rituals to make sure gang members evade bullets fired at them by police. According to eyewitnesses, the charms are successful and have contributed to minimal police presence in areas ... The political elite also protect gangs and ethnic militia members, making it difficult for the police to effectively enforce the law ... As a result, ethnic conflict from the past remains a dimension of contemporary political life.[10]

—Jane Lumumba, 'Impossible Possibilities'

---

8   Diefendorf, *In the Wake of War*, 19; and Reader, *Cities*, 193–94.
9   Jean Yves Barcelo, Ansa Masaud and Anne Davies, *Meeting Humanitarian Challenges in Urban Areas: Review of Urban Humanitarian Challenges in Port-au-Prince, Manila, Nairobi, Eldoret*, UN-Habitat Report, Nairobi: United Nations Human Settlement Programme, 2011, iv, available from: www.calpnetwork.org/wp-content/uploads/2020/01/humanitarianchallengesurbancasestudies-1.pdf.
10   Jane Lumumba, 'Impossible Possibilities: The Fragility and Resilience of Lagos', in *Building Resilience in Cities under Stress*, Francesco Mancini and Andrea Ó Súilleabháin (eds), New York, NY: International Peace Institute, June 2016, 38–49, at 38, 40, 41.

The tangled web of interconnections within and between megacities means the tremors of decisions made during recovery and rebuilding will reach far in terms of time and wide in terms of the numbers of people affected. Returning to our metaphor of rocks cast into a pond, appropriate decisions and resulting actions cause mere ripples that little disrupt the surface, pleasurably rocking canoes and gently shifting sands to more favourable locations. Poor decisions cause waves that overturn boats, erode the shore and reflect back and forth, inflicting further damage. The dangers of post-disaster inflation have been mentioned above—dangers that, depending on the reach of the crisis, could be urban area–wide, limited to only some communities or sectors of its economy or reverberate around the world. Too much money injected too rapidly or into some segments of the population and not others drives up prices and passions. The first makes money worth less and thus can waste and diminish the value of aid. The second can deepen existing social divides or undermine backing from previously supportive communities. As with so much in an urban area, specific second and higher-order effects can be hard to forecast and impossible to predict. Whether in terms of inflation or other factors, a more appropriate metaphor when the urban area is a megacity would be many separate ponds, each representing a nearby rural area, town or small city, the country of which the megacity is a part, part of the immediate international region or further afield—all impacted by stones cast from the disaster site.

There is money—lots of money—to be made in a disaster's wake. There will never be an absence of unsavoury types wanting to take advantage of that truth. Money is sticky; a bit (or more) stays in the hands of the unscrupulous at every level through which it passes. Chances are some donors will refuse to accept a single centralised manager for setting procedures and distributing money. Others will prefer to fund government officials directly, their intentions having as much to do with gaining influence or future funding as assisting recovery. Nevertheless, administering aid logically and effectively benefits receiver and giver alike even if not all play by the rules. It is a lesson yet to be gleaned from US funding for Iraq's and Afghanistan's national recoveries, which takes us to the subject of governing and control in a disaster's aftermath.

Control in the wake of urban catastrophe

> Bombing tore away the city's skin, revealing tunnels carrying water and human filth, pipes delivering flammable gas, and wires crackling with deadly electricity, but it also gutted and consumed the papers that recorded financial contracts, family links, and personal history.[11]
>
> —Aaron William Moore, *Bombing the City*

> Good government requires an interactive two-way process between the government and the governed.[12]
>
> —Robert Orr, 'Governing When Chaos Rules'

Humankind has been a tad remiss in accepting history's offerings when it comes to managing post-catastrophe recoveries. Commanders and their staff arriving in Los Angeles during and in the aftermath of the 1992 riots drew boundaries between military units as they had been trained to do during combat: along broad streets, city waterways and other obvious terrain features so soldiers could tell where the limits of their responsibilities were even in the dark. Within those boundaries they had to coordinate only with their own leaders. Anything beyond those limits required communicating and carefully coordinating activities with the unit on the other side of the boundary. A boundary should never go down the middle of a street, river or other linear feature, for example, but rather along its edge so that one unit 'owns' the feature. Otherwise, one unit might fire on those approaching thinking them enemy when in fact they are soldiers from the adjacent organisation.

Such obvious features generally make good sense in wartime—less so in 1992 in Los Angeles. Those roads and rivers might be valuable *physical* features, but in urban areas when the worst of combat is past (if there was any), *social* features are the most important. In choosing freeways to bound its subordinate units, staff multiplied the number of police, fire and precinct, district, city, county, neighbourhood and other organisations with which those units had to coordinate. It would have been better to have aligned boundaries with political, administrative, neighbourhood or community limits.[13] These problems were quickly

---

11 Moore, *Bombing the City*, 101.
12 Robert Orr, 'Governing When Chaos Rules: Enhancing Governance and Participation', in *The Battle for Hearts and Minds: Using Soft Power to Undermine Terrorist Networks*, Alexander T.J. Lennon (ed.), Cambridge, MA: MIT Press, 2003, 232–48, at 233.
13 Medby and Glenn, *Street Smart*, 44.

rectified in Los Angeles by the redesignation of boundaries, but a decade later, coalition forces in Baghdad initially made the same mistake. Life could be even more interesting if the soldiers found themselves in a city like Dubai, in the United Arab Emirates, where the desire to draw foreign investment, expertise and commerce means different parts of the city have very different legal codes and occupants in some areas use the US dollar as official currency rather than the Emirati dirham as for the rest of the city.[14] Even remembering to use administrative lines for unit boundaries does not mean headaches won't exist. Pakistan's largest city, Karachi, suffers from poor infrastructure and national government support. Squabbles between the leaders of the Muttahida Qaumi Movement who consider Karachi their base and provincial leaders from the Pakistan People's Party call into question just who is in charge in various locations. The situation is even tougher in that some neighbourhoods are administered by neither provincial nor city authorities; the army, port authority or a rail company instead has responsibility.[15] That said, there is no reason to make the challenges greater than they must be. Those in charge in Los Angeles or Iraq would have saved themselves headaches with a look over their shoulders at the occupation of Germany after World War II. The US Third Army failed to recognise the wisdom of the British and French, both of which drew boundaries for their military governments along German administrative lines.[16]

NGOs and other relief organisations can draw from these examples as well. Physical features will likely delineate city authorities like police precincts (though the streets in question might be less prominent ones). There will still be advantages in drawing the demarcations between organisations such that one of the two 'owns' the road or other feature when actions such as moving refugees in one direction or supplies in the other are necessary. Likewise, the owner of a route would assume responsibility for coordinating debris clearing, garbage pickup and the like, avoiding confusion as to who is responsible. Depending on what an organisation seeks to achieve, drawing on unofficial divides when establishing boundaries can be equally important. Invisible lines (at least ones invisible to the unwitting outsider) might separate gang turfs, religious communities with long-held antipathies, clans with years-old

---

14   Brook, *A History of Future Cities*, 359–60.
15   'King of the heap: Karachi', *The Economist*, [London], 26 October 2019, 35–36, at 36.
16   Schadlow, *War and the Art of Governance*, 69.

revenge obligations or organised crime territories previously held in check but now begging for expansion given the collapse of normalcy thanks to natural disaster or war.

Post-disaster recovery operations are fertile ground for innovation and creativity as well as insights such as these. Where to shelter the thousands, tens of thousands or hundreds of thousands who might be de-housed? If authorities maintain a frequently updated list of vacant properties before the event or have a ready way of compiling such a list in disaster's immediate aftermath, the number of individuals who might be accommodated in existing facilities rather than temporary tent cities or trailers could save millions of dollars in logistical costs. These could include Airbnb and other properties, as mentioned previously, encompassing those held as investments (called 'land banking') but rarely if ever occupied. Almost one-third of the apartments in Midtown Manhattan between Fifth Avenue and Park Avenue and 49th and 70th streets are vacant for 10 or more months a year. Hong Kong and London are likewise popular with wealthy real estate investors.[17] It won't be easy. Real estate companies and politicians will join property owners in screaming foul as regulations requiring sharing in times of crisis could take cash from pockets and re-election coffers should real estate markets become less popular because of such laws. Incentives such as tax breaks or assurances regarding repair of damages could mitigate resistance.

Post-disaster comprehensive approaches

> There is still a tendency in each separate unit ... to be a one-handed puncher. By that I mean the rifleman wants to shoot, the tanker to charge, the artilleryman to fire ... That is not the way to win battles. If the band played a piece first with the piccolo, then with the brass horn, then with the clarinet, and then with the trumpet, there would be a hell of a lot of noise but no music. To get harmony in music, each instrument must support the others. To get harmony in battle, each weapon must support the other. Team play wins. You musicians of Mars ... must come into the concert at the proper place and at the proper time.[18]
>
> —George S. Patton, Jr, addressing 2nd Armored Division, Fort Benning, GA, 8 July 1941

17 Baker, 'The death of a once great city'.
18 George S. Patton, Jr, address to the 2nd Armored Division, Fort Benning, GA, 8 July 1941, cited in Center for Army Lessons Learned (CALL), *Musicians of Mars II*, Handbook, Fort Leavenworth, KS: CALL, April 2016, iii, available from: usacac.army.mil/sites/default/files/publications/16-12_Musicians_of_Mars_II.pdf.

The planners commissioned libraries for several poor districts of the city, specifying maximum costs and minimum construction standards; but they left it to individual communities and architects to work out what the individual libraries would look like. The result is [that] very different structures are used in very different ways.[19]

—Richard Sennett, *Building and Dwelling*

'Team play wins'. Whether soldiers or disaster responders, the musicians must be the right ones and join the concert at the proper place and time. This is the elusive but worthy pursuit of orchestration we have previously set as the mark on the wall. But that mark eludes in another sense as well. One might envision all participants following the same sheet music and looking to a single conductor. The reality will be quite different. Conditions change quickly during and after disasters. Rather than a symphony, the preferred approach will be one of jazz improvisation, with one player complementing or replacing another as the situation dictates. Once again, mission command's decentralisation comes to the fore. Orchestration is desirable but unattainable. Improvisation and tolerance of some players being off key will be imperfect yet good enough under even the best conditions.

The importance of even imperfect orchestration is obvious when history shows us the cost of its absence. Mosul, Iraq, tells us that disasters attract both legitimate NGOs and posers whose inexperience, illegitimate agendas or inadequate logistical support mean they offer little other than a burden. Dissatisfied when refused, these mock aid providers will bypass local authorities and neighbourhood representatives to ply their persuasive efforts with politicians or the media, with the worst putting their own agendas before the people they are allegedly there to assist. Legitimate outsiders will not be blameless as some uncarefully vet those joining them locally, hiring individuals who then pass sensitive information to criminals and others with agendas that do not include aiding residents in need. Afghan NGOs were regularly infiltrated by Taliban for information-collection purposes. Somali 'guards' turning on those they were hired to protect remind us that international representatives need to exercise caution when looking for local assistance. Yet, such caution presents something of a conundrum. NGO struggles in the DRC similarly inform us that failing to hire people from local communities can do more harm than the aid provided does

---

19 Sennett, *Building and Dwelling*, 236.

good. When asked, religious and other leaders might prevent an outsider from making well-intentioned but serious missteps in terms of hiring or otherwise. Melding outsiders' medical knowledge with awareness of local customs could help an international partner in determining how best to handle corpses, for example. While some diseases such as cholera and haemorrhagic fever favour rapid cremation or burial, risk of infection from the dead is generally low. Rapid burial makes later identification difficult and can deny families cultural obligations in treating their deceased.[20] Aid providers will at other times have to find ways of working around potentially deadly practices such as sharing a last meal with the deceased, as was the case with Ebola in 2014 in West Africa.

Deciding on whom to rely for accurate information will undoubtedly be challenging. The problem of outsiders relying on local officials untrusted by the local population initially challenged RAMSI members in Honiara, Solomon Islands, during the summer of 2003. Locals were happy to assist police if they weren't part of the Solomon Islands force. The foreigners appreciated the trust, but it conflicted with RAMSI leaders' hopes of restoring confidence in government authorities who had deservedly lost citizens' favour. RAMSI leaders acted quickly to root out the worst of the police, often asking junior (and therefore less likely to be tainted) members of the force to accompany patrols (Solomon Islands has no military, relying on its law enforcement personnel for security). Individuals approaching the foreign soldiers or police were then directed to take their issues to these 'liaisons' as a first step towards restoring local police legitimacy. Domestic US officials sometimes confront the same hesitation. Knowing residents of select San Francisco communities would be unwilling to deal with less familiar faces, the city's Department of Health assigned restaurant inspectors to gauge the needs of damaged communities after a severe deluge of rain in January 2004.[21] The benefits gained through such wise but careful partnering work both ways. Locals are more likely to have their needs addressed; aid providers can better allocate their resources by avoiding falling victim to con artists.

Though we might tend to think of recovery in terms of individuals or families, what might be called 'mass aid' can be both more efficient and more effective. In the words of former dean of the Johns Hopkins School of Public Health Al Sommer: 'Medicine saves lives retail, one at

20   Sanderson et al., *Responding to urban disasters*.
21   Rodin, *The Resilience Dividend*, 17.

a time, [while] public health saves them wholesale, millions at a time.'[22] Sommer's wisdom extends beyond medicine. Importing bottled water might seem the logical option when addressing a megacity community's lack of drinking water. Author Judith Rodin instead found Coca-Cola's Slingshot program provides systems that can filter and purify water from any source—freshwater, saltwater, even sewage—to make it safely drinkable. One Slingshot filter unit uses less electricity than an ordinary hairdryer and can produce 800 litres of clean water a day—enough to serve 300 people.[23]

There will be problems to overcome no matter how good the plans or how many the pre-event rehearsals. Confronted with gangs, looters, insurgents or corrupt officials, the military will seek to immediately capitalise on any information that helps them get such miscreants off the streets. Police tend to be more deliberate. They must preserve forensic evidence that will stand up in court to put the lowlifes in jail. Appropriately orchestrated mission command guidance that identifies how to resolve potential friction is too often absent. Guidance from international organisations' leaders and from local government can differ. Deployed leaders will at other times find themselves having to 'best guess' as they try to find a workable balance between vague policies from home and requirements on the ground. Partnerships with NGO, IGO and commercial representatives can at times provide options otherwise unavailable. While government officials must toe the political line, these less-constrained partners can make things happen that they cannot.

Post-combat recovery

As long as people want shelter over their heads, we are going to fight in buildings.[24]

—Sergeant Major David Wilson

Urban combat magnifies the effects of battle.[25]

—General Stephen J. Townsend, US Army

22   McNickle, *Bloomberg*, 173.
23   Rodin, *The Resilience Dividend*, 289.
24   David Wilson, remarks at Analysis of Urban Warfare, Military Operations Research Society Conference, Quantico, VA, 2 April 2019.
25   Stephen J. Townsend [General, US Army], 'Megacity scenarios, foundations, and convergence', Presentation to MDB in Megacities Conference, Fort Hamilton, NY, 3 April 2018.

Warsaw was 80 per cent destroyed and lost 800,000 of its 1.3 million residents during World War II.[26] One-third of (a then much smaller) New York City was destroyed during Revolutionary War fighting in 1776.[27] Manila saw 100,000 of its 1945 population of 1.1 million killed and many more injured during fighting that year. Dresden and Coventry, Hiroshima and Nanking, Jerusalem and Rome—war has gutted cities and slain their occupants wholesale for centuries. More recently, 'no one even bothered to count how many civilians were killed' during fighting in Grozny and other parts of Chechnya in the 1990s.[28]

Recovery after a disaster regardless of cause provides opportunities to address the otherwise unaddressable. Recovering from the 1871 fire that ravaged Chicago provided an opportunity—one the city seized to become the world's skyscraper king. Hydraulic elevators became commonplace. Less known: steam heating replaced fireplaces as the primary means of warding off Chicago's winter cold in the aftermath of the conflagration.[29] As would be the case in Warsaw nearly 300 years later, the 1666 Great Fire of London destroyed 80 per cent of the city's buildings.[30] As in Chicago, in London:

> [D]estruction caused by the Great Fire provided a major opportunity for the redesign of London … Parliament enacted a number of … schemes. These included: minimum street widths of 14 feet [4.3 metres]; regulations governing the height of buildings in relation to street width; special fire courts to resolve disputes during the rebuilding; straightening of roads; [and] the London Rebuilding Act made (fire-proof) stone and brick compulsory construction materials. Thatched roofs were also replaced with tiled ones.[31]

Megacity officials may suddenly find themselves running engines of great change in the aftermath of catastrophe. Recent lessons from the combat arena have much to offer those facing decisions with consequences lasting decades.

---

26   Vale and Campanella, 'Introduction', 4, 10.
27   Page, 'The City's End', 77.
28   Knezys and Sedlickas, *The War in Chechnya*, 260.
29   Neal Bascomb, *Higher: A Historic Race to the Sky and the Making of a City*, New York, NY: Doubleday, 2003, 95–97.
30   Vale and Campanella, 'Introduction', 4, 10.
31   Parker, 'Disaster Response in London', 191.

Getting post-combat right

We are measuring how much we spend or how many miles of pipeline we lay. That isn't really measuring what's important.[32]

—Colonel John Hurley, US Army

When General Chiarelli was moving into Sadr City [Iraq], they needed to have water. One of the questions he asked was, 'How do we get water into the neighborhood?' And the solution was to put spigots on the outside of houses. We didn't have the time to run the lines into the houses.

—Anonymous interviewee

'We tend to measure inputs, not outputs', Major General David Perkins observed while commanding the US Army's 4th Infantry Division in Iraq in 2011—years after he suspended patrols in Fallujah. Perkins's observation reinforces Colonel Hurley's just above:

I believe the coalition's was the largest purchase of electrical generators in the history of the world, a multi-billion dollar contract to buy generators … We were measuring how many generators we ordered and their delivery status. That included the mother of all generators—the MOAG, we called it—this huge thing that came through on a flatbed truck. We tracked it as it moved to wherever its final resting place was. The graph we used to track it started when the generator entered Iraq and we followed it to wherever it was going. At that point the bar was green: MOAG had arrived. Well, just getting a generator to where it's going is maybe 20% of the problem. You've got to build the electrical generation plant. You have to fuel the electric generator. You have to install the transmission lines. And once the transmission lines are installed, you have to distribute the electricity to the houses. We were focused very much on buying electrical generators. But buying generators is not a solution to the problem. The problem is getting electricity into houses. There's a distribution aspect to that. There's a transmission aspect. There's a generation problem. There's a fueling the generator problem. We have a proclivity to focus in on what we understand, what is manageable, what is easily measured. So buying a generator and tracking delivery tends to draw our attention more than a discussion about sub-district distribution of electrical lines and the like. These are the types

---

32   John Hurley (Colonel, US Army), Interview with Dr Russell W. Glenn, Winchester, VA, 8 November 2011.

of challenges that I seem to have to deal with again and again. We sometimes make very big decisions and spend a lot of money without having what's last in mind.[33]

Knowing how to measure progress during a megacity recovery is a less-than-obvious enterprise. The number of dollars allocated to projects was an infamous metric of 'progress' in Iraq during US operations from 2003. The demand to spend money resulted in tens of millions of dollars squandered to corruption. It also resulted in focusing on large projects as that meant committing huge amounts in one fell swoop rather than many smaller projects involving more paperwork, management and quality control personnel. Our previous example of installing various parts of a sewage disposal system without considering the whole system brings the point home. Focus on the inputs (dollars spent) rather than the intended effect (in this case, the literal output of removing sewage from homes and neighbourhoods) resulted in wasted funds and waste not moved.[34] Big projects take months or years to build. Smaller projects with impact in a matter of days or weeks are the smart move when popular perceptions are important. It's even smarter if they are tied into a longer-term plan so that small projects flow into large like fingers into a glove.

Solutions do not need to be all or nothing. US Army Corps of Engineers officer Carl Strock recalled his time in Iraq when people were complaining that US efforts were failing because Baghdad did not have electricity 24/7—an impractical standard given the long neglect of power infrastructure under Saddam's regime. Strock realised that the Iraqis weren't asking for constant, all-day power. Eventually perhaps, but in the short run they wanted predictability so that they knew when they would have power and could adjust schedules accordingly.[35] Another project in Iraq saw $18.4 billion committed to building 147 medical facilities. The structures were built and filled with state-of-the-art equipment. Unfortunately, there were not enough people who knew how to maintain the equipment in many locations. Elsewhere there were no staff to train the personnel who would have to run the facilities.[36] The result was both

33 Perkins, Interview.
34 Peter Chiarelli (General, US Army), Interview with Dr Russell W. Glenn, Pentagon, Washington, DC, 9 November 2011, [as appears in Russell W. Glenn, *Core Counterinsurgency Asset: Lessons from Iraq and Afghanistan for United States Army Corps of Engineers Leaders*, Study sponsored by the United States Army Corps of Engineers, 31 May 2012 (revised 8 December 2016), 273–81].
35 Carl A. Strock (Lieutenant General, US Army, retired), Interview with Dr Russell W. Glenn and Dave Dilegge, Frederick, MD, 29 July 2011.
36 Chiarelli, Interview.

a waste of money and a blackeye for the coalition as it rightly appeared someone had failed to think through more than the physical structures that are only one part of a larger medical care system. As with General Perkins's generators, focusing on parts of a system in isolation failed as a measure of success. General Perkins was not alone with his observations:

> For those assisting in humanitarian assistance or similar efforts, General Perkins' outputs (measures of effect) are likely to be what really tells leaders what's being accomplished. [Colonel (US Army, retired)] Greg Fontenot provided two examples from his military career to demonstrate the point. One cited the removal of 2,962 mines by his soldiers when he was a brigade commander in Bosnia-Herzegovina. His immediate senior was quite impressed, but Fontenot told him it wasn't the number of mines removed that was really important to the people … [The area] was seeded with tens if not hundreds of thousands of mines. What was important: the removal of those mines cleared forty-five routes previously closed to pedestrian or vehicle traffic, more than doubling 'freedom of movement' for local citizens. The second example provides what would be an even more misleading example of mistaking an input for a meaningful measure of results. Fontenot used the example of tons of information leaflets dropped in an attempt to convince enemy soldiers that they should surrender. Measuring tons of leaflets dropped would reveal nothing about how much they influenced anyone to no longer fight. A valuable measure of effect might be the number of enemy soldiers who surrendered due to having seen a leaflet, an estimate of which could be obtained by asking a sample of the prisoners why they gave up or counting the number who brought a leaflet with them (if the leaflet directed them to bring one when surrendering).[37]

Rebuilding megacity capacity

In the immediate aftermath of 9/11, Wall Street profits fell 60 percent and the city lost 130,000 private sector jobs.[38]

—Chris McNickle, *Bloomberg*

---

37   Russell W. Glenn, *Considering Urban Control: A Summary of the 2006 Israeli Defense Forces–US Joint Forces Command Urban Operations Conference*, Santa Monica, CA: RAND Corporation, February 2007, xiii, 31.
38   McNickle, *Bloomberg*, 135.

> Not only do you need a mass of people to re-establish a neighborhood. Their homes need to be in proximity to one another in order to build and maintain relationships, establish organizations, and pursue group activities.[39]
>
> —Judith Rodin, *The Resilience Dividend*

While Japan annually has more people exposed to the dangers of typhoons than the Philippines, history suggests fatalities in the latter would be an estimated 17 times greater than in Japan should storms of like types strike both countries.[40] Richer nations tend to have better building regulations than poorer ones. They tend to enforce them more stringently. They also are likely to better prepare for disasters in other ways. Tokyo's Metropolitan Government has designated 56,553 hectares (565 square kilometres, or 95 per cent) of the Tokyo Ward Area into two types of special districts: fireproof districts and quasi-fireproof districts.[41] In fireproof districts, any building with more than three storeys or over 100 square metres of floor space must be constructed of nonflammable materials such as reinforced concrete. Standards in the quasi-fireproof district require fireproofing of only some larger and taller structures. We have already mentioned other preparations such as the requirement for local governments to prepare disaster preparedness maps and the city's many official evacuation sites that include parks, other open spaces or nonflammable buildings. No resident is supposed to have to travel more than 2 kilometres to reach such a site.[42]

Standards like these explain why Tokyo's losses and recovery demands should be less than for similar disasters in megacities less aggressive with their preparations. There are additional benefits when an urban area is served by competent, noncorrupt officials who ensure these standards are more than paper deep. Urban areas with officials who keep track of where community members live, work or go to school add to readiness. Accounting for residents should be far quicker in such cases—a boon to first responders wanting to determine which homes or other structures might have individuals trapped beneath rubble and to families awaiting news about loved ones. Armed with disaster preparedness maps and knowledge of where their family members are to go when evacuating, men and women returning home from work can plot safer routes and find

---

39   Rodin, *The Resilience Dividend*, 248.
40   IFRC, *World Disasters Report 2010*, 13.
41   The Tokyo Ward Area comprises the 23 wards that are traditionally considered to make up the 'City of Tokyo'. This is only a small portion of the megacity and contains roughly one-quarter of its population.
42   Kumagai and Nojima, 'Urbanization and Disaster Mitigation in Tokyo', 79, 80.

loved ones more readily. These represent thousands, tens of thousands or more who will less burden overtasked mobile phone systems or government officials with demands to determine family status.

These preparations are even more important when the urban area in question is hyperconnected worldwide. Select commodity markets could conceivably come to a standstill were Manhattan to suffer damage even more extensive than that of 9/11; New York City is the planet's primary hub for coffee trading. These sometimes-unexpected connections (for those of us less familiar with coffee or other commodity markets) are not unusual. Megacities are inherently crucial to financial sectors; other urban areas can be likewise. Frankfurt leads trading for British treasuries—and did so even before Brexit (who would have thought?). Chicago is the top financial centre for futures.[43]

Laying sewer pipes and intermediate pumps in Baghdad without providing connections to a treatment facility was an obvious failure—one understandable if not forgivable given pressures to spend large amounts of relief funds quickly. A second example reinforces the need to plan for the social as well as the physical infrastructure aspects of any project. In this case, it was a $20 million water treatment facility paid for with US funds, successfully completed, but never opened because competing Iraqi factions disagreed on who would run it—something that should have been part of preliminary evaluations (and a reminder of the criticality of knowing both what to ask and how to acquire the answers).[44] Such stumbles wasted funds and bruised reputations. The second is no small matter when insurgent or other parties seek to convince residents that present governments and any party associated with them are unworthy of popular support. Partnering with local government or community organisations should help in early identification of lurking problems. Unfortunately, knowing what questions to ask can be harder than one might think. The right question might be no more than: 'What local issues do we need to be aware of before we start this project?' The earlier quotation regarding libraries in Medellín, Colombia, reflects the fact that asking those affected helps get

43   Saskia Sassen, 'Cities in Today's Global Age', in *Connecting Cities: Networks. A Research Publication for the 9th World Congress of Metropolis*, Chris Johnson, Richard Hu and Shanti Abedin (eds), Barcelona: Metropolis Secretariat General, 2008, 22–43, at 31, available from: www.metropolis. org/sites/default/files/network_complete_0.pdf.
44   Raymond Odierno (General, US Army, retired), Speech to 'Operating in Dense Urban Environments' Class of 1978 Student Workshop for Civil–Military Operations, West Point, NY, 18 April 2018.

it right. Similar meetings, held before making plans or committing funds, would also provide outsiders with a chance to gauge local capacity to manage a project once it is done. Representatives of outside organisations often depart for home while construction, hiring or other elements of a project are still in progress. Knowing if anyone local can see the work through to completion is a guessing game unless someone has determined the lie of the social landscape.

A caution is in order. While strengthening the influence of community organisations seems like a win-win, some city, national or party officials may see grassroots empowerment as a threat to their influence (recall Mexico City government officials' unease when neighbourhood leaders stepped forward in the aftermath of the 1985 earthquake). Communities may see catastrophe as a long-awaited chance to marginalise corrupt or otherwise untrusted authorities. Collective action by refugee camp occupants in Gaza resulted in protests when the UN Relief and Works Agency for Palestine Refugees in the Near East sought to turn over sanitation responsibilities to local officials.[45] On the positive side, pre-existing social ties can serve as a magnet that reunites communities fractured by misfortune. Vietnamese-Americans displaced by Hurricane Katrina re-formed around their Mary Queen of Vietnam Church on return to New Orleans—pieces reuniting like an explosion shown in reverse.[46] Focusing on pieces alone without recognition of previous ties would be like trying to construct a house from random parts of separate structures. The result may be a building but one far from the home it once was. Getting residents back into houses quickly without thought to their once-community—locating them randomly and remotely from longstanding religious, commercial, club, school, neighbourhood and other social links—returns people but fails to reconstruct a city.

As in Hamburg and Berlin after World War II, both the physical and the social elements for rebuilding will lie among the depressing ugliness of post-disaster rubble. The trained eye sees resources where another looks on seeming waste. Designs can take advantage of the shattered pieces by filling wire-mesh containers to form walls. Crushing bricks provides

---

45   Haysom, *Sanctuary in the City?*.
46   Wei Li, Christopher A. Airriess, Angela Chia-Chen Chen, Karen J. Leong and Verna Keith, 'Katrina and migration: Evacuation and return by African Americans and Vietnamese Americans in an eastern New Orleans suburb', *The Professional Geographer* 62(1) (2010): 103–18, at 116, doi.org/10.1080/00330120903404934.

aggregate for concrete or mortar.[47] Chances are good that the bonds of a city's social structure are only temporarily broken if action is taken with sufficient speed. Some will see opportunity for renewal where others find only ruin, as with the case of Queen of Vietnam Church.

Jakarta suffered the one–two punch of the 1997–98 El Niño's effects on crops and Indonesia's economic crisis in the closing years of the twentieth century. Though calamities of a sort different to this book's focus on sudden shocks, they nonetheless suggest how a megacity can reorient shattered parts and fractured bonds to new purposes. Economic problems were made worse by a third blow: urban violence that disrupted the city in May and November of 1998.[48] NGOs sought to address critical food shortages resulting from this trio of jolts but lacked the infrastructure due to commitments in suffering rural areas and an inability to deal with the magnitude of demand from the megacity's needy millions. A lack of transparency at Indonesia's national level led US Government officials to fear that what aid was available would not reach those poor who were suffering most.

From misery rose innovation, but it came from the commercial rather than the government sector. Rice is the number one cereal consumed by Jakartans. Much of the food aid sent to address El Niño's ravages on agriculture was, however, in the form of wheat. Aid providers saw opportunity where others saw crisis. Noodles had long been popular among Jakarta's poor before the economic crisis. Though that had become less the case when economic crisis reduced incomes, enlightened aid managers recognised that a twofer offered itself: a way not only to feed the poor but also to stimulate portions of the capital's food distribution system, which was lagging as was so much else in the economy. They created a 'market-targeted food assistance program' that included the following parts:

- Imported wheat was ground into flour by one of Indonesia's three flour mills.
- Wheat had earlier been processed by companies later forced to lay off workers when noodle demand dropped. Rejuvenation of wheat availability thus constituted a twofer in a twofer as both the companies and the many economically disadvantaged who were rehired benefited given the new demand.

---

47 Sanderson et al., *Responding to urban disasters.*
48 Material in this vignette relies on Kelly, *Acute food insecurity in mega-cities,* 10–15.

- Noodles were sold through commercial outlets with prices and packaging designed to accommodate the communities most in need. A quality-control program sought to ensure noodle products met acceptable standards. Managers turned to existing noodle-producing companies' stock management systems to limit corruption by monitoring product movements. A discrepancy between tonnage produced and tonnage sold would result in a fine for the responsible party. Organisations involved in production, distribution and sales were permitted to make a normal profit, however.

- Jakarta delivery companies distributed products throughout the massive urban area, forgoing reliance on government vehicles or limited NGO transport resources. An added benefit: these companies knew where street vendors had operated when noodles were popular before the downturn.

- Other organisations such as marketing and sales companies benefited by helping to identify buyers.

- Recognising that limiting sales to Jakarta would disrupt commercial markets supplying megacity residents, managers expanded the program to other parts of Java, the island on which the capital is located.

The initiative was not without flaws—a major one being the lag between conception and delivery of nearly a year. Nevertheless, the aid community's use of recent history (knowing noodles had been a staple for the poor before the economic crisis), understanding of the megacity's existing capacity for production, distribution and marketing and positive impact on the labour market are remarkable.

More on systems awareness during recovery

> Three weeks after I left [Lagos,] Nigeria, police entered a nearby slum and burned it to the ground, leaving 20,000 people—mostly families with young children—homeless.[49]
> —Jeff Goodell, *The Water Will Come*

> Cops hate two things—change and status quo.[50]
> —James P. O'Neill, 'Preparing for and managing megacity crises'

49 Goodell, *The Water Will Come*, 231.
50 James P. O'Neill, 'Preparing for and managing megacity crises (the NYPD perspective): 9/11 and Hurricane Sandy lessons for US military leaders', Presentation to Multi-Domain Battle in Megacities Conference, Fort Hamilton, NY, 3 April 2018.

Bukit Ho Swee was where many new arrivals to Singapore settled.[51] Chinese triad splinter groups were among those finding the crowded ramshackle housing and twisting byways a shelter from the police. Youths not in school and lacking parental supervision were willing gang recruits. It should not surprise that the slum had a bad reputation among government authorities. Aware of the criminals, residents nevertheless did not consider their community a crime haven. The gangs provided protection. The doors of homes were left unlocked so people could cut through them to shorten journeys or avoid unwanted contacts. Owners of legitimate businesses, gambling establishments, opium dens and street vendors did not appreciate paying protection money but understood the necessity. Gang members provided what police would not. Intergang violence could at times put those hoping to remain uninvolved at risk, but it was not unusual for one of the gangs to warn residents of the fighting to come. City officials had made it clear they held no love for the poor who lived in the community. Their police were untrusted. Like the Lagos community in the quote above, Bukit Ho Swee would burn to the ground. But unlike the Nigerian fire, it appears an accident rather than the police was the perpetrator that rendered homeless 16,000 people from Bukit Ho Swee and nearby neighbourhoods.

In the Lagos slum of Badia East, many of those forcibly evicted in early 2013 were homeless two and a half years later. Housing for more than 80 per cent of the displaced was worse than what had been demolished. Half were separated from their families and one-third of the children had yet to resume schooling.[52] In Manila, officials housed forcibly displaced residents in locations so distant from their jobs as to make commuting grossly time-consuming if not impractical.

These are brutal but not unusual cases. There are gradations of how punishing neighbourhood destruction can be. Often the ousted receive nothing in the way of land or structures to re-establish themselves. Gradual removal of housing or allowing residents time to move on their own can reduce the pain of displacement. Not turning housing into unusable rubble means families can take materials from their previous residences

51 Material in this vignette comes from Loh Kah Seng, *Squatters into Citizens: The 1961 Bukit Ho Swee Fire and the Making of Modern Singapore*, Singapore: NUS Press, 2013, 65–67, 16–17, doi.org/10.2307/j.ctv1qv3g0.
52 Megan Chapman and Andrew Maki, 'The Cities We Create Depend on the Choices We Make: Lagos', in *Know Your City: Slum Dwellers Count*, Janet Byrne (ed.), Cape Town, South Africa: Slum Dwellers International, 2018, 20–22, at 20, available from: sdinet.org/wp-content/uploads/2018/02/SDI_StateofSlums_LOW_FINAL.pdf.

to rebuild elsewhere. Further, they are more likely to build a structure meeting their needs if they are not forcibly allotted shelter provided by government authorities.[53]

The cause of displacement is often landowners looking for a way to clear the unwanted from their properties when more economically attractive alternatives beckon. As we saw in Karachi, city officials can be in cahoots with landlords. On the other hand, accident or not, Bukit Ho Swee was the lighting of a fuse that exploded into Singapore's highly regarded public housing program—a program that at once improved property standards and brought multitudes in the informal economy into the ranks of taxpaying citizens. Gaining a home in a government-sponsored property required proof of an income from a steady job. Ownership required salary contributions. Both state and individual benefited as the policy forced those wanting housing into the formal rather than the casual workforce.[54] The housing program spawned in the aftermath of the Bukit Ho Swee fire is now the norm for the city-state's residents.

Megacity fragmentation can mollify the negative effects of displacement. Instead of a single CBD with a nearly exclusive hold on select job types, lesser CBDs sprout up at various locations throughout the urban area, as in Los Angeles, where the phenomenon is so common it could be called the 'LA effect'. This dispersal has several benefits, including reducing the length and expense of worker commutes, traffic congestion and pollution (many in Los Angeles might question the comment about traffic congestion. Bottom line: it could be even worse, LA). For Los Angeles, the sprouting of smaller CBDs and cores has been a natural evolution. There is the possibility that similar dispersion could be a deliberate response motivated either by conscious government policy or as an opportunity seized in the wake of a major disaster.

Tokyo in 1995, New York in 2001, London in 2005, Mumbai in 2008, Paris in 2015—there is no lack of evidence that megacities make attractive targets for terrorists. Centralised power, water distribution, communications and other vital infrastructure elements are vulnerable to interruption via assaults that no longer require a physical strike, as cyberattacks have already made clear. The potential value of decentralising select infrastructure despite sacrifices in economies of scale in doing so has already been mentioned. Nature's own means of reducing the severity of her storms merits consideration as well.

---

53 Acción Contra El Hambre, *Urban Disaster Lessons Learnt*.
54 Seng, *Squatters into Citizens*, 207.

Wetlands and additional natural features act to dampen the worst effects of typhoons and tidal surges, but these are features too often ravaged due to ignorance, carelessness or in the service of greed. It is estimated that storm surges in New Orleans that once ranged from 3 to 3.6 metres have increased to between 5.5 and 6 metres due to the destruction of marshes and other tidal lands near the city.[55] Oyster beds stood metres high in New York City's Hudson River estuary many years ago, acting to breakup waves before they reached shore. Harvesting of the molluscs combined with water pollution to all but eliminate these protective barriers (efforts are under way to replace some of these natural storm-effect mitigators).[56] In times of rising sea levels, examples of past devastation bode ill for any urban area casual about maintaining its natural guardians. In other cases, it is urban pollution combined with high temperatures related to climate change that is the culprit; the causes together have done much to exacerbate Miami's soon-to-be-legendary flooding challenges.[57] Choosing to partner with instead of abusing Mother Nature could save much that otherwise will eventually have to be spent in moving the forward line of buildings to higher ground (if available); constructing seawalls, dykes or other barriers; raising structures on pillars; returning those ravaged areas to wetlands; or simply surrendering to the inevitability of more frequent and damaging floods and increased financial punishment. In developing-world urban areas in particular, that damage and those punishments are more likely to be suffered by the poor living in areas the wealthier avoid. Unfortunately, viable alternative locations may not exist for those in exposed slums. Also unfortunate: the limited political influence such communities generally wield means little will be done other than to leave residents to suffer with little promise of help in the aftermath of a disaster.

It is unlikely Jakarta's program to develop a 'noodle economy' would have succeeded had NGO managers not been aware of the previous noodle system, including the dishes' popularity, drivers' knowledge of where previous markets were and awareness of a need to rein in corruption. Understanding the many parts of the megacity's commercial, social and economic systems made the venture a success (if a someone belated one). Our example of constructing a sewerage system without ensuring connection to a water treatment facility provides a counterexample. A more thorough look would have considered not only the pipe system

55   Brinkley, *The Great Deluge*, 13.
56   Roman Mars and Kurt Kohlstedt, *The 99% Invisible City: A Field Guide to the Hidden World of Everyday Design*, Boston, MA: Houghton Mifflin Harcourt, 2020, 118–19.
57   Ariza, *Disposable City*, 54.

and local pumps, but also power supply for treatment pumps; chemicals essential for purification; availability of talent for maintaining pipes, pumps and power supply; who, where and how those with the necessary talents would be educated; and so much more. And these considerations only touch on that portion of the system within or near the Iraqi capital. The quality of water released from treatment facilities influences the health of those downstream and of the Persian Gulf. So it is with any urban area along a shore or river, as so many are.

More on the ties that bind: Renewing or creating systems capacity

In 1919 at the Jerusalem Court of Appeals, presided over by Judge Muhammad Yusif al Kahlidi, widely known for both his eccentricity and fairness … a well-known Old City prostitute was brought before him on charges of 'disturbing the peace.' Judge Khalidi apparently had been drinking heavily the night before and was still in a daze when the woman was ushered screaming into the court. [The judge said:] 'Shut up, you whore, and control yourself.' Prostitute: (enraged by the insult) 'My lord, I may be a prostitute at home, but here I am a citizen in the court of the state.' Judge Khalidi: (sobering and taken aback) 'You are absolutely right.' [Judge to the court secretary:] 'Write this down. In the new case of slander … I hereby fine the accused [myself] five Palestinian pounds.'[58]

—Salim Tamari, 'Confessionalism and Public Space in Ottoman and Colonial Jerusalem'

The cities most at risk are those where these events are already common—although there is some evidence of the geographic range of some extreme weather events expanding. Coastal cities will be doubly at risk as sea-level rise increases hazards from coastal flooding and erosion. For any city, the scale of the risk from these extreme weather events is also much influenced by the quality of housing and infrastructure in that city and the level of preparedness among the city's population and key emergency services.[59]

—David Satterthwaite et al., *Adapting to climate change in urban areas*

---

58   Salim Tamari, 'Confessionalism and Public Space in Ottoman and Colonial Jerusalem', in *Cities & Sovereignty: Identity Politics in Urban Spaces*, Diane E. Davis and Nora Libertun de Duren (eds), Bloomington, IN: Indiana University Press, 2011, 59–82, at 74.

59   Satterthwaite et al., *Adapting to climate change in urban areas*, 17.

Depending on the extent of the punishment inflicted on an urban area, all or parts of it form a vacuum when existing authorities are removed. Such was the case in Medellín, Colombia, with the killing of drug lord Pablo Escobar, with other criminal elements fighting for control given his sudden absence. The British Army and Royal Ulster Constabulary combined forces to free East Belfast's Ballymacarrett neighbourhood of the Provisional Irish Republican Army (PIRA) in late 1971. They, and civil authorities, succeeded in ousting the PIRA but failed to backfill the resulting void. Within six weeks, the PIRA had re-established its sway; Ballymacarrett was once again other-governed.[60] There is no reason to think megacities are exempt in this regard. First-generation gangs were greatly weakened after a slum-clearing initiative in Mumbai, India, during the 1970s and 1980s. Planning only for initial purges of criminal elements again opened the door to a second generation who took up where the previous had left off. The same happened a second time in the aftermath of religious riots and another round of crackdowns in 1992–93, with the new breed of organised crime becoming even more sophisticated as it added to previous controls over real estate development and commerce, legitimising its status by putting hand-selected representatives in the state legislature.[61]

Again and again, a lesson presents itself: a systems approach is essential to lasting success. That means not only removing criminal elements but also readying effective and legitimate capabilities to step into the void. It means not only training a megacity police force but also comprehensively addressing legal system requirements. It should be a collective effort. Just short of three-quarters of Dhaka's slums benefit from services provided by NGOs; they are an invaluable asset.[62] Their offerings can be even more beneficial if orchestrated with government assets … given the government is effective.

The underlying assumption is that there exists a legitimate government to backfill a vacuum following any removal of other-governed capabilities, to create and maintain an effective legal system or provide services to citizens. Janice Perlman provides 10 ingredients she found common to violence in Rio de Janeiro's *favelas*. These included 'underpaid,

---

60   Aaron Edwards, 'Misapplying lessons learned? Analysing the utility of British counterinsurgency strategy in Northern Ireland, 1971–76', *Small Wars & Insurgencies* 21(2) (June 2010): 303–30, at 316, doi.org/10.1080/09592318.2010.481427.

61   Brugmann, *Welcome to the Urban Revolution*, 127.

62   Nazrul Islam, A.Q.M. Mahbub and Nurul Islam Nazem, 'Urban slums of Bangladesh', *The Daily Star*, [Dhaka], 20 June 2009, available from: www.thedailystar.net/news-detail-93293.

understaffed, unaccountable police forces; a weak government indifferent to the "rule of law;" [and] a sensationalist mass media empire fomenting fear to … justify police brutality'.[63]

Just as each megacity is unique, an approach successful in one situation might not provide a solution acceptable in another, barring adaptation. Singapore's former long-time president Lee Kuan Yew explained that policies aimed at integrating Chinese, Indian and Malay citizens in the state-sponsored housing program were being defeated when buyers sold their properties. Initial sales designated what percentage of each demographic group could buy into a building, but there were no constraints on who could buy on resale. The result was a drift towards segregation that flew in the face of the original sales policies and the government's objectives. Singapore adapted, setting limits on what percentage of each demographic could own in a neighbourhood. Lee was not ignorant of the fact that his efforts at social engineering imposed costs borne directly by homeowners. 'When a Malay or Indian is not allowed to sell to a Chinese because the Chinese quota has already been filled, the apartment invariably sells at a price lower than the market rate,' Lee wrote. However, he continued, 'this is a small cost for achieving our larger objective of getting the races to intermingle'.[64] Workable in Singapore, it is less likely to be a solution accepted in less authoritarian societies. Then again, acceptance might be forthcoming were dictates replaced with tax or other incentives promoting integration and other desirable ends.

Concluding thoughts on post-disaster relief, recovery and rebuilding

In designing the Imperial Hotel in Tokyo, which opened in 1922, Frank Lloyd Wright and his engineer Paul Mueller put in an exterior reflecting pool that could also serve as a water source when earthquakes broke water mains needed for firefighting. [They also] exposed and suspended plumbing and electrical components instead of encasing them in walls or floors where they could be damaged.[65]

—Judith Rodin, *The Resilience Dividend*

---

63   Perlman, *Favela*, 174.
64   Lee Kuan Yew, *From Third World to First: Singapore and the Asian Economic Boom*, New York, NY: HarperCollins, 2000, 209.
65   Rodin, *The Resilience Dividend*, 33–34.

[Following the 1995 great Hanshin–Awaji earthquake,] the most prevalent answers to the question of why citizens have not had seismic retrofitting work carried out on their dwellings [included]: Such a large earthquake will not occur again. If such an earthquake occurs again, then I will do it.[66]

—City of Kobe, *Comprehensive Strategy for Recovery*

'Make the training harder than the game' should apply regardless of the type of urban disaster for which authorities are planning. A well-run exercise conducted in a major US city not too long before this book was published brought an international array of federal, state and city officials, academics and commercial-world experts together to deal with the challenges of a weapon of mass destruction attack—but the scenario left the urban area's emergency operations centre just outside the area affected by the notional blast. Exercises shouldn't sidestep the toughest challenges. New York City's former transportation commissioner Janette Sadik-Khan wrote that 'a massive contingent of [her] transportation department itself was shut out of its headquarters for nearly two months' after Hurricane Sandy thanks to it being in the low-lying confines of southern Manhattan.[67] In the early 1980s, the IDF found itself fighting in Beirut's 50 square kilometres and among the city's population of more than 1 million—an undertaking characterised by missteps and adhockery. 'The war was a disaster for Israel', one expert noted. Most of the 344 killed and more than 2,000 other Israeli military casualties were in the capital or other urban areas. The damage to Beirut was devastating. Some 17,000 noncombatants were killed, deeply wounding Israel's legitimacy among that population.[68] The Hayward Fault Zone in the San Francisco Bay Area is notorious for the number of public facilities lying on or close to it as commercial builders look elsewhere. Pipes beneath the University of California Golden Bears football stadium require regular repair as the fault's creep pulls them apart. Hayward City Hall suffers frequent cracks for similar reasons. Other facilities exposed include the Contra Costa Community College campus, the Chabot Dam and Fairmont Hospital— all of which are sure to offer significant challenges in the aftermath of a future rupture.[69]

---

66   City of Kobe, *Comprehensive Strategy for Recovery*, 317.

67   Sadik-Khan, *Street Fight*, 279.

68   Charles Dick, 'FIBUA: Lessons from history', *British Army Review Special Report: Urban Operations Report 1* (Winter 2018): 10–27, at 16, 17.

69   Steven Newton, 'The most dangerous fault in America', *Earth: The Science behind the Headlines*, 9 May 2016, available from: www.earthmagazine.org/article/most-dangerous-fault-america/.

Bringing as many people as possible together to plan, practise and otherwise prepare for crisis is one of the intermediate marks on the wall at the top of which is an orchestrated effort that synchronises the many disparate efforts and objectives. That is not to say that every exercise must take on a mega-challenge like Japan's earthquake, tsunami and nuclear reactor failure trifecta of horrors. Starting small and later cranking up the challenge thermostat allow for small-lesson bites of the disaster elephant without becoming overwhelmed. Preparations will never be ideal. People move from position to position too quickly—political leaders, in particular. But establishing a progression of exercises, rehearsals and revisits to incorporate insights into plans means that adapting to the challenge will be less a panicked leap than a reasoned step. Closer ties between those responsible for megacities' security mean more people will benefit from this ratchetting up of challenges as each urban area learns from both practice and events, then shares with contemporaries elsewhere. Smaller urban and even rural areas will likewise benefit given upgrades of national urban response standards and procedures. After the debacle that was the reaction to Hurricane Katrina, US Department of Health and Human Services officials dictated rules requiring that facilities receiving Medicare or Medicaid have emergency plans and provide training in their implementation. Movement of nursing home and hospital residents when Hurricane Harvey later struck Houston, Texas, saw far better coordination of ambulances than had occurred in New Orleans.[70] Lessons had been observed and shared. Yet, the dubious performances of too many mayors, governors and federal officials during the 2020 Covid-19 crisis showed regulations, preparations, inspection standards, enforcement, leader training and cooperation have a long way to go. Readiness is never a state attained but rather a constant process.

Smart money will underlie successful recoveries both at home and abroad. Once again, lessons from smaller urban areas offer truths of value to the world's largest. Efforts to assist Iraq and Afghanistan recover from twenty-first-century economic, wartime and social catastrophes showed that the best technology might not be the right technology. We recall that ceiling fans or building design to maximise natural ventilation better link ambition to reality in Afghanistan. Building with local materials means less profit for contractors from aid providing countries but makes maintenance and

---

70   Philipps, 'Seven hard lessons federal responders to Harvey learned from Katrina'.

replacement easier and less expensive once NGOs return home.[71] Just as taking a breath before forging ahead during recovery helps balance short and longer-term city needs, avoiding undue haste in awarding building contracts aids in sidestepping poorly advised construction. Even locality-appropriate construction can prove ill advised if designs fail to consider full lifecycles. Apartments built for the 1972 Olympics in Munich, Germany, served visiting athletes well. Once those very fit and generally unmarried individuals had spent their few days occupying the properties, however, the tiny living spaces and awkward stairwells proved less attractive for the elderly and families having to regularly navigate them with crutches, groceries or small children. Megacities are already suffering increased frequency and severity of flooding due to climate change and accompanying sea-level rise. Coastal storms cause more damage than wildfires, earthquakes and tornadoes combined—a sobering statistic given that 17 of the world's most destructive hurricanes in history have struck since 2000.[72] Individuals responsible for megacity disaster preparedness need to recognise that history is a helpful but, when it comes to climate change–related matters, increasingly poor reference when looking forward. Developing disaster preparations based on historical norms rather than future projections assures a future of excessive losses and recovery costs in these cases.[73] A 2013 look at an area of New York City's Brooklyn identified more than 5,000 buildings in flood zones; 30 years before, only 26 were thought to be at risk. Hurricane Sandy's 2012 waters inundated areas in both Brooklyn and neighbouring Queens that were twice the size of the floodplains identified at the time of the storm's visit. Nonetheless, Sandy spared America's largest megacity from what could have been considerably greater suffering. The Hunts Point Food Distribution Center in the Bronx handled some 60 per cent of the urban area's produce and much of its fish and meat. Just as Tokyo's escape from devastation was a near-run thing, only because Hurricane Sandy struck a few hours after high tide was the food security of 22 million people never in serious danger.[74] Across the Atlantic, the Thames Barrier that was designed to protect London from flooding needed to close only

71   CALL, 'Operation United Assistance', 18.
72   Gilbert M. Gaul, 'The homes in Dorian's path are in a high-risk area. Why do they cost so much?', *The New York Times*, 3 September 2019, available from: www.nytimes.com/2019/09/04/books/review/gilbert-gaul-the-geography-of-risk.html.
73   Jonathan D. Woodruff, Jennifer L. Irish and Suzana J. Camargo, 'Coastal flooding by tropical cyclones and sea-level rise', *Nature* 504 (2013): 44–52, at 50, doi.org/10.1038/nature12855.
74   Rodin, *The Resilience Dividend*, 241.

four times between 1982 and 1990 and 35 times in the 1990s; it was closed on 144 occasions from 2000 to mid-2019. The Greater London Authority states that 17 per cent of the city is at medium to high risk of flooding; more than 1 million residents live on a floodplain. How long the barrier will be able to continue to spare London severe flooding is a matter of debate,[75] but it's a sucker's bet to put money on fewer closures per year.

A 24-hour water supply for Hong Kong's residents was recognised as unrealistic during the city's recovery from World War II.[76] Yet, 60 years later, all-day electricity for Baghdad and other Iraqi urban areas was the expectation of many despite years of sanctions and the failure of Saddam Hussein's regime to maintain critical infrastructure. It was less a failure of engineering than a case of not making it clear that such expectations were unrealistic. Authorities giving social considerations too little attention in the aftermath of a disaster risk instability. Pay government officials less than they can make in the private sector and city administrations find themselves filled with less-qualified officials or those relying on bribes and other forms of corruption to augment meagre salaries. One may view Singapore's more authoritarian approach to governing with a jaundiced eye, but the city-state's policies on pegging public salaries to those of private-sector counterparts ceased practices such as judges earning S$300,000 while the lawyers in their courtrooms earned six to seven times as much.[77] The importance of hiring qualified officials in positions responsible for disaster preparedness is hard to overstate.

Fortunately, many in the commercial and nonprofit worlds are willing to step forward as partners in readying a megacity for crises. Others will unfortunately put profit before public welfare, as was the case with a mid-nineteenth-century foreign landlord in Shanghai. His view on building: 'Within two or three years at the most, I hope to leave. What do I care if

---

75   David W. Chen, 'In New York, drawing flood maps is a "game of inches"', *The New York Times*, 7 January 2018, available from: www.nytimes.com/2018/01/07/nyregion/new-york-city-flood-maps-fema.html; NYC Special Initiative for Rebuilding and Resiliency, *PlaNYC*, 11, 13; 'Higher tide', *The Economist*, [London], 17 August 2019, 15–18, at 17; Carbon Brief Staff, 'Risk and uncertainty: Calculating the Thames Barrier's future', *Carbon Brief*, [London], 25 February 2014, available from: www.carbonbrief.org/risk-and-uncertainty-calculating-the-thames-barriers-future/; and Ivana Kottasová, 'Floods in London are the latest sign big cities aren't ready for climate change', *CNN*, 26 July 2021, available from: www.cnn.com/2021/07/26/europe/london-flooding-infrastructure-climate-intl-cmd/index.html.

76   Monnery, *Architect of Prosperity*, 190.

77   Lee, *From Third World to First*, 169.

Shanghai is subsequently engulfed in fire or floods?'[78] Fast forward to the twenty-first century when a Miami real estate mogul was reported to have dismissed the dangers of sea-level rise with his comment in 2016 that:

> in 20 or 30 years, someone is going to find a solution for this. If it is a problem in Miami, it will also be a problem for New York and Boston—so where are people going to go … Besides, by that time, I'll be dead, so what does it matter?[79]

Relying on responsible decisions from politicians (or, obviously, some real estate types) may prove disappointing. One author looking at the threat of disasters related to sea-level rise pointed to a harsh but unfortunate truth: 'Nobody wants to spend money to build a more resilient city because nobody owns the risk.'[80] All but the exceptional politician will seek to push expensive programs down the road while real estate developers and private property owners figure they can make their sales before the next catastrophe strikes. History provides some measure of hope. It is well known that Napoleon III and Baron Haussmann revamped portions of Paris for both civil control and aesthetic purposes. Less known: their destruction of tenements to open passageways where previously only dead-ends existed and widening of roads to create boulevards had the additional aim of reducing the spread of disease.[81] Some megacities around the world have plans to deal with sea-level rise and the related magnification of disasters' effects. Some have begun to put those plans into effect. Their residents are among the more fortunate.

---

78 Brook, *A History of Future Cities*, 64.
79 Goodell, *The Water Will Come*, 93; and Rene Rodriguez, 'Miami condo king breaks silence on sea level rise comment: "Maybe I had too many drinks"', *Miami Herald*, 31 May 2018, available from: www.miamiherald.com/news/business/real-estate-news/article210857319.html.
80 Goodell, *The Water Will Come*, 103.
81 'Microbes and the metropolis: How diseases shape cities', *The Economist*, [London], 25 April 2020, 78–79, at 79.

9

Leaning forward:
What can be

Urban warfare is a key trend that will define combat for years
to come.[1]

—Yaakov Lappin, *The IDF's momentum plan aims to create a new
type of war machine*

Cities and Thrones and Powers
Stand in Time's eye,
Almost as long as flowers,
Which daily die:
But, as new buds put forth
To glad new men,
Out of the spent and unconsidered Earth,
The Cities rise again.[2]

—Rudyard Kipling, 'A Centurion of the Thirtieth'

Our definition of megacity tells us that large-scale catastrophes have the
potential to devastate a country and wreak havoc regionally if not planet-
wide. More than one-third of Bangladesh's urban-dwellers live in Dhaka.[3]
Not a megacity, perhaps, but the urban area is fundamental to the social,
economic and political welfare of the country. In the richest country in
the world, one urban area (New York City) nonetheless accounts for 8

1   Yaakov Lappin, *The IDF's momentum plan aims to create a new type of war machine*, Perspectives
Paper No. 1497, Ramat Gan, Israel: Begin-Sadat Center for Strategic Studies, 22 March 2020.
2   In Rudyard Kipling, *The Works of Rudyard Kipling*, Ware, UK: Wordsworth Poetry Library,
1994, 487.
3   Islam et al., 'Urban slums of Bangladesh'.

per cent of its total economic output.[4] The shock of a catastrophe beyond a 9/11, Hurricane Sandy or Covid-19 would reach far beyond Wall Street, lasting for months if not years. Thankfully, post–Hurricane Sandy New York City did take steps to plan for future flood threats. In the future, according to its *PlaNYC*:

> water that makes its way inland will find hardened and, in some cases, elevated homes, making it more difficult to knock buildings off their foundations or knock out mechanical and electrical systems ... Power, liquid fuels, telecommunications, transportation, water and wastewater, healthcare, and other networks will operate largely without interruption, or will return to service quickly when preventative shutdowns or localized interruptions occur.[5]

New York City has dramatically enhanced preparations for interdicting the worst other calamities can impose, though Covid-19 reminds us that readiness is never an end but rather an ongoing activity. Planning is good. Planning tied to rehearsals and exercises challenging specious assumptions and dubious policies is better. Effective preparations put into effect are better yet, especially if the interval is short.[6] Mother Nature won't wait.

---

4   Oliver Schelske, Lukas Sundermann and Peter Hausmann, *Mind the Risk: A Global Ranking of Cities Under Threat from Natural Disasters*, Zürich: Swiss Re, 18 September 2013, 5, available from: www.researchgate.net/publication/329450315_Mind_the_risk_-_A_global_ranking_of_cities_under _threat_from_natural_disasters.
5   NYC Special Initiative for Rebuilding and Resiliency, *PlaNYC*, 'Foreword'.
6   Several conferences, publications and other initiatives have had varying degrees of influence on the approaches to addressing megacity disasters and those more generally urban. Valuable for raising consciousness and inspiring action, observations from these range from the general to a focus on specific communities. Readers interested in further investigating the history of urban disaster policy or particular initiatives might find the following interesting: Yuki Matsuoka and Rajib Shaw (eds), *Hyogo Framework for Action and Urban Disaster Resilience*, Community, Environment and Disaster Risk Management Vol. 16, Bingley, UK: Emerald Publishing Limited, 2014, doi.org/10.1108/S2040-7262201416; William J. Mitchell, *e-topia: 'Urban Life, Jim—But Not as We Know It'*, Cambridge, MA: MIT Press, 1999, doi.org/10.7551/mitpress/2844.001.0001; Rockefeller Foundation 100 Resilient Cities initiative, available from: www.rockefellerfoundation.org/100-resilient-cities/; Juhan I. Uitto, 'The geography of disaster vulnerabilities in megacities: A theoretical framework', *Applied Geography* 18(1) (1998): 7–16, doi.org/10.1016/S0143-6228(97)00041-6; the United Nations' Making Cities Resilient 2030 (MCR 2030) and related initiatives, such as the Sendai Framework for Disaster Risk Reduction 2015–30; Wenzel Friedemann, Fouad Bendimerad and Ravi Sinha, 'Megacities: Megarisks', *Natural Hazards* 42 (2007): 481–91, doi.org/10.1007/s11069-006-9073-2.

Tomorrow's megacity catastrophes: Context

The Bosphorus … was a stretch of water that in c. AD 1506 Leonardo [da Vinci] would come to include in his 'Gaia Scheme'—a prescient theory about the danger of rising sea-levels and subsequent global, environmental destruction.[7]

—Bettany Hughes, *Istanbul*

Everyone has eyes, young man. Not everyone can see.[8]

—Greg Iles, *Deep Sleep*

Looking back on her duties during the period 16 October 2016 to 20 July 2017, Lise Grande recalled how the UN Office for the Coordination of Humanitarian Affairs worked closely with the Iraqi Government, approximately 270 NGOs, Kurdish representatives, US military and many other parties during the evacuation of Mosul. The task was carried out during what was, in the words of the senior US general in Iraq at the time, 'the most significant urban combat to take place since World War II'.[9] Even so, Grande recalled that 'protection of civilians in Mosul was the central strategic aim for the Iraqi security forces. Civilian infrastructure was second. Destruction of the enemy was third.'[10] Far from a megacity in terms of our definition, Mosul's population of 1,905,000 people was still nearly twice that confronted by the US and its allies either in 1945 in Manila (1.1 million) or in 1950 in Seoul (1 million).[11] The challenges related to humanitarian assistance during combat operations in Mosul therefore provide some degree of understanding about similar operations in a megacity. Reinforcing the value of drawing on such historical offerings, Iraqi Security Force operations in Mosul 'benefitted from the lessons learned in Ramadi and Fallujah' during previous months.

---

7   Hughes, *Istanbul*, 416.
8   Greg Iles, *Deep Sleep*, New York, NY: Penguin, 2002, 160.
9   Jim Michaels, 'Iraqi forces in Mosul see deadliest urban combat since World War II', *USA Today*, 29 March 2017, [Updated 30 March 2017], available from: www.usatoday.com/story/news/world/2017/03/29/united-states-mosul-isis-deadly-combat-world-war-ii/99787764/.
10   United States Agency for International Development (USAID), 'Iraq: Complex Emergency', Fact Sheet #4, Fiscal year 2017, Washington, DC: USAID, 9 June 2017, 1, available from: www.usaid.gov/sites/default/files/2022-05/2021-09-30_USG_Iraq_Complex_Emergency_Fact_Sheet_4.pdf.
11   Mosul population taken from *Demographia World Urban Areas*, 15th edn, 27. Not surprisingly given recent and ongoing security challenges in Iraq, estimates of Mosul's population vary considerably, from just above 1.6 million to more than 2 million.

Though casualties inflicted on Iraqi Security Force units in East Mosul would result in greater reliance on firepower when attention turned to the city's western environs:

> in Mosul, the Iraqi military constrained the use of airstrikes and artillery fire; limited the role of PMF [Popular Mobilization Forces, which had been accused of abusing Sunni members of the population in Fallujah]; and put in place a 'humanitarian concept of operations' intended to ensure that internally displaced persons (IDPs) received life-saving assistance and respectful treatment.[12]

Nearly 531,000 of the city's residents had already been displaced as the battle continued in its final weeks.[13] Removing these urban refugees from danger was only the first step. Months of abuse and deprivation under the ISIS regime meant children had to be screened for malnutrition and the population in general checked for and vaccinated against disease, provided safe drinking water and protected from personal violations such as forced evictions, arbitrary detention, collective punishment and restricted freedom of movement as various parties sought to pursue their political and ethnic agendas.[14] Most NGO personnel worked in IDP camps somewhat distant from the fighting. We know willingness to cooperate varied considerably. Médecins Sans Frontières was among the organisations that reportedly refused to assist in trauma centres on the front lines because they would have had to rely on military transport or otherwise work with armed forces' assets. They did support relief efforts elsewhere. Other individuals and organisations fortunately recognised that military assets were insufficient to address the massive scale of IDP needs and understood the value of closer civil–military cooperation. Medical personnel from New York City hospitals were notable for their service at Mosul's front lines. Grande reflected that most such frontline medical personnel were not from traditional or legacy NGOs but from those formed explicitly for responding to the disaster at hand.

Relief activities during the fighting ultimately included construction of 19 emergency camps on the outskirts of the city. Establishing and maintaining routes between the camps and Iraqi combat forces were essential to safe evacuations. Coordinating with military officials to reduce the chances the tempo of battle would overwhelm screening, medical

---

12   SREO Consulting, 'Lessons Learned Study on UN Humanitarian, Civil–Military Coordination and Stabilization Efforts in Mosul', January 2019, 4.
13   USAID, 'Iraq', 1.
14   ibid., 3–4.

care or camp capacity meant dealing with a system of many parts. Camps were more than merely places of refuge, shelter, medical assistance and sustenance. Additional services included preventative healthcare, education and jobs. Yet, the distance between these locations and the front lines meant anyone wounded or injured would exceed the 'golden hour' threshold deemed vital to timely treatment if they awaited completion of their move to camp facilities. Civilian providers staffed stabilisation and triage points closer to the fighting, providing interim care. These medical nodes moved when necessary to stay as close as feasible to advancing fighting forces.

Grande highlighted three factors underlying this approximation of successful orchestration. First, UN civil–military officials directly embedded with Iraqi Security Force civil affairs cells. They additionally worked closely with Iraqi Security Force planners and representatives from units in the field to ensure combatant and aid provider efforts were synchronised in terms of timing, movements and allocation to facilities with available capacity. Second, early establishment of personal connections with Iraqi Security Force and other personnel helped smooth the wrinkles that are inevitable when many organisations work together— an end accomplished even under the intense pressure of ongoing combat and mass IDP movements. Finally, military representatives and civilian humanitarian providers shared a concept of how to conduct operations— an exceptional situation that demonstrated the extent to which the various parties sought to meld their very different functions. Unfortunately, the number of casualties among the better-trained units fighting in East Mosul meant those committed to the twisted-street, hyper-dense urban environment of West Mosul were less prepared for urban combat. Though the Iraqi Prime Minister's Office repeatedly called for its armed forces to prioritise noncombatant protection, including restraint in the use of heavy weaponry, these calls were not accompanied by rules of engagement specifying which weapons the Iraqi Security Forces should restrain from using. The result, articulated by an Iraqi colonel in his army's 15th Division, was that those doing the fighting 'were told to reduce civilian casualties but [were] not told how to achieve that'. The lack of training in some units committed to West Mosul meant their members were also unaware of the effects of various munitions on urban structures, further complicating estimates of damage before calling for support.[15]

---

15   Center for Civilians in Conflict (CIVIC), *Policies and Practices to Protect Civilians: Lessons from ISF Operations against ISIS in Urban Areas*, Report, Washington, DC: CIVIC, 1 October 2019, available from: civiliansinconflict.org/publications/research/policies-practices-to-protect-civilians/.

Despite these variations during combat operations, civil–military cooperation continued during post-fighting recovery. The conditions encountered merit recalling in some detail given the likelihood of them being confronted again. Pehr Lodhammar's experiences while a UN mine-clearing manager reinforced Lise Grande's description of the mutual support between NGOs, IGOs and members of the Iraqi Security Forces while providing a vivid description of the conditions under which he and his colleagues worked:

> Mosul was my first urban experience. It was a shock given the amount of debris … It was very different than what we had seen and the industry at large had seen. Mine-detecting is normally flat, two-dimensional. In Mosul, we were working with debris, human remains and many devices we had never seen before, mostly improvised explosive devices … Let me focus on Al Shifa Hospital. It used to be the second most modern hospital in Iraq. It was actually a hospital complex with a blood bank, teaching hospital and other facilities. It was initially used as a hospital by ISIS for its warriors and their families only, then as a headquarters as it could look from the old city in Western Mosul into Eastern Mosul. That is the first time we encountered human remains. When we first started clearing debris, we found the remains of ISIS fighters, often with suicide vests still on … There were a lot of technical challenges with debris … We had to use armoured machinery. We are very conservative in the mine-clearing community and I had to force contractors to use it. Now we use it everywhere. And we had to use hook-and-line sets to move doors, furniture [as a precaution against booby traps]. It was extremely time-consuming. Highrise buildings [were another challenge]. Normally you clear by square metres. How do you do it in a building like the nine-storey Al Shifa Hospital?
>
> There were also technology challenges. I wanted to use drones with cameras to look around corners and buildings. Because ISIS had used explosives dropped from the air, I couldn't get permission. People began to twitch when they saw drones. The government didn't allow them to be imported because they might be misused, though ISIS also built their own. The Iraqi Government didn't want drones flying along filming everything. The Iraqi Government is very cautious about how they manage information.
>
> I would come back and shower and would still stink. I had seen bodies before, but never to that extent … Mosul was apocalyptic.[16]

---

16 Lodhammar, Skype interview.

These collective efforts represent a far cry from that comment 10 years earlier when a fellow conference attendee declared that achieving a comprehensive approach during an operation is impossible. Maybe it's the passage of time. Maybe it's recognition after missteps in Iraq and Afghanistan that pursuing such an approach is no longer optional. Then again, maybe the effort at orchestration in and around Mosul was a one-time achievement rather than an emerging trend.

Both the frequency and the severity of urban catastrophes will worsen. We can blame Mother Nature's cruel streak for Hurricane Sandy, the Fukushima Daiichi nuclear disaster or the devastation Covid-19 wrought on urban areas, but we'd be fooling ourselves. In the first case, it was a failure to recognise (or admit) that the consequences of climate change are already on us, that sea levels are rising, will continue to rise and thus will make bad storms worse. It is unquestionably a red flag given the United Nations tells us 14 of the world's most populous 19 cities are on the coast.[17] In the case of Fukushima, we saw the all-too-common shared neglect of not recognising that generators, electrical power panels and other features key to flood prevention or mitigation are an invitation to failure when not positioned well above historical 100-year flood levels. In the third case—the devastation wreaked by Covid-19—evidence suggests that acting on exercise recommendations, awareness of historical events such as SARS and better leadership could have saved thousands if not tens of thousands of lives nationwide, many in urban concentrations.

The developing world's urban populations grew by an average of 1.2 million people a week in the first decade of this century. That's just a tad less than Europe's urban growth for an entire year.[18] And while declarations that megacities in these countries exist on the razor's edge of chaos may be overstated, there are undoubtedly challenges. It took the United Kingdom 120 years to see its population go from 17 per cent to 39 per cent urbanised. The United States took 80 years. China took 40, reaching that mark in 2003;[19] by 2019, it was 60 per cent urbanised.[20] Many of the developing world's megacities have had similarly frantic rates of growth compared with the gradual development of Tokyo or Europe's largest urban areas. Though the newly arrived may not suffer from

17   UN-Habitat, *State of the World's Cities 2012/2013*, 90.

18   ibid., 28.

19   ibid., 44.

20   Joel Kotkin, 'China's urban crisis', *City Journal* (Spring 2019), available from: www.city-journal.org/chinas-urban-crisis.

deliberate and official exclusionary policies as do urban immigrants in China, they are likely to share that country's unemployment (or frustrating underemployment) of educated youth. Real estate costs and the inability to secure confirmation of landownership are other potential sources of friction. More an issue in China's larger cities than in most countries is the fact that a severe drop in property values could precipitate unrest in years to come (as Chinese tend to invest in property in lieu of stockmarkets). China's exceptionalism in this instance is again extreme, with roughly one in every five housing units in some cities owned but unoccupied. A potential upside: as in London, New York and other investment-popular megacities, those vacant properties could house the displaced were disaster to strike.

Parts to wholes: The future megacity as a system and subsystem

Megacities add an incredible layer of complexity to all operations.[21]
—General Robert B. Brown, US Army

When you build a thing you cannot merely build that thing in isolation, but must also repair the world around it, and within it, so that the larger world at that one place becomes more coherent, and more whole; and the thing which you make takes its place in the web of nature.[22]
—Christopher Alexander et al., *A Pattern Language*

Megacities are growing ever more complex. Links within and between them span the spectrum from individual ties to those involving international conglomerates and heads of government. It was but a few decades ago that communications supporting these interconnections were measured in terms of days, the exceptions being pricey telephone calls, couriers and a few other means of communication limited by inconvenience or cost. Now the world's billions communicate one-on-one, one-on-many (think Twitter, Zoom or Teams) or many-on-many formally and informally—with information factual or fabricated, legitimate or criminal—all

---

21   Robert B. Brown [General, US Army], Presentation to Current and Future Operations in Megacities Conference, US Army Pacific Command, Tokyo, 18 July 2019.
22   Christopher Alexander, Sara Ishikawa and Murray Silverstein, *A Pattern Language: Towns, Buildings, Construction*, New York, NY: Oxford University Press, 1977, 13.

but instantaneously. Economic, social and diplomatic ties promote interdependency even as they inform, inspire, misinform or mislead. Increasing societal complexity has complements in the physical arena that are sometimes hidden from view and thus less recognised. Recall the previous description of underground features in Tokyo, which has an uninterrupted 4 kilometres of commercial and public facilities beneath the megacity's surface.

Improved and expanded ways of communicating can ease disaster preparations. Other evolutions are not as helpful. Those subterranean features add another dimension to post-calamity recovery. When breaks occurred in those waterlines that remained largely intact after World War II bombings, it tended to be where the lines joined buildings rather than long stretches elsewhere. Urban areas' outward spread means megacities are likely to be built on—and through—many soil types. Features spanning these differences are especially vulnerable to tearing or twisting as shock waves affect unalike materials differently. Flooding will have its own varying effects, devastating underground commercial spaces while having less effect on many aboveground properties.

Viewing recovery from a systems perspective should ease calamity's costs. Tokyo's massive flood-control system north of the city has dramatically reduced the risk of damage in the megacity's low-lying areas even as buildings, streets and sidewalks seal more ground with impermeable materials such as concrete and asphalt. The Metropolitan Area Outer Underground Discharge Channel, as it is known, routes excessive rainwater away from the downtown area via 6.3 kilometres of underground channels with pumps that can evacuate the equivalent of a large swimming pool every second, eventually dumping the water into the Edo River.[23] Hong Kong has a similar underground system, with one of its subterranean drainage tunnels running for 10.5 kilometres—roughly half the length of Manhattan.[24] But the impressive flood-control system cannot completely undo the local effects of humankind ignoring the need for rainwater runoff. Localised events known as 'guerilla rainstorms' still submerge parts

23   David Wogan, 'This massive underground complex protects Tokyo from floods', [*Plugged In Blog*], *Scientific American*, 29 October 2013, available from: blogs.scientificamerican.com/plugged-in/this-massive-underground-complex-protects-tokyo-from-floods/; and 'Floods in Tokyo and safety tips and preparation', *realestate-tokyo.com*, 28 February 2020, [Updated 18 May 2022], available from: www.realestate-tokyo.com/living-in-tokyo/emergency-disaster/flood-in-tokyo-japan/.
24   James Griffiths, 'Hong Kong's vast $3.8 billion rain-tunnel network', *CNN Style*, 26 July 2020, available from: www.cnn.com/style/article/hong-kong-tunnels-climate-crisis-intl-hnk-dst/index.html.

of Tokyo when heavy downfalls overwhelm drainage. Miami is among the other cities similarly suffering from these severe microbursts, which are defined by one source as extreme rainfall totalling between 50 and 100 millimetres (2 to 4 inches) falling in a concentrated area within an hour.[25]

The future of control in megacities

Polarized politics also reproduce the power of the *mastans*. Motiar Rahman, a police officer, describes the *mastans* as 'thugs committing a wide range of crimes such as taking meals in restaurants without payment [and] forcible extraction of tolls and subscriptions ... Some of them have made [a] fortune by grabbing real estate property, shops, buses and trucks ... [They] extort huge amount[s] of money from businessmen, contractors and others [and] no one dare[s] to oppose [them] or to lodge complaint[s] with the law enforcement authorit[ies] for fear of retaliation.' The power of *mastans* ... mainly comes from their impunity ... Politicians make constant use of the *mastans* to enforce conformity or obedience within parties.[26]

—Imtiaz Ahmed, 'Dhaka'

The young consume.[27]

—Darrell Bricker and John Ibbitson, *Empty Planet*

The income gap between rural and urban residents in the United States is 4 per cent, with those living in urban areas being that much richer.[28] In China, the difference is 63 per cent. When you read of the rise of the Chinese middle class, you are reading overwhelmingly of those who possess the highly desirable urban *hukou* ('household registration', or residence permits) that allows them to take full advantage of city living. If you are reading of the country's millionaires, chances are nine in 10 that the person mentioned has a senior family member occupying a high-level government position. The best Chinese universities (the top 1 per cent) are in the country's largest and wealthiest cities such as Shanghai and Beijing. They provide those with local *hukou* a disproportionate number

---

25   Ariza, *Disposable City*, 43; Kumagai and Nojima, 'Urbanization and Disaster Mitigation in Tokyo', 67; and realestate-tokyo.com, 'Floods in Tokyo and safety tips and preparation'.
26   Ahmed, 'Dhaka', 19.
27   Bricker and Ibbitson, *Empty Planet*, 82.
28   Material in this paragraph is primarily drawn from Kotkin, 'China's urban crisis'; and 'Worlds apart: Hukou reform', *The Economist*, [London], 23 August 2020, 35–36.

of places. In general, only 0.3 per cent of rural students are accepted by those top 1 per cent of institutions while 2.8 per cent of those with urban papers get a slot.[29]

Internal migration brings Chinese to cities in search of fame and fortune, or simply survival, and those not granted urban *hukou* are not legal residents of their chosen urban area. They can expect to be denied healthcare, housing subsidies and unemployment insurance. They and their families are unlikely to have access to formal education. Children adopted from the countryside can be denied education even if the adopting family has urban *hukou*.[30] Only a little more than one in every four of these disenfranchised has insurance should they be injured—despite them tending to be less likely to be able to afford care and often being employed in dangerous jobs like construction or manufacturing as other work is denied them. Of the estimated 850 million urban-dwellers in China, more than one-quarter (roughly 230 million) lacks *hukou* for the city in which they reside. Others might live in a town or city but hold *hukou* for a different urban location. Overall, an estimated 376 million Chinese live in a location other than that listed on their paperwork.[31] Yet, the allure of urban living is popular even for those handicapped by national policy. A decades-long research effort measured rural Chinese youngsters' cognitive development and found more than half were delayed due to undernourishment, anaemia (impacting concentration) or intestinal worms (which can make the victim lethargic). Intellectual development can also be impaired in life's earliest stages. Whereas urban infants and toddlers have frequent and substantive interaction with adults, the very young in rural areas are often strapped to their grandmother's back as the adults toil all day, allowing little intellectual stimulation. The combined result: many of the cognitively delayed 50 per cent are unlikely to achieve an IQ of 90 (only 16 per cent score as poorly in typical populations). Other obstacles compound these disadvantages further. One-third of children aged 11 or 12 with poor vision did not wear glasses. The fact that schools in rural areas are often second class in terms of quality exacerbates the problems. Private schools in cities (often the only alternative for children lacking urban *hukou*) tend to be expensive and substandard compared with both public facilities available to urban *hukou*-holders and those in rural areas, meaning children are left behind in rural areas when

---

29 'Serve the rich: Inequality in education', *The Economist*, [London], 29 May 2021, 36–37, at 36.
30 Chaguan, 'Crossing blood lines', *The Economist*, [London], 6 June 2020, 34.
31 Chaguan, 'New life for an old tradition', *The Economist*, [London], 22 May 2021, 36.

one or both parents moves to take advantage of better-paying urban work or seeks employment when none is available rurally.[32] National officials have tried to lure many of these 230 million to lesser cities with promises of *hukou* there. Their efforts have met limited success. Megacities like Beijing and some provincial but booming larger urban areas such as Xi'an (population 13 million) and Chengdu (more than 16 million) offering big-city amenities are the ones that instead attract. China's nosedive from 'highly egalitarian' to equality ratings lower than for almost all of Europe, the United States, Brazil and Kenya is by and large an urban-based phenomenon.

Efforts to control aspects of urban life are rarely so heavy-handed in the developed world's megacities. The largely voluntary nature of attempts to control abuses on social media provides a case in point. Despite the potential benefits of social media as a source of understanding and guidance, its use in post-Fukushima Tokyo and confusion during US efforts to inform about Covid-19 remind us of the challenges that remain in providing consistent guidance if public and private authorities fail to coordinate their messaging. There are steps that can be taken to improve consistency—for example, designating a single point of contact in a city's emergency operations centre as the purveyor of information. Without consistency from trusted sources, rumours will be believed as fact, criminals will manipulate audiences for profit or political or diplomatic gain and simple irresponsibility will undermine effective responses. This misinformation and disinformation are potentially far more damaging than crying 'Fire!' in a crowded theatre. Yet, both laws and effective means of controlling irresponsible communication lag the tools available to protect the naive or ignorant and rein in the malicious. Fellow social media users—including those from traditional media—constitute the first line of defence. Akin to *first* first responders in neighbourhoods, responsible platform users need to step (or finger) forward and draw attention to falsehoods or other misuse. They can also serve fellow residents by spreading rebuttals or corrections to information found to be untrue. Such reactions cannot hope to completely undo the damage, but they will

---

32 'Trouble in the country: Human capital', *The Economist*, [London], 23 January 2021, 66–67; Ai Yue, Yaojiang Shi, Renfu Luo, Jamie Chen, James Garth, Jimmy Zhang, Alexis Medina, Sarah Kotb and Scott Rozelle, 'China's invisible crisis: Cognitive delays among rural toddlers and the absence of modern parenting', *The China Journal* (78) (2017), doi.org/10.1086/692290; and Scott Rozelle and Natalie Hell, *Invisible China: How the Urban–Rural Divide Threatens China's Rise*, Chicago, IL: University of Chicago Press, 2020, 8–9, 156–57, doi.org/10.7208/chicago/9780226740515.001.0001.

help to mitigate misinformation having far longer and faster legs than its less-intriguing truthful companions. (A Hong Kong newspaper drew on an article in *Practical Preventative Medicine* to report that 'coronavirus can travel twice as far as official safe distance'. The journal retracted the article the day after it appeared in the newspaper. Only 1,000 readers re-sent the newspaper's immediate publication of the *Practical Preventative Medicine* retraction versus the original information having been shared 53,000 times on social media.)[33]

Traditional media representatives still reach audiences social media does not. Unfortunately, they too often fall victim to 'if it's on the internet it must be true' gullibility no less than wrong-headed smartphone re-broadcasters. The challenge is not to control social media. Rather, it is to make it as much a power for good in times of crisis as it is day to day in providing a way for individuals to reconnect with friends and relatives. A bit of good news: younger smartphone users tend to be more discerning than those in older age groups. They should thus be able to act as a brake on social media misuse if they so choose—or be convinced of the importance of doing so by urban officials.

Success in controlling corruption in the aftermath of a megacity calamity remains an unmet challenge. Medusa's head has fewer snakes than the serpents that sprout post catastrophe. Measuring success by the number of dollars spent, as was the case in Iraq and Afghanistan, was fundamentally flawed, just as was the United States measuring progress in Vietnam by counting the number of enemy killed. Both inspired behaviours that were counterproductive to strategic objectives. Measures of effectiveness are great motivators—for ill or good. Humans want to be recognised. They therefore find ways to stand out in meeting their seniors' standards of excellence. Unfortunately, for some, this encourages deliberately misleading actions like counting civilian deaths in addition to those of the enemy when the measure is body-count or being less discriminating than should be the case when it is dollars spent. Zero corruption is an unattainable goal even in more honest societies, but there is a need to set limits on what is tolerated.

---

33 'Reaping from the whirlwind: How Covid-19 is changing science', *The Economist*, [London], 9 May 2020, 62–63, at 63.

The preceding pages suggest that prevention of another sort can reduce the number of megacity disasters and the consequences of those that cannot be avoided. Jakarta's maximum rate of ground subsidence in the mid-1990s nearly tripled from that of the decade before, from 9 centimetres a year to 25 (from about 3.5 inches to 10 inches). Little wonder the national government is looking to move its capital. Yet, Jakarta has been Indonesia's strongest attractor of foreign investment in part due to higher-quality infrastructure, access to local and international markets, concentration of skilled labour and its spirit of entrepreneurship in addition to the presence of the country's decision-makers. Duplicating all but the last will not be easy. Foreign investment goes where there is money to be made. Perhaps it is too late to recover from bad decisions in Jakarta (the capital's green space went from more than 35 per cent of the city in 1965 to less than 10 per cent in 2011).[34] Some of the most important lessons one megacity can offer another are mistakes to avoid.

The future of the megacity comprehensive approach

Cities have been perceived as the 'engines' of national economies and there is no reason to depart from that view.[35]

UN-Habitat, *State of the World's Cities 2012/2013*

Support of noncombatants can divert resources from mission-related activities. For instance, a combat operation that displaces a significant number of residents, or disrupts critical public works functions, might necessitate redirecting unit resources away from their originally intended recipients, as it did when Allied Forces liberated Paris in 1944. During that operation, fuel supplies and supply aircraft scheduled to be used for an Air Transport Command training exercise had to be diverted in order to haul necessary commodities to the city.[36]

—Jamison Jo Medby and Russell W. Glenn, *Street Smart*

---

34   Hasanuddin Z. Abidin, Heri Andreas, Irwan Gumilar, Yoichi Fukuda, Yusuf E. Pohan and T. Deguchi, 'Land subsidence of Jakarta (Indonesia) and its relation with urban development', *Natural Hazards* 59(1753) (December 2011), doi.org/10.1007/s11069-011-9866-9. Also see Sausan Atika, 'Amid shortage of land, Jakarta eyes more green spaces', *The Jakarta Post*, 21 October 2019, available from: www.thejakartapost.com/news/2019/10/21/amid-limited-land-availability-jakarta-eyes-more-green-spaces.html.
35   UN-Habitat, *State of the World's Cities 2012/2013*.
36   Medby and Glenn, *Street Smart*, 34.

Cities—and megacities in particular—hold our attention, sometimes to the detriment of other areas that are in greater need of assistance. NATO forces focused their early relief efforts on Sarajevo during the violence that wracked Bosnia-Herzegovina after it broke away from the former Yugoslavia during the late 1990s. The same characteristics that motivated the new capital receiving much of the early disaster support made it attractive to the media: a high concentration of people, better lodging, the density of newsworthy stories, communications superior to those in more remote areas and other features or comforts. A prominent television reporter from a US network positioned herself in front of a cemetery and spoke of the city's depravations. The problem was that Sarajevo was by that point in better shape than Bosnia-Herzegovina's smaller cities, towns and other regions. Priorities for aid delivery had already begun to shift to those more in need. The pressures resulting from the news broadcast nevertheless saw the redirected aid redirected again—this time, back to the capital.

There was likely good reason to give Sarajevo initial primacy. That time had passed. The first quotation opening this section rightly notes that a nation's welfare is closely tied to its dominant urban areas. That should not mean ignoring the larger system of which the urban area is a part. Media sources are ideally part of efforts to create a comprehensive approach when dealing with the consequences of a megacity disaster. Responsible members of that community should adapt their reporting to conditions on the ground just as will other instruments in the response orchestra. Their representatives travelling within and beyond the urban area are potential sources of information that could benefit aid allocation.

Future megacity capacity

Success in a campaign and victory over one's enemies are great things. It requires much greater skill and caution to use such successes well. Accordingly, you will find that those who have gained victories are many times more numerous than those who have made good use of them.[37]

—Polybius, *On Roman Imperialism*

---

37   Polybius, *On Roman Imperialism*, trans. Evelyn S. Shuckburgh, Lake Bluff, IL: Regnery Gateway, 1987, 268.

Brilliance attracts brilliance.[38]

—Garth Gibson, Toronto Vector Institute

Jeopardy answer no. 1: 'This European megacity is the continent's most prone to tidal flooding.' Correct question: 'What is London?' We have already noted that by 2030, the Thames Barrier's ability to protect the UK capital against extreme surges will be dubious.[39]

Jeopardy answer no. 2: 'Two million of this Indian megacity's current population is exposed to coastal flooding.' Correct question: 'What is Kolkata?' By 2070, that number is projected to increase sevenfold.[40]

A partial list of megacities similarly threatened by sea-level rise: our already-mentioned New York City, Tokyo, Dhaka, Lagos, Shanghai, Bangkok and Jakarta. Ho Chi Minh City is another.[41] We know it's not sea-level rise that kills you (not yet for any megacity anyway). It's when the effects of those skulking parts-of-a-millimetre increase over time and combine with a typhoon, hurricane, micro-storm, tsunami or earthquake that nature and humankind's missteps bring the full brunt of devastation to bear. The 'sea-level rise effect' might be thought of in the same light as the butterfly effect. Those millimetre rises in ocean levels year to year help to flood your second floor during a storm, but the link between those millimetres and your floating furniture is far more direct than that between insect and tornado. How much of a megacity is on higher ground is a factor. So, too, is how much lies below sea level. Sea-level rise is not equally distributed around the globe; some places will see dramatic increases in the decades to come while others will experience but a fraction of what the less lucky suffer.[42] Previous estimates of which megacities will see how much rise cannot be trusted. Changes in the rate of global warming combine with other factors, meaning estimates (and any plans based on those estimates) need to be checked and rechecked to ensure the original assumptions

---

38   As quoted in Clive Thompson, 'North Star: The American dream is alive and well—in Canada', *WIRED*, September 2020, 16–17, at 17.

39   Parker, 'Disaster Response in London', 214.

40   Williams and Selle, *Military Contingencies in Megacities and Sub-Megacities*, 23.

41   ibid., 23.

42   For one analysis of variable sea-level rise affecting the United States, see W.V. Sweet, Robert E. Kopp, Christopher P. Weaver, Jayantha Obeysekera, Radley M. Horton, E. Robert Thieler and Chris Zervas, *Global and Regional Sea Level Rise Scenarios for the United States*, NOAA Technical Report NOS CO-OPS 083, Silver Spring, MD: National Oceanic and Atmospheric Administration, January 2017, vii, available from: tidesandcurrents.noaa.gov/publications/techrpt83_Global_and_Regional_SLR_Scenarios_for_the_US_final.pdf.

remain valid.[43] Nine of the top-20 urban areas thought to be vulnerable to the greatest economic losses due to flooding have populations that exceed 10 million: Guangzhou (1), New York City (3), Mumbai (5), Shenzen (9), Osaka (10), Tianjin (12), Ho Chi Minh City (13), Kolkata (14) and Jakarta (20).[44] Several of these qualify for our definition of megacities. Knowing the extent of a threat can help the responsible official deny building permits for vulnerable land and take other precautions before the combination of sea level's slow rise and a sudden shock of nature's choosing next occur. Adding to the risk: we expect global warming to worsen the consequences of future hurricanes and cyclones as well as the number and severity of future rainstorms generally.[45] Tie this to ageing populations and the expected extent of harm starts climbing. The fact that Covid-19 disproportionately ravaged the old and underserved in the United States is well known. It should not have been shocking news; three-quarters of those dying in conjunction with Hurricane Katrina were aged over 60; half were over 75 years of age.[46] Pre-existing health issues and limited mobility account for most of that vulnerability. Human nature plays a role as well. As with Tokyoites who claim they will ready their homes for an earthquake after the next one comes, individuals worldwide tend to believe that because they survived the last disaster they will do so during the next.[47]

Residents refuse to leave for many reasons in addition to the 'it won't happen to me' syndrome. One is the justified fear that their vacant home will become a magnet for thieves—another form of a vacuum attracting humankind's bottom-feeders. Pre-disaster exercises should reveal how long the mobilisation of the National Guard or international equivalents will take such that evacuated neighbourhoods are not left open to criminals. Those rehearsals are also opportunities to identify relevant laws that will affect tough decisions. Rules of engagement allowing soldiers to shoot armed looters suppress the problem as the unarmed fear the consequences of continuing. Some will surely find this solution extreme. Failing to deal

---

43   ibid., 9.
44   Stephane Hallegatte, Colin Green, Robert J. Nicholls and Jan Corfee-Morlot, 'Future flood losses in major coastal cities', *Nature Climate Change* 3 (2013): 802–6, at 803, doi.org/10.1038/nclimate1979.
45   Union of Concerned Scientists, *Overwhelming Risk: Rethinking Flood Insurance in a World of Rising Seas*, Report, Cambridge, MA: UCSUSA, August 2013, [Revised February 2014], available from: www.ucsusa.org/global_warming/science_and_impacts/impacts/flood-insurance-sea-level-rise.html#.WZsrCXeGO8o.
46   Ripley, *The Unthinkable*, 28.
47   Miles, *Super Storm*, 187.

with looting that resulted in setbacks to recovery measured in months and sometimes years in 2003 in Iraq suggests that such harsh measures may be justified in the interest of longer-term stability and lives saved thanks to preserving essential public services. The decisions will always be difficult. Crisis-savvy leaders know that at times even the best course of action available is a poor one.

Well-written plans and other preparations mean leaders make these tough judgements armed with better information. Being savvy means avoiding mistakes based on misguided assumptions. Sending ambulances and other full-size vehicles to an urban area where motorbikes and bicycles rule the roads finds aid providers sitting in traffic as those in need expire. Getting there quicker with less could be the better choice. Rehearsals and plans must consider how to handle evacuations. Estimates are that only about 10 per cent of residents go to shelters. The rest head out of a city—another argument for keeping megacity populations informed so that some can opt for early departure, hopefully reducing the worst traffic jams. One estimate suggests roughly 24 hours is a 'safe clearance time' for New York City residents relying on cars or mass transit. The time needed for the city's hospitals, assisted care facilities and other facilities to evacuate the less mobile is more like 72 hours.[48] Actual times for New York and other megacities will depend on the extent of notice given, the portion of the population owning cars, the quality of public transportation systems and the day of the week (workday, weekend or holiday). Preparing a megacity population for no-warning or short-warning events such as tsunamis, earthquakes or volcanic eruptions is equally important but more difficult. Pre-event rehearsals are not for officials alone. Schoolchildren in one community were not evacuated to nearby high ground despite early warning of the approaching tsunami that struck communities north of Tokyo in 2011—with tragic results. In contrast, those practise evacuations of highrise apartment buildings in Mexico City mean residents know how to exit their building and where to go to reduce the chances of injury. Similarly, initiatives like that of forming and regularly holding meetings of key emergency planners and responders promote common understanding and standards across many of the authorities that together make up the megacity. The governor of New Jersey directed evacuation before Hurricane Sandy's landfall. We noted that the mayor of New York City was less timely with his

---

48 ibid., 271.

decision, undermining rather than underlining the decision made by an authority whose area of responsibility (the State of New Jersey) included parts of what is the megacity of New York.[49] A further caution: simply providing information is no guarantee that those on the receiving end will know what to do with it. A study into Tokyo's excellent and potentially very valuable disaster hazard maps revealed that 9 per cent of residents had a copy posted on their wall at home, while 11 per cent often checked their map. The remainder had a map but never looked at it, had not bothered to get a copy but knew they could or—despite public awareness campaigns—had never seen or heard of this resource.[50] Efforts to keep a megacity's population in the know about how to respond to disasters must be a constant process.

Technology: Part of the solution … but not the solution

After a devastating earthquake rocked Haiti in January 2010, a Canadian woman trapped in rubble … was rescued after her text message for help reached Canada's Foreign Affairs Department and was relayed back to Canadian authorities on the ground. The Canadian Foreign Affairs minister in his daily briefings told reporters, 'We know where this woman is, exactly.'[51]

—American Red Cross, *The case for integrating crisis response with social media*

Ion mobility spectrometry (IMS) is used to sniff swabs taken from baggage, clothing, and personal items in searches for those carrying drugs or explosives … In theory, IMS could quickly determine from a sample of breath if someone had an illness such as tuberculosis or diphtheria … If airport trials prove the technology to be reliable, they hope to close the loop by offering it back to hospitals and clinics for the rapid analysis of infectious diseases.[52]

—'Grounding bugs', *The Economist*

49   ibid., 261.
50   Junko Sagara and Keiko Saito, *Risk Assessment and Hazard Mapping*, Learning from Megadisasters Knowledge Note 5-1, Washington, DC: Global Facility for Disaster Reduction and Recovery, 1 July 2012, 12, available from: www.gfdrr.org/en/publication/learning-megadisasters-knowledge-note-5-1.
51   American Red Cross, *The case for integrating crisis response with social media*.
52   'Grounding bugs: Public health', *The Economist*, [London], 20 October 2018, 73.

We know urban areas conspire to defeat technology. Structures break lines of sight, making it hard for rescuers, aid providers or security personnel to see a building only a block away or a passageway but a few inches below their feet. Intersections swirl with channelled breezes, making UAVs vulnerable to drafts that can drive them into the ground or nearest wall. Summer heat can cook the innards of earthbound or flying robots. The variety of materials in walls, ceilings and floors not only cripples voice communications, but also disrupts signals between operators and those UAVs and unmanned ground systems, defeating efforts to overcome the urban blindness caused by visual barriers. Warmer days saturate layers of clothing and fog face shields for humans draped in firefighting or protective gear guarding against hazardous materials or disease. Sweat that cannot be wiped runs into eyes. Add post-quake tumbled-down structures or collapsed subsurface features and even the most sophisticated of human or robot finds the going hard if not impossible.

Technology can help first responders find, get to and save victims' lives regardless of the handicaps. Despite their limitations, ground-based or flying robots can go where no human can go. Should war impose itself, the innocent benefit from weapons able to strike only the target in the fifth window from the left on the eighth floor of a building, unlike during previous conflicts in which the entire structure would have to come down. Increasingly, rescuers and soldiers alike can 'see' through walls or beneath tonnes of debris thanks to x-ray, acoustic, chemical-detection or other technology designed to overcome building materials' efforts to deny rescuers information. Software already helps filter data to separate information-rich wheat from irrelevant chaff. AI will soon make that software even savvier. Which parts of the megacity will be worst hit by the ash plume from the volcano? Which parts are downwind from a drifting radiation cloud? How might damage to the water supply be overcome to supply neighbourhoods currently deprived? Being able to quickly compile information during or after a catastrophe and mine the ore contained therein mean not only having the hardware and software in place before it is needed but also knowing what questions to ask.

Getting the information to the right audiences will be tougher yet. Even a large chemical release will not threaten an entire megacity. It could be deadly for thousands in its path, however. Timely guidance to the potentially exposed will be vital. The panic following a blanket warning to an entire megacity population could result in more injuries and deaths than suffered among potential downwind victims. Recalling the roughly

80 per cent of sympathetic casualties during the Tokyo nerve agent attack, population-wide messaging could also cause an overwhelming of medical facilities, depriving the truly needy of care. The IDF works with telecommunications companies to provide pinpoint messaging to individuals or neighbourhoods,[53] but not everyone has a mobile phone. Some people do not use Facebook, Twitter, Instagram or other platforms (I know, Gen Xers; it's hard to believe). Others will be deaf or blind. Touching select audiences means using multiple ways of getting the word out when power and mobile phone services are up and otherwise (the 'how' of messaging). It will also require the expertise needed to design effective message content (which is fundamental to maintaining control, avoiding panic and distributing aid burdens across available assets) and determine who gets what information and when they need to get it. Political advisors and marketers will have a role. Michael Bloomberg's 2001 run for mayor of New York City demonstrated:

> a much finer level of detail in his telephone survey than most campaigns can afford. In turn, the team could develop direct mail pieces targeted to small demographic groups with very specific concerns [to include] pamphlets and fliers with carefully considered images and messages to individual voters chosen to receive them.[54]

Social media and more sophisticated use of data now provide new ways of reaching out to chosen audiences—ways that might complement or replace those tried and true from previous generations. The future holds possibilities already under consideration but thus far only the stuff of movies or television: holograms able to wander neighbourhood streets providing guidance—perhaps featuring national or local personalities pertinent to local demographics or changing depending on the age, gender or other audience features as the hologram walks its beat. Elsewhere it might be police using flawless portable voice translators or 'god voice' area delivery of information. Theme-park experts and others used to dealing with multicultural audiences have insights regarding effectively addressing both individuals and mass gatherings. As Fukushima again reminds us, achieving (and maintaining) consistency in those messages and defeating deliberate misinformation and disinformation efforts adds to the challenges.

---

53   Glenn, *Short war in a perpetual conflict*, 15, 53.
54   McNickle, *Bloomberg*, 35.

We are able only to dip a toe into technology's future in these pages. Some capabilities will be adaptations of those already on hand. The use of binary explosives (where two separate components need to be combined to cause an explosion but neither by itself is combustible) minimises the chances of accidental detonation as occurred in the Port of Beirut with the devastation wrought by ammonium nitrate on the Russian-leased ship MV *Rhosus* on 4 August 2020. Binary vehicle fuels would offer obvious benefits.[55] Driverless supply and passenger vehicles, ambulances (air and ground), information collectors and other means of transport will reduce manpower demands and accidents. They might also make finding parking locations more difficult for relief providers as previous lots and garages needed when everyone was driving give way to buildings with better profit margins. These vehicles could be—should be—multipurpose. 'Patrolbots' have already established themselves as security guards;[56] the robots' 'eyes' and 'ears' provide information that reduces dependence on humans. Linking security cameras to ways of communicating with the public (to include, possibly, commercial GPS systems such as Waze or Google Maps) will permit responders and city leaders to cut down on traffic jams during emergencies while routing vehicles and pedestrian traffic away from dangerous hotspots. Capitalising on mobile phone location signals and other real-time data feeds could likewise aid in steering people away from fires and areas known to pose disease or contamination risks or instead direct them to aid distribution points.

AI linked to weather sensors might instantly update chemical or radioactive plume movements and generate warning messages (putting our opening pages' Haruki Akamatsu at ease should the radiation be negligible). Linked to additional sensors, AI's calculations could also account for urban micro-weather phenomena that impact plume direction and potency. Studies in Singapore found that urban vegetation, proximity to water, shade in the lee of tall buildings and other factors determine an urban area's localised heat-island effect and air movement.[57] AI should eventually be able to help in maximising the value of residents' post-disaster inputs that provide information such as the location of individuals

---

55   Glenn et al., *Urban Combat Service Support Operations*, 77.

56   Jeremy D. McLain, 'Match made in heaven? Or hell?: Megacities and autonomous systems', *Small Wars Journal*, 25 August 2018, available from: smallwarsjournal.com/jrnl/art/match-made-heaven-or-hell-megacities-and-autonomous-systems.

57   Winston T.L. Chow and Matthias Roth, 'Temporal dynamics of the urban heat island of Singapore', *International Journal of Climatology* 26(15) (December 2006): 2243–60, at 2255–56, doi.org/10.1002/joc.1364.

in need of medical care, looting or other crime, fractures in waterpipes or other infrastructure, loved ones or friends looking for lost people or pets and suspicious activities, all while filtering out inputs seeking to deceive. AI to date is better at focusing on single tasks (monitoring and directing water allocation or automobile traffic, for example) than taking into consideration multiple systems' considerations. The potential to take on other tasks is there. Those concerned about access to personal data even for the greater good should find comfort when looking at Barcelona, Spain. Residents in that city have control over what personal information the city government can hold.[58] Participation in Singapore's Ministry of Health–sponsored Bluetooth contact-tracing TraceTogether software (part of a wider epidemiological monitoring system) is likewise voluntary.[59] We earlier noted that Virginia, US, residents can voluntarily download the COVIDWISE app that notifies them if they have been exposed to someone who has tested positive for the virus.

It might be surprising to read that Los Angeles, New York City and other US urban areas lag cities in Japan, Taiwan, China, Mexico, Italy and elsewhere when it comes to earthquake early warning. Reminiscent of the 'Yo!' app used in Israel to warn citizens of an incoming missile or rocket, Japanese mobile phone users are sent text messages warning of impending quakes. California, Oregon and Washington State have a similar but limited system in place that will eventually include smartphone early warning notices via the MyShake app for everyone in potentially affected areas.[60] This is progress, but progress that needs to be shared beyond its current reach. One of the potentially most devastating earthquake zones on the North American continent is that along the New Madrid Fault in the US Midwest. It has a particularly disturbing history. During the eight weeks after an initial quake on 16 December 1811 that struck near Blytheville, Arkansas, the epicentres of subsequent shakes crept progressively north-eastward over a distance of 89 kilometres to New Madrid, Missouri.[61] Currently, MyShake services none of the states or cities along that path.

---

58   'Digital plurality: Are data more like oil or sunlight?', *The Economist*, [London], 22 February 2020: [Special report] 4–6.
59   Gideon Lewis-Kraus, 'Trust fails', *WIRED*, July–August 2020, 62–67, at 65–66.
60   'Ten per cent: Earthquake preparedness', *The Economist*, [London], 3 February 2018, 26; and United States Geological Survey, *ShakeAlert: An Earthquake Early Warning System for the West Coast of the United States*, Reston, VA: USGS, 2016, available from: www.shakealert.org.
61   Barrett K. Parker and H. Quinton Lucie, 'Secondary earthquakes: New Madrid Seismic Zone response during an ongoing emergency', *HDIAC Journal* 4 (Spring 2017): 23–27, at 23–24.

How bright is the future? Megacity disasters to come

> Mexico's populist president, Andres Manuel Lopez Obrador, is doing little to prepare Mexicans for what is coming [during the Covid-19 crisis]. He continued to travel and hug supporters and encouraged families to visit restaurants, as 'this strengthens the economy.' Other officials are taking the virus more seriously. On March 22nd the mayor of Mexico City shut bars and banned large gatherings.[62]
>
> —'Distancing neighbors', *The Economist*

> Even though danger signs abound in the environment, we believe that no harm can come to us ... Our best method for combating drama is to think it already happened ... This strange collective delusion allows us to think that we're beyond the apocalypse.[63]
>
> —Juan Villoro, *Horizontal Vertigo*

> History suggests that it is foolish to bet against big cities.[64]
>
> —'Microbes and the metropolis', *The Economist*

We are at a fork in the world's road as I pen these words. Globalisation took one on the chin with Covid-19. SARS had cast a light on the path ahead. That light was apparently too dim to catch the attention of any other than the more astute such as leaders in Taiwan who learned from and adapted policies thanks to history's offerings. That both diseases had their origins in China is not lost on the world. Some believe it is time to reconsider dependency on a country from which promises can prove hollow and partnership dangerous given faulty personal protective equipment, less-effective pharmaceuticals and disrupted supply lines. Ties won't be severed, but near-complete reliance on a partner proven to be less than reliable suggests that the once white-hot vehicle of globalisation might need a tune-up.

Does the world continue business as it was in late 2019 or turn down the thermostat to lend regional rather than global relationships a bit more influence, if not primacy?[65] It's unwise to bet against megacities either

---

62 'Distancing neighbors: Mexican–American relations', *The Economist*, [London], 28 March 2020, 30, 32.
63 Villoro, *Horizontal Vertigo*, 276.
64 *The Economist*, 'Microbes and the metropolis', 79.
65 'The global list', *The Economist*, [London], 26 January 2019, 19–22, at 22.

way. While ties with select fellow global influencers might fade, others will remain if not strengthen. Covid-19 did not undermine Tokyo's, London's or New York City's status as world financial hubs—though it may have made their stock markets more wary of that in Shanghai as it has with Hong Kong's economic system given recent political machinations there. Regional relationships look more attractive amid the pandemic, but regional isn't what it used to be when it comes to sustainment and access to goods and services. For megacities and other influential urban areas in the coming years of the twenty-first century, 'regional' may imply less in the way of nearby geography and more in terms of partners among the world's primary urban players. New York and London will remain regional partners with the European Union (Brexit notwithstanding). Singapore's region will include much of Asia, Africa and a good part of the world beyond thanks to its dominant role as an international maritime fuel provider on one of the globe's most travelled shipping routes. While South Korea and Japan may warily circle each other on the diplomatic front, their megacities will continue to provide much of what Manila, Ho Chi Minh City and South Asia's most influential urban areas require. Some residents and governing officials in Rio de Janeiro, São Paulo, Buenos Aires, Bogotá and Lima will see less value in dependence on national ties than on those farther reaching. These physically separate but more or less economically, socially and diplomatically linked urban areas often have more in common than they do with other urban areas in their own countries. Plato observed that Greek city-states were scattered along the Mediterranean's shores 'like frogs on a pond'[66] with ties less ethnic than urban and cultural.

Physical dispersion does have its advantages. Where national leaders made (and often mishandled) decisions as they tried to find the balance between protecting their citizens and controlling economic losses during the 2020 pandemic, a global strengthening of ties between megacities—something akin to international urban treaties—offers the possibility of communal support during disasters to come. Cities less affected at one point in time might lend a hand to others during a crisis, knowing those now suffering are likely to return the favour when Mother Nature or humankind turns pandemic, earthquake, flooding, tsunami, terrorism, war or some other screw on their residents and economies. You may say I'm a dreamer, but existing interurban ties show I'm not the only one. Those ties also have

---

66   Reader, *Cities*, 238.

much to offer in addressing the creeping threats that have taken only a supporting role in the preceding pages. Sea levels are rising. Developed nations' populations are ageing. Pollution and water shortages threaten. Closer ties should reduce the costly learning of lessons already in hand in other megacities. Another rebalancing may be needed to take full advantage of these lessons—one addressing what binds those urban areas to their nation-states.

Going it alone ... sort of: Megacities as semiautonomous substates

[A]dministratively it would be good for the country's development (to) create city-states and give them the power to undertake development. They should not be under the state governments but rather under their own chief minister or chief administrator or whatever you want to call the position.[67]

—Sheila Dikshit, chief minister of Delhi

In the world of independence, sovereignty works; in the world of interdependence, it is dysfunctional.[68]

—Benjamin R. Barber, *If Mayors Ruled the World*

New York City, Los Angeles and other large US cities received little aid and even less guidance from Washington during the spread of Covid-19. The federal government was more competitor for resources than facilitator, less a source of insight than of confusion and delay while urban leaders dealt with the crisis. Countries are suffering a loss of productive workers due to low birthrates and ageing populations. Megacities suffer less given their populations are younger than the national average and their attractiveness to educated workers from both their own countries and—immigration laws allowing—others. But those laws too often impede rather than promote megacity (and, by extension, national) progress. Why, then, does Tokyo remain part of Japan, Shanghai of China or London of the United Kingdom—the last, in particular, given its residents strongly favoured remaining in the European Union only to be forced out due to so many non-Londoners favouring Brexit? Given the wealth they generate, the expertise they possess and their role locally, nationally and globally,

---

67   As quoted in Barber, *If Mayors Ruled the World*, 238–39.
68   ibid., 147.

many megacities could flourish with less interference by state, provincial or national governments. It's not like their country is going to give birth to another megacity that will steal their thunder. On the contrary, as a separate—or semi-separate—city-state, a megacity could control the price of goods and services flowing through its ports, airfields and railyards enough to make any ambitious lesser city fear for its existence. City-states in the Middle Ages worked with power bases such as the Catholic Church and the aristocracy to limit monarchs' power.[69] Some in New York City, including its mayor, contemplated becoming an independent urban republic in 1861 as the Civil War loomed—one that would favour neither North nor South but remain open for business with both and the rest of the world.[70] Singapore was not originally granted independence. The British expected it would remain part of newly freed Malaysia after World War II. Singapore instead opted for separation. When the US Congress refused to fund a Port of Los Angeles expansion and adaptation, City of Los Angeles mayor Antonio Villaraigosa flew to China and received funding not only for the port but also for other infrastructure, casting doubt on those who think megacities rely exclusively on their state or national governments in times of need.[71] As the US population became more urban than rural between the two world wars, historian Arthur M. Schlesinger noted that 'these urban provinces, new to the American scene, possess greater economic, social, and cultural unity than most of the states'.[72] We've already seen that many major urban areas have city-to-city ties independent of the countries of which they are a part. Major urban areas across the United States, disgusted by a White House that backed out of the Paris Agreement on climate change, declared they would ignore federal back-peddling and uphold the agreement's standards. Nor is this assertiveness limited to US mayors. Anies Baswedan, Jakarta's governor, sought to lockdown the world's second-largest urban area despite Indonesia's president refusing such action.[73] While Colombia's capital of Bogotá struggled with Covid-19, the mayor of Medellín, its second-largest

---

69   Francis Fukuyama, *The Origins of Political Order: From Prehuman Times to the French Revolution*, London: Profile, 2012, 125–26.

70   Timothy Egan, *The Immortal Irishman*, Boston, MA: Mariner Books, 2016, 171. It was not the first time New York City had contemplated leaving New York State. While in 1861 the separation envisioned the city 'becoming a free and open port city', some in 1857 suggested breaking away to become a separate state in the United States to escape Republicans stripping the Democratic mayor of his power. See John Strausbaugh, *City of Sedition: The History of New York City during the Civil War*, New York, NY: Hachette, 2016, 137–38.

71   Barber, *If Mayors Ruled the World*, 97.

72   As quoted in Katz and Bradley, *The Metropolitan Revolution*, 41.

73   'Viral marketing: Indonesian politics', *The Economist*, [London], 6 June 2020, 30–31, at 30.

city, collected data to provide residents with aid and protect communities by denying anyone exposed to the virus use of the subway. The mayor also relied on such information to decide when shops could reopen. Medellín's Covid-19 performance proved exceptional even in a country that initially excelled in its response and despite protests about the data collection.[74] Urban areas' bondage to nation-states can seem more burden than benefit. Preparing for, responding to and recovering from disaster could be better served were megacities more the masters of their own fates. Why not fracture the tie—at least in part? It should not surprise that talk of New York City as a state has again merited consideration in years since the Civil War.

Sure, there would be obstacles. Though the risk of civil war were New York or Los Angeles to declare itself semiautonomous is all but zero—at least in the military sense—the same might be less true in other countries. But negotiations could identify benefits for both megacity and nation-state when ties are not completely severed. Rich as they are, megacities could afford to pay a fee to their former national government for military support when threatened by foreign powers rather than trying to create militaries of their own (though a citizen volunteer corps might be able to handle some of what militaries provide now, including emergency response capabilities). A sufficiently professional law enforcement system would address all but the most extreme challenges from internal or external threats. The megacity–country relationship would ultimately be something like that of cities centuries ago when capitalist merchants provided money that their countries used to raise and maintain armed forces. These agreements benefited the urban wealthy both in terms of interest paid and in the security status provided them as a national banker.[75] Intelligence could be another arena for sharing. We have noted that such exchanges already exist both between megacities themselves (New York and London, for example) and with the countries of which they are a part, though at times the urban area believes it gives more than it receives.

Breaking away, even partially, will sometimes not be an option. The national governments of West Africa's Côte d'Ivoire and Senegal took direct control of their largest urban areas on independence, fearing the

---

74 'Medellín's medical marvel: Colombia', *The Economist*, [London], 6 June 2020, 25–26.
75 Charles Tilly, 'Cities and states in Europe, 1000–1800', *Theory and Society* 18 (1989): 563–84, at 571, doi.org/10.1007/BF00149492.

cities would de facto replace the state government as the primary hub of power.[76] The same would surely be true of totalitarian governments. China is not about to allow Shanghai or Hong Kong to go it alone (as Beijing's increasingly authoritarian subjugation of the latter shows). Not too far from the control exercised by Côte d'Ivoire and Senegal, China is a country in which party or state authorities appoint mayors (France, interestingly, is another).[77] Despite Moscow's mayors occasionally flashing a bit of in-your-face to the country's plutocrats, the Red Army would be unlikely to stand by as the Republic of Moscow asked for UN recognition or semiautonomy.

More subtle forms of coercion also constrain megacity opportunities to flex independent muscles. Much of how New York City's budget is spent lies not within the purview of its mayor or city council but within the state legislature and the governor in Albany.[78] The city's education system and many other functions are funded (and therefore in great part controlled) not by officials elected by the city's residents but by others answerable to a far broader set of voters—voters unlikely to tolerate the megacity breaking away given the tax revenues they receive from the cash cow that is the five boroughs and other nearby urban authorities. Given the role of the state, it is not surprising that the private Police Foundation of New York pays for the NYPD's international liaison and similar programs while London receives funding from the national government that supports such activities.[79] In both instances, the officers are, in a sense, law enforcement ambassadors to other cities around the globe.

There would be other obstacles making partial autonomy rather than complete independence the logical alternative—for example, tariffs and border controls and the newly semi-free urban government's swollen payrolls as it assumes responsibilities currently paid for by state or country. Probably toughest of all: getting the many (many, many, many in some cases) parts that together make up the whole of a megacity to agree on the character of the semi-separate replacement government. Some of the subauthorities within the megacity will be less attractive than others to the whole of a semiautonomous urban state. Taxes paid will not always equal

---

76 Warren Smit and Edgar Pieterse, 'Decentralisation and Institutional Reconfiguration in Urban Africa', in *Africa's Urban Revolution*, Susan Parnell and Edgar Pieterse (eds), New York, NY: Bloomsbury Academic, 2014, 148–66, at 150, doi.org/10.5040/9781350218246.ch-008.

77 Barber, *If Mayors Ruled the World*, 83.

78 McNickle, *Bloomberg*, 45.

79 Nussbaum, 'Protecting global cities', 223.

taxes returned to better-off communities, but the binds that tie will likely be closer than those elsewhere in a state or halfway across a country. It is true the various parts are not likely to find themselves singing 'We Are the City-State', but they'll be better at humming the tune once they are part of a larger urban whole offering benefits that give them more bang for their tax dollar. The result might be a city-state in which its parts agree to key functions such as diplomacy (for example, treaty-making) and military security remaining with the federal government while assuming rights to retain more tax revenue, dictate select regulatory authorities and enhance professional licensing requirements. City-states would then capitalise on their megacity interconnectedness, ensuring initiatives such as those licensing requirements promote commercial and professional intercourse.

Additional benefits in increasing a megacity's autonomy include luring multinational (and national) companies via tax agreements unhindered by state governments, creating burden-sharing agreements with other independent or semiautonomous cities to mitigate the consequences of major disasters (a 'shared pot' insurance scheme to cover recovery, for example) and control over their own budgets by administrators better able to predict future cash flows as tax income goes directly to the urban area's coffers. As urban–rural political divides deepen throughout the world, megacity folk will be able to elect governments more in keeping with urban priorities and social norms such as infrastructure development and gun control while knowing that their basic needs such as food and water from outside sources are virtually guaranteed given their purchasing power. (Pittsburgh approved strict restrictions on military-style assault weapons and high-capacity magazines after killings at its Tree of Life Synagogue despite threats of a challenge in state courts. Pennsylvania forbids urban authorities from establishing gun regulations. Philadelphia has joined Pittsburgh in challenging the state's restrictions. As I write, a lawsuit challenging the two cities' right to establish independent gun-control policies is pending a hearing in the state supreme court.)[80]

---

80   Ramesh Santanam, 'Pittsburgh approves gun restrictions; lawsuits expected', *Associated Press*, 3 April 2019, 20, available from: apnews.com/article/3f4ffc8f307d46499b824dbf47467fe3; Associated Press, 'Pittsburgh appeals ruling that blocks gun violence prevention measures', *CBS Pittsburgh*, 4 May 2020, available from: pittsburgh.cbslocal.com/2020/05/04/pittsburgh-appeals-judges-rejection-of-firearm-restrictions/; and Angela Couloumbus and Stephen Caruso, 'Pennsylvania's highest court could give cities the go-ahead to craft their own gun laws', *Spotlight PA*, [Harrisburg], 1 June 2022, available from: www.spotlightpa.org/news/2022/06/uvalde-shooting-pennsylvania-gun-laws/.

Urban areas' willingness to uphold Paris Agreement climate standards reminds us that cities have also chosen to chart their own path in the face of national policies thought to be flawed. These stricter urban regulations need not cause businesses to flee thanks to urban wealth, increasing public support for greater accountability and the more autonomous urban area granting tax or other benefits to individual commercial entities. Several decades ago, the United Nations tagged the Japanese city of Kitakyushu as one of the world's worst pollution hubs. Kitakyushu spent a good part of the latter half of the twentieth century addressing the challenge—without significant national involvement. It was local housewives who motivated the turnaround. Major commercial players like Hitachi, Nippon Steel and Mitsubishi voluntarily entered into agreements. By the early 1990s, Kitakyushu had come back from the grey and could brag of air and water quality among the country's best. Residents worked with city officials to support the return of pollution-ravaged firefly populations. Success led to the reintroduction of a former cultural icon: the annual children's firefly festival.[81]

Differences in urban and national priorities are becoming more pronounced in many developed countries. Whether it was accurate or not, America's rural areas were long perceived as the country's moral bastion. Recent evidence suggests many such areas have failed to keep pace with social change, with communities taking on a reactionary character in the face of socially progressive and increasingly accepted norms regarding human rights and common-good standards. When California refused to pay for nonessential state-employee travel to states thought to have anti-gay policies, the mayors of Lexington and Louisville, Kentucky—one of the states so judged—requested exception to the policy. 'It does not fit us,' the mayor of Lexington wrote, 'We're a university city, open, welcoming, inclusive.'[82] The pair was not alone. In the face of state legislatures passing anti-LGBTQ bills in 2017, 68 American cities were putting strong LGBTQ guarantees in place[83]—more evidence that the champions of human rights tend to reside in the country's urban areas. Pressures for more equitable representation than that provided by US gerrymandering and Electoral College distortions may increase as

---

81   Brugmann, *Welcome to the Urban Revolution*, 245.
82   'The longest flush: California against the rest', *The Economist*, [London], 8 July 2017, 26.
83   Susan Miller, 'Record number of cities advance LGBT rights this year', *USA Today Weekend*, 20–22 October 2017, 4A.

America's urban majority flexes its economic and social muscles to redress the artificialities of disproportionate influence by select states and rural communities generally.

It would be expected that the world's megacities will be a part if not the leader of this transition. Carrying the banner for social initiatives like women's voting has long been an urban phenomenon. New York City already has preschool for four-year-olds and is expanding the offering to include those a year younger. Less populous cities are similarly assuming social leadership. Texas as a state does not provide full-day preschool; the City of San Antonio does.[84] Such forward-looking inventiveness is not limited to US or developed-world urban areas. The negative consequences of tribal, clan and other cultural ties have undermined sectarian African political processes for decades. Urbanisation offers hope of a brighter future in that regard. Ethnic ties tend to weaken in larger urban areas. Even in Kenya, where tribal ties have long dictated voting preferences and underlain brutal, often fatal, election violence, voting by Nairobi residents suggests tribal links are loosening within the city.[85] Late twentieth-century predictions of Mexico City becoming the world's most populous urban area have fallen by the wayside as declining national birthrates and the attractiveness of other cities slowed growth. Others instead prophesised Lagos as the population champion come the middle decades of the new century, but as we have seen, women living in urban areas tend to have lower birthrates than those in the countryside. Further, fertility rates in larger cities are apt to fall more sharply than those in smaller ones.[86] Some megacities being among the most expensive places to live worldwide acts as an additional suppressor of family size. From social norms to cultural impact to political standards and ethnic tolerance, urban areas—once considered dens of iniquity—are in many cases doing much to change the world for the better.

With increased control over their own destinies and in a world in which multinational companies, IGOs such as the United Nations and the European Union and even some NGOs dramatically influence or even make policy, these urban areas could negotiate agreements securing priority of recovery assistance before disaster strikes. A Londoner or resident of Rio de Janeiro might agree with standards that do not

---

84 'Young Americans: Early education', *The Economist*, [London], 26 January 2019, 23–24, at 24.
85 'First we take Nairobi: Democracy in Africa', *The Economist*, [London], 24 June 2017, 44.
86 'Baby bust: The birth rate', *The Economist*, [London], 24 November 2018, 23–24.

recognise a Chinese medical licence in their country. That reticence could fall by the wayside were Shanghai to join those two megacities in establishing mutually agreeable regulatory policies based on interurban standards rather than less rigorously designed or loosely enforced national ones.[87] Relationships already exist for the exchange of urban-specific innovations. Mayors' interest in the CoolRoofs initiative, which involves painting urban roofs with reflective white paint to lower cooling costs and related carbon emissions, resulted in the founding of a nonprofit that is now part of Bloomberg Philanthropies.[88] Cities have demonstrated that they can bring relevant parties together both before and during crises to outperform federal and state endeavours. Our example of the Los Angeles TEWG is one. Another reaches back to 2013 when San Francisco created a partnership with BayShare—an organisation committed to facilitating the sharing of goods and services—that seeks to address the three phases of preparing for, reacting to and recovering from the Bay Area's next major earthquake.[89] BayShare does so through its network of regional businesses, among them Airbnb (which could coordinate shelter for those who lose their homes), RelayRides (which facilitates privately owned car rental), Trove (an online site previously named 'Yerdle', where individuals can sell unwanted items for a credit to acquire other Trove offerings) and nonprofit media outlets.[90] With great potential for coordinating these resources across the San Francisco Bay Area's many towns and cities, the connections that BayShare (and the San Francisco–Oakland–San Jose urban aggregation) has with national ventures make them an obvious point of contact for other major urban areas nationwide.

Further insights regarding the challenges and benefits of increasing megacity autonomy can be found when considering several such urban areas around the world. We've mentioned Singapore with its striking growth but limits on social freedoms and political representation. Might the residents of more autonomous urban areas suffer increased restrictions on social freedoms given wealthy plutocrats dominating the government—

---

87   *The Economist*, 'The global list', 20.

88   Ben Paynter, 'Why Bloomberg Philanthropies' James Anderson tops our list of the most creative people in business 2017', *Fast Company*, 15 May 2017, available from: www.fastcompany.com/40412383/why-bloomberg-philanthropies-james-anderson-tops-our-list-of-the-most-creative-people-in-business-2017.

89   Sarah Rich, 'San Francisco embraces sharing economy for emergency preparedness', *Government Technology*, 14 June 2013, available from: www.govtech.com/public-safety/San-Francisco-Embraces-Sharing-Economy-for-Emergency-Preparedness.html.

90   Rodin, *The Resilience Dividend*, 274.

or would they see political liberalisation instead? Hong Kong once gained much and now stands to lose much since rejoining China (including, possibly, megacity status by our definition). By early 2020, it ranked third among the world's financial centres. It was a climb reliant on the former colony maintaining excellent fiscal credentials that provided exceptional access to developed-world financial systems.[91] China's coercive influence threatens to curtail that access. Others stand ready to step in. While urban areas might assist one another in times of calamity, their political and commercial leaders are ever ready to take advantage of weakness. Singapore understandably is already looking to capitalise on Hong Kong's diminishing status as a global financial hub; it was in hungry pursuit of the territory's arbitration lawyers as of mid-2020.[92] Germany's Berlin, Hamburg and Bremen represent the other end of the autonomy scale. Each can introduce legislation as a separate representative at the federal level while remaining very much part of the country.[93]

What are the risks for megacity residents should theirs seek greater autonomy? There is no guarantee that a city government will be superior to those of states, provinces or nations. Several twentieth-century US mayors succeeded in adding themselves to prison populations. Detroit, for example, had three mayors sent to prison and one recalled after less than a year in office between 1930 and 2008. Atlanta's mayoral office was tainted with a similar number of scandals during a like period. Mayoral performance during the Covid-19 crisis varies considerably (so, too, of course, has that of governors and various federal officials). That megacities are magnets for the very wealthy's real estate investments means there are those who would use the full potential of their resources to protect those interests at the expense of the less well-to-do. Nor are mayors or city board members immune to uninspired thinking. While a more enjoyable cure than injecting disinfectant as suggested by Donald Trump,[94] Nairobi's governor distributed equally useless (but less dangerous) bottles of Hennessy cognac as what he called 'throat sanitizer'.[95]

---

91   'Electrical storm: Hong Kong's future', *The Economist*, [London], 6 June 2020, 58–60, at 58–59.
92   'The darkness behind: Hong Kong's companies', *The Economist*, [London], 18 July 2020, 32.
93   Emanuel, *The Nation City*, 234.
94   Dartunorro Clark, 'Trump suggests "injection" of disinfectant to beat coronavirus and "clean" the lungs', *NBC News*, 23 April 2020, available from: www.nbcnews.com/politics/donald-trump/trump-suggests-injection-disinfectant-beat-coronavirus-clean-lungs-n1191216.
95   'Leaders and misleaders', *The Economist*, [London], 2 May 2020, 36. Since 2010, Kenya's constitution has replaced local governments such as mayors with county authorities.

Increased autonomy could threaten access to essentials from nearby regions of the country despite a megacity's economic influence. Climate change, swelling world populations and a generally increasing demand for resources mean some megacities would have new competitors for food, water and other necessities now procured from nearby (and not so nearby) communities. Roughly 40 per cent of Singapore's water comes from outside its borders.[96] Lagos already suffers continuous water shortages.[97] Increased autonomy could also make it difficult for urban areas to expand outward rather than the more expensive upward or below ground. Mexico City expanded its geographic area by an average of more than 7 per cent annually in the two decades spanning the end of the past and the beginning of this century.[98] Delhi, India, more than doubled its spread across the landscape in only 14 years, from 67.71 square kilometres in 1998 to 181.97 square kilometres in 2011 (that expansion provides insights into just how much urban terrain acts as a heat island. What was primarily agricultural land in 1998 is now part of Delhi's north. The surface temperature of the area ranged between 20°C and 30°C that year; by 2011, the variation was between 30°C and 35°C. The increase is greater in the centre of another Indian megacity, Mumbai, which saw average surface temperatures increase 15–20°C between 1998 and 2009).[99]

There is a financial risk as well for megacities considering going it alone. The US federal government pays from 75 to 100 per cent of disaster response bills when FEMA issues a disaster declaration.[100] Increased control over taxation would cast this dependency in a different light, but supplemental 'insurance' such as the aforementioned megacity cooperative for such contingencies would probably still be necessary for the worst disasters—and even then recovery funding could fall short. Nor can megacities rely on their countries as fountains of youth. Current demographic trends suggest those wells have already begun to dry. It is estimated that the administrative entity that is the City of Tokyo will lose half its 2010 population by 2100—a point at which the portion of that population over the age of 65 will be approaching the 50 per cent mark

96   Zahra Jamshed, 'How Singapore is using technology to solve its water shortage', *CNN*, 25 September 2019, available from: www.cnn.com/2019/09/25/tech/singapore-water-technology-innovative-cities/index.html.
97   UN-Habitat, *State of the World's Cities 2012/2013*, 50.
98   ibid., 30.
99   Richa Sharma and P.K. Joshi, 'Rapidly urbanizing Indian cities: The problem of local heat but a global challenge', *UGEC Viewpoints*, July 2013, 28–32, at 29, 30.
100   Bucci et al., *After Hurricane Sandy*, 2.

(assuming current population trends continue. These estimates saw 2020 as the peak for Tokyo's population—the last year before the decline was to begin).[101] As for Shanghai, it has had negative growth in terms of birth and death rates for two decades but has managed annual double-digit growth during that same period except for the recession years of 2008 and 2009.[102] How? The stream of immigration into Shanghai has made it a growth dynamo despite the already apparent effects on ageing of China's One-Child Policy and refusal to grant rights to many migrating from rural areas. But how long can that last? It is a challenge Chinese Government officials seem to be aware of given their 2015 objective of moving 260 million people from rural to urban areas after years of attempting to hamstring the influx. 'Domestic demand is the fundamental impetus for China's development', the relevant government plan states, 'and the greatest potential for expanding domestic demand lies in urbanisation'.[103] On the other hand, many are the Chinese cities that have seen far lower growth rates since 2010 than had been projected.[104] For both Japan and China, looking to new sources of workers will require significant changes in immigration policies and cultural norms. The two countries see only a small percentage of newcomers from other ethnic groups coming to settle permanently. With greater autonomy, megacities might maintain their youthfulness by casting aside national government dictates like those that have limited China to only 0.22 foreign immigrants per 1,000 population and South Korea and Japan to ratios of 0.03 and 0.02, respectively.[105]

As most of the world ages, Africa will not.[106] The majority of today's Africans were born in the twenty-first century; most of those in European Union countries were born before 1978.[107] The once Dark Continent might turn out to be the source of new light as young migrants spur innovation via immigration, their education funded by international

101 World Population Review, 'Tokyo Population 2020', [Online], Walnut, CA: World Population Review, 2020, [Updated 2022], available from: worldpopulationreview.com/world-cities/tokyo-population/.

102 World Population Review, 'Shanghai Population 2020', [Online], Walnut, CA: World Population Review, 2020, [Updated 2022], available from: worldpopulationreview.com/world-cities/shanghai-population/.

103 Chris Weller, 'Here's China's genius plan to move 250 million people from farms to cities', *Business Insider*, [New York, NY], 5 August 2015, available from: www.businessinsider.com/heres-chinas-big-plan-to-move-a-population-the-size-of-the-phillippines-from-farms-to-cities-2015-7.

104 *Demographia World Urban Areas*, 15th edn, 2.

105 Bricker and Ibbitson, *Empty Planet*, 88.

106 ibid., 237.

107 'Generation game: Democracy in Africa', *The Economist*, [London], 7 March 2020, 46.

megacities hungry for promising and ambitious youths. (Africa's young urban-dwellers are better educated and have access to more sources of information than their rural counterparts. Their countries' economies are also proving unable to provide many of them with the employment opportunities they seek.)[108] Countries with high birthrates have at least two pressures working to encourage emigration. First, the once common phenomenon of children dying before the age of five is increasingly rare.[109] Second, education and healthcare in major urban areas tend to be better than in smaller cities, towns or rural areas. More educated youth unable to find work means more people looking to emigrate to more welcoming pastures (or, perhaps we should say, streets)—or looking for ways to challenge national governments that deny them their ambitions.

Readying for the 'Big One': Not if, but when

> The morning of December 16th, 1707 there arose from Mount Fuji a column of what looked like belching black smoke to an altitude of some 20 kilometers accompanied by loud sounds of explosions … [What is] present-day Tokyo was covered with several centimeters of fallout and the population suffered from the noxious fumes of the eruption … Since then Fuji has been dormant for longer than during any period in recorded history. Volcanologists predict an eruption during the next fifty years and are studying the events of 1707 to assess the damage this might cause.[110]
>
> —'The 1707 eruption of Mount Fuji as blueprint for events to come'

> Our founder perceived that a site on the seacoast is not the most desirable for cities founded in the hope of long life and extended dominion.[111]
>
> —Cicero, *The Republic*

---

108 ibid.
109 Bollyky, *Plagues and the Paradox of Progress*, 2.
110 Beatrice M. Bodart-Bailey, 'The 1707 eruption of Mount Fuji as blueprint for events to come', Flyer for Beatrice M. Bodart-Bailey presentation, The Australian National University, Canberra, 6 October 2015.
111 Cicero, *The Republic*, as quoted in Piero Boitani, *A New Sublime: Ten Timeless Lessons of the Classics*, trans. Ann Goldstein, New York, NY: Europa, 2020, 215.

No one apparently had thought that an event fierce enough to damage a reactor might also disrupt basic communications.[112]
—David Lochbaum et al., *Fukushima*

Dense concentrations of people and buildings; reliance on consistent flows of power, water, food and money; locations among the most vulnerable on the planet—what could go wrong?

Japan's three largest urban areas are at risk from floods, earthquakes, high winds, storm surges or tsunamis. Those five hazards—in that order—are what inflict the greatest harm on humankind when Mother Nature plays a significant role. The three cities and their immediate surrounding areas— Tokyo (57.1 million population), the Osaka–Kobe area (32.1 million) and Nagoya (22.9 million)—are, respectively, first, fourth and sixth in terms of the number of people in danger according to a recent insurance analysis,[113] which means a total of 112.1 million in a country with a population of 127 million at the time these numbers were calculated. Large urban areas at risk in terms of being near significant volcanoes include Tokyo, Mexico City and Manila.[114] The last eruption of Mount Fuji described in the above passage came 49 days after an earthquake of magnitude 8.7 that badly damaged Nagoya, reminding us that the 2011 earthquake–tsunami–nuclear reactor failure isn't alone as a potential multiple-disaster threat to Tokyo.[115] Popocatépetl ('Smoking Mountain'), approximately 80 kilometres south-east of Mexico City, remains active. Like Mount Fuji and Tokyo, it can be seen by those in Mexico's capital on clear days. About 20 centimetres (approximately 8 inches) of ash could blanket the entire city should a major eruption occur and winds blow towards Mexico City, making air unbreathable, poisoning water supplies, clogging drainage and damaging power generation facilities.[116]

---

112 Lochbaum et al., *Fukushima*, 16.
113 Schelske et al., *Mind the Risk*, 11. Note that Schelske's numbers include significant portions of the population beyond our definition of urban area.
114 Jean-Claude Thouret, 'Urban hazards and risks; consequences of earthquakes and volcanic eruptions: An introduction', *GeoJournal* 49 (1999): 131–35, at 131, doi.org/10.1023/A:1007118027266; and Chester et al., 'The increasing exposure of cities to the effects of volcanic eruptions', 94, 97.
115 Beatrice M. Bodart-Bailey, 'Pyroclastic Rivers: The Hōei Fuji Eruption (1707)', in *Local Realities and Environmental Changes in the History of East Asia*, Ts'ui-Jung Liu (ed.), London: Routledge, 2015, 157–80, at 158, available from: www.taylorfrancis.com/books/edit/10.4324/9781315695655/local-realities-environmental-changes-history-east-asia-ts-ui-jung-liu.
116 Mark Oprea, 'What will Mexico do when its deadliest volcano erupts?', *Pacific Standard*, [Santa Barbara, CA], 30 October 2018, available from: psmag.com/environment/what-will-mexico-do-if-its-deadliest-volcano-erupts; and Patrick J. McDonnell, 'As it recovers from earthquakes, Mexico City looks nervously at its (very) active volcano', *Los Angeles Times*, 27 September 2017, available from: www.latimes.com/world/mexico-americas/la-fg-mexico-volcano-20170927-story.html.

Though the 'after' period of a megacity disaster is a time of considerable opportunity, recovery and rebuilding, plans too often focus on speed in returning to the pre-event situation rather than balancing those demands with taming the impact of the next disaster to come. Sir Christopher Wren proposed improvements to London in the wake of the 1666 Great Fire. City leaders dragged their feet rather than acting. Others with more initiative rebuilt the capital along its medieval roads before Wren's and others' proposals could be brought to bear.[117] Perhaps London today would be gridlock-free had that opportunity not been forgone, with cars flowing smoothly through roundabouts and along wide, tree-lined avenues with nary a pause. Or perhaps not.

Recovery considerations ought to be organic to disaster plans. A poll of readers who manage to make it through this book might choose 'system' as the word that mercilessly beat them about the head and shoulders throughout its pages, yet repeated references to backup generators and circuit-breaker panels installed beneath flood lines and recovery plans that look backward in time rather than towards the future also remind us that both government and commercial representatives repeatedly forget (or choose to overlook) the interconnected consequences of threats yet to come. Author Jeff Goodell found that New York City utility Consolidated Edison (ConEd) was ready to spend $1 billion after Hurricane Sandy without taking the effects of climate change into account.[118] This need not be the case. I was told that my Virginia licence had reciprocity in most other states when I passed my professional engineer examination. There were exceptions. California's licensed engineers had to have exceptional expertise in earthquake design. Professional engineers in New York had to be especially proficient in dealing with wind loads and other features of skyscrapers; I was told it was part of their licensing examination. The events of 9/11 suggest that building standards in that city and elsewhere need to include surviving more than what nature might throw at them. Designing to allow for partial failures would probably have done nothing to reduce the losses on that fateful day. Yet, constructing a bridge so that spans fail individually rather than the entire structure collapsing catastrophically should the bridge be struck by a ship or tremor seems a good idea. 'Failure' in such cases would mean buckling rather than complete collapse barring the most cataclysmic of incidents. Designing for such 'graceful failure' has parallels in other disaster preparedness

---

117 'The great land grab: Transport', *The Economist*, [London], 23 May 2020, 45.
118 Goodell, *The Water Will Come*, 160.

arenas. The decentralisation of water or power supply systems would offer the additional benefit of limiting the number of those going without in a crisis. New standards and common sense on the part of architects and builders need to account for the seemingly little things. Those placements of backup generators and related components provide only one example of details repeatedly overlooked—or in need of looking at again given climate change's adroitness in magnifying nature's effects. Just as some professions require continuing education to make sure those licensed stay up-to-date, cities should require that buildings and other infrastructure are inspected and reinspected with an eye to new threats such as the second and higher-order effects of sea-level rise. Meeting revised standards should not be voluntary. Voters would be wise to consider alternatives to political ostriches who refuse to face realities like climate change and the value of vaccines. Urban residents are already key to the security of their cities thanks to their recognition and reporting of 'absence of the normal or presence of the abnormal'. They are the *first* first responders who save tens if not hundreds and thousands of lives because of both their reporting of the unusual to authorities and their service in the immediate aftermath of catastrophes. Megacities' men, women and children are the first line of preparedness much as was Dr Stella Ameyo Adadevoh, the physician who stood firm in the face of pressure to release Lagos's Ebola patient zero.

Cities continue to attract our planet's best, brightest, most ambitious and most forward-looking. More than one-third of New York City's population is foreign-born.[119] Chicago in 1880 could claim that almost nine of every 10 residents were first or second-generation immigrants.[120] The rapid growth that can accompany influxes of either domestic or international arrivals is not without its challenges. A full third of Dhaka's residents either rely on surface latrines or have no sewage disposal at all. They also must deal with political neglect, as is evident in the lack of concern shown for clothing labourers during the Covid-19 pandemic. As ably said by one of my former students, cities 'are about the people'. Those fleeing serfdom in Middle Ages towns or cities that offered freedom to anyone not retaken in a year and a day did so not only to escape servitude. They, like their successors today, also pursued the irresistible lure of economic opportunity and a life offering more than drudgery. The magnet has not weakened with the passage of centuries. A Pakistani arriving in 1950s Karachi revelled in a 'city of free hard work', unlike elsewhere in the

119 Katz and Bradley, *The Metropolitan Revolution*, 24.
120 Rybczynski, *City Life*, 121.

Province of Sindh, where bonded labour was regularly practised, or the Frontier and Punjab provinces, in which tribal ties dictated social interactions. Karachi belonged to 'the workers and the middle classes'. Women, too, could experience 'their first opportunity to breathe freely'.[121]

Learning from the past, preparing for the future: Making megacities safer

Particularly in an urban context, exposure to disaster risk and to violence is more closely interrelated than is often assumed.[122]
—Elizabeth Ferris, 'Urban disasters, conflict and violence'

We are reminded that training of private sector security personnel and first responders is an essential element of securing our nation's critical infrastructure. As many possible soft targets are controlled by private organizations, the private sector must be a full partner in efforts to protect the homeland.[123]
—Charles E. Allen, under secretary for intelligence and analysis, US Department of Homeland Security

It would be too obvious at this point to relate that 'an ounce of prevention is worth a pound of cure'. Better even than preparations when misfortune visits are capabilities that also provide routine value. State-of-the-art megacity operations centres fall into that category. The United Nations raved that in Brazil:

Rio de Janeiro's newly established operations centre offers a glimpse of the way cities might be managed in the future. Conceived as a city-wide decision-making mechanism for emergency situations based on real-time information, the centre integrates information from multiple departments and government agencies; visual displays of data from various urban systems, including surveillance cameras; together with maps, news updates, information about incidents and even simulations [to] facilitate real-time monitoring and analysis. Although initially designed for forecasting floods and other emergencies, the centre is also used for day-to-day management of urban functions.[124]

---

121 As quoted in Gayer, *Karachi*, 17–18.
122 Ferris, 'Urban disasters, conflict and violence'.
123 Quoted in US Senate, *Lessons from the Mumbai Terrorist Attacks*.
124 UN-Habitat, *State of the World's Cities 2012/2013*, 42.

Public information programs can likewise serve daily functions while also helping an urban population prepare for that coming storm, blackout, quake, flood or otherwise less-than-everyday event. Designing and trialling various ways of getting word only to targeted groups (the elderly, those with a specific illness or a particular neighbourhood or community, for example) put the pieces in place for when those muscles need to be flexed during an emergency. History can help in readying both authorities and citizens. Several US cities studied the challenges of Seattle, Washington, during the 1999 World Trade Organization gathering—later referred to as the 'Battle of Seattle' due to the extent of anarchist-inspired violence—and adapted their pre-event crowd-control plans to deal with manipulated demonstrations that might come to their own streets. Chechens fighting Russian invaders during the last decade of the twentieth century are said to have studied Germany's World War II defence of Berlin before badly bloodying the invader's nose in Grozny.[125]

We hear much about 'smart cities' and their high-speed surveillance cameras, ubiquitous internet and AI-assisted functions to save energy, control traffic flow and otherwise improve efficiency, lower costs and enhance quality of life. We posited that maybe the smartest of urban areas will in the future be thought to merit that status less because of their technologies and more because of how they meld these capabilities with those of humans working together to serve the public good. A megacity's internal towns, cities and agencies will have to sacrifice a bit of autonomy in the interest of the totality of which they are a part. Such is the goal behind the New York area Regional Plan Association seeking 'to improve the prosperity, sustainability, and quality of life in the New York–New Jersey–Connecticut metropolitan region through work in transportation, economic development and real estate, environment and open space and more'. It does so by working with 31 counties spanning those three states 'to recommend the best outcomes for individual communities and the region as a whole'.[126]

Individual residents, too, will have to find that sweet spot between self-service and sacrificing for the greater good. Personal information-sharing and public surveillance have been sore rather than sweet spots in that regard. It is admittedly disturbing to know your movements are tracked

---

125 Knezys and Sedlickas, *The War in Chechnya*, 51.
126 Regional Plan Association, 'Our work', [Online], New York, NY: RPA, 2022, available from, www.rpa.org/programs.

and personal contacts recorded, even when those doing the collecting insist the data remain separate from identities. Covid-19 is among the emergencies demonstrating the value of tolerating what some consider treading on privacy. Tracking smartphones can save lives, mitigate the worst of unemployment and reduce the negative economic impacts of a pathogen's rampage. Perhaps an opt in – opt out option as exists in Barcelona would be satisfactory for lesser contingencies, but when some future Patrick Sawyer fails to conveniently collapse on arrival in a megacity airport, being able to track his phone and that of those with whom he came in contact (and those with whom they come in contact …) could mean the difference between mere hundreds being exposed with tens of deaths and a far worse exposure of millions and proportional loss of life. At some point, even opting out should be pushed aside in the interest of the greater good, if only temporarily.

Information collection, monitoring and data-mining will continue. The extent to which that is true, the benefits gained or unacceptable costs accrued will depend on many factors. They include the authoritarianism of the using government, the willingness of urban residents to share (Barcelona), links to locations beyond the megacity itself (New York and highway toll collection cameras) and the sophistication of information analysis technologies.

Less sure is the continued growth of megacity populations. Those in sub-Saharan Africa are likely to continue growing for years, likely decades. Tokyo's will shrink thanks to Japan's combination of ageing and limited immigration. Shrinkage in several other megacities was already in progress before the arrival of Covid-19. Occurrences like that virus can speed emigration. The pandemic caused a surge in New York City residents looking to rent or buy in surrounding communities, though most searches were for locations close enough that the megacity of New York would not lose numbers. How many leave, whether the relocations are permanent and the significance of the migration remain to be seen. Los Angeles sees a swell of departures to Arizona, Utah or other more distant, less quake-threatened locations after its occasional major-ish tremors but not enough to have a noticeable long-term effect on its population. Among other reasons for megacity shrinkage are those declining birthrates and greater willingness to support cybercommuting (working from home). Previous improvements and better-quality emergency services in some megacity communities might act as attractors after a future disaster. Writing for *GeoJournal*, author James Mitchell observed:

The locus of hazard is shifting, often rapidly. For example, in Tokyo the inner and outer suburbs are now increasingly at risk both because of rapid expansion of the city's periphery and lack of attention to hazard-sensitive design in the newer developments. By contrast, the central city and adjacent neighborhoods have been the focus of major investments in emergency preparedness, hazard mitigation, and other disaster reduction alternatives.[127]

Disaster readiness will continue to vary dramatically not only within megacities but also between them. Mitchell continues:

> Some cities (e.g., Tokyo) have adopted multiple reinforcing public adjustments involving sophisticated technologies backed up by high levels of training and self-reliance on the part of civilian populations that together are designed to address all parts of the disaster cycle (i.e., preparedness, emergency management, recovery, mitigation). Others possess no effective formal programs for natural hazard management (e.g., Dhaka).[128]

How bad can it be? Dhaka, it turns out, is not only hyper-vulnerable to frequent flooding. Two other authors reveal that:

> Dhaka is one of the most vulnerable cities to earthquake … In some areas, construction according to official building codes was followed for less than 10 per cent of buildings … 78,000 out of 326,000 buildings in Dhaka are vulnerable to collapse … There are concerns regarding the city's readiness to respond to disaster. Though there are contingency plans for the threat of earthquakes, there are none for floods or fires. Which parts of the city government have which responsibilities is also a question … [On a more positive note,] the nonprofit Oxfam facilitates interaction between a wide range of partners including civil society organizations, NGOs, media organizations, foreign and local universities.[129]

Nearly one in five of the migrants living in Dhaka moved there to avoid catastrophes elsewhere.[130] There will be plenty of work for Oxfam and its partners in the years ahead.

---

127 James K. Mitchell, 'Coping with natural hazards and disasters in megacities: Perspectives on the twenty-first century', *GeoJournal* 37 (1995): 303–11, at 305, doi.org/10.1007/BF00814009.
128 ibid., 305.
129 Stott and Nadiruzzaman, *Disaster Risk Reduction in Dhaka City*, 15, 33, 43.
130 Asif Ishtiaque and Nurul Islam Nazem, 'Household-level disaster-induced losses and rural–urban migration: Experience from world's one of the most disaster-affected countries', *Natural Hazards* 86 (2017): 315–26, at 324, doi.org/10.1007/s11069-016-2690-5.

Mother Nature cares no more for the poor than do some megacity administrators. Yet, with wealth comes an ability to ensure greater security against her unladylike whimsies. We have noted that most megacity growth is not in the city core but in its suburbs or slums. Manila's downtown in 1950 had something less than 1 million of the larger urban area's population of just over 1.5 million—about 60 per cent of the total. Sixty years later, the core's population had increased by 700,000 while the rest expanded by almost 20 million residents.[131] The megacity of Jakarta saw 75 per cent of its overall growth in its suburbs between 1971 and 2000 and 84 per cent in the decade that followed.[132] Similar growth in other megacities means that many of the additional millions are in slums where formal building standards may be unheard of and other-governing authorities reign. It is in these areas that outsiders offering post-disaster relief are likely to find themselves most needed, rather than in posh neighbourhoods or among skyscrapers. A further reason aid providers are unlikely to be rubbing shoulders with a megacity elite (despite political pressures to favour wealthier neighbourhoods): not only are the better off more likely to be able to pay for needed services once they have built their homes and businesses; they also probably built on land more suitable for the structure's survival. Such is true even in megacities where massive expanses of slums are not an issue. Tokyo's Ministry of Construction promoted the building of wide, flat-topped 'super banks'—berms with excellent earthquake resistance and flood protection. Real estate developers greeted the initiative with open arms, seeing the raised land as both highly survivable and providing views where otherwise there would be little to see beyond the building across the street.[133]

Re-envisioning disaster response relationships would constitute another stride in the right direction. National governments tend to view coalitions only in terms of governmental organisations. The US Army, for example, views a coalition as 'an ad hoc arrangement between two or more nations for common action'.[134] This definition fails to recognise an inevitable truth: governments will find everything from nonprofits to fortune-seeking companies to IGOs such as the United Nations competing for

131 Wendell Cox, 'The evolving urban form: Manila', *New Geography*, 24 April 2011, available from: www.newgeography.com/content/002198-the-evolving-urban-form-manila.
132 Cox, 'The evolving urban form: Jakarta'.
133 Kumagai and Nojima, 'Urbanization and Disaster Mitigation in Tokyo', 83.
134 Department of the Army, *Terms and Military Symbols*, ADP 1-02, Washington, DC: Headquarters, Department of the Army, August 2018, 1–18, available from: irp.fas.org/doddir/army/adp1_02.pdf.

space, funds, bandwidth, local political attention and other resources during crises. It would be better to delimit our understanding of coalition, defining it instead as 'an ad hoc arrangement between two or more organisations in the interest of supporting a common action', as suggested previously.[135] This broadened understanding promotes incorporation of local and more far-flung governments, but also NGO, IGO, faith-based, industry, neighbourhood and individual volunteers and other resources in the service of sought-after ends during not only execution but also planning and preparation for megacity disaster relief.

How much reasons to leave will ultimately affect megacity populations remains to be seen. Even as some cities shrink, the lure of the world's greatest urban areas will continue to entice. Commercial symbiosis (the benefits of being close to other organisations possessing valuable talent or expertise), 'coolness' factors (cultural offerings, access to better restaurants, concerts, theatre and professional sporting events) and the value of physical proximity for social life (online dating only takes a guy or gal so far) will maintain their allure. The continued existence of megacities is not in doubt, but flight during Covid-19's ravages tells us that ignoring the potential for disaster will cause some existing or potential residents to reconsider whether these attractions are worth the risks. Cyberattacks on urban power distribution, water supply or internet connectivity could cause loss of services for days or weeks. The devastation in terms of millions affected will be needlessly high until city leaders and utility providers question the wisdom of relying on only a few mutually dependent infrastructure nodes. Focusing on quicker recoveries and designing for partial versus catastrophic failures could be key to keeping urban residents in their cities should these assaults transpire.[136] The same is true if a city suffers a nuclear or large-scale chemical, biological or radiological terrorist attack. Ultimately, however, whether a megacity begins to age or continues to drink from the fountain of youth, whether it grows or trims its numbers, depends on leadership and the dynamism of its residents, government and commercial ventures. Unfortunately, the destiny of megacities is only partially in the hands of those living and working within their bounds. Seeing opportunity, much as does Singapore in the erosion of Hong Kong's economic legitimacy, Toronto has quietly emerged as one of North America's premier tech centres. It added more

---

135 Glenn, *Band of Brothers or Dysfunctional Family?*, 41.
136 Andy Greenberg, *Sandworm: A New Era of Cyberwar and the Hunt for the Kremlin's Most Dangerous Hackers*, New York, NY: Doubleday, 2019, 134, 305.

technology jobs in 2017 than Seattle, Washington, DC, and the San Francisco Bay Area combined. Only the last outhired it in the tech sector the following year. Toronto's secret? It is in part a willingness to welcome those with talent. Almost half of the city's residents are foreign-born.[137]

Glimpses of possible futures

More than any other trace we will leave behind … our cities will form the most concentrated and revealing archive of who we were and how we lived.[138]

—David Farrier, *Footprints*

Two-thirds of the world's population growth in the next thirty years will occur in just fourteen large, lower-income nations: India, Pakistan, Nigeria, Indonesia, Bangladesh, Ethiopia, Democratic Republic of the Congo, the Philippines, Tanzania, Uganda, Sudan, Afghanistan, Iraq, and Kenya.[139]

—Thomas J. Bollyky, *Plagues and the Paradox of Progress*

Seven of the 14 countries mentioned in the previous quote have one or more cities of over 10 million in population, some of which meet our definition of megacity. Virtually all those urban areas are under threat of catastrophes singly or in combination. One (Lagos) used to be its country's capital. Another (Jakarta) has a national government that wants to move that status elsewhere due to the challenges nature and humankind have cooperated on to cause frequent disasters of increasing scale.[140] Egypt hopes to do the same, fleeing Cairo's narrow, twisting passageways and compressed masses of impoverished slums by creating a city with an expanse all but matching that of Singapore.[141] Like picnickers climbing into their car and leaving their waste behind, those wealthy enough to abandon a mess largely of their own making believe they can solve problems simply by departing—except in these cases, they abandon millions less able to depart the waste they lacked the care or wisdom to address.

---

137 Thompson, 'North star', 16–17.
138 David Farrier, *Footprints: In Search of Future Fossils*, New York, NY: Farrar, Straus & Giroux, 2020, 62–63.
139 Bollyky, *Plagues and the Paradox of Progress*, 105.
140 Bianca Britton, 'Indonesia plans to relocate its capital from Jakarta', *CNN*, 29 April 2019, available from: www.cnn.com/2019/04/29/asia/indonesia-relocate-jakarta-intl/index.html.
141 'An elephant in the desert: Egypt's new capital', *The Economist*, [London], 26 January 2019, 40.

Relocating Indonesia's capital will do nothing to halt the sinking landscape that worsens the severity of Jakarta's floods any more than Lagos or Cairo has or will escape the more gradual challenges to security and welfare when national authorities run from rather than confront the challenges facing their largest urban areas. National governments are not alone in failing to recognise that urbanisation is not the pending trend; it is already the defining characteristic of human expansion. The urban future is already here and has been for some time. Humanity has 145 million of its members living on coastlines less than 1 metre above sea level. Most of those are residents of the world's most populous urbans areas—New York City, Jakarta, Mumbai, Lagos and suffering Dhaka among them.[142] This reality will not be solved by moving capitals or averting one's eyes by gating wealthy communities. Relocating a capital is likely to result in some of the most qualified people leaving government service. Even decades after the move, the purpose-built capitals of Brasília and Canberra remain small in comparison with their countries' long-established and more cosmopolitan urban centres. The same is true of South Korea's new administrative capital of Sejong, a city created from a few rural buildings that now claims about 300,000 residents. Many choose to remain in the more vibrant, larger urban areas that offer a higher—and more interesting—quality of life. The challenges in creating anew what already exists elsewhere are evident in a plaque at the base of Canberra's National Carillon bell tower installed in celebration of the fiftieth anniversary of the capital's founding. The inscriptions provide three popular early descriptions of the capital, one of which is 'a cemetery with lights'.[143]

There are many futures in terms of what should be just as today's megacities are victims or beneficiaries of what could have been. Reducing the negative consequences and seizing the opportunities offered by

---

142 Farrier, *Footprints*, 59, 63.

143 When my wife and I lived in Canberra, residents frequently stated that it was a great place for families with children though it admittedly lacked the vibrancy and breadth of offerings of life in Melbourne or Sydney. The same might well be true of South Korea's Sejong, the administrative city not far south of the national capital. With a population comparable with Canberra's (roughly 300,000), its fertility rate is significantly higher than the national average and higher yet than that in Seoul—in the country with the lowest reported fertility rate in the world. Unsurprisingly, Sejong's population also has the youngest average age of any administrative district in the Republic of Korea. Maybe there's something to be said for less vibrancy and fewer urban distractions for countries suffering ageing populations. See Yonhap News Agency, 'S. Korean population slightly grows, becomes older in 2019', *Yonhap News Agency*, [Seoul], 15 August 2020, available from: en.yna.co.kr/view/AEN20200814002200315; 'Cradle to desk: Sexual politics in South Korea', *The Economist*, [London], 17 October 2020, 31–32; and World Bank, 'Fertility rate, total (births per woman)—Korea, Rep.', *Data*, [Online], Washington, DC: The World Bank, 2018, available from: data.worldbank.org/indicator/SP.DYN.TFRT.IN?locations=KR.

future disasters will inevitably clash with economic and political goals. Recent rather than more distant history will tend to dominate decisions. Preparing for the next pandemic rather than readying for Mount Fuji's pending eruption better suits those with short-term memories, unlike the wiser with an understanding of history's arbitrariness. Just as soldiers are often accused of preparing for the last war, humankind tends to pay less attention to what are sometimes more likely future calamities than others fresher in the mind.

M. Mitchell Waldrop's well-written *Complexity* uses the analogy of a sandpile to describe how hard it is to predict events in a complex system (hopefully, we all agree at this point in the book that megacities are complex systems). It is a useful metaphor when thinking about the difference between predicting and forecasting. Waldrop's sandpile builds on a tabletop as a container of sand above drops one grain at a time. The pile grows tall and wide in the shape of a cone. Eventually, a grain will cause a part of the cone to slough like a mini avalanche. Some amount of sand will cascade from some location on the pile at some point in time. It will be impossible to *predict* how much of, where and when the sand will slip downward. Yet, based on the history of sandpiles and the size of our pile, we can *forecast* how much, where and when with some degree of accuracy and give a range of probabilities for the event. We're unlikely to be exactly correct (in fact, the probability of that is zero, but never mind; it's the former maths instructor in me trying to assert itself). Megacities are, to be sure, more complex than sandpiles. That makes prediction even more impossible—an impossible on top of an impossible. The greater complexity does not make forecasting any easier either. But histories of a megacity's storms and their frequency and ferocity tell us that our forecasts need to reflect growing chances that storms will be bigger, more damaging and cause greater suffering than in past decades if little is done to diminish the effects of sea-level rise. Preparations ought to go far in making sure future sand-slides on the pile are smaller. In the case of acts of terrorism and even some nature-triggered events, they could also be fewer in number.

'Not going to happen in my neighbourhood', you might reply regarding the chances of multiple disasters occurring simultaneously—unless you live in Tokyo. You might also be a believer if you hail from Utah, where communities found their pandemic hotline knocked out when a 5.7 magnitude earthquake struck on 20 March 2020 just as Covid-19 was hitting its stride in the United States.[144] Students of history could refrain from such belief as well if they fail to recall that Athens was ravaged by plague for three years just as the city-state began the decades-long Peloponnesian War with Sparta in the fifth century BCE. You might remember Constantinople's double whammy of earthquakes in 557 and 558 CE followed by a Hun attack in early 559 that took advantage of the resultant damage to the city's walls.[145] An offshore earthquake estimated at magnitude 9.0 or more devastated Lisbon, Portugal, on 1 November 1755. It was at the time one of the world's wealthiest cities. Thousands not killed by the quake died when the accompanying tsunami washed ashore, then receded, dragging its victims out to sea much as would happen two and a half centuries later in Fukushima Province. Misery's visit was not over; an ensuing firestorm raged in the city's ruins for weeks afterwards, killing thousands more and burning much of what the earthquake and sea had spared.[146]

Utah's example involving Covid-19 is particularly relevant to larger urban areas. Believe it or not, the air and water pollution that plague many megacities can offer an advantage when it comes to holding some diseases at bay thanks to their reducing the reproduction of mosquitoes and other vectors. Perhaps for similar reasons, malaria infection rates tend to be lower in sub-Saharan urban than rural areas. The flipside of the sickness coin is less encouraging. Dengue fever is primarily an urban problem. We need only look at New York City, Wuhan, London, Los Angeles and other major urban locations during the Covid-19 pandemic to realise that megacities' concentrations of humans make them attractive hosts for other forms of disease as well.[147]

The world's most connected urban areas are mega-creators of positive synergy. The future of the world *is* an urban one, and megacities will be at its centre in terms of influence. They will continue to offer what the less connected cannot. Other urban areas will provide select top-echelon, cutting-edge offerings. Megacities will have them in great numbers. They are what push the edges of cultural, intellectual and economic envelopes.

---

144 Steven Levy, 'Has the Coronavirus killed the Techlash?', *WIRED*, 20 March 2020, available from: www.wired.com/story/plaintext-has-the-coronavirus-killed-the-techlash/.
145 Hughes, *Istanbul*, 252.
146 A book-length review of Lisbon's disaster is available in Mark Molesky, *This Gulf of Fire: The Destruction of Lisbon, or Apocalypse in the Age of Science and Reason*, New York, NY: Alfred A. Knopf, 2015.
147 Alirol et al., 'Urbanisation and infectious diseases in a globalized world', 134–36.

Chinese sports footwear maker Anta concentrates its shops in medium-sized urban areas. It finds it can better compete there than in richer Shanghai or Beijing where the allure of global (and more expensive) brands like Adidas and Nike makes them more popular.[148] Just as medieval urban areas granted freedom to the serf and were richer soil for women's rights, today's larger cities are where India's caste system breaks down in addition to being where Africans find sanctuary from tribal and clan narrow-mindedness. 'No one knows who you are in the city,' observed Mumbai factory worker Tawwai Ali, 'so there's less conflict.' His fellow countryman Chinmay Tumbe agreed: 'Strict rules about "untouchability" are impossible to enforce in a jam-packed Mumbai train.'[149]

The future of megacity combat

According to our analysis, the likelihood of interstate conflict drops sharply (to around one-quarter to one-third below the peak values) once countries reach the following thresholds: (1) a median age above 30 years, (2) a youth-bulge ratio below 20 percent of the adult population, (3) a fertility level below two births per woman, and (4) a life expectancy above 75 years … China … will be one of the very oldest societies on Earth in just a few decades … It is also true that much of the developing world, including the Middle East, is likely to be more conflict prone in the next few decades given the currently youthful profiles of countries in their region.[150]

—Deborah Jordan Brooks et al., 'The demographic transition theory of war'

Rising levels of urbanization and education … have been associated with the spread of more doctrinaire forms of Islam in other countries.[151]

—'A long shadow', *The Economist*

---

148 'Upping the Anta: Chinese brands', *The Economist*, [London], 16 May 2020, 54.
149 Quoted in 'City air makes you free: Domestic migration', *The Economist*, [London], 16 November 2019, 10–11, at 10; and 'Melting pots', *The Economist*, [London], 21 December 2019, 63–65, at 63, 65.
150 Deborah Jordan Brooks, Stephen G. Brooks, Brian D. Greenhill and Mark L. Haas, 'The demographic transition theory of war: Why young societies are conflict prone and old societies are the most peaceful', *International Security* 43(3) (2018–19): 53–95, at 94, 95, doi.org/10.1162/isec _a_00335.
151 'A long shadow: Islam and politics in Bangladesh', *The Economist*, [London], 3 June 2017, 31–32, at 32.

> The attack jumped off at 0715 on 24 January [1945] following a fifteen-minute preparation by the 25th Division artillery ... The right company failed to reach the edge of town because of sniper fire ... The left company reached the north edge of town under the artillery preparation. This company was halted about fifty yards into town by machine gun crossfire and then driven back out of town by a prompt counterattack led by three tanks ... For the succeeding four days the operations consisted of a block-by-block advance south through the town ... On 27 January a coordinated attack on a two-battalion front was made against the southern half of the town. It was preceded by a 105-mm preparation of two battalions and supported by a similar concentration advanced by time schedule. Though several tanks were eliminated, no more than 100 yards was gained along the front. Casualties were heavy. Fatigue was becoming apparent in attacking units.[152]
>
> —Colonel James L. Dalton II, 'Commentary on Reduction of Strong Point San Manuel, Luzon, P.I.'

As with so much in this consideration of megacities, the possibility of future combat presents a mixture of challenge and opportunity, concern and—dare it be said—promise. The first quotation above lends hope for reduced chances of war given worldwide ageing (with exceptions such as sub-Saharan Africa and portions of the Middle East) and the lower birthrates in urban areas. The second suggests that other trends creating educated but less enlightened youths unable to find employment have an opposite effect. Finally, quotation three reminds us that the costs promise to be high should warfare come to these urban areas. The loss of noncombatant lives during fighting in 1945 in Manila was more than five times that of the combined deaths among the combatants, forcibly reminding us that the penalties are far greater than a focus on military casualties alone suggests.

We recall that an underlying premise of this book has been that urban disasters brought about by war can provide lessons for responses to disasters with human-aggravated natural or other humanmade causes and that the reverse is likewise true. War it was not, but reviewing the findings from the previously mentioned exercise in which the emergency operations centre was left outside the notional area affected by a nuclear attack reinforces the above lessons or presents others:

---

152 Colonel James L. Dalton II, Commander, 161st Infantry Regiment, 25th Infantry Division, 'Commentary on Reduction of Strong Point San Manuel, Luzon, P.I.', 8 February 1945. 'P.I.' refers to 'Philippine Islands'.

- Focus on the urban system, not just its individual parts.

- Rehearsing for disaster relief along pristine streets or in empty training buildings instead of roads and rooms strewn with debris and the scattered residue of daily life is like playing T-ball and hoping to make the major leagues.

- Inviting only cooperative organisations to planning and rehearsal sessions means failing to include all those with necessary capabilities and potentially missing out on their resources in times of need.

- Though having all relevant parties involved makes planning, rehearsing and the possibility of agreeing to a single orchestrating authority more difficult, gaining the cooperation of as many of those parties as possible for at least part of the orchestra's performance beats the chaos of noncooperation. If creating a single orchestra is impossible, consider forming quintets, quartets, jazz ensembles or several smaller orchestras. It beats everyone playing their instrument on their own.

- The same can be said for an orchestra's string, brass, woodwind and percussion sections. The conductor succeeds only if the sections know and play their parts effectively. The same applies to new arrivals; community volunteers add a fifth section to the orchestra's normal four. Outside aid and service providers expand it further yet. Without music (the plan) and practise (rehearsals), the result is noise rather than a symphony. Unfortunately, there will be those who prefer cacophony to music as it better suits their taste (criminals, enemy forces, purveyors of misinformation).

- Megacities can be more like sports stadiums than concert halls during disaster responses. Chance, friction and (in time of war) enemy actions will work to disrupt the orchestra. Good plans, mutual familiarity and rehearsals that include improvisation-ready responders give conductor and orchestra a shot at prevailing.

- Terrorists will place second, third or more bombs to kill first responders or innocents fleeing from initial attack locations. Calls for help unrelated to an attack such as those on the World Trade Center or Taj Mahal Palace Hotel are also inevitable in a city of millions. Over-response to attention-grabbing events threatens lives and a megacity's general security. Mission command plays a role here.

- Having some grasp of probable initial priorities is better than starting from scratch amid the wreckage. Plan. Rehearse. Learn from other megacity disasters. Revise plans. Rehearse again. And again.

The crawl–walk–run approach to disaster response will tend to be most effective. Simple or routine activities are a good place to start when preparing. Parts perfecting their roles (crawl), then gradually coming together and cooperatively adapting those near perfection (walk), so that their orchestration better serves the collective effort (run), take advantage of individual capabilities while never losing focus on the readiness of the whole.

10

Conclusion

citizen (n.)

c. 1300, citisein (fem. citeseine) 'inhabitant of a city or town,' from Anglo-French citesein, citezein 'city-dweller, town-dweller, citizen' (Old French citeien, 12c., Modern French citoyen), from cite (see city) + -ain (see -ian).[1]

—'Citizen', *Online Etymology Dictionary*

Cars helped drive huge change in the mid-20th century, including entirely unexpected knock-on effects such as the fact that 25% of the US's agricultural land, which had been used for rearing horses, was then freed up for human food production … City authorities are also playing a part as they introduce inducements to ditching cars … Most driverless vehicles will be more used than typical manual cars which typically spend 95% of their time parked up. As the need for parking space and potential bus lanes tails off, city authorities will find new public space to play with.[2]

—Kevin McCullagh, 'Cities are about to change forever'

Forget Washington—Cities will win or lose the future.[3]

—Benjamin R. Barber, *If Mayors Ruled the World*

---

1   Douglas R. Harper, 'Citizen', in *Online Etymology Dictionary*, 2001–22, available from: www.etymonline.com/word/citizen.
2   Kevin McCullagh, 'Cities are about to change forever: Here are three key decisions they must make', *Fast Company*, 5 May 2017, available from: www.fastcompany.com/90123848/cities-are-about-to-change-forever-here-are-3-key-decisions-they-must-make.
3   Barber, *If Mayors Ruled the World*.

Two recent undertakings help to reinforce several of the observations from previous pages. One is from Iraq in the early years of this century, the second from New York City.

The strikingly successful early 2003 military operation that defeated Iraq's armed forces in a matter of weeks will long stand in combination with the years that followed as an example of the dictum that one can win the war but lose the peace. Coalition military forces swept northward from Kuwait and Saudi Arabia into Baghdad and beyond, ousting Saddam Hussein from power and—for several months—taking control of the country. Preparations to bring about recovery from the social disaster of war were minimal, poorly and inconsistently organised and fundamentally flawed at the highest levels. The result was a series of insurgencies that continued to percolate two decades after the original combat assaults.

There are plenty of sources relating the details behind the failed preparations and flawed decisions for anyone who is unfamiliar. They include descriptions of US Government departments failing to take advantage of one another's capabilities, an apparent ignorance of history's lessons resulting in outright disbandment of Iraq's military structure and an unwillingness to recognise that battlefield success is only a table setting for the feast of challenges to come.

The experiences of then Major General James N. Mattis serve in microcosm to reveal the broader consequences of the inability to win the peace.[4] Recognising that a combat force eventually assumes responsibility for an occupied population, previous commander in chief of US Central Command, retired General Anthony C. Zinni, called Mattis and his fellow 1st Marine Division commanders together just before the 10 November 2002 Marine Corps ball, knowing they would be part of the coalition invading Iraq the following year. 'You'll go through the Iraqi Army within the first six weeks,' he told the assembled group, 'Then the real work begins.' At the same time, the US Army's chief of staff, General Eric K. Shinseki, was making it clear that it would probably take more military personnel to occupy Iraq than to win the fight to defeat its armed forces. Both men would be proven right.

The first weeks of the occupation seemed to signal that concerns about violence during the occupation were overblown. Soldiers walked city streets with little worry of being attacked. The leadership of 1st Marine

---

4   Material in this vignette is supported by that from Mattis, Interview.

Division was meeting with members of the Iraqi Army, working through the initial awkwardness of victor and defeated, Westerner and Iraqi. The men shared coffee. Relations improved to the point that they shared a professional education seminar during which the Iraqis discussed the differences between fighting Iranians and fighting Americans. Additional Iraqi military personnel were called in and paid as the Marines sought to continually improve the working relationship (casting doubt on senior US political leaders who claimed the Iraqi Army had disbanded itself and their formal order directing that action was simply recognising an established reality). In the meantime, Mattis requested that the senior US organisation in Iraq, the Coalition Provisional Authority (CPA), send civilian experts to help re-establish control in his division's urban areas. The CPA refused, claiming they were unable to spare any of their 240 personnel. Fortunately, UK Government representative Cheryl Plumridge in southern Iraq's Basra, part of the United Kingdom's occupation zone, offered two individuals for each city Mattis felt could benefit. Plumridge's response to his initial request for just one: 'No, no. I think you need two in each city because if I call one back I don't want to leave you uncovered.'[5] Plumridge had 13 people in her organisation at the time.

Ensuing weeks saw the formal disbanding of the Iraqi Army. Occupation policies were largely ad hoc. US Department of Defense leaders chose to ignore Department of State post-combat plans and offers of expertise. Far from bringing the Iraqi people and its military onside as part of a comprehensive approach to recovery, internal US Government squabbles strained even US intragovernmental relationships. Opportunities to win the peace were lost in no small part because urban security could not be guaranteed. British General Graham Lamb observed: 'There are only two kinds of people here: reconcilable and irreconcilable.'[6] Lacking the cooperation from many of Iraq's soldiers, police and population, it was virtually impossible to discern who was who until they started attacking coalition personnel and fellow Iraqis. Mattis drew on his knowledge of history in concluding his discussion of the frustrations he felt regarding the lack of US efforts to successfully occupy Iraq. 'Great empires don't go out with a bang,' he observed, 'They go out with a whimper.' The same is true of great nations.

---

5   The words are Mattis's recollection of the conversation.
6   Again, the words are as recollected by Mattis.

We have already touched on our second example. It is one offering a more encouraging response while unfortunately reflecting the fact that government squabbles continue to plague disaster reaction. New York City was hit particularly hard by Covid-19 in the opening months of 2020. By April, more than 700 of its residents were dying every day. The state of the city's health system and inability to manage the bodies of the dead led to what were then extraordinary actions: public properties converted into temporary hospitals, freezer vans parked outside medical facilities to store the deceased before burial or cremation and calls for federal assistance—some of which was forthcoming, some of which was not. By far the hardest hit location in the United States at the time, the number of dead would exceed 21,000 in a little more than 14 weeks after the city's first diagnosis on 29 February 2020.[7] Both New York City's mayor and the state's governor struggled with a lack of accurate and consistent federal guidance and Washington's decision to be a competitor for dangerously short supplies of equipment such as personal protective gear. There were notable successes despite the lack of support. Many listened and took the precautions advised. Photos showed Hollywood-like post-apocalyptic streets vacant of vehicles and people. Online offerings featured a ghostly quiet Manhattan devoid of car horns, vehicle sirens and its normal 24/7 hum of activity. By mid-August 2020, six and a half months after detection of the city's first cases, more than 27 per cent of the five boroughs' population tested positive for the Covid-19 antibody.[8] Infectious disease epidemiologist Dr Maureen Miller at once described the situation and revealed New Yorkers' underlying distress:

> They stopped all businesses. They insisted that there be no social gatherings. They had shelter-in-place laws in place and enforced by fear … We had watched what had happened in Europe and then suddenly it's happening in New York City, our home.[9]

---

7   Wan Yang, Sasikiran Kandula, Mary Huynh, Sharon K. Greene, Gretchen Van Wye, Wenhui Li, Hiu Tai Chan, Emily McGibbon, Alice Yeung, Don Olson, Anne Fine and Jeffrey Shaman, 'Estimating the infection-fatality risk of SARS-CoV-2 in New York City during the spring 2020 pandemic wave: A model-based analysis', *The Lancet* 21(2) (February 2021): 203–12, at 203, doi.org/10.1016/S1473-3099(20)30769-6; and NYC Health, 'Trends and totals', *COVID-19 Data*, City of New York, 11 March 2021, [Updated 2022], available from: www1.nyc.gov/site/doh/covid/covid-19-data-totals.page.
8   Joseph Goldstein, '1.5 million antibody tests show what parts of N.Y.C. were hit hardest', *The New York Times*, 20 August 2020, available from: www.nytimes.com/2020/08/19/nyregion/new-york-city-antibody-test.html.
9   Quoted in Amy Jamieson, 'How New York City got control of COVID-19—and where it goes from here', *Healthline*, 20 July 2020, available from: www.healthline.com/health-news/how-new-york-city-got-control-of-covid19.

It was a healthy fear, or at least a fear in the service of staying healthy. The residents of America's largest megacity—aside from the foolish few—toed the line, thereby playing a major role benefiting their personal welfare, that of their neighbours and, by extension, a quicker return to work for the many suddenly unemployed. It was a struggle, nonetheless. More than half of those residing in (ironically) the Corona, Queens, zip code tested positive at one point, this from a population in which for many, every dollar was critical to meeting essentials (much of the Corona area's population relies on construction or restaurant service work—jobs requiring close contact with others and often lengthy travel to places of work).[10] The next hardest hit community was one consisting principally of Hasidic Jews, where large and multigenerational households are common and some resisted both social distancing and wearing masks.[11]

Federal help in the form of military medical and other personnel arrived to assist those in need. The publicly owned Jacob K. Javits Center became a medical facility in four days thanks to US Army Corps of Engineers modifications and the infusion of armed forces nurses, lab technicians, pharmacists and doctors. Elsewhere, newly erected tents sheltered medical procedures and patients. A crash initiative converted 'portable on demand storage' containers into surgical facilities.[12] Partnership for New York City, a nonprofit organisation that brings the private sector and government together, supported the public information campaign and encouraged support for struggling businesses. It lent assistance to the vulnerable, first responders and healthcare personnel while at the same time arranging for essential support from businesses, linking the local population with federal help in another step towards a comprehensive approach in combating the virus's spread.[13] Companies suspended demands for payment from residents who could not afford internet or other services, which was particularly critical as schools instituted distance learning and adults increasingly worked from home. Groups voluntarily provided food, other goods and assistance to benefit megacity area residents.

10   Amanda Rosa, 'What N.Y.C.'s antibody test results show us', *The New York Times*, 20 August 2020, available from: www.nytimes.com/2020/08/20/nyregion/nyc-coronavirus-antibody-testing.html.
11   ibid.
12   Paige Williams, 'Urgent care from the Army Corps of Engineers', *The New Yorker*, 27 July 2020, available from: www.newyorker.com/magazine/2020/08/03/urgent-care-from-the-army-corps-of-engineers.
13   For a similar example of services provided by New York City, see City of New York, 'COVID-19 guidance for business owners and FAQs', [Online], New York City Small Business Services, n.d., available from: www1.nyc.gov/site/sbs/businesses/covid19-business-tips-faqs.page.

The New York megacity response reflected the good and bad and the opportunities and challenges that catastrophe brings to the world's biggest, most connected and hyper-influential urban areas. Basic functions continued—at times constrained but continuous nevertheless—softening the impact for those domestic and international residents who depended on the city for critical functions. Orchestration involving high-level government officials, commercial enterprises, volunteers and cooperation by the men, women and children who live in the city was key to containing the first wave of Covid-19 as lessons were relearned.

Calamity capitalises on the vulnerability of those in particular economic, cultural, ethnic or other conditions, putting them at greater risk. Consistent, frequent, high-quality and accessible guidance makes responses and recovery more effective. It is a shield deflecting rumour, misinformation and disinformation—and, by extension, panic. Insights available from New York's battle with Covid-19 join the many from other crises described in these pages and offer fodder for megacity preparations worldwide. So will disasters yet to come.

We have made some generalities in the preceding chapters even as we recognise that each megacity is unique. These urban areas individually trend in different directions. In many cases, the direction of that trend depends on whether the megalopolis is part of the developing or the developed world. Growing wealth in the former means residents can increasingly afford automobiles even as others rely on more traditional forms of transportation. Congestion increases such that some cities— Bangkok among them—are among the most traffic-intense on the planet, as cars compete with scooters, motorcycles, bicycles, pedestrians and, sometimes, oxcarts, rickshaws or horse carriages. Industrialisation is often the trigger. Factories bring wealth, wealth brings automobiles, automobiles and industry bring pollution at levels not seen since executives in early industrial Pittsburgh had to change shirts over lunch, their morning white turning grey before noon. Residents of Mumbai and Beijing today are among those who can relate.

Meanwhile, the developed world's megacities look towards a not-too-distant decade in which self-driving cars diminish the number of vehicles on which residents rely. Relying on others for intra-urban area transit (for example, Uber, Lyft, traditional taxis and public transportation), costly automobile insurance and congestion charges and limited and expensive workplace parking are among the factors reversing the trends of early industrial urbanisation. Populations age. Megacities shrink, barring sufficient immigration. A pandemic makes working from home the norm for many. Those long commutes in heavy traffic and too little time with family are happily avoided for some even as others pine for the vibrancy of in-person exchanges with office colleagues, the variety of lunch options and the higher RPM of megacity living compared with the idling pace of the 'burbs.

What such trends and choices mean in readying for future megacity disasters is yet to receive much scrutiny. Recent working from home trends notwithstanding, developing and developed-world megacity residents alike could find themselves sympathising with our Haruki Akamatsu as he sat traffic-bound in this book's opening pages: too many cars and lingering danger as the population attempts to flee. As time moves on, developed-world cities' evacuees will instead deal with the slim pickings among driverless rides or public transport thanks to disrupted service should disaster strike. A positive note: the costs of living closer to megacity commercial cores are likely to remain prohibitive for first responders, meaning there will be a yin for the yang as those aid providers responding to disaster bring driverless vehicles to areas from which others are trying to escape. How desperate the transport shortage will be will depend considerably on the when of a catastrophe. We remember that many of Tokyo's 20 million workday commuters were hard pressed to get home after the earthquake of 11 March 2011.

Traditional federal–local government partnerships are less likely to find solutions to these challenges than cooperatives of a new ilk. Urban areas have discovered richer relationships among the innovative and youthful within their jurisdictions. Cutting-edge companies, universities, imaginative and publicly oriented nonprofits, fellow urban governments and citizens' groups offer expertise, passion and—sometimes—money. The more than 100 cities in California's Bay Area range from north of San Francisco to south beyond San Jose and east well distant from saltwater. Depending on who is defining (and therefore counting), it is home to between 6.5 and nearly 10 million people. Many of those cities have agreements to provide mutual assistance in times of need, understanding that while all may suffer somewhat, some will suffer more than others. Those authorities are not unique in this regard either within the United States or beyond, combining as they do private as well as government partners in their readying for future catastrophes. The previous pages make it clear that grassroots intermegacity relationships have much to offer in the way of best-practice exchanges and helping one another close capability gaps. Tokyo's citizen-level preparations put it in an elite class. New York's interorganisational ties within the megacity and beyond complement its intelligence competencies to similarly guarantee it a premier position when it comes to providing vital information. Both megacities have much to offer each other and those elsewhere given these complementary proficiencies. Such bilateral or multilateral links could see the world's most influential urban areas conducting a series of future exercises, each offering participants a promise of better readiness when calamity next visits. One wonders how the tragic mishandling of Mumbai's 2008 terrorist attack might have gone differently had that city's officials seized the opportunity to learn from other, better-prepared megacities and their law enforcement organisations. Paris's response to a similar multilocation attack in 2015 demonstrates the value of learning from disasters elsewhere.

Little wonder that citizens of the world's wealthier urban areas seek more say over their fates by declaring themselves sanctuaries from what are for them detrimental immigration, environmental, social or other federally, state or provincially dictated policies. Nearly two-thirds of residents from the City of Los Angeles—the core of the United States' second megacity— are first or second-generation immigrants. Support for wiser policies regarding those wishing to come to the United States makes economic sense. As observed by former Chicago mayor Rahm Emanuel, half of the US tech companies valued at $1 billion or more in 2020 were founded by recent arrivals from other countries (44 of 87).[14] Toronto, Canada, has capitalised on the lesson; some federal officials in the United States seem set on not doing so.

If the lady on Liberty Island is to be believed, her 'beacon hand glows world-wide welcome' to those 'huddled masses yearning to breathe free'—many of whom continue to bring genius, ambition, wealth and, thus far, eternal youth to America's megacities, other urban areas and the country at large. Imperfect though they may be, cities in the United States remain melting pots for races, genders, cultures, religions, politics and economic status. Urban values are the ones evolving in line with the tolerance and acceptance long treasured (if not always practised) as signature American traits. US cities in the twenty-first century represent a more welcoming, broader-minded set of values better in keeping with the nation's Constitution.

---

14   Emanuel, *The Nation City*, 90.

The growth of the world's collective mind is elsewhere similarly reliant on its urban citizens. Recent efforts to impose narrowmindedness on Türkiye's citizenry—the antithesis of Kemal Atatürk's ambitions for his people—suffered a blow when the country's megacity of Istanbul had partners in four of its five other largest cities in voting against the ruling Justice and Development Party.[15] Demonstrations in the world's most influential cities are the ones that draw our attention. Beijing, Hong Kong, Moscow, Jakarta and Lagos are among them—despite repressive national regimes in some.

No few of our planet's most influential urban areas were losing population even before the Covid-19 pandemic. The causes were varied. Intolerable crime was the problem in some, too much congestion and too little open space the problems elsewhere. For parents, it was the cost of raising children—a cost on top of the already punishing prices of rent and essential needs. For the youngish but getting older, the call of a place of one's own rather than continued sharing to make ends meet motivates flight. Often that flight is internal; while the core city that gives its name to a megacity might see numbers diminish, the larger whole simply experiences a shift in numbers among its parts. Lewis Mumford considered the transition to America's larger urban areas the third of the country's great migrations, the first being expansion west to the Pacific and the second a shift from agrarian living to small towns. Despite the opportunities offered by remote working thanks to internet technologies and the pressure to flee when earthquake, virus or another of the four horsemen visits (or one or more of their recently emerged cronies), megacities will for decades and likely centuries remain disproportionate sources of wealth, innovation, youth, power and coolness. It is increasingly accepted that we are now living in an era best tagged with the label 'Anthropocene'. Never before has the world's environment been so influenced by a single species. That species is predominantly an urban one and, for better or for ill, the largest and most influential of those urban areas are the ones that have the greatest impact on our planet's population. That it is for the better remains a goal still inadequately addressed. We have yet to show we possess the wisdom to learn from the lessons offered us by megacity disasters.

---

15 'Revolt of the cities: Turkey's local elections', *The Economist*, [London], 6 April 2019, 41.

Within weeks of the 2018 Camp Fire—the deadliest and most destructive wildfire in the history of California—the County of Los Angeles approved a 19,000-home development in areas designated by the state's fire agency as being particularly vulnerable to fires.[16] 'We see the impacts of fires, then turn around and rebuild largely in the same way and the same place, but expect things to go differently next time,' says David Shew, a former staff chief at the California Department of Forestry and Fire Protection. 'That's the definition of insanity.'[17]

16   Alice Hill and Leonardo Martinez-Diaz, 'Adapt or perish: Preparing for the inescapable effects of climate change', *Foreign Affairs* 99(1) (January–February 2020): 107–17, at 110. A similar self-inflicted wound exists in the flood insurance arena where 'the National Flood Insurance Program … has kept flood insurance prices artificially low for almost three generations', meaning homeowners are incentivised to buy (and, more importantly, real estate developers are incentivised to build) where flood damage is likely. The problem is made worse by FEMA's flood maps being optimistic in terms of current threats and short-sighted in that they fail to account for sea-level rise. Ariza, *Disposable City*, 86, 93.
17   Quoted in 'Learning to live with it: Natural disasters', *The Economist*, [London], 12 September 2020, 67–68, at 68.

Bibliography

Abidin, Hasanuddin Z., Heri Andreas, Irwan Gumilar, Yoichi Fukuda, Yusuf E. Pohan and T. Deguchi, 'Land subsidence of Jakarta (Indonesia) and its relation with urban development', *Natural Hazards* 59(1753) (December 2011). doi.org/10.1007/s11069-011-9866-9.

Abrams Urban Quick Reference Guide, Publication No. ST 3-20.12-1, Fort Eustis, VA: US Army Training and Doctrine Command, December 2002.

Acción Contra El Hambre [Action Against Hunger], *Urban Disaster Lessons Learnt*, Paris, n.d., available from: silo.tips/download/urban-disaster-lessons-learnt.

ActionAid International, *Unjust Waters: Climate Change, Flooding and the Protection of Poor Urban Communities*, Report, 5 March 2007, Johannesburg, South Africa: ActionAid International, available from: actionaid.org/publications/ 2007/unjust-waters-climate-change-flooding-and-protection-poor-urban-communities.

Adkin, Mark, *Urgent Fury: The Battle for Grenada*, London: Leo Cooper, 1989.

Ahmed, Imtiaz, 'Dhaka: Stressed but Alive!', in *Building Resilience in Cities under Stress*, Francesco Mancini and Andrea Ó Súilleabháin (eds), New York, NY: International Peace Institute, June 2016, 13–23, available from: www. academia.edu/27153738/Building_Resilience_in_Cities_under_Stress.

Ai, Yue, Yaojiang Shi, Renfu Luo, Jamie Chen, James Garth, Jimmy Zhang, Alexis Medina, Sarah Kotb and Scott Rozelle, 'China's invisible Crisis: Cognitive delays among rural toddlers and the absence of modern parenting', *The China Journal* 78 (2017). doi.org/10.1086/692290.

Albiges, Marie, 'Wastewater could be indicator of where virus will strike: Surges noticed in water prior to spike in cases', *The Virginia Gazette*, [Williamsburg, VA], 12 August 2020, 2A.

Alexander, Christopher, Sara Ishikawa and Murray Silverstein, *A Pattern Language: Towns, Buildings, Construction*, New York, NY: Oxford University Press, 1977.

Alford, Stephen, *London's Triumph: Merchants, Adventurers, and Money in Shakespeare's City*, New York, NY: Bloomsbury, 2017.

Alirol, Emilie, Laurent Getaz, Beat Stoll, François Chappius and Louis Loutan, 'Urbanisation and infectious diseases in a globalized world', *The Lancet* 11(2) (1 February 2011): 131–41. doi.org/10.1016/S1473-3099(10)70223-1.

A.M., Jacob, A. Allen and Larry P. Graham, Megacities and the proposed urban intervention model, Thesis, Monterey, CA: Naval Postgraduate School, June 2016, available from: apps.dtic.mil/sti/pdfs/AD1026697.pdf.

American Public Transportation Association, *Public Transportation Facts*, Washington, DC: APTA, 2022, available from: www.apta.com/news-publications/public-transportation-facts/.

American Red Cross, *The case for integrating crisis response with social media*, Paper, Washington, DC: American Red Cross, August 2010.

Ariza, Mario Alejandro, *Disposable City: Miami's Future on the Shores of Climate Catastrophe*, New York, NY: Bold Type, 2020.

Arnold, Thomas D. and Nicolas Fiore, 'Five operational lessons from the battle for Mosul', *Military Review: The Professional Journal of the US Army* 99 (January–February 2019): 56–71, Fort Leavenworth, KS: Army University Press, available from: www.armyupress.army.mil/Journals/Military-Review/English-Edition-Archives/Jan-Feb-2019/Arnold-Mosul/.

Arthur, W. Brian, 'On the Evolution of Complexity', in *Complexity: Metaphors, Models, and Reality*, George A. Cowan, David Pines and David Meltzer (eds), SFI Studies in the Sciences of Complexity, Proc. Vol. XIX, Boston, MA: Addison-Wesley, 1994, 65–78, available from: sites.santafe.edu/~wbarthur/Papers/Evol%20of%20Complexity.pdf.

Asar, Mohamed, 'Going Formal in Egypt: A Way Out for the Urban Poor—Land Titling versus Upgrading in Informal Settlements', in *Shelter for the Urban Poor: Proposals for Improvements—Inspired by World Urban Forum III*, Karin Gundström and Annette Wong Jere (eds), Lund, Sweden: Grahns Tryckeri AB, 2007, 95–110.

Associated Press, 'Pittsburgh appeals ruling that blocks gun violence prevention measures', *CBS Pittsburgh*, 4 May 2020, available from: pittsburgh.cbslocal.com/2020/05/04/pittsburgh-appeals-judges-rejection-of-firearm-restrictions/.

Atika, Sausan, 'Amid shortage of land, Jakarta eyes more green spaces', *The Jakarta Post*, 21 October 2019, available from: www.thejakartapost.com/news/2019/10/21/amid-limited-land-availability-jakarta-eyes-more-green-spaces.html.

Atlas of Urban Expansion: Monitoring Global Urban Expansion Program, [Online], Paris: Sciences Po Urban School, n.d., available from: www.sciencespo.fr/ecole-urbaine/en/actualites/atlas-urban-expansion.html.

Attack on a Fortified Position and Combat in Towns, Field Manual 31-50, War Department Basic Field Manual, Washington, DC: US Government Printing Office, 31 January 1944.

Australian Army, *Land Warfare Doctrine 1: The Fundamentals of Land Power*, Canberra: Commonwealth of Australia, 2014, available from: researchcentre. army.gov.au/sites/default/files/2020-01/lwd-1_b5_190914.pdf.

Australian Defence Force (ADF), *ADF Concept for Command and Control of the Future Force*, Version 1.0, Canberra: Commonwealth of Australia, 13 May 2019.

Australian Public Service Commission, *Tackling Wicked Problems: A Public Service Perspective*, Canberra: Commonwealth of Australia, 2007, available from: www.apsc.gov.au/tackling-wicked-problems-public-policy-perspective [page discontinued].

Azuonwu, Obioma, 'Emergence and re-emergence of 2014 Ebola outbreak in sub-Sahara Africa: "Challenges and lessons learned" from Nigerian epidemic outbreak', *Scholars Journal of Applied Medical Sciences* 3(8A) (2015): 2802–14, available from: www.researchgate.net/publication/326381400_Emergence_ and_Re-emergence_of_2014_Ebola_outbreak_in_Sub-_Sahara_Africa_%27 Challenges_and_lessons_learned%27_from_Nigerian_epidemic_outbreak.

Bagehot, 'England speaks up: A radical new force is reshaping the country', *The Economist*, [London], 20 March 2021, 52.

Bodart-Bailey, Beatrice M., 'The 1707 eruption of Mount Fuji as blueprint for events to come', Flyer for Beatrice M. Bodart-Bailey presentation, The Australian National University, Canberra, 6 October 2015.

Baker, Kevin, 'The death of a once great city: The fall of New York and the urban crisis of affluence', *Harper's Magazine*, 8 July 2018, available from: harpers. org/archive-2018/07/the-death-of-new-york-city-gentrification/.

Banyan, 'When the Earth wobbled: An earthquake in Japan', *The Economist*, [London], 11 March 2011, available from: www.economist.com/banyan/2011/ 03/11/when-the-earth-wobbled.

Barber, Benjamin R., *If Mayors Ruled the World: Dysfunctional Nations, Rising Cities*, New Haven, CT: Yale University Press, 2013.

Barcelo, Jean Yves, Ansa Masaud and Anne Davies, *Meeting Humanitarian Challenges in Urban Areas: Review of Urban Humanitarian Challenges in Port-au-Prince, Manila, Nairobi, Eldoret*, UN-Habitat Report, Nairobi: United Nations Human Settlement Programme, 2011, available from: www.calpnetwork.org/wp-content/uploads/2020/01/humanitarianchallengesurbancasestudies-1.pdf.

Barnard, Anne, 'How a caliphate ends: On the frontline of the fight against ISIS', *Foreign Affairs* 98(6) (November–December 2019), available from: www.foreignaffairs.com/reviews/review-essay/2019-10-15/how-caliphate-ends.

Barry, John M., 'How the horrific 1918 flu spread across America', *Smithsonian Magazine*, November 2017, available from: www.smithsonianmag.com/history/journal-plague-year-180965222/.

Bartolucci, Andrea, Darren Walter and Tony Redmond, 'Comparative review on the cost-effectiveness analysis of relief teams' deployment to sudden-onset disasters', *Prehospital and Disaster Medicine* 34(4) (12 July 2019): 415–21. doi.org/10.1017/S1049023X19004540.

Bascomb, Neal, *Higher: A Historic Race to the Sky and the Making of a City*, New York, NY: Doubleday, 2003.

BBC News, 'Paris attacks: What happened on the night', *BBC News*, 9 December 2015, available from: www.bbc.com/news/world-europe-34818994.

Beall, Jo and Tom Goodfellow, 'Conflict and Post-War Transition in African Cities', in *Africa's Urban Revolution*, Susan Parnell and Edgar Pieterse (eds), New York, NY: Bloomsbury Academic, 2014, 18–34. doi.org/10.5040/9781350218246.ch-002.

Becker, David C., 'Gangs, netwar, and "community counterinsurgency" in Haiti', *PRISM: The Journal of Complex Operations* 2(3) (June 2011): 137–54, [Washington, DC: National Defence University], available from: cco.ndu.edu/Portals/96/Documents/prism/prism_2-3/Prism_137-154_Becker.pdf.

Beinart, Julian, 'Resurrecting Jerusalem', in *The Resilient City: How Modern Cities Recover from Disaster*, Lawrence J. Vale and Thomas I. Campanella (eds), New York, NY: Oxford University Press, 2005, 181–210. doi.org/10.1093/oso/9780195175844.003.0014.

Benton-Short, Lisa, Marie D. Price and Samantha Friedman, 'Globalization from below: The ranking of global immigrant cities', *International Journal of Urban and Regional Research* 29(4) (December 2005): 945–59. doi.org/10.1111/j.1468-2427.2005.00630.x.

Bettencourt, Luís M.A., *The kind of problem a city is: New perspectives on the nature of cities from complex systems theory*, SFI Working Paper 2013-03-008, Santa Fe, NM: Santa Fe Institute, 2013, available from: studylib.net/doc/8927135/the-kind-of-problem-a-city-is.

Birmingham, Lucy and David McNeill, *Strong in the Rain: Surviving Japan's Earthquake, Tsunami, and Fukushima Nuclear Disaster*, New York, NY: Palgrave, 2012.

Bodart-Bailey, Beatrice M., 'Pyroclastic Rivers: The Hôei Fuji Eruption (1707)', in *Local Realities and Environmental Changes in the History of East Asia*, Ts'ui-Jung Liu (ed.), London: Routledge, 2015, 157–80, available from: www.taylorfrancis.com/books/edit/10.4324/9781315695655/local-realities-environmental-changes-history-east-asia-ts-ui-jung-liu.

Bogan, Joseph and Aimee Feeney, *Future Cities: Trends and Implications*, Fareham, UK: Defence and Security Analysis, Defence Science and Technology Laboratory, 17 February 2020, available from: assets.publishing.service.gov.uk/government/uploads/system/uploads/attachment_data/file/875528/Dstl_Future_Cities_Trends___Implications_OFFICIAL.pdf.

Boitani, Piero, *A New Sublime: Ten Timeless Lessons of the Classics*, trans. Ann Goldstein, New York, NY: Europa, 2020.

Bollyky, Thomas J., *Plagues and the Paradox of Progress: Why the World is Getting Healthier in Worrisome Ways*, Cambridge, MA: MIT Press, 2018. doi.org/10.7551/mitpress/11750.001.0001.

Boo, Katherine, *Behind the Beautiful Forevers: Life, Death, and Hope in a Mumbai Undercity*, New York, NY: Random House, 2012.

Bowden, Mark, *Black Hawk Down: A Story of Modern War*, New York, NY: Atlantic Monthly Press, 1999.

Bowers, Christopher O., 'Future megacity operations: Lessons from Sadr City', *Military Review* (May–June 2015): 8–16, available from: www.armyupress.army.mil/Portals/7/Primer-on-Urban-Operation/Documents/MilitaryReview_20150630_art006.pdf.

Boyd, Emily, Aditya Ghosh and Maxwell T. Boykoff, 'Climate Change Adaptation in Mumbai, India', in *The Urban Climate Challenge: Rethinking the Role of Cities in the Global Climate Regime*, Craig Johnson, Noah Toly and Heike Schroeder (eds), Abingdon, UK: Routledge, 2015.

Brasser, Ramon, 'Tokyo's rush hour by the numbers', *ELSI Blog*, Tokyo: Earth–Life Science Institute, Tokyo Institute of Technology, 26 November 2015, available from: old.elsi.jp/en/blog/2015/11/blog1126.html.

Braszko, Alexander, 'Military implications of smart cities', *Mad Scientist Blog*, 4 June 2020, available from: madsciblog.tradoc.army.mil/242-military-implications-of-smart-cities/.

Breitmeier, Helmut, Judith Kuhn and Sandra Schwindenhammer, 'Analyzing urban adaptation strategies to climate change: A comparison of the coastal cities of Dhaka, Lagos and Hamburg', Paper contributed to DVPW Congress 21: Politics in Climate Change—No Power for Just Solutions?, 2009.

Bricker, Darrell and John Ibbitson, *Empty Planet: The Shock of Global Population Decline*, New York, NY: Crown, 2019.

Brinkley, Douglas, *The Great Deluge: Hurricane Katrina, New Orleans, and the Mississippi Gulf Coast*, New York, NY: William Morrow, 2006.

Britton, Bianca, 'Indonesia plans to relocate its capital from Jakarta', *CNN*, 29 April 2019, available from: www.cnn.com/2019/04/29/asia/indonesia-relocate-jakarta-intl/index.html.

Brook, Daniel, *A History of Future Cities*, New York, NY: Norton, 2013.

Brooks, Deborah Jordan, Stephen G. Brooks, Brian D. Greenhill and Mark L. Haas, 'The demographic transition theory of war: Why young societies are conflict prone and old societies are the most peaceful', *International Security* 43(3) (2018–19): 53–95. doi.org/10.1162/isec_a_00335.

Brooks, Johnny W., Personal communication, Subject: Looters in Panama, 13 September 2004.

Brottman, Makita, 'Richard Gere and Hachiko, the most faithful dog in history', *The Telegraph*, [London], 25 October 2014, available from: www.telegraph.co.uk/lifestyle/pets/11183010/Richard-Gere-and-Hachiko-the-most-faithful-dog-in-history.html.

Brown, James H., 'Complex Ecological Systems', in *Complexity: Metaphors, Models, and Reality*, George A. Cowan, David Pines and David Meltzer (eds), SFI Studies in the Sciences of Complexity, Proc. Vol. XIX, Boston, MA: Addison-Wesley, 1994, 419–49.

Brown, Robert B., Presentation to Current and Future Operations in Megacities Conference, US Army Pacific Command, Tokyo, 18 July 2019.

Brugmann, Jeb, *Welcome to the Urban Revolution: How Cities Are Changing the World*, New York, NY: Bloomsburg, 2009.

Bucci, Steven, David Inserra, Jonathan Lesser, Matt Mayer, Jack Spencer, Brian Slattery and Katie Tubb, *After Hurricane Sandy: Time to Learn and Implement the Lessons in Preparedness, Response, and Resilience*, Homeland Security Report, Washington, DC: The Heritage Foundation, 24 October 2013, available from: www.heritage.org/homeland-security/report/after-hurricane-sandy-time-learn-and-implement-the-lessons-preparedness.

Bunker, Robert J. and Pamela Ligouri Bunker (eds), *Plutocratic Insurgency Reader*, A Small Wars Journal Book, Bloomington, IN: Xlibris, 2019.

Bunker, Robert J. and Pamela Ligouri Bunker, 'Plutocratic Insurgency Note No. 5: The Techno-Palaces of the Global Elite', in *Plutocratic Insurgency Reader*, Robert J. Bunker and Pamela Ligouri Bunker (eds), A Small Wars Journal Book, Bloomington, IN: Xlibris, 2019, 128–40.

Burch, Lauren, 'What's the difference between predicting and forecasting earthquakes?', *Blog*, Seattle, WA: Pacific Northwest Seismic Network, 23 May 2016, available from: pnsn.org/blog/2016/05/23/what-s-the-difference-between-predicting-and-forecasting-earthquakes.

Calder, Kent E., *Singapore: Smart City, Smart State*, Washington, DC: Brookings Institution Press, 2016.

Campbell, John, 'Nigeria's political and security crises boiling over across the country', *Blog Post*, New York, NY: Council on Foreign Relations, 6 August 2019, available from: www.cfr.org/blog/nigerias-political-and-security-crises-boiling-over-across-country.

Canella, Charles J., *The defense of small towns and villages by infantry*, US Army Advanced Infantry Officers Course 1948–1949 paper, Fort Benning, GA, n.d.

Canton, James, 'The extreme future of megacities', *Significance* 8(2)[SI: Megacities] (June 2011): 53–56. doi.org/10.1111/j.1740-9713.2011.00485.x.

Carbon Brief Staff, 'Risk and uncertainty: Calculating the Thames Barrier's future', *Carbon Brief*, [London], 25 February 2014, available from: www.carbonbrief.org/risk-and-uncertainty-calculating-the-thames-barriers-future/.

Carp, Benjamin, *Rebels Rising: Cities and the American Revolution*, Oxford, UK: Oxford University Press, 2007. doi.org/10.1093/acprof:oso/9780195304022.001.0001.

Center for Army Lessons Learned (CALL), *Musicians of Mars II*, Handbook, Fort Leavenworth, KS: CALL, April 2016, available from: usacac.army.mil/sites/default/files/publications/16-12_Musicians_of_Mars_II.pdf.

Center for Army Lessons Learned (CALL), *Dense urban environment analysis from Operation Eagle Strike: Mosul, IZ*, CALL Information Paper, Fort Leavenworth, KS: US Army Center for Army Lessons Learned, 31 May 2017.

Center for Civilians in Conflict (CIVIC), *Policies and Practices to Protect Civilians: Lessons from ISF Operations against ISIS in Urban Areas*, Report, Washington, DC: CIVIC, 1 October 2019, available from: civiliansin conflict.org/publications/research/policies-practices-to-protect-civilians/.

Centers for Disease Control and Prevention (CDC), 'Signs and symptoms', *Ebola Virus Disease*, [Online], Washington, DC: US Department of Health and Human Services, 22 May 2018, available from: www.cdc.gov/vhf/ebola/symptoms/index.html.

Centers for Disease Control and Prevention (CDC), *2014–2016 Ebola Outbreak in West Africa*, Washington, DC: US Department of Health and Human Services, 8 March 2019, available from: www.cdc.gov/vhf/ebola/history/2014-2016-outbreak/index.html.

Chaguan, 'Crossing blood lines', *The Economist*, [London], 6 June 2020, 34.

Chaguan, 'New life for an old tradition', *The Economist*, [London], 22 May 2021, 36.

Chan, Serena, *Complex adaptive systems*, ESD.83 Research Seminar in Engineering Systems Paper, Cambridge, MA: Massachusetts Institute of Technology, 31 October – 6 November 2001, available from: web.mit.edu/esd.83/www/notebook/Complex%20Adaptive%20Systems.pdf.

Chapman, Megan and Andrew Maki, 'The Cities We Create Depend on the Choices We Make: Lagos', in *Know Your City: Slum Dwellers Count*, Janet Byrne (ed.), Cape Town, South Africa: Slum Dwellers International, 2018, 20–22, available from: sdinet.org/wp-content/uploads/2018/02/SDI_State ofSlums_LOW_FINAL.pdf.

Chen, David W., 'In New York, drawing flood maps is a "game of inches"', *The New York Times*, 7 January 2018, available from: www.nytimes.com/2018/01/07/nyregion/new-york-city-flood-maps-fema.html.

Chester, D.K., M. Degg, A.M. Duncan and J.E. Guest, 'The increasing exposure of cities to the effects of volcanic eruptions: A global survey', *Environmental Hazards* 2(3) (2001): 89–103. doi.org/10.3763/ehaz.2000.0214.

Chiarelli, Peter (General, US Army), Interview with Dr Russell W. Glenn, Pentagon, Washington, DC, 9 November 2011 [as appears in Russell W. Glenn, *Core Counterinsurgency Asset: Lessons from Iraq and Afghanistan for United States Army Corps of Engineers Leaders*, Study sponsored by the United States Army Corps of Engineers, 31 May 2012 (Revised 8 December 2016), 273–81].

Chow, Fiona, 'Underground space: The final frontier?', *Ingenia* (14) (November 2002): 15–20, available from: www.ingenia.org.uk/ingenia/14/underground-space-the-final-frontier.

Chow, Winston T.L. and Matthias Roth, 'Temporal dynamics of the urban heat island of Singapore', *International Journal of Climatology* 26(15) (December 2006): 2243–60. doi.org/10.1002/joc.1364.

Churchman, C. West, 'Wicked problems', *Management Science* 14(4) Application Series (December 1967): B-141–42, available from: www.jstor.org/stable/2628678.

City of Kobe, *Comprehensive Strategy for Recovery from the Great Hanshin–Awaji Earthquake*, Kobe, Japan, March 2010.

City of New York, 'COVID-19 guidance for business owners and FAQs', [Online], New York City Small Business Services, n.d., available from: www1.nyc.gov/site/sbs/businesses/covid19-business-tips-faqs.page.

Clark, Dartunorro, 'Trump suggests "injection" of disinfectant to beat coronavirus and "clean" the lungs', *NBC News*, 23 April 2020, available from: www.nbcnews.com/politics/donald-trump/trump-suggests-injection-disinfectant-beat-coronavirus-clean-lungs-n1191216.

CNN Wire Staff, 'US Coast Guard sinks Japanese fishing trawler near Alaska', *CNN*, 5 April 2012, [Updated 6 April 2012], available from: www.cnn.com/2012/04/05/us/japan-tsunami-ship/index.html.

Cohen, Eliot and John Gooch, *Military Misfortune: The Anatomy of Failure in War*, New York, NY: Free Press, 1990.

Colley, Linda, *The Gun, the Ship, and the Pen: Warfare, Constitutions, and the Making of the Modern World*, New York, NY: Liveright, 2021.

Commins, Stephen, 'Urban fragility and security in Africa', *Africa Security Brief* (12) (April 2011).

Commons, Austin G., 'Cyber is the new air domain superiority in the megacity', *Military Review* (January–February 2018): 120–30.

Conlin, Jonathan, *Tales of Two Cities: Paris, London, and the Birth of the Modern City*, Berkeley, CA: Counterpoint, 2013.

Conservation Action Trust, *Mumbai Marooned: An Enquiry into Mumbai Floods 2005*, Final Report, Mumbai, India: Conservation Action Trust, 26 July 2006.

Coté, Andrew, *Honey and Venom: Confessional of an Urban Beekeeper*, New York, NY: Ballantine, 2020.

Couloumbus, Angela and Stephen Caruso, 'Pennsylvania's highest court could give cities the go-ahead to craft their own gun laws', *Spotlight PA*, [Harrisburg], 1 June 2022, available from: www.spotlightpa.org/news/2022/06/uvalde-shooting-pennsylvania-gun-laws/.

Courage, Katherine Harmon, 'How did Nigeria quash its Ebola outbreak so quickly?', *Scientific American*, 18 October 2014, available from: www.scientific american.com/article/how-did-nigeria-quash-its-ebola-outbreak-so-quickly/.

Cox, Wendell, 'The evolving urban form: Manila', *New Geography*, 24 April 2011, available from: www.newgeography.com/content/002198-the-evolving-urban-form-manila.

Cox, Wendell, 'The evolving urban form: Jakarta (Jabotabek)', *New Geography*, 30 May 2011, available from: www.newgeography.com/content/002255-the-evolving-urban-form-jakarta-jabotabek.

Cox, Wendell, 'Largest 1,000 cities on Earth: World urban areas—2015 edition', *New Geography*, 2 February 2015, available from: www.newgeography.com/content/004841-largest-1000-cities-earth-world-urban-areas-2015-edition.

Culbertson, Shelly and Linda Robinson, *Making Victory Count after Defeating ISIS: Stabilization Challenges in Mosul and Beyond*, Santa Monica, CA: RAND Corporation, 2017. doi.org/10.7249/RR2076.

Dalton, Colonel James L. II, Commander, 161st Infantry Regiment, 25th Infantry Division, 'Commentary on Reduction of Strong Point San Manuel, Luzon, P.I.', 8 February 1945.

da Silva, Jo, Sam Kernaghan and Andrés Luque, 'A systems approach to meeting the challenges of urban climate change', *International Journal of Urban Sustainable Development* 4(2) (2012): 125–45. doi.org/10.1080/19463138. 2012.718279.

Dasgupta, Rana, *Capital: The Eruption of Delhi*, New York, NY: Penguin.

Davis, Diane E., 'Reverberations: Mexico City's 1985 Earthquake and the Transformation of the Capital', in *The Resilient City: How Modern Cities Recover from Disaster*, Lawrence J. Vale and Thomas I. Campanella (eds), New York, NY: Oxford University Press, 2005, 255–80. doi.org/10.1093/oso/9780195175844.003.0018.

de Boar, John, 'Resilience and the fragile city', *Stability: International Journal of Security & Development* 4(1) (2015), Art. 17. doi.org/10.5334/sta.fk.

De Landa, Manuel, 'The Nonlinear Development Cities', in *ECO-TEC: Architecture of the In-Between*, Amerigo Marras (ed.), New York, NY: Princeton Architectural Press, 1999, 23-31.

Delk, James, 'MOUT: A Domestic Case Study—The 1992 Los Angeles Riots', in Russell W. Glenn (ed.), *The City's Many Faces: Proceedings of the RAND Arroyo-MCWL-J8 UWG Urban Operations Conference, April 13–14, 1999*, Santa Monica, CA: RAND Corporation, 2000, 79–156.

Delk, James D., *Fires & Furies: The L.A. Riots*, Palm Springs, CA: ETC, 1995.

De Manuel, *A Thousand Years of Nonlinear History*, New York, NY: Swerve, 2014.

Demarest, Geoffrey, 'Urban Land Use by Illegal Armed Groups in Medellin', in *Blood and Concrete: 21st Century Conflict in Urban Centers and Megacities*, Dave Dilegge, Robert J. Bunker, John P. Sullivan and Alma Keshavarz (eds), A Small Wars Journal Book, Washington, DC: Xlibris, 2019, 102–20.

Demographia, *Demographia World Urban Areas*, 13th annual edition, Belleville, IL: Wendell Cox Consultancy, April 2017.

Demographia, *Demographia World Urban Areas*, 15th annual edition, Belleville, IL: Wendell Cox Consultancy, April 2019.

Demographia, *Demographia World Urban Areas*, 16th annual edition, Belleville, IL: Wendell Cox Consultancy, April 2020.

Demographia, *Demographia World Urban Areas*, 17th annual edition, Belleville, IL: Wendell Cox Consultancy, June 2021, available from: www.demographia.com/db-worldua.pdf.

Department of the Army, *Military Operations on Urbanized Terrain (MOUT)*, Field Manual 90-10, Washington, DC: US Government Printing Office, 15 August 1979.

Department of the Army, *An Infantryman's Guide to Urban Combat*, Field Manual 90-10-1 [Advance copy], Washington, DC: US Government Printing Office, 12 May 1993.

Department of the Army, *Terms and Military Symbols*, ADP 1-02, Washington, DC: Headquarters, Department of the Army, August 2018, available from: irp.fas.org/doddir/army/adp1_02.pdf.

Department of Defense (DOD), *Department of Defense Dictionary of Military and Associated Terms*, Arlington, VA: US Department of Defense, 1972.

Desmet, Klaus and Esteban Rossi-Hansberg, *Analyzing urban systems: Have megacities become too large?*, Paper, Princeton University, 20 October 2014, available from: www.princeton.edu/~erossi/WBChapterKD%26ERH.pdf.

Dick, Charles, 'FIBUA: Lessons from history', *British Army Review Special Report: Urban Operations Report 1*, Winter 2018, 10–27.

Dickey, Christopher, *Securing the City: Inside America's Best Counterterror Force— The NYPD*, New York, NY: Simon & Schuster, 2009.

Diefendorf, Jeffry M., *In the Wake of War: The Reconstruction of German Cities after World War II*, New York, NY: Oxford University Press, 1993.

Dijkstra, Lewis, Ellen Hamilton, Somik Lall and Sameh Wahba, 'How do we define cities, towns, and rural areas?', *Sustainable Cities Blog*, Washington, DC: The World Bank, 10 March 2020, available from: blogs.worldbank.org/sustainablecities/how-do-we-define-cities-towns-and-rural-areas.

Dobbs, Richard, Jaana Remes, Sven Smit, James Manyika, Jonathan Woetzel and Yaw Agyenim-Boateng, *Urban World: The Shifting Global Business Landscape*, McKinsey Global Institute Report, Washington, DC: McKinsey Global Institute, 1 October 2013, available from: www.mckinsey.com/featured-insights/urbanization/urban-world-the-shifting-global-business-landscape.

Doyle, Arthur Conan, *A Study in Scarlet*, London: Ward Lock & Co., 1887.

D'Souza, Shanthie Mariet, 'Mumbai Terrorist Attacks of 2008', *Encyclopaedia Britannica*, [Online], n.d., available from: www.britannica.com/event/Mumbai-terrorist-attacks-of-2008.

Dueker, Ken (Director, Emergency Services, City of Palo Alto Office of Emergency Services), Interview with Dr Russell W. Glenn, 14 April 2016.

Dunn, Rob, *Never Out of Season: How Having the Food We Want When We Want It Threatens Our Food Supply and Our Future*, NY: Little, Brown & Company, 2017.

Dwyer, Jim and Kevin Flynn, 'Fatal confusion: A troubled emergency response; 9/11 exposed deadly flaws in rescue plan', *The New York Times*, 7 July 2020, available from: www.nytimes.com/2002/07/07/nyregion/fatal-confusion-troubled-emergency-response-9-11-exposed-deadly-flaws-rescue.html.

Dwyer, Sarah, 'Why Nigeria's response to Ebola succeeded', *CapacityPlus Blog*, October 2014, available from: www.capacityplus.org/why-nigerias-response-to-ebola-succeeded.

Edwards, Aaron, 'Misapplying lessons learned? Analysing the utility of British counterinsurgency strategy in Northern Ireland, 1971–76', *Small Wars & Insurgencies* 21(2) (2010): 303–30. doi.org/10.1080/09592318.2010.481427.

Egan, Timothy, *The Immortal Irishman*, Boston, MA: Mariner Books, 2016.

Elkhamri, Mounir, Lester W. Grau, Laurie King-Irani, Amanda S. Mitchell and Lenny Tasa-Bennett, 'Urban population control in a counterinsurgency', *Small Wars Journal*, n.d., available from: smallwarsjournal.com/documents/urbanpopulationcontrol.pdf.

Emanuel, Kerry, 'Edward Norton Lorenz, 1917–2008', *Science* 320(5879) (23 May 2008): 1025. doi.org/10.1126/science.1159438.

Emanuel, Rahm, *The Nation City: Why Mayors are Now Running the World*, New York, NY: Alfred A. Knopf, 2020.

Engelke, Peter, *The Security of Cities: Ecology and Conflict On an Urbanizing Planet*, Report, Washington, DC: Atlantic Council, 18 November 2013, available from: www.atlanticcouncil.org/in-depth-research-reports/report/the-security-of-cities-ecology-and-conflict-on-an-urbanizing-planet/.

Epstein, Dr Aaron, Telephone interview with Dr Russell W. Glenn, 25 September 2019.

Espinosa, Benjamin, 'Operation United Assistance: The Department of Defense response to the West African Ebola virus epidemic', Presentation to MDB in Megacities Conference, Fort Hamilton, NY, 4 April 2018.

Fair, C. Christine, *Urban Battle Fields of South Asia: Lessons Learned from Sri Lanka, India, and Pakistan*, Santa Monica, CA: RAND Corporation, 2004. doi.org/10.7249/MG210.

Fairries, Bertram, Interview with Dr Russell W. Glenn, San Francisco, CA, 12 April 2016.

Farmer, Paul, *Fevers, Feuds, and Diamonds: Ebola and the Ravages of History*, New York, NY: Farrar, Straus & Giroux, 2020.

Farrier, David, *Footprints: In Search of Future Fossils*, New York, NY: Farrar, Straus & Giroux, 2020.

Fasina, F.O., A. Shittu, D. Lazarus, O. Tomori, L. Simonsen, C. Viboud and G. Chowell, 'Transmission dynamics and control of Ebola virus disease outbreak in Nigeria, July to September 2014', *Euro Surveillance* 19(40) (9 October 2014). doi.org/10.2807/1560-7917.ES2014.19.40.20920.

Federal Emergency Management Agency (FEMA), *National Incident Management System, Third Edition*, Washington, DC: Department of Homeland Security, October 2017, available from: www.fema.gov/sites/default/files/2020-07/fema_nims_doctrine-2017.pdf.

Felbab-Brown, Vanda, *Bringing the State to the Slum: Confronting Organized Crime and Urban Violence in Latin America—Lessons for Law Enforcement and Policymakers*, Latin America Initiative at Brookings, Washington, DC: Brookings Institution, December 2011, available from: www.brookings.edu/wp-content/uploads/2016/06/1205_latin_america_slums_felbabbrown.pdf.

Felix, Kevin M. and Frederick D. Wong, 'The case for megacities', *The US Army War College Quarterly: Parameters* 45(1) (Spring 2015): 19–32. doi.org/10.55540/0031-1723.2798.

Ferris, Elizabeth, 'Urban disasters, conflict and violence: Implications for humanitarian work', *On the Record*, Washington, DC: The Brookings Institution, 28 February 2012, available from: www.brookings.edu/on-the-record/urban-disasters-conflict-and-violence-implications-for-humanitarian-work/.

Finch, Gavin, 'London retains its crown as world's top financial center', *Bloomberg*, 11 September 2017, available from: www.bloomberg.com/news/articles/2017-09-11/london-still-tops-financial-centers-despite-brexit-survey-says.

Fink, Sheri, 'Beyond hurricane heroics: What Sandy should teach us all about preparedness', *Stanford Medicine*, Special Report (Summer 2013), available from: sm.stanford.edu/archive/stanmed/2013summer/article5.html.

Finz, Stacy, 'HOSED/S.F. hydrants don't fit equipment from other fire departments. In a disaster, the city could be …', *SFGate*, [San Francisco, CA], 21 September 2005, available from: www.sfgate.com/news/article/HOSED-S-F-hydrants-don-t-fit-equipment-from-2568046.php.

Fisch, Michael, *An Anthropology of the Machine: Tokyo's Commuter Train Network*, Chicago, IL: University of Chicago Press, 2018. doi.org/10.7208/chicago/9780226558691.001.0001.

Fitzgerald, Robert B. (Master Chief US Navy, 1st Force Reconnaissance Company, 1st Reconnaissance Battalion, 1st Marine Division), Interview with Russell W. Glenn, Camp Pendleton, CA, 12 July 2001.

Florida, Richard, 'The economic power of cities compared to nations', [*CityLab*], *Bloomberg*, 17 March 2017, available from: www.citylab.com/life/2017/03/the-economic-power-of-global-cities-compared-to-nations/519294/.

Florida Health, 'Surveillance systems', [Online], Tallahassee: Florida Department of Health, 2020, available from: www.floridahealth.gov/diseases-and-conditions/disease-reporting-and-management/disease-reporting-and-surveillance/surveillance-systems.html.

Foege, William H., *House on Fire: The Fight to Eradicate Smallpox*, Berkeley, CA: University of California Press, 2011.

Foggatt, Tyler, 'Protocols: Who gets a ventilator?', *The New Yorker*, 20 April 2020, 13–14.

Ford, Paul, 'Tech support', *WIRED*, September 2020, 14–15.

Ford, Peter, 'Best practices for securing a megacity during a major world event 2: The 2016 Rio de Janeiro Summer Olympics', Presentation to Current and Future Operations in Megacities Conference, Tokyo, 18 July 2016.

Fox, Robert, Los Angeles Joint Regional Intelligence Center, Los Angeles Police Department Briefing, n.d., available from: docplayer.net/3600423-Los-angeles-joint-regional-intelligence-center-lieutenant-robert-fox-los-angeles-police-department-jric-co-program-manager-562-345-1102.html.

Fox, Sean, 'Urbanisation as a Global Historical Process: Theory and Evidence from Sub-Saharan Africa', in *Africa's Urban Revolution*, Susan Parnell and Edgar Pieterse (eds), New York, NY: Bloomsbury Academic, 2014, 257–83. doi.org/10.5040/9781350218246.ch-014.

Franco, Joseph, *The battle for Marawi: Urban warfare lessons for the AFP*, SRI Working Paper, Manila: Security Reform Initiative, 4 October 2017, available from: www.researchgate.net/publication/337076300_The_Battle_for_Marawi_Urban_Warfare_Lessons_for_the_AFP.

Frater, Alexander, *Chasing the Monsoon*, New York, NY: Alfred A. Knopf, 1991.

Frerichs, Ralph R., 'John Snow's Map 1 (Broad Street Pump Outbreak, 1854)', [Online], Los Angeles, CA: UCLA Department of Epidemiology, n.d.[a], available from: www.ph.ucla.edu/epi/snow/snowmap1_1854.html.

Frerichs, Ralph R., John Snow Site, [Online], Los Angeles, CA: UCLA Department of Epidemiology, n.d.[b], available from: www.ph.ucla.edu/epi/snow.html.

Frewen, John J., 'The Solomon Islands Intervention: The Regional Assistance Mission 2003', in *Trust and Leadership: The Australian Army Approach to Mission Command*, Russell W. Glenn (ed.), Dahlonega, GA: University of North Georgia Press, 2020, 206–40.

Frey, William H. and Zachary Zimmer, 'Defining the City', in *Handbook of Urban Studies*, Ronan Paddison (ed.), London: Sage, 2001, 15–35. doi.org/10.4135/9781848608375.n2.

Fukuyama, Francis, *The Origins of Political Order: From Prehuman Times to the French Revolution*, London: Profile, 2012.

Fuller, J.F.C., *The Generalship of Alexander the Great*, New York, NY: Da Capo, 1960.

Garrett, Laurie, 'Welcome to the first war zone Ebola crisis', *Foreign Policy*, 18 October 2018, available from: foreignpolicy.com/2018/10/18/welcome-to-the-first-war-zone-ebola-crisis/.

Gaul, Gilbert M., 'The homes in Dorian's path are in a high-risk area. Why do they cost so much?', *The New York Times*, 3 September 2019, available from: www.nytimes.com/2019/09/04/books/review/gilbert-gaul-the-geography-of-risk.html.

Gayer, Laurent, *Karachi: Ordered Disorder and the Struggle for the City*, Noida, India: HarperCollins, 2014.

Gell-Mann, Murray, 'Complex Adaptive Systems', in *Complexity: Metaphors, Models, and Reality*, George A. Cowan, David Pines and David Meltzer (eds), SFI Studies in the Sciences of Complexity, Proc. Vol. XIX, Boston, MA: Addison-Wesley, 1994, 17–45.

Gies, Francis and Joseph Gies, *Life in a Medieval City*, New York, NY: Harper Perennial, 2016.

Gilbert, Jackie, 'CDC RFP: Electronic Surveillance System of the Early Notification of Community-based Epidemics (ESSENCE) operations and maintenance support', *FedHealthIT.com*, 7 April 2020, available from: www.fedhealthit.com/2020/04/cdc-to-award-contract-for-electronic-surveillance-system-for-the-early-notification-of-community-based-epidemics-essence-operations-and-maintenance-support/ [page discontinued].

Gilligan, Andrew, 'Fukushima: Tokyo was on the brink of nuclear catastrophe, admits former prime minister', *The Telegraph*, [London], 4 March 2016, available from: www.telegraph.co.uk/news/worldnews/asia/japan/12184114/Fukushima-Tokyo-was-on-the-brink-of-nuclear-catastrophe-admits-former-prime-minister.html.

Glaeser, Edward, *Triumph of the City: How Our Greatest Invention Makes Us Richer, Smarter, Greener, Healthier, and Happier*, New York, NY: Penguin, 2011.

Glenn, Russell W., *Combat in Hell: A Consideration of Constrained Urban Warfare*, Santa Monica, CA: RAND Corporation, 1996.

Glenn, Russell W., *Heavy Matter: Urban Operations' Density of Challenges*, Santa Monica, CA: RAND Corporation, 2000.

Glenn, Russell W., *Honing the Keys to the City: Refining the United States Marine Corps Reconnaissance Force for Urban Ground Combat Operations*, Santa Monica, CA: RAND Corporation, 2003.

Glenn, Russell W., *Managing complexity during military urban operations: Visualizing the elephant*, Documented Briefing No. DB-430-A, Santa Monica, CA: RAND Corporation, January 2004, available from: www.rand.org/pubs/documented_briefings/DB430.readonline.html.

Glenn, Russell W., 'Terrorism and cities: A target rich environment', *Small Wars Journal*, 1 April 2005, 8–12, available from: smallwarsjournal.com/documents/swjmag/v1/glenn.htm.

Glenn, Russell W., *Considering Urban Control: A Summary of the 2006 Israeli Defense Forces–US Joint Forces Command Urban Operations Conference*, Santa Monica, CA: RAND Corporation, February 2007.

Glenn, Russell W., *All Glory is Fleeting: Insights from the Second Lebanon War*, Santa Monica, CA: RAND Corporation, February 2008.

Glenn, Russell W., *Band of Brothers or Dysfunctional Family? A Military Perspective on Coalition Challenges during Stability Operations*, Santa Monica, CA: RAND Corporation, 2011.

Glenn, Russell W., *Core Counterinsurgency Asset: Lessons from Iraq and Afghanistan for United States Army Corps of Engineers Leaders*, Study sponsored by the United States Army Corps of Engineers, 31 May 2012 [Revised 8 December 2016].

Glenn, Russell W., *Rethinking Western Approaches to Counterinsurgency: Lessons from Post-Colonial Conflict*, London: Routledge, 2015. doi.org/10.4324/9781315744650.

Glenn, Russell W., 'Megacities: The good, the bad, and the ugly', *Small Wars Journal*, 17 February 2016, available from: smallwarsjournal.com/jrnl/art/megacities-the-good-the-bad-and-the-ugly.

Glenn, Russell W., *Short war in a perpetual conflict: Implications of Israel's 2014 Operation Protective Edge for the Australian Army*, Army Research Paper No. 9, Canberra: Australian Army, June 2016, available from: researchcentre.army.gov.au/sites/default/files/arp9_glen_short_war_in_a_perpetual_conflict.pdf.

Glenn, Russell W., 'Ten million is not enough: Coming to grips with megacities, challenges and opportunities', *Small Wars Journal*, 25 January 2017, available from: smallwarsjournal.com/jrnl/art/ten-million-is-not-enough-coming-to-grips-with-megacities%E2%80%99-challenges-and-opportunities.

Glenn, Russell W., 'Terrorism and Cities: A Target Rich Environment', in *Blood and Concrete: 21st Century Conflict in Urban Centers and Megacities*, Dave Dilegge, Robert J. Bunker, John P. Sullivan and Alma Keshavarz (eds), A Small Wars Journal Book, Washington, DC: Xlibris, 2019.

Glenn, Russell W. (ed.), *Trust and Leadership: The Australian Army Approach to Mission Command*, Dahlonega, GA: University of North Georgia Press, 2020.

Glenn, Russell W., Sidney W. Atkinson, Michael Barbero, Frederick J. Gellert, Scott Gerwehr, Steven Hartman, Jamison Jo Medby, Andrew O'Donnell, David Owen and Suzanne Pieklik, *Ready for Armageddon: Proceedings of the 2001 RAND Arroyo–Joint ACTD-CETO-USMC Nonlethal and Urban Operations Program Urban Operations Conference*, Santa Monica, CA: RAND Corporation, 2002, available from: www.rand.org/pubs/conf_proceedings/CF179.html.

Glenn, Russell W., Eric L. Berry, Colin C. Christopher, Thomas A. Kruegler and Nicholas R. Marsella, *Where None Have Gone Before: Operational and Strategic Perspectives on Multi-Domain Operations in Megacities. Proceedings of the 'Multi-Domain Battle in Megacities' Conference, April 3–4, 2018, Fort Hamilton, New York*, Fort Eustis, VA: US Army Training and Doctrine Command, 20 July 2018, available from: community.apan.org/wg/tradoc-g2/mad-scientist/m/multi-domain-battle-mdb-in-megacities/244661.

Glenn, Russell W., Colin Christopher, Caleb Dexter, David Norton and Robert Nussbaumer (eds), *Achieving Convergence during Humanitarian Assistance and Disaster Relief Operations in the World's Largest Urban Areas: Proceedings of the 'Current and Future Operations' in Megacities Conference, Tokyo, Japan, July 16–18, 2019*, Fort Eustis, VA: US Army Training and Doctrine Command, 1 October 2019, available from: community.apan.org/wg/tradoc-g2/mad-scientist/m/tokyo-megacities-conference-2019/294569.

Glenn, Russell W., Steven L. Hartman and Scott Gerwehr, *Urban Combat Service Support Operations: The Shoulders of Atlas*, Santa Monica, CA: RAND Corporation, 2003, available from: www.rand.org/content/dam/rand/pubs/monograph_reports/2005/MR1717.pdf.

Glenn, Russell W., Colin Holland, Alasdair W.G. Mackie, Brenda Oppermann, Deborah Zubow Prindle and Myra Speelmans, *Evaluation of USAID's Community Stabilization Program (CSP) in Iraq: Effectiveness of the CSP Model as a Non-Lethal Tool for Counterinsurgency*, Washington, DC: United States Agency for International Development, 2009, available from: pdf.usaid.gov/pdf_docs/PDACN461.pdf.

Glenn, Russell W. and Gina Kingston, *Urban Battle Command in the 21st Century*, Santa Monica, CA: RAND Corporation, 2005, available from: www.rand.org/content/dam/rand/pubs/monographs/2005/RAND_MG181.pdf.

Glenn, Russell W., Randall Steeb and John Matsumura, *Corralling the Trojan Horse: A Proposal for Improving U.S. Urban Operations Preparedness in the Period 2000–2025*, Santa Monica, CA: RAND Corporation, 2001.

Glenny, Misha, 'Cocaine, sex and social media: The untold story of Rio's most notorious cartel boss', *WIRED*, 26 October 2015, available from: www.wired.co.uk/article/rocinha-brazil-drug-cartel-antonio-lopes-nem.

Glenny, Misha, *Nemesis: One Man and the Battle for Rio*, New York, NY: Alfred A. Knopf, 2016.

Goldstein, Joseph, '1.5 million antibody tests show what parts of N.Y.C. were hit hardest', *The New York Times*, 20 August 2020, available from: www.nytimes.com/2020/08/19/nyregion/new-york-city-antibody-test.html.

Goodell, Jeff, *The Water Will Come: Rising Seas, Sinking Cities, and the Remaking of the Civilized World*, NY: Little, Brown & Company, 2017.

Grande, Lise, 'Humanitarian assistance and disaster relief: Lessons from a combat zone', Presentation to Achieving Convergence during Humanitarian Assistance and Disaster Relief Operations in the World's Largest Urban Areas Conference, Tokyo, 18 July 2019.

Greenberg, Andy, *Sandworm: A New Era of Cyberwar and the Hunt for the Kremlin's Most Dangerous Hackers*, New York, NY: Doubleday, 2019.

Griffiths, James, 'Hong Kong's vast $3.8 billion rain-tunnel network', *CNN Style*, 26 July 2020, available from: www.cnn.com/style/article/hong-kong-tunnels-climate-crisis-intl-hnk-dst/index.html.

Guest, Robert, 'The Anglosphere and the Sinosphere drift apart', [*The World in 2020*], *The Economist*, [London], December 2019, 19, available from: worldin. economist.com/article/17310/edition2020anglosphere-and-sinosphere-drift-apart.

Hall, Nathan, 'Fukushima-Daiichi: Multinational disaster response & longterm crisis management', Briefing slides, Santa Monica, CA: RAND Corporation, 14 May 2013.

Hallegatte, Stephane, Colin Green, Robert J. Nicholls and Jan Corfee-Morlot, 'Future flood losses in major coastal cities', *Nature Climate Change* 3 (2013): 802–6. doi.org/10.1038/nclimate1979.

Hammer, Joshua, 'The great Japan earthquake of 1923', *Smithsonian Magazine*, May 2011, available from: www.smithsonianmag.com/history/the-great-japan-earthquake-of-1923-1764539/.

Hand, Marcus, 'Malacca and S'pore Straits traffic hits new high in 2016, VLCCs fastest growing segment', *Seatrade Maritime News*, 13 February 2017, available from: www.seatrade-maritime.com/news/asia/malacca-and-s-pore-strait-traffic-hits-new-high-in-2016-vlccs-fastest-growing-segment.html.

Harmsen, Peter, *Shanghai 1937: Stalingrad on the Yangtze*, Havertown, PA: Casemate, 2013.

Harper, Douglas R., 'Citizen', in *Online Etymology Dictionary*, 2001–22, available from: www.etymonline.com/word/citizen.

Harris, Marc, Robert Dixon, Nicholas Melin, Daniel Hendrex, Richard Russo and Michael Bailey, *Megacities and the United States Army: Preparing for a Complex and Uncertain Future*, Chief of Staff of the Army Strategic Studies Group, June 2014, available from: www.army.mil/e2/c/downloads/351235.pdf.

Harrison, Dustin (Lieutenant Commander, US Navy), Interview with Dr Russell W. Glenn, Fort Detrick, MD, 30 March 2018.

Hartrich, John P., 'Adapting the army to win decisively in megacities', *Military Review: The Professional Journal of the US Army*, 18 December 2015, available from: www.armyupress.army.mil/Journals/Military-Review/Online-Exclusive/2015-Online-Exclusive-Articles/Win-Decisively/.

Hassett, Brenna, *Built on Bones: 15,000 Years of Urban Life and Death*, New York, NY: Bloomsbury Sigma, 2017. doi.org/10.5040/9781472948311.

Haysom, Simone, *Sanctuary in the City? Urban Displacement and Vulnerability: Final Report*, HPG Report 33, London: Humanitarian Policy Group, Overseas Development Institute, June 2013, available from: cdn.odi.org/media/documents/8444.pdf.

Heal, Charles S., Email to Russell W. Glenn, Subject: Megacities research, 17 March 2016.

Heal, Charles S., 'Best practices for securing a megacity during a major world event 1', Presentation to Current and Future Operations in Megacities Conference, Tokyo, 18 July 2019.

Hein, Carola, 'Resilient Tokyo: Disaster and Transformation in the Japanese City', in *The Resilient City: How Modern Cities Recover from Disaster*, Lawrence J. Vale and Thomas I. Campanella (eds), New York, NY: Oxford University Press, 2005, 213–34. doi.org/10.1093/oso/9780195175844.003.0016.

Helfand, David J., *A Survival Guide to the Misinformation Age: Scientific Habits of Mind*, New York, NY: Columbia University Press, 2016. doi.org/10.7312/helf16872.

Hempel, Sandra, *Medical Detective: John Snow and the Mystery of Cholera*, London: Granta, 2006.

Hesiod, *Works and Days*, trans. Hugh G. Evelyn-White, 1914, available from: people.sc.fsu.edu/~dduke/lectures/hesiod1.pdf.

Hill, Alice and Leonardo Martinez-Diaz, 'Adapt or perish: Preparing for the inescapable effects of climate change', *Foreign Affairs* 99(1) (January–February 2020): 107–17.

Hirsch, Martin, Pierre Carli, Rémy Nizard, Bruno Riou, Barouyr Baroudjian, Thierry Baubet, Vibol Chhor, Charlotte Chollet-Xemard, Nicolas Dantchev, Nadia Fleury, Jean-Paul Fontaine, Youri Yordanov, Maurice Raphael, Catherine Paugam Burtz and Antoine Lafont, 'The medical response to multisite terrorist attacks in Paris', *The Lancet* 386(10012) (19 December 2015): 2535–38. doi.org/10.1016/S0140-6736(15)01063-6.

Hongo, Jun, 'Tokyo underground: Taking property development to new depths', *The Japan Times*, [Tokyo], 12 April 2014, available from: www.japantimes.co.jp/life/2014/04/12/lifestyle/tokyo-underground/#.XDp77M9KgWo.

Hornak, Leo, 'It's not just a soap opera, it's a "radio movie"', *The World*, [Boston, MA], 8 September 2014, available from: www.pri.org/stories/2014-09-08/its-not-just-soap-opera-its-radio-movie.

Hudson-Edwards, Karen and Noah Raford, *Humanitarian Crisis Drivers of the Future: Urban Catastrophes—The Wat/San Dimension*, Humanitarian Futures Programme Report, London: King's College London, 2009, available from: www.humanitarianfutures.org/wp-content/uploads/2013/06/Humanitarian-Crisis-Drivers-of-the-Future-Urban-Catastrophes-the-WatSan-Dimension.pdf.

Hughes, Bettany, *Istanbul: A Tale of Three Cities*, London: Weidenfeld & Nicolson, 2017.

Huq, Saleemul, 'Environmental Hazards in Dhaka', in *Crucibles of Hazard: Mega-Cities and Disasters in Transition*, James K. Mitchell (ed.), New York, NY: United Nations University, 1999.

Hurley, John (Colonel, US Army), Interview with Dr Russell W. Glenn, Winchester, VA, 8 November 2011.

Hurst, Daniel, 'This is not a "what if" story: Tokyo braces for the earthquake of a century', *The Guardian*, 11 June 2019, available from: www.theguardian.com/cities/2019/jun/12/this-is-not-a-what-if-story-tokyo-braces-for-the-earthquake-of-a-century.

Iles, Greg, *Deep Sleep*, New York, NY: Penguin, 2002.

Immigration and Refugee Board of Canada, 'Responses to Information Requests (RIRs)', Document KEN103225.E, Toronto: IRB, 16 November 2009, available from: www.justice.gov/sites/default/files/eoir/legacy/2013/11/07/KEN103225.E.pdf.

Imran, Muhammad, Shady Elbassuoni, Carlos Castillo, Fernando Diaz and Patrick Meier, 'Practical Extraction of Disaster-Relevant Information from Social Media', in *WWW '13 Companion: Proceedings of the 22nd International World Wide Web Conference*, New York, NY: Association for Computing Machinery, 2013, 1021–24. doi.org/10.1145/2487788.2488109.

Inam, Aseem, *Planning for the Unplanned: Recovering from Crises in Megacities*, London: Routledge, 2005.

Ingersoll, Geoffrey, 'General James "Mad Dog" Mattis email about being "too busy to read" is a must-read', *Business Insider*, 10 May 2013, available from: www.businessinsider.com/viral-james-mattis-email-reading-marines-2013-5.

Ingram, Kiriloi M., 'Revisiting Marawi: Women and the struggle against the Islamic State in the Philippines', *Lawfare*, 4 August 2019, available from: www.lawfareblog.com/revisiting-marawi-women-and-struggle-against-islamic-state-philippines.

Inskeep, Steve, *Instant City: Life and Death in Karachi*, New York, NY: Penguin, 2011.

Institute of Governance Studies, *State of Cities: Urban Governance in Dhaka*, Report, Dhaka: BRAC University, May 2012, available from: www.academia.edu/35811593/STATE_OF_CITIES_Urban_Governance_in_Dhaka.

Intergovernmental Panel on Climate Change (IPCC), 'Urban Areas', in *Climate Change 2014: Impacts, Adaptation, and Vulnerability. Part A: Global and Sectoral Aspects. Working Group II Contribution to the IPCC Fifth Assessment Report*, Cambridge, UK: Cambridge University Press, 2014, 535–612.

Internal Displacement Monitoring Centre, *Global Report on Internal Displacement 2018: Part 1. On the GRID: The Global Displacement Landscape*, Geneva: IDMC, 2018, available from: www.internal-displacement.org/global-report/grid2018/downloads/report/2018-GRID-part-1.pdf.

International Committee of the Red Cross (ICRC), 'Syria: ICRC works to avoid massive water crisis in Aleppo', *News*, Geneva: ICRC, 10 November 2015, available from: www.icrc.org/en/document/syria-icrc-water-crisis-aleppo.

International Committee of the Red Cross (ICRC), 'New research shows urban warfare 8 times more deadly for civilians in Syria and Iraq', News release, Geneva: ICRC, 1 October 2018, available from: www.icrc.org/en/document/new-research-shows-urban-warfare-eight-times-more-deadly-civilians-syria-iraq.

International Federation of Red Cross and Red Crescent Societies (IFRC), *World Disasters Report 2010: Focus on Urban Risk*, Geneva: IFRC, 2010, available from: www.theisrm.org/public-library/IFRC%20(2010)%20World%20Disaster%20Report%20-%20Urban%20Risk.pdf.

International Federation of Red Cross and Red Crescent Societies (IFRC), *Emergency Plan of Action Final Report: Nigeria—Ebola Virus Disease*, Geneva: IFRC, 2 September 2014, available from: reliefweb.int/sites/reliefweb.int/files/resources/MDRNG017FR.pdf.

International Organization for Migration (IOM), *Migrants and Cities: New Partnerships to Manage Mobility*, World Migration Report 2015, Geneva: IOM, 2015, available from: www.iom.int/world-migration-report-2015.

Ishtiaque, Asif and Nurul Islam Nazem, 'Household-level disaster-induced losses and rural–urban migration: Experience from world's one of the most disaster-affected countries', *Natural Hazards* 86 (2017): 315–26. doi.org/10.1007/s11069-016-2690-5.

Ishtiaque, Asif and Md. Sofi Ullah, 'The influence of factors of migration on the migration status of rural–urban migrants in Dhaka, Bangladesh', *Human Geographies* 7(2) (2013): 45–52. doi.org/10.5719/hgeo.2013.72.45.

Islam, Nazrul, A.Q.M. Mahbub and Nurul Islam Nazem, 'Urban slums of Bangladesh', *The Daily Star*, [Dhaka], 20 June 2009, available from: www.thedailystar.net/news-detail-93293.

Jacobs, Jane, *The Death and Life of Great American Cities*, New York, NY: Vintage, 1992.

Jamieson, Amy, 'How New York City got control of COVID-19—and where it goes from here', *Healthline*, 20 July 2020, available from: www.healthline.com/health-news/how-new-york-city-got-control-of-covid19.

Jamshed, Zahra, 'How Singapore is using technology to solve its water shortage', *CNN Business*, 25 September 2019, available from: www.cnn.com/2019/09/25/tech/singapore-water-technology-innovative-cities/index.html.

Japan Joint Staff, 'Lessons learned from the Great East Japan Earthquake', Briefing slides, Disaster Relief Operation, J-3, Japan Joint Staff, 7 February 2012.

Jefferson, Mark, 'The law of the primate city', *Geographical Review* 29(2) (April 1939): 226–32. doi.org/10.2307/209944.

Jenkins, R.D., 'Some notes on fighting in built-up areas (FIBUA)', *British Army Review Special Report: Urban Operations Report 1*, Winter 2018, 28–37.

Jennings, Steve, Julian Cottee, Tom Curtis and Simon Miller, *Food in an Urbanised World: The Role of City Region Food Systems in Resilience and Sustainable Development*, International Sustainability Unit Report, Long Hanborough, UK: 3Keel, April 2015, available from: www.3keel.com/wp-content/uploads/reports/CRFS%20Final%20Draft_0.pdf.

Jha, Abbas, Jessica Lamond, Robin Bloch, Namrata Bhattacharya, Ana Lopez, Nikolaos Papachristodoulou, Alan Bird, David Proverbs, John Davies and Robert Barker, *Five feet high and rising: Cities and flooding in the 21st century*, Policy Research Working Paper 5648, Washington, DC: The World Bank, May 2011. doi.org/10.1596/1813-9450-5648.

JLee, 'No more skipping 4, 13, 14, or 24 in Vancouver floor numbers', *Vancouver Sun*, 14 November 2015, available from: vancouversun.com/news/local-news/no-more-skipping-4-13-14-24-in-vancouver-floor-numbers.

Joint and Coalition Operational Analysis (JCOA), *Operation UNITED ASSISTANCE: The DOD Response to Ebola in West Africa*, Suffolk, VA: JCOA, US Joint Staff J-7, 6 January 2016, available from: www.jcs.mil/Portals/36/Documents/Doctrine/ebola/OUA_report_jan2016.pdf.

Jones, Colin, *Paris: The Biography of a City*, New York, NY: Penguin, 2006.

Josephus, *The Jewish War*, London: Penguin, 1959.

Katz, Bruce and Jennifer Bradley, *The Metropolitan Revolution: How Cities and Metros Are Fixing Our Broken Politics and Fragile Economy*, Washington, DC: Brookings Institution Press, 2013.

Katz, Jesse, 'The geography of getting by: Vendors in Los Angeles' MacArthur Park fight for their right to sell', *The American Prospect*, 19 June 2012, available from: prospect.org/article/geography-getting.

Kautzman, Janette L., Managing internally displaced persons (IDP) in an urban fight, Unpublished paper, n.d.

Kelly, Charles, 'Assessing disaster needs in megacities: Perspectives from developing countries', *GeoJournal* 37 (November 1995): 381–85. doi.org/10.1007/BF00814020.

Kelly, Charles, *Acute food insecurity in mega-cities: Issues and assistance options*, Disaster Studies Working Paper 7, London: Benfield Hazard Research Centre, University College London, July 2003, available from: www.ucl.ac.uk/hazard-centre/sites/hazard_centre/files/wp7.pdf.

Kelly, Raymond W., 'Testimony by Raymond W. Kelly, Police Commissioner, City of New York', in *Lessons from the Mumbai Terrorist Attacks: Parts I and II*, Hearings before the Committee on Homeland Security and Governmental Affairs, United States Senate, 111th Congress, 1st Session, 8 and 28 January 2009, Washington, DC: US Government Printing Office, available from: www.govinfo.gov/content/pkg/CHRG-111shrg49484/html/CHRG-111shrg49484.htm.

Kennedy, Kelly, *They Fought for Each Other: The Triumph and Tragedy of the Hardest Hit Unit in Iraq*, New York, NY: St Martin's Press, 2010.

Kennedy, Ross (1st Lieutenant, British Army), Interview with Russell W. Glenn and Todd Helmus, Upavon, UK, 8 December 2003.

Kenny, Alice, 'Ecosystem services in the New York City watershed', *The Ecosystem Marketplace*, 10 February 2006, available from: www.forest-trends.org/ecosystem_marketplace/ecosystem-services-in-the-new-york-city-watershed-1969-12-31/.

Khambatta, Michael, Interview with Dr Russell W. Glenn, Washington, DC, 26 February 2008.

Khanna, Parag, 'When cities rule the world', *Featured Insights*, McKinsey & Company, 1 February 2011, available from: www.mckinsey.com/featured-insights/urbanization/when-cities-rule-the-world.

Kiger, Patrick J., 'How 9/11 became the deadliest day in history for US firefighters', *History Channel*, 20 May 2019, available from: www.history.com/news/9-11-world-trade-center-firefighters.

Kilcullen, David, *The Australian Army in the urban, networked littoral*, Australian Army Research Paper No. 2, Canberra: Australian Army Research Centre, 2014, available from: researchcentre.army.gov.au/sites/default/files/kilcullen_b5_web_11august_0.pdf.

Kilcullen, David, *Out of the Mountains: The Coming Age of the Urban Guerrilla*, Oxford, UK: Oxford University Press, 2015.

Kipling, Rudyard, *The Works of Rudyard Kipling*, Ware, UK: Wordsworth Poetry Library, 1994.

Klay, Phil, *Redeployment*, New York, NY: Penguin, 2015.

Knezys, Stasys and Romanas Sedlickas, *The War in Chechnya*, College Station, TX: Texas A&M Press, 1999.

Knight, Charles and Katja Theodorakis, *The Marawi Crisis: Urban Conflict and Information Operations*, Special Report, Canberra: Australian Strategic Policy Institute, 31 July 2019, available from: www.aspi.org.au/report/marawi-crisis-urban-conflict-and-information-operations.

Koerner, Brendan I., 'Street life', *WIRED*, 27 October 2019, 72–85.

Kolbert, Elizabeth, 'The spread: How pandemics shape human history', *The New Yorker*, 6 April 2020, 58–61.

Kotkin, Joel, 'China's urban crisis', *City Journal* (Spring 2019), available from: www.city-journal.org/chinas-urban-crisis.

Kottasová, Ivana, 'Floods in London are the latest sign big cities aren't ready for climate change', *CNN*, 26 July 2021, available from: www.cnn.com/2021/07/26/europe/london-flooding-infrastructure-climate-intl-cmd/index.html.

Kötter, Theo and Frank Friesecke, *Developing urban indicators for managing mega cities*, Paper, Copenhagen: International Federation of Surveyors, 2009, available from: www.fig.net/resources/proceedings/2009/fig_wb_2009/papers/urb/urb_2_koetter.pdf.

Krulak, Charles C., 'The strategic corporal: Leadership in the three block war', *Marines Magazine*, January 1999, available from: apps.dtic.mil/sti/pdfs/ADA399413.pdf.

Kumagai, Yoshio and Yoshiteru Nojima, 'Urbanization and Disaster Mitigation in Tokyo', in *Crucibles of Hazard: Mega-Cities and Disasters in Transition*, James K. Mitchell (ed.), New York, NY: United Nations University, 1999, 56–91.

Lacey, Sharon Tosi, 'How the invasion of Grenada was planned with a tourist map and a copy of "The Economist"', *Military Times*, [Arlington, VA], 26 October 2018, available from: www.militarytimes.com/veterans/military-history/2018/10/25/how-the-invasion-of-grenada-was-planned-with-a-tourist-map-and-a-copy-of-the-economist/.

Lall, Somik V. and Uwe Deichmann, *Density and disasters: Economics of urban hazard risk*, Policy Research Working Paper No. 5161, Washington, DC: The World Bank, January 2010. doi.org/10.1596/1813-9450-5161.

Langford, Ian, 'Mission command during megacity HADR operations', Presentation to Current and Future Operations in Megacities Conference, Tokyo, 16 July 2019.

Lappin, Yaakov, *The IDF's momentum plan aims to create a new type of war machine*, Perspectives Paper No. 1497, Ramat Gan, Israel: Begin-Sadat Center for Strategic Studies, 22 March 2020.

Le Drian, Jean-Yves, *Who Is the Enemy?*, trans. Sandra Smith, Paris: Les Éditions du Cerf, 2016.

Lee Kuan Yew, *From Third World to First: Singapore and the Asian Economic Boom*, New York, NY: HarperCollins, 2000.

Levy, Steven, 'Has the Coronavirus killed the Techlash?', *WIRED*, 20 March 2020, available from: www.wired.com/story/plaintext-has-the-coronavirus-killed-the-techlash/.

Lewis, James, 'The battle of Marawi: Small team lessons learned for the close fight', *Small Wars Journal*, 23 January 2019, available from: smallwarsjournal.com/index.php/blog/battle-marawi-small-team-lessons-learned-close-fight.

Lewis-Kraus, Gideon, 'Trust fails', *WIRED*, July–August 2020, 62–67.

Li, Enjie, Joanna Endter-Wada and Shujuan Li, 'Characterizing and contextualizing the water challenges of megacities', *Journal of the American Water Resources Association* 51(3) (2016): 589–613. doi.org/10.1111/1752-1688.12310.

Lochbaum, David, Edwin Lyman and Susan Q. Stranahan, *Fukushima: The Story of a Nuclear Disaster*, New York, NY: The New Press, 2014.

Lodhammar, Pehr, Skype interview with Dr Russell W. Glenn, 7 June 2021.

Loh Kah Seng, *Squatters into Citizens: The 1961 Bukit Ho Swee Fire and the Making of Modern Singapore*, Singapore: NUS Press, 2013. doi.org/10.2307/j.ctv1qv3g0.

Lombardo, Joseph, Howard Burkom, Eugene Elbert, Steven Magruder, Sheryl Happel Lewis, Wayne Loschen, James Sari, Carol Sniegoski, Richard Wojcik and Julie Pavlin, 'A systems overview of the Electronic Surveillance System for the Early Notification of Community-Based Epidemics (ESSENCE II)', *Journal of Urban Health* 80(Supp. 1) (2003): i32–i42, available from: pubmed.ncbi.nlm.nih.gov/12791777/.

Lorenz, Edward N., 'Predictability: Does the flap of a butterfly's wings in Brazil set off a tornado in Texas?', Paper presented to American Association for the Advancement of Science 139th Meeting, Washington, DC, 29 December 1972, available from: eapsweb.mit.edu/sites/default/files/Butterfly_1972.pdf.

Los Angeles Almanac, 'Municipal Police Departments Los Angeles County', *Los Angeles Almanac*, 2022, available from: www.laalmanac.com/crime/cr69.php.

Los Angeles Police Department (LAPD), 'Gangs', [Online], Los Angeles Police Department, 8 September 2019, available from: www.lapdonline.org/get_informed/content_basic_view/1396.

Lowe, Keith, *Inferno: The Fiery Destruction of Hamburg, 1943*, New York, NY: Scribner, 2007.

Lumumba, Jane, 'Impossible Possibilities: The Fragility and Resilience of Lagos', in *Building Resilience in Cities under Stress*, Francesco Mancini and Andrea Ó Súilleabháin (eds), New York, NY: International Peace Institute, June 2016, 38–49.

Machado, James (Major, US Army), Discussion with Russell W. Glenn, Republic of Korea, 7 November 2018.

Machold, Rhys, 'Militarising Mumbai? The "politics of response"', *Contexto Internacional* 39(03) (September–December 2017): 477–98. doi.org/10.1590/s0102-8529.2017390300002.

Madad, Syra, Nicholas V. Cagliuso, Sr, Dave A. Chokshi, Machelle Allen, Remle Newton-Dame and Jesse Singer, 'NYC Health + Hospitals' rapid responses to COVID-19 were built on a foundation of emergency management, incident command, and analytics', *Health Affairs*, 11 June 2020, available from: www.healthaffairs.org/do/10.1377/hblog20200609.171463/full/.

Mahoney, Dan (Northern California Regional Intelligence Center), Interview with Dr Russell W. Glenn, San Francisco, CA, 12 April 2016.

Malpezzi, Stephen, Urban growth and development at six scales, Second draft, University of Wisconsin James A. Graaskamp Center for Real Estate, 29 January 2008.

Manaugh, Geoff and Nicola Twilley, Until Proven Safe: The History and Future of Quarantine, NY: Farrar, Straus & Giroux, 2021.

Maritime and Port Authority of Singapore, 'Port statistics', [Online], Singapore: MPA, 2021, available from: www.mpa.gov.sg/who-we-are/newsroom-resources/research-and-statistics.

Markel, Howard, Harvey B. Lipman, J. Alexander Navarro, Alexandra Sloan, Joseph R. Michalsen, Alexandra Minna Stern and Martin S. Cetron, 'Nonpharmaceutical interventions implemented by US cities during the 1918–1919 influenza pandemic', *Journal of the American Medical Association* 298(6) (2007): 644–54. doi.org/10.1001/jama.298.6.644.

Mars, Roman and Kurt Kohlstedt, *The 99% Invisible City: A Field Guide to the Hidden World of Everyday Design*, Boston, MA: Houghton Mifflin Harcourt, 2020.

Mask, Deirdre, *The Address Book: What Street Addresses Reveal about Identity, Race, Wealth, and Power*, New York, NY: St Martin's Press, 2020.

Matsuda, Iware, 'Two surveys for taking measures to cope with the coming earthquake to the Tokyo metropolis', *GeoJournal* 38 (March 1996): 349–53. doi.org/10.1007/BF00204728.

Matsuoka, Yuki and Rajib Shaw (eds), *Hyogo Framework for Action and Urban Disaster Resilience*, Community, Environment and Disaster Risk Management Vol. 16, Bingley, UK: Emerald Publishing Limited, 2014. doi.org/10.1108/S2040-7262201416.

Mattis, James N., Interview with Russell W. Glenn, Palo Alto, CA, 31 August 2014.

Maxey, Levi, 'Preparing for the urban future of counterinsurgency', *Indian Strategic Studies Blog*, 10 March 2018, available from: strategicstudyindia. blogspot.com/2018/03/preparing-for-urban-future-of.html.

Mayakovsky, Vladimir, 'Great Big Hell of a City', in *Imagining America: Influence and Images in Twentieth-Century Russia*, Alan M. Ball (ed.), Oxford, UK: Rowman & Littlefield, 2003.

McAvoy, Jennifer L., Telephone interview with Dr Russell W. Glenn, 4 February 2021.

McCarthy, Dayton, *The worst of both worlds: An analysis of urban littoral combat*, Australian Army Occasional Paper: Conflict Theory and Strategy 002, Canberra: Australian Army Research Centre, April 2018, available from: researchcentre. army.gov.au/sites/default/files/the_worst_of_both_worlds.pdf.

McCullagh, Kevin, 'Cities are about to change forever: Here are three key decisions they must make', *Fast Company*, 5 May 2017, available from: www. fastcompany.com/90123848/cities-are-about-to-change-forever-here-are-3-key-decisions-they-must-make.

McCullough, David, *The Path between the Seas: The Creation of the Panama Canal, 1870–1914*, New York, NY: Touchstone, 1977.

McCurry, Justin, 'Tokyo "has 70% chance of powerful earthquake within four years"', *The Guardian*, 23 January 2012, available from: www.theguardian. com/world/2012/jan/23/tokyo-powerful-earthquake-four-years.

McDonald, Robert I., *Conservation for Cities: How to Plan & Build Natural Infrastructure*, Washington, DC: Island Press, 2015. doi.org/10.5822/978-1-61091-523-6.

McDonnell, Patrick J., 'As it recovers from earthquakes, Mexico City looks nervously at its (very) active volcano', *Los Angeles Times*, 27 September 2017, available from: www.latimes.com/world/mexico-americas/la-fg-mexico-volcano-20170927-story.html.

McGeehan, Timothy, 'A war plan orange for climate change', *Proceedings* 143(10) (October 2017): 48–53, [Annapolis, MD: US Naval Institute], available from: www.usni.org/magazines/proceedings/2017-10/war-plan-orange-climate-change.

McLain, Jeremy D., 'Match made in heaven? Or hell?: Megacities and autonomous systems', *Small Wars Journal*, 25 August 2018, available from: smallwarsjournal. com/jrnl/art/match-made-heaven-or-hell-megacities-and-autonomous-systems.

McNickle, Chris, *Bloomberg: A Billionaire's Ambition*, New York, NY: Skyhorse, 2017.

McWilliams, Timothy S., *US Marines in Battle: Fallujah, November–December 2004*, Quantico, VA: Marine Corps History Division, 2014.

Medby, Jamison Jo and Russell W. Glenn, *Street Smart: Intelligence Preparation of the Battlefield*, Santa Monica, CA: RAND Corporation, 2002.

Meerow, Sara, 'Double exposure, infrastructure planning, and urban climate resilience in coastal megacities: A case study of Manila', *Environment and Planning A: Economy and Space* 49(11) (2017): 2649–72. doi.org/10.1177/0308518X17723630.

Mehrota, Shagun, Claudia E. Natenzon, Ademola Omojola, Regina Folorunsho, Joseph Gilbride and Cynthia Rosenzweig, 'Framework for City Climate Risk Assessment', in *Cities and Climate Change: Responding to an Urgent Agenda. Volume 2*, Daniel Freire Hoornweg, Mila Lee, Marcus J. Bhada-Tata and Belinda Perinaz Yuen (eds), Washington, DC: The World Bank, 2013, 182–241, available from: documents1.worldbank.org/curated/en/321111468182335037/pdf/626960PUB0v20B0iesClimateChangeVol2.pdf.

Melvin, Mungo, *Sevastopol's Wars: Crimea from Potemkin to Putin*, New York, NY: Osprey, 2017.

Metzel, Matthew N., Todd J. McCubbin, Heidi B. Fouty, Ken G. Morris, John J. Gutierrez and John Lorenzen, 'Failed megacities and the joint force', *JFQ* 96 (1st Quarter 2020): 109–14, available from: ndupress.ndu.edu/Portals/68/Documents/jfq/jfq-96/JFQ-96_109-114_Metzel-et-al.pdf?ver=2020-02-07-150502-647.

Michaels, Jim, 'Iraqi forces in Mosul see deadliest urban combat since World War II', *USA Today*, 29 March 2017, [Updated 30 March 2017], available from: www.usatoday.com/story/news/world/2017/03/29/united-states-mosul-isis-deadly-combat-world-war-ii/99787764/.

Miles, Kathryn, *Super Storm: Nine Days Inside Hurricane Sandy*, New York, NY: Dutton, 2014.

Miller, Susan, 'Record number of cities advance LGBT rights this year', *USA Today Weekend*, 20–22 October 2017, 4A.

Milner, Greg, 'Nobody knows what lies beneath New York City', *Bloomberg Businessweek*, 10 August 2017, available from: www.bloomberg.com/news/features/2017-08-10/nobody-knows-what-lies-beneath-new-york-city.

Ministry of Defence (MOD), *Operation Banner: An Analysis of Military Operations in Northern Ireland*, Army Code 71842, London: Chief of the General Staff, British Army, July 2006, available from: wikileaks.cash/uk-operation-banner-2006.pdf.

Mitchell, Ellen, 'Foreign powers test US defenses amid coronavirus pandemic', *The Hill*, [Washington, DC], 19 April 2020, available from: thehill.com/policy/defense/493490-foreign-powers-test-us-defenses-amid-coronavirus-pandemic.

Mitchell, James K., 'Coping with natural hazards and disasters in megacities: Perspectives on the twenty-first century', *GeoJournal* 37 (1995): 303–11. doi.org/10.1007/BF00814009.

Mitchell, James K. (ed.), *Crucibles of Hazard: Mega-Cities and Disasters in Transition*, New York, NY: United Nations University, 1999.

Mitchell, James K., 'Introduction', in *Crucibles of Hazard: Mega-Cities and Disasters in Transition*, James K. Mitchell (ed.), New York, NY: United Nations University, 1999.

Mitchell, James K., 'Natural Disaster in the Context of Mega-Cities', in *Crucibles of Hazard: Mega-Cities and Disasters in Transition*, James K. Mitchell (ed.), New York, NY: United Nations University, 1999.

Mitchell, William J., *e-topia: 'Urban Life, Jim—But Not as We Know It'*, Cambridge, MA: MIT Press, 1999. doi.org/10.7551/mitpress/2844.001.0001.

Mogul, Rhea and Swati Gupta, 'At least 31 people killed after Mumbai hit with torrential rain', *CNN*, 19 July 2021, [Updated 20 July 2021], available from: www.cnn.com/2021/07/19/india/mumbai-heavy-rain-landslide-intl-hnk/index.html.

Molesky, Mark, *This Gulf of Fire: The Destruction of Lisbon, or Apocalypse in the Age of Science and Reason*, New York, NY: Alfred A. Knopf, 2015.

Molteni, Megan, 'Fatal flaw', *WIRED*, July–August 2021, 62–73.

Monnery, Neil, *Architect of Prosperity: Sir John Cowperthwaite and the Making of Hong Kong*, London: London Publishing Partnership, 2017.

Moore, Aaron William, *Bombing the City: Civilian Accounts of the Air War in Britain and Japan, 1939–1945*, Cambridge, UK: Cambridge University Press, 2018. doi.org/10.1017/9781108552479.

Mougeot, Luc J.A., *Urban Food Production: Evolution, Official Support and Significance*, Cities Feeding People Series Report 8, Ottawa: International Development Research Centre, 1994, available from: idl-bnc-idrc.dspacedirect.org/bitstream/handle/10625/14949/103013.pdf?sequence=1.

Mourby, Adrian, 'Where are the world's most war-damaged cities?', *The Guardian*, 17 December 2015, available from: www.theguardian.com/cities/2015/dec/17/where-world-most-war-damaged-city.

Mumford, Lewis, *The City in History: Its Origins, Its Transformations, and Its Prospects*, New York, NY: MJF, 1961.

Myhre, Janell (Regional Program Manager, Bay Area Urban Area Security Initiative), Interview with Russell W. Glenn, San Francisco, CA, 13 April 2016.

Nanto, Dick K., William H. Cooper, J. Michael Donnelly and Renée Johnson, *Japan's 2011 Earthquake and Tsunami: Economic Effects and Implications for the United States*, CRS Report for Congress R41702, Washington, DC: Congressional Research Service, 6 April 2011, available from: sgp.fas.org/crs/row/R41702.pdf.

Narvekar, Mahesh and Gita Kewalramani, *City Profile: Greater Mumbai*, Mumbai, India: Municipal Corporation of Greater Mumbai Disaster Risk Management Master Plan, 2010.

National Defense University, CAPSTONE General and Flag Officer Course, Washington, DC: NDU, n.d., available from: capstone.ndu.edu.

National Diet of Japan, *The Official Report of the Fukushima Nuclear Accident Independent Investigation Commission: Executive Summary*, Tokyo: Government of Japan, 2012.

National Geographic, 'Walking Tokyo', *National Geographic* 235 (April 2019): 38–65.

Neuwirth, Robert, *Shadow Cities: A Billion Squatters, A New Urban World*, New York, NY: Routledge, 2005.

Newton, Steven, 'The most dangerous fault in America', *Earth: The Science behind the Headlines*, 9 May 2016, available from: www.earthmagazine.org/article/most-dangerous-fault-america/.

Norman, Donald A., *Living with Complexity*, Cambridge, MA: MIT Press, 2011.

Norton, Richard J., 'Feral cities: Problems today, battlefields tomorrow', *Marine Corps University Journal* 1 (Spring 2010): 50–77.

NPR Staff and Wires, 'Food, gas shortages amid relief efforts in Japan', *KPBS*, [San Diego, CA], 17 March 2011, available from: www.kpbs.org/news/2011/mar/17/food-gas-shortages-amid-relief-efforts-japan/.

Nuclear Energy Agency of the Organisation for Economic Co-operation and Development (NEA), 'Timeline for the Fukushima Daiichi nuclear power plant accident', *News*, Paris: NEA, 7 March 2012, available from: www.oecd-nea.org/news/2011/NEWS-04.html.

Nussbaum, Brian, 'Protecting global cities: New York, London and the internationalization of municipal policing for counter terrorism', *Global Crime* 8(3) (2007): 213–32. Doi.org/10.1080/17440570701507745.

NYC Health, 'Trends and totals', *COVID-19 Data*, City of New York, 11 March 2021, [Updated 2022], available from: www1.nyc.gov/site/doh/covid/covid-19-data-totals.page.

NYC Special Initiative for Rebuilding and Resiliency, *PlaNYC: A Stronger, More Resilient New York*, City of New York, 2013, available from: www1.nyc.gov/site/sirr/report/report.page.

Odierno, Raymond (General, US Army, retired), Speech to 'Operating in Dense Urban Environments' Class of 1978 Student Workshop for Civil–Military Operations, West Point, NY, 18 April 2018.

Okumura, Tetsu, Kouichiro Suzuki, Atsuhiro Fukuda, Akitsugu Kohama, Nobukatsu Takasu, Shinichi Ishimatsu and Shigeaki Hinohara, 'The Tokyo subway sarin attack: Disaster management, part 1—Community emergency response', *Academic Emergency Medicine* 5(6) (1998): 613–17. doi.org/10.1111/j.1553-2712.1998.tb02470.x.

Olshansky, Robert B., Laurie A. Johnson and Kenneth C. Topping, with Yoshiteru Murosaki, Kazuyoshi Ohnishi, Hisako Koura and Ikuo Kobayashi, *Opportunity in Chaos: Rebuilding After the 1994 Northridge and 1995 Kobe Earthquakes*, Urbana-Champaign, IL, and San Francisco, CA: Department of Urban and Regional Planning, University of Illinois, and Laurie Johnson Consulting & Research, 2005 [Online 2011], available from: docs.wixstatic.com/ugd/0b4d51_a073dddfe4f0474ba7b91f1d5572dfa6.pdf.

Olson, Wyatt, 'After 2011 Japan earthquake, US military learned to play supporting role in disaster relief', *Stars and Stripes*, [Washington, DC], 8 March 2016, available from: www.stripes.com/news/after-2011-japan-earthquake-us-military-learned-to-play-supporting-role-in-disaster-relief-1.396953 [page discontinued].

O'Neill, James P., 'Preparing for and managing megacity crises (the NYPD perspective): 9/11 and Hurricane Sandy lessons for US military leaders', Presentation to Multi-Domain Battle in Megacities Conference, Fort Hamilton, NY, 3 April 2018.

O'Neill, R.V., Donald Lee Deangelis, J.B. Waide and Timothy F.H. Allen, *A Hierarchical Concept of Ecosystems*, Monographs in Population Biology Vol. 23, Princeton, NJ: Princeton University Press, 1986.

Oosterveld, Willem, Reinier Bergema, Rianne Siebenga and Bernhard Schneider, *Resilient Cities, Safe Societies: How Cities and States Can Cooperate to Combat the Violence Nexus and Promote Human Security*, The Hague, Netherlands: The Hague Centre for Strategic Studies, 2018.

Oprea, Mark, 'What will Mexico do when its deadliest volcano erupts?', Pacific Standard, [Santa Barbara, CA], 30 October 2018, available from: psmag. com/environment/what-will-mexico-do-if-its-deadliest-volcano-erupts.

Oriki, Ryoichi, Keynote presentation to Current and Future Operations in Megacities Conference, Tokyo, 17 July 2019.

Orr, Robert, 'Governing When Chaos Rules: Enhancing Governance and Participation', in *The Battle for Hearts and Minds: Using Soft Power to Undermine Terrorist Networks*, Alexander T.J. Lennon (ed.), Cambridge, MA: MIT Press, 2003, 232–48.

Osaragi, Toshihiro, 'Modeling a spatiotemporal distribution of stranded people returning home on foot in the aftermath of a large-scale earthquake', *Natural Hazards* 68 (2013): 1385–98. doi.org/10.1007/s11069-012-0175-8.

Osborne, Robin and Andrew Wallace-Hadrill, 'Cities of the Ancient Mediterranean', in *The Oxford Handbook of Cities in World History*, Peter Clark (ed.), Oxford, UK: Oxford University Press, 2016, 49–65.

Oshinsky, David, *Bellevue: Three Centuries of Medicine and Mayhem at America's Most Storied Hospital*, New York, NY: Doubleday, 2016.

Oskin, Becky, 'Japan earthquake & tsunami of 2011: Facts and information', *Live Science*, [New York], 13 September 2017, [Updated 26 February 2022], available from: www.livescience.com/39110-japan-2011-earthquake-tsunami-facts.html.

Otu, Akaninyene, Soter Ameh, Egbe Osifo-Dawodu, Enoma Alade, Susan Ekuri and Jide Idris, 'An account of the Ebola virus disease outbreak in Nigeria: Implications and lessons learnt', *BMC Public Health* 18(3) (2018). doi.org/ 10.1186/s12889-017-4535-x.

Packer, George, 'The megacity: Decoding the chaos of Lagos', *The New Yorker*, 13 November 2016, 62–75.

Page, Max, 'The City's End: Past and Present Narratives of New York's Destruction', in *The Resilient City: How Modern Cities Recover from Disaster*, Lawrence J. Vale and Thomas I. Campanella (eds), New York, NY: Oxford University Press, 2005, 75–93. doi.org/10.1093/oso/9780195175844.003.0008.

Parker, Barrett K. and H. Quinton Lucie, 'Secondary earthquakes: New Madrid Seismic Zone response during an ongoing emergency', *HDIAC Journal* 4 (Spring 2017): 23–27.

Parker, Dennis J., 'Disaster Response in London: A Case of Learning Constrained by History and Experience', in *Crucibles of Hazard: Mega-Cities and Disasters in Transition*, James K. Mitchell (ed.), New York, NY: United Nations University, 1999.

Paulovich, Michael J. (Lieutenant Colonel, US Marine Corps), Email to Russell W. Glenn, Subject: Force recon and STA [surveillance and target acquisition] teams, 13 November 2001.

Paynter, Ben, 'Why Bloomberg Philanthropies' James Anderson tops our list of the most creative people in business 2017', *Fast Company*, 15 May 2017, available from: www.fastcompany.com/40412383/why-bloomberg-philanthropies-james-anderson-tops-our-list-of-the-most-creative-people-in-business-2017.

Peilin, Wu and Minghong Tan, 'Challenges for sustainable urbanization: A case study of water shortage and water environment changes in Shandong, China', *Procedia Environmental* Sciences 13 (2012): 919–27. doi.org/10.1016/j.proenv.2012.01.085.

Perkins, David G. (Commanding General, US Division—North), Interview with Dr Russell W. Glenn, Tikrit, Iraq, 28 June 2011 [as appears in Russell W. Glenn, *Core Counterinsurgency Asset: Lessons from Iraq and Afghanistan for United States Army Corps of Engineers Leaders*, Study sponsored by the US Army Corps of Engineers, 31 May 2012 (Revised 8 December 2016), 261–271].

Perlman, Janice, *Favela: Four Decades of Living on the Edge in Rio de Janeiro*, New York, NY: Oxford University Press, 2010.

Perry, Andre M., 'New Orleans is still learning from the lessons of Katrina—Houston should too', *The Avenue Blog*, Washington, DC: The Brookings Institution, 29 August 2017, available from: www.brookings.edu/blog/the-avenue/2017/08/29/new-orleans-is-still-learning-from-the-lessons-of-katrina-houston-should-too/.

Perry, Suzanne, Dale Cox, Lucile Jones, Richard Bernknopf, James Goltz, Kenneth Hudnut, Dennis Mileti, Daniel Ponti, Keith Porter, Michael Reichle, Hope Seligson, Kimberley Shoaf, Jerry Treiman and Anne Wein, *The Shakeout Earthquake Scenario: A Story That Southern Californians Are Writing*, USGS Circular 1324, Reston, VA: US Geological Survey, 2008. doi.org/10.3133/cir1324.

Petraeus, David, 'Reflections on wars in Iraq and Afghanistan', *PRISM: The Journal of Complex Operations* 7(1) (14 September 2017), [Washington, DC: National Defence University], available from: cco.ndu.edu/News/Article/1299605/reflections-on-wars-in-iraq-and-afghanistan/.

Philipps, Dave, 'Seven hard lessons federal responders to Harvey learned from Katrina', *The New York Times*, 7 September 2017, available from: www.nytimes.com/2017/09/07/us/hurricane-harvey-katrina-federal-responders.html.

Polybius, *On Roman Imperialism*, trans. Evelyn S. Shuckburgh, Lake Bluff, IL: Regnery Gateway, 1987.

Pont, M.Y. Berghauser, P.G. Perg, P.A. Haupt and A. Heyman, 'A systematic review of the scientifically demonstrated effects of densification', *IOP Conference Series: Earth and Environmental Science* 588 (2020): 1.15–1.19. doi.org/10.1088/1755-1315/588/5/052031.

Postings, Robert, 'A guide to the Islamic State's way of urban warfare', Article, West Point, NY: Modern War Institute, 9 July 2018, available from: mwi.usma.edu/guide-islamic-states-way-urban-warfare/.

PricewaterhouseCoopers (PwC), 'Which are the largest city economies in the world and how might this change by 2025?', *PricewaterhouseCoopers UK Economic Outlook*, November 2019, London: PwC, available from: pwc.blogs.com/files/global-city-gdp-rankings-2008-2025.pdf.

Puente, Sergio, 'Social vulnerability to disasters in Mexico City: An assessment method', in *Crucibles of Hazard: Mega-Cities and Disasters in Transition*, James K. Mitchell (ed.), New York, NY: United Nations University, 1999.

Rabasa, Angel, Robert D. Blackwill, Peter Chalk, Kim Cragin, C. Christine Fair, Brian A. Jackson, Brian Michael Jenkins, Seth G. Jones, Nathaniel Shestak and Ashley J. Tellis, *The lessons of Mumbai*, Occasional Paper 249, Santa Monica, CA: RAND Corporation, 2009, available from: www.rand.org/content/dam/rand/pubs/occasional_papers/2009/RAND_OP249.pdf.

Rakodi, Carole, 'Religion and Social Life in African Cities', in *Africa's Urban Revolution*, Susan Parnell and Edgar Pieterse (eds), New York, NY: Bloomsbury Academic, 2014, 82–109. doi.org/10.5040/9781350218246.ch-005.

Rasmussen, Jacob, '"We Are the True Blood of the Mau Mau": The Mungiki Movement in Kenya', in *Global Gangs: Street Violence Across the World*, Jennifer M. Hazen and Dennis Rodgers (eds), Minneapolis, MN: University of Minnesota Press, 2014, 213–35. doi.org/10.5749/minnesota/9780816691470.003.0011.

Rawlence, Ben, *City of Thorns: Nine Lives in the World's Largest Refugee Camp*, New York, NY: Picador, 2017.

Reader, John, *Cities*, New York, NY: Atlantic Monthly, 2004.

realestate-tokyo.com, 'Floods in Tokyo and safety tips and preparation', *realestate-tokyo.com*, 28 February 2020, [Updated 18 May 2022], available from: www.realestate-tokyo.com/living-in-tokyo/emergency-disaster/flood-in-tokyo-japan/.

Reeves, Robert W., 'Edward Lorenz revisiting the limits of predictability and their implications: An interview from 2007', *Bulletin of the American Meteorological Society* 95(5) (2014): 681–87. doi.org/10.1175/BAMS-D-13-00096.1.

Regional Plan Association, 'Our work', [Online], New York, NY: RPA, 2022, available from: www.rpa.org/programs.

Reid, T.R., *Confucius Lives Next Door: What Living in the East Teaches Us about Living in the West*, New York, NY: Vintage, 1999.

Renn, Aaron M., 'What is a global city?', *New Geography*, 6 December 2012, available from: www.newgeography.com/content/003292-what-is-a-global-city.

Revelli, Philippe, 'Singapore, Malaysia, and Indonesia: A triangle of growth or a triangle of inequality?', *Equal Times*, [Brussels], 4 October 2016, available from: www.equaltimes.org/singapore-malaysia-and-indonesia-a?lang=en#.Xzr AIEl7kyk.

Reynolds, Cory (Regional Project Manager, Whole of Community and Communications, Bay Area Urban Area Security Initiative), Interview with Russell W. Glenn, San Francisco, CA, 13 April 2016.

Rich, Sarah, 'San Francisco embraces sharing economy for emergency preparedness', *Government Technology*, 14 June 2013, available from: www.govtech.com/public-safety/San-Francisco-Embraces-Sharing-Economy-for-Emergency-Preparedness.html.

Richards, David (General, British Army), Interview with Russell W. Glenn, Wilton, UK, 2 April 2008.

Ripley, Amanda, *The Unthinkable: Who Survives When Disaster Strikes—and Why*, New York, NY: Crown, 2008.

Ritchie, Hannah and Max Roser, 'Urbanization', *Our World in Data*, 2018, [Updated 2019], available from: ourworldindata.org/urbanization.

Roberts, Brian H., 'Risk and resilience in Asian cities: Case study of Manila', n.d., available from: www.academia.edu/9265596/Risk_and_Resilience_in_Asian _Cities_Case_Study_of_Manila.

Roberts, Nancy, 'Wicked problems and network approaches to resolution', *International Public Management Review* 1(1) (2000), available from: ipmr. net/index.php/ipmr/article/view/175.

Robinson, Wayne A., Eradicating organized criminal gangs in Jamaica: Can lessons be learnt from a successful counterinsurgency?, Master's thesis, United States Marine Corps Command and Staff College, Quantico, VA, 2008.

Rodin, Judith, *The Resilience Dividend: Being Strong in a World Where Things Go Wrong*, New York, NY: PublicAffairs, 2014.

Rodriguez, Rene, 'Miami condo king breaks silence on sea level rise comment: "Maybe I had too many drinks"', *Miami Herald*, 31 May 2018, available from: www.miamiherald.com/news/business/real-estate-news/article210857 319.html.

Rosa, Amanda, 'What N.Y.C.'s antibody test results show us', *The New York Times*, 20 August 2020, available from: www.nytimes.com/2020/08/20/ nyregion/nyc-coronavirus-antibody-testing.html.

Rose, Gideon, 'The fourth founding: The United States and the liberal order', *Foreign Affairs* 98(1) (January–February 2019): 10–21.

Ross, Will, 'Ebola crisis: How Nigeria's Dr Adadevoh fought the virus', *BBC News*, 20 October 2014, available from: www.bbc.com/news/world-africa-29696011.

Rozelle, Scott and Natalie Hell, *Invisible China: How the Urban–Rural Divide Threatens China's Rise*, Chicago, IL: University of Chicago Press, 2020. doi.org/ 10.7208/chicago/9780226740515.001.0001.

Rubin, Louis D., Jr (ed.), *The Quotable Baseball Fanatic*, Guilford, CT: Lyons Press, 2000.

Rukmana, Deden, 'The megacity of Jakarta: Problems, challenges and planning efforts', *Indonesia's Urban Studies Blog*, 29 March 2014, available from: indonesia urbanstudies.blogspot.com/2014/03/the-megacity-of-jakarta-problems.html.

Rybczynski, Witold, *City Life: Urban Expectations in a New World*, New York, NY: Scribner, 1995.

Sadik-Khan, Janette, *Street Fight: Handbook for an Urban Revolution*, New York, NY: Viking, 2016.

Sadler, A.L., *Japanese Architecture: A Short History*, Tokyo: Tuttle Publishing, 2009.

Sagara, Junko and Keiko Saito, *Risk Assessment and Hazard Mapping*, Learning from Megadisasters Knowledge Note 5-1, Washington, DC: Global Facility for Disaster Reduction and Recovery, 1 July 2012, available from: www.gfdrr. org/en/publication/learning-megadisasters-knowledge-note-5-1.

Samaniego, Horacio and Melanie E. Moses, 'Cities as organisms: Allometric scaling of urban road networks', *Journal of Transport and Land Use* 1(1) (2008): 21–39. doi.org/10.5198/jtlu.v1i1.29.

Sampaio, Antonio and Eleanor Beevor, *Urban Drivers of Political Violence: Declining State Authority and Armed Groups in Mogadishu, Nairobi, Kabul and Karachi*, IISS Research Report, London: International Institute for Strategic Studies, May 2020, available from: www.urban-response.org/system/files/content/ resource/files/main/Urban%20drivers%20of%20political%20violence%20 -%20IISS%20Research%20Report.pdf.

Sanderson, D., P. Knox Clarke and L. Campbell, *Responding to urban disasters: Learning from previous relief and recovery operations*, ALNAP Lessons Paper, London: ALNAP, 2012, available from: www.alnap.org/help-library/ responding-to-urban-disasters-learning-from-previous-relief-and-recovery-operations.

Santanam, Ramesh, 'Pittsburgh approves gun restrictions; lawsuits expected', *Associated Press*, 3 April 2019, 20, available from: apnews.com/article/3f4ffc 8f307d46499b824dbf47467fe3.

Sassen, Saskia, *The Global City: New York, London, Tokyo*, Princeton, NJ: Princeton University Press, 2001. doi.org/10.2307/j.ctt2jc93q.

Sassen, Saskia, 'Cities in Today's Global Age', in *Connecting Cities: Networks. A Research Publication for the 9th World Congress of Metropolis*, Chris Johnson, Richard Hu and Shanti Abedin (eds), Barcelona: Metropolis Secretariat General, 2008, 22–43, available from: www.metropolis.org/sites/default/ files/network_complete_0.pdf.

Satterthwaite, David, 'How urban societies can adapt to resource shortage and climate change', *Philosophical Transactions of the Royal Society A: Mathematical, Physical and Engineering Sciences* 369(1942) (2011): 1762–83. doi.org/ 10.1098/rsta.2010.0350.

Satterthwaite, David, Saleemul Huq, Mark Pelling, Hannah Reid and Patricia Romero Lankao, *Adapting to climate change in urban areas: The possibilities and constraints in low- and middle-income nations*, Human Settlements Discussion Paper Series, London: International Institute for Environment and Development, January 2007, available from: pubs.iied.org/pdfs/10549 IIED.pdf.

Schadlow, Nadia, *War and the Art of Governance: Consolidating Combat Success into Political Victory*, Washington, DC: Georgetown University Press, 2017.

Schelske, Oliver, Lukas Sundermann and Peter Hausmann, *Mind the Risk: A Global Ranking of Cities Under Threat from Natural Disasters*, Zürich: Swiss Re, 18 September 2013, available from: www.researchgate.net/publication/329450315_Mind_the_risk_-_A_global_ranking_of_cities_under_threat_from_natural_disasters.

Schilthuizen, Menno, *Darwin Comes to Town: How the Urban Jungle Drives Evolution*, New York, NY: Picador, 2018.

Schmeltz, Michael T., Sonia K. González, Liza Fuentes, Amy Kwan, Anna Ortega-Williams and Lisa Pilar Cowan, 'Lessons from Hurricane Sandy: A community response in Brooklyn, New York', *Journal of Urban Health* 90 (2013): 799–809. doi.org/10.1007/s11524-013-9832-9.

Schumpeter, 'Global cities revisited: Where businesses locate now—and where they will go', *The Economist*, [London], 3 October 2013, available from: www.economist.com/blogs/schumpeter/2013/10/geography-business.

Scott-Clark, Cathy and Adrian Levy, *The Siege: 68 Hours Inside the Taj Hotel*, New York, NY: Penguin, 2013.

Scruggs, Gregory, 'How much public space does a city need?', *Next City*, [Philadelphia, PA], 7 January 2015, available from: nextcity.org/daily/entry/how-much-public-space-does-a-city-need-UN-Habitat-joan-clos-50-percent.

Seidensticker, Edward, *Tokyo from Edo to Showa, 1867–1989: The Emergence of the World's Greatest City*, Singapore: Tuttle, 2010.

Sennett, Richard, *The Uses of Disorder: Personal Identity & City Life*, New York, NY: Alfred A. Knopf, 1970.

Sennett, Richard, *Building and Dwelling: Ethics for the City*, New York, NY: Farrar, Straus & Giroux, 2018.

Shackle, Samira, *Karachi Vice: Life and Death in a Contested City*, London: Granta, 2001.

Shakespeare, William, 'The Tragedy of Coriolanus', in *Shakespeare, The Complete Works*, G.B. Harrison (ed.), New York, NY: Harcourt, Brace & World, 1968.

Sharkey, Patrick, *Uneasy Peace: The Great Crime Decline, the Renewal of City Life, and the Next War on Violence*, New York, NY: Norton, 2018.

Sharma, Richa and P.K. Joshi, 'Rapidly urbanizing Indian cities: The problem of local heat but a global challenge', *UGEC Viewpoints*, July 2013, 28–32.

Sheldrake, Merlin, *Entangled Life: How Fungi Make Our Worlds, Change Our Minds, & Shape Our Futures*, New York, NY: Random House, 2020.

Shepherd, J. Marshall, Harold Pierce and Andrew J. Negri, 'Rainfall modification by major urban areas: Observations from spaceborne rain radar on the TRMM satellite', *Journal of Applied Meteorology and Climatology* 41(7) (2002): 689–701. doi.org/10.1175/1520-0450(2002)041<0689:RMBMUA>2.0.CO;2.

Sherly, Mazhuvanchery Avarachen, Subhankar Karmakar, Devanathan Parthasarathy, Terence Chan and Christian Rau, 'Disaster vulnerability mapping for a densely populated coastal urban area: An application to Mumbai, India', *Annals of the Association of American Geographers* 105(6) (2015): 1198–220. doi.org/10.1080/00045608.2015.1072792.

Ship & Bunker News Team, '6 countries are responsible for almost 60% of all bunker sales', *Ship & Bunker*, [Vancouver, BC], 5 January 2016, available from: shipandbunker.com/news/world/608701-6-countries-are-responsible-for-almost-60-of-all-bunker-sales.

Shuaib, Faisal, Rajni Gunnala, Emmanuel O. Musa, Frank J. Mahoney, Olukayode Oguntimehin, Patrick M. Nguku, Sara Beysolow Nyanti, Nancy Knight, Nasir Sani Gwarzo, Oni Idigbe, Abdulsalam Nasidi and John F. Vertefeuille, 'Ebola virus disease outbreak—Nigeria, July–September 2014', *Morbidity and Mortality Weekly Report* 63(39) (3 October 2014): 867–72, Atlanta, GA: Centers for Disease Control and Prevention, available from: www.cdc.gov/mmwr/preview/mmwrhtml/mm6339a5.htm.

Singer, P.W. and Emerson T. Brooking, *Like War: The Weaponization of Social Media*, Boston, MA: Houghton Mifflin, 2018.

Skates, Jesse L., Interview with Dr Russell W. Glenn, Fort Eustis, VA, 21 January 2020.

Smit, Warren and Edgar Pieterse, 'Decentralisation and Institutional Reconfiguration in Urban Africa', in *Africa's Urban Revolution*, Susan Parnell and Edgar Pieterse (eds), New York, NY: Bloomsbury Academic, 2014, 148–66. doi.org/10.5040/9781350218246.ch-008.

Smith, Monica L., *Cities: The First 6,000 Years*, New York, NY: Viking, 2019.

Snow, John, 'Instances of the Communications of Cholera through the Medium of Polluted Water in the Neighborhood of Broad Street, Golden Square', in *On the Mode of Communication of Cholera*, London: John Churchill, 1855, available from: www.ph.ucla.edu/epi/snow/snowbook_a2.html.

Special Inspector General for Afghanistan Reconstruction, *Corruption in Conflict: Lessons from the US Experiences in Afghanistan*, Arlington, VA: SIGAR, September 2016, available from: www.sigar.mil/pdf/lessonslearned/SIGAR-16-58-LL-Executive-Summary.pdf.

Spillane, Mickey, *The Mike Hammer Collection. Volume 1*, New York, NY: New American Library, 2001.

SREO Consulting, 'Lessons Learned Study on UN Humanitarian, Civil–Military Coordination and Stabilization Efforts in Mosul', January 2019.

Statistics Japan, 'Railway passenger transport', *Prefecture Comparisons*, [Online], Tokyo: Statistics Japan, 2010, available from: stats-japan.com/t/kiji/10796.

Stillman, Sarah, 'Ebola and the culture makers', *The New Yorker*, 11 November 2014, available from: www.newyorker.com/news/daily-comment/ebola-culture-makers.

Stott, Clare and Mohammed Nadiruzzaman, *Disaster Risk Reduction in Dhaka City: From Urban Landscape Analysis to Opportunities for DRR Integration*, Uxbridge, UK: World Vision, 2014.

Strausbaugh, John, *City of Sedition: The History of New York City during the Civil War*, New York, NY: Hachette, 2016.

Strausbaugh, John, *Victory City: A History of New York and New Yorkers during World War II*, New York, NY: Hachette, 2018.

Strock, Carl A. (Lieutenant General, US Army, retired), Interview with Dr Russell W. Glenn and Dave Dilegge, Frederick, MD, 29 July 2011.

Suhartono, Muktita and Russell Goldman, 'Flash floods in Indonesia leave hundreds of thousands homeless', *The New York Times*, 2 January 2020, available from: www.nytimes.com/2020/01/02/world/asia/indonesia-jakarta-rain-floods.html.

Sullivan, John (Los Angeles County Sheriff's Department, retired), Discussion with Russell W. Glenn, Los Angeles, CA, 20 October 2021.

Sullivan, John P. and Alain Bauer, *Terrorism Early Warning: 10 Years of Achievement in Fighting Terrorism and Crime*, Los Angeles, CA: Los Angeles County Sheriff's Office, October 2008.

Sun, Tzu, *The Art of War*, trans. Samuel B. Griffith, New York, NY: Oxford University Press, 1982.

Sundermann, Lukas, Oliver Schelske and Peter Hausmann, *Mind the Risk: A Global Ranking of Cities Under Threat from Natural Disasters*, Zürich: Swiss Re, 2014, available from: www.swissre.com/dam/jcr:1609aced-968f-4faf-beeb-96e6a2969d79/Swiss_Re_Mind_the_risk.pdf.

Sweet, William V., Robert E. Kopp, Christopher P. Weaver, Jayantha Obeysekera, Radley M. Horton, E. Robert Thieler and Chris Zervas, *Global and Regional Sea Level Rise Scenarios for the United States*, NOAA Technical Report NOS CO-OPS 083, Silver Spring, MD: National Oceanic and Atmospheric Administration, January 2017, available from: tidesandcurrents.noaa.gov/publications/techrpt83_Global_and_Regional_SLR_Scenarios_for_the_US_final.pdf.

Szepesy, James E., The strategic corporal and the emerging battlefield: The Nexus between the USMC's three block war concept and network centric warfare, Master's thesis, The Fletcher School at Tufts University, Medford, MA, March 2005, available from: www.dtic.mil/dtic/tr/fulltext/u2/a575338.pdf [page discontinued].

Takemoto, Ryuji, 'The JGSDF role in megacity security operations', Presentation to Achieving Convergence during Humanitarian Assistance and Disaster Relief Operations in the World's Largest Urban Areas Conference, Tokyo, 16–18 July 2019.

Tamari, Salim, 'Confessionalism and Public Space in Ottoman and Colonial Jerusalem', in *Cities & Sovereignty: Identity Politics in Urban Spaces*, Diane E. Davis and Nora Libertun de Duren (eds), Bloomington, IN: Indiana University Press, 2011, 59–82.

Teng, Paul, Margarita Escaler and Mely Caballero-Anthony, 'Urban food security: Feeding tomorrow's cities', *Significance* 8(2) (2011): 57–60. doi.org/10.1111/j.1740-9713.2011.00486.x.

The Economist, 'A magic moment for the city of God: Security in Brazil', *The Economist*, [London], 12 June 2010, 42–43.

The Economist, 'Onward and upward: Shanty life in Brazil', *The Economist*, [London], 24 July 2010, 81.

The Economist, 'Conquering Complexo do Alemão: Organised crime in Brazil', *The Economist*, [London], 4 December 2010, 49.

The Economist, 'Golding goes: Jamaica's prime minister', *The Economist*, [London], 1 October 2011, 40.

The Economist, 'Mission impossible: Fukushima Dai-ichi', *The Economist*, [London], 7 February 2015, 22–23.

The Economist, 'Free exchange: Hard-nosed compassion', *The Economist*, [London], 26 September 2015, 70.

The Economist, 'Disaster foretold: Planning for El Nino', *The Economist*, [London], 7 November 2015, 55–56.

The Economist, 'The great urban racket: Africa's slums', *The Economist*, [London], 22 April 2017, 39–40.

The Economist, 'A long shadow: Islam and politics in Bangladesh', *The Economist*, [London], 3 June 2017, 31–32.

The Economist, 'First we take Nairobi: Democracy in Africa', *The Economist*, [London], 24 June 2017, 44.

The Economist, 'The longest flush: California against the rest', *The Economist*, [London], 8 July 2017, 26.

The Economist, 'The global property business tries to adapt to e-commerce', *The Economist*, 14 December 2017, 58–59, available from: www.economist.com/business/2017/12/14/the-global-property-business-tries-to-adapt-to-e-commerce.

The Economist, 'Vacant spaces: Retail property', *The Economist*, [London], 16 December 2017, 58.

The Economist, 'Ten per cent: Earthquake preparedness', *The Economist*, [London], 3 February 2018, 26.

The Economist, 'Into the urban maw: Cities and farming', *The Economist*, [London], 17 February 2018, 53–54.

The Economist, 'Beating the bugs: Sanitation in Bangladesh', *The Economist*, [London], 24 March 2018, 33–34.

The Economist, 'Shining some light: Latin America's homicide problem is a harbinger for the developing world', *The Economist*, [London], 7 April 2018, 16–18.

The Economist, 'Algorithm blues: Predictive policing and sentencing', *The Economist*, [London], 2 June 2018, [Technology Quarterly] 9–11.

The Economist, 'Villas and slums: Housing in the Middle East,' *The Economist*, [London], 16 June 2018, 37–38.

The Economist, 'Tragedy of the commons: Land in South Asia', *The Economist*, [London], 25 August 2018, 38.

The Economist, 'The anti-Lagos: Nigerian cities', *The Economist*, [London], 20 October 2018, 47.

The Economist, 'Grounding bugs: Public health', *The Economist*, [London], 20 October 2018, 73.

The Economist, 'Underneath the lamplight: Evolution', *The Economist*, [London], 10 November 2018, 77–78.

The Economist, 'Baby bust: The birth rate', *The Economist*, [London], 24 November 2018, 23–24.

The Economist, 'Brekekekex koax koax: Animal behavior', *The Economist*, [London], 15 December 2018, 17.

The Economist, 'Less than the sum of their parts: Municipal limits', *The Economist*, [London], 22 December 2018, 41–42.

The Economist, 'Four wheels better: Transport in Myanmar', *The Economist*, [London], 19 January 2019, 39.

The Economist, 'The global list', *The Economist*, [London], 26 January 2019, 19–22.

The Economist, 'Young Americans: Early education', *The Economist*, [London], 26 January 2019, 23–24.

The Economist, 'An elephant in the desert: Egypt's new capital', *The Economist*, [London], 26 January 2019, 40.

The Economist, 'First, wash your hands: Battling superbugs', *The Economist*, [London], 26 January 2019, 43–44.

The Economist, 'A school for small families: Demography', *The Economist*, [London], 2 February 2019, 50–52.

The Economist, 'Geography lessons', *The Economist*, [London], 23 February 2019, 50.

The Economist, 'Fighting Ebola, and myths: Congo', *The Economist*, [London], 23 March 2019, 42–43.

The Economist, 'Revolt of the cities: Turkey's local elections', *The Economist*, [London], 6 April 2019, 41.

The Economist, 'Chairbound but seated: Japanese with disabilities', *The Economist*, [London], 3 August 2019, 29.

The Economist, 'Seeing red: Turmoil in Hong Kong', *The Economist*, [London], 10 August 2019, 16–18.

The Economist, 'Higher tide', *The Economist*, [London], 17 August 2019, 15–18.

The Economist, 'King of the heap: Karachi', *The Economist*, [London], 26 October 2019, 35–36.

The Economist, 'City air makes you free: Domestic migration', *The Economist*, [London], 16 November 2019, 10–11.

The Economist, 'The age of mechanical reproduction as a work of art', *The Economist*, [London], 21 December 2019, 23–25.

The Economist, 'Melting pots', *The Economist*, [London], 21 December 2019, 63–65.

The Economist, 'The incredible sinking city: Jakarta submerged', *The Economist*, [London], 11 January 2020, 32.

The Economist, 'The long game: The road', *The Economist*, [London], 8 February 2020, 7–9.

The Economist, 'Digital plurality: Are data more like oil or sunlight?', *The Economist*, [London], 22 February 2020, [Special report] 4–6.

The Economist, 'Flu jabs: Japan may have to cancel the Olympics', *The Economist*, [London], 7 March 2020, 36.

The Economist, 'Generation game: Democracy in Africa', *The Economist*, [London], 7 March 2020, 46.

The Economist, 'An island at the ready', *The Economist*, [London], 28 March 2020, 35.

The Economist, 'Distancing neighbors: Mexican–American relations', *The Economist*, [London], 28 March 2020, 30, 32.

The Economist, 'Hand-to-mouth to lockdown: Covid-19 in South Asia', *The Economist*, [London], 28 March 2020, 36.

The Economist, 'The drifters', *The Economist*, [London], 4 April 2020, 31.

The Economist, 'Corona-speak', *The Economist*, [London], 4 April 2020, 70.

The Economist, 'Tall tales of the city: Kenya', *The Economist*, [London], 11 April 2020, 39.

The Economist, 'Microbes and the metropolis: How diseases shape cities', *The Economist*, [London], 25 April 2020, 78–79.

The Economist, 'Leaders and misleaders', *The Economist*, [London], 2 May 2020, 36.

The Economist, 'Reaping from the whirlwind: How Covid-19 is changing science', *The Economist*, [London], 9 May 2020, 62–63.

The Economist, 'Upping the Anta: Chinese brands', *The Economist*, [London], 16 May 2020, 54.

The Economist, 'The great land grab: Transport', *The Economist*, [London], 23 May 2020, 45.

The Economist, 'Medellín's medical marvel: Colombia', *The Economist*, [London], 6 June 2020, 25–26.

The Economist, 'Viral marketing: Indonesian politics', *The Economist*, [London], 6 June 2020, 30–31.

The Economist, 'Electrical storm: Hong Kong's future', *The Economist*, [London], 6 June 2020, 58–60.

The Economist, 'On every street: Urban society', *The Economist*, [London], 13 June 2020, 31–32.

The Economist, 'Missions impossible: Global firefighting', *The Economist*, [London], 20 June 2020, [Special report] 6–9.

The Economist, 'Who you gonna call? Civil society', *The Economist*, [London], 11 July 2020, 32–33.

The Economist, 'The darkness behind: Hong Kong's companies', *The Economist*, [London], 18 July 2020, 32.

The Economist, 'Class acts: The socioeconomics of sewage', *The Economist*, [London], 18 July 2020, 65–66.

The Economist, 'An outsized punch', *The Economist*, [London], 25 July 2020, 3–4.

The Economist, 'Hold on: Life on furlough', *The Economist*, [London], 25 July 2020, 38.

The Economist, 'Cleanliness is next to growth: Hygiene', *The Economist*, [London], 1 August 2020, 69–71.

The Economist, 'Worlds apart: Hukou reform', *The Economist*, [London], 23 August 2020, 35–36.

The Economist, 'The high-rise life: Housing in Seoul', *The Economist*, [London], 29 August 2020, 60–61.

The Economist, 'Parcels, plots and power: Property rights', *The Economist*, [London], 12 September 2020, 37–39.

The Economist, 'Learning to live with it: Natural disasters', *The Economist*, [London], 12 September 2020, 67–68.

The Economist, 'Cradle to desk: Sexual politics in South Korea', *The Economist*, [London], 17 October 2020, 31–32.

The Economist, 'Picking up the pieces: Turkey', *The Economist*, [London], 5 December 2020, 52.

The Economist, 'Country bumpkins and city slickers', *The Economist*, [London], 23 January 2021, 65.

The Economist, 'Trouble in the country: Human capital', *The Economist*, [London], 23 January 2021, 66–67.

The Economist, 'Build it and they will go', *The Economist*, [London], 27 February 2021, 35.

The Economist, 'Urbs prima in Indis: City administration in India', *The Economist*, [London], 8 May 2021, 38–39.

The Economist, 'Serve the rich: Inequality in education', *The Economist*, [London], 29 May 2021, 36–37.

The Economist, 'Rich slum, poor slum: Poverty', *The Economist*, [London], 19 June 2021, 57–58.

The Economist, 'A midsummer bug hunt: Microecology', *The Economist*, [London], 19 June 2021, 76.

The Economist, 'Soaking it up: Flood-proofing cities', *The Economist*, [London], 20 November 2021, 42–43.

The Japan Times, '"Indirect" deaths from disasters', [Editorial], *The Japan Times*, [Tokyo], 23 March 2019, available from: www.japantimes.co.jp/opinion/2019/03/23/editorials/indirect-deaths-disasters/#.XLz2v-tKhn4.

The Saskawa Peace Foundation (SPF), *The Fukushima Nuclear Accident and Crisis Management: Lessons for Japan–US Alliance Cooperation*, Tokyo: SPF, September 2012, available from: www.spf.org/jpus/img/investigation/book_fukushima.pdf.

The Washington Post, 'The battle for hearts and minds', *The Washington Post*, Fog of War Vignette No. 8, 1998, available from: www.washingtonpost.com/wp-srv/inatl/longterm/fogofwar/vignettes/v8.htm?noredirect=on.

The White House, 'Chapter Five: Lessons Learned', in *The Federal Response to Hurricane Katrina: Lessons Learned*, Washington, DC: The White House, 2006, available from: georgewbush-whitehouse.archives.gov/reports/katrina-lessons-learned/chapter5.html.

Thompson, Clive, 'North star: The American dream is alive and well—in Canada', *WIRED*, September 2020, 16–17.

Thouret, Jean-Claude, 'Urban hazards and risks; consequences of earthquakes and volcanic eruptions: An introduction', *GeoJournal* 49 (1999): 131–35. doi.org/10.1023/A:1007118027266.

Thucydides, *History of the Peloponnesian War*, trans. Rex Warner, New York, NY: Penguin, 1972.

Tilly, Charles, 'Cities and states in Europe, 1000–1800', *Theory and Society* 18 (1989): 563–84. doi.org/10.1007/BF00149492.

Tinniswood, Adrian, *Visions of Power: Ambition and Architecture from Ancient Times to the Present*, New York, NY: Steward, Tabori & Chang, 1998.

Tokyo Metropolitan Government, 'About our city', [Online], 2006, available from: www.metro.tokyo.lg.jp/english/about/index.html.

TomTom International BV, 'TomTom Traffic Index: Ranking 2019', [Online], Amsterdam: TomTom, 2019, [Updated 2021], available from: www.tomtom.com/en_gb/traffic-index/ranking/.

Townsend, Anthony M., *Smart Cities: Big Data, Civic Hackers, and the Quest for a New Utopia*, New York, NY: W.W. Norton, 2013.

Townsend, Stephen J., 'Megacity scenarios, foundations, and convergence', Presentation to MDB in Megacities Conference, Fort Hamilton, NY, 3 April 2018.

Traas, Adrian G., *Turning Point, 1967–1968*, Washington, DC: US Army Center of Military History, 2017.

Turoc, Ivan, 'Linking Urbanisation and Development to Africa's Economic Revival', in *Africa's Urban Revolution*, Susan Parnell and Edgar Pieterse (eds), New York, NY: Bloomsbury Academic, 2014, 60–81. doi.org/10.5040/9781350218246.ch-004.

Twain, Mark, *The Innocents Abroad*, Ware, UK: Wordsworth, 2010.

Uitto, Juha I., 'The geography of disaster vulnerabilities in megacities: A theoretical framework', *Applied Geography* 18(1) (1998): 7–16. doi.org/10.1016/S0143-6228(97)00041-6.

Union of Concerned Scientists, *Overwhelming Risk: Rethinking Flood Insurance in a World of Rising Seas*, Report, Cambridge, MA: UCSUSA, August 2013, [Revised February 2014], available from: www.ucsusa.org/global_warming/science_and_impacts/impacts/flood-insurance-sea-level-rise.html#.WZsrCXeGO8o.

United Nations, 'Goal 11: Make Cities Inclusive, Safe, Resilient and Sustainable', *Sustainable Development Goals*, New York, NY: United Nations, 2015, available from: www.un.org/sustainabledevelopment/cities/.

United Nations Conference on Housing and Sustainable Urban Development (Habitat III), *Urban ecosystems and resource management*, Habitat III Issue Paper 16, New York, NY: United Nations, 31 May 2015, available from: habitat3.org/wp-content/uploads/Habitat-III-Issue-Paper-16_Urban-Ecosystem-and-Resource-Management-2.0.pdf.

United Nations Human Settlement Programme (UN-Habitat), *State of the World's Cities 2012/2013: Prosperity of Cities*, World Urban Forum edn, Nairobi: UN-Habitat, 2012, available from: sustainabledevelopment.un.org/content/documents/745habitat.pdf.

United Nations Human Settlement Programme (UN-Habitat), *Urbanization and Development: Emerging Futures*, World Cities Report 2016, Nairobi: UN-Habitat, 2016, available from: unhabitat.org/sites/default/files/download-manager-files/WCR-2016-WEB.pdf.

United States Agency for International Development (USAID), 'Iraq: Complex Emergency', Fact Sheet #4, Fiscal year 2017, Washington, DC: USAID, 9 June 2017, available from: www.usaid.gov/sites/default/files/2022-05/2021-09-30_USG_Iraq_Complex_Emergency_Fact_Sheet_4.pdf.

United States Army Center for Army Lessons Learned (CALL), 'Operation United Assistance: Report for follow-on forces', *Bulletin: Lessons and Best Practices*, No. 15-16, Fort Leavenworth, KS: US Army Center for Army Lessons Learned, September, 2015, available from: usacac.army.mil/sites/default/files/publications/15-16.pdf.

United States Army Training and Doctrine Command (TRADOC), *The Changing Character of Warfare: The Urban Operational Environment*, TRADOC Pamphlet 525-92-1, Fort Eustis, VA: TRADOC, April 2020, available from: adminpubs.tradoc.army.mil/pamphlets/TP525-92-1.pdf.

United States Geological Survey, *ShakeAlert: An Earthquake Early Warning System for the West Coast of the United States*, Reston, VA: USGS, 2016, available from: www.shakealert.org.

United States Marine Corps, *Urban Operations I: Introduction*, Basic Officer Course Student Handout B4R5359, Camp Barrett, VA: The Basic School, Marine Corps Training Command.

United States Senate, *Lessons from the Mumbai Terrorist Attacks: Parts I and II*, Hearings before the Committee on Homeland Security and Governmental Affairs, United States Senate, 111th Congress, 1st Session, 8 and 28 January 2009, Washington, DC: US Government Printing Office, 2009, available from: www.govinfo.gov/content/pkg/CHRG-111shrg49484/html/CHRG-111 shrg49484.htm.

Vale, Lawrence J. and Thomas I. Campanella, 'Introduction: The Cities Rise Again', in *The Resilient City: How Modern Cities Recover from Disaster*, Lawrence J. Vale and Thomas I. Campanella (eds), New York, NY: Oxford University Press, 2005, 3–23. doi.org/10.1093/oso/9780195175844.003.0004.

Van Duyn, Donald N., 'Testimony by Donald N. Van Duyn, Chief Intelligence Officer, Directorate of Intelligence, National Security Branch, Federal Bureau of Investigation', in *Lessons from the Mumbai Terrorist Attacks: Parts I and II*, Hearings before the Committee on Homeland Security and Governmental Affairs, United States Senate, 111th Congress, 1st Session, 8 and 28 January 2009, Washington, DC: US Government Printing Office, available from: www.govinfo.gov/content/pkg/CHRG-111shrg49484/html/CHRG-111shrg 49484.htm.

van Heerden, Ivor, *The Storm: What Went Wrong and Why during Hurricane Katrina—The Insider Story from One Louisiana Scientist*, New York, NY: Penguin, 2007.

van Rijn, Nina, Urbanization in sub-Saharan Africa, Bachelor's thesis, University of Amsterdam, 16 December 2014.

Varro, Marcus Tarentius, *On Agriculture. Book III*, London: Loeb Classical Library, 1934, available from: penelope.uchicago.edu/Thayer/E/Roman/ Texts/Varro/de_Re_Rustica/3*.html.

Verini, James, *They Will Have to Die Now: Mosul and the Fall of the Caliphate*, New York, NY: W.W. Norton, 2019.

Villoro, Juan, *Horizontal Vertigo: A City Called Mexico*, New York, NY: Pantheon, 2021.

von Clausewitz, Carl, *On War*, ed. and trans. by Michael Howard and Peter Paret, Princeton, NJ: Princeton University Press, 1976.

Wan, Yang, Sasikiran Kandula, Mary Huynh, Sharon K. Greene, Gretchen Van Wye, Wenhui Li, Hiu Tai Chan, Emily Mcgibbon, Alice Yeung, Don Olson, Anne Fine and Jeffrey Shaman, 'Estimating the infection-fatality risk of SARS-CoV-2 in New York City during the spring 2020 pandemic wave: A model-based analysis', *The Lancet* 21(2) (February 2021): 203–12, doi.org/10.1016/S1473-3099(20)30769-6.

Warr, Nicholas and Scott A. Nelson, 'Lessons Learned: Operation "Hue City", 1968', in *Ready for Armageddon: Proceedings of the 2001 RAND Arroyo–Joint ACTD-CETO-USMC Nonlethal and Urban Operations Program Urban Operations Conference*, Russell W. Glenn, Sidney W. Atkinson, Michael Barbero, Frederick J. Gellert, Scott Gerwehr, Steven Hartman, Jamison Jo Medby, Andrew O'Donnell, David Owen and Suzanne Pieklik (eds), Santa Monica, CA: RAND Corporation, 2002, available from: www.rand.org/pubs/conf_proceedings/CF179.html.

Wei, Li, Christopher A. Airriess, Angela Chia-Chen Chen, Karen J. Leong and Verna Keith, 'Katrina and migration: Evacuation and return by African Americans and Vietnamese Americans in an eastern New Orleans suburb', *The Professional Geographer* 62(1) (2010): 103–18. doi.org/10.1080/00330120903404934.

Weller, Chris, 'Here's China's genius plan to move 250 million people from farms to cities', *Business Insider*, [New York, NY], 5 August 2015, available from: www.businessinsider.com/heres-chinas-big-plan-to-move-a-population-the-size-of-the-phillippines-from-farms-to-cities-2015-7.

Wenzel, Friedemann, Fouad Bendimerad and Ravi Sinha, 'Megacities: Megarisks', *Natural Hazards* 42 (2007): 481–91. doi.org/10.1007/s11069-006-9073-2.

West, Geoffrey, *Scale: The Universal Laws of Growth, Innovation, Sustainability, and the Pace of Life in Organisms, Cities, Economies, and Companies*, New York, NY: Penguin, 2017.

Whalen, Jeanne, Loveday Morris, Tom Hamburger and Terrence McCoy, 'White House scrambles to scoop up medical supplies worldwide, angering Canada, Germany', *The Washington Post*, 4 April 2020, available from: www.washingtonpost.com/business/2020/04/03/white-house-scrambles-scoop-up-medical-supplies-angering-canada-germany/.

Wikimedia, 'Snow Cholera Map 1' [from Snow, John, *On the Mode of Communication of Cholera*, C.F. Cheffins, London, 1854], available from: upload.wikimedia.org/wikipedia/commons/2/27/Snow-cholera-map-1.jpg.

Will, George F., 'Winning the "three-block war"', *The Washington Post*, 14 April 2004, available from: www.washingtonpost.com/archive/opinions/2004/04/14/winning-the-three-block-war/f72ecf07-870b-4d5c-8ce1-a54562d1546c/?noredirect=on&utm_term=.8a82c56fb9bb.

Willacy, Mark, *Fukushima: Japan's Tsunami and the Inside Story of the Nuclear Meltdowns*, Sydney: Macmillan, 2013.

Willemer, Wilhelm, *The German Defense of Berlin*, trans. R.D. Young, Historical Division, Headquarters, United States Army, Europe MS No. P-136, 1953.

Williams, Paige, 'Urgent care from the Army Corps of Engineers', *The New Yorker*, 27 July 2020, available from: www.newyorker.com/magazine/2020/08/03/urgent-care-from-the-army-corps-of-engineers.

Williams, Phil and Werner Selle, *Military Contingencies in Megacities and Sub-Megacities*, Carlisle, PA: Strategic Studies Institute and US Army War College Press, December 2016.

Wilson David, Remarks at Analysis of Urban Warfare, Military Operations Research Society Conference, Quantico, VA, 2 April 2019.

Wiltshire, Susan Ford, *Greece, Rome, and the Bill of Rights*, Norman, OK: University of Oklahoma Press, 1992.

WIRED, 'Internet providers to the dispossessed', *WIRED Business Special*, [UK edition], November–December 2018, 28–29.

Wisner, Ben and Henry R. Luce, 'Bridging "expert" and "local" knowledge for counter-disaster planning in urban South Africa', *GeoJournal* 37 (1995): 335–48. doi.org/10.1007/BF00814014.

Wogan, David, 'This massive underground complex protects Tokyo from floods', [*Plugged In Blog*], *Scientific American*, 29 October 2013, available from: blogs.scientificamerican.com/plugged-in/this-massive-underground-complex-protects-tokyo-from-floods/.

Woodruff, Jonathan D., Jennifer L. Irish and Suzana J. Camargo, 'Coastal flooding by tropical cyclones and sea-level rise', *Nature* 504 (2013): 44–52. doi.org/10.1038/nature12855.

Woolf, Greg, *The Life and Death of Ancient Cities: A Natural History*, New York, NY: Oxford University Press, 2020.

World Bank, *East Asia's Changing Urban Landscape: Measuring a Decade of Spatial Growth*, Urban Development Series, Washington, DC: The World Bank, 2015, available from: www.worldbank.org/content/dam/Worldbank/Publications/Urban%20Development/EAP_Urban_Expansion_full_report_web.pdf. doi.org/10.1596/978-1-4648-0363-5.

World Bank, 'Fertility rate, total (births per woman)—Korea, Rep.', *Data*, [Online], Washington, DC: The World Bank, 2018, available from: data.worldbank.org/indicator/SP.DYN.TFRT.IN?locations=KR.

World Economic Forum (WEF), *Global Risks 2015: 10th edition*, Insight Report, Geneva: World Economic Forum, 2015, available from: www3.weforum.org/docs/WEF_Global_Risks_2015_Report15.pdf.

World Nuclear Association, 'Fukushima Daiichi Accident', *Information Library*, London: World Nuclear Association, June 2018, [Updated May 2022], available from: www.world-nuclear.org/information-library/safety-and-security/safety-of-plants/fukushima-accident.aspx.

World Population Review, 'Berlin population 2018', Walnut, CA: World Population Review, [Online], 19 October 2018, available from: worldpopulationreview.com/world-cities/berlin-population/.

World Population Review, 'Lagos Population 2020', [Online], Walnut, CA: World Population Review, 2020, [Updated 2022], available from: worldpopulationreview.com/world-cities/lagos-population/.

World Population Review, 'Shanghai Population 2020', [Online], Walnut, CA: World Population Review, 2020, [Updated 2022], available from: worldpopulationreview.com/world-cities/shanghai-population/.

World Population Review, 'Tokyo Population 2020', [Online], Walnut, CA: World Population Review, 2020, [Updated 2022], available from: worldpopulationreview.com/world-cities/tokyo-population/.

World Shipping Council, 'About Liner Shipping', [Online], Washington, DC: World Shipping Council, 2018, available from: www.worldshipping.org/about-liner-shipping.

World Vision, *Cities Prepare! Reducing Vulnerabilities for the Urban Poor*, Asia Pacific Disaster Report, Bangkok: World Vision Asia Pacific, 2013, available from: www.worldvision.jp/about/item_img/13_12_en.pdf.

Worrall, Simon, 'Two years after Hurricane Sandy hit the US, what lessons can we learn from the deadly storm?', *National Geographic*, 19 October 2014, available from: www.nationalgeographic.com/adventure/article/141019-hurricane-sandy-katrina-coast-guard-hunters-ngbooktalk.

Wright, Lawrence, *The Plague Year: America in the Time of Covid*, New York, NY: Alfred A. Knopf, 2021.

Yale-Tulane ESF-8 Planning and Response Network, *Yale/Tulane ESF-8 Planning and Response Program Special Report (Japan Earthquake and Tsunami), as of 2200 hours EST, March 25, 2011*, [Online], available from: slideplayer.com/slide/5350222/.

Yeung, Jessie, Swati Gupta and Michael Guy, 'Experts: India has just five years to solve its water crisis—Groundwater has been steadily decreasing', *CNN*, 27 June 2019, [Updated 4 July 2019], available from: edition.cnn.com/2019/06/27/india/india-water-crisis-intl-hnk/index.html.

Yonhap News Agency, 'S. Korean population slightly grows, becomes older in 2019', *Yonhap News Agency*, [Seoul], 15 August 2020, available from: en.yna.co.kr/view/AEN20200814002200315.

Yudhistira, Geradi, Muhammad Iqbal Firdaus and Lira Agushinta, 'Transportation system in Japan: A literature study', *Journal of Management and Logistics* 2(3) (2015): 333–52. doi.org/10.25292/j.mtl.v2i3.108.

Yukalov, V.I. and D. Sornette, 'Statistical outliers and dragon-kings as Bose-condensed droplets', *Physics and Society*, 7 May 2012, available from: arxiv.org/abs/1205.1364.

Zavis, Alexandra and Christine Mai-Duc, 'Clashes erupt as Liberia seals off slum to prevent spread of Ebola', *Los Angeles Times*, 20 August 2014, available from: www.latimes.com/world/africa/la-fg-africa-liberia-ebola-quarantine-curfew-20140820-story.html.

Ziegler, Philip, *London at War: 1939–1945*, New York, NY: Alfred A. Knopf, 1995.

Zucchino, David, *Thunder Run: The Armored Strike to Capture Baghdad*, New York, NY: Atlantic Monthly Press, 2004.

Index

Page number in bold represents an image.

www.ingramcontent.com/pod-product-compliance
Lightning Source LLC
Chambersburg PA
CBHW050806270326
41926CB00026B/4559